PEARSON  ALWAYS LEARNING

D1541064

Multicultural Film
An Anthology
for Florida State University

Fall 2015-Spring/Summer 2016

Selected by Kathryn Karrh Cashin and Lauren C. Martilli

Pearson Learning Solutions, 330 Hudson Street, New York, New York 10013
A Pearson Education Company
www.pearsoned.com

Printed in the United States of America

1 2 3 4 5 6 7 8 9 10 VOCR 18 17 16 15

000200010271972458

SK/KE

ISBN 10: 1-323-13415-8
ISBN 13: 978-1-323-13415-3

Copyright Acknowledgments

"Ten Things You Should Know About Selma Before You See the Film," by Emilye Crosby, reprinted by permission from *Zinn Education Project* 3, (January 3, 2015).

"Racial Microaggressions in Everyday Life: Implications for Clinical Practice," by Derald Wing Sue et al., reprinted by permission from *American Psychologist* 62, no. 4 (May 2007).

"Naturalizing Racial Differences through Comedy: Asian, Black, and White Views on Racial Stereotypes in 'Rush Hour 2'," by Ji Hoon Park, Nadine G. Gabbadon and Ariel R. Chemin, reprinted from the *Journal of Communication* 56, no. 1 (2006), by permission of John Wiley & Sons, Inc.

"The Meritocracy Myth," by Stephen J. McNamee and Robert K. Miller Jr., reprinted by permission from *Sociation Today* 2, no. 1 (Spring 2004).

"Business as Usual: The American Dream in Hollywood Business Films," by Mary S. Pileggi et al., reprinted from *Mass Communication and Society* 3, no. 2 (2000), by permission of Taylor & Francis.

Excerpt from "The Destructive Power of Money," by Karl Marx, reprinted from *Marx's Concept of Man*, edited by Erich Fromm (1963), by permission of Robin Feuer Miller.

"Gender as a Social Structure: Theory Wrestling with Activism," by Barbara J. Risman, reprinted from *Gender and Society* 18, no. 4 (August 2004), by permission of Sage Publications, Inc.

"We (Still) Need a Woman for the Job: The Warrior Woman, Feminism, and Cinema in the Digital Age," by Lee-Jane Bennion-Nixon, reprinted by permission from *Senses of Cinema* 56, no. 3 (2010).

"Sexual Orientations in Perspective," by Linda D. Garnets, reprinted by permission from *Cultural Diversity and Ethnic Minority Psychology* 8, no. 2 (May 2002).

"Queer Feelings," by Sara Ahmed, reprinted from *The Politics of Emotion* (2004), by permission of Edinburgh University Press.

"To Commend or To Critique?: The Question of Religion and Film Studies," by John Lyden, reprinted by permission from the *Journal of Religion and Film Studies* 1, no. 2 (October 1997).

"Real or Not Real: The Hunger Games as Transmediated Religion," by Yonah Ringlestein, reprinted from the *Journal of Religion and Popular Culture* 25, no. 3 (2013), University of Toronto Press.

"The Sigh of the Oppressed?: Marxism and Religion in America Today," by Kathryn Lofton, reprinted from *New Labor Forum* 21, no. 3 (October 1, 2012), by permission of Taylor & Francis.

"Treat Students Right by Valuing Their Diversity," by Matthew Mueleners (2001), by permission of the author.

"A Revolution of Values: The Promise of Multicultural Change," by bell hooks, reprinted from the *Journal of the Midwest Modern Language Association* 26, no. 1 (1993).

"National Identity and the Politics of Multiculturalism," by Henry A. Giroux, reprinted from *College Literature* 22, no. 2 (1995), by permission of the author.

Table of Contents

Introduction

When was the last time a Hollywood movie inspired you or captivated your attention? Were you particularly drawn to the actors, imagery, storyline, or special effects? Each of us likely has preferences about the cultural products we consume, especially movies—whether we enjoy comedy, drama, horror, musicals, or any variety of film genres, the movies impact our lives in profound ways. Hollywood movies convey ideas about how to behave or what to wear. Beyond entertainment value, movies teach us valuable lessons; they inform our understanding of American culture, and portray images of the nation or what constitutes 'ideal' citizenship. Thus, to participate meaningfully in our communities, we must acquire conceptual tools to analyze, interpret, and negotiate the many messages and meanings in Hollywood film.

I remember watching the political thriller *Blood Diamond* (2006) starring Leonardo DiCaprio, Jennifer Connelly, and Djimon Hounsou. When American journalist Maddie Bowen (Connelly) exclaims, "Americans wouldn't buy a diamond if they knew it cost someone their hand," it resonated with me, yet the final courtroom scene implies a resolution to the corruption and terror of the conflict diamond trade. For me, it provoked further research into the issue of conflict diamonds as well as child soldiers; both are exceptionally complex issues, and far more widespread than I initially imagined, yet very few Hollywood movies seem to adequately confront such social injustices.

Given the structure and commercial imperatives of the Hollywood feature film, the omissions are understandable, but our awareness of social issues must not cease when the movie ends. We must remain cognizant of the formal techniques and devices filmmakers choose in their construction of meaning. Mise en scène elements such as lighting, scenery, props, and wardrobe are intentional choices that must be considered in the context of each film. Moreover, the construction of meaning in film extends to socially accepted (and contested) meanings such as nationality, race, class, gender, and sexuality.

Consider a few exemplars of Hollywood drama: *Forrest Gump* (1994), *The Blind Side* (2009), or *The Help* (2011). Each story involves a main character, an American individual who pursues equal rights for all citizens regardless of race, class, physical or mental ability. Symbolic of progress and equanimity, Forrest (Tom Hanks), the Touhy family (Sandra Bullock et al.), and Skeeter (Emma Stone) portray presumably ideal qualities of American citizenship—they aspire to help others through compassionate acts of courage and generosity. Yet, when we examine the representation of race, ethnicity, class, gender, or sexuality in each film, what more might we uncover? In movies that tell stories about triumph and empowerment in the face of racism and prejudice, why are leading protagonists almost always white? We might also consider which individuals and social groups appear privileged at the expense of those marginalized or exploited. The concept of white privilege and, what critics refer to as, the "white savior film" offer useful conceptual tools to facilitate a critical exploration of cultural representation.

Furthermore, Hollywood movies often follow established patterns. We frequently see familiar character types and similar narrative structure across a wide variety of films. For example, the "happily ever after" ending is a Hollywood favorite, especially in comedy and romance films. A comparison of the popular Disney animated film *Cinderella* (1950) with *Sex and the City* (2008), for instance, offers some insight.

Cinderella represents the quintessential "fair maiden" and "damsel in distress" character type. Endowed with beauty (portrayed as thin, fair-skinned, blond hair, and blue eyes) and charming compassion, she overcomes oppression with elegance and grace, and by winning the heart of Prince Charming. The glass slipper fits, followed by a royal wedding, and, *naturally*, the couple lives happily ever after. Are we convinced? Do we believe in the fairytale love story? We may even imagine ourselves in one of these roles.

Fast-forward several decades to the movie *Sex and the City* (2008), based on the popular television series, which recycles familiar patterns. Blonde-haired, blue-eyed Carrie Bradshaw (Sara Jessica Parker) is a modern Cinderella—she is a writer living in New York City who socializes and shops with friends. In the movie, Carrie plans the wedding of her dreams to her version of Prince Charming, Mr. Big who has (finally) divorced his wife. Like Cinderella, she overcomes obstacles to "live happily ever after," albeit the social conditions have changed, but ultimately the shoe fits, only this time it's a Manolo Blahnick (a very expensive designer brand).

While *Cinderella* (1950) and *Sex and the City* (2008) are merely two examples from a plethora of Hollywood feature films, they follow similar formulas. Arguably, they perpetuate a myth that happiness involves love and wealth, more specifically heterosexual marriage and an upper-class lifestyle. Both leading characters—Cinderella and Carrie—are white, wealthy, 'feminine' heterosexual women who pursue white, wealthy 'masculine' heterosexual men. While social conditions have significantly changed, both stories feature similar narrative patterns and convey similar messages about American identities that are often accepted as *natural*. Yet, how might these narratives underrepresent or silence certain individuals or social groups in American culture?

Approaching cinematic representations through the lens of cultural studies provides the tools necessary for these types of analyses. A cultural studies framework offers meaningful conceptual tools for interpreting and evaluating the construction of American identities in Hollywood film. This course and the articles in this edition of *Multicultural Film: An Anthology* aim to broaden your awareness of and engagement with representations of multicultural meanings in Hollywood film. In an age of unprecedented technological advancement, our ability to respond critically to the visual texts we encounter regularly is paramount to living a productive life within our individual communities, and as members of a global audience.

—Lauren C. Martilli

1

Cultural Studies, Multiculturalism, and Media Culture

Douglas Kellner

Radio, television, film, and the other products of media culture provide materials out of which we forge our very identities; our sense of selfhood; our notion of what it means to be male or female; our sense of class, of ethnicity and race, of nationality, of sexuality; and of "us" and "them." Media images help shape our view of the world and our deepest values: what we consider good or bad, positive or negative, moral or evil. Media stories provide the symbols, myths, and resources through which we constitute a common culture and through the appropriation of which we insert ourselves into this culture. Media spectacles demonstrate who has power and who is powerless, who is allowed to exercise force and violence, and who is not. They dramatize and legitimate the power of the forces that be and show the powerless that they must stay in their places or be oppressed.

We are immersed from cradle to grave in a media and consumer society and thus it is important to learn how to understand, interpret, and criticize its meanings and messages. The media are a profound and often misperceived source of cultural pedagogy: They contribute to educating us how to behave and what to think, feel, believe, fear, and desire—and what not to. The media are forms of pedagogy that teach us how to be men and women. They show us how to dress, look, and consume; how to react to members of different social groups; how to be popular and successful and how to avoid failure; and how to conform to the dominant system of norms, values, practices, and institutions. Consequently, the gaining of critical media literacy is an important resource for individuals and citizens in learning how to cope with a seductive cultural environment. Learning how to read, criticize, and resist socio-cultural manipulation can help empower oneself in relation to dominant forms of media and culture. It can enhance individual sovereignty vis-à-vis media culture and give people more power over their cultural environment.

In this chapter, I will discuss the potential contributions of a cultural studies perspective to media critique and literacy. In recent years, cultural studies has emerged as a set of approaches to the study of culture and society. The project was inaugurated by the University of Birmingham Centre for Contemporary Cultural Studies, which developed a variety of critical methods for the analysis, interpretation,

Reprinted from *Gender, Race, and Class in Media,* Second Edition, edited by Jean M. Humez and Gail Dines (2002), by permission of Sage Publications.

and criticism of cultural artifacts.[1] Through a set of internal debates, and responding to social struggles and movements of the 1960s and the 1970s, the Birmingham group came to focus on the interplay of representations and ideologies of class, gender, race, ethnicity, and nationality in cultural texts, including media culture. They were among the first to study the effects of newspapers, radio, television, film, and other popular cultural forms on audiences. They also focused on how various audiences interpreted and used media culture differently, analyzing the factors that made different audiences respond in contrasting ways to various media texts.

Through studies of youth subcultures, British cultural studies demonstrated how culture came to constitute distinct forms of identity and group membership. For cultural studies, media culture provides the materials for constructing views of the world, behavior, and even identities. Those who uncritically follow the dictates of media culture tend to "mainstream" themselves, conforming to the dominant fashion, values, and behavior. Yet cultural studies is also interested in how subcultural groups and individuals resist dominant forms of culture and identity, creating their own style and identities. Those who obey ruling dress and fashion codes, behavior, and political ideologies thus produce their identities within the mainstream group, as members of specific social groupings (such as white, middle-class conservative Americans). Persons who identify with subcultures, like punk culture, or black nationalist subcultures, look and act differently from those in the mainstream, and thus create oppositional identities, defining themselves against standard models.

Cultural studies insists that culture must be studied within the social relations and system through which it is produced and consumed and that thus study of culture is intimately bound up with the study of society, politics, and economics. Cultural studies shows how media culture articulates the dominant values, political ideologies, and social developments and novelties of the era. It conceives of U.S. culture and society as a contested terrain with various groups and ideologies struggling for dominance (Kellner, 1995). Television, film, music, and other popular cultural forms are thus often liberal or conservative, although they occasionally articulate more radical or oppositional positions and are often ideologically ambiguous, combining various political positions.

Cultural studies is valuable because it provides some tools that enable one to read and interpret one's culture critically. It also subverts distinctions between "high" and "low" culture by considering a wide continuum of cultural artifacts ranging from novels to television and by refusing to erect any specific cultural hierarchies or canons. Previous approaches to culture tended to be primarily literary and elitist, dismissing media culture as banal, trashy, and not worthy of serious attention. The project of cultural studies, by contrast, avoids cutting the field of culture into high and low, or popular against elite. Such distinctions are difficult to maintain and generally serve as a front for normative aesthetic valuations and, often, a political program (i.e., either dismissing mass culture for high culture, or celebrating what is deemed "popular" while scorning "elitist" high culture).

Cultural studies allows us to examine and critically scrutinize the whole range of culture without prior prejudices toward one or another sort of cultural text, institution, or practice. It also opens the way toward more differentiated political, rather than aesthetic, valuations of cultural artifacts in which one attempts to distinguish critical and oppositional from conformist and conservative moments in a cultural artifact. For instance, studies of Hollywood film show how key 1960s films promoted the views of radicals and the counterculture and how film in the 1970s was a battleground between liberal and conservative positions; late 1970s films, however, tended toward conservative positions that helped elect Ronald Reagan as president (see Kellner & Ryan, 1988).

There is an intrinsically critical and political dimension to the project of cultural studies that distinguishes it from objectivist and apolitical academic approaches to the study of culture and society. British cultural studies, for example, analyzed culture historically in the context of its societal origins effects. It situated culture within a theory of social production and reproduction, specifying the ways that cultural forms served either to further social domination or to enable people to resist and struggle against domination. It analyzed society as a hierarchical and antagonistic set of social relations characterized by the oppression of subordinate class, gender, race, ethnic, and national strata. Employing Gramsci's (1971) model of hegemony and counterhegemony, it sought to analyze "hegemonic," or ruling, social and cultural forces of domination and to seek "counterhegemonic" forces of resistance and struggle. The project as aimed at social transformation and attempted to specify forces of domination and resistance in order to aid the process of political struggle and emancipation from oppression and domination.

For cultural studies, the concept of ideology is of central importance, for dominant ideologies serve to reproduce social relations of domination and subordination.[2] Ideologies of class, for instance, celebrate upper-class life and denigrate the working class. Ideologies of gender promote sexist representations of women and ideologies of race utilize racist representations of people of color and various minority groups. Ideologies make inequalities and subordination appear natural and just, and thus induce consent to relations of domination. Contemporary societies are structured by opposing groups who have different political ideologies (liberal, conservative, radical, etc.) and cultural studies specifies what, if any, ideologies are operative in a given cultural artifact (which could involve, of course, the specification, of ideological contradictions). In the course of this study, I will provide some examples of how different ideologies are operative in media cultural texts and will accordingly provide examples of ideological analysis and critique.

Because of its focus on representations of race, gender, and class, and its critique of ideologies that promote various forms of oppression, cultural studies lends itself to a multiculturalist program that demonstrates how culture reproduces certain forms of racism, sexism, and biases against members of subordinate classes, social groups, or alternative lifestyles. Multiculturalism affirms the worth of different types of culture and cultural groups, claiming, for instance, that black, Latino, Asian, Native American, gay and lesbian, and other oppressed and marginal voices have their own validity and importance. An insurgent multiculturalism attempts to show how various people's voices and experiences are silenced and omitted from mainstream culture and struggles to aid in the articulation of diverse views, experiences, and cultural forms, from groups excluded from the mainstream. This makes it a target of conservative forces who wish to preserve the existing canons of white male, Eurocentric privilege and thus attack multiculturalism in cultural wars raging from the 1960s to the present over education, the arts, and the limits of free expression.

Cultural studies thus promotes a multiculturalist politics and media pedagogy that aims to make people sensitive to how relations of power and domination are "encoded" in cultural texts, such as those of television or film. But it also specifies how people can resist the dominant encoded meanings and produce their own critical and alternative readings. Cultural studies can show how media culture manipulates and indoctrinates us, and thus can empower individuals to resist the dominant meanings to media cultural products and to produce their own meanings. It can also point to moments of resistance and criticism within media culture and thus help promote development of more critical consciousness.

A critical cultural studies—embodied in many of the chapters collected in this reader—thus develops concepts and analyses that will enable readers to analytically dissect the artifacts of contemporary media culture and to gain power over their cultural environment. By exposing the entire field of culture to knowledgeable scrutiny, cultural studies provides a broad, comprehensive framework to undertake studies of culture, politics, and society for the purposes of individual empowerment and social and political struggle and transformation. In the following pages, I will therefore indicate some of the chief components of the type of cultural studies that I find most useful.

Components of a Critical Cultural Studies

At its strongest, cultural studies contains a threefold project of analyzing the production and political economy of culture, cultural texts, and the audience reception of those texts and their effects. This comprehensive approach avoids too narrowly focusing on one dimension of the project to the exclusion of others. To avoid such limitations, I would thus propose a multiperspectival approach that (a) discusses production and political economy, (b) engages in textual analysis, and (c) studies the reception and use of cultural texts.[3]

Production and Political Economy

Because it has been neglected in many modes of recent cultural studies, it is important to stress the importance of analyzing cultural texts within their system of production and distribution, often referred to as the political economy of culture.[4] Inserting texts into the system of culture within which they are produced and distributed can help elucidate features and effects of the texts that textual analysis alone might miss or downplay. Rather than being antithetical approaches to culture, political economy can actually contribute to textual analysis and critique. The system of production often determines what sort of artifacts will be produced, what structural limits there will be as to what can and cannot be said and shown, and what sort of audience effects the text may generate.

Study of the codes of television, film, or popular music, for instance, is enhanced by studying the formulas and conventions of production. These cultural forms are structured by well-defined rules and conventions, and the study of the production of culture can help elucidate the codes actually in play. Because of the demands of the format of radio or music television, for instance, most popular songs are three to five minutes, fitting into the frames of the distribution system. Because of their control by giant corporations oriented primarily toward profit, film and television production in the United States is dominated by specific genres such as talk and game shows, soap operas, situation comedies, action/adventure series, reality TV, and so on. This economic factor explains why there are cycles of certain genres and subgenres, sequelmania in the film industry, crossovers of popular films into television series, and a certain homogeneity in products constituted within systems of production marked by rigid generic codes, formulaic conventions, and well-defined ideological boundaries.

Likewise, study of political economy can help determine the limits and range of political and ideological discourses and effects. My study of television in the United States, for instance, disclosed that takeover of the television networks by major transnational corporations and communications conglomerates was part of a "right turn" within U.S. society in the 1980s whereby powerful corporate groups won control of the state and the mainstream media (Kellner, 1990). For example, during the 1980s all three networks were taken over by major corporate conglomerates: ABC was bought out in 1985 by Capital Cities, NBC was absorbed by GE, and CBS was purchased by the Tisch Financial Group. Both ABC and NBC sought corporate mergers and this motivation, along with other benefits derived from Reaganism, might well have influenced them to downplay criticisms of Reagan and to generally support his conservative programs, military adventures, and simulated presidency.

Corporate conglomeratization has intensified further and today AOL and Time Warner, Disney, and other global media conglomerates control ever more domains of the production and distribution of culture (McChesney, 2000). In this global context, one cannot really analyze the role of the media in the Gulf war, for instance, without analyzing the production and political economy of news and information, as well as the actual text of the Gulf war and its reception by its audience (see Kellner, 1992). Likewise, the ownership by conservative corporations of dominant media corporations helps explain mainstream media support of the Bush administration and their polities, such as the 2000 U.S. presidential election (Kellner, 2001).

Looking toward entertainment, one cannot fully grasp the Madonna phenomenon without analyzing her marketing strategies, her political environment, her cultural artifacts, and their effects (Kellner, 1995). In a similar fashion, younger female pop music stars and groups such as Mariah Carey, Britney Spears, Jennifer Lopez, or N'Sync also deploy the tools of the glamour industry and media spectacle to make certain stars the icons of fashion, beauty, style, and sexuality, as well as purveyors of music. And in appraising the full social impact of pornography, one needs to be aware of the sex industry and the production process of, say, pornographic films, and not just dwell on the texts themselves and their effects on audiences.

Furthermore, in an era of globalization, one must be aware of the global networks that produce and distribute media culture in the interests of profit and corporate hegemony. Yet political economy alone does not hold the key to cultural studies and important as it is, it has limitations as a single approach. Some political economy analyses reduce the meanings and effects of texts to rather circumscribed and reductive ideological functions, arguing that media culture merely reflects the ideology of the ruling economic elite that controls the culture industries and is nothing more than a vehicle for capitalist ideology. It is true that media culture overwhelmingly supports capitalist values, but it is also a site of intense struggle between different races, classes, gender, and social groups. Thus, in order to fully grasp the nature and effects of media culture, one needs to develop methods to analyze the full range of its meanings and effects.

Textual Analysis

The products of media culture require multidimensional close textual readings to analyze their various forms of discourses, ideological positions, narrative strategies, image construction, and effects. There have been a wide range of types of textual criticism of media culture, ranging from quantitative content analysis that dissects the number of, say, episodes of violence in a text, to qualitative study that examines images of women, blacks, or other groups, or that applies various critical theories to unpack the meanings of the texts or to explicate how texts function to produce meaning. Traditionally, the qualitative analysis of texts has been the task of formalist literary criticism, which explicates the central meanings, values, symbols, and ideologies in cultural artifacts by attending to the formal properties of imaginative literature texts—such as style, verbal imagery, characterization, narrative structure and point of view, and other formal elements of the artifact. From the 1960s on, however, literary-formalist textual analysis has been enhanced by methods derived from semiotics, a critical approach for investigating the creation of meaning not only in written languages but also in other, nonverbal codes, such as the visual and auditory languages of film and TV.

Semiotics analyzes how linguistic and nonlinguistic cultural "signs" form systems of meanings, as when giving someone a rose is interpreted as a sign of love, or getting an A on a college paper is a sign of mastery of the rules of the specific assignment. Semiotic analysis can be connected with genre criticism (the study of conventions governing established types of cultural forms, such as soap operas) to reveal how the codes and forms of particular genres follow certain meanings. Situation comedies, for instance, classically follow a conflict/resolution model that demonstrates how to solve certain social problems by correct actions and values, and thus provide morality tales of proper and improper behavior. Soap operas, by contrast, proliferate problems and provide messages concerning the endurance and suffering needed to get through life's endless miseries, while generating positive and negative models of social behavior. And advertising shows how commodity solutions solve problems of popularity, acceptance, success, and the like.

A semiotic and genre analysis of the film *Rambo* (1982) for instance, would show how it follows the conventions of the Hollywood genre of the war film that dramatizes conflicts between the United States and its "enemies" (see Kellner, 1995). Semiotics describes how the images of the villains are constructed according to the codes of World War II movies and how the resolution of the conflict and happy ending follows the traditional Hollywood classical cinema, which portrays the victory of good over evil. Semiotic analysis would also include study of the strictly cinematic and formal elements of a film like *Rambo*, dissecting the ways that camera angles present Rambo as a god, or slow-motion images of him gliding through the jungle code him as a force of nature. Semiotic analysis of the 2001 film *Vanilla Sky* could engage how Cameron Crowe's film presents a remake of a 1997 Spanish film, and how the use of celebrity stars Tom Cruise and Penelope Cruz, involved in a real-life romance, provides a spectacle of modern icons of beauty, desire, sexuality, and power. The science fiction theme and images present semiotic depictions of a future in which techno-science can make everyone beautiful and we can live out our culture's dreams and nightmares.

The textual analysis of cultural studies thus combines formalist analysis with critique of how cultural meanings convey specific ideologies of gender, race, class, sexuality, nation, and other ideological dimensions. Ideological textual analysis should deploy a wide range of methods to fully explicate each dimension and to show how they fit into textual systems. Each critical method focuses on certain features of a text from a specific perspective: The perspective spotlights some features of a text while ignoring others. Marxist methods tend to focus on class, for instance, while feminist approaches will highlight gender, critical race theory spotlights race and ethnicity, and gay and lesbian theories explicate sexuality.

More sophisticated critical Marxism, feminisms, or semiotics articulate their own method with the other approaches to develop multiperspectivist positions. Yet each critical method on its own has its particular strengths and limitations, with specific optics and blindspots. Traditionally, Marxian ideology critiques have been strong on class and historical contextualization and weak on formal analysis, while some versions are highly "reductionist," reducing textual analysis to denunciation of ruling class ideology. Feminism excels in gender analysis and in some versions is formally sophisticated, drawing on such methods as psychoanalysis and semiotics, although some versions are reductive and early feminism often limited itself to analysis of images of gender. Psychoanalysis in turn calls for the interpretation of unconscious contents and meaning, which can articulate latent meanings in a text, as when Alfred Hitchcock's dream sequences in films like *Spellbound* (1945) or *Vertigo* (1958) project cinematic symbols that illuminate his characters' dilemmas, or when the image of the female character in *Bonnie and Clyde* (1967) framed against the bars of her bed suggests her sexual frustration, imprisonment in lower-middle-class family life, and need for revolt.

Of course, each reading of a text is only one possible reading from one critic's subject position, no matter how multiperspectival, and may or may not be the reading preferred by audiences (which themselves will be significantly different according to their class, race, gender, ethnicity, ideologies and so on). Because there is a split between textual encoding and audience decoding, there is always the possibility of a multiplicity of readings of any text of media culture (Hall, 1980b). There are limits to the openness or polysemic nature of any text, of course, and textual analysis can explicate the parameters of possible readings and delineate perspectives that aim at illuminating the text and its cultural and ideological effects. Such analysis also provides the materials for criticizing misreadings, or readings that are one-sided and incomplete. Yet to further carry through a cultural studies analysis, one must also examine how diverse audiences actually read media texts, and attempt to determine what effects they have on audience thought and behavior.

Audience Reception and Use of Media Culture

All texts are subject to multiple readings depending on the perspectives and subject positions of the reader. Members of distinct genders, classes, races, nations, regions, sexual preferences, and political ideologies are going to read texts differently, and cultural studies can illuminate why diverse audiences interpret texts in various, sometimes conflicting, ways. It is indeed one of the merits of cultural studies to have focused on audience reception in recent years and this focus provides one of its major contributions, though there are also some limitations and problems with the standard cultural studies approaches to the audience.[5]

A standard way to discover how audiences read texts is to engage in ethnographic research, in an attempt to determine how texts affect audiences and shape their beliefs and behavior. Ethnographic cultural studies have indicated some of the various ways that audiences use and appropriate texts, often to empower themselves. Radway's (1983) study of women's use of Harlequin novels, for example, shows how these books provide escapism for women and could be understood as reproducing traditional women's roles, behavior, and attitudes. Yet they can also empower women by promoting fantasies of a different life and may thus inspire revolt against male domination. Or they may enforce, in other audiences, female submission to male domination and trap women in ideologies of romance, in which submission to Prince Charming is seen as the alpha and omega of happiness for women.

Media culture provides materials for individuals to create identities and meanings and cultural studies detects specific ways that individuals use cultural forms. Teenagers use video games and music television as an escape from the demands of a disciplinary society. Males use sports as a terrain of fantasy identification, in which they feel empowered as "their" team or star triumphs. Such sports events also generate a form of community, currently being lost in the privatized media and consumer culture of our time. Indeed, fandoms of all sorts, ranging from *Star Trek* fans ("Trekkies") to devotees of *Buffy the Vampire Slayer*, or various soap operas, also form communities that enable people to relate to others who share their interests and hobbies. Some fans, in fact, actively recreate their favorite cultural forms, such as rewriting the scripts of preferred shows, sometimes in the forms of "slash," which redefine characters' sexuality, or in the forms of music poaching or remaking such as "filking" (see examples in Lewis, 1992, and Jenkins, 1992).

This emphasis on audience reception and appropriation helps cultural studies overcome the previous one-sided textualist orientations to culture. It also directs focus on the actual political effects that texts have and how audiences use texts. In fact, sometimes audiences subvert the intentions of the producers or managers of the cultural industries that supply them, as when astute young media users laugh at obvious attempts to hype certain characters, shows, or products (see de Certeau, 1984, for more examples of audiences constructing meaning and engaging in practices in critical and subversive ways). Audience research can reveal how people are actually using cultural texts and what sort of effects they are having on everyday life.

Yet there are several problems that I see with reception studies as they have been constituted within cultural studies, particularly in the United States. First, there is a danger that class will be downplayed as a significant variable that structures audience decoding and use of cultural texts. Cultural studies in England were particularly sensitive to class differences—as well as subcultural differences—in the use and reception of cultural texts, but I have noted many dissertations, books, and articles in cultural studies in the United States where attention to class has been downplayed or is missing altogether. This is not surprising as a neglect of class as a constitutive feature of culture and society is an endemic deficiency in the American academy in most disciplines.

There is also the reverse danger, however, of exaggerating the constitutive force of class, and downplaying, or ignoring, such other variables as gender or ethnicity. Staiger (1992) notes that Fiske (1989a, 1989b), building on Hartley, lists seven "subjectivity positions" that are important in cultural reception, "self, gender, age-group, family, class, nation, ethnicity," and proposes adding sexual orientation. All of these factors, and no doubt more, interact in shaping how audiences receive and use texts and must be taken into account in studying cultural reception, for audiences decode and use texts according to the specific constituents of their class, race or ethnicity, gender, sexual preferences, and so on.

Furthermore, I would warn against a tendency to romanticize the "active audience," by claiming that all audiences produce their own meanings and denying that media culture may have powerful manipulative effects. Some individuals who do cultural studies (tradition of) reception research distinguish between dominant and oppositional readings (Hall, 1980b), a dichotomy that structures much of Fiske's work. "Dominant" readings are those in which audiences appropriate texts in line with the interests of the hegemonic culture and the ideological intentions of a text, as when audiences feel pleasure in the restoration of male power, law and order, and social stability at the end of a film like *Die Hard*, after the hero and representatives of authority eliminate the terrorists who had taken over a high-rise corporate headquarters. An "oppositional" reading, by contrast, celebrates the resistance to this reading in audience appropriation of a text; for example, Fiske (1993) observes resistance to dominant readings when homeless individuals in a shelter cheered the destruction of police and authority figures, during repeated viewings of a videotape of *Die Hard*.

Although this can be a useful distinction, there is a tendency in cultural studies to celebrate resistance per se without distinguishing between types and forms of resistance (a similar problem resides with indiscriminate celebration or audience pleasure in certain reception studies). For example, resistance to social authority by the homeless evidenced in their viewing of *Die Hard* could serve to strengthen brutal masculist behavior and encourage manifestations of physical violence to solve social problems. Jean-Paul Sartre, Frantz Fanon, and Herbert Marcuse, among others, have argued that violence can be either emancipatory, when directed at forces of oppression, or reactionary, when directed at popular forces struggling against oppression. Many feminists, by contrast, or those in the Gandhian tradition, see all violence as forms of brute masculist behavior and many people see it as a problematical form of conflict resolution. Resistance and pleasure cannot therefore be valorized per se as progressive elements of the appropriation of cultural texts, but difficult discriminations must be made as to whether the resistance, oppositional reading, or pleasure in a given experience is progressive or reactionary, emancipatory or destructive.

Thus, while emphasis on the audience and reception was an excellent correction to the one-sidedness of purely textual analysis, I believe that in recent years cultural studies has overemphasized reception and textual analysis, while underemphasizing the production of culture and its political economy. This type of cultural studies fetishizes audience reception studies and neglects both production and textual analysis, thus producing populist celebrations of the text and audience pleasure in its use of cultural artifacts. This approach, taken to an extreme, would lose its critical perspective and would lead to a positive gloss on audience experience of whatever is being studied. Such studies also might lose sight of the manipulative and conservative effects of certain types of media culture and thus serve the interests of the cultural industries as they are presently constituted.

A new way, in fact, to research media effects is to use the databases that collect media texts such as Nexis/Lexis, or search engines like Google, and to trace the effects of media artifacts like *The X-Files*, *Buffy the Vampire Slayer*, or advertising corporations like Nike and McDonald's, through analysis of references to them in the media. Likewise, there is a new terrain of Internet audience research that studies how fans act in chat rooms devoted to their favorite artifacts of media culture, create their own fan-sites, or construct artifacts that disclose how they are living out the fantasies and scripts of the culture industries. Previous studies of the audience and the reception of media privileged ethnographic studies that selected slices of the vast media audiences, usually from the site where researchers themselves lived. Such studies are invariably limited and broader effects research can indicate how the most popular artifacts of media culture have a wide range of effects. In my book *Media Culture* (1995), I studied some examples of popular cultural artifacts that clearly influenced behavior in audiences throughout the globe. Examples include groups of kids and adults who imitated Rambo in various forms of asocial behavior, or fans of *Beavis and Butt-Head* who started fires or tortured animals in the modes practiced by the popular MTV cartoon characters. Media effects are complex and controversial and it is the merit of cultural studies to make their study an important part of its agenda.

Toward a Cultural Studies Approach That Is Critical, Multicultural, and Multiperspectival

To avoid the one-sidedness of textual analysis approaches, or audience and reception studies, I propose that cultural studies itself be multiperspectival, getting at culture from the perspectives of political economy, text analysis, and audience reception, as outlined above. Textual analysis should utilize a multiplicity of perspectives and critical methods, and audience reception studies should delineate the wide range of subject positions, or perspectives, through which audiences appropriate culture. This requires a multicultural approach that sees the importance of analyzing the dimensions of class, race and ethnicity, and gender and sexual preference within the texts of media culture, while studying as well their impact on how audiences read and interpret media culture.

In addition, a critical cultural studies attacks sexism, racism, or bias against specific social groups (i.e., gays, intellectuals, and so on), and criticizes texts that promote any kind of domination or oppression. As an example of how considerations of production, textual analysis and audience readings can fruitfully intersect in cultural studies, let us reflect on the Madonna phenomenon. Madonna first appeared in the moment of Reaganism and embodied the materialistic and consumer-oriented ethos of the 1980s ("Material Girl"). She also appeared in a time of dramatic image proliferation, associated with MTV, fashion fever, and intense marketing of products. Madonna was one of the first MTV music video superstars who consciously crafted images to attract a mass audience. Her early music videos were aimed at teenage girls (the Madonna wanna-be's), but she soon incorporated black, Hispanic, and minority audiences with her images of interracial sex and multicultural "family" in her concerts. Madonna also appealed to gay and lesbian audiences, as well as to feminist and academic audiences, as her videos became more complex and political (i.e., "Like a Prayer," "Express Yourself," "Vogue," and so on).

Thus, Madonna's popularity was in large part a function of her marketing strategies and her production of music videos and images that appealed to diverse audiences. To conceptualize the meanings and effects in her music, films, concerts, and public relations stunts requires that her artifacts be interpreted within the context of their production and reception, which involves discussion of MTV, the music industry, concerts, marketing, and the production of images (see Kellner, 1995). Understanding Madonna's popularity also requires focus on audiences, not just as individuals but as members of specific groups, such as teenage girls, who were empowered in their struggles for individual identity by Madonna, or gays, who were also empowered by her incorporation of alternative images of sexuality within popular mainstream cultural artifacts. Yet appraising the politics and effects of Madonna also requires analysis of how her work might merely reproduce a consumer culture that defines identity in terms of images and consumption. It would make an interesting project to examine how former Madonna fans view the evolution and recent incarnations of the superstar, such as her second marriage and 2001 Drowned World tour, as well as to examine how contemporary fans view Madonna in an age that embraces younger teen pop singers like Britney Spears or Mariah Carey.

In short, a cultural studies that is critical and multicultural provides comprehensive approaches to culture that can be applied to a wide variety of artifacts from pornography to Madonna, from MTV to TV news, or to specific events like the 2000 U.S. presidential election (Kellner, 2001), or media representations of the 2001 terrorist attacks on the United States and the U.S. response. Its comprehensive perspectives encompass political economy, textual analysis, and audience research and provide critical and political perspectives that enable individuals to dissect the meanings, messages, and effects of dominant cultural forms. Cultural studies is thus part of a critical media pedagogy that enables individuals to resist media manipulation and to increase their freedom and individuality. It can empower people to gain sovereignty over their culture and to be able to struggle for alternative cultures and political change. Cultural studies is thus not just another academic fad, but can be part of a struggle for a better society and a better life.

Notes

1. For more information on British cultural studies, see Hall (1980b), Hall et al. (1980), Johnson (1986/1987), Fiske (1986), O'Conner (1989), Turner (1990), Grossberg (1989), Agger (1992), and the articles collected in Grossberg, Nelson, and Triechler (1992), During (1992, 1998), and Durham and Kellner (2000). I might note that the Frankfurt school also provided much material for a critical cultural studies in their works on mass culture from the 1930s through the present; on the relation between the Frankfurt school and British cultural studies, see Kellner (1997).

2. On the concept of ideology, see Kellner (1978, 1979), Centre for Contemporary Cultural Studies (1980), Kellner and Ryan (1988), and Thompson (1990).

3. This model was adumbrated in Hall (1980a) and Johnson (1986/1987) and guided much of the early Birmingham work. Around the mid-1980s, however, the Birmingham group began to increasingly neglect the production and political economy of culture (some believe that this was always a problem with their work) and much of their studies became more academic, cut off from political struggle. I am thus trying to recapture the spirit of the early Birmingham project, reconstructed for our contemporary moment. For a fuller development of my conception of cultural studies, see Kellner (1992, 1995, 2001).

4. The term *political economy* calls attention to the fact that the production and distribution of culture take place within a specific economic system, constituted by relations between the state and economy. For instance, in the United States a capitalist economy dictates that cultural production is governed by laws of the market, but the democratic imperatives of the system mean that there is some regulation of culture by the state. There are often tensions within a given society concerning how many activities should be governed by the imperatives of the market, or economics, alone and how much state regulation or intervention is desirable, to assure a wider diversity of broadcast programming, for instance, or the prohibition of phenomena agreed to be harmful, such as cigarette advertising or pornography (see Kellner, 1990).

5. Cultural studies that have focused on audience reception include Brunsdon and Morley (1978), Radway (1983), Ang (1985, 1996), Morley (1986), Fiske (1989a, 1989b), Jenkins (1992), and Lewis (1992).

References

Agger, B. (1992). *Cultural studies*. London: Falmer.

Ang, I. (1985). *Watching* Dallas. New York: Methuen.

Ang, I. (1996). *Living room wars: Rethinking media audiences for a postmodern world*. London and New York: Routledge.

Brunsdon, C., & Morley, D. (1978). *Everyday television: "Nationwide."* London: British Film Institute.

Centre for Contemporary Cultural Studies. (1980). *On ideology*. London; Hutchinson.

de Certeau, M. (1984). *The practice of everyday life*. Berkeley: University of California Press.

Durham, M. G., & Kellner, D. (Eds.). (2001). *Media and cultural studies: Keyworks.* Malden, MA, and Oxford, UK: Basil Blackwell.

During, S. (1992). *Cultural studies.* London and New York: Routledge.

During, S. (1998). *Cultural studies.* (2nd ed.). London and New York: Routledge.

Fiske, J. (1986). British cultural studies and television. In R. C. Allen (Ed.), *Channels of discourse* (pp. 254–289). Chapel Hill: University of North Carolina Press.

Fiske, J. (1987). *Television culture.* New York and London: Routledge.

Fiske, J. (1989a). *Reading the popular.* Boston: Unwin Hyman.

Fiske, J. (1989b). *Understanding popular culture.* Boston: Unwin Hyman.

Fiske, J. (1993). *Power plays, power works.* London: Verso.

Gramsci, A. (1971). *Selections from the prison notebooks.* New York; International.

Grossberg, L. (1989). The formations of cultural studies: An American in Birmingham. *Strategies, 22,* 114–149.

Grossberg, L., Nelson, C., & Treichler, P. (1992). *Cultural studies.* New York: Routledge.

Hall, S. (1980a). Cultural studies and the Centre: Some problematics and problems. In S. Hall et al., *Culture, media, language* (pp. 15–47). London: Hutchinson.

Hall, S. (1980b). Encoding/decoding. In S. Hall et al., *Culture, media, language* (pp. 128–138). London: Hutchinson.

Hall, S. et al. (1980). *Culture, media, language.* London: Hutchinson.

Jenkins, H. (1992). *Textual poachers.* New York: Routledge.

Johnson, R. (1986/1987). What is cultural studies anyway? *Social Text, 16,* 38–80.

Kellner, D. (1978, November-December). Ideology, Marxism, and advanced capitalism. *Socialist Review, 42,* 37–65.

Kellner, D. (1979, May-June). TV, ideology, and emancipatory popular culture. *Socialist Review, 45,* 13–53.

Kellner, D. (1990). *Television and the crisis of democracy.* Boulder, CO: Westview.

Kellner, D. (1992). *The Persian Gulf TV war.* Boulder, CO: Westview.

Kellner, D. (1995). *Media culture. Cultural studies, identity, and politics between the modern and the postmodern.* London and New York: Routledge.

Kellner, D. (1997). Critical theory and British cultural studies: The missed articulation. In J. McGuigan (Ed.), *Cultural methodologies* (pp. 12–41). London: Sage.

Kellner, D. (2001). *Grand theft 2000.* Lanham, MD: Rowman & Littlefield.

Kellner, D., & Ryan, M. (1988). *Camera politica: The politics and ideology of contemporary Hollywood film.* Bloomington: Indiana University Press.

Lewis, L. A. (1992). *Adoring audience: Fan culture and popular media.* New York: Routledge.

McChesney, R. (2000). *Rich media, poor democracy: Communications politics in dubious times.* New York: New Press.

Morley, D. (1986). *Family television.* London: Comedia.

O'Connor, A. (1989, December), The problem of American cultural studies. *Critical Studies in Mass Communication,* pp. 405–413.

Radway, J. (1983). *Reading the romance.* Chapel Hill: University of North Carolina Press.

Staiger, J. (1992). Film, reception, and cultural studies. *Centennial Review, 26*(1), 89–104.

Thompson, J. (1990). *Ideology and modern culture.* Cambridge, UK, and Stanford, CA: Polity Press and Stanford University Press.

Turner, G. (1990). *British cultural studies: An introduction.* New York: Unwin Hyman.

2 | *Representation, Meaning, and Language*

Stuart Hall

In this chapter we will be concentrating on one of the key processes in the 'cultural circuit'—the practices of *representation*. The aim of this chapter is to introduce you to this topic, and to explain what it is about and why we give it such importance in cultural studies.

The concept of representation has come to occupy a new and important place in the study of culture. Representation connects meaning and language to culture. But what exactly do people mean by it? What does representation have to do with culture and meaning? One common-sense usage of the term is as follows: 'Representation means using language to say something meaningful about, or to represent, the world meaningfully, to other people.' You may well ask, 'Is that all?' Well, yes and no. Representation is an essential part of the process by which meaning is produced and exchanged between members of a culture. It does involve the use of language, of signs and images which stand for or represent things. But this is a far from simple or straightforward process, as you will soon discover.

How does the concept of representation connect meaning and language to culture? In order to explore this connection further, we will look at a number of different theories about how language is used to represent the world. Here we will be drawing a distinction between three different accounts or theories: the *reflective*, the *intentional* and the *constructionist* approaches to representation. Does language simply reflect a meaning which already exists out there in the world of objects, people and events *(reflective)*? Does language express only what the speaker or writer or painter wants to say, his or her personally intended meaning *(intentional)*? Or is meaning constructed in and through language *(constructionist)*? You will learn more in a moment about these three approaches.

Most of the chapter will be spent exploring the *constructionist* approach, because it is this perspective which has had the most significant impact on cultural studies in recent years. This chapter chooses to examine two major variants or models of the constructionist approach—the *semiotic* approach, greatly influenced by the great

Reprinted from *Representation: Cultural Representations and Signifying Practices* (1997), by permission of Sage Publications.

Swiss linguist, Ferdinand de Saussure, and the *discursive* approach, associated with the French philosopher and historian, Michel Foucault. Now, we turn to the principle of representation.

Making Meaning, Representing Things

What does the word **representation** really mean, in this context? What does the process of representation involve? How does representation work?

To put it briefly representation is the production of meaning through language. *The Shorter Oxford English Dictionary* suggests two relevant meanings for the word:

1. To represent something is to describe or depict it, to call it up in the mind by description or portrayal or imagination, to place a likeness of it before us in our mind or in the senses; as for example, in the sentence, 'This picture represents the murder of Abel by Cain.'

2. To represent also means to symbolize, stand for, to be a specimen of, or to substitute for; as in the sentence, 'In Christianity, the cross represents the suffering and crucifixion of Christ.'

The figures in the painting *stand in the place of,* and at the same time, *stand for* the story of Cain and Abel. Likewise, the cross simply consists of two wooden planks nailed together; but in the context of Christian belief and teaching, it takes on, symbolizes or comes to stand for a wider set of meanings about the crucifixion of the Son of God, and this is a concept we can put into words and pictures.

Activity I

Here is a simple exercise about representation. Look at any familiar object in the room. You will immediately recognize what it is. But how do you *know* what the object is? What does 'recognize' mean?

Now try to make yourself conscious of what you are doing—observe what is going on as you do it. You recognize what it is because your thought-processes decode your visual perception of the object in terms of a concept of it which you have in your head. This must be so because, if you look away from the object, you can still *think* about it by conjuring it up, as we say, 'in your mind's eye'. Go on—try to follow the process as it happens: There is the object . . . and there is the concept in your head which tells you what it is, what your visual image of it *means*.

Now, tell me what it is. Say it aloud: 'It's a lamp'—or a table or a book or the phone or whatever. The concept of the object has passed through your mental representation of it to me *via* the word for it which you have just used. The word stands for or represents the concept, and can be used to reference or designate either a 'real' object in the world or indeed even some imaginary object, like angels dancing on the head of a pin, which no one has ever actually seen.

This is how you give meaning to things through language. This is how you 'make sense of' the world of people, objects and events, and how you are able to express a complex thought about those things to other people, or communicate about them through language in ways which other people are able to understand.

Why do we have to go through this complex process to represent our thoughts? If you put down a glass you are holding and walk out of the room, you can still *think* about the glass, even though it is no longer physically there. Actually, you can't think with a glass. You can only think with *the concept of the* glass. As the linguists are fond of saying, 'Dogs bark. But the concept of "dog" cannot bark or bite.' You can't speak with the actual glass, either. You can only speak with the *word* for glass—GLASS—which is the linguistic sign which we use in English to refer to objects which you drink water out of. This is where *representation* comes in. Representation is the production of the meaning of the concepts in our minds through language. It is the link between concepts and language which enables us to *refer to* either the 'real' world of objects, people or events, or indeed to imaginary worlds of fictional objects, people and events.

So there are *two* processes, two **systems of representation** involved. First, there is the 'system' by which all sorts of objects, people and events are correlated with a set of concepts or *mental representations* which we carry around in our heads. Without them, we could not interpret the world meaningfully at all. In the first place, then, meaning depends on the system of concepts and images formed in our thoughts which can stand for or 'represent' the world, enabling us to refer to things both inside and outside our heads.

Before we move on to look at the second 'system of representation', we should observe that what we have just said is a very simple version of a rather complex process. It is simple enough to see how we might form concepts for things we can perceive—people or material objects, like chairs, tables and desks. But we also form concepts of rather obscure and abstract things, which we can't in any simple way see, feel or touch. Think, for example, of our concepts of war, or death, or friendship or love. And, as we have remarked, we also form concepts about things we never have seen, and possibly can't or won't ever see, and about people and places we have plainly made up. We may have a clear concept of, say, angels, mermaids, God, the Devil, or of Heaven and Hell, or of Middlemarch (the fictional provincial town in George Eliot's novel), or Elizabeth (the heroine of Jane Austen's *Pride and Prejudice).*

We have called this a *'system* of representation'. That is because it consists, not of individual concepts, but of different ways of organizing, clustering, arranging and classifying concepts, and of establishing complex relations between them. For example, we use the principles of similarity and difference to establish relationships between concepts or to distinguish them from one another. Thus I have an idea that in some respects birds are like planes in the sky, based on the fact that they are similar because they both fly—but I also have an idea that in other respects they are different, because one is part of nature whilst the other is man-made. The mixing and matching of relations between concepts to form complex ideas and thoughts is possible because our concepts are arranged into different classifying systems. In this example, the first is based on a distinction between flying/not flying and the second is based on the distinction between natural/man-made. There are other principles of organization like this at work in all conceptual systems: for example, classifying according to sequence—which concept follows which—or causality—what causes what—and so on. The point here is that we are talking about, not just a random collection of concepts, but concepts organized, arranged and classified into complex relations with one another. That is what our conceptual system actually is like. However, this does not undermine the basic point. Meaning depends on the relationship between things in the world—people, objects and events, real or fictional—and the conceptual system, which can operate as *mental representations* of them.

Now it could be the case that the conceptual map which I carry around in my head is totally different from yours, in which case you and I would interpret or make sense of the world in totally different ways. We would be incapable of sharing our thoughts or expressing ideas about the world to each other. In fact, each of us probably does understand and interpret the world in a unique and individual way. However, we are able to communicate because we share broadly the same conceptual maps and thus make sense of or interpret the world in roughly similar ways. That is indeed what it means when we say we 'belong to the same culture'. Because we interpret the world in roughly similar ways, we are able to build up a shared culture of meanings and thus construct a social world which we inhabit together. That is why 'culture' is sometimes defined in terms of 'shared meanings or shared conceptual maps' (see du Gay, Hall et al., 1997).

However, a shared conceptual map is not enough. We must also be able to represent or exchange meanings and concepts, and we can only do that when we also have access to a shared language. Language is therefore the second system of representation involved in the overall process of constructing meaning. Our shared conceptual map must be translated into a common language, so that we can correlate our concepts and ideas with certain written words, spoken sounds or visual images. The general term we use for words, sounds or images which carry meaning is *signs*. These signs stand for or represent the concepts and the conceptual relations between them which we carry around in our heads and together they make up the meaning-systems of our culture.

Signs are organized into languages and it is the existence of common languages which enable us to translate our thoughts (concepts) into words, sounds or images, and then to use these, operating as a language, to express meanings and communicate thoughts to other people. Remember that term 'language' is being used here in a very broad and inclusive way. The writing system or the spoken system of a particular language are both obviously 'languages'. But so are visual images, whether produced by hand, mechanical, electronic, digital or some other means, when they are used to express meaning. And so are other things which aren't 'linguistic' in any ordinary sense: the 'language' of facial expressions or of gesture, for example, or the 'language' of fashion, of clothes, or of traffic lights. Even music is a 'language', with complex relations between different sounds and chords, though it is a very special case since it can't easily be used to reference actual things or objects in the world (a point further elaborated in du Gay, ed., 1997, and Mackay, ed., 1997). Any sound, word, image or object which functions as a sign, and is organized with other signs into a system which is capable of carrying and expressing meaning is, from this point of view, 'a language'. It is in this sense that the model of meaning which I have been analysing here is often described as a 'linguistic' one; and that all the theories of meaning which follow this basic model are described as belonging to 'the linguistic turn' in the social sciences and cultural studies.

At the heart of the meaning process in culture, then, are two related 'systems of representation'. The first enables us to give meaning to the world by constructing a set of correspondences or a chain of equivalences between things—people, objects, events, abstract ideas, etc.—and our system of concepts, our conceptual maps. The second depends on constructing a set of correspondences between our conceptual map and a set of signs, arranged or organized into various languages which stand for or represent those concepts. The relation between 'things', concepts and signs lies at the heart of the production of meaning in language. The process which links these three elements together is what we call 'representation'.

Language and Representation

Just as people who belong to the same culture must share a broadly similar conceptual map, so they must also share the same way of interpreting the signs of a language, for only in this way can meanings be effectively exchanged between people. But how do we know which concept stands for which thing? Or which word effectively represents which concept? How do I know which sounds or images will carry, through language, the meaning of my concepts and what I want to say with them to you? This may seem relatively simple in the case of visual signs, because the drawing, painting, camera or TV image of a sheep bears a resemblance to the animal with a woolly coat grazing in a field to which I want to refer. Even so, we need to remind ourselves that a drawn or painted or digital version of a sheep is not exactly like a 'real' sheep. For one thing, most images are in two dimensions whereas the 'real' sheep exists in three dimensions.

Visual signs and images, even when they bear a close resemblance to the things to which they refer, are still signs: they carry meaning and thus have to be interpreted. In order to interpret them, we must have access to the two systems of representation discussed earlier: to a conceptual map which correlates the sheep in the field with the concept of a 'sheep'; and a language system which in visual language, bears some resemblance to the real thing or 'looks like it' in some way. This argument is clearest if we think of a cartoon drawing or an abstract painting of a 'sheep', where we need a very sophisticated conceptual and shared linguistic system to be certain that we are all 'reading' the sign in the same way. Even then we may find ourselves wondering whether it really is a picture of a sheep at all. As the relationship between the sign and its referent becomes less clear-cut, the meaning begins to slip and slide away from us into uncertainty. Meaning is no longer transparently passing from one person to another. . . .

So, even in the case of visual language, where the relationship between the concept and the sign seems fairly straightforward, the matter is far from simple. It is even more difficult with written or spoken language, where words don't look or sound anything like the things to which they refer. In part, this is because there are different kinds of signs. Visual signs are what are called *iconic* signs. That is, they bear, in their form, a certain resemblance to the object, person or event to which they refer. A photograph of a tree reproduces some of the actual conditions of our visual perception in the visual sign. Written or spoken signs, on the other hand, are what is called *indexical*.

They bear no obvious relationship at all to the things to which they refer. The letters T,R,E,E, do not look anything like trees in Nature, nor does the word 'tree' in English sound like 'real' trees (if indeed they make any sound at all!). The relationship in these systems of representation between the sign, the concept and the object to which they might be used to refer is entirely *arbitrary*. By 'arbitrary' we mean that in principle any collection of letters or any sound in any order would do the trick equally well. Trees would not mind if we used the word SEERT—'trees' written backwards—to represent the concept of them. This is clear from the fact that, in French, quite different letters and a quite different sound is used to refer to what, to all appearances, is the same thing—a 'real' tree—and, as far as we can tell, to the same concept—a large plant that grows in nature. The French and English seem to be using the same concept. But the concept which in English is represented by the word, TREE, is represented in French by the word, ARBRE.

Sharing the Codes

The question, then, is: how do people who belong to the same culture, who share the same conceptual map and who speak or write the same language (English) know that the arbitrary combination of letters and sounds that makes up the word, TREE, will stand for or represent the concept 'a large plant that grows in nature'? One possibility would be that the objects in the world themselves embody and fix in some way their 'true' meaning. But it is not at all clear that real trees *know* that they are trees, and even less clear that they know that the word in English which represents the concept of themselves is written TREE whereas in French it is written ARBRE! As far as they are concerned, it could just as well be written COW or VAGHE or indeed XYZ. The meaning is *not* in the object or person or thing, nor is it *in* the word. It is we who fix the meaning so firmly that, after a while, it comes to seem natural and inevitable. The meaning is *constructed by the system of representation*. It is constructed and fixed by the *code*, which sets up the correlation between our conceptual system and our language system in such a way that, every time we think of a tree, the code tells us to use the English word TREE, or the French word ARBRE. The code tells us that, in our culture—that is, in our conceptual and language codes—the concept 'tree' is represented by the letters T,R,E,E, arranged in a certain sequence, just as in Morse code, the sign for V (which in World War II Churchill made 'stand for' or represent 'Victory') is Dot, Dot, Dot, Dash, and in the 'language of traffic lights', Green=Go! and Red=Stop!

One way of thinking about 'culture', then, is in terms of these shared conceptual maps, shared language systems and the *codes which govern the relationships of translation between them.* Codes fix the relationships between concepts and signs. They stabilize meaning within different languages and cultures. They tell us which language to use to convey which idea. The reverse is also true. Codes tell us which concepts are being referred to when we hear or read which signs. By arbitrarily fixing the relationships between our conceptual system and our linguistic systems (remember, 'linguistic' in a broad sense), codes make it possible for us to speak and to hear intelligibly, and establish the translatability between our concepts and our languages which enables meaning to pass from speaker to hearer and be effectively communicated within a culture. This translatability is not given by nature or fixed by the gods. It is the result of a set of social conventions. It is fixed socially, fixed in culture. English or French or Hindi speakers have over time, and without conscious decision or choice, come to an unwritten agreement, a sort of unwritten cultural covenant that, in their various languages, certain signs will stand for or represent certain concepts. This is what children learn, and how they become, not simply biological individuals but cultural subjects. They learn the system and conventions of representation, the codes of their language and culture, which equip them with cultural 'know-how' enabling them to function as culturally competent subjects. Not because such knowledge is imprinted in their genes, but because they learn its conventions and so gradually *become* 'cultured persons'—i.e. members of their culture. They unconsciously internalize the codes which allow them to express certain concepts and ideas through their systems of representation—writing, speech, gesture, visualization, and so on—and to interpret ideas which are communicated to them using the same systems.

You may find it easier to understand, now, why meaning, language and representation are such critical elements in the study of culture. To belong to a culture is to belong to roughly the same conceptual and linguistic universe, to know how concepts and ideas translate into different languages, and how language can be interpreted to refer to or *reference* the world. To share these things is to see the world from within the same conceptual map and to make sense of it through the same language systems. Early anthropologists of language, like Sapir and Whorf, took this insight to its logical extreme when they argued that we are all, as it were, locked into our cultural perspectives or 'mind-sets', and that language is the best clue we have to that conceptual universe. This observation, when applied to all human cultures, lies at the root of what, today we may think of as cultural or linguistic *relativism.*

Activity 2

You might like to think further about this question of how different cultures conceptually classify the world and what implications this has for meaning and representation.

The English make a rather simple distinction between sleet and snow. The Inuit (Eskimos) who have to survive in a very different, more extreme and hostile climate, apparently have many more words for snow and snowy weather. Consider the list of Inuit terms for snow from the Scott Polar Research Institute in Table 1. There are many more than in English, making much finer and more complex distinctions. The Inuit have a complex classificatory conceptual system for the weather compared with the English. The novelist Peter Hoeg, for example, writing about Greenland in his novel, *Miss Smilla's Feelings for Snow* (1994, pp. 5–6), graphically describes 'frazzil ice' which is 'kneaded together into a soapy mash called porridge ice, which gradually forms free-floating plates, pancake ice, which one, cold, noonday hour, on a Sunday, freezes into a single solid sheet'. Such distinctions are too fine and elaborate even for the English who are always talking about the weather! The question however, is—do the Inuit actually experience snow differently from the English? Their language system suggests they conceptualize the weather differently. But how far is our experience actually bounded by our linguistic and conceptual universe?

Table 1 Inuit Terms for Snow and Ice

snow		ice	siku
blowing—	piqtuluk	—pan, broken—	siqumniq
is snowstorming	piqtuluktuq	—ice water	immiugaq
falling—	qanik	melts—to make water	immiuqtuaq
—is falling:—is snowing	qaniktuq	candle—	illauyiniq
light falling—	qaniaraq	flat—	qaimiq
light—is falling	qaniaraqtuq	glare—	quasaq
first layer of—in fall	apilraun	piled—	ivunrit
deep soft—	mauya	rough—	iwuit
packed—to make water	aniu	shore—	tugiu
light soft—	aquluraq	shorefast—	uvaq
sugar—	pukak	slush—	quna
waterlogged. mushy—	masak	young—	sikuliaq
—is turning into masak	masaguqtuaq		
watery—	maqayak		
wet—	misak		
wet falling—	qanikkuk		
wet—is falling	qanikkuktuq		
—drifting along a surface	natinivik		
—is drifting along a surface	natiruviktuaq		
—lying on a surface	apun		
snowflake	qanik		
is being drifted over with—	apiyuaq		

One implication of this argument about cultural codes is that, if meaning is the result, not of something fixed out there, in nature, but of our social, cultural and linguistic conventions, then meaning can never be *finally* fixed. We can all 'agree' to allow words to carry somewhat different meanings—as we have for example, with the word 'gay', or the use, by young people, of the word 'wicked!' as a term of approval. Of course, there must be some fixing of meaning in language, or we would never be able to understand one another. We can't get up one morning and suddenly decide to represent the concept of a 'tree' with the letters or the word VYXZ, and expect people to follow what we are saying. On the other hand, there is no absolute or final fixing of meaning. Social and linguistic conventions do change over time. In the language of modern managerialism, what we used to call 'students', 'clients', 'patients' and 'passengers' have all become 'customers'. Linguistic codes vary significantly between one language and another. Many cultures do not have words for concepts which are normal and widely acceptable to us. Words constantly go out of common usage, and new phrases are coined: think, for example, of the use of 'down-sizing' to represent the process of firms laying people off work. Even when the actual words remain stable, their connotations shift or they acquire a different nuance. The problem is especially acute in translation. For example, does the difference in English between *know* and *understand* correspond exactly to and capture exactly the same conceptual distinction as the French make between *savoir* and *connaitre?* Perhaps; but can we be sure?

The main point is that meaning does not inhere *in* things, in the world. It is constructed, produced. It is the result of a signifying practice—a practice that *produces* meaning, that *makes things mean.*

Theories of Representation

There are broadly speaking three approaches to explaining how representation of meaning through language works. We may call these the reflective, the intentional and the constructionist or constructivist approaches. You might think of each as an attempt to answer the questions, 'where do meanings come from?' and 'how can we tell the "true" meaning of a word or image?'

In the **reflective approach**, meaning is thought to lie in the object, person, idea or event in the real world, and language functions like a mirror, to *reflect* the true meaning as it already exists in the world. As the poet Gertrude Stein once said, 'A rose is a rose is a rose'. In the fourth century BC, the Greeks used the notion of *mimesis* to explain how language, even drawing and painting, mirrored or imitated Nature; they thought of Homer's great poem, *The Iliad,* as 'imitating' a heroic series of events. So the theory which says that language works by simply reflecting or imitating the truth that is already there and fixed in the world is sometimes called 'mimetic'.

Of course there is a certain obvious truth to mimetic theories of representation and language. As we've pointed out, visual signs do bear some relationship to the shape and texture of the objects which they represent. But, as was also pointed out earlier, a two-dimensional visual image of a *rose* is a sign—it should not be confused with the real plant with thorns and blooms growing in the garden. Remember also that there are many words, sounds and images which we fully well understand but which are entirely fictional or fantasy and refer to worlds which are wholly imaginary—including, many people now think, most of *The Iliad!* Of course, I can use the word 'rose' to *refer* to real, actual plants growing in a garden as we have said before. But this is because I know the code which links the concept with a particular word or image. I cannot *think* or *speak* or *draw* with an actual rose. And if someone says to me that there is no such word as 'rose' for a plant in her culture, the actual plant in the garden cannot resolve the failure of communication between us. Within the conventions of the different language codes we are using, we are both right—and for us to understand each other, one of us must learn the code linking the flower with the word for it in the other's culture.

The second approach to meaning in representation argues the opposite case. It holds that it is the speaker, the author, who imposes his or her unique meaning on the world through language. Words mean what the author intends they should mean. This is the **intentional approach**. Again, there is some point to this argument since we all, as individuals, do use language to convey or communicate things which are special or unique to us, to our way of seeing the world. However, as a general theory of representation through language, the intentional approach is also flawed. We cannot be the sole or unique source of meanings in language, since that would mean that we could express ourselves in entirely private languages. But the essence of language is communication and that, in turn, depends on shared linguistic conventions and shared codes. Language can never be wholly a private game. Our private intended meanings, however personal to us, have to *enter into the rules, codes and conventions of language* to be shared and understood. Language is a social system through and through. This means that our private thoughts have to negotiate with all the other meanings for words or images which have been stored in language which our use of the language system will inevitably trigger into action.

The third approach recognizes this public, social character of language. It acknowledges that neither things in themselves nor the individual users of language can fix meaning in language. Things don't *mean:* we *construct* meaning, using representational systems—concepts and signs. Hence it is called the constructivist or **constructionist approach** to meaning in language. According to this approach, we must not confuse the *material* world, where things and people exist, and the *symbolic* practices and processes through which representation, meaning and language operate. Constructivists do not deny the existence of the material world. However, it is not the material world which conveys meaning: it is the language system or whatever system we are using to represent our concepts. It is social actors who use the conceptual systems of their culture and the linguistic and other representational systems to construct meaning, to make the world meaningful and to communicate about that world meaningfully to others.

Of course, signs may also have a material dimension. Representational systems consist of the actual *sounds* we make with our vocal chords, the *images* we make on light-sensitive paper with cameras, the *marks* we make with paint on canvas, the digital *impulses* we transmit electronically. Representation is a practice, a kind of 'work', which uses material objects and effects. But the *meaning* depends, not on the material quality of the sign, but on its *symbolic function*. It is because a particular sound or word *stands for, symbolizes or represents a* concept that it can function, in language, as a sign and convey meaning—or, as the constructionists say, signify (sign-i-fy).

The Language of Traffic Lights

The simplest example of this point, which is critical for an understanding of how languages function as representational systems, is the famous traffic lights example. A traffic light is a machine which produces different coloured lights in sequence. The effect of light of different wavelengths on the eye—which is a natural and material phenomenon—produces the sensation of different colours. Now these things certainly do exist in the material world. But it is our culture which breaks the spectrum of light into different colours, distinguishes them from one another and attaches names—Red, Green, Yellow, Blue—to them. We use a way of *classifying* the colour spectrum to create colours which are different from one another. We *represent* or symbolize the different colours and classify them according to different colour-concepts. This is the conceptual colour system of our culture. We say 'our culture' because, of course, other cultures may divide the colour spectrum differently. What's more, they certainly use different actual *words* or *letters* to identify different colours: what we call 'red', the French call 'rouge' and so on. This is the linguistic code—the one which correlates certain words (signs) with certain colours (concepts), and thus enables us to communicate about colours to other people, using 'the language of colours'.

But how do we use this representational or symbolic system to regulate the traffic? Colours do not have any 'true' or fixed meaning in that sense. Red does not mean 'Stop' in nature, any more than Green means 'Go'. In other settings, Red may stand for, symbolize or represent 'Blood' or 'Danger' or 'Communism'; and Green may represent 'Ireland' or 'The Countryside' or 'Environmentalism'. Even these meanings can change. In the 'language of electric plugs', Red used to mean 'the connection with the positive charge' but this was arbitrarily and without explanation changed to Brown! But then for many years the producers of plugs had to attach a slip of paper telling people that the code or convention had changed, otherwise how would they know? Red and Green work in the language of traffic lights because 'Stop' and 'Go' are the meanings which have been assigned to them in our culture by the code or conventions governing this language, and this code is widely known and almost universally obeyed in our culture and cultures like ours—though we can well imagine other cultures which did not possess the code, in which this language would be a complete mystery.

Let us stay with the example for a moment, to explore a little further how, according to the constructionist approach to representation, colours and the 'language of traffic lights' work as a signifying or representational system. Recall the *two* representational systems we spoke of earlier. First, there is the conceptual map of colours in our culture—the way colours are distinguished from one another, classified and arranged in our mental universe. Secondly, there are the ways words or images are correlated with colours in our language—our linguistic colour-codes. Actually, of course, a *language* of colours consists of more than just the individual words for different points on the colour spectrum. It also depends on how they function in relation to one another—the sorts of things which are governed by grammar and syntax in written or spoken languages, which allow us to express rather complex ideas. In the language of traffic lights, it is the sequence and position of the colours, as well as the colours themselves, which enable them to carry meaning and thus function as signs.

Does it matter which colours we use? No, the constructionists argue. This is because what signifies is not the colours themselves but (a) the fact that they are different and can be distinguished from one another; and (b) the fact that they are organized into a particular sequence—Red followed by Green, with sometimes a warning Amber in between which says, in effect, 'Get ready! Lights about to change'. Constructionists put this point in the following way. What signifies, what carries meaning—they argue—is not each colour in itself nor even the concept or word for it. It is *the difference between Red and Green* which signifies. This is a very important principle, in general, about representation and meaning, and we shall return to it on more than one occasion in the chapters which follow. Think about it in these terms. If you couldn't differentiate between Red and Green, you couldn't use one to mean 'Stop' and the other to mean 'Go'. In the same way, it is only the difference between the letters P and T which enable the word SHEEP to be linked, in the English language code, to the concept of 'the animal with four legs and a woolly coat', and the word SHEET to 'the material we use to cover ourselves in bed at night'.

In principle, any combination of colours—like any collection of letters in written language or of sounds in spoken language—would do, provided they are sufficiently different not to be confused. Constructionists express this idea by saying that all signs are 'arbitrary'. 'Arbitrary' means that there is no natural relationship between the sign and its meaning or concept. Since Red only means 'Stop' because that is how the code works, in principle any colour would do, including Green. It is the code that fixes the meaning, not the colour itself. This also has wider implications for the theory of representation and meaning in language. It means that signs themselves cannot fix meaning. Instead, meaning depends on *the relation between* a sign and a concept which is fixed by a code. Meaning, the constructionists would say, is 'relational'.

Activity 3

Why not test this point about the arbitrary nature of the sign and the importance of the code for yourself? Construct a code to govern the movement of traffic using two different colours—Yellow and Blue—as in the following:

When the yellow light is showing, . . .

Now add an instruction allowing pedestrians and cyclists only to cross, using Pink.

Provided the code tells us clearly how to read or interpret each colour, and everyone agrees to interpret them in this way, any colour will do. These are just colours, just as the word SHEEP is just a jumble of letters. In French the same animal is referred to using the very different linguistic sign MOUTON. Signs are arbitrary. Their meanings are fixed by codes.

As we said earlier, traffic lights are machines, and colours are the material effect of light-waves on the retina of the eye. But objects—things—can also function as signs, provided they have been assigned a concept and meaning within our cultural and linguistic codes. As signs, they work symbolically —they represent concepts, and signify. Their effects, however, are felt in the material and social world. Red and Green function in the language of traffic lights as signs, but they have real material and social effects. They regulate the social behaviour of drivers and, without them, there would be many more traffic accidents at road intersections.

Summary

We have come a long way in exploring the nature of representation. It is time to summarize what we have learned about the constructionist approach to representation through language.

Representation is the production of meaning through language. In representation, constructionists argue, we use signs, organized into languages of different kinds, to communicate meaningfully with others. Languages can use signs to symbolize, stand for or reference objects, people and events in the so-called 'real' world. But they can also reference imaginary things and fantasy worlds or abstract ideas which are not in any obvious sense part of our material world. There is no simple relationship of reflection, imitation or one-to-one correspondence between language and the real world. The world is not accurately or otherwise reflected in the mirror of language. Language does not work like a mirror. Meaning is produced within language, in and through various representational systems which, for convenience, we call 'languages'. Meaning is produced by the practice, the 'work', of representation. It is constructed through signifying—i.e. meaning-producing—practices.

How does this take place? In fact, it depends on two different but related systems of representation. First, the concepts which are formed in the mind function as a system of mental representation which classifies and organizes the world into meaningful categories. If we have a concept for something, we can say we know its 'meaning'. But we cannot communicate this meaning without a second system of representation, a language. Language consists of signs organized into various relationships. But signs can only convey meaning if we possess codes which allow us to translate our concepts into language —and vice versa. These codes are crucial for meaning and representation. They do not exist in nature but are the result of social conventions. They are a crucial part of our culture—our shared 'maps of meaning'—which we learn and unconsciously internalize as we become members of our culture. This constructionist approach to language thus introduces the symbolic domain of life, where words and things function as signs, into the very heart of social life itself.

3

Hegemony

James Lull

Hegemony is the power or dominance that one social group holds over others. This can refer to the "asymmetrical interdependence" of political-economic-cultural relations between and among nation-states (Straubhaar, 1991) or differences between and among social classes within a nation. Hegemony is "dominance and subordination in the field of relations structured by power" (Hall, 1985). But hegemony is more than social power itself; it is a method for gaining and maintaining power.

Classical Marxist theory, of course, stresses economic position as the strongest predictor of social differences. Today, more than a century after Karl Marx and Friedrich Engels wrote their treatises about capitalist exploitation of the working class, economic disparities still underlie and help reproduce social inequalities in industrialized societies. In that important, basic sense, Marxism and Marxist critical theory, which have been so badly maligned in the rhetoric surrounding the recent political transformation of communist nations, remain fundamentally on target. Technological developments in the twentieth century, however, have made the manner of social domination much more complex than before. Social class differences in today's world are not determined solely or directly by economic factors. Ideological influence is crucial now in the exercise of social power.

The Italian intellectual Antonio Gramsci—to whom the term hegemony is attributed—broadened materialist Marxist theory into the realm of ideology. Persecuted by his country's then fascist government (and writing from prison), Gramsci emphasized society's "super structure," its ideology-producing institutions, in struggles over meaning and power (1971, 1973, 1978; see also Boggs, 1976; Sassoon, 1980; and Simon, 1982). A shift in critical theory thus was made away from a preoccupation with capitalist society's "base" (its economic foundation) and towards its dominant dispensaries of ideas. Attention was given to the structuring of authority and dependence in symbolic environments that correspond to, but are not the same as, economically determined class-based structures and processes of industrial production. Such a theoretical turn seems a natural and necessary development in an era when communications technology is such a pervasive and potent ideological medium. According to Gramsci's theory of ideological hegemony, mass media are tools that

Reprinted from *Media, Communication, Culture: A Global Approach* (1995), by permission of Columbia University Press.

ruling elites use to "perpetuate their power, wealth, and status [by popularizing] their own philosophy, culture and morality" (Boggs, 1976: 39). The mass media uniquely "introduce elements into individual consciousness that would not otherwise appear there, but will not be rejected by consciousness because they are so commonly shared in the cultural community" (Nordenstreng, 1977: 276). Owners and managers of media industries can produce and reproduce the content, inflections, and tones of ideas favorable to them far more easily than other social groups because they manage key socializing institutions, thereby guaranteeing that their points of view are constantly and attractively cast into the public arena.

Mass-mediated ideologies are corroborated and strengthened by an interlocking system of efficacious information-distributing agencies and taken-for-granted social practices that permeate every aspect of social and cultural reality. Messages supportive of the status quo emanating from schools, businesses, political organizations, trade unions, religious groups, the military, and the mass media all dovetail together ideologically. This inter-articulating, mutually reinforcing process of ideological influence is the essence of hegemony. Society's most entrenched and powerful institutions—which all depend in one way or another on the same sources for economic support—fundamentally agree with each other ideologically.

Hegemony is not a *direct* stimulation of thought or action, but, according to Stuart Hall, is a "framing [of] all competing definitions of reality within [the dominant class's] range, bringing all alternatives within their horizons of thought. [The dominant class] sets the limits—mental and structural—within which subordinate classes 'live' and make sense of their subordination in such a way as to sustain the dominance of those ruling over them" (1977: 333). British social theorist Philip Elliott suggested similarly that the most potent effect of mass media is how they subtly influence their audiences to perceive social roles and routine personal activities. The controlling economic forces in society use the mass media to provide a "rhetoric [through] which these [concepts] are labeled, evaluated, and explained" (1974: 262). Television commercials, for example, encourage audiences to think of themselves as "markets rather than as a public, as consumers rather than citizens" (Gitlin, 1979: 255).

But hegemony does not mature strictly from ideological articulation. Dominant ideological streams must be subsequently reproduced in the activities of our most basic social units—families, workplace networks, and friendship groups in the many sites and undertakings of everyday life. Gramsci's theory of hegemony, therefore, connects ideological representation to culture. Hegemony requires that ideological assertions become self-evident cultural assumptions. Its effectiveness depends on subordinated peoples accepting the dominant ideology as "normal reality or common sense . . . in active forms of experience and consciousness" (Williams, 1976: 145). Because information and entertainment technology is so thoroughly integrated into the everyday realities of modern societies, mass media's social influence is not always recognized, discussed, or criticized, particularly in societies where the overall standard of living is relatively high. Hegemony, therefore, can easily go undetected (Bausinger, 1984).

Hegemony implies a willing agreement by people to be governed by principles, rules, and laws they believe operate in their best interests, even though in actual practice they may not. Social consent can be a more effective means of control than coercion or force. Again, Raymond Williams: "The idea of hegemony, in its wide sense, is . . . especially important in societies [where] electoral politics and public opinion are significant factors, and in which social practice is seen to depend on consent to certain dominant ideas which in fact express the needs of a dominant class" (1976: 145). Thus, in the words of Colombian communication theorist Jesús Martín-Barbero, "one class exercises hegemony to the extent that the dominating class has interests which the subaltern classes recognize as being in some degree their interests too" (1993: 74).

Relationships between and among the major information-diffusing, socializing agencies of a society and the interacting, cumulative, socially accepted ideological orientations they create and sustain is the essence of hegemony. The American television industry, for instance, connects with other large industries, especially advertising companies but also national and multinational corporations that produce, distribute, and market a wide range of commodities. So, for example, commercial TV networks no longer buy original children's television shows. Network executives only want new program ideas associated with successful retail products already marketed to children. By late 1990 more than 20 toy-based TV shows appeared on American commercial TV weekly. Television also has the ability to absorb other major social institutions—organized religion, for instance—and turn them into popular culture. The TV industry also connects with government institutions, including especially the federal agencies that are supposed to regulate telecommunications. The development of American commercial broadcasting is a vivid example of how capitalist economic forces assert their power. Evacuation of the legislatively mandated public service ideal could only have taken place because the Federal Communications Commission stepped aside while commercial interests amassed power and expanded their influence. Symptomatic of the problem is the fact that government regulators typically are recruited from, and return to, the very industries they are supposed to monitor.

Transmedia and transgenre integrations with mutually reinforcing ideological consequences are also commonplace. Popular radio and video songs, for example, can also be commercials. . . . Commercial logos become products themselves and are reproduced on tee-shirts, posters, beach towels, and other informal media. The rhetoric of TV commercials and programs is recycled in the lyrics of rap music and in the routines of stand-up comedians performing live and on television. . . . There are films made for television, magazines published about television, and television news magazines. The most well-known national newspaper in the United States, *USA Today*, is sold nationwide in vending boxes that resemble TV sets. Television commercials appear on Channel One, an educational news channel shown to students in American elementary school classrooms. Logos that advertise only national gasoline, food, and motel chains appear on government highway signs, advising travelers of their availability at upcoming freeway exits. Expensive public relations campaigns of major corporations distribute "informational" supplementary textbooks to elementary and secondary school systems. Major business organizations send digests of their annual reports and other promotional materials to college instructors, hoping this biased information will be incorporated into teaching and research. Similar materials are sent to political and religious leaders so they will pass the information along to their constituencies and congregations.

In the United States, advocacy of alternative political ideologies, parties, and candidates, or suggestions of viable consumer alternatives to the commercial frenzy stimulated and reinforced by advertising and other marketing techniques, are rarely seen on the popular media. Radical ideas typically appear only on underfinanced, non-commercial radio and TV stations and in low-budget print media. These media have tiny public followings compared to commercial television and video outlets, metropolitan daily newspapers, and national magazines. When genuinely divergent views appear on mainstream media, the information is frequently shown in an unfavorable light or is modified and co-opted to surrender to the embrace of mainstream thought. . . . The mass media help create an impression that even society's roughest edges ultimately must conform to the conventional contours of dominant ideologies.

Hegemony has been central to the management of ideology in communist nations too, though it develops differently. Central ideological planning and the creation of propaganda to advise "the people" represent the same intention—to protect the interests of ruling elites. . . .

The collapse of political authority in Eastern and Central Europe and the former Soviet Union was a breakdown in communist ideological hegemony. Conflict between culture producers and young audiences in East Germany and Hungary is typical of what happened in the Soviet bloc (Wicke, 1992; Szemere, 1985). Young rock musicians and their enthusiastic audiences led a cultural and political struggle against the repressive institutions and the ideology behind them. Trying to contain and control rebellious youth, the former communist governments attempted in sinister ways to defuse the politically charged musical and cultural activity of youth by incorporating and sponsoring them. Young people and other dissenters saw through the strategy, however, challenged the hegemony, and stimulated policy changes that later contributed to the dramatic downfall of the European communist governments. In China, the extraordinary student and worker uprising in 1989 is but the most visible sign of wide-spread resistance among that country's disaffected urban population.[1] Recent popular revolutions in communist countries developed from widespread discontent with an interacting spectrum of economic, political, and cultural conditions. Ironically, the workers' uprising that Marx and Engels theorized would take place in repressive, class-based capitalist economies developed instead in communist nations which had proven in many respects to be even more repressive.

Hegemony as an Incomplete Process

Two of our leading critical theorists, Raymond Williams and Stuart Hall, remind us that hegemony in any political context is indeed fragile. It requires renewal and modification through the assertion and reassertion of power. Hall suggests that "it is crucial to the concept that hegemony is not a 'given' and permanent state of affairs, but it has to be actively won and secured; it can also be lost" (1977: 333). Ideological work is the winning and securing of hegemony over time. . . . Ideology is composed of "texts that are not closed" according to Hall, who also notes that ideological "counter-tendencies" regularly appear in the seams and cracks of dominant forms (Hall, 1985). Mediated communications ranging from popular television shows to rap and rock music, even graffiti scrawled over surfaces of public spaces, all inscribe messages that challenge central political positions and cultural assumptions.

Counter-hegemonic tendencies do not inhere solely in texts. They are formulated in processes of communication—in the interpretations, social circulation, and uses of media content. As with the American soldiers' use of military gas masks as inhaling devices to heighten the effect of marijuana smoke, or the homeless's transformation of supermarket shopping carts into personal storage vehicles, ideological resistance and appropriation frequently involve reinventing institutional messages for purposes that differ greatly from their creators' intentions. Expressions of the dominant ideology are sometimes reformulated to assert alternative, often completely resistant or contradictory messages. . . .

Furthermore, resistance to hegemony is not initiated solely by media consumers. Texts themselves are implicated. Ideology can never be stated purely and simply. Ways of thinking are always reflexive and embedded in a complex, sometimes contradictory, ideological regress. . . .

Audience interpretations and uses of media imagery also eat away at hegemony. Hegemony fails when dominant ideology is weaker than social resistance. Gay subcultures, feminist organizations, environmental groups, radical political parties, music-based formations such as punks, B-boys, Rastafarians, and metal heads all use media and their social networks to endorse counter-hegemonic values and lifestyles. Indeed, we have only just begun to examine the complex relationship between ideological representation and social action.

Note

1. It's important to realize that the military suppression of the student-worker uprising in Beijing in 1989 did not stop the Chinese revolutionary movement. It made possible the dramatic and far-reaching (if less visually spectacular) economic and cultural changes that characterize the People's Republic today.

References

Bausinger, H. (1984). Media, technology, and everyday life. *Media, Culture & Society*, 6, 340–52.

Boggs, C. (1976). *Gramsci's Marxism.* London: Pluto.

Elliott, P. (1974). Uses and gratifications research: A critique and a sociological alternative. In J. G. Blumler and E. Katz (eds.), *The Uses of Mass Communications: Current Perspectives on Gratifications Research.* Beverly Hills, CA; Sage.

Gitlin, T. (1979). Prime-time ideology: the hegemonic process in television entertainment. *Social Problems*, 26, 251–66.

Gramsci, A. (1971). *Selections from the Prison Notebooks.* New York: International.

Gramsci, A. (1973). *Letters from Prison.* New York: Harper and Row.

Gramsci, A. (1978). *Selections from Cultural Writings.* Cambridge, MA: Harvard University Press.

Hall, S. (1977). Culture, media, and the "ideological effect." In J. Curran, M. Gurevitch, and J. Woollacott (eds.), *Mass Communication and Society.* London: Edward Arnold.

Hall, S. (1985). Master's session. International Communication Association. Honolulu, Hawaii.

Martin-Barbero, J. (1993). *Communication, Culture and Hegemony.* Newbury Park, CA: Sage.

Nordenstreng, K. (1977). From mass media to mass consciousness. In G. Gerbner (ed.), *Mass Media Policies in Changing Cultures.* New York: Wiley.

Sassoon, A. S. (1980). *Gramsci's Politics.* New York: St. Martin's.

Simon, R. (1982). *Gramsci's Political Thought.* London: Lawrence and Wishart.

Straubhaar, J. (1991). Beyond media imperialism: asymmetrical interdependence and cultural proximity. *Critical Studies in Mass Communication*, 8, 39–59.

Szemere, A. (1985). Pop music in Hungary. *Communication Research*, 12, 401–11.

Wicke, P. (1992). The role of rock music in the political disintegration of East Germany. In J. Lull (ed .), *Popular Music and Communication.* Newbury Park, CA: Sage.

Williams, R. (1976). *Key Words: A Vocabulary of Culture and Society.* New York: Oxford University Press.

4 | Ideology and Ideological State Apparatuses (Notes toward an Investigation)

Louis Althusser

On the Reproduction of the Conditions of Production[1]

I must now expose more fully something which was briefly glimpsed in my analysis when I spoke of the necessity to renew the means of production if production is to be possible. That was a passing hint. Now I shall consider it for itself.

As Marx said, every child knows that a social formation which did not reproduce the conditions of production at the same time as it produced would not last a year.[2] The ultimate condition of production is therefore the reproduction of the conditions of production. This may be "simple" (reproducing exactly the previous conditions of production) or "on an extended scale" (expanding them). Let us ignore this last distinction for the moment.

What, then, is *the reproduction of the conditions of production?*

Here we are entering a domain which is both very familiar (since *Capital* Volume Two) and uniquely ignored. The tenacious obviousnesses (ideological obviousnesses of an empiricist type) of the point of view of production alone, or even of that of mere productive practice (itself abstract in relation to the process of production) are so integrated into our everyday "consciousness" that it is extremely hard, not to say almost impossible, to raise oneself to the *point of view of reproduction.* Nevertheless, everything outside this point of view remains abstract (worse than one-sided: distorted)—even at the level of production, and, *a fortiori,* at that of mere practice.

Let us try and examine the matter methodically.

To simplify my exposition, and assuming that every social formation arises from a dominant mode of production, I can say that the process of production sets to work the existing productive forces in and under definite relations of production.

Reprinted from *Lenin and Philosophy and Other Essays* (1991), by permission of Monthly Review Magazine.

It follows that, in order to exist, every social formation must produce the conditions of its production at the same time as it produces, and in order to be able to produce. It must therefore reproduce:

1. the productive forces,
2. the existing relations of production.

Reproduction of the Means of Production

Everyone (including the bourgeois economists whose work is national accounting, or the modern "macro-economic" "theoreticians") now recognizes, because Marx compellingly proved it in *Capital* Volume Two, that no production is possible which does not allow for the reproduction of the material conditions of production: the reproduction of the means of production.

The average economist, who is no different in this than the average capitalist, knows that each year it is essential to foresee what is needed to replace what has been used up or worn out in production: raw material, fixed installations (buildings), instruments of production (machines), etc. I say the average economist = the average capitalist, for they both express the point of view of the firm, regarding it as sufficient simply to give a commentary on the terms of the firm's financial accounting practice.

But thanks to the genius of Quesnay who first posed this "glaring" problem, and to the genius of Marx who resolved it, we know that the reproduction of the material conditions of production cannot be thought at the level of the firm, because it does not exist at that level in its real conditions. What happens at the level of the firm is an effect, which only gives an idea of the necessity of reproduction, but absolutely fails to allow its conditions and mechanisms to be thought.

A moment's reflection is enough to be convinced of this: Mr. X, a capitalist who produces woollen yarn in his spinning-mill, has to "reproduce" his raw material, his machines, etc. But *he* does not produce them for his own production—other capitalists do: an Australian sheep-farmer, Mr. Y, a heavy engineer producing machine-tools, Mr. Z, etc., etc. And Mr. Y and Mr. Z, in order to produce those products which are the condition of the reproduction of Mr. X's conditions of production, also have to reproduce the conditions of their own production, and so on to infinity—the whole in proportions such that, on the national and even the world market, the demand for means of production (for reproduction) can be satisfied by the supply.

In order to think this mechanism, which leads to a kind of "endless chain," it is necessary to follow Marx's "global" procedure, and to study in particular the relations of the circulation of capital between Department I (production of means of production) and Department II (production of means of consumption), and the realization of surplus-value, in *Capital,* Volumes Two and Three.

We shall not go into the analysis of this question. It is enough to have mentioned the existence of the necessity of the reproduction of the material conditions of production.

Reproduction of Labour Power

However, the reader will not have failed to note one thing. We have discussed the reproduction of the means of production—but not the reproduction of the productive forces. We have therefore ignored the reproduction of what distinguishes the productive forces from the means of production, i.e. the reproduction of labour power.

From the observation of what takes place in the firm, in particular from the examination of the financial accounting practice which predicts amortization and investment, we have been able to obtain an approximate idea of the existence of the material process of reproduction, but we are now entering a domain in which the observation of what happens in the firm is, if not totally blind, at least almost entirely so, and for good reason: the reproduction of labour power takes place essentially outside the firm.

How is the reproduction of labour power ensured?

It is ensured by giving labour power the material means with which to reproduce itself: by wages. Wages feature in the accounting of each enterprise, but as "wage capital,"[3] not at all as a condition of the material reproduction of labour power.

However, that is in fact how it "works," since wages represent only that part of the value produced by the expenditure of labour power which is indispensable for its reproduction: sc. indispensable to the reconstitution of the labour power of the wage-earner (the wherewithal to pay for housing, food and clothing, in short to enable the wage-earner to present himself again at the factory gate the next day—and every further day God grants him); and we should add: indispensable for raising and educating the children in whom the proletarian reproduces himself (in n models where n = 0, 1, 2, etc. . . . .) as labour power.

Remember that this quantity of value (wages) necessary for the reproduction of labour power is determined not by the needs of a "biological" Guaranteed Minimum Wage (*Salaire Minimum Interprofessionnel Garanti*) alone, but by the needs of a historical minimum (Marx noted that English workers need beer while French proletarians need wine)—i.e. a historically variable minimum.

I should also like to point out that this minimum is doubly historical in that it is not defined by the historical needs of the working class "recognized" by the capitalist class, but by the historical needs imposed by the proletarian class struggle (a double class struggle: against the lengthening of the working day and against the reduction of wages).

However, it is not enough to ensure for labour power the material conditions of its reproduction if it is to be reproduced as labour power. I have said that the available labour power must be "competent," i.e. suitable to be set to work in the complex system of the process of production. The development of the productive forces and the type of unity historically constitutive of the productive forces at a given moment produce the result that the labour power has to be (diversely) skilled and therefore reproduced as such. Diversely: according to the requirements of the socio-technical division of labour, its different "jobs" and "posts."

How is this reproduction of the (diversified) skills of labour power provided for in a capitalist regime? Here, unlike social formations characterized by slavery or serfdom, this reproduction of the skills of labour power tends (this is a tendential law) decreasingly to be provided for "on the spot" (apprenticeship within production itself), but is achieved more and more outside production: by the capitalist education system, and by other instances and institutions.

What do children learn at school? They go varying distances in their studies, but at any rate they learn to read, to write and to add—i.e. a number of techniques, and a number of other things as well, including elements (which may be rudimentary or on the contrary thoroughgoing) of "scientific" or "literary culture," which are directly useful in the different jobs in production (one instruction for manual workers, another for technicians, a third for engineers, a final one for higher management, etc.). Thus they learn "know-how."

But besides these techniques and knowledges, and in learning them, children at school also learn the "rules" of good behaviour, i.e. the attitude that should be observed by every agent in the division of labour, according to the job he is "destined" for: rules of morality, civic and professional conscience, which actually means rules of respect for the sociotechnical division of labour and ultimately the rules of the order established by class domination. They also learn to "speak proper French," to "handle" the workers correctly, i.e. actually (for the future capitalists and their servants) to "order them about" properly, i.e. (ideally) to "speak to them" in the right way, etc.

To put this more scientifically, I shall say that the reproduction of labour power requires not only a reproduction of its skills, but also, at the same time, a reproduction of its submission to the rules of the established order, i.e. a reproduction of submission to the ruling ideology for the workers, and a reproduction of the ability to manipulate the ruling ideology correctly for the agents of exploitation and repression, so that they, too, will provide for the domination of the ruling class "in words."

In other words, the school (but also other State institutions like the Church, or other apparatuses like the Army) teaches "know-how," but in forms which ensure *subjection to the ruling ideology* or the mastery of its "practice." All the agents of production, exploitation and repression, not to speak of the "professionals of ideology" (Marx), must in one way or another be "steeped" in this ideology in order to perform their tasks "conscientiously"—the tasks of the exploited (the proletarians), of the exploiters (the capitalists), of the exploiters' auxiliaries (the managers), or of the high priests of the ruling ideology (its "functionaries"), etc.

The reproduction of labour power thus reveals as its *sine qua non* not only the reproduction of its "skills" but also the reproduction of its subjection to the ruling ideology or of the "practice" of that ideology, with the proviso that it is not enough to say "not only but also," for it is clear that *it is in the forms and under the forms of ideological subjection that provision is made for the reproduction of the skills of labour power.*

But this is to recognize the effective presence of a new reality: *ideology.*

Here I shall make two comments.

The first is to round off my analysis of reproduction.

I have just given a rapid survey of the forms of the reproduction of the productive forces, i.e., of the means of production on the one hand, and of labour power on the other.

But I have not yet approached the question of the *reproduction of the relations of production*. This is a *crucial question* for the Marxist theory of the mode of production. To let it pass would be a theoretical omission—worse, a serious political error.

I shall therefore discuss it. But in order to obtain the means to discuss it, I shall have to make another long detour.

The second comment is that in order to make this detour, I am obliged to re-raise my old question: what is a society?

The State

The Marxist tradition is strict, here: in the *Communist Manifesto* and the *Eighteenth Brumaire* (and in all the later classical texts, above all in Marx's writings on the Paris Commune and Lenin's on *State and Revolution*), the State is explicitly conceived as a repressive apparatus. The State is a "machine" of repression, which enables the ruling classes (in the nineteenth century the bourgeois class and the "class" of big landowners) to ensure their domination over the working class, thus enabling the former to subject the latter to the process of surplus-value extortion (i.e. to capitalist exploitation).

The State is thus first of all what the Marxist classics have called *the State apparatus.* This term means: not only the specialized apparatus (in the narrow sense) whose existence and necessity I have recognized in relation to the requirements of legal practice, i.e. the police, the courts, the prisons; but also the army, which (the proletariat has paid for this experience with its blood) intervenes directly as a supplementary repressive force in the last instance, when the police and its specialized auxiliary corps are "outrun by events"; and above this ensemble, the head of State, the government and the administration.

Presented in this form, the Marxist-Leninist "theory" of the State has its finger on the essential point, and not for one moment can there be any question of rejecting the fact that this really is the essential point. The State apparatus, which defines the State as a force of repressive execution and intervention "in the interests of the ruling classes" in the class struggle conducted by the bourgeoisie and its allies against the proletariat, is quite certainly the State, and quite certainly defines its basic "function."

The State Ideological Apparatuses

Thus, what has to be added to the "Marxist theory" of the State is something else.

Here we must advance cautiously in a terrain which, in fact, the Marxist classics entered long before us, but without having systematized in theoretical form the decisive advances implied by their experiences and procedures. Their experiences and procedures were indeed restricted in the main to the terrain of political practice.

In fact, i.e., in their political practice, the Marxist classics treated the State as a more complex reality than the definition of it given in the "Marxist theory of the State," even when it has been supplemented as I have just suggested. They recognized this complexity in their practice, but they did not express it in a corresponding theory.[4]

I should like to attempt a very schematic outline of this corresponding theory. To that end, I propose the following thesis.

In order to advance the theory of the State it is indispensable to take into account not only the distinction between *State power* and *State apparatus*, but also another reality which is clearly on the side of the (repressive) State apparatus, but must not be confused with it. I shall call this reality by its concept: *the ideological State apparatuses.*

What are the ideological State apparatuses (ISAs)?

They must not be confused with the (repressive) State apparatus. Remember that in Marxist theory, the State Apparatus (SA) contains: the Government, the Administration, the Army, the Police, the Courts, the Prisons, etc., which constitute what I shall in future call the Repressive State Apparatus. Repressive suggests that the State Apparatus in question "functions by violence"—at least ultimately (since repression, e.g. administrative repression, may take non-physical forms).

I shall call Ideological State Apparatuses a certain number of realities which present themselves to the immediate observer in the form of distinct and specialized institutions. I propose an empirical list of these which will obviously have to be examined in detail, tested, corrected and reorganized. With all the reservations implied by this requirement, we can for the moment regard the following institutions as Ideological State Apparatuses (the order in which I have listed them has no particular significance):

- the religious ISA (the system of the different Churches),
- the educational ISA (the system of the different public and private "Schools"),
- the family ISA,[5]
- the legal ISA,[6]
- the political ISA (the political system, including the different Parties),
- the trade-union ISA,
- the communications ISA (press, radio and television, etc.),
- the cultural ISA (Literature, the Arts, sports, etc.).

I have said that the ISAs must not be confused with the (Repressive) State Apparatus. What constitutes the difference?

As a first moment, it is clear that while there is *one* (Repressive) State Apparatus, there is a *plurality* of Ideological State Apparatuses. Even presupposing that it exists, the unity that constitutes this plurality of ISAs as a body is not immediately visible.

As a second moment, it is clear that whereas the—unified—(Repressive) State Apparatus belongs entirely to the public domain, much the larger part of the Ideological State Apparatuses (in their apparent dispersion) are part, on the contrary, of the *private* domain. Churches, parties, trade unions, families, some schools, most newspapers, cultural ventures, etc., etc., are private.

We can ignore the first observation for the moment. But someone is bound to question the second, asking me by what right I regard as Ideological *State* Apparatuses, institutions which for the most part do not possess public status, but are quite simply *private* institutions. As a conscious Marxist, Gramsci already forestalled this objection in one sentence. The distinction between the public and the private is a distinction internal to bourgeois law, and valid in the (subordinate) domains in which bourgeois law exercises its "authority." The domain of the State escapes it because the latter is "above the law": the State, which is the State *of* the ruling class, is neither public nor private; on the contrary, it is the precondition for any distinction between public and private. The same thing can be said from the starting-point of our

State Ideological Apparatuses. It is unimportant whether the institutions in which they are realized are "public" or "private." What matters is how they function. Private institutions can perfectly well "function" as Ideological State Apparatuses. A reasonably thorough analysis of any one of the ISAs proves it.

But now for what is essential. What distinguishes the ISAs from the (Repressive) State Apparatus is the following basic difference: the Repressive State Apparatus functions "by violence," whereas the Ideological State Apparatuses *function "by ideology."*

I can clarify matters by correcting this distinction. I shall say rather that every State Apparatus, whether Repressive or Ideological, "functions" both by violence and by ideology, but with one very important distinction which makes it imperative not to confuse the Ideological State Apparatuses with the (Repressive) State Apparatus.

This is the fact that the (Repressive) State Apparatus functions massively and predominantly *by repression* (including physical repression), while functioning secondarily by ideology. (There is no such thing as a purely repressive apparatus.) For example, the Army and the Police also function by ideology both to ensure their own cohesion and reproduction, and in the "values" they propound externally.

In the same way, but inversely, it is essential to say that for their part the Ideological State Apparatuses function massively and predominantly *by ideology,* but they also function secondarily by repression, even if ultimately, but only ultimately, this is very attenuated and concealed, even symbolic. (There is no such thing as a purely ideological apparatus.) Thus Schools and Churches are suitable methods of punishment, expulsion, selection, etc., to "discipline" not only their shepherds, but also their flocks. The same is true of the Family. . . . The same is true of the cultural IS Apparatus (censorship, among other things), etc.

It is necessary to add that this determination of the double "functioning" (predominantly, secondarily) by repression and by ideology, according to whether it is a matter of the (Repressive) State Apparatus or the Ideological State Apparatuses, makes it clear that very subtle explicit or tacit combinations may be woven from the interplay of the (Repressive) State Apparatus and the Ideological State Apparatuses. Everyday life provides us with innumerable examples of this, but they must be studied in detail if we are to go further than this mere observation.

Nevertheless, this remark leads us towards an understanding of what constitutes the unity of the apparently disparate body of the ISAs. If the ISAs "function" massively and predominantly by ideology, what unifies their diversity is precisely this functioning, insofar as the ideology by which they function is always in fact unified, despite its diversity and its contradictions, *beneath the ruling ideology,* which is the ideology of "the ruling class." Given the fact that the "ruling class" in principle holds State power (openly or more often by means of alliances between classes or class fractions), and therefore has at its disposal the (Repressive) State Apparatus, we can accept the fact that this same ruling class is active in the Ideological State Apparatuses insofar as it is ultimately the ruling ideology which is realized in the Ideological State Apparatuses, precisely in its contradictions. Of course, it is a quite different thing to act by laws and decrees in the (Repressive) State Apparatus and to "act" through the intermediary of the ruling ideology in the Ideological State Apparatuses. We must go into the details of this difference—but it cannot mask the reality of a profound identity. To my knowledge, *no class can hold State power over a long period without at the same time exercising its hegemony over and in the State Ideological Apparatuses.* I only need one example and proof of this: Lenin's anguished concern to revolutionize the educational Ideological State Apparatus (among others), simply to make it possible for the Soviet proletariat, who had seized State power, to secure the future of the dictatorship of the proletariat and the transition to socialism.[7]

One ideological State apparatus certainly has the dominant role, although hardly anyone lends an ear to its music: it is so silent! This is the school.

It takes children from every class at infant-school age, and then for years, the years in which the child is most "vulnerable," squeezed between the family State apparatus and the educational State apparatus, it drums into them, whether it uses new or old methods, a certain amount of "know-how" wrapped in the ruling ideology (French, arithmetic, natural history, the sciences, literature) or simply the ruling ideology in its pure state (ethics, civic instruction, philosophy). Somewhere around the age of sixteen, a huge mass of children are ejected "into production": these are the workers or small peasants. Another portion of scholastically adapted youth carries on: and, for better or worse, it goes somewhat further, until it falls by the wayside and fills the posts of small and middle technicians, white-collar workers, small and middle executives, petty bourgeois of all kinds. A last portion reaches the summit, either to fall into intellectual semi-employment, or to provide, as well as the "intellectuals of the collective labourer," the agents of exploitation (capitalists, managers), the agents of repression (soldiers, policemen, politicians, administrators, etc.) and the professional ideologists (priests of all sorts, most of whom are convinced "laymen").

Each mass ejected *en route* is practically provided with the ideology which suits the role it has to fulfill in class society: the role of the exploited (with a "highly-developed" "professional," "ethical," "civic," "national" and a-political consciousness); the role of the agent of exploitation (ability to give the workers orders and speak to them: "human relations"), of the agent of repression (ability to give orders and enforce obedience "without discussion," or ability to manipulate the demagogy of a political leader's rhetoric), or of the professional ideologist (ability to treat consciousnesses with the respect, i.e. with the contempt, blackmail, and demagogy they deserve, adapted to the accents of Morality, of Virtue, of "Transcendence," of the Nation, of France's World Role, etc.).

Of course, many of these contrasting Virtues (modesty, resignation, submissiveness on the one hand, cynicism, contempt, arrogance, confidence, self-importance, even smooth talk and cunning on the other) are also taught in the Family, in the Church, in the Army, in Good Books, in films and even in the football stadium. But no other ideological State apparatus has the obligatory (and not least, free) audience of the totality of the children in the capitalist social formation, eight hours a day for five or six days out of seven.

But it is by an apprenticeship in a variety of know-how wrapped up in the massive inculcation of the ideology of the ruling class that the *relations of production* in a capitalist social formation, i.e. the relations of exploited to exploiters and exploiters to exploited, are largely reproduced. The mechanisms which produce this vital result for the capitalist regime are naturally covered up and concealed by a universally reigning ideology of the School, universally reigning because it is one of the essential forms of the ruling bourgeois ideology: an ideology which represents the School as a neutral environment purged of ideology (because it is . . . lay), where teachers respectful of the "conscience" and "freedom" of the children who are entrusted to them (in complete confidence) by their "parents" (who are free, too, i.e. the owners of their children) open up for them the path to the freedom, morality and responsibility of adults by their own example, by knowledge, literature and their "liberating" virtues.

I ask the pardon of those teachers who, in dreadful conditions, attempt to turn the few weapons they can find in the history and learning they "teach" against the ideology, the system and the practices in which they are trapped. They are a kind of hero. But they are rare and how many (the majority) do not even begin to suspect the "work" the system (which is bigger than they are and crushes them) forces them to do, or worse, put all their heart and ingenuity into performing it with the most advanced awareness (the famous new methods!). So little do they suspect it that their own devotion contributes to the maintenance and nourishment of this ideological representation of the School, which makes the School today as "natural," indispensable, useful and even beneficial for our contemporaries as the Church was "natural," indispensable and generous for our ancestors a few centuries ago.

In fact, the Church has been replaced today *in its role as the dominant Ideological State Apparatus* by the School. It is coupled with the Family just as the Church was once coupled with the Family. We can now claim that the unprecedentedly deep crisis which is now shaking the education system of so many States across the globe, often in conjunction with a crisis (already proclaimed in the *Communist Manifesto*) shaking the family system, takes on a political meaning, given that the School (and the School-Family couple) constitutes the dominant Ideological State Apparatus, the Apparatus playing a determinant part in the reproduction of the relations of production of a mode of production threatened in its existence by the world class struggle.

Ideology Is a "Representation" of the Imaginary Relationship of Individuals to Their Real Conditions of Existence

In order to approach my central thesis on the structure and functioning of ideology, I shall first present two theses, one negative, the other positive. The first concerns the object which is "represented" in the imaginary form of ideology, the second concerns the materiality of ideology.

THESIS I: Ideology represents the imaginary relationship of individuals to their real conditions of existence.

We commonly call religious ideology, ethical ideology, legal ideology, political ideology, etc., so many "world outlooks." Of course, assuming that we do not live one of these ideologies as the truth (e.g., "believe" in God, Duty, Justice, etc. . . .), we admit that the ideology we are discussing from a critical point of view, examining it as the ethnologist examines the myths of a "primitive society," that these "world outlooks" are largely imaginary, i.e., do not "correspond to reality."

However, while admitting that they do not correspond to reality, i.e. that they constitute an illusion, we admit that they do make allusion to reality, and that they need only be "interpreted" to discover the reality of the world behind their imaginary representation of that world (ideology = *illusion/allusion*).

There are different types of interpretation, the most famous of which are the *mechanistic* type, current in the eighteenth century (God is the imaginary representation of the real King), and the *"hermeneutic"* interpretation, inaugurated by the earliest church Fathers, and revived by Feuerbach and the theologico-philosophical school which descends from him, e.g., the theologian Barth (to Feuerbach, for example, God is the essence of real Man). The essential point is that on condition that we interpret the imaginary transposition (and inversion) of ideology we arrive at the conclusion that in ideology "men represent their real conditions of existence to themselves in an imaginary form."

Unfortunately, this interpretation leaves one small problem unsettled: why do men "need" this imaginary transposition of their real conditions of existence in order to "represent to themselves" their real conditions of existence?

The first answer (that of the eighteenth century) proposes a simple solution: Priests or Despots are responsible. They "forged" the Beautiful Lies so that, in the belief that they were obeying God, men would in fact obey the Priests and Despots, who are usually in alliance in their imposture, the Priests acting in the interests of the Despots or *vice versa*, according to the political positions of the "theoreticians" concerned. There is therefore a cause for the imaginary transposition of the real conditions of existence: that cause is the existence of a small number of cynical men who base their domination and exploitation of the "people" on a falsified representation of the world which they have imagined in order to enslave other minds by dominating their imaginations.

The second answer (that of Feuerbach, taken over word for word by Marx in his Early Works) is more "profound," i.e. just as false. It, too, seeks and finds a cause for the imaginary transposition and distortion of men's real conditions of existence, in short, for the alienation in the imaginary of the representation of men's conditions of existence. This cause is no longer Priests or Despots, nor their active imagination and the passive imagination of their victims. This cause is the material alienation which reigns in the conditions of existence of men themselves. This is how, in *The Jewish Question* and elsewhere, Marx defends the Feuerbachian idea that men make themselves an alienated (= imaginary) representation of their conditions of existence because these conditions of existence are themselves alienating (in the *1844 Manuscripts:* because these conditions are dominated by the essence of alienated society—*alienated labour*).

All these interpretations thus take literally the thesis which they presuppose, and on which they depend, i.e. that what is reflected in the imaginary representation of the world found in an ideology is the conditions of existence of men, i.e. their real world.

Now I can return to a thesis which I have already advanced: it is not their real conditions of existence, their real world, that "men" "represent to themselves" in ideology, but above all it is their relation to those conditions of existence which is represented to them there. It is this relation which is at the centre of every ideological, i.e. imaginary, representation of the real world. It is this relation that contains the "cause" which has to explain the imaginary distortion of the ideological representation of the real world. Or rather, to leave aside the language of causality it is necessary to advance the thesis that it is the *imaginary nature of this relation* which underlies all the imaginary distortion that we can observe (if we do not live in its truth) in all ideology.

To speak in a Marxist language, if it is true that the representation of the real conditions of existence of the individuals occupying the posts of agents of production, exploitation, repression, ideologization, and scientific practice, does in the last analysis arise from the relations of production, and from relations deriving from the relations of production, we can say the following: all ideology, represents in its necessarily imaginary distortion not the existing relations of production (and the other relations that derive from them), but above all the (imaginary) relationship of individuals to the relations of production and the relations that derive from them. What is represented in ideology is therefore not the system of the real relations which govern the existence of individuals, but the imaginary relation of those individuals to the real relations in which they live.

If this is the case, the question of the "cause" of the imaginary distortion of the real relations in ideology disappears and must be replaced by a different question: why is the representation given to individuals of their (individual) relation to the social relations which govern their conditions of existence and their collective and individual life necessarily an imaginary relation? And what is the nature of this imaginariness? Posed in this way, the question explodes the solution by a "clique,"[8] by a group of individuals (Priests or Despots) who are the authors of the great ideological mystification, just as it explodes the solution by the alienated character of the real world. We shall see why later in my exposition. For the moment I shall go no further.

I can now come to my central thesis.

Ideology Interpellates Individuals as Subjects

This thesis is simply a matter of making my last proposition explicit: there is no ideology except by the subject and for subjects. Meaning, there is no ideology except for concrete subjects, and this destination for ideology is only made possible by the subject: meaning, *by the category of the subject* and its functioning.

By this I mean that, even if it only appears under this name (the subject) with the rise of bourgeois ideology, above all with the rise of legal ideology,[9] the category of the subject (which may function under other names: e.g., as the soul in Plato, as God, etc.) is the constitutive category of all ideology, whatever its determination (regional or class) and whatever its historical date—since ideology has no history.

I say: the category of the subject is constitutive of all ideology, but at the same time and immediately I add that *the category of the subject is only constitutive of all ideology insofar as all ideology has the function (which defines it) of "constituting" concrete individuals as subjects.* In the interaction of this double constitution exists the functioning of all ideology, ideology being nothing but its functioning in the material forms of existence of that functioning.

In order to grasp what follows, it is essential to realize that both he who is writing these lines and the reader who reads them are themselves subjects, and therefore ideological subjects (a tautological proposition), i.e. that the author and the reader of these lines both live "spontaneously" or "naturally" in ideology in the sense in which I have said that "man is an ideological animal by nature."

That the author, insofar as he writes the lines of a discourse which claims to be scientific, is completely absent as a "subject" from "his" scientific discourse (for all scientific discourse is by definition a subject-less discourse, there is no "Subject of science" except in an ideology of science) is a different question which I shall leave on one side for the moment.

As St. Paul admirably put it, it is in the "Logos," meaning in ideology, that we "live, move and have our being." It follows that, for you and for me, the category of the subject is a primary "obviousness" (obviousnesses are always primary): it is clear that you and I are subjects (free, ethical, etc. . . . .). Like all obviousnesses, including those that make a word "name a thing" or "have a meaning" (therefore including the obviousness of the "transparency" of language), the "obviousness" that you and I are subjects—and that that does not cause any problems—is an ideological effect, the elementary ideological effect.[10] It is indeed a peculiarity of ideology that it imposes (without appearing to do so, since these are "obviousnesses") obviousnesses as obviousnesses, which we cannot *fail to recognize* and before which we have the inevitable and natural reaction of crying out (aloud or in the "still, small voice of conscience"): "That's obvious! That's right! That's true!"

At work in this reaction is the ideological *recognition* function which is one of the two functions of ideology as such (its inverse being the function of *misrecognition—méconnaissance*).

To take a highly "concrete" example, we all have friends who, when they knock on our door and we ask, through the door, the question "Who's there?," answer (since "it's obvious") "It's me." And we recognize that "it is him," or "her." We open the door, and it's true, it really was she who was there. To take another example, when we recognize somebody of our (previous) acquaintance (*(re)-connaissance*) in the street, we show him that we have recognized him (and have recognized that he has recognized us) by saying to him "Hello, my friend," and shaking his hand (a material ritual practice of ideological recognition in everyday life—in France, at least; elsewhere, there are other rituals).

In this preliminary remark and these concrete illustrations, I only wish to point out that you and I are *always already* subjects, and as such constantly practice the rituals of ideological recognition, which guarantee for us that we are indeed concrete, individual, distinguishable and (naturally) irreplaceable subjects. The writing I am currently executing and the reading you are currently[11] performing are also in this respect rituals of ideological recognition, including the "obviousness" with which the "truth" or "error" of my reflections may impose itself on you.

But to recognize that we are subjects and that we function in the practical rituals of the most elementary everyday life (the hand-shake, the fact of calling you by your name, the fact of knowing, even if I do not know what it is, that you "have" a name of your own, which means that you are recognized as a unique subject, etc.)—this recognition only gives us the "consciousness" of our incessant (eternal) practice of ideological recognition—its consciousness, i.e. its *recognition*—but in no sense does it give us the (scientific) *knowledge* of the mechanism of this recognition. Now it is this knowledge that we have to reach, if you will, while speaking in ideology, and from within ideology we have to outline a discourse which tries to break with ideology, in order to dare to be the beginning of a scientific (i.e. subjectless) discourse on ideology.

Thus in order to represent why the category of the "subject" is constitutive of ideology, which only exists by constituting concrete subjects as subjects, I shall employ a special mode of exposition: "concrete" enough to be recognized, but abstract enough to be thinkable and thought, giving rise to a knowledge.

As a first formulation I shall say: *all ideology hails or interpellates concrete individuals as concrete subjects,* by the functioning of the category of the subject.

This is a proposition which entails that we distinguish for the moment between concrete individuals on the one hand and concrete subjects on the other, although at this level concrete subjects only exist insofar as they are supported by a concrete individual.

I shall then suggest that ideology "acts" or "functions" in such a way that it "recruits" subjects among the individuals (it recruits them all), or "transforms" the individuals into subjects (it transforms them all) by that very precise operation which I have called *interpellation* or hailing, and which can be imagined along the lines of the most commonplace everyday police (or other) hailing: "Hey, you there!"[12]

Assuming that the theoretical scene I have imagined takes place in the street, the hailed individual will turn round. By this mere one-hundred-and-eighty-degree physical conversion, he becomes a *subject*. Why? Because he has recognized that the hail was "really" addressed to him, and that "it was *really him* who was hailed" (and not someone else). Experience shows that the practical telecommunication of hailings is such that they hardly ever miss their man: verbal call or whistle, the one hailed always recognizes that it is really him who is being hailed. And yet it is a strange phenomenon, and one which cannot be explained solely by "guilt feelings," despite the large numbers who "have something on their consciences."

Naturally for the convenience and clarity of my little theoretical theatre I have had to present things in the form of a sequence, with a before and an after, and thus in the form of a temporal succession. There are individuals walking along. Somewhere (usually behind them) the hail rings out: "Hey, you there!" One individual (nine times out of ten it is the right one) turns round, believing/suspecting/knowing that it is for him, i.e. recognizing that "it really is he" who is meant by the hailing. But in reality these things happen without any succession. The existence of ideology and the hailing or interpellation of individuals as subjects are one and the same thing.

I might add: what thus seems to take place outside ideology (to be precise, in the street), in reality takes place in ideology. What really takes place in ideology seems therefore to take place outside it. That is why those who are in ideology believe themselves by definition outside ideology: one of the effects of ideology is the practical *denegation* of the ideological character of ideology by ideology: ideology never says, "I am ideological." It is necessary to be outside ideology, i.e. in scientific knowledge, to be able to say: I am in ideology (a quite exceptional case) or (the general case): I was in ideology. As is well known, the accusation of being in ideology only applies to others, never to oneself (unless one is really a Spinozist or a Marxist, which, in this matter, is to be exactly the same thing). Which amounts to saying that ideology *has no outside* (for itself), but at the same time *that it is nothing but outside* (for science and reality).

Spinoza explained this completely two centuries before Marx, who practiced it but without explaining it in detail. But let us leave this point, although it is heavy with consequences, consequences which are not just theoretical, but also directly political, since, for example, the whole theory of criticism and self-criticism, the golden rule of the Marxist-Leninist practice of the class struggle, depends on it.

Thus ideology hails or interpellates individuals as subjects. As ideology is eternal, I must now suppress the temporal form in which I have presented the functioning of ideology, and say: ideology has always-already interpellated individuals as subjects, which amounts to making it clear that individuals are always-already interpellated by ideology as subjects, which necessarily leads us to one last proposition: *individuals are always-already subjects*. Hence individuals are "abstract" with respect to the subjects which they always-already are. This proposition might seem paradoxical.

That an individual is always-already a subject, even before he is born, is nevertheless the plain reality, accessible to everyone and not a paradox at all. Freud shows that individuals are always "abstract" with respect to the subjects they always-already are, simply by noting the ideological ritual that surrounds the expectation of a "birth," that "happy event." Everyone knows how much and in what way an unborn child is expected. Which amounts to saying, very prosaically, if we agree to drop the "sentiments," i.e. the forms of family ideology (paternal/maternal/conjugal/fraternal) in which the unborn child is expected: it is certain in advance that it will bear its Father's Name, and will therefore have an identity and be irreplaceable. Before its birth, the child is therefore always-already a subject, appointed as a subject in and by the specific familial ideological configuration in which it is "expected" once it has been conceived. I hardly need add that this familial ideological configuration is, in its uniqueness, highly structured, and that it is in this implacable and more or less "pathological" (presupposing that any meaning can be assigned to that term) structure that the former subject-to-be will have to "find" "its" place, i.e., "become" the sexual subject (boy or girl) which it already is in advance. It is clear that this ideological constraint and preappointment, and all the rituals of rearing and then education in the family, have some relationship with what Freud studied in the forms of the pre-genital and genital "stages" of sexuality, i.e., in the "grip" of what Freud registered by its effects as being the unconscious. But let us leave this point, too, on one side.

Let me go one step further. What I shall now turn my attention to is the way the "actors" in this *mise en scène* of interpellation, and their respective roles, are reflected in the very structure of all ideology.

Notes

1. This text is made up of two extracts from an ongoing study. The sub-title "Notes toward an Investigation" is the author's own. The ideas expounded should not be regarded as more than the introduction to a discussion.

2. Marx to Kugelmann, 11 July 1868, *Selected Correspondence,* Moscow, 1955, p. 209.

3. Marx gave it its scientific concept: *variable capital.*

4. To my knowledge, Gramsci is the only one who went any distance in the road I am taking. He had the "remarkable" idea that the State could not be reduced to the (Repressive) State Apparatus, but included, as he put it, a certain number of institutions from *"civil society"*: the Church, the Schools, the trade unions, etc. Unfortunately, Gramsci did not systematize his institutions, which remained in the state of acute but fragmentary notes (cf. Gramsci, *Selections from the Prison Notebooks,* International Publishers, 1971, pp. 12, 259, 260–3); see also the letter to Tatiana Schucht, 7 September 1931, in *Lettre del Carcere,* Einaudi, 1968, p. 479. English-language translation in preparation.

5. The family obviously has other "functions" than that of an ISA. It intervenes in the reproduction of labour power. In different modes of production it is the unit of production and/or the unit of consumption.

6. The "Law" belongs both to the (Repressive) State Apparatus and to the system of the ISAs.

7. In a pathetic text written in 1937, Krupskaya relates the history of Lenin's desperate efforts and what she regards as his failure.

8. I use this very modern term deliberately. For even in Communist circles, unfortunately, it is a commonplace to "explain" some political deviation (left or right opportunism) by the action of a "clique."

9. Which borrowed the legal category of "subject in law" to make an ideological notion: man is by nature a subject.

10. Linguists and those who appeal to linguistics for various purposes often run up against difficulties which arise because they ignore the action of the ideological effects in all discourses—including even scientific discourses.

11. NB: this double "currently" is one more proof of the fact that ideology is "eternal," since these two "currentlys" are separated by an indefinite interval; I am writing these lines on 6 April 1969, you may read them at any subsequent time.

12. Hailing as an everyday practice subject to a precise ritual takes a quite "special" form in the policeman's practice of "hailing" which concerns the hailing of "suspects."

5

Reel Bad Arabs: How Hollywood Vilifies a People

Jack G. Shaheen

Live images on big screen and television go beyond a thousand words in perpetuating stereotypes and clichés. This article surveys more than a century of Hollywood's projection of negative images of the Arabs and Muslims. Based on the study of more than 900 films, it shows how moviegoers are led to believe that all Arabs are Muslims and all Muslims are Arabs. The moviemakers' distorted lenses have shown Arabs as heartless, brutal, uncivilized, religious fanatics through common depictions of Arabs kidnapping or raping a fair maiden; expressing hatred against the Jews and Christians; and demonstrating a love for wealth and power. The article compares the stereotype of the hook-nosed Arab with a similar depiction of Jews in Nazi propaganda materials. Only five percent of Arab film roles depict normal, human characters.

Introduction

> Al tikrar biallem il hmar *(By repetition even the donkey learns).*

This Arab proverb encapsulates how effective repetition can be when it comes to education: how we learn by repeating an exercise over and over again until we can respond almost reflexively. A small child uses repetition to master numbers and letters of the alphabet. Older students use repetition to memorize historical dates and algebraic formulas.

For more than a century Hollywood, too, has used repetition as a teaching tool, tutoring movie audiences by repeating over and over, in film after film, insidious images of the Arab people. I ask the reader to study in these pages the persistence of this defamation, from earlier times to the present day, and to consider how these slanderous stereotypes have affected honest discourse and public policy.

Reprinted by permission from *Annals of the American Academy of Political and Social Science* 588 (July 2003).

Genesis

In [my book *Reel Bad Arabs*], I document and discuss virtually every feature that Hollywood has ever made—more than 900 films, the vast majority of which portray Arabs by distorting at every turn what most Arab men, women, and children are really like. In gathering the evidence for this book, I was driven by the need to expose an injustice: cinema's systematic, pervasive, and unapologetic degradation and dehumanization of a people.

When colleagues ask whether today's reel Arabs are more stereotypical than yesteryear's, I can't say the celluloid Arab has changed. That is the problem. He is what he has always been—the cultural "other." Seen through Hollywood's distorted lenses, Arabs look different and threatening. Projected along racial and religious lines, the stereotypes are deeply ingrained in American cinema. From 1896 until today, filmmakers have collectively indicted all Arabs as Public Enemy #1—brutal, heartless, uncivilized religious fanatics and money-mad cultural "others" bent on terrorizing civilized Westerners, especially Christians and Jews. Much has happened since 1896—women's suffrage, the Great Depression, the civil rights movement, two world wars, the Korean, Vietnam, and Gulf wars, and the collapse of the Soviet Union. Throughout it all, Hollywood's caricature of the Arab has prowled the silver screen. He is there to this day—repulsive and unrepresentative as ever.

What is an Arab? In countless films, Hollywood alleges the answer: Arabs are brute murderers, sleazy rapists, religious fanatics, oil-rich dimwits, and abusers of women. "They [the Arabs] all look alike to me," quips the American heroine in the movie *The Sheik Steps Out* (1937). "All Arabs look alike to me," admits the protagonist in *Commando* (1968). Decades later, nothing had changed. Quips the U.S. Ambassador in *Hostage* (1986), "I can't tell one [Arab] from another. Wrapped in those bed sheets they all look the same to me." In Hollywood's films, they certainly do.

Pause and visualize the reel Arab. What do you see? Black beard, headdress, dark sunglasses. In the background—a limousine, harem maidens, oil wells, camels. Or perhaps he is brandishing an automatic weapon, crazy hate in his eyes and Allah on his lips. Can you see him?

Think about it. When was the last time you saw a movie depicting an Arab or an American of Arab heritage as a regular guy? Perhaps a man who works ten hours a day, comes home to a loving wife and family, plays soccer with his kids, and prays with family members at his respective mosque or church. He's the kind of guy you'd like to have as your next door neighbor, because—well, maybe because he's a bit like you.

But would you want to share your country, much less your street, with any of Hollywood's Arabs? Would you want your kids playing with him and his family, your teenagers dating them? Would you enjoy sharing your neighborhood with fabulously wealthy and vile oil sheikhs with an eye for Western blondes and arms deals and intent on world domination, or with crazed terrorists, airplane hijackers, or camel-riding bedouins?

Real Arabs

Who exactly are the Arabs of the Middle East? When I use the term "Arab," I refer to the 265 million people who reside in, and the many more millions around the world who are from, the 22 Arab states.[1] The Arabs have made many contributions to our civilization. To name a few, Arab and Persian physicians and scientists inspired European thinkers like Leonardo da Vinci. The Arabs invented algebra and the concept of zero. Numerous English words—algebra, chemistry, coffee, and others—have Arab roots. Arab intellectuals made it feasible for Western scholars to develop and practice advanced educational systems.

In astronomy Arabs used astrolabes for navigation, star maps, celestial globes, and the concept of the center of gravity. In geography, they pioneered the use of latitude and longitude. They invented the water clock; their architecture inspired the Gothic style in Europe. In agriculture, they introduced oranges, dates, sugar, and cotton, and pioneered water works and irrigation. And, they developed a tradition of legal learning, of secular literature and scientific and philosophical thought, in which the Jews also played an important part.

There exists a mixed ethnicity in the Arab world—from 5000 BC to the present. The Scots, Greeks, British, French, Romans, English, and others have occupied the area. Not surprisingly, some Arabs have dark hair, dark eyes, and olive complexions. Others boast freckles, red hair, and blue eyes.

Geographically, the Arab world is one-and-a-half times as large as the United States, stretching from the Strait of Hormuz to the Rock of Gibraltar. It's the point where Asia, Europe, and Africa come together. The region gave the world three major religions, a language, and an alphabet.

In most Arab countries today, 70 percent of the population is under age 30. Most share a common language, cultural heritage, history, and religion (Islam). Though the vast majority of them are Muslims, about 15 million Arab Christians (including Chaldean, Coptic, Eastern Orthodox, Episcopalian, Roman Catholic, Melkite, Maronite, and Protestant), reside there as well.

. . . Their dress is traditional and Western. The majority are peaceful, not violent; poor, not rich; most do not dwell in desert tents; none are surrounded by harem maidens; most have never seen an oil well or mounted a camel. Not one travels via "magic carpets." Their lifestyles defy stereotyping.

. . . Through immigration, conversion, and birth, . . . Muslims are America's fastest growing religious group; about 500,000 reside in the greater Los Angeles area. America's six to eight million Muslims frequent more than 2,000 mosques, Islamic centers, and schools. They include immigrants from more than 60 nations, as well as African-Americans. In fact, most of the world's 1.1 billion Muslims are Indonesian, Indian, or Malaysian. Only 12 percent of the world's Muslims are Arab. Yet, moviemakers ignore this reality, depicting Arabs and Muslims as one and the same people. Repeatedly, they falsely project all Arabs as Muslims and all Muslims as Arabs. As a result, viewers, too, tend to link the same attributes to both peoples.

. . . Hollywood's past omission of "everyday" African-Americans, American Indians, and Latinos unduly affected the lives of these minorities. The same holds true with the industry's near total absence of regular Arab-Americans. Regular Mideast Arabs, too, are invisible on silver screens. Asks Jay Stone, "Where are the movie Arabs and Muslims who are just ordinary people?"[2]

Why is it important for the average American to know and care about the Arab stereotype? It is critical because dislike of "the stranger," which the Greeks knew as xenophobia, forewarns that when one ethnic, racial, or religious group is vilified, innocent people suffer. History reminds us that the cinema's hateful Arab stereotypes are reminiscent of abuses in earlier times. Not so long ago—and sometimes still—Asians, American Indians, blacks, and Jews were vilified.

Ponder the consequences. In February 1942, more than 100,000 Americans of Japanese descent were displaced from their homes and interred in camps; for decades blacks were denied basic civil rights, robbed of their property, and lynched; American Indians, too, were displaced and slaughtered; and in Europe, six million Jews perished in the Holocaust.

This is what happens when people are dehumanized.

Mythology in any society is significant. And, Hollywood's celluloid mythology dominates the culture. No doubt about it, Hollywood's renditions of Arabs frame stereotypes in viewer's minds. The problem is peculiarly American. Because of the vast American cultural reach via television and film—we are the world's leading exporter of screen images—the all-pervasive Arab stereotype has much more of a negative impact on viewers today than it did thirty or forty years ago.

Nowadays, Hollywood's motion pictures reach nearly everyone. Cinematic illusions are created, nurtured, and distributed worldwide, reaching viewers in more than 100 countries, from Iceland to Thailand. Arab images have an effect not only on international audiences, but on international movie makers as well. No sooner do contemporary features leave the movie theaters than they are available in video stores and transmitted onto TV screens. Thanks to technological advances, old silent and sound movies impugning Arabs, some of which were produced before I was born, are repeatedly broadcast on cable television and beamed directly into the home.

Check your local guides and you will see that since the mid-1980s, appearing each week on TV screens, are fifteen to twenty recycled movies projecting Arabs as dehumanized caricatures: *The Sheik* (1921), *The Mummy* (1932), *Cairo* (1942), *The Steel Lady* (1953), *Exodus* (1960), *The Black Stallion* (1979), *Protocol* (1984), *The Delta Force* (1986), *Ernest in the Army* (1997), and *Rules of Engagement* (2000). Watching yesteryear's stereotypical Arabs on TV screens is an unnerving experience, especially when pondering the influence celluloid images have on adults and our youth.

. . . Arabs, like Jews, are Semites, so it is perhaps not too surprising that Hollywood's image of hook-nosed, robed Arabs parallels the image of Jews in Nazi-inspired movies such as *Robert and Bertram* (1939), *Die Rothschilds Aktien von Waterloo* (1940), *Der Ewige Jude* (1940), and *Jud Süss* (1940). Once upon a cinematic time, screen Jews boasted exaggerated nostrils and dressed differently—in yarmulkes and dark robes—than the films' protagonists. In the past, Jews were projected as the "other"—depraved and predatory money-grubbers who seek world domination, worship a different God, and kill innocents. Nazi propaganda also presented the lecherous Jew slinking in the shadows, scheming to snare the blonde Aryan virgin.

Yesterday's Shylocks resemble today's hook-nosed sheikhs, arousing fear of the "other." Reflects William Greider, "Jews were despised as exemplars of modernism," while today's "Arabs are depicted as carriers of primitivism—[both] threatening to upset our cozy modern world with their strange habits and desires."[3]

. . . Because of Hollywood's heightened cultural awareness, producers try not to demean most racial and ethnic groups. They know it is morally irresponsible to repeatedly bombard viewers with a regular stream of lurid, unyielding, and unrepentant portraits of a people. The relation is one of cause and effect. Powerful collages of hurtful images serve to deepen suspicions and hatreds. Jerry Mander observes, screen images "can cause people to do what they might otherwise never [have] thought to do."[4]

One can certainly make the case that movie land's pernicious Arab images are sometimes reflected in the attitudes and actions of journalists and government officials. Consider the aftermath of the 19 April 1995 bombing of the federal building in Oklahoma City. Though no American of Arab descent was involved, they were instantly targeted as suspects. Speculative reporting, combined with decades of harmful stereotyping, resulted in more than 300 hate crimes against them.[5]

A Basis for Understanding

. . . [I have reviewed] more than 900 feature films displaying Arab characters. Regrettably, in all these I uncovered only a handful of heroic Arabs; they surface in a few 1980s and 1990s scenarios. In *Lion of the Desert* (1981), righteous Arabs bring down invading fascists. Humane Palestinians surface in *Hanna K* (1983) and *The Seventh Coin* (1992). In *Robin Hood, Prince of Thieves* (1991), a devout Muslim who "fights better than twenty English knights," helps Robin Hood get the better of the evil Sheriff of Nottingham. In *The 13th Warrior* (1999), an Arab Muslim scholar befriends Nordic warriors, helping them defeat primitive cavemen. And in *Three Kings* (1999), a movie celebrating our commonalities and differences, we view Arabs as regular folks, with affections and aspirations. This anti-war movie humanizes the Iraqis, a people who for too long have been projected as evil caricatures.

Most of the time I found moviemakers saturating the marketplace with all sorts of Arab villains. Producers collectively impugned Arabs in every type of movie you can imagine, targeting adults in well-known and high-budgeted movies such as *Exodus* (1960), *Black Sunday* (1977), *Ishtar* (1987), and *The Siege* (1998); and reaching out to teenagers with financially successful schlock movies such as *Five Weeks in a Balloon* (1962), *Things Are Tough All Over* (1982), *Sahara* (1983), and *Operation Condor* (1997). One constant factor dominates all the films: Derogatory stereotypes are omnipresent, reaching youngsters, baby boomers, and older folk.

I am not saying an Arab should never be portrayed as the villain. What I am saying is that almost all Hollywood depictions of Arabs are bad ones. This is a grave injustice. Repetitious and negative images of the reel Arab literally sustain adverse portraits across generations. The fact is that for more than a century producers have tarred an entire group of people with the same sinister brush.

Villains

. . . Beginning with *Imar the Servitor* (1914), up to and including *The Mummy Returns* (2001), a synergy of images equates Arabs from Syria to the Sudan with quintessential evil. In hundreds of movies "evil" Arabs stalk the screen. We see them assaulting just about every imaginable foe—Americans, Europeans, Israelis, legionnaires, Africans, fellow Arabs, even— for heaven's sake—Hercules and Samson.

Scores of comedies present Arabs as buffoons, stumbling all over themselves. Some of our best known and most popular stars mock Arabs: Will Rogers in *Business and Pleasure* (1931); Laurel and Hardy in *Beau Hunks* (1931); Bob Hope and Bing Crosby in *Road to Morocco* (1942); the Marx Brothers in *A Night in Casablanca* (1946); Abbott and Costello in *Abbott and Costello in the Foreign Legion* (1950); the Bowery Boys in *Bowery to Bagdad* (1955); Jerry Lewis in *The Sad Sack* (1957); Phil Silvers in *Follow That Camel* (1967); Marty Feldman in *The Last Remake of Beau Geste* (1977); Harvey Korman in *Americathon* (1979); Bugs Bunny in *1001 Rabbit Tales* (1982); Dustin Hoffman and Warren Beatty in *Ishtar* (1987); Pauly Shore in *In the Army Now* (1994); and Jim Varney in *Ernest in the Army* (1997).

Some protagonists even refer to Arabs as "dogs" and "monkeys." As a result, those viewers laughing at bumbling reel Arabs leave movie theaters with a sense of solidarity, united by their shared distance from these peoples of ridicule.

In dramas, especially, Hollywood's stars contest and vanquish reel Arabs. See Emory Johnson in *The Gift Girl* (1917); Gary Cooper in *Beau Sabreur* (1928); John Wayne in *I Cover the War* (1937); Burt Lancaster in *Ten Tall Men* (1951); Dean Martin in *The Ambushers* (1967); Michael Caine in *Ashanti* (1979); Sean Connery in *Never Say Never Again* (1983); Harrison Ford in *Frantic* (1988); Kurt Russell in *Executive Decision* (1996); and Brendan Frasier in *The Mummy* (1999).

Perhaps in an attempt to further legitimize the stereotype, as well as to attract more viewers, in the mid-1980s studios presented notable African-American actors facing off against, and ultimately destroying, reel Arabs. Among them, Eddie Murphy, Louis Gossett Jr., Robert Guillaume, Samuel Jackson, Denzel Washington, and Shaquille O'Neal.[6]

In the Disney movie *Kazaam* (1996), O'Neal pummels three Arab Muslims who covet "all the money in the world." Four years later, director William Friedkin has actor Samuel Jackson exploiting jingoistic prejudice and religious bigotry in *Rules of Engagement* (2000). The effects of ethnic exploitation are especially obvious in scenes revealing egregious, false images of Yemeni children as assassins and enemies of the United States.

To my knowledge, no Hollywood WWI, WWII, or Korean War movie has ever shown America's fighting forces slaughtering children. Yet, near the conclusion of *Rules of Engagement*, US marines open fire on the Yemenis, shooting 83 men, women, and children. During the scene, viewers rose to their feet, clapped and cheered. Boasts director Friedkin, "I've seen audiences stand up and applaud the film throughout the United States."[7] Some viewers applaud Marines gunning down Arabs in war dramas not necessarily because of cultural insensitivity, but because for more than 100 years Hollywood has singled out the Arab as our enemy. Over a period of time, a steady stream of bigoted images does, in fact, tarnish our judgment of a people and their culture.

Rules of Engagement not only reinforces historically damaging stereotypes, but promotes a dangerously generalized portrayal of Arabs as rabidly anti-American. Equally troubling to this honorably discharged US Army veteran is that *Rules of Engagement*'s credits thank for their assistance the Department of Defense (DOD) and the US Marine Corps. More than fourteen feature films, all of which show Americans killing Arabs, credit the DOD for providing needed equipment, personnel, and technical assistance. Sadly, the Pentagon seems to condone these Arab-bashing ventures, as evidenced in *True Lies* (1994), *Executive Decision* (1996), and *Freedom Strike* (1998).

On November 30, 2000, Hollywood luminaries attended a star-studded dinner hosted by Defense Secretary William Cohen in honor of Motion Picture Association President Jack Valenti, for which the Pentagon paid the bill—$295,000. Called on to explain why the DOD personnel were fraternizing with imagemakers at an elaborate Beverly Hills gathering, spokesman Kenneth Bacon said: "If we can have television shows and movies that show the excitement and importance of military life, they can help generate a favorable atmosphere for recruiting."

The DOD has sometimes shown concern when other peoples have been tarnished on film. For example, in the late 1950s, DOD officials were reluctant to cooperate with moviemakers attempting to advance Japanese stereotypes. When *The Bridge over the River Kwai* (1957) was being filmed, Donald Baruch, head of the DOD's Motion Picture Production Office, cautioned producers not to overemphasize Japanese terror and torture, advising:

> In our ever-increasing responsibility for maintaining a mutual friendship and respect among the people of foreign lands, the use of disparaging terms to identify ethnic, national or religious groups is inimical to our national interest, particularly in motion pictures sanctioned by Government cooperation.[8]

Arabs are almost always easy targets in war movies. From as early as 1912, decades prior to the 1991 Gulf War, dozens of films presented allied agents and military forces—American, British, French, and more recently Israeli—obliterating Arabs. In the World War I drama *The Lost Patrol* (1934), a brave British sergeant (Victor McLaughlin) guns down "sneaky Arabs, those dirty, filthy swine." An American newsreel cameraman (John Wayne) helps wipe out a "horde of [Arab] tribesmen" in *I Cover the War* (1937).

In *Sirocco* (1951), the first Hollywood feature film projecting Arabs as terrorists, Syrian "fanatics" assail French soldiers and American arms dealer Harry Smith (Humphrey Bogart). *The Lost Command* (1966) shows French Colonel Raspeguy's (Anthony Quinn) soldiers killing Algerians. And, Israelis gun down sneaky bedouins in two made-in-Israel films, *Sinai Guerrillas* (1960) and *Sinai Commandos* (1968).

Arabs trying to rape, kill, or abduct fair-complexioned Western heroines is a common theme, dominating scenarios from *Captured by Bedouins* (1912), to *The Pelican Brief* (1993). In *Brief*, an Arab hit man tries to assassinate the protagonist, played by Julia Roberts. In *Captured*, desert bandits kidnap a fair American maiden, but she is eventually rescued by a British officer. As for her bedouin abductors, they are gunned down by rescuing US Cavalry troops.

Arabs enslave and abuse Africans in about ten films, including *A Daughter of the Congo* (1930), *Drums of Africa* (1963), and *Ashanti* (1979). Noted African-American filmmaker Oscar Micheaux, who made "race movies" from 1919 to 1948, also advanced the Arab-as-abductor theme in his *A Daughter of the Congo*. Though Micheaux's movies contested Hollywood's Jim Crow stereotypes of blacks, *A Daughter of the Congo* depicts lecherous Arab slavers abducting and holding hostage a lovely Mulatto woman and her maid. The maiden is eventually rescued by the heroic African-American officers of the 10th US Cavalry.

Anti-Christian Arabs appear in dozens of films. When the US military officer in *Another Dawn* (1937) is asked why Arabs despise Westerners, he barks: "It's a good Moslem hatred of Christians." Islam is also portrayed as a violent faith in *Legion of the Doomed* (1959). Here, an Arab is told, "Kill him before he kills you." Affirms the Arab as he plunges a knife into his foe's gut, "You speak the words of Allah." And, in *The Castilian* (1963), Spanish Christians triumph over Arab Muslim zealots. How? By releasing scores of squealing pigs! Terrified of the pigs, the reel Arabs retreat.

Arabs invade the United States and terrorize innocents in *Golden Hands of Kurigal* (1949), *Terror Squad* (1988), *True Lies* (1994), and *The Siege* (1998). *The Siege* is especially alarming. In it, Arab immigrants methodically lay waste to Manhattan. Assisted by Arab-American auto mechanics, university students, and a college teacher, they blow up the city's FBI building, kill scores of government agents, blast theatergoers, and detonate a bomb in a crowded bus.

. . . Oily Arabs and robed thugs intent on acquiring nuclear weapons surface in roughly ten films. See *Fort Algiers* (1958) and *Frantic* (1988).

At least a dozen made-in-Israel and Golan-Globus movies, such as *Eagles Attack at Dawn* (1970), *Iron Eagle* (1986), and *Chain of Command* (1993), show Americans and/or Israelis crushing evil-minded Arabs, many of whom are portrayed by Israeli actors.

More than 30 French Foreign Legion movies, virtually a sub-genre of boy's-own-adventure films, show civilized legionnaires obliterating backward desert bedouin. These legion formula films cover a span of more than 80 years, from *The Unknown* (1915) to *Legionnaire* (1998). Scenarios display courageous, outnumbered legionnaires battling against, and ultimately overcoming, unruly Arabs. Even Porky Pig as a legionnaire and his camel join in the melee, beating up bedouins in the animated cartoon, *Little Beau Porky* (1936).

. . . Observes William Greider of the Washington Post, "Much of what Westerners 'learned' about Arabs sounds similar to what nineteenth-century Americans 'discovered' about Indians on this continent . . . acceptable villains make our troubles so manageable." In the past, imagemakers punctuated "anti-human qualities in these strange people," American Indians. They projected them as savages, not thinking like us, "not sharing our aspirations." Once one has concluded that Indians thrive on violence, disorder, and stealth, it becomes easier to accept rather than challenge "irrational" portraits. Today, says Greider, "The Arab stereotypes created by British and French colonialism are still very much with us."[9]

Film producers, broadcast journalists, and military leaders echo Greider's Arab-as-Indian analogy. Seeing marauding desert Arabs approach, the American protagonist in the war movie *The Steel Lady* (1953) quips, "This is bandit area, worse than Arizona Apache." In talking up his film *Iron Eagle* (1986), producer Ron Samuels gushed: Showing an American teen hijacking a jet and wiping out scores of Arabs "was just the kind of story I'd been looking for. . . . It reminded me of the old John Wayne westerns."

Sheikhs

The word "sheikh" means, literally, a wise elderly person, the head of the family, but you would not know that from watching any of Hollywood's "sheikh" features, more than 160 scenarios, including the Kinetoscope short *Sheik Hadj Tahar Hadj Cherif* (1894) and the Selig Company's *The Power of the Sultan* (1907)—the first movie to be filmed in Los Angeles. Throughout the Arab world, to show respect, people address Muslim religious leaders as sheikhs.

Moviemakers, however, attach a completely different meaning to the word. As Matthew Sweet points out, "The cinematic Arab has never been an attractive figure . . . in the 1920s he was a swarthy Sheik, wiggling his eyebrows and chasing the [Western] heroine around a tiled courtyard. After the 1973 oil crisis . . . producers revitalized the image of the fabulously wealthy and slothful sheikh, only this time he was getting rich at the expense of red-blooded Americans; he became an inscrutable bully—a Ray-Ban-ed variation of the stereotypes of the Jewish money lender."[10]

Instead of presenting sheikhs as elderly men of wisdom, screenwriters offer romantic melodramas portraying them as stooges-in-sheets, slovenly, hook-nosed potentates intent on capturing pale-faced blondes for their harems. Imitating the stereotypical behavior of their lecherous predecessors—the "bestial" Asian, the black "buck," and the "lascivious" Latino—slovenly Arabs move to swiftly and violently deflower Western maidens. Explains Edward Said, "The perverted sheikh can often be seen snarling at the captured Western hero and blonde girl . . . [and saying] 'My men are going to kill you, but they like to amuse themselves before.' "[11]

Early silent films, such as *The Unfaithful Odalisque* (1903), *The Arab* (1915), and *The Sheik* (1921), all present bearded, robed Arab rulers as one collective stereotypical lecherous cur. In *The Unfaithful Odalisque*, the sheikh not only admonishes his harem maiden, he directs a Nubian slave to lash her with a cat-o'-nine-tails. In *The Sheik* (1921), Sheikh Ahmed (Valentino) glares at Diana, the kidnapped British lovely and boasts: "When an Arab sees a woman he wants, he takes her!"

Flash forward 33 years. Affirms the sheikh in *The Adventures of Hajji Baba* (1954): "Give her to me or I'll take her!"

Moving to kidnap and/or seduce the Western heroine, clumsy moneyed sheikhs fall all over themselves in more than 60 silent and sound movies, ranging from *The Fire and the Sword* (1914) to *Protocol* (1984). Sheikhs disregard Arab women, preferring instead to ravish just one Western woman.

But Hollywood's silent movies did not dare show Western women bedding sheikhs. Why? Because America's movie censors objected to love scenes between Westerners and Arabs. Even producers experiencing desert mirages dared not imagine such unions.

Some viewers perceived Valentino's *The Sheik* (1921) to be an exception to the rule. Not true. Valentino's Sheikh Ahmed, who vanquishes Diana, the Western heroine in the movie, is actually a European, not an Arab. This helps explain why the European lover-boy dressed in Arab garb was viewed so positively by his essentially female audience. Note the dialogue, revealing Ahmed to be a European:

Diana, the heroine: "His [Ahmed's] hand is so large for an Arab."

Ahmed's French friend: "He is not an Arab. His father was an Englishman, his mother a Spaniard."

Other desert scenarios followed suit, allowing the hero and heroine to make love, but only after revealing they were actually Western Christians!

In Europe, it was otherwise. As early as 1922, a few European movies such as *The Sheikh's Wife* (1922) countered fixed themes, showing Western heroines embracing dashing Arab sheikhs.

Both good and evil sheikhs battle each other in about 60 Arabian Nights fantasies, animated and non-animated. A plethora of unsavory characters, wicked viziers, slimy slavers, irreverent magicians, and shady merchants contest courageous princes, princesses, lamp genies, and folk heroes such as Ali Baba, Sinbad, Aladdin and, on occasion, the benevolent caliph. You can see some of them in the four Kismet fantasies (1920, 1930, 1944, 1955), *Prisoners of the Casbah* (1955), and *Aladdin* (1992).

Even animated cartoon characters thump Arabs. My childhood hero, Bugs Bunny, clobbers nasty Arabs in *1001 Rabbit Tales* (1982). Bugs trounces an ugly genie, a dense sheikh, and the ruler's spoiled son. My other cartoon hero, Popeye, also trounces Arabs. In the early

1930s, Fleischer Studios' lengthy Popeye cartoons presented Arab folk heroes as rogues, not as champions. Popeye clobbers, not befriends, Ali Baba and Sinbad in *Popeye the Sailor Meets Ali Baba's Forty Thieves*, and *Popeye the Sailor Meets Sinbad the Sailor.*

Beginning in the mid-1970s, fresh directors also projected Arab leaders through warped prisms. Emulating their predecessors' stereotypes they, too, displayed Western heroines fending off over-sexed desert sheikhs.

Yet, there are dramatic differences in sheikh images. Once-upon-a-time Arabian Nights movies, such as *Ali Baba Goes to Town* (1937) and *Aladdin and His Lamp* (1952), show indolent sheikhs lounging on thrones. But, contemporary films present oily, militant, ostentatious sheikhs reclining in Rolls Royces, aspiring to buy up chunks of America.

Today's films present anti-Christian, anti-Jewish Arab potentates perched atop missile bases, armed with nuclear weapons, plenty of oil, and oodles of cash. Using Islam to justify violence, today's reel mega-rich hedonists pose a much greater threat to the West, to Israel, and to fellow Arabs than did their predecessors. You can catch a few of their kind in *Rollover* (1981), *Wrong Is Right* (1982), *The Jewel of the Nile* (1985), and *American Ninja 4: The Annihilation* (1991).

Scantily clad harem maidens attend sheikhs in more than 30 scenarios. The rulers shrug off some, torture others, and enslave the rest. Enslaving international beauties in the X-rated movie, *Ilsa: Harem Keeper of the Oil Sheikhs* (1976), is a depraved Arab ruler and his cohort—Ilsa, the "She-Wolf of the S.S." Depraved sheikhs also subjugate dwarfs and Africans; see *Utz* (1992) and *Slavers* (1977).

Often, producers falsify geopolitical realities. During WWII many Arab nations actively supported the Allies. Moroccan, Tunisian, and Algerian soldiers, for example, fought alongside French troops in North Africa, Italy, and France. Also, Jordanian and Libyan troops assisted members of the British armed services. And, late in the conflict, Egypt, Saudi Arabia, and Iraq declared war on Germany.[12]

Yet, most movies fail to show Arabs fighting alongside the good guys. Instead, burnoosed pro-Nazi potentates, some belonging to the "Arabian Gestapo," appear in more than ten sheikh movies; see, for example, *A Yank in Libya* (1942), *Action in Arabia* (1944), and *The Steel Lady* (1953). As early as 1943, about fifty years before the Gulf War, *Adventure in Iraq* (1943) depicts the US Air Force bombing the pro-German Iraqi ruler's "devil-worshiper" minions into oblivion.

From the start, protagonists ranging from Samson to 007 have battled burnoosed chieftains. Flashback to the 1900s. Two 1918 films, *Tarzan of the Apes* and *Bound in Morocco*, show Tarzan and Douglas Fairbanks, respectively, trouncing shifty sheikhs.

Cut to the 1940s. Abbott and Costello, Bing Crosby, and Bob Hope follow suit by belittling Arabs in *Lost in a Harem* (1944) and *Road to Morocco* (1942).

Advance to the 1950s. The Bowery Boys and Tab Hunter thrash robed rulers in *Looking for Danger* (1957) and *The Steel Lady* (1953), respectively.

Flash forward to the 1960s and the 1970s. Elvis Presley, Pat Boone, and Jerry Lewis deride Arabs in: *Harum Scarum* (1965), *The Perils of Pauline* (1967), and *Don't Raise the Bridge, Lower the River* (1968). Other stars bashing sheikhs were Ron Ely in *Slavers* (1977), Michael Douglas in *The Jewel of the Nile* (1985), Cheech and Chong in *Things Are Tough All Over* (1982), and Eddie Murphy in *Best Defense* (1984). And I almost forgot—Burt Braverman drubs two of movie land's ugliest sheikhs in *Hollywood Hot Tubs 2: Educating Crystal* (1990).

The movies of the 1980s are especially offensive. They display insolent desert sheikhs with thick accents threatening to rape and/or enslave starlets: Brooke Shields in *Sahara* (1983), Goldie Hawn in *Protocol* (1984), Bo Derek in *Bolero* (1984), and Kim Basinger in *Never Say Never Again* (1986).

Finally, five made-in-Israel films lambast sheikhs. Particularly degrading is Golan and Globus' *Paradise* (1981). A combination of Western teenagers and chimpanzees finish off the "jackal," a Christian-hating bedouin chieftain, and his cohorts.

Maidens

Arab women, meanwhile, are humiliated, demonized, and eroticized in more than 50 feature films.

Half-Arab heroines as well as mute enslaved Arab women appear in about sixteen features, ranging from foreign legion films to Arabian Nights fantasies. "The Arabian Nights never end," writes William Zinsser. It is a place where young slave girls lie about on soft couches, stretching their slender legs, ready to do a good turn for any handsome stranger who stumbles into the room. Amid all this décolletage sits the jolly old Caliph, miraculously cool to the wondrous sights around him, puffing his water pipe. . . . This is history at its best.[13]

Stereotypical idiosyncrasies abound, linking the Arab woman to several regularly repeated "B" images:

1. They appear as bosomy bellydancers leering out from diaphanous veils, or as disposable "knick-knacks," scantily-clad harem maidens with bare midriffs, closeted in the palace's women's quarters.

2. Background shots show them as Beasts of Burden, carrying jugs on their heads. Some are "so fat, no one would touch them."

3. In films such as *The Sheltering Sky* (1990) they appear as shapeless Bundles of Black, a homogeneous sea of covered women trekking silently behind their unshaven mates.

4. Beginning in 1917 with Fox's silent *Cleopatra*, starring Theda Bara, studios labeled Arab women "serpents" and "vampires." Subsequently, the word "vamp," a derivation of that word, was added to English dictionaries. Advancing the vampire image are movies such as *Saadia* (1953) and *Beast of Morocco* (1966). Both display Arab women as Black magic vamps, or enchantresses "possessed of devils."

5. In *The Leopard Woman* (1920) and *Nighthawks* (1981) they are Bombers intent on killing Westerners.

When those dark-complexioned femmes fatales move to woo the American/ British hero, they are often disappointed. The majority of movies, such as *Outpost in Morocco* (1949), posit that an Arab woman in love with a Western hero must die.

A few films allow Arab maidens to embrace Western males. In *A Café in Cairo* (1925) and *Arabesque* (1966), actresses Priscilla Dean and Sophia Loren appear as bright and lovely Arab women. Only after the women ridicule and reject Arab suitors, does the scenario allow them to fall into the arms of Western protagonists.

Regrettably, just a handful of movies—*Anna Ascends* (1922), *Princess Tam Tam* (1935), *Bagdad* (1949), *Flame of Araby* (1951), and *Flight from Ashiya* (1964), present brave and compassionate Arab women, genuine heroines. There are also admirable queens and princesses in several Cleopatra films and Arabian fantasy tales.

. . . Taken together, her mute on-screen non-behavior and black-cloaked costume serve to alienate the Arab woman from her international sisters, and vice versa. Not only do the reel Arab women never speak, but they are never in the work place, functioning as doctors, computer specialists, school teachers, print and broadcast journalists, or as successful, well-rounded electric or domestic engineers. Movies don't show charitable Arab women such as those who belong to the Mosaic Foundation, which donates millions to American hospitals. Points out Camelia Anwar Sadat, Syria and Egypt gave women the right to vote as early as Europe did—and much earlier than Switzerland. Today, women make up nearly one-third of the Egyptian parliament. You would never guess from Hollywood's portrayal of Arab women that they are as diverse and talented as any others. Hollywood has not yet imagined a woman as interesting as Ivonne Abdel-Baki, the daughter of Lebanese immigrants and Ecuador's ambassador to Washington. Abdel-Baki, a specialist in conflict resolution, graduated from

Harvard University's Kennedy School of Government and is fluent in five languages. Or De' Al-Mohammed, the University of Missouri's blind fencing star.[14] And many, many more.

Egyptians

... Egyptian caricatures appear in more than 100 films, from mummy tales to legends of pharaohs and queens to contemporary scenarios. Reel Egyptians routinely descend upon Westerners, Israelis, and fellow Egyptians. Interspersed throughout the movies are souk swindlers as well as begging children scratching for baksheesh. An ever-constant theme shows devious Egyptians moving to defile Western women; see Cecil B. DeMille's *Made for Love* (1926) and *Sphinx* (1981).

Stephen Spielberg's films *Raiders of the Lost Ark* (1981), *Young Sherlock Holmes* (1986), and *Indiana Jones and the Last Crusade* (1989) merit special attention, as do Golan-Globus' 1960s scenarios, made-in-Israel: *Cairo Operation* (1965) and *Trunk to Cairo* (1965). The producers paint Egyptians as nuclear-crazed and pro-Nazi. Their scenarios are particularly objectionable given the real-life heroics of the Arab Brotherhood of Freedom, a group of brave Egyptians who sided with the Allies during World War II.

Imagemakers are not so harsh with Queen Cleopatra. Beginning with Helen Gardner's *Cleopatra* (1912), Hollywood enlisted stars such as Ava Gardner, Theda Bara, Vivian Leigh, Sophia Loren, Claudette Colbert, and Elizabeth Taylor to portray Egypt's seductive queen. Approximately fifteen movies show Egypt's queen, encircled by stereotypical maidens, pining over Roman leaders. Only four movies display Egyptian queens romancing Egyptians. The majority display Egyptian royals feuding with fellow Egyptians as well as Rome's soldiers.

A few movies, such as Cecil B. DeMille's *The Ten Commandments* (1923) and Dream-Works' Jeffrey Katzenberg's *The Prince of Egypt* (1998), feature Egyptian rogues trying to crush heroic Israelites. I found the animated *Prince of Egypt* to be less offensive than DeMille's scenarios. Though Katzenberg's movie displays plenty of Egyptian villains, *Prince of Egypt* offers more humane, balanced portraits than do DeMille's 1923 and 1956 versions of *The Ten Commandments*. DeMille's 1923 film shows Egyptian guards beating "the dogs of Israel" and Pharaoh's ten-year-old son whipping Moses.

From the start, moviemakers linked Egypt with the undead. In Georges Méliès's film *The Monster* (1903), the camera reveals a bearded Egyptian magician removing a skeleton from its casket. Presto! He transforms the bony thing into a lovely maiden. But, not for long. The cunning magician changes the woman back into a skeleton.

Say "Egypt" and producers think "Mummies" and "Money." Beginning with Vitagraph's *The Egyptian Mummy* (1914) and *Dust of Egypt* (1915), Hollywood presented about 26 mummy films. In order to spook viewers, cinematographers placed gauze over the camera's lens, creating chilling, dreamlike, and exotic moods. Topping the list is Universal's *The Mummy* (1932). Due to a fine screenplay and Boris Karloff's performance as the mummy Imhotep, this classic stands the test of time as the mummy film. Other popular mummy movies are *The Mummy's Hand* (1940), *The Mummy's Tomb* (1942), and *The Mummy's Revenge* (1973).

Mummy plots are relatively simple: Revived mummies and their caretaker "priests" contest Western archaeologists. In most scenarios, the ambitious gravediggers ignore tomb curses. So of course they suffer the consequences for daring to reawaken Egypt's sleeping royals. Meanwhile, the Westerners dupe ignorant, superstitious, and two-timing Egyptians.

Once fully revived, the bandages-with-eyes mummy lusts after the archaeologist's fair-skinned daughter. And, the mummy crushes panicked Egyptian workers and all crypt violators—"infidels," "unbelievers," and "heretics." Occasionally, movies like *The Awakening* (1980) pump up the action by offering decomposed horrors; also in this one, a queen's evil spirit so contaminates the Western heroine, she kills her father.

Obviously, there's more to the state of Egypt, the most heavily populated of all Arab countries, than pyramids and curses. Egypt is comprised of a people who take pride in their culture and their long and honorable history. Moving to modernize its economy and to improve the living standards of its population, Egypt now boasts more than fourteen state universities. The likes of scholarly students or noted Egyptian archaeologists, men like the celebrated Kamal El Malakh, are absent from movie screens.

Nor do screenwriters present scenarios patterned after Egypt's renowned journalists and authors, like Rose El-Yousef and Nobel Laureate Naguib Mahfouz. Egyptians, like most other Arabs, are deeply religious and are noted for their warm hospitality. In villages and throughout cosmopolitan cities like Cairo and Alexandria, *Ahlan wa Sahlan* (Welcome, this is your home) is spoken as often as "good morning."

Palestinians

. . . Observed Mark Twain, "We are all ignorant, just about different things." When it comes to the Middle East, many Americans are ignorant about the history and plight of the Palestinian people. One reason is that moviegoers may mistakenly believe reel Palestinians, those ugly make-believe film "terrorists," are real Palestinians. Should this be true, then what must viewers think of Palestinians after exiting movie theaters?

To assume viewers acquire some true knowledge of Palestinians after watching the 45 Palestinian fiction films that I discuss here is both dangerous and misleading. It's the same as thinking that you could acquire accurate knowledge of Africans by watching Tarzan movies, or that you would know all about Americans after watching movies about serial killers.

More than half of the Palestinian movies were released in the 1980s and 1990s; nineteen from 1983–1989; nine from 1990–1998. Absent from Hollywood's Israeli-Palestinian movies are human dramas revealing Palestinians as normal folk—computer specialists, domestic engineers, farmers, teachers, and artists. Never do movies present Palestinians as innocent victims and Israelis as brutal oppressors. No movie shows Israeli soldiers and settlers uprooting olive orchards, gunning down Palestinian civilians in Palestinian cities. No movie shows Palestinian families struggling to survive under occupation, living in refugee camps, striving to have their own country and passports stating "Palestine." Disturbingly, only two scenarios present Palestinian families.

. . . One year after the state of Israel was born, the film, *Sword of the Desert* (1949), presented Palestine according to the popular Zionist slogan, as a land without a people—even though the vast majority of people living in Palestine at the time were, in fact, Palestinians. This myth—no-Palestinians-reside-in-Palestine—is also served up in *Cast a Giant Shadow* (1966) and *Judith* (1966).

A decade after *Sword of the Desert* Paul Newman declared war on the Palestinians in *Exodus* (1960). Hollywood's heroes followed suit. In *Prisoner in the Middle* (1974), David Janssen links up with Israeli forces; together they gun down Palestinian nuclear terrorists. Films from the 1980s such as *The Delta Force* (1986) and *Wanted: Dead or Alive* (1987) present Lee Marvin, Chuck Norris, and Rutger Hauer blasting Palestinians in the Mideast and in Los Angeles. In the 1990s, Charlie Sheen and Kurt Russell obliterate Palestinians in Lebanon and aboard a passenger jet, in *Navy SEALs* (1990) and *Executive Decision* (1996).

In *Ministry of Vengeance* (1989) filmmakers dishonor Palestinians and American military chaplains as well. In lieu of presenting the chaplain, a Vietnam veteran, as a devout, non-violent man, the minister exterminates Palestinians. The minister's parishioners approve of the killings, applauding him.

Seven films, including *True Lies* (1994) and *Wanted: Dead or Alive* (1987), project the Palestinian as a nerve-gassing nuclear terrorist. In more than eleven movies, including *Half-Moon Street* (1986), *Terror in Beverly Hills* (1988), and *Appointment with Death* (1988), Palestinian evildoers injure and physically threaten Western women and children.

The reader should pay special attention to *Black Sunday* (1977), Hollywood's first major movie showing Palestinians terrorizing and killing Americans on US soil. Telecast annually the week of Super Bowl Sunday, the movie presents Dahlia, a Palestinian terrorist, and her cohort Fasil. They aim to massacre 80,000 Super Bowl spectators, including the American President, a Jimmy Carter look-alike.

Dictating numerous Palestinian-as-terrorist scenarios is the Israeli connection. More than half (28) of the Palestinian movies were filmed in Israel. Nearly all of the made-in-Israel films, especially the seven Cannon movies, display violent, sex-crazed Palestinian "bastards [and] animals" contesting Westerners, Israelis, and fellow Arabs.

I believe Cannon's poisonous scenarios are not accidental, but rather propaganda disguised as entertainment. Even in the early 1900s studio moguls knew that motion pictures could serve propagandists. Following WWI, Adolph Zukor, the head of Paramount Pictures affirmed this film-as-propaganda fact, saying fiction films should no longer be viewed as simply "entertainment and amusement." The war years, he said, "register[ed] indisputably the fact that as an avenue of propaganda, as a channel for conveying thought and opinion, the movies are unequaled by any form of communication."[15]

Why the Stereotype?

. . . Ask a film industry executive, director, or writer whether it is ethical to perpetuate ethnic or racial stereotypes and you can expect a quick negative response. How then, to explain that since 1970, these very same individuals produced, directed, and scripted more than 350 films portraying Arabs as insidious cultural "others"?

Either filmmakers are perpetuating the stereotype unknowingly, and would immediately disassociate themselves from such activities were they to realize the implications of their actions, or they are doing so knowingly and will only stop when sufficient pressure is brought to bear on them.

It is difficult to imagine that screenwriters who draft scenes of fat, lecherous sheikhs ogling Western blondes, or crazed Arab terrorists threatening to blow up America with nuclear weapons, are not precisely aware of what they are doing. But we sometimes forget that one of the elements that makes stereotyping so powerful, and so hard to eliminate, is that it is self-perpetuating. Filmmakers grew up watching Western heroes crush hundreds of reel "bad" Arabs. Some naturally repeat the stereotype without realizing that, in so doing, they are innocently joining the ranks of the stereotypes' creators.

Huge inroads have been made toward the elimination of many racial and ethnic stereotypes from the movie screen, but Hollywood's stereotype of Arabs remains unabated. Over the last three decades stereotypical portraits have actually increased in number and virulence.

The Arab stereotype's extraordinary longevity is the result, I believe, of a collection of factors. For starters, consider print and broadcast "if it bleeds it leads" news reports. Like most Americans, creators of popular culture (including novelists, cartoonists, and filmmakers), form their opinions of a people, in part, based on what they read in print, hear on the radio, and see on television. Like the rest of us, they are inundated and influenced by a continuous flow of "seen one, seen 'em all" headlines and sound bites.

. . . The image began to intensify in the late 1940s when the state of Israel was founded on Palestinian land. From that preemptive point on—through the Arab-Israeli wars of 1948, 1967, and 1973, the hijacking of planes, the disruptive 1973 Arab oil embargo, along with the rise of Libya's Muammar Qaddafi and Iran's Ayatollah Khomeini—shot after shot delivered the relentless drum beat that all Arabs were and are Public Enemy No. 1.

Right through the 1980s, the 1990s, and into the twenty-first century, this "bad people" image prevailed, especially during the Palestinian intifada and the Israeli invasion of Lebanon. In 1980, the rabid followers of Iran's Ayatollah Khomeini held 52 Americans hostage at the US Embassy in Teheran for 444 days. Nightly, TV cameras blazoned across the planet Khomeini's supporters chanting "Death to America!" and calling our country "the Great Satan" as they burned our flag and, in effigy, Uncle Sam himself.

At the height of the Iranian hostage crisis anti-Arab feelings intensified, as 70 percent of Americans wrongly identified Iran as an Arab country. Even today, most Americans think of Iranians as Arabs. In fact, Iranians are Persians, another people altogether.

. . . It got worse in the 1990s. Two major events, the Iraqi invasion of Kuwait that led to the Gulf War, and the bombing of New York City's World Trade Center, combined to create misguided mindset, leading some Americans to believe all Arabs are terrorists and that Arabs do not value human life as much as we do. As a result, some of us began even perceiving our fellow Americans of Arab descent as clones of Iraq's Saddam Hussein and the terrorist Osama bin Laden. Well, I think you get the picture.

. . . Not only do these violent news images of extremists reinforce and exacerbate already prevalent stereotypes, but they serve as both a source and excuse for continued Arab-bashing by those filmmakers eager to exploit the issue. In particular, the news programs are used by some producers and directors to deny they are actually engaged in stereotyping. "We're not stereotyping," they object. "Just look at your television set. Those are real Arabs."

Such responses are disingenuous and dishonest. As we know, news reports by their very nature cover extraordinary events. We should not expect reporters to inundate the airwaves with the lives of ordinary Arabs. But filmmakers have a moral obligation not to advance the news media's sins of omission and commission, not to tar an entire group of people on the basis of the crimes and the alleged crimes of a few.

. . . Why would anyone take part in the denigration of a people knowingly? I think one answer is the Arab-Israeli conflict. Though the majority of moviemakers are fair-minded professionals, there are some who, in the interests of pursuing their own political or personal agenda, are willing to perpetuate hate. These individuals may be expected to continue to indict Arabs on movie screens for as long as unjust images are tolerated.

New York Times columnist Maureen Dowd offers another answer: "[S]tereotypes are not only offensive [but] they are also comforting. They . . . exempt people from any further mental or emotional effort. They wrap life in the arch toastiness of fairy tale and myth. They make complicated understandings unnecessary."[16] Convenient stereotypes make everyone's job easier. Rather than having to pen a good joke, the writer inserts a stumbling, bumbling sheikh. Looking for a villain? Toss in an Arab terrorist—we all know what they look like from watching movies and TV. No thought required. As for the audience? Well, it also makes some of us feel better to see ourselves as superior to someone else. If one is no longer allowed to feel superior to Asians, Jews, Latinos, or blacks, at least we can feel superior to those wretched Arabs.

. . . Certainly, the Department of Defense's rubber-stamping of motion pictures that lambaste Arabs plays a role. The fact is, the government has a history of playing a role in what movies do and don't get made. As early as 1917, the federal government not only acknowledged the power of film to influence political thought, it took on the wrongful role of censor. As soon as the United States declared war on Germany, the government declared that no Hollywood movie could arouse prejudice against friendly nations. The 1917 film *The Spirit of '76* reveals heroic American revolutionaries such as Patrick Henry and Paul Revere. But, some frames show British soldiers committing acts of atrocities. As England was our World War I ally, the government protested; a judge declared producer Robert Goldstein's movie advanced anti-British sentiments. Calling the film "potent German propaganda,"[17] the judge sentenced Goldstein to prison.

Greed, too, is an incentive. Bash-the-Arab movies make money. Thus, some producers exploit the stereotype for profit.

. . . The absence of vibrant film criticism is another cause. A much-needed recourse against harmful Arab images would be more vigorous criticism emanating from industry executives and movie critics. I recall, still, Bosley Crowther's *New York Times* review of *Adventure in Sahara* (1938). Instead of criticizing stereotypes, Crowther advanced them, writing: "We know the desert is no picnic and you can't trust an Arab very far."

Another factor is silence. No significant element of public opinion has yet to oppose the stereotype; even scholars and government officials are mum. If we are ever to illuminate our common humanity, our nation's leaders must challenge all hateful stereotypes. Teachers need to move forward and incorporate, at long last, discussions of Arab caricatures in schools, colleges, military, and government classrooms.

Ethnic stereotypes do not die off on their own, but are hunted down and terminated by those whom the stereotypes victimize. Other groups, African-Americans, Asian-Americans and Jewish-Americans, have acted aggressively against discriminatory portraits. Arab-Americans as a group, however, have been slow to mobilize and, as a result, their protests are rarely heard in Hollywood and even when heard, are heard too faintly to get the offenders to back off.

Another reason is lack of presence. With the exception of a few movies, *Party Girl* (1995) and *A Perfect Murder* (1998), Arab-Americans are invisible on movie screens. One reason, simply put, is that there are not many Arab-Americans involved in the film industry; not one is a famous Hollywood celebrity.

What does their absence have to do with contesting stereotypes? Well, one answer is that movie stars have clout. Consider how Brad Pitt altered the scenario, *The Devil's Own* (1996). After reading the initial script, Pitt protested, telling the studio the screenplay made him "uneasy" because it was loaded with stereotypes—"full of leprechaun jokes and green beer." The dialogue, he argued, unfairly painted his character as a stereotypical Irish "bad" guy. Explains Pitt, "I had the responsibility to represent somewhat these [Irish] people whose lives have been shattered. It would have been an injustice to Hollywood-ize it." Unless changes were made to humanize the Irish people, especially his character, Pitt "threatened to walk." The studio acquiesced, bringing in another writer to make the necessary changes.

Also, when it comes to studio moguls, not one Arab American belongs to the media elite. The community boasts no communication giants comparable to Disney's Michael Eisner, DreamWorks' Jeffrey Katzenberg, Fox's Rupert Murdoch, or Time-Warner's Ted Turner.

The lack of an Arab-American presence impacts the stereotype in another way. The industry has a dearth of those men and women who would be the most naturally inclined to strive for accurate and balanced portrayals of Arabs. But a number of high-level Arab Americans in the industry over the course of time would rectify the situation. It's difficult to demean people and their heritage when they're standing in front of you, especially if those persons are your bosses.

. . . Regrettably, America's Arabs do not yet have an organized and active lobby in Los Angeles. To bring about fundamental changes in how motion pictures project Arabs, a systematic lobbying effort is needed. Though the Arab-American and Muslim-American presence is steadily growing in number and visibility in the United States, only a few Arab-Americans meet with and discuss the stereotype with filmmakers. When dialogue does occur, some discriminatory portraits are altered. Declares a February 3, 2001, Council on American-Islamic Relations (CAIR) fax: "The villains in Paramount's upcoming film, The Sum of All Fears, were changed to European neo-Nazis." CAIR officials acknowledged Paramount for this important change, as Tom Clancy's book, on which the movie is based, presents Arab Muslims detonating a nuclear device at the Super Bowl in Denver. In a letter to CAIR, the film's director, Phil Alden Robinson, wrote: "I hope you will be reassured that I have no intention of portraying negative images of Arabs or Muslims."

Ongoing informal and formal meetings with movie executives are essential. Such sessions enable community members to more readily explain to producers the negative effects misperceptions of Arabs have on their children as well as on American public opinion and policy. Also, Arab-Americans need to reach out and expand their concerns with well-established ethnic and minority lobbying groups—with Asians, blacks, Jews, Latinos, gays and lesbians, and others.

Positives

To see is to make possible new ways of seeing. . . . I have tried to be uncompromisingly truthful, and to expose the Hollywood stereotype of Arabs for all to see. While it is true that most filmmakers have vilified the Arab, others have not. Some contested harmful stereotypes, displaying positive images—that is, casting an Arab as a regular person.

In memorable well-written movies, ranging from the Arabian Nights fantasy *The Thief of Bagdad* (1924), to the World War II drama *Sahara* (1943), producers present Arabs not as a threateningly different people but as "regular" folks, even as heroes. In *Sahara,* to save his American friends, a courageous Arab soldier sacrifices his life.

Note this father and son exchange from the film *Earthbound* (1980):

Son: "Why do they [the police] hate us so?"

Father: "I guess because we're different."

Son: "Just because somebody's different doesn't mean they have to hate 'em. It's stupid."

Father: "It's been stupid for a long time."

At first, I had difficulty uncovering "regular" and admirable Arab characters—it was like trying to find an oasis in the desert. Yet, I discovered more than 50 motion pictures sans Arab villains, five percent of the total number reviewed here. Refreshingly, the movies debunk stale images, humanizing Arabs.

As for those Arabian Nights fantasies of yesteryear, only a few viziers, magicians, or other scalawags lie in ambush. Mostly fabulous Arabs appear in *The Desert Song* (1929), *Ali Baba and the Forty Thieves* (1944), *Son of Sinbad* (1955), and *Aladdin and His Magic Lamp* (1969). The movies present viewers with brave and moral protagonists: Aladdin, Ali Baba, and Sinbad. Emulating the deeds of Robin Hood and his men of Sherwood Forest, Arabs liberate the poor from the rich, and free the oppressed from corrupt rulers.

Worth noting is the presence of glittering Arabs in non-fantasy movies. A heroic Egyptian princess appears in the movie serial, *Chandu the Magician* (1932). A courageous Egyptian innkeeper assists British troops in *Five Graves to Cairo* (1943). *Gambit* (1966) displays a compassionate Arab entrepreneur. In *King Richard and the Crusaders* (1954), Saladin surfaces as a dignified, more humane leader than his counterpart, Richard.

Some independent Israeli filmmakers, notably those whose movies were financed by the Fund for the Promotion of Israeli Quality Films, allow viewers to empathize with Palestinians, presenting three-dimensional portraits. To their credit, producers of *Beyond the Walls* (1984) and *Cup Final* (1992) contest the self-promotional history and Palestinian stereotypes spun out by most other filmmakers. Both movies show the Palestinian and the Israeli protagonist bonding; the two men are projected as soul-mates, innocent victims of the Arab-Israeli conflict.

Notes

1. The 22 Arab states are Algeria, Bahrain, Chad, Comoros, Djibouti, Egypt, Iraq, Jordan, Lebanon, Libya, Mauritania, Morocco, Oman, Palestine, Qatar, Saudi Arabia, Somalia, Sudan, Syria, Tunisia, United Arab Emirates, and Yemen.

2. Jay Stone, *Ottawa Citizen* 16 March 1996.

3. William Greider, "Against the Grain," *Washington Post* 15 July 1979: 4E.

4. Jerry Mander, *Four Arguments for the Elimination of Television* (New York: William Morrow, 1978).

5. See ADC, "The Anti-Discrimination Hate Crimes," (Washington, DC, 1996).

6. For movies featuring African-American actors destroying reel Arabs, see *Best Defense* (1984), *Iron Eagle* (1986), *The Delta Force* (1986), *Wanted: Dead or Alive* (1987), *Firewalker* (1986), *Kazaam* (1996), *The Siege* (1998), and *Rules of Engagement* (2000).

7. Matthew Sweet, "Movie Targets: Arabs Are the Latest People to Suffer the Racial Stereotyping of Hollywood," *The Independent* 30 July 2000.

8. Lawrence Suid, *Sailing on the Silver Screen: Hollywood and the U.S. Navy* (Annapolis, MD: Naval Institute Press, 1996): 151.

9. Greider 1E.

10. Sweet.

11. Edward W. Said, *Orientalism* (New York: Pantheon, 1978): 125.

12. I.C.B. Dear and M.R.D. Foot, eds., *The Oxford Companion to World War II* (Oxford: Oxford University Press, 1995).

13. William Zinsser, "In Search of Lawrence of Arabia," *Esquire* June 1961: 72.

14. "Fencing by Ear," *Missou* Fall 1997: 11.

15. Adolph Zukor, "Most Important Events of the Year," *Wid's Year Book* 1918. For more on Palestinian portraits, see my essay "Screen Images of Palestinians in the 1980s," *Beyond the Stars, Volume 1: Stock Characters in American Film*, ed. Paul Loukides and Linda K. Fuller (Bowling Green, OH: Bowling Green State University Press, 1990).

16. Maureen Dowd, "Cuomos vs. Sopranos," *New York Times* 22 April 2001.

17. *Censored!*, documentary, American Movie Classics, 7 December 1999.

Jack G. Shaheen is a professor emeritus of mass communications at Southern Illinois University. Dr. Shaheen is the world's foremost authority on media images of Arabs and Muslims. He regularly appears on national programs such as Nightline, Good Morning America, 48 Hours, *and* The Today Show. *He is the author of* Arab and Muslim Stereotyping in American Popular Culture, Nuclear War Films, *and the award-winning* TV Arab. Los Angeles Times *TV critic Howard Rosenberg calls* Reel Bad Arabs: How Hollywood Vilifies a People *"a groundbreaking book that dissects a slanderous history dating from cinema's earliest days to contemporary Hollywood blockbusters that feature machine-gun wielding and bomb-blowing 'evil' Arabs."*

6

How to Read Iron Man: *The Economics, Geopolitics and Ideology of an Imperial Film Commodity*

Tanner Mirrlees

Iron Man (2008) is a Hollywood film produced by Marvel Studios and distributed by Viacom-owned Paramount Pictures. Based on the Cold War-era Marvel comic by the same name, the film is about Tony Stark (Robert Downey, Jr.), a multi-millionaire engineer whose Stark Industries (inherited from his father) researches, develops and sells weapons technologies to the U.S. Department of Defense (DOD). In the opening scene, Stark is escorted to U.S.-occupied Afghanistan by a friendly DOD liaison, Lieutenant Colonel James Rhodes (Terrence Howard). There, Stark demonstrates the killing power of a new commercialized weapon system (the "Jericho Missile") but is soon after ambushed and taken captive in a cave by a jihadist group called The Ten Rings. Stark is almost killed by IED shrapnel, which is lodged close to his heart. But Yinsen, Stark's fellow captive, saves him by grafting an electromagnet into Stark's chest to keep the shrapnel from reaching his heart. The terrorist leader Raza then forces Stark and Yinsen to make weapons of mass destruction (WMDs) for them from the cave. But instead of doing so, they engineer an electric generator (the arc reactor) and a weaponized armoured battle-suit, which Stark uses to escape. Yinsen is killed, but Stark fights his way to freedom and is then rescued by the DOD, which takes him back to the U.S. There, Stark announces that he will no longer sell WMDs, but Obadiah Stane, the manager of Stark Industries, advises him against this decision. To his dismay, Stark learns that the weapons Stark Industries sells are being used by the Ten Rings to kill peasant Afghanis and also, that Stane wants to cut him out of Stark Industries. Stark engineers a new weaponized armour suit, flies back to Afghanistan, kills the terrorists and saves the Afghani villagers. Pepper Potts (Gwyneth Paltrow), Stark's assistant, discovers that Stane supplied the Ten Rings with WMDs and also, hired the terrorist group to kill Stark. At the film's climax, Stark battles Stane (who dons his own battle-suit) atop his Stark Industries and defeats him with a massive energy blast. The film ends with Stark revealing his super-hero identity to the press.

Reprinted from *Cineaction* 92 no. 2 (summer 2013).

Iron Man was made in a world system in which the U.S. is the dominant imperial power. Since at least WWII, the U.S. state and U.S. corporations have struggled to rule markets across territories by building, promoting and policing a world system of states that share the U.S.'s core features: the capitalist mode of production, the liberal democratic state form, and the consumerist "way of life." The U.S. fights for "hegemony" in the world system through the incorporation of others, using strategies of coercion and ideological persuasion, brute force and consent building. In the early 21st century, the U.S. continues to be a dominant imperial power, economically, militarily and media-culturally. The U.S. economy is three times the size of the world's next largest, Japan. With only 4.6% of the world population, the U.S. accounts for about 27.5% of the world's total Gross Domestic Product (GDP). *Iron Man* exists in a world in which U.S.-based corporations are backed by the U.S. Department of Defense (DOD)—the Army, Navy, Marine Corps, Air Force, and Coast Guard—which controls more than half a million troops, is equipped with nearly half of the world's total weapons and has more than eight hundred and sixty five military bases in more than forty foreign countries. *Iron Man* is also part of globalizing Hollywood, major film companies that are located in Los Angeles, California, but have business operations that encircle the planet. Hollywood studios, distribution networks and exhibition platforms are largely controlled by six U.S.-based transnational media conglomerates (TNMCs): the Walt Disney Company, Comcast-NBC-Universal, News Corporation, Viacom, Time-Warner and Sony Entertainment of America. TNMC-controlled Hollywood exerts asymmetrical influence over the internal structure, ownership patterns, distribution and exhibition process and standards of film of other national film industries without proportionate reciprocation of influence by them. Hollywood's worldwide box office revenues climbed in 2011 to $32.6 billion and in 2012, rose even higher to $34.7 billion.[1] Hollywood adds nearly $180 billion to the U.S. economy each year and sustains a near one-way flow of film commodities between the U.S. and other countries. Hollywood TNMCs control the property rights to the top 30 all-time worldwide highest grossing films and in 2012, Hollywood made all of the top ten highest grossing films: *The Avengers, Skyfall, The Dark Knight Rises, The Hobbit: An Unexpected Journey, Ice Age: Continental Drift, The Twilight Saga, The Amazing Spider-Man, Madagascar 3,* and *The Hunger Games*. In terms of its economic size, military preponderance and cultural power, the U.S. is an Empire.

In this article, I argue that *Iron Man* is one small but important part of the U.S. Empire. While much has been made of *Iron Man*'s spectacle as Hollywood entertainment media, this article examines how *Iron Man* is shaped by and supportive of the economic, military and ideological power of the U.S. Empire. I argue that *Iron Man* supports U.S. economic power (as a Hollywood blockbuster and synergistic franchise), U.S. military power (as DOD-Hollywood co-produced militainment) and cultural power (as a national and global relay for U.S. imperial ideologies). The nexus of the actual world of U.S. Empire and the reel world of Hollywood film expressed by *Iron Man* highlights how popular film is not "just entertainment" that circulates in apolitical theatre markets, but is linked to and supportive of the geopolitical-economy and ideology of the U.S. Empire. Combining the political-economy of communications and critical cultural studies methods, I explore the nexus of the U.S. security state, Hollywood and film so as to critically interpret *Iron Man* with respect to the broad economic, geopolitical and ideological forces and relations that shape it.

The Economic Power of *Iron Man*: A Synergistic Blockbuster for the Walt Disney Company

Iron man is a blockbuster film and synergistic franchise that supports the U.S. Empire's economic power by extending Hollywood's global market dominance, adding to the Walt Disney Company's profits and perpetuating the class power of Robert I. Ager, Disney's CEO, Chairman and major shareholder.

Like all blockbuster films, *Iron Man* was made with a big budget ($140,000,000) with the goal of making Hollywood as much money as possible. To cultivate consumer demand for this film and attract viewers to theatres, Marvel Studios and Paramount Pictures mass marketed *Iron Man* using in-cinema previews, TV ad spots (one during halftime of Super Bowl XLII), ads in newspapers and on billboards, buses, benches and websites, soft news interviews with actors, tie-ins at thousands of 7-Eleven stores and Burger King chains and via social media platforms like Facebook. After creating global hype, buzz and intrigue, Paramount Pictures mass-released *Iron Man* to theatres worldwide. Between April 14, 2008 and May 14, 2008, the *Iron Man* commodity flowed across and was consumed in eighty countries including Argentina, Brazil, China, Germany, Estonia, Iceland, India, Israel, Malaysia, Mexico, New Zealand, Pakistan, Russia, South Africa, Ukraine, the United Arab Emirates and Vietnam. As *Iron Man* crossed the borders of these and other countries, the title was translated or dubbed into local languages. In Argentina, *Iron Man* became *El Hombre de hierro*; in Brazil, *Homem de Ferro*; in Estonia, *Raudmees*; in Greece, *O atsalenios anthropos*; in Japan, *Aian Man*; in Russia, *Железный человек*, in Vietnam, *Nguoi Sat*. *Iron Man's* box office returns quadrupled the amount the film cost to make. Overall, *Iron Man* took a total of $585.2 million: $318.4 at the "North American" box office (54.5% of the total) and $266.8 million at the worldwide box office (45.6% of the total).[2] *Iron Man's* production budget was approximately $140 million, meaning the film generated a little more than $445 million at the box office. This box office return made *Iron Man* the 89th highest grossing worldwide film of all time and set in motion Marvel Studios' production of *Iron Man 2* (2010) (the 74th highest grossing worldwide film of all time) and *Iron Man 3* (2013), the 3rd highest grossing film of all time. Clearly, *Iron Man* contributed to Hollywood's global market dominance.

In addition to being a global blockbuster, *Iron Man* is a synergistic entertainment franchise, designed to generate as much revenue for its owners as possible, not only through the accumulation of box office receipts, but also, through the sale of ancillary commodities. At the core of the *Iron Man* franchise is the comic book (stories and characters), which prior to the film, already had a big fan base and whose "high concept" was widely recognized by people. Spreading from the core of the *Iron Man* concept are brand extensions that expand a consumable *Iron Man* experience through commodities, screens, platforms and stores. Accompanying the "pre-sold" release of the *Iron Man* film to the world was a CD soundtrack (composed by Ramin Djawadi, an *Iron Man* fan) and an *Iron Man* Video game (published by Sega and released on Playstation 3, Xbox 360, Playstation 2, Playstation Portable, Nintendo DS, Wii, and PCs). In the lead up to and following this multi-platform release, *Iron Man* merchandise (action figures, coffee mugs, T-shirts, candy, trading cards) was sold by retailers at shopping malls around the world. Four months following its theatrical release, *Iron Man* DVDs and Blue-ray discs started filling the shelves of more retailers and rental stores and soon after, the film was licensed to broadcast and cable TV networks and pay-per-view providers in the U.S. and elsewhere, generating even more revenue for *Iron Man's* owners. To generate long-term engagement with the *Iron Man* brand, Marvel Studios built an *Iron Man* Web site that invites users to interactively "learn more" about the film, read character profiles, view stills, watch preview trailers, sign up to receive emails, deals and "insider info" and download desktop *Iron Man* themed wallpaper, screensavers and skins. The website uses its users to extend the *Iron Man* brand through their own lives, bodies and screens and also, uses its users' creativity and love of the story and characters to generate *Iron Man* fan art, which it co-opts and showcases to add further value to the overall franchise. *Iron Man* is not just a blockbuster, but a synergistic entertainment property designed to move consumers from medium to medium, commodity to commodity, transaction to transaction. With each user gaze, click, move, download and turn, additional revenue is generated for *Iron Man's* owners.

While spinning out branded commodities based upon itself, the *Iron Man* also cross-promotes brands for other products. Hollywood has been fused with branding and the result is "branded entertainment": films that try to cultivate goodwill for brands by associating them with the positive attributes of scripted protagonists. *Iron Man* is an example of branded entertainment. For example, after battling his way out of an Afghan cave and crash landing in an Afghan desert, Stark talks about longing for "a real American cheeseburger." In the next scene, Stark has been rescued from Afghanistan, returned to the U.S. and has had his appetite sated by Burger King, whose Whopper wrapper he dangles in the face of journalists at a press conference. *Iron Man* celebrates the liberation of Stark from Afghan terrorists, but places its own viewers in a cage of corporate brand culture: Pepper Potts drives an Audi; Stark uses a Mac computer and reads *Vanity Fair, Rolling Stone,* and *Wired* magazines; other characters fashion Bulgari watches, LG phones and Dell computers.

Though *Iron Man* made money for Marvel Studios and Paramount Pictures in 2008, since 2009, the film has been exploited as a revenue source by the Walt Disney Company, which acquired *Iron Man* from Marvel Studios in 2009 by merging this studio into its ownership portfolio. Since mid-1990s, Marvel Studios had operated as a semi-independent production company that made and licensed content for the majors. Marvel Studios generated revenue by making TV shows and films based on the content of its comic book collection and then selling distribution rights to these media commodities to bigger conglomerates. It also licensed the film production rights to comics like *The Avengers, Daredevil, The Incredible Hulk, Iron Man, The Fantastic Four, Spider-Man, X-Men* to bigger studios, which developed them into films and then sold the distribution rights to other companies, which rented them to theatre chains and other exhibitors. Noticing the popular appeal and box of returns accruing to Marvel comic book films like *X-Men, The Incredible Hulk* and *Iron Man*, the Walt Disney Company launched a takeover of the company. On August 31, 2009, the Walt Disney Company bought Marvel Studios and with it, an archive of at least 5,000 comic book characters, each a potential source of a new synergistic franchise to be spread, cross-promoted and sold across films, TV series, video games, toys, rides and more. The Walt Disney Company's CEO, Robert A. Iger, said that by buying Marvel, he gained control of a "treasure trove" of intellectual property and that this comic world offered "so many opportunities to mine [for value] both characters that are known and characters that are not widely known."[3] Stan Lee, Marvel's founder, enthused that the Walt Disney and Marvel convergence would "be extremely beneficial to both companies" and be a "perfect synergy."[4] This synergy has served the Walt Disney Company well, as it has made Marvel characters into two of the world's top five highest grossing films of all time: *The Avengers* (#3) and *Iron Man 3* (#5). The Walt Disney Company's Marvel feature films, including *Iron Man*, contribute to its annual revenue. In 2012, the Walt Disney Company generated $42.3 billion in revenue, a sum greater than the combined 2012 GDP of the world's six poorest countries: the Democratic Republic of the Congo (17.87 billion), Liberia (1.767 billion), Zimbabwe ($10.81 billion), Burundi (2.472 billion), Eritrea (3.092 billion) and the Central African Republic (2.139 billion). Moreover, the Walt Disney Company's control of *Iron Man* supports the class power of Robert A. Iger, Disney's Chairman, Chief Executive Office (CEO) and holder of 1,159,675 Disney shares. In 2007, *Fortune* magazine ranked Iger as one of the "25 Most Powerful People in Business" and he is one of the top ten highest paid people in the U.S. In 2011, Iger took home $28 million.

In sum, *Iron Man* supports the economic power of the U.S. Empire by sustaining the global market dominance of Hollywood and its cross-border trade in blockbuster films, synergistically cross-promoting itself and other U.S. commodities through itself and other derivative goods, and generating revenue for the Walt Disney Company and its U.S. ruler and owner, Iger.

The Military Power of *Iron Man*: The DOD-Hollywood Complex and Militainment

In addition to supporting U.S. economic power, *Iron Man* supports the U.S. Empire's military power as a form of DOD-Hollywood complex "militainment" that serves DOD public relations goals (PR).

The DOD-Hollywood complex refers to the symbiotic (mutually beneficial) relationships between the DOD and Hollywood studios which encourage the production of films which glorify militarism as a way of life. For the past hundred years, the DOD has supported the business of Hollywood and many Hollywood war films have aligned with the DOD's use of PR to engineer public support for militarism and state violence. DOD-Hollywood complex militainment is designed to make the DOD look good and to make Hollywood money. In the 21st century, the DOD controls a centralized Hollywood liaison office that links every branch of the DOD. Headed by Phil Strub and located in the Pentagon, Washington, D.C., the Department of Defense Special Assistant for Entertainment Media (DODSAEM) is the "go to" place for Hollywood studios that wish to produce war films with the DOD. The Army's Hollywood liaison is called the Office of Army Chief of Public Affairs; the Navy's is called the Navy Office of Information West; the Air Force's is the Office of Public Affairs-Entertainment Liaison Office; the Marine Corps' is the Public Affairs Motion Picture and Television Liaison; the Coast Guard's is called the Motion Picture and TV Office.

The DODSAEM, a DOD-film policy agency, grants war filmmakers access to military locations (bases, barracks, battlefields), personnel (U.S. officers and soldiers), software (knowledge about military protocol, chain of command, systems operation, troop lingo, drill routines), and most importantly, hardware (actual battleships, jet fighters, tanks, helicopters and guns), so long as their war scripts meet DOD content requirements. Hollywood war scripts that promote the DOD's image to the public, cast the DOD in a positive light, align with DOD policy objectives and link with the DOD's ongoing recruitment efforts tend to get DOD support while those that fail to meet these content stipulations, do not. Since 9/11, the DOD has helped Hollywood studios make a number of blockbuster war films such as *Pearl Harbor* (2001), *Enemy At the Gates* (2001), *Black Hawk Down* (2001), *Bad Company* (2002), *Behind Enemy Lines* (2002), and *Windtalkers* (2002), *Transformers* (2007), *Transformers: Revenge of the Fallen* (2009). *Iron Man* is thus one among many examples of DOD-Hollywood complex militainment. The DODSAEM supported *Iron Man*'s production by linking Marvel Studios to the U.S. Air Force, which turned its Edwards Air Force Base into a Hollywood set piece for three days of shooting. The Air Force allowed Marvel Studios to cast over one hundred Airmen as extras in the film, flew its F-22 Raptor aircraft for the camera to help Marvel create high altitude action combat sequences, provisioned helicopters, Humvees and jumbo jets, and even let its service-people act in the film. Technical Sergeant Thoshiya Jones played a pilot; Second Lieutenant Carsten Stahr played an Army special operations soldier; and Staff Sergeant Joe Gambles of the 31st Test and Evaluation Squadron acted as an Air Force pilot in a scene with Rhodie. "No other Air Force base has this opportunity", enthused Gambles. "We're near Hollywood and we work with Hollywood all the time."[5] The Air Force also supported *Iron Man*'s production by giving acting lessons to Terrence Howard by embedding him on its base and letting him observe, train with and learn about the way the Air Force operates and communicates.

By working with the Air Force, Marvel Studios saved on production costs (associated with acquiring and flying an F-22 Raptor, paying extras to play as soldiers, renting locations to shoot and more). For director Jon Favreau, his DOD-Hollywood synergy also enhanced the "realism" of *Iron Man*: "This is the best back lot you could ever have. Every angle you shoot is authentic: desert, dry lake beds, hangars." The Air Force is full of "tremendous professionals," he said. "Every background performer is a bit of technical advisor. So there's a plethora of information available to you." The Air Force was happy to help Favreau make *Iron Man* seem "realistic," so long as its comic book fantasy helped promote a positive image of itself to the public and to the world. Master Sergeant Larry Belen described *Iron Man*'s contribution to Air Force PR: "I want people to walk away from this movie with a really good impression of the Air Force, like they got about the Navy seeing Top Gun." Air Force Captain Christian Hodge, *Iron Man*'s DOD Project Officer, said the film was also "good for [troop] morale" as it made its airmen look "like rock stars." Furthermore, the Air Force chose to help Marvel Studios make

Iron Man because it believed the character Rhodie conveyed its key values. According to Lt. Colonel Stephen Clutter, the Air Force Entertainment Liaison Office director, "The character of Rhodes reflects our warrior ethos and the professionalism that is so important to our Air Force culture."[6] Clutter continued: "Mr. Howard worked very hard to ensure Airmen would be proud of his character. [. . .] We're also proud of the fact that the airman battle uniform made its Hollywood debut in the film."

In addition to serving Air Force PR goals, *Iron Man* promotionally interfaces with the DOD's attempt to make a cyborg-soldier suit capable of enhancing the strength, speed, security and intellect of U.S. war-fighters. Since the 1990s, DOD proponents of a revolution in military affairs (RMA) have argued that information and communication technologies (ICTs) are transforming war and that the DOD must prepare itself to fight 21st century Network Centric Warfare (NCW) by integrating ICTs into every facet of what it does and networking its soldiers with weapon systems and the hardware and software of the information age: computers, mobile devices, the World Wide Web.[7] The DOD also strives to enhance the physical, cognitive and sensorial powers of its soldiers by equipping them with combinations of ICTs, artificial intelligence (AI) supports, augmented reality interfaces (ARIs) and wearable exoskeletons. To generate buzz about these "cyborg-soldier" R&D projects, the DOD is linking them to the *Iron Man* film. Since *Iron Man*'s debut, DOD-sponsored university researchers and defense companies have been "working to turn *Iron Man* fiction into real technology."[8] As the military analyst Max Boot says, the DOD is designing suits that aim to "give ordinary mortals many of the attributes of comic book superheroes."[9] At the University of Utah and the University Berkeley, for example, DARPA-funded researchers say they aim to create an "Iron Man" suit that would "protect soldiers in combat by giving them increased strength and endurance."[10] At MIT, the Army-supported Future Force Warrior project intends to make *Iron Man* into a new innovation. U.S. journalists have echoed this excitement, simultaneously promoting the *Iron Man* film and the DOD's cyborg-soldier R&D. The Popular Science magazine story "Building the Real *Iron Man*," forwards the headline: "While audiences flood theaters this month to see the comic-book-inspired *Iron Man*, a real-life mad genius toils in a secret mountain lab to make the mechanical superhuman more than just fantasy."[11] A September 10, 2012 CNNMoney news segment avers: "*Iron Man* is a prized military asset in the movie, the ultimate soldier. Hollywood styles it as futuristic fantasy, but decades of research, development and considerable investment have made bionic technology a reality."[12] A Slate video declares "Yes, the U.S. Military is building real *Iron Man* suits"[13] while a YouTube video says "US Army test real life *Iron Man* exoskeleton."[14]

These stories and videos promote the idea that the suit worn by Stark in *Iron Man* has become or one day will become a reality, and this is what the DOD hopes will one day happen. *Iron Man* offers the DOD's researchers a way to promote their cyborg-soldier R&D to the public and also, a fictional model to inspire their present-day prototypes. The *Iron Man* suit and MIT's Future Force Warrior prototype, for example, have much in common. In addition to being battery powered, they are equipped with flexible armor that protects the wearer's body from bullet fire, Heads Up Display Units (HUDs) that extend the wearer's vision across many screens and tactical imaging systems, ear-pieces that extend the wearer's hearing through global telecommunication systems, physiological monitoring devices that record and track wearer's heart rate, temperature and hydration, and a variety of personalized impact-heavy but physically light weapons systems the wearer can kill with. Like Stark's Iron Man suit, the actual suits being designed by the DOD are designed to augment or enhance the wearer's experience of reality so they may more effectively and efficiently defend America and attack its enemies. The *Iron Man* film sequences which show off the military capabilities of Stark's suit not only prefigure the DOD's cyborg-soldier, but also, encourage viewers to expect a future of cyborgian soldier warfare ruled by the U.S. By doing this, *Iron Man* normalizes a future that is yet to be while cultivating public compliance with present-day DOD expenditure on R&D that aims to make *Iron Man*'s cyborgian weapons system real.

In sum, *Iron Man* serves the U.S. DOD as a form of DOD-Hollywood militainment that glorifies the Air Force and promotes the military-industrial-academic-complex's R&D on cyborg-soldier weapons technology.

The Cultural Power of *Iron Man*: The Imperial Ideology of the *Iron Man* Text

Iron Man gives cultural and ideological support to the U.S. Empire by affirming post-9/11 U.S. foreign policy in Afghanistan, U.S. exceptionalism, and a distinctly U.S. military-industrial-complex (MIC).

Following 9/11, the U.S. launched an invasion and prolonged occupation of Afghanistan, a country from which Osama bin Laden and Al-Qaeda allegedly planned and orchestrated the 9/11 attacks. *Iron Man* supports the U.S. state's post-9/11 foreign policy in Afghanistan by depicting it as a space of threat to America, a space that must be contained and controlled with military might. In the film's opening scene, Stark is being toured around Afghanistan by the DOD and is then ambushed by the Ten Rings jihadist terrorist group, which kills U.S. soldiers and nearly kills Stark. By representing Afghanistan as a place full of fanatical terrorists that wish to kill Americans and conquer the region, the film affirms the U.S.'s post-9/11 occupation of this country. Moreover, *Iron Man*, like the Bush Administration, contends that proper response to the terrorist threat is violence, not diplomacy. In an early scene, Stark demonstrates the destructive power of his Jericho missile to the DOD: "They say the best weapon is one you never have to fire. I respectfully disagree. I prefer the weapon you only have to fire once. That's how dad did it, that's how America does it, and it's worked out pretty well so far" says Stark. "Find an excuse to let one of these off the chain and I personally guarantee you the bad guys won't want to come out of their caves." Stark then launches the Jericho at an Afghan mountain. Stark and the DOD are delighted and viewers are invited to enjoy the spectacle of Afghan caves and terrorists being obliterated by U.S. WMDs. In another scene, Stark escapes the Afghan cave-prison and uses his new suit to pummel terrorists and smash them into cave walls while incinerating them with a flamethrower. In these and other scenes, *Iron Man* gives popular support to the post-9/11 U.S. state's violence in Afghanistan.

In addition to glorifying violence as the proper U.S. state response to terrorism, *Iron Man* intersects with and perpetuates post-9/11 nation-making processes that construct a positive American self by distinguishing it from a negative Arab-Muslim Other. For over one-hundred years, Hollywood has made Orientalist films that define America by othering Arabs and Muslims as "heartless, brutal, uncivilized, religious fanatics."[15] *Iron Man* participates in this process by casting the majority of Arabs and Muslims as villainous terrorists set against the heroic American Stark. The terrorists are dumb while Stark is a genius (Stark is able to make the first *Iron Man* suit while under the surveillance of the terrorists, who don't understand what he's doing). The terrorists are emotional and lack the scientific knowledge required to engineer weapons while Stark is rational, possesses scientific knowledge and can innovate weapons in a short period of time with limited resources. The terrorists are passive consumers of U.S. weapons technology; Stark Industries is the seller. While *Iron Man* perpetuates the post-9/11 stereotype of Arabs and Muslims as bad and inferior Others to define a good and superior American self, the film does depict some Arab-Muslim characters as good and intelligent, but not quite as good or intelligent as Stark. Yinsen, Stark's friend, designs the technology that keeps Stark alive. But Stark improves upon this technology upon his return to the U.S. Yinsen even sacrifices himself to save Stark's life, perhaps perceiving Stark to be more integral to scientific progress than he is. Other "good" Muslim characters appear in the film, but they are cast in passive, weak and dependent roles, in need of U.S. military help. In one scene, the Ten Rings attacks an Afghan village, killing men and taking women and children hostage. Stark is made aware of this by the news, which says "no political or international pressure means no hope for

[Afghan] refugees and villagers—who will help them?" Stark decides that he is the only one that can help, so dons his new suit for the first time, flies to Afghanistan and destroys the Ten Rings, saving the poor and helpless good Afghanis from the bad terrorist ones. *Iron Man* thereby gives popular credence to the post-9/11 liberal imperialist idea that the U.S. has a responsibility, obligation or mission to use it's military power to liberate or save other peoples living in other countries that are suffering from some kind of oppression. As an allegorical figure of the U.S. state, *Iron Man*'s protagonist Stark personifies the U.S.'s exceptionalist state and the post-9/11 state of exception. To secure America, Stark must play by his own rules and pursue goals he deems just, free of external constraints on his power.

 Iron Man also promotes the existence of a distinctly U.S. military-industrial-complex in the guise of a critique of it. Hollywood studios often take account of the problems of the time and incorporate some of the potentially explosive and resonant political issues of the day when scripting films, opening some space in film texts for liberal, sometimes even radical, criticism of the world. While *Iron Man* addresses some of the anxieties viewers may have about the U.S. MIC, it efficiently defuses them. In an early scene, a female journalist accuses Stark of being a "war profiteer" but Stark deflects this label by saying that "peace means having a bigger stick than the bad guys" and that Stark Industries and the DOD's expenditure on weapons R&D "helped defeat the Nazis." Here, the MIC is represented as an "arsenal of democracy," something that serves world peace. Stark further deracinates the journalist's questions by seducing her, having sexual intercourse with her and then allowing his servant Pepper Potts, who proudly claims to do "anything and everything for Mr. Stark," to call the journalist "trash" as she takes her out of Stark's mansion the morning after. *Iron Man* addresses and then silences criticisms of the MIC by allowing its super-hero to outwit, penetrate and then humiliate a caricature of a liberal-minded female journalist. *Iron Man* also addresses post-9/11 fears that U.S. weapons corporations are selling weapons to terrorist groups that use these weapons to kill non-U.S. civilians and U.S. soldiers. A terrorist calls Stark "the most famous mass murderer in the history of America," noting how Stark Industry sells weapons that fuel violent conflicts between peoples in his "part of the world." Stark is shocked to discover that there is some truth in this claim, as Stark Industries manufactured the Ten Rings' entire weapons supply, including the shrapnel bomb that nearly killed him. At a press conference in the U.S., Stark says that while in Afghanistan, he "saw Americans killed by the very weapons I created to protect them. And I saw that I had become part of a system that had become comfortable with zero accountability." In response to this discovery, Stark attempts to close down the weapons manufacturing division of Stark Industries, but this leads to a conflict with Obadiah Stane, whose main goal is to please the firm's shareholders and Wall Street. When Stark fails to step back or step down from Stark Industries, Stane goes into a rage, dawns the behemoth Iron Monger suit and tries to kill Stark, but is defeated.

 Iron Man addresses worries that the U.S. MIC is controlled by greedy CEOs, who, motivated by profit, make and sell weapons to whoever will buy them (including the U.S.'s terrorist enemies). The potential of this framing of the U.S. MIC to become a structural critique of militarized capitalism, however, is not realized. *Iron Man* individualizes the MIC in Stark and Stane. Stark is a well-intentioned but naïve war profiteer who is oblivious to the harm his company causes until feeling and seeing this harm up close. Stane is a callous and realist minded war profiteer who is aware that the weapons he makes and sells kill people, but he only cares about the bottom line. *Iron Man*'s division of the MIC into individuals—a good war profiteer (Stark) and a bad one (Stane)—obscures how the system of capitalist-imperialism relies on near permanent war and the MIC. The film implies there are a few bad apples that need to be removed from the MIC, but the system which needs it is fine. Furthermore, *Iron Man* tries to placate concerns about the MIC with a plea for state regulation and by pushing the idea that the DOD should be the exclusive consumer of its weapons. Having realized that a global free-market in weapons and the free use of any weapons by anyone threaten the U.S. and its allies, Stark, by the end of the narrative, concedes to work with the U.S. state, thereby legitimizing its claim to the monopoly of physical violence. *Iron Man*'s potential for critique of the MIC slides into an argument for a distinctly U.S. MIC and affirms the need for a firm structural alliance between the DOD, U.S. weapons companies and military-minded engineers. *Iron Man* does not call for the abolishment of corporate weapons manufacture, but for regulations that make sure the U.S.'s war profiteers only sell their commodities to the U.S. state. *Iron Man* is not opposed to corporations prospering by selling weapons to the DOD or the DOD using such weapons to kill non-Americans; it is against profiteering by selling weapons to non-U.S. state and non-state actors that might use these commodities to kill Americans. Overall, it is a popular affirmation of the U.S. Empire's military-industrial-complex.

Conclusion

This article's analysis of the geopolitical-economic conditions and text of *Iron Man* show how the capitalist accumulation logics of global Hollywood intersect with the strategic, promotional and ideological imperatives of the U.S. state, the DOD in particular. Although Hollywood and the DOD are not "fused" and Hollywood studios and the DOD are different kinds of organizations, this difference does not mean there is never any symbiotic interaction between the two. Though Hollywood and the DOD are motivated by different priorities, *Iron Man*—a new imperial film commodity—illustrates how economic and geopolitical interests interact and intertwine in support of the U.S. Empire and the broader culture of U.S. imperialism. *Iron Man* is part and product of the global market dominance of Hollywood, the DOD's promotional and R&D goals and imperial ideology. As the Walt Disney Company's *Iron Man* franchise flies across borders through various commodity platforms and brand extensions, it may, in addition to helping global Hollywood profit-maximize, elicit trans-national identification with an imagined U.S. community and shore up popular support for an expanding but always contested U.S. Empire.

Notes

1. J. Kay, "Global box office hit $34.7 billion in 2012," www.screendaily.com (March 22, 2013).

2. Box Office Mojo (October 20, 2013).

3. A. Clark, "Disney Buys Marvel Entertainment," www.theguardian.com (August 31, 2009).

4. The Economist, "Of Mouse and *X-men*," www.economist.com (September 3, 2009).

5. D. Miles, "Movie Makers Team with Military to create Realism," U.S. Airforce, www.af.mil (June 21, 2007).

6. I. Spencer, "*Iron Man's* Wingman, Terrence Howard Talks" U.S. Air Force, www.af.mil (June 4, 2008).

7. P. W. Singer, "How To Be All That You Can Be: A Look At The Pentagon's Five Step Plan for Making *Iron Man* Real," www.brookings.edu (May 2, 2008).

8. I. Pederson and L. Simcoe, "The *Iron Man* Phenomenon, participatory Culture, & Future Augmented Reality Technologies," CHI'12: 5–10. (2012).

9. M. Boot, *War Made New: Technology, Warfare and the Course of History, 1500 to Today.* New York: Gotham Books. 449. (2006).

10. J. Winston, "U Researchers Develop *Iron Man* Suit," *Daily Utah Chronicle,* www.dailyutahchronicle.com (October 25, 2008).

11. G. Mone, "Building the Real Iron Man," www.popsci.com (September 4, 2008).

12. Video, "Building a real life Iron Man," www.youtube.com.

13. Video, "Yes, the U.S. Military Is Building Real Iron Man Suits," www.slate.com.

14. Video, "US army test real life 'Iron Man' exoskeleton," www.youtube.com.

15. J. Shaheen, *Reel Bad Arabs: How Hollywood Vilifies a People,* Annals, 171–197. (2003).

7 Stereotypes: Conceptual and Normative Considerations

Judith Andre

A familiar battle is raging. The current skirmish involves a comic strip character, Miss Buxley, in "Beetle Bailey." Her portrayal has been called sexist: she's a dumb blonde, physically well-endowed, whose every move leaves her boss panting and unable to think. The author of the strip admits that the situation is stereotypical, but claims that "Miss Buxleys do get preferential treatment. I'm just telling the truth."[1]

Both the attack ("This is an offensive stereotype") and the defense ("I'm just telling the truth") are familiar.[2] The same battle is fought over illustrations in schoolbooks, characters in commercials, situations in sitcoms. Sometimes the battle is an inner one: realizing how blacks have been victimized by stereotypes, one may be reluctant to state some simple truth about, say, blacks and welfare.

Sometimes the question is best resolved by looking at the specific situation. The Miss Buxley character raises many interesting questions: Why is the sexual power of women over men considered funny? Why is the power of men over women—physical, economic, emotional, and political—never considered funny? What is life really like for a buxom young woman in the contemporary United States? Is it true that the Miss Buxleys of the world are treated preferentially in an office? Many stereotypes have fallen once the social scientists examined them.

In this paper, however, I will be interested in the broader question: Is there something in the nature of a stereotype that makes it objectionable, even when it (roughly) represents the truth? My discussion begins with the concept of a stereotype. How does it differ, say, from other generalizations?

The word "stereo" first meant a metal printing plate. The Greek prefix "stereo" means "solid, hard, firm." As Rosemary Gordon points out, "The idea of unchangeability, of monotonous regularity and formalisation was very soon abstracted from the material object itself and applied in a more metaphorical sense . . . The use of 'stereotype' as a verb in the sense of fixing something and perpetuating it in an unchanging form can be traced back to the nineteenth century."[3] Today

Reprinted from *Racism and Sexism: An Integrated Study,* edited by Paula S. Rothenberg (1987), by permission of the author.

the term means: "a conventional, formulaic, and usually oversimplified conception, opinion, or belief; a person, group, event or issue considered to typify or conform to an unvarying pattern. . . ."[4] As psychologists use the term, the central characteristic of a stereotype is its rigidity: it persists in spite of evidence.[5] Like most beliefs it filters the evidence, so that inconsistent information is less likely to be assimilated. But why do some beliefs have the particular inflexibility that makes them stereotypes?[6] Because stereotypes as I will define them are commonly held (rather than simply individually held) beliefs, discussion of subconscious motivation is particularly problematic. Inflexible opinions in the general public might result from conscious inflexibility on the part of relatively few opinion-makers (in other words, from deliberate indoctrination). But I will assume otherwise: my discussion here will be valid to the extent that general stereotypes are a function of individual resistance to changes of mind.

An unwillingness to face something is a form of self-deception; it results from a sense of danger to oneself: a fear that the unfaced fact itself will turn out to be unpleasant, or at least that the facing of it will be. Thinking is work; an unpredictable world is frightening. Stereotypes, like other generalizations, protect us from both effort and fear. But stereotypes differ from other generalizations in their greater immunity to revision; they are not just handy but disposable rules of thumb. Why are we so particularly unwilling to think about some things? Both logical and psychological reasons are possible. As Quine describes the web of belief, privileged beliefs are those whose denial would bring about the most change in our conceptual scheme. A principle of economy leads us, when beliefs conflict, to keep those which are more fundamental. Psychologically, some beliefs are privileged because they keep us happy (or less unhappy). Their denials are threatening. Now there are only a few kinds of situations where a belief as such makes us happy *overall*; ordinarily it is true beliefs which, in the long run, help us. Flame burns, and burns are painful, soup nourishes; gravity is constant. Believing these true things will make our lives better. But some beliefs make life better whether or not they are true: self-esteem is the central case. My belief that I am attractive, intelligent, and honest makes my life pleasant even if I am wrong on all counts. In fact, I may be much happier than the objectively attractive, intelligent and honest person who doesn't know her own worth. Here the content of the belief is more important than its congruence with reality (although even here that congruence also matters).

In two other areas the content of a belief is more important than its well foundedness: where the belief itself changes the world around me, and where the world around me is invulnerable to any attempt to cope. Our beliefs about other people, for instance, shape their behavior; and our lack of awareness of impending inexorable doom is a blessing if there's nothing we could do about it anyway. (Only rarely would that be true; we might at least want to get our affairs in order. But this is nevertheless a logically possible category.)

This analysis suggests that a stereotype—which we retain in the face of contradictory evidence—must function in one of the following ways: it may be relatively fundamental to our conceptual scheme; it may protect our self-esteem; it may help bring about some desirable situation; or it may shield us from facing an unchangeable, unpleasant fact, when facing it would accomplish nothing. (I'm assuming here quite a rational subconscious; it might be safer to say that the belief *appears* to us, feels to us, important in one of the ways just mentioned, and so we resist questioning it.)

But even among rigid, logically or psychologically privileged beliefs, stereotypes form a subset. To begin with, they concern classes of people rather than the whole human race. Rigid beliefs about human beings in general are not stereotypes (except perhaps in science fiction, where "heroic Terrans" confront extraterrestrials); nor are inflexible beliefs about individuals—about celebrities or historical figures. These are myths, perhaps, but not stereotypes. This may explain why there are relatively few stereotypes about white men; white men are, in this culture, unreflectively taken to be the standard human being from whom women and other races deviate. What stereotypes there are concern not men as such, but men in relation to women: men are naturally polygamous or domestically clumsy.

In addition, stereotypes concern behavioral or psychological attributes. Fat people are believed to be jolly *and* to be bad health risks, but only the belief about their personality counts as a stereotype. A stereotype is usually a belief that members of a group will behave in certain ways—it's an expectation that something observable will happen.

A stereotype is also simple and general. The more complex and specific a statement, the less likely it is to express a stereotype. Compare, for instance, "Most great jazz musicians have been black" (a nonstereotypical claim) with "Blacks are so musical" (a stereotypical claim). This characteristic of a stereotype—generality—complements the first characteristic (rigidity); for a general statement is hard to falsify. If this particular black child is tone-deaf, he may still be good on the drums—or an inspired dancer. If he fails at all these activities, well, he's "the exception that proves the rule"—the original belief may refer to all blacks, almost all, or just a majority of them.

Simplicity is a related characteristic. The categories invoked are not only broad, they are few. Fat people are jolly, priests are dedicated, the Irish are garrulous and hard-drinking.

Finally, stereotypes ignore, or falsify, or oversimplify the causes of this behavior. Because of this, a stereotype at least suggests that the attributed behavior is inevitable; this, too, contributes to the rigidity of the belief. When a cause for the behavior is mentioned, claims gain empirical content and become falsifiable. Thus, beliefs or portrayals that include beliefs about the causes of the behavior are less likely to count as stereotypes. A nagging wife is a stereotype; a wife who nags because her only route to success is through her husband is less so. Even a false or farfetched causal claim—sociobiological speculation, for instance—at least calls attention to the question of cause, and is to that extent better than a free-floating claim such as "women are monogamous, men polygamous; they just are." But unfounded claims about genetic causes are only slightly better than what I have called "free-floating" claims (those which make no reference to cause at all). Stereotypes, in one way or the other, suggest that the behavior in question is an unalterable given. Stereotypes, then, are a subset of commonly believed generalizations about the way certain kinds of people feel and act. Stereotypes are inflexible beliefs; they involve a few broad categories only; and they imply that what they describe is inevitable.

Stereotypes as Undesirable

"Stereotype" is pejorative; there is always something objectionable in the beliefs and images to which the word refers. Once the concept of stereotype has been analyzed, the nature of that objectionableness is clearer. To begin with, a stereotype is particularly resistant to change; it keeps us from seeing the truth, should the truth be at odds with our beliefs. The truth is a good thing to know, ordinarily, since we can deal more effectively with what we see than with what we don't. The habit of seeking the truth is therefore also a good thing; it's useful, and—I will not try to defend this here—morally preferable. Ceteris paribus, then, a stereotype is a bad thing because it is unfriendly to truth.

The analysis in Part I also helps illuminate the role of stereotypes in unjust social arrangements. Remember that a stereotypical portrayal reinforces two beliefs at once: that X's are Y, and that X's are inevitably Y. If these beliefs are particularly privileged, then they must (at least seem to our subconscious) do one of the following: protect our self-esteem; underlie many other significant beliefs; help perpetual situations pleasing to us; shield us from knowledge which is better not known. Stereotypes about minorities do all of this. They protect the self-esteem of the majority in two ways. First, some assure the majority of its superiority. ("Blacks are ignorant.") Secondly, they protect the ruling class from seeing its moral turpitude. ("Blacks are like happy children. They don't need what we need." Or, "Women haven't succeeded because they're naturally frivolous.") The realization that something could and should be changed is a moral burden. Once enlightened, I cannot think well of myself *and* remain inactive. What makes the burden worse is that stereotypes about minorities often do have a central place in our conceptual scheme. The possibility of their falsehood or mutability threatens our beliefs about many other things. When stereotypes fall, beliefs about myself—in particular, about my worth—may fall; as may beliefs about how society actually works, why it works that way, and what alternatives are available. Finally, of course, stereotypes about the disadvantaged are self-fulfilling prophecies. People act as they are expected to act, for a variety of familiar reasons.

Stereotypes concerning minorities, then, may well help perpetuate injustices. Interesting questions remain, however: are all stereotypes about minorities objectionable? For that matter, are all stereotypes as such morally objectionable? Or instead must each be examined for its possible role in perpetuating injustice?

As mentioned earlier, at least one thing counts against all stereotypes: their inflexibility. Truth is endangered, and truth is a good thing. But truth isn't the only good thing; its sacrifice is sometimes justified. And as there are arguments to be given in favor of stock figures in literature, so there are advantages to culturally shared expectations about people. These expectations make the world more predictable and hence more manageable; since they are commonly shared, they make communication easier. A stereotype may even enshrine an attribute of which the people in question are truly and proudly the possessors. Perhaps most Irish *are* religious, most nurses dedicated, most Italians warm and loving.

But "stereotype" remains a pejorative. When, then, would a portrayal of, say, a dedicated physician become objectionable? The objection might be aesthetic rather than moral; stale writing fails to do what literature should do: make us see more clearly. The aesthetic criticism, however, leads directly to the moral one. Stereotypes prevent us from seeing clearly, not only in the sense that they filter out conflicting information, but also in the sense that they keep us from understanding what they do allow us to see. This is true even of positive stereotypes about nonminorities. Suppose most physicians are in fact dedicated. What is the harm in the portrayal of one more selfless doctor? The portrayal keeps us from attending to the uniqueness of each individual. He may be heroic in some respects, conscientious in others, but occasionally imperfect. He, and we, are reluctant to admit the imperfection, and unduly shocked when we do see it; in either case we will not cope well with the problem. We are, ironically, less likely to appreciate his heroism, too—for it is simply expected. All doctors are like that.

Stereotypes, then, are bad things even when the image they convey is a positive one. Their patronizing romanticism keeps us from coping with reality, and from appreciating the individual troubles and successes of the people we meet.

What Is to Be Done?

Stereotypes are avoidable. There are many ways to portray ordinary conventional people without descending into stereotype. We need not be afraid of telling the truth. The guidelines for doing so are found in the description of a stereotype given in Part I. Stereotypes are simple, general, and causally agnostic. A portrayal of a carping mother-in-law is not stereotypical if her individuality shows. What does she complain about? What doesn't she complain about? What other characteristics does she have? Most importantly, why is she so unpleasant? A stereotyped portrayal would focus on just two facts: she is a mother-in-law; she carps. *That* picture reinforces the connection which most people make already and automatically. But even a portrayal that is congruent with a stereotype can challenge that stereotype by calling attention to its limited, specific applicability, and by encouraging thought about the origins of the behavior. The criminals on the TV show *Hill Street Blues* are primarily black and Hispanic. But each is shown as an individual; blacks are seen in many noncriminal roles; and the social factors that promote criminality are obvious. Only for the least discerning of viewers would the show encourage the identification: "young black" = "thug."

To answer the questions which began this paper: there's a great difference between a true generalization and a stereotype. And there's nothing wrong with telling the truth; just make sure it's the whole truth. Responsible portrayals encourage us to see in one another both our individuality and our roles in a social system. Stereotypes blind us to the first, and keep us enlightened about the second. The world of the stereotype is a world of free-floating stock figures, whose behavior has no explanation (except, perhaps, in their genes). It may be a humorous world (although that's a subject for a different paper) but it is not a happy world. Nor is it a true one.

Notes

1. Mort Walker, quoted by Sheryl Jones, "Sexism Draws Some New Battle Lines," *The Ledger-Star* (Norfolk, Virginia), December 28, 1982.

2. Another line of defense is equally familiar: "Your attempt at censorship is worse than anything I've done." However common, the defense is confused. Attempts to influence editorial discretion through reason are not censorship. If legal threats are used (say, the threat of a boycott) the question becomes more complicated. See my "'Censorship': Some Distinctions," in *The International Journal of Applied Philosophy,* vol. 1, no. 4 (Fall 1983), pp. 25–37.

3. Rosemary Gordon, *Stereotypy of Imagery and Belief as an Ego Defense* (Cambridge: University Press, 1962), pp. 2–3.

4. *American Heritage Dictionary* (Boston: Houghton Mifflin, 1979).

5. Gordon, p. 4.

6. The dictionary speaks of community stereotypes, and does not include inflexibility as a defining characteristic. The psychologists are speaking of individually held stereotypes, and give inflexibility as their major defining characteristic. I discuss in this paper those commonly held stereotypes which are relatively inflexible; I assume that most are. Some of the objections I will make, however, apply only to those formulaic beliefs which are relatively rigid; others apply to all formulaic beliefs (about the behavior and feelings of classes of people).

8

Team Apatow and the Tropes of Geek-Centered Romantic Comedy

Carter Soles

"Nowadays, schlubs play schlubs and audiences are expected to accept that geeky males can win over classically beautiful women. What does it tell us about the state of gender relations, sexual fantasy, and desire that a physically average geek like Seth Rogen can trump an iconically attractive and glamorous star like Cary Grant?"

In 2008, *Vanity Fair* ran a tongue-in-cheek photo spread depicting geeky, overweight comedy star Seth Rogen reenacting the crop duster scene from *North by Northwest* (1959), thereby equating the likeable if schlubbish Rogen to debonair screwball comedy star Cary Grant. This parodic photo represents a provocative moment in the evolution of the romantic comedy, one of Hollywood's most enduringly popular and profitable genres. It suggests that in the new millennium, suave and attractive male protagonists like Grant can be dismissed in favor of a new breed of male romantic lead: the geeky, slackerish underachiever. How could such a drastic substitution have taken place? Actors like Grant have long played the role of the feminized geek or "professor hero" for comedic purposes, but underneath the glasses and the mawkish behavior, *Bringing Up Baby*'s Dr. David Huxley is still Cary Grant, always dashing underneath his awkwardness, and always emerging from his feminized pedantry to become a more virile and adventurous Ideal Male.[1] Nowadays, schlubs play schlubs and audiences are expected to accept that geeky males can win over classically beautiful women. What does it tell us about the state of gender relations, sexual fantasy, and desire that a physically average geek like Rogen can trump an iconically attractive and glamorous star like Grant?

To answer this, we must examine the rise of the pop-cultural geek since the 1970s. At that time, responding to the crisis in white, masculine hegemony brought about by the rise of feminism, the civil rights movement, and, later, queer activism, pop-cultural texts began foregrounding sensitive, intellectual (but still white) males as protagonists.

Reprinted from *Bright Lights Film Journal* (October 31, 2013).

Schlubby geeks like Woody Allen (*Annie Hall, Manhattan*), Dustin Hoffman (*The Graduate, Midnight Cowboy*) and Richard Dreyfuss (*Jaws, Close Encounters of the Third Kind*) functioned as trojan horses for white masculinity, maintaining white male centrality while seeming to deconstruct traditional masculine paradigms via their intellectual, non-materialistic, underdog status. Hailing from the bottom of the traditional masculine hierarchy vis-à-vis their jockish predecessors, the geeks swept onto the scene and by the early 1980s were dominant in practically every popular film genre. Their rise was abetted by a concomitant ascension of geeks into real-life positions of cultural and economic power: the 1980s saw the rise of Bill Gates, Steve Jobs, Steven Spielberg, George Lucas, and James Cameron, to name just a few prevalent examples. These technological innovators and filmmakers paved the way for the rise of the next generation of geek cultural producers such as Joss Whedon, Zack Snyder, Kevin Smith, Christopher Nolan, and Judd Apatow.

The pop-cultural rise of the geek supposedly introduces intellect and sensitivity to the dominant masculine paradigm, but it is not truly progressive because white male privilege, and the deeply ingrained sense of entitlement that accompanies it, have simply expanded from the figure of the insensitive jock or classically appealing male lead to include the figure of the "sensitive" geek or undesirable schlub. The geek, as promoted most recently and successfully by the works of Team Apatow and others, has done nothing to smash or subvert patriarchal privilege; he has merely taken it over as his own. Using Team Apatow's film comedies as textual examples, this essay elucidates the recurring tropes that express the pop-cultural dominance of the white male geek.

The films of Team Apatow, which carry on the "nervous romance" tradition and additionally incorporate aspects of the male-centered buddy film, subvert the feminist potential of the classic rom-com by claiming the genre as the territory of the male geek.[2] They achieve this by pervasively applying the eight tropes of geek-centered film narratives: (1) Conflict with Jocks, the fundamental wedge by which a geek's intellectual and creative capacities are valorized above the physical and sexual powers of his more traditionally appealing and attractive male rivals; (2) Geek Melodrama, in which victimhood is invoked to generate feelings of sympathy for geeks, despite their culturally privileged status; (3) Simulated Ethnicity, a name given to the appropriation of blackness and the discourses of racial oppression by white geeks; (4) Voyeurism and Stalkerism, two key activities in which geeks engage that their narratives wish to condone and naturalize; (5) Creativity and Vivid Fantasy Life, an integral quality of geeks that allows them to carry out their melodramatized fantasies and claim access to beautiful women "out of their league"; (6) Bromance, the term designating the millennial male-centered buddy comedy, elements of which pervade all the geek comedies, romantic or otherwise; (7) Marginalized and/or Masculine Women, the strategy by which women are shunted aside, vilified, and turned into objects of ridicule, fear, and/or objectification in geek narratives; and (8) Slackerism and Underemployment, a crucial trope that dominates geek comedies since the 1990s (i.e., the rise of Generation X) due to its powerful enabling of geek melodrama.

While the tropes analyzed in this essay are applicable to all film genres in which geek narratives appear—i.e., all contemporary genres—their gendered and raced reversals are staged in particularly dramatic fashion in the romantic comedy genre, that being a genre in which women traditionally achieve narrative dominance or at least parity with their male counterparts. Further, while Apatow himself is the figurehead of a diversified media empire—Apatow Productions—that produces geek centered films and television programs across many genres, Apatow's auteur persona and directorial efforts strongly identify him with the bromance-influenced rom-com of the new millennium. Since the success of *The 40-Year-Old Virgin* in 2005, Apatow's name has become synonymous with film comedies built around groups of male geeks and slackers, usually portrayed by the same repertory company of recurring players including Seth Rogen, Jonah Hill, Jay Baruchel, Jason Segel, Martin Starr, and Paul Rudd. As Apatow's star has risen, he has helped many of his creative collaborators to realize their own film projects, serving as a producer on a great many successful comedies written, directed, and performed by writer/actors Rogen, Segel, and Hill; actors Baruchel, Starr, Kristen Wiig, and Bill Hader; musician/actor Loudon Wainwright III; writer/directors Paul Feig and Nicholas Stoller; and directors Greg Mottola, John Hamburg, Jake Kasdan, and Bryan Gordon. This group, plus a few extended outliers like Mike White (writer/producer on *Dawson's Creek* and *Freaks and Geeks*), have become known as "Team Apatow" in pop-cultural parlance. Team Apatow, which, as of this writing, has its own subheading under the "Frat Pack" entry on wikipedia, denotes both the wide array of media productions made by this network of confederates, usually under the official Apatow Productions brand, but also, as I argue here, any number of geek-centered films influenced by the trend spearheaded by the enormously successful Apatow and company.

While acknowledging that generic analysis is crucial to understanding these geek-centered films, a tropic analysis is equally if not more useful in getting at the specific thematic moves these movies make and the cultural ideologies they disseminate. Tropic analysis offers a different kind of analytic flexibility than genre analysis, retaining the historical specificity of the former while cutting across generic categories to highlight specific features of a cultural trend—in this case, the rise of the pop-cultural geek—present across multiple, sometimes widely disparate genres. This helps account for the genre-hybridizing work of Team Apatow as well as many films outside Apatow's purview. For example, many of the tropes discussed here are found in contemporary action/adventure films: e.g., computer geek Matt Farrell (Justin Long) competes with the jockish John McClane (Bruce Willis) in *Live Free or Die Hard* (2007), exemplifying the "Conflict with Jocks" trope, and geek protagonist Sam Witwicky (Shia LaBeouf) is paired with an out-of-his-league female striver (Megan Fox) in the first two *Transformers* films (2007, 2009), which evinces the "Vivid Fantasy Life" and "Marginalized Women" tropes. Similarly, the Oscar-winning film adaptation of J. R. R. Tolkien's *Return of the King* pours on the homosocial melodrama between Frodo (Elijah Wood) and Sam (Sean Astin), forcing the latter to weep his way through much of the film as he pines for his suffering buddy, thus enacting the "Geek Melodrama" and "Bromance" tropes. These tropes are also found pervasively in contemporary geek-centered TV situation comedies like *The Big Bang Theory* (2007–present), *Arrested Development* (2003–06), and *Party Down* (2009–10).

This essay explicates the eight tropes of geek film comedy via analysis of three Team Apatow-produced romantic comedies: *The 40-Year-Old Virgin* (2005, dir. Apatow), *Knocked Up* (2007, dir. Apatow), and *Forgetting Sarah Marshall* (2008, dir. Nicholas Stoller). While my sole focus on Apatow productions is to some extent arbitrary, I have chosen this focus for my textual sample in part because Team Apatow's rom-coms cut across many relevant geek-centered genres and hybridize them in more unexpected ways than many other works produced by so-called "frat pack" filmmakers such as Adam MacKay and Will Ferrell, Danny McBride and Jody Hill, and Todd Phillips. All the films in my sample carry the Apatow Productions (sometimes Apatow Company) label and are distributed by Universal Studios. In my analysis I refer only to content appearing in the theatrical versions of the films, *not* extended DVD edition or deleted-scene material.

Further related research on geeks and their tropes surely remains to be done: to cite two prominent examples, the massive popularity of cinematic blockbusters based upon superhero comic properties such as Batman, Spider-Man and Iron Man is clearly tied to the rise of pop-cultural geekdom, yet receives no analysis here. Furthermore, I focus my analysis upon the incursion of white, male geeks into the genre-hybridized romantic comedy; female geeks and geeks of non-white ethnicities also warrant critical attention.[3] But my hope is that these eight geek tropes will serve as useful analytical tools for other researchers investigating the rise of geekdom in other genres and modes besides romantic comedy.

Revenge of the Nerds: Grotesque to Ambivalent

Leger Grindon locates the male-centered striver-slacker comedies in the "grotesque to ambivalent" cycle of romantic comedies that began in 1997 with *There's Something About Mary* and *Chasing Amy*.[4] His analysis is accurate, yet many of these striver-slacker films, especially those produced by members of Team Apatow, elide generic boundaries, frequently hybridizing the romantic comedy, the raunchy sex comedy, and/or the male buddy film with something else: e.g., the sex comedy/rom-com (*The 40-Year-Old Virgin* and *Knocked Up*), the sex comedy/buddy cop film (*Pineapple Express*), the male buddy film/rom-com (*Role Models*), the male melodrama/rom-com (*Forgetting Sarah Marshall*), plus a few examples of relatively "pure" sex comedies (*Superbad*), buddy films or "bromances" (*I Love You, Man*), and romantic comedies (*Adventureland*). Of course, *all* of these films are male-centered, a point Denby emphasizes when he argues that "the perilous new direction of the slacker-striver genre reduces the role of women to vehicles. Their only real function is to make the men grow up."[5] I agree with Denby yet I want to use tropic analysis to expand his definition of the "slacker-striver genre" to embrace more than just the "classic" romantic comedy. A broader interpretive model is called for; the unbalanced generic conventions caused by geek-centered tropes is what enables a critical analysis of these tropes to create a more expansive, useful definition of the slacker-striver motif across multiple subgenres and hybridized genres. Thus, while my own focus will be mainly upon ostensible romantic comedies, I will gesture toward the ways in which these geek tropes extend into other related films and film genres.

Both *There's Something About Mary* and *Chasing Amy* feature geek protagonists, and Judd Apatow himself has publicly acknowledged the enormous influence Kevin Smith, writer/director of *Amy* and contemporary geek culture icon, exerted upon his own work.[6] Yet along with *Amy* and *Mary*, one other key film stands as a precursor to Apatow's cycle of hybridized, geek-centered film comedies: *American Pie* (1999), itself a near-perfect hybrid of Animal Comedy—defined by William Paul as a 1980s cycle of male-centered, sex-obsessed, gross-out comedies launched by the success of *Animal House* (1979)—and romantic comedy elements.[7] While retaining a male focus, centering upon a group of four buddies attempting to lose their virginity by prom night, *American Pie* takes this sex-comedic premise and infuses it with some surprisingly emotional touches of genuine romance, particularly between Oz (Chris Klein) and Heather (Mena Suvari).[8] Of course, *Pie* displays copious amounts of sexual hijinks and grotesquery, and more than one of the central couples bears an ambivalent relationship toward love: in a nod to *The Graduate*, Paul Finch (Eddie Kaye Thomas) has great, obligation-free sex with the much older mother of one of his companions, whilst longtime romantic steadies Kevin (Thomas Ian Nicholas) and Vicky (Tara Reid) lose their virginity to each other only to break up immediately afterward.[9]

American Pie ultimately grossed less than *There's Something About Mary*—$102.5 million versus *Mary*'s $176.5 million—but it did so on half the budget ($11 million to *Mary*'s $23 million) and with no known stars except Eugene Levy in a small role. By contrast, *Mary* had Ben Stiller and Cameron Diaz in the leads, and other industry names like Matt Dillon in supporting roles. *American Pie* also launched a highly successful and enduring franchise, including three theatrical sequels and numerous straight-to-DVD spinoffs. So in terms of return on its investment and overall economic and cultural impact, *Pie* is an important prototype of the geek-centered R-rated comedy, and points even more emphatically than *Mary* to the increased male-centeredness and genre mixing to follow in the millennial sex comedy/romantic comedy hybrids of Team Apatow and others.

American Pie and *There's Something About Mary* both foreground an explicitly Jewish geek protagonist, Jim Levenstein (Jason Biggs) and Ted Stroehmann (Ben Stiller) respectively. This deployment of a coded-Jewish hero aligns these films with the rise of key romantic comedy geeks like Dustin Hoffman's Ben Braddock in *The Graduate*, the characters played by Richard Dreyfuss in the early works of George Lucas and Steven Spielberg, the onscreen persona of Woody Allen, and Harry Burns (Billy Crystal) in *When Harry Met Sally. . .* (1989), placing Jim and Ted in a long tradition of nebbish romantic comedy leads, a move that would influence (or at least resonate with) all of the Team Apatow works that followed in the wake of *Mary*'s and *Pie*'s enormous success. Like Steven Spielberg before him, Judd Apatow began his career in television, first working as an executive producer and occasional sketch writer on

The Ben Stiller Show (1992–1993), then catching a break as consulting producer, episode writer, and, in its final season, co-executive producer on Garry Shandling's *The Larry Sanders Show* (1993–1998), both for HBO. Apatow then co-created (with Paul Feig) the critically beloved but short-lived Fox drama series *Freaks and Geeks* (1999–2000), executive producing the show and writing and directing several of its episodes. After helming one more short-lived series, *Undeclared* (2001–2003), and producing the hit comedy film *Anchorman* in 2004, Apatow made his feature film directorial debut with *The 40-Year-Old Virgin* in 2005.

Before commencing the trope-by-trope analysis of Team Apatow's geek film comedies, I will introduce the specific generic affiliation(s), narrative structure, and major themes of each of the films under discussion. While structured as romantic comedies, all three—*The 40-Year-Old Virgin, Knocked Up*, and *Forgetting Sarah Marshall*—contain pervasive elements of male-centered buddy comedy, that is, "bromance," though each film incorporates bromantic tropes to a different degree.

All of these films bear some relationship to Oedipal trajectory, whether it primarily be to embrace a classic Oedipal narrative or to reject it in favor of a pre-Oedipal celebration of grotesquery and arrested development. While all these comedies begin in the realm of the pre-Oedipal, all of them ultimately reform the slacker, allowing male homosociality to give way to heterosexual coupling, moving the male protagonist out of his state of arrested development and resolving his Oedipal crisis.

While *The 40-Year-Old Virgin* is inflected with a certain amount of grotesquery and ambivalence, it is the least sex comedyish and most traditionally romantic comedyish of any Apatow production.[10] *Virgin* is a classic boy-meets-girl film with two Team Apatow-ish distinguishing features: (1) its male protagonist, Andy (Steve Carell) is extremely geeky and sexually naive, and (2) the film includes intermittent episodes of raunchy, lower-stratum humor infused into the proceedings by Andy's male co-workers. The first quarter of the film, until Trish (Catherine Keener) is introduced at the twenty eight-minute mark, is more or less an Animal comedy (raunchy sex comedy with a male-dominated ensemble cast) focused upon Andy's new-found male buddy group trying to get him laid. Yet while the male pack of buddies learning of Andy's virginal status sets the film's narrative in motion, and while the buddy coworkers' advice functions as one of the key obstacles to the heterosexual pairing between Andy and Trish, ultimately the romantic love plot drives *The 40-Year-Old Virgin* film to its climax and conclusion, which centers upon Andy and Trish's marriage and long-awaited consummation thereof.

Virgin is romantic in tone and ends with Andy and Trish marrying, yet the focus of that final marriage is placed upon Andy's sexual conquest of Trish. That is, like all sex comedies/Animal comedies, *The 40-Year-Old Virgin* is finally about sex, about the geeky male protagonist getting laid: see also Pinto in *Animal House* and Jim in *American Pie*. What Apatow achieves here is to successfully romanticize the male-centered sex comedy, much as *American Pie* successfully added rom-com components to its Animal comedy antics six years earlier.

Knocked Up is structurally identical to *Virgin*, a male-centered sex comedy or Animal comedy fused with a romantic comedy.[11] Its conformity to the *Virgin* formula is evident in its close adherence to the "reform the slacker" plotline. In *Virgin*, Andy goes on an Oedipal journey in which he must learn to forsake childhood things, symbolized by his action figure collection which he sells off on ebay, but really indicating his deep fear of sex. Similarly, *Knocked Up*'s Ben Stone (Seth Rogen) learns to overcome his resistance to getting a real job, leaving the house where he lives with his bromantic male buddies, and committing fully to Alison (Katherine Heigl) and the imminent parenthood indicated by her unplanned pregnancy.

There are further parallels between *Knocked Up* and *Virgin*: for example, Ben's first serious discussion with Alison about her pregnancy takes place at the thirty minute mark, the same point at which *Virgin* introduces Andy to Trish. However, in contrast to *The 40-Year-Old Virgin*, which has an overtly romantic-comedic tone, *Knocked Up* is more ambivalent. This tonal shift is due in large part to *Knocked Up*'s provocative, sex-and-unplanned-pregnancy-before-romantic-love plot. *Knocked Up*'s relative emphasis on non-sentimental sex comedy is abetted by reversing the gender roles of its heterosexual protagonists vis-à-vis geekiness and slackerism: Ben, the male lead, is a sexually aware, vulgar slacker rather than a high-strung, naive virgin like Andy, and Alison is a type-A, careerist achiever, having more in common with *Sarah Marshall*'s driven title character (or *Election*'s Tracy Flick) than *Virgin*'s laid-back, slackerish Trish. Whereas Andy's sexual naiveté allows *Virgin* to take a more idealistically romantic view toward sex, *Knocked Up* makes no bones about the accidental and casual nature of its lead duo's first intimate coupling nor about the difficulties they face as a potentially mismatched couple. *Knocked Up* and *Virgin* are both raunchy, male-centered sex comedies that turn into heterosexual romantic comedies, but *Knocked Up* builds its romantic charge a bit later in the narrative than *Virgin* does and is much more "nervous" about that romance's outcome until it resolves in the last reel. It is actually more melodramatic than *Virgin* in part because it deals with the weighty issue of new parenthood, which Ben's slackerism (shown in the earthquake scene in which he rescues his bong rather than Alison from the shaking house) and the tenuousness of their romantic bond both threaten. Despite Alison's insistence that "I really do love you" an hour into the film, her accompanying admission that "I don't know what that love means" expresses the fragility of her and Ben's very new relationship.

Despite its deep ambivalence about romance, *Knocked Up* devotes more screen time to its principal female characters than any other film in my sample. Unlike *Virgin*, which spends its first half-hour integrating Andy into his newfound group of work buddies, *Knocked Up* begins with its bromantic group already intact, thereby downplaying their narrative importance. *Knocked Up* gives Alison's home life, family relationships, and point of view far more narrative attention than *Virgin* does Trish's. Alison's relationship with her sister Debbie (Leslie Mann) is a driving force and highlight of *Knocked Up*, and has no correlate in any other Team Apatow film under discussion. As a point of comparison, John Hamburg's bromance *I Love You, Man* (2009) devotes narrative time to showing Zooey's (Rashida Jones') interactions with her female friends, but not as extensively as *Knocked Up* depicts Alison's work life and relationship with her sister.[12]

The relative importance of women in *Knocked Up* is emphasized by the film's climax, in which Ben must convince *Debbie* of his competence to be a good father before the delivery of his baby with Alison may occur: Debbie says "I think he's going to be a good dad. I think I like him." All that said, *Knocked Up* is still fundamentally male-centered and participates in structural misogyny, particularly in its privileging of Ben's point of view and in its unfortunate vilification of Alison's mother; see trope 7.

Forgetting Sarah Marshall is a romantic comedy with extreme doses of male melodrama, or possibly a male melodrama "rescued" by a romantic-comedy happy ending, a kind of "nervous romance" in reverse.[13] Written by Jason Segel, its star, the film is structured around sad-sack protagonist Peter Bretter's long emotional recovery from being dumped by Sarah Marshall (Kristen Bell), a famous and beautiful woman who is way out of his league in both looks and career success. Bretter spends the bulk of the film pining for Sarah, literally crying his way through several early scenes. He leaves Los Angeles for Hawaii, and once there, spends his time bonding with bromantic buddies like Chuck (Paul Rudd), and finally healing his wounds with the help of new romantic interest Rachel (Mila Kunis). *Forgetting Sarah Marshall*'s Rachel is a key example of the "Manic Pixie Dream Girl" type described by film critic Nathan Rabin as a female character who "exists solely in the fevered imaginations of sensitive writer-directors to teach broodingly soulful young men to embrace life and its infinite mysteries and adventures."[14] *Sarah Marshall* uses Rachel to stage a climactic showdown wherein both she and a remorseful Sarah compete for the slackerish Peter's affections, exemplifying the "one geek/two female suitors" setup (see trope 5).

Forgetting Sarah Marshall is structurally similar to Woody Allen's *Manhattan*, only with an unambiguously happier ending. Both films document the geek hero's passing from one romantic obsession to another, and both stage the geek's recovery from a breakup via his reconnection with creativity and art: Allen's Isaac Davis through Tracy's gift of a harmonica, and Peter via Rachel's encouragement of his inspiration to write his Dracula-themed puppet musical. However, whereas even Kevin Smith's geek-friendly early films like *Clerks* and *Chasing Amy* preserve the ambivalence of the nervous romances, denying the geek his ultimate romantic consummation, in line with the cultural shift toward valorizing geeks now underway, millennial geek-centered comedies like *Sarah Marshall* always give the geek protagonist exactly what he wants.

Eight Tropes of Geek-Centered Romantic Comedy[15]

1. Conflict with Jocks

Conflict with jocks is one of the defining tropes of nerddom and geekdom, so central to the formation of the geek type that it is constitutive of it. The geek is always in conflict with jocks, and in geek-centered comedies geeks are frequently embarrassed, attacked, and humiliated by jocks. The term "jocks" is not synonymous with "athletes"—in fact, many athletes are geeks of the sports they practice—but constitutes its own category of anti-intellectual, sexually confident individuals whose main role in geek narratives is to best geeks sexually and to bully them verbally and/or physically. The terms "jock" and "geek" are interdependent, best defined relative to each other: the geek merely has to be physically or sexually deficient and intellectually better endowed with respect to his jock oppressor(s), and to feel threatened or be made insecure by the jock's presence. This fundamental geek-jock opposition is strongly connected to trope 2, geek melodrama, in that the geek's fundamental antagonism with people he deems less intelligent than he gives his melodramatized victimhood its raison d'etre. However, despite its strong ties to melodramatic geek suffering, the geek-jock conflict can also be played for straight comedy, as in the Delta vs. inter-house rivalry in *Animal House*, or turned around on the geek, as in the Roman vs. Kyle rivalry on *Party Down*, in which handsome girl-magnet Kyle (Ryan Hansen) is frequently allowed to best misogynistic geek Roman (Martin Starr). Regardless of specific tone, in geek-centered comedies the jock acts as a catalyst for the geek males' sexual anxiety, which is especially central to the sex comedies, i.e., *American Pie*, *The 40-Year-Old Virgin*, *Superbad*, and *Pineapple Express*.

The most prevalent geek-jock rivalries in our film sample are those seen in *Forgetting Sarah Marshall*. In this film, the main jock, Aldous Snow (Russell Brand), is both more narratively prevalent and more complex than the average jock character. A British pop star whose entire persona revolves around his voracious, over-the-top sexuality, Snow is the very embodiment of everything the schlubby, sensitive geek Peter Bretter fears. Knowing himself to be sexually inadequate and way out of Sarah's league, Peter spends the bulk of the film being (comedically) tortured by Snow's public displays of erotic affection toward Sarah, and listening to him regale her with sexually explicit love songs like "Inside of You" at a luau. All of Snow's songs remind of us of his jockish orientation to sexuality and the body: even his ostensibly "political" hit song, "Do Something," proposes that the solution to all world problems is simply to *do* something, a nebulous call to action reminiscent of the Nike "Just Do It" campaign, its indeterminate use of the verb "do" also being suggestive of the sexual act in and of itself.

Yet *Sarah Marshall* humanizes Snow more so than do most geek-centered films, even allowing Peter to recognize how cool and relatable the British rocker is by the end of the film. In part this takes place because Peter's real struggle is with Sarah herself, and having him make peace with Snow sets the stage for his final showdown with his (by then demonized) ex-girlfriend—see trope 7 below. But Snow's sympathetic position may also relate to his ties to the rock and roll industry, for creative types, no matter how jockish, hold a special place in the world of geeks: see also William Miller's (Patrick Fugit's) adoration of rocker Russell Hammond (Billy Crudup) in Cameron Crowe's semi-autobiographical geek odyssey *Almost Famous* (2000).

Despite the absence of prevalent jock characters in *Knocked Up* and *The 40-Year-Old Virgin*, their implied presence and sexual threat is nevertheless felt by these films' insecure geek protagonists, or is embodied in unusual ways by supporting characters. *Knocked Up*'s Ben is well aware that Alison is out of his league—he admits to her early in their relationship that he is "the guy that girls fuck over"—and his slackerish resistance to her could be seen as displaced anger toward jockish "beautiful people" like her. This point is clearly made when Alison shows embarrassment at being seen with Ben in front of her beautiful female friends outside a department store. Ben is not overtly humiliated by this—he is too good-natured and clueless to pick up on it—but it is clear to the viewer, and Ben does note in an immediately subsequent scene that he thinks Alison has grown uneasy with him because he hasn't proposed marriage to her, again misinterpreting the cause of their strained relations. He also goes on an enraged rant against Dr. Howard, their jockish, smooth-talking gynecologist, when the latter disappears to an out-of-town Bar Mitzvah just before Alison goes into labor.

Virgin makes interesting use of the geek vs. jock trope by incorporating a seemingly friendly jock into the male buddy group that takes Andy under its wing. Jockish black man Jay (Romany Malco) gives Andy all kinds of dating advice premised upon an exclusively sexual, objectifying approach to women: e.g., that Andy must go have meaningless sex with a "hoodrat" before trying to have sex with someone he actually cares about. This jockish advice echoes that of Trent (Vince Vaughn) to Mike (Jon Favreau) in *Swingers*, and is ultimately proven wrong when the geek protagonist finds his one true love, and his jockish adviser is ridiculed and infantilized, by film's end. In these cases the geek and jock remain friends but the film still champions earnest geek values over slick jock ones.

2. Geek Melodrama

This is a form of male melodrama wherein the geek justifies his rage toward his jock oppressors by framing it as melodramatic suffering on his own part. Linda Williams defines the melodramatic mode as a loose set of tropes that generate "pathos for protagonists beset by forces more powerful than they and who are perceived as victims." According to Williams, melodramatic narratives "[consist] of a story that generates sympathy for a hero who is also a victim and that [lead] to a climax that permits an audience, and usually other characters, to recognize that character's moral value."[16] Geek-centered film narratives across all genres place the geek in the role of long-suffering victim vis-à-vis jocks and women, therefore activating viewer sympathy for his plight and placing him in the melodramatized position of moral righteousness: in *Forgetting Sarah Marshall*, Peter Bretter suffers through the entire film at the hands of his cheating ex-girlfriend and her new paramour, Aldous Snow. While played to excess for comedic purposes, Peter's many scenes of unabashed sobbing and suffering align viewer sympathies with him, as does the film's insistence upon depicting all events strictly from his point of view. By film's end, it is clear that Peter is the "victim" here, and that Sarah, as Peter himself puts it, is "the Devil."

The geek protagonist's morally charged victim status allows him to freely vent his rage at jocks and women, and for the audience to accept this rage as justified, as when *Knocked Up*'s Ben Stone leaves a wildly inappropriate and threatening message on Dr. Howard's answering machine: "You know what I'm going to have to do now? I'm going to have to kill you! I am going to pop a fucking cap in your ass! You're dead, you're Tupac, you are fucking Biggie, you piece of shit!" Ben's racialized anger (see also trope 3) is justified emotionally and morally by his own geeky underdog status as well as his narrative position of defending the rights of a suffering pregnant woman.

This melodramatization of the privileged geek has been a dominant trope in mainstream Hollywood cinema since the 1970s, when filmmakers like Woody Allen, George Lucas, and Steven Spielberg placed geeks at the center of their science-fiction, action-adventure, and romantic comedy films. A paradigmatic example much discussed by comedy critics is *Annie Hall*, a comedian comedy that plays upon male melodrama (Alvy's suffering at having lost Annie) to defang the power of women's laughter—indeed, diegetically Alvy "smothers" Annie.[17]

Films like *Chasing Amy*, *The 40-Year Old Virgin*, and *Forgetting Sarah Marshall* mimic the structure of Allen's nervous romances, placing a traditional romantic comedy narrative within the larger frame story of a male-centered comedy, replete with heavy doses of male melodrama.[18] Whereas classic romantic comedies tend to privilege female laughter and unruliness over male suffering, as in the bakery scene in *Moonstruck* in which Ronnie's suffering at the hands of his brother is rendered comedic and ridiculous, the geek-centered films take their melodrama seriously, using romantic comedy tropes not so much to empower women but instead to provide happy endings for stories about male suffering and redemption.[19] Exemplary in this regard is the Las Vegas scene in *Knocked Up* in which Ben and Pete realize, while tripping on mushrooms, that they are not worthy of the women they love. Their melodramatic suffering paired with drug use in this sequence renders Ben and Pete comedic and yet vulnerable at the same time: Pete muses "Do you ever wonder how somebody can even like you? How could Debbie like me? She likes me. She *loves* me. The biggest problem in our marriage is that she wants me around. She loves me so much that she wants me around all the time. *That's* our biggest problem." The buddies return to L.A. intent on doing whatever it takes to win their respective women back, a melodramatic turn that sets up the film's climax wherein Ben literally rescues Alison from her missing obstetrician and the other difficulties of reaching the hospital and having her baby. These films deploy melodrama in order to ensure that audience loyalties ultimately lie with the male, rather than female, protagonists.

Additionally, regardless of the geek protagonist's actual ethnicity, his victimhood and suffering is often raced, as when Jewish geek Neal Schweiber commiserates with an unnamed black kid about being racially stereotyped in an episode of *Freaks and Geeks* (see trope 3).[20]

3. Simulated Ethnicity

Simulated ethnicity refers to the process by which privileged white geeks simulate/claim a "marked" (and therefore broadly "raced") identity, a trope tightly connected to the well-documented white fascination with imagined blackness that cultural critics from Leslie Fiedler to Norman Mailer to Eric Lott have argued constitutes white male adolescence in America.[21] White appropriation of imagined blackness contributes to the marginalization of black characters by deploying the strategy of exclusion, whereby "repetition of black absence from locations of autonomy and importance creates the presence of the idea that blacks belong in positions of obscurity and dependence."[22] Instead, white characters remain central while appropriating simulated blackness with impunity. Of course, the white geek always has the option of abandoning his simulated ethnic status, which is why it must be designated as merely simulated; in fact, it is central to the geek myth that he will eventually rise above his socially abject status and, with the help of his intellect and education, claim his white masculine privilege like Scott (Keanu Reeves) does in *My Own Private Idaho*, cruelly leaving his homeless life and companions behind, or like *Clerks'* Dante, who becomes co-owner of the Qwik Stop convenience store at the end of *Clerks 2*.

The most common manifestation of this trope is in the figure of the white geek who acts black, indulging—and usually socially benefiting from—his imagined blackness. Everything about the Apatow-produced teen sex comedy *Superbad* flaunts this trope: right from its 1970s style opening credits, the film's title and blaxploitation soundtrack frame the geeky white boys' sexual misadventures in black pop-cultural terms, much like the frat parties in *Animal House* are accompanied by the music and performance of Otis Day and the Knights. However, where *Animal House* at least tries to point out, in its heavy handed and somewhat racist roadhouse bar scene, that the band and the black community do not appreciate the white frat boys' adoration, *Superbad* never questions its white protagonists' appropriation of imagined blackness. Fogell names himself "McLovin" on his fake ID, prompting Evan to ask him: "Are you trying to be an Irish R and B singer?" Yet when Evan, far from aware of his own simulation of ethnicity, successfully offers to buy Becca's alcohol, he says he feels "pimp," a raced term referring to blaxploitation-based stereotypes. Similarly, *Virgin*'s Andy emulates the mannerisms of black friend Jay in attempting to pick up "hoodrats," and Jay even tells Andy early in the film that "Your dick is my dick!"—a line which surely cuts to the core of the white fascination with imagined black masculinity. Simulated ethnicity is also seen in non-Apatow films: *I Love You, Man*'s Peter Klaven loosens up and discovers his own coolness by playing bass guitar and, as he puts it, "Slappin' da bass," thereby emulating his imagined version of a black Rastafarian; *Road Trip*'s Kyle Edwards (DJ Qualls) joins a hip-hop crew onstage at an all-black frat party and ends up dating black girlfriend Rhonda (Mia Amber Davis); and *Office Space*'s geeky white protagonist Peter Gibbons (Ron Livingston) liberatingly slacks off at his off job as the Geto Boys' "Damn It Feels Good to Be a Gangsta" plays on the soundtrack. All these instances exemplify the white fantasy of blackness as strongly associated with the body, sexuality, and easygoing slackerism or laziness—the precise qualities that geeks in particular lack.[23]

The uptight geek's raced attraction to sexual and bodily looseness draws him to his frequent cinematic companion, the slacker. Slackers, while usually white, live in the moment and are more clownish and carefree than geeks. They are less introspective and sensitive than their geek buddies, though they share the geek's love of comic books and other geek-cultural products. Geek-slacker buddy duos proliferate in the films of Team Apatow: *Sarah Marshall*'s Peter and Chuck, *Superbad*'s Evan and Seth, and *Pineapple Express*'s Dale and Saul all embody such pairings. In *Virgin* and *Knocked Up*, whole gangs of underachieving buddies act as conglomerate slacker sidekicks to geek protagonists Andy and Ben.

It should be noted that the Jewishness of many geek protagonists is obviously not simulated, and that Jewishness is a legitimate, historically oppressed identity, but in these films that identity is usually flaunted by characters who are themselves privileged. Key in this regard is the geek buddy group's discussion of Jewish action star Eric Bana in the dance club scene in *Knocked Up*, wherein Ben prophetically declares "If any of us get laid tonight, it's because of Eric Bana in *Munich*!" In addition to foreshadowing Ben's own imminent successful hookup with Alison, this brief talk foregrounds the Jewish identity of all these young men, and allows them to bemoan their difficulties with women as a result (see trope 2, geek melodrama). Yet the *Munich* talk, echoing the narrative move *Knocked Up* is itself about to make, simultaneously shows via its example of Bana that Jewish men can be accepted as romantic leading men and viable protagonists in mainstream Hollywood cinema.

However, the most pernicious dimension of simulated ethnicity is that it does not require the simulator to have or invoke *any* connection to a specific, real-world ethnic identity: the geek imagines that his social marginalization alone, especially in light of his superior intelligence and sensitivity vis-à-vis his jock rivals, justifies his claiming a marginalized or oppressed status. This explains why geeks are often the most virulent defenders of the fiction of "Post-Racialism," that is, the insistence that race and ethnicity are not valid cultural or societal issues anymore. Despite their prolific engagement with racial appropriation, Team Apatow's films rarely tackle (or critique) post-racialism head-on. However, edgier geek fare such as Kevin Smith's *Clerks 2* pushes the boundaries, offering geek protagonist Randal (Jeff Anderson) wearing a shirt with the words "Porch Monkey 4 Ever" and having him unleash a tirade about his right to call himself a "porch monkey" in an obviously misguided attempt to reclaim the term back from racist hate-mongers. Similarly, *Party Down*'s Roman (Martin Starr) claims to be "post-racial" after asking black funeral guests highly inappropriate questions about the nature and etymology of the term "jungle fever" in the "James Ellison Funeral" episode.

4. Voyeurism and Stalkerism

The geek is usually a connoisseur of visual media, such as film and comic books, and this emphasis upon visual consumption extends to his tendencies toward voyeurism, stalkerism, and interest in porn. A great many pre-Oedipal geek comedy narratives involve the geek protagonist and/or his buddies pruriently spying upon women; Blutarsky's extended sequence of climbing a ladder to peep into a sorority house in *Animal House* provides the template here, and *American Pie* brilliantly updated the trope for twenty first century audiences by having Jim's buddies watch foreign exchange student Nadia undress and masturbate via an internet webcam he set up in his bedroom for the purpose. The films often conclude these sequences by poking fun at the geeks—Blutarsky falls off his ladder, and Jim embarrasses himself by prematurely ejaculating during an attempt to seduce Nadia—yet they never seriously question the ethics of peeping tomism, never depict serious social or legal consequences for the person(s) committing the deed, and in fact reward voyeurism by always providing the "payoff" of nude women put on overt display for the characters and the viewer. They also sign off on these deeds diegetically by pairing Blutarsky off with his voyeurism target, Mandi Pepperidge, in *Animal House*'s denouement; Jim is similarly rewarded when Nadia confesses her longtime crush on him in *American Pie 2*. *Superbad* extends this tradition by having Fogell follow Nicola down a school hallway, voyeuristically ogling her ass, then walking away uncomfortably when she notices him; yet he has sex with her during their only other encounter at the end of the film.

In addition to spying on women in general, geeks often feel no compunction against stalking the women they supposedly love. A key film in this regard is Cameron Crowe's Gen X romance *Say Anything . . .*, in which Lloyd Dobler famously lurks outside Diane Court's house playing "In Your Eyes" very loudly on a portable boom box.[24] In this iconic moment, Lloyd's melodramatic suffering at having been broken up with by Diane is supposed to justify his standing outside in the wee hours of the night blasting music in an upscale suburban neighborhood. Another variant on the stalkerism trope, best exemplified by Mike in *Swingers*, is the geek's leaving of endless neurotic answering machine messages, to the point of his talking himself out of the possibility of a successful relationship even before the other party ever picks up. This exposes the geek's underlying conceit: that stalking itself counts as a relationship, or as a legitimate phase in a relationship he imagines is transpiring (see also trope 5). For example, in *The 40-Year-Old Virgin*, Andy makes a phone call to Trish only to pose as a telemarketer when he loses the nerve to identify himself. Viewers are supposed to empathize with Andy for his extreme nervousness in the face of the potentially true romance Trish represents, but not ask themselves why this immature man is repeatedly calling Trish if he is incapable of mustering the honesty to conduct a simple conversation with her. Sure, this is comedy, but the film further endorses stalkerism by showing Andy watching Trish through her store window and accepting dating advice from Dave, a man who, like Andy, assumes the role of a sensitive "nice guy" yet obsessively stalks his own ex-girlfriend. Similarly, *Forgetting Sarah Marshall* excuses Peter's stalkerism by landing him at the same Hawaiian hotel as his ex-girlfriend purely by random chance, and by having his brother-in-law Brian specifically warn him not to stalk her; yet Peter deliberately spies on her anyway, and Brian's admonishment has more to do with Peter's pain over what he sees—Sarah making love with her new beau—rather than the inherent ethical questionability of his voyeurism.[25]

5. Creativity and Vivid Fantasy Life

Geeks are highly imaginative fellows, and in their comedies the viewer is often given direct access to their imaginings, be they positive (struggling film director Nick Reve envisioning himself winning a "Best Film Ever Made By a Human Being" award in *Living in Oblivion*), prurient (Jay picturing himself kissing and fondling Justice in *Jay and Silent Bob Strike Back*), or nightmarish (Matthew Kidman imagining the fatal car crash that might result if he tries to skip school in *The Girl Next Door*). This trope is frequently expressed via geeks who are directly involved (or aspire to be involved) with media creation/production, for in addition to being avid consumers ("fanboys") of contemporary media, geek protagonists are quite often filmmakers, comic book artists, writers, and the like.

Annie Hall's Alvy Singer is surely the principal template for this trope. The entirety of *Annie Hall* is presented to the viewer as a series of flashbacks told from comedian/writer Alvy's point of view. The episodes that make up Alvy and Annie's relationship unfold in an associative fashion, introduced by Alvy and mimicking the format of one of his standup routines.[26] Further, the snippet of Alvy's stage play seen in the film's penultimate sequence, in which Annie stays with Alvy rather than leaving him as in the film's diegesis, exposes Alvy's (and the film's) awareness that the geek protagonist is manipulating viewer perception of the events depicted, coloring his recollections, perhaps, to shift outcomes in his favor.

Explicit depiction of the geek's imaginings gives the viewer direct access to the geek protagonist's inner thoughts and point of view, reinforcing the male-centeredness of these films. An insidious corollary of this male focus is that geek comedies quite frequently pair the geek protagonist with a classically beautiful woman, who would be "way out of his league" in real life. This tendency may originate with Woody Allen's *Manhattan*, in which Allen's Isaac Davis is paired with Mariel Hemingway's very young and angelically beautiful Tracy. Yet Allen's film displays an awareness of the implausibility of their union—Isaac comments on it frequently—and ends fairly ambiguously, with Tracy headed off to Europe and the couple's fate uncertain. That uncertainty has been dismissed in the contemporary geek films inspired by Allen's work: it is hard to see either Sarah *or* Rachel developing sexual feelings for the awkward, schlubby Peter in *Forgetting Sarah Marshall*, yet they do, and *Knocked Up*'s insistence that Ben and Alison will stay together as a couple is the limit case of this geek-gets-the-girl wish fulfillment.

The geeky guy coupled with an out-of-his-league beauty motif demonstrates how the rise of the geek protagonist is bound up with the emergence of the "Manic Pixie Dream Girl," a pernicious stereotype described by *Onion AV Club* writer Nathan Rabin as a sensitive, quirky, attractive girl who exists solely to teach emotionally damaged men to love again. She is a purely male fantasy projection of desirable traits, a figure "defined by secondary status and lack of an inner life" who is "on hand to lift a gloomy male protagonist out of the doldrums, not to pursue her own happiness."[27] The Manic Pixie Dream Girl proliferates in contemporary geek media: see Heather Graham in *Swingers, Arrested Development, Scrubs*, and *The Hangover*, Mila Kunis in *Sarah Marshall* and *Extract*, Natalie Portman in *Garden State*, Kaley Cuoco in *The Big Bang Theory*, Shannon Elizabeth in *American Pie* and *Jay and Silent Bob Strike Back*, Elisha Cuthbert in *The Girl Next Door*, and even Catherine Keener as Trish in *Virgin*. In calling Cameron Diaz's Mary "an exaggerated confection of male desire" in *There's Something About Mary*, Leger Grindon implies this same stereotype.[28]

In many cases, male geek fantasies of hyper-exaggerated potency and desirability extend beyond simply being paired with one beautiful woman. Quite often the geek finds himself the object of affection of *two* such women at the same time: the "one geek/two female suitors" motif appears in *Clerks, Dawson's Creek, Scott Pilgrim vs. The World*, and, most dramatically, *Forgetting Sarah Marshall*, wherein Peter's harsh rejection of Sarah after she attempts to fellate him provides the film with its climax.

Geek fantasizing can also take the form of power fantasies involving guns, violence, and excessive action. Many geek comedies thrust their protagonists into highly exaggerated "action movie" situations only to have them prevail against far stronger and better trained opponents. Jay and Silent Bob escape mall security guards by enacting Batman-inspired fantasies in *Mallrats*, Ronnie beats up multiple policemen in *Observe and Report*, Dale, Saul, and Red wipe out a gang of well-armed drug dealers in *Pineapple Express*, and a group of four geeks do the same in the recent *30 Minutes or Less*.

In short, if the geek can imagine it, it's real to him since he lives mostly in his head anyway. His potential for vivid imagination is what enables him to feel justified in committing acts of voyeurism and stalkerism as substitutes for real relationships (see trope 4). Sometimes geek comedies ridicule the geek for this behavior, the classic example here being Brad's masturbation fantasy in *Fast Times at Ridgemont High*, which ends with the real woman he's fantasizing about walking in on him and humiliating him. But more often geek comedies sign off on the geek's fantasy, making it come true. This is a disturbing trend.

6. Bromance

"Bromances" are an extension of the male buddy film tradition analyzed by Robin Wood.[29] The buddy road movie cycle hit its apex during the 1970s with films like *Midnight Cowboy, Butch Cassidy and the Sundance Kid*, and *Scarecrow*, then was largely subsumed into the buddy cop/action film cycle of the 1980s which included the *Lethal Weapon* films, *Midnight Run*, and *48 Hours*. The buddy films and the more recent bromances all center upon narratives of male bonding (bromance) and the concomitant suggestion and homophobic repudiation of homoeroticism between closely bonded male friends. Even when these bromantic films feature a larger "pack" of male friends, usually specific buddy pairs (in the form of geek/slacker duos) are emphasized. For example, in the paradigmatic *Animal House*, two distinct buddy duos are foregrounded against the backdrop of the larger ensemble: Otter (Tim Matheson) and Boone (Peter Riegert), and Pinto (Thomas Hulce) and Flounder (Stephen Furst). Similarly, while in *Virgin* Andy technically befriends the entire group of Smart Tech guys all at once, he takes turns bonding with each of them episodically and learning different (usually self-sabotaging) dating lessons from each of them. *Knocked Up* begins with a male buddy group much like the one that coalesces around Andy in *Virgin*, but the film's attention rapidly shifts from Ben's original somewhat homogeneous buddy group to the new, intense bromantic bond he forms with Alison's brother-in-law Pete.

Of course, objectifying women and graphically discussing sex are key bonding rituals in which these boys-only groups engage: Andy and Jay discuss strategies for picking up "Hoodrats" in *Virgin*, and the opening minutes of *Superbad* consist of an extended vignette in which Evan and Seth discuss porn sites, their past sexual exploits, and bits of adolescent wisdom such as Seth's oddly worded claim that "You don't want girls thinking you suck dick at fucking pussy." Further, pursuit of women-as-sex-objects takes up the whole plot of *American Pie*, much as it did that film's precursors like *Animal House* and *Porky's*. However, as Eve Sedgwick has documented in her groundbreaking literary study *Between Men*, this male rallying around the pursuit of heterosexual love (or lust) ultimately leads to a stronger narrative focus on the homosocial and homoerotic love-bonds between the men themselves.[30] For example, in *Knocked Up* the love-bond between Ben and Pete develops over the course of the double-date dinner sequence, in which the two men bond over their shared love of *Back to the Future* and Ben declares that he finds Pete "cute," and their subsequent trip to Las Vegas, a paradigmatic bromantic destination since the original 1950s Rat Pack and 1996's indie landmark *Swingers*. Ben and Pete explicitly refer to the latter film by yelling "You're so money!" at each other on their way into Vegas.

In line with this focus on the (possibly homoerotic) relations between men, many of these contemporary bromances are punctuated with explicit declarations of male homosocial love: in addition to Ben's comments about Pete noted above, *Superbad* concludes with its male buddy duo vocally gushing about their love for each other. John Hamburg's non-Team Apatow bromance *I Love You, Man* (2009) ends with a heterosexual wedding ceremony in which the usual climax is usurped by its two male leads, Peter (Paul Rudd) and Seymour (Jason Segel), spouting the film's titular phrase at one another before Peter exchanges vows with his bride.

The underlying thrust of all these films is the homoerotic yet (usually) homophobic dance the narratives play around the bond between the central buddy pair. Steven Cohan has documented how the buddy road movie cycle has depended upon homoerotic triangles and coded queerness since the 1940s, stating that "the comedic framework of the [subgenre] plays upon intimations of homoeroticism,"[31] and Robin Wood links the popularity of the buddy movie in the 1970s to the emergence of explicitly homosexual film narratives like *Victor Victoria* and *Making Love* in the 1980s.[32] Wood notes that the more overtly homosexually themed 1980s buddy films contain the threat of male-male homoeroticism by eliminating sexual ambiguity and fluidity, instead presenting a milieu in which "sexual orientation is separated out; there are heterosexuals and homosexuals, but they are two distinct species."[33] This is likewise true of the 1990s and millennial bromances: their buddy duos embrace a kind of platonic and even semi-romantic *love* for each other, yet their heterosexual interests are never remotely called into question, and uneasy homophobic joking permeates these films, as when Seth repeatedly calls Fogell "Faggle" in *Superbad*. Yet the 1990s emergence of the mainstream bromance has been accompanied by independent films like *My Own Private Idaho* (1991), *Chuck & Buck* (2000), and *Y Tu Mama Tambien* (2001) more willing to explore the queerness constitutive of the male buddy relation.[34]

7. Marginalized and/or Masculine Women

This trope has a long history in Hollywood cinema, and a tenacious presence in the male-centered buddy film tradition delineated by Robin Wood. Wood argues that women in the buddy film genre are "merely present for casual encounters en route, 'chicks' for the boys to pick up and put down," which presages Denby's concerns about millennial bromance-influenced romcoms and their inability to provide women protagonists of much depth or interest.[35]

Falling squarely within this tradition of Hollywood misogyny, the films of Team Apatow tend to depict women characters as either two-dimensional objects of male sexual desire (e.g., Beth in *Virgin,* Becca and Jules in *Superbad*) or as asexualized/hyper-sexualized objects of fear and revulsion, in the form of domineering mother figures (Debbie in *Knocked Up*, Liz Bretter in *Sarah Marshall*), awkward, asexualized female geeks (Jodi in *Knocked Up*), and/or scary, masculinized butches (Paula in *Virgin,* Carol the female cop in *Pineapple Express*).[36]

This trope also takes in the "unappreciated woman" motif that is prevalent in many geek narratives: perhaps intended as an indicator of the geek's pre-Oedipal status and sexual naiveté, many geek-centered films feature an obviously attractive and sexually available female character who is nevertheless not recognized as such by the geek protagonist. This character is often regarded as "just one of the boys" until late in the film, when the male geek finally sees her for what she is and becomes romantically interested in her. Classic examples include Veronica (Marilyn Ghigliotti) in *Clerks*, Zoe (Kristen Bell) in *Fanboys*, Jenny (Michelle Trachtenberg) in *Eurotrip*, and Joey (Katie Holmes) in the long-running, geek-centered television melodrama *Dawson's Creek*.[37]

In addition to relegating most of their secondary female characters to longstanding stereotypes, geek-centered films usually vilify or sell short their female leads as well. *Virgin's* Trish is likeable, almost to a fault, but remains underdeveloped relative to Andy and his group of male buddies. *Forgetting Sarah Marshall's* titular character is presented as a careerist achiever who, while justified in breaking up with the slovenly, unmotivated Peter, nevertheless fails to appreciate his unflagging love and support of her over time: numerous flashbacks from his point of view show her receiving public adulation and accolades while he stands humiliated and overlooked by her side. By the end, the film asks us to side with the vindicated Peter when he refuses Sarah's sexual advances and shouts at her: "You're the goddamned Devil!"

However, whereas Sarah Marshall's ultimately thankless role in Peter's narrative of recovery is anticipated by her dumping him in the first place, and her subsequent replacement by Manic Pixie Dream Girl Rachel (Mila Kunis), *Knocked Up's* Alison has an even harder road to travel. As Ben Stone's love interest, Alison needs to remain sympathetic and on roughly equal terms with Ben, yet narrative events conspire to render her subservient to him and a villain of sorts as well. Much of Alison's villainy comes via her relationships with other women, whose harsh advice stands in stark contrast to the warm, touchy-feely proclamations of the film's various men. For example, *Knocked Up* features Alison's mother (Joanna Kerns) in only one short scene, depicting her as an unsympathetic woman who calls the pregnancy "a big, big mistake" and icily suggests an abortion as the only solution to Alison's "problem." After a short sequence showing Ben with his father, Alison is next seen on the phone in a highly agitated state, telling Ben that she's absolutely keeping the baby: the strong implication of the paired "talk with mother"/"decide to keep the baby" sequences is that Alison keeps her baby mainly to spite her unsupportive mother. By contrast, Ben's dad (Harold Ramis) is totally supportive of, even thrilled about the pregnancy, and Ben's friend Jay cannot even pronounce the word "abortion" aloud because the very notion offends his tender, life-affirming sensibilities.[38] Finally, when Alison calls Ben, he, like his father, offers unqualified commitment and support, saying that "I know my job is to just support you in whatever it is you want to do, and I'm in, you know, so—whatever you want to do, I'm gonna do, you know. I'm on board." In essence, Ben provides Alison the "maternal" support she could not get from her own mother.

In these examples, men (Ben's father, Jay, Ben himself) usurp the maternal role, a trope with a long history in film comedy: as Lucy Fischer observes, comedy films since Chaplin's *The Kid* (1920) frequently "substitute the clown for the mother," staging a scenario "in which men [supplant] the female parent."[39] Indeed, male groups usually take on the maternal role in the geek comedies: Andy's friends "mother" him through his journey of sexual maturation in *Virgin*, Chuck (Paul Rudd) and Kemo (Taylor Wily) emotionally nurture Peter in *Sarah Marshall*, and Evan and Seth frequently act as surrogate mothers to each other in *Superbad*, rescuing each other from dangerous situations.

In perhaps the most drastic and disturbing iteration of this men-as-mothers substitution, *Knocked Up* ultimately reclaims the act of childbirth for the man: in the film's climactic sequence, it is revealed that Ben knows more about pregnancy than Alison by having read three baby books, and it is *his* reception of his daughter into the world that is given melodramatic weight, that takes up screen time, that "matters." Similarly, the marriage in *Virgin* is centered upon Andy carrying his bride to bed and *his* first sexual experience—closing credits "Aquarius" song is an expression of *his* sexual awakening and post-coital ecstasy. The geek-centered comedies often treat marriage in similar ways: *I Love You, Man* reclaims the typically bride-centered institution of marriage for masculinity by making the site of Paul's marriage double as the site of his bromantic reconciliation with Sidney. *Wedding Crashers* and *The Hangover* also use weddings as a mere pretense or backdrop to raunchy, anarchic male fun.

See also trope 5 and the framing of women characters as projections of male fantasy.

8. Slackerism and Underemployment

This trope, an outgrowth of the experiences of Generation X in the 1990s, depicts geeks as almost always working at mcjobs and suffering from various forms of un- or underemployment. The classic embodiment of this trope, and the melodrama that accompanies it, is found in Kevin Smith's generation-defining *Clerks*, in which geeky convenience store worker Dante suffers when he is called into work on his day off, and spends the whole day repeating the phrase: "I'm not even supposed to be here today!" Indeed, lousy, demeaning, boring day jobs provide the backdrop to a great many geek-centered comedies, for example, the tech firm Initech in *Office Space*, the convenience store in *Clerks*, the underpaying catering gigs in *Party Down*, and the entire setting of *The Office*.

It is important to note that while underemployed geeks may legitimately suffer for being intelligent people under-deployed at menial jobs, these guys are primarily *not* working-class: they are white, middle-class, college educated (or at least have the potential for college enrollment) and work these undemanding jobs because they are caught in a pre-Oedipal, deliberately melodramatized developmental phase wherein they are misusing their own potential while simultaneously bemoaning how the world at large does not appreciate them. What gets elided in their narratives is that the geek's refusal to grow up depends upon his possessing a high degree of socioeconomic privilege to begin with.

Examples of this trope abound in the Team Apatow films. *Virgin* has guys who work at a Best Buy-style electronics shop called Smart Tech. The members of the male gang in *Knocked Up* are unemployed: they loaf around their shared rental house getting stoned, playing ping-pong, and discussing their "business," a porn-related website that never launches. Even *Sarah Marshall*'s Peter, who has a "real" job as a soundtrack composer for a prime time television show, hates that job and is creatively unfulfilled by it. He is relieved when the show is canceled midway through the film and a major part of his emotional recovery in the wake of his breakup is the restoration of his faith in his own talents: with Rachel's help and encouragement he undergoes a kind of vocational rehab during the course of the film to believe in himself and put his musical talents to proper use writing and producing his own Dracula-themed musical.

This trope sets up geek melodrama by positioning the geek protagonist as a suffering victim (no one appreciates what he has to offer) and implying that, by dint of his intelligence, unexploited potential, and other advantages, the geek will rise again in the future.

A close relative of slackerism and underemployment in the contemporary cultural paradigm, stonerism is often present here: there is almost always at least one stoner among the geek's group of friends: Reuben in *Road Trip*, Jay and Silent Bob in *Clerks*, Saul and Dale in *Pineapple Express*, and the whole male gang in *Knocked Up*. Stonerism is also subtly raced, with strong ties to stereotypical depictions of black gangster culture (see trope 3).

Conclusion

The rise of the geek protagonist is troubling because under the guise of offering a kinder, more intelligent, more sensitive alternative to the traditional jockish male, the geek acts as a trojan horse for rampant misogyny, racism, infantilism, and reification of white male centrality and privilege. The eight tropes elucidated here are tools the textual analyst may use to intervene in these areas, exposing the mechanisms by which geek protagonists and narratives are "sold" to consumers of film and pop-culture across many genres. It is my hope that these tools may be used to combat the structural inequities repeated and reified by these films and to lambaste texts that do not support feminist, anti-racist, socially just points of view.

Notes

1. Kathleen Rowe Karlyn, *The Unruly Woman: Gender and the Genres of Laughter* (Austin: UT Press, 1995), 146–7.

2. For a thorough discussion of the 1970s "nervous romance," see Frank Krutnik, "The Faint Aroma of Performing Seals: The 'Nervous' Romance and the Comedy of the Sexes," *The Velvet Light Trap* Number 26 (Fall 1990): 57–72.

3. Geek race is discussed in my co-authored article "Postmodern Geekdom as Simulated Ethnicity," *Jump Cut* 54 (Summer 2012).

4. Leger Grindon, *The Hollywood Romantic Comedy: Conventions, History, Controversy* (Malden, MA: Wiley-Blackwell, 2011), 61–66, 171–180.

5. David Denby, "A Fine Romance: The New Comedy of the Sexes," *The New Yorker* (July 23, 2007), 65.

6. Asked about his cinematic influences at a San Diego Comic-Con panel in 2008, Apatow replied that "Kevin Smith laid down the tracks [. . .] I remember seeing *Clerks* and thinking 'You can do that?!'"

7. William Paul, "The Rise and Fall of Animal Comedy," *The Velvet Light Trap* Number 26 (Fall 1990): 73–86.

8. *American Pie*'s Oz is a key example of the geek-friendly jock, a good-looking and otherwise jockish character who is close friends with a group of nerds or geeks. The geek-friendly jock is a staple of many Animal comedies—see Otter (Tim Matheson) in *Animal House*—and appears sporadically in the 1990s and 2000s as the feminized geek assumes increasing dominance. Key examples include Charles Jefferson (Forest Whitaker) in *Fast Times at Ridgemont High* (1982), Wooderson (Matthew McConaughey) and Pink (Jason

London) in *Dazed and Confused* (1993), T.S. (Jeremy London) in *Mallrats* (1995), and the characters played by Vince Vaughn in *Rudy* (1993), *Swingers* (1996), *Old School* (2003), and *Dodgeball* (2004).

9. *American Pie*, directed by Paul Weitz (1999; Universal City, CA: Universal Home Entertainment, 1999), DVD.

10. *The 40-Year-Old Virgin*, directed by Judd Apatow (2005; Universal City, CA: Universal Studios Home Entertainment, 2005), DVD. The plot of the male virgin being too nervous to have sex with the woman he loves was previously explored by Apatow in "Parent's Weekend," an episode of *Undeclared* he executive produced for the Fox Network in 2002. That episode's director was John Hamburg, who would later direct the Paul Rudd-Jason Segel bromance *I Love You, Man* (2009).

11. *Knocked Up*, directed by Judd Apatow (2007; Universal City, CA: Universal Studios Home Entertainment, 2007), DVD.

12. Apatow and Judge have both directed and/or produced female-geek-centered projects: *Freaks and Geeks* and *Bridesmaids* for the former (collaborating with Paul Feig as creator and director on both), and the animated series *Daria* for the latter.

13. *Forgetting Sarah Marshall*, directed by Nicholas Stoller (2008; Universal City, CA: Universal Studios Home Entertainment, 2008), DVD.

14. Nathan Rabin, "The Bataan Death March of Whimsy Case File #1: *Elizabethtown*," Onion AV Club, January 25, 2007.

15. Special thanks to Kom Kunyosying for his integral role in developing the tropes list. Note also that tropes 6 and 7 overlap with two of Wood's features of 1970s buddy films; see Robin Wood, *Hollywood from Vietnam to Reagan . . . and Beyond* (New York: Columbia UP, 2003), 198–218.

16. Linda Williams, "Melodrama Revised," in *Refiguring American Film Genres*, ed. Nik Browne (Berkeley: U Cal Press, 1998), 42, 58.

17. For an example of this argument, see Thomas Schatz, "*Annie Hall* and the Issue of Modernism," *Literature/Film Quarterly* Vol. 10 (1982): 180–187.

18. Schatz, "Modernism," 183.

19. Kathleen Rowe Karlyn, "Comedy, Melodrama and Gender: Theorizing the Genres of Laughter," in *Classical Hollywood Comedy*, ed. Kristine Brunovska Karnick and Henry Jenkins (New York: Routledge, 1995), 53.

20. *Freaks and Geeks*, created by Paul Feig, executive produced by Judd Apatow (1999–2000; Los Angeles,CA: Shout! Factory, 2004), DVD.

21. The interracial buddy fantasy at the heart of white adolescence in America has a long history that, according to Leslie Fiedler, sees an early and influential iteration in the relationship between Huck and Jim in Mark Twain's *Huckleberry Finn*. Eric Lott has traced the same white fascination with and appropriation of imagined blackness in the twentieth century minstrel show, and Norman Mailer's "The White Negro" documents the same phenomenon among white fans of jazz music in the 1950s. The concept of geeks' simulated ethnicity is discussed more fully in Kom Kunyosying and Carter Soles, " Postmodern Geekdom as Simulated Ethnicity," *Jump Cut* 54 (Fall 2012).

22. James Snead, *White Screens Black Images: Hollywood from the Dark Side* (New York: Routledge, 1994), 6.

23. For an in-depth discussion of the assumed uptightness of white people, see Richard Dyer, *White* (London: Routledge, 1997), 21, 23–24.

24. *Say Anything. . . ,* directed by Cameron Crowe. (1989; Century City, CA: Twentieth Century Fox, 2003), DVD.

25. In the Judd Apatow series *Undeclared,* Ken (Seth Rogen) stalks Kelly (Busy Phillips) and idealizes that stalking as a quasi-relationship, and *The Big Bang Theory* shows Leonard obsessing over Penny for a year or more before they actually date, endorsing stalking as a legitimate form of relationship or courtship. True to form, McBride and Hill take this to its squirmy extreme with Fred Simmons in *The Foot Fist Way,* exposing the delusional misogyny at the heart of the stalkerism trope. As I have written elsewhere, *Chuck & Buck* also queers and partially deconstructs this trope.

26. Schatz, "Modernism," 183.

27. Donna Bowman, Amelie Gillette, Steven Hyden, Noel Murray, Leonard Pierce, and Nathan Rabin, "Wild Things: 16 Films Featuring Manic Pixie Dream Girls," Onion AV Club, August 4, 2008.

28. Grindon, *The Hollywood Romantic Comedy,* 174.

29. Wood, *Hollywood from Vietnam to Reagan,* 203–4.

30. Eve Kosofsky Sedgwick, *Between Men: English Literature and Male Homosocial Desire* (New York: Columbia UP, 1985).

31. Steven Cohan, "Queering the Deal: On the Road with Hope and Crosby," in *Out Takes: Essays on Queer Theory and Film,* ed. Ellis Hanson (Durham: Duke UP, 1999), 25.

32. Wood, *Hollywood from Vietnam to Reagan,* 199, 218.

33. Ibid., 213.

34. Perhaps in response to these queer independent buddy films, many recent bromances beyond those already mentioned include explicit and emotional declarations of love between the male buddies: *Clerks 2, Role Models,* also J.D. and Turk, who perform a musical number about their shared (insistently non-sexual) love on an episode of *Scrubs.* See my queer analysis of *Chuck & Buck* in Carter Soles, "A Stalker's Odyssey: Arrested Development, Gay Desire, and Queer Comedy in Chuck & Buck," *Jump Cut* 49 (Spring 2007).

35. Wood, *Hollywood from Vietnam to Reagan,* 203.

36. As Leger Grindon has documented, sexually assertive women, like Paula (Jane Lynch), Nicky (Leslie Mann) and Beth (Elizabeth Banks) in *Virgin,* are presented as grotesque and "freaky," an obstacle to true love and romance in geek comedies. As representatives of the grotesque, which is always closely aligned with sexuality, these women provide "a source of contrast between a demeaning physicality versus the grace of passion" (Grindon 63), showing Andy what he does *not* want so he can eventually realize that Trish is who he *does* want.

37. A related but less frequently occurring trope is the "she turned lesbian after he slept with her" motif, seen with Randal in the *Clerks* cartoon and Andy Millman in *Extras.* This motif signifies male fear of lesbian sexuality and the false assumption that any woman who rejects or mistreats the male protagonist must be a lesbian.

38. In this regard, *Knocked Up* played an influential role, alongside *Juno* (2007), in reinforcing the religious right's anti-feminist stance against abortion and women's reproductive rights.

39. Lucy Fischer, "Sometimes I Feel Like a Motherless Child: Comedy and Matricide," in *Comedy/Cinema/Theory,* ed. Andrew Horton (Berkeley: U of California P, 1991), 67, 69.

Carter Soles is Assistant Professor of Film Studies and Director, Interdisciplinary Film Studies Minor in the Department of English at The College at Brockport, State University of New York.

9 | *Women in Film Noir*

Janey Place

Place discusses film noir as a movement (e.g., German Expressionism, Soviet Formalism, Italian Neo-Realism) rather than genre and as a national myth that secures the existence of the social structure within the precise polemics of WWII. She describes the visual stylization and motifs of two gender scripts in film noir: "spider woman" (independence via a particularly sexual self-knowledge and masquerade) and "nurturing woman" (offering integration for alienated, lost men into stable "values," "roles" and "identities"). This article is pedagogically useful because it considers a number of films, is careful to note atypical examples and explores the continuing popularity of film noir on college campuses, television and film retrospectives due to its "sensuality."

The dark lady, the spider woman, the evil seductress who tempts man and brings about his destruction is among the oldest themes of art, literature, mythology and religion in western culture. She is as old as Eve, and as current as today's movies, comic books and dime novels. She and her sister (or *alter ego*), the virgin, the mother, the innocent, the redeemer, form the two poles of female archetypes.

Film noir is a male fantasy, as is most of our art. Thus woman here as elsewhere is defined by her sexuality: the dark lady has access to it and the virgin does not. That men are not so deterministically delineated in their cultural and artistic portrayal is indicative of the phallocentric cultural viewpoint; women are defined *in relation* to men, and the centrality of sexuality in this definition is a key to understanding the position of women in our culture. The primary crime the "liberated" woman is guilty of is refusing to be defined in such a way, and this refusal can be perversely seen (in art, or in life) as an attack on men's very existence. Film noir is hardly "progressive" in these terms—it does not present us with role models who defy their fate and triumph over it. But it does give us one of the few periods of film in which women are active, not static symbols, are intelligent and powerful, if destructively so, and derive power, not weakness, from their sexuality.

Reprinted from *Women in Film Noir*, edited by E. Ann Kaplan (1980), by permission of Macmillan Press.

Myth

Our popular culture functions as myth for our society: it both expresses and reproduces the ideologies necessary to the existence of the social structure. Mythology is remarkably responsive to changing needs in the society: in sex roles for example—when it was necessary for women to work in factories during World War II and then necessary to channel them back into the home after the war.

We can look at our historic film heroines to demonstrate these changing attitudes: the strong women of 40s films such as Katharine Hepburn and Rosalind Russell (whose strength was none the less often expressed by their willingness to stand *behind* their men in the last reel) were replaced by the sex goddesses (Marilyn Monroe), virtuous wife types (Jane Wyman), and professional virgins (Doris Day) of the 50s as the dominant cultural heroines. This is not to assert that these were the *only* popular movie stars of their times, but by the shift in relative importance of an archetype can be observed the corresponding change in the needs of the culture which produced them all.

Myth not only expresses dominant ideologies, it is also responsive to the *repressed* needs of the culture. It gives voice to the unacceptable archetypes as well; the myths of the sexually aggressive woman (or criminal man) first allows sensuous expression of that idea and then destroys it. And by its limited expression, ending in defeat, that unacceptable element is controlled. For example, we can see pornography as expressing unacceptable needs which are created by the culture itself, and allowed limited (degraded) expression to prevent these socially induced tensions from erupting in a more dangerous form.

Two aspects of the portrayal of women in film noir are remarkable. First, the particular mix and versions of the more general archetypes that recur in films noirs; and second the style of that expression. Visually, film noir is fluid, sensual, extraordinarily expressive, making the sexually expressive woman, which is its dominant image of woman, extremely powerful. It is not their inevitable demise we remember but rather their strong, dangerous and, above all, exciting sexuality. In film noir we observe both the social action of myth which damns the sexual woman and all who become enmeshed by her, and a particularly potent stylistic presentation of the sexual strength of woman which man fears. This operation of myth is so highly stylised and conventionalised that the final "lesson" of the myth often fades into the background and we retain the image of the erotic, strong, unrepressed (if destructive) woman. The style of these films thus overwhelms their conventional narrative content, or interacts with it to produce a remarkably potent image of woman.

This expression of the myth of man's "right" or need to control women sexually is in contrast to the dominant version of it in "A" films of the 30s, 40s, and 50s, which held that women are so weak and incapable that they need men's "protection" to survive. In these films, it is the woman who is portrayed benefiting from her dependence on men; in film noir, it is clear that men need to control women's sexuality in order not to be destroyed by it. The dark woman of film noir had something her innocent sister lacked: access to her own sexuality (and thus to men's) and the power that this access unlocked.

Movement and Genre

Any claims for film noir's special significance in portraying fear of women (which is both ancient and newly potent, today and during the period which produced film noir) must account for the particularly valid ties between film noir and the cultural obsessions of the United States during the 40s and early 50s. Film noir has been considered a genre, but it has more in common with previous film movements (e.g., German Expressionism, Soviet Socialist Realism, Italian neo-realism) and, in fact, touches every genre. For a consideration of women in film noir, this is more than a semantic dispute. Film movements occur in specific historical periods—at times of national stress and focus of energy. They express a consistency of both thematic and formal elements which makes them particularly expressive of those times, and are uniquely able to express the homogeneous hopes (Soviet Socialist Realism and Italian Neo-Realism) and fears (German Expressionism and film noir) brought to the fore by, for example, the upheaval of war.

The attitudes towards women evidenced in film noir—i.e., fear of loss of stability, identity and security—are reflective of the dominant feelings of the time.

Genres, on the other hand, exist through time: we have had Westerns since the early 1900s and, in spite of rises and falls in their popularity, Westerns are with us today. Genres are characterised more by their subject matter and their iconography than movements, and they can express a wide and changing range of ideologies. The convention of the railroad in the Western, for example, has changed radically from 1924 (*The Iron Horse*) when it symbolised man's hopes for progress, the uniting of the continent, and the building of a peaceful community in the West, to 1972 (Sergio Leone's *Once Upon a Time in the West*), when it was the economic imperative causing exploitation of the poor. Many gangster pictures now champion the criminals, and Westerns depict the West as corrupt and lawless instead of an innocent refuge from corrupt Eastern values and a pure environment in which to build a virtuous society. -

Unlike genres, defined by objects and subjects, but like other film movements, film noir is characterised by the remarkably homogeneous visual style with which it cuts across genres: this can be seen in the film noir influence on certain Westerns, melodramas (even musicals) and particularly the detective genre. This style indicates a similarly homogeneous cultural attitude, and is only possible within an isolated time period, in a particular place, in response to a national crisis of some kind.

The characteristics of film noir style, however, are not "rules" to be enforced,[1] nor are they necessarily the most important aspects of each film in which they appear; and no attempt to fix and categorise films will be very illuminating if it prescribes strict boundaries for a category. This leads to suppression of those elements which do not "fit," and to exclusion of films which have strong links but equally strong differences from a particular category. Often the most exceptional examples of these films will be exceptional *because* of the deviations from the general "norms" of the movement.

For example, in the classic film noir, *They Live By Night,* the strain of romanticism is far more important than that of the spider woman, who is in this film a minor character. The "evil" Mattie who turns Bowie over to the police is even psychologically sympathetic—through love and loyalty to her imprisoned husband she is "trading" Bowie for him. On the other hand, in an equally central a film, *Kiss Me Deadly,* no one, male or female, enjoys any of the transcending benefits of the romantic aspects of film noir. Only the victims Christina (Cloris Leachman) and Nick (the mechanic) are sympathetic: the rest are doomed only by their own greed. But after acknowledging that *every* film worth discussing is going to be "exceptional" in *some* way and that their visual styles are going to vary, we can then go on to identify the visual and narrative themes that dominate film noir and influence countless other films made during the 40s and early to mid-50s in the United States.

The detective/thriller genre, whose subjects are generally the lawless underworld, the fringes of society, crimes of passion and of greed, is particularly well suited to the expression of film noir themes. The movement affected other genres: melodrama particularly, but there are Westerns and even musicals that have distinctly noir elements. When the themes of the genre are not conducive to the noir mood, an interesting and confused mix results. *Ramrod* (1947, directed by André de Toth) is one such Western. Veronica Lake plays the typically aggressive, sexual "dark lady" of film noir who causes the murders; Arleen Whelan is her opposite, the nurturing, stay-at-home good woman. The usual stable moral environment of the typical Western is lacking, and the noir influence is evident in the murky moral confusion of the male characters and in their inability to control the direction of the narrative. *Ramrod* has the open, extreme long shots characteristic of the genre, but the clarity they generally signify is undercut by the noir ambiguity.

The dominant world view expressed in film noir is paranoid, claustrophobic, hopeless, doomed, predetermined by the past, without clear moral or personal identity. Man has been inexplicably uprooted from those values, beliefs and endeavours that offer him meaning and stability, and in the almost exclusively urban landscape of film noir (in pointed contrast to the pastoral, idealised, remembered past) he is struggling for a foothold in a maze of right and wrong. He has no reference points, no moral base from which to confidently operate. Any previous framework is cut loose and morality becomes relative, both externally (the world) and internally (the character and his relations to his work, his friends, his sexuality). Values, like identities, are constantly shifting and must be redefined at every turn. Nothing—especially woman—is stable, nothing is dependable.

The visual style conveys this mood through expressive use of darkness: both real, in predominantly underlit and night-time scenes, and psychologically through shadows and claustrophobic compositions which overwhelm the character in exterior as well as interior settings. Characters (and we in the audience) are given little opportunity to orient themselves to the threatening and shifting shadowy environment. Silhouettes, shadows, mirrors and reflections (generally darker than the reflected person) indicate his lack of both unity and control. They suggest a *doppelganger,* a dark ghost, *alter* ego or distorted side of man's personality which will emerge in the dark street at night to destroy him. The sexual, dangerous woman lives in this darkness, and she is the psychological expression of his own internal fears of sexuality, and his need to control and repress it.

The characters and themes of the detective genre are ideal for film noir. The moral and physical chaos is easily expressed in crime: the doomed, tortured souls seem to be at home in the violent, unstable milieu of the underworld. The dark woman is comfortable in the world of cheap dives, shadowy doorways and mysterious settings. The opposite archetype, the woman as redeemer, as agent of integration for the hero into his environment and into himself, is found in the innocent victim who dies for the hero (*The Big Combo*), the longsuffering and faithful lover of the loser hero (*Pick-up on South Street, They Live By Night, Night and the City*) or as a contrast to the fringe world itself (*The Big Heat, On Dangerous Ground, Out of the Past*).

The Spider Woman

The meaning of any film image is a complex function of its visual qualities (composition, angle, lighting, screen size, camera movement, etc.), the content of the image (acting, stars, iconography, etc.), its juxtaposition to surrounding images, and the context of the narrative. Even more broadly, meaning is affected by ever-enlarging contexts, such as the conventions of a particular genre, of film generally, and of the time in which the film is made and in which it is viewed. It would be presumptuous and an impossible undertaking to attempt to establish a "dictionary" of meanings within a system which is so bound for specific meaning to such complex elements and their interaction. Nevertheless, film noir is a movement, and as such is remarkably stylistically consistent. It thus becomes possible to identify recurrent visual motifs and their general range of meanings. Within these recurrent patterns, some drawn from conventions not specifically filmic, others specific to film generally, and still others to film noir or the detective film genre, the source and operation of the sexual woman's dangerous power is expressed visually.

The following illustrations are all made up of these visual motifs, but the consistent meaning is not necessarily the entire meaning in any single image. A director—consciously or unconsciously—can use a convention against its usual meaning for expressive effect, as for example in *Laura.* The power to incite murder which is visually ascribed to Laura's magnificent portrait is revealed to be a product of the neuroses of the men around her, not of the power she wields. Norma Desmond in *Sunset Boulevard* is the most highly stylised "spider woman" in all of film noir as she weaves a web to trap and finally destroy her young victim, but even as she visually dominates him, she is presented as caught by the same false value system. The huge house in which she controls camera movement and is constantly centre frame is also a hideous trap which requires from her the maintenance of the myth of her stardom: the contradiction between the reality and the myth pull her apart and finally drive her mad. The complete meaning of any single image is complex and multidimensional, but we can identify motifs whose meaning proceeds initially from common origins.

The source and the operation of the sexual woman's power and its danger to the male character is expressed visually both in the iconography of the image and in the visual style. The iconography is explicitly sexual, and often explicitly violent as well: long hair (blond or dark), make-up, and jewellery. Cigarettes with their wispy trails of smoke can become cues of dark and immoral sensuality, and the iconography of violence (primarily guns) is a specific symbol (as is perhaps the cigarette) of her "unnatural" phallic power. The *femme fatale* is characterised by her long, lovely legs: our first view of the elusive Velma in *Murder My Sweet* (*Farewell My Lovely*) and of Cora in *The Postman Always Rings Twice* is a significant, appreciative shot of their bare legs, a *directed* glance (so directed in the latter film that the shot begins on her calves, cuts to a shot of her whole body, cuts back to the man looking, then finally back to Lana Turner's turban-wrapped angelic face) from the viewpoint of the male character who is to be seduced. In *Double Indemnity* Phyllis's legs (with a gold anklet significantly bearing her name) dominate Walter's and our own memory of her as the camera follows her descent down the stairs, framing only her spike heels and silk-stockinged calves. Dress—or lack of it—further defines the woman: Phyllis first is viewed in *Double Indemnity* wrapped in a towel, and the sequinned, tight, black gown of the fantasy woman in *Woman in the Window* and the nameless "dames" of film noir instantly convey the important information about them and their role in the film.

The strength of these women is expressed in the visual style by their dominance in composition, angle, camera movement and lighting.[2] They are overwhelmingly the compositional focus, generally centre frame and/or in the foreground, or pulling focus to them in the background. They control camera movement, seeming to direct the camera (and the hero's gaze, with our own) irresistibly with them as they move. (In contrast, the "good" women of film noir and many of the seduced, passive men are predominantly static, both within the frame and in their ability to motivate camera movement and composition.) The *femme fatale* ultimately loses physical movement, influence over camera movement, and is often actually or symbolically imprisoned by composition as control over her is exerted and expressed visually: sometimes behind visual bars (*The Maltese Falcon*), sometimes happy in the protection of a lover (*The Big Sleep*), often dead (*Murder My Sweet, Out of the Past, Gun Crazy, Kiss Me Deadly, Double Indemnity*), sometimes symbolically rendered impotent (*Sunset Boulevard*). The ideological operation of the myth (the absolute necessity of controlling the strong, sexual woman) is thus achieved by first demonstrating her dangerous power and its frightening results, then destroying it.

Often the original transgression of the dangerous lady of film noir (unlike the vamp seductress of the 20s) is ambition expressed metaphorically in her freedom of movement and visual dominance. This ambition is inappropriate to her status as a woman, and must be confined. She wants to be the owner of her own nightclub, not the owner's wife (*Night and the City*). She wants to be a star, not a recluse (*Sunset Boulevard*). She wants her husband's insurance money, not her comfortable, middle-class life (*Double Indemnity*). She wants the "great whatsit," and ends up destroying the world (*Kiss Me Deadly*). She wants independence, and sets off a chain of murders (*Laura*). She wants to win an uninterested lover, and ends up killing him, herself, and two other people (*Angel Face*). She wants money, and succeeds only in destroying herself and the man who loves her (*Gun Crazy, The Killers*). She wants freedom from an oppressive relationship, and initiates events that lead to murder (*The Big Combo, The Postman Always Rings Twice*). Whether evil (*Double Indemnity, Gun Crazy, Kiss Me Deadly, Night and the City, The Maltese Falcon, The Postman Always Rings Twice*), or innocent (*Laura, The Big Combo*), her desire for freedom, wealth or independence ignites the forces which threaten the hero.

Independence is her goal, but her nature is fundamentally and irredeemably sexual in film noir. The insistence on combining the two (aggressiveness and sensuality) in a consequently dangerous woman is the central obsession of film noir, and the visual movement which indicates unacceptable activity in film noir women represents the man's own sexuality, which must be repressed and controlled if it is not to destroy him.

The independence which film noir women seek is often visually presented as self-absorbed narcissism: the woman gazes at her own reflection in the mirror, ignoring the man she will use to achieve her goals.[3] This attention to herself instead of the man is the obvious narrative transgression of Norma Desmond whose images—both reflected and pictures—dominate her mansion in *Sunset Boulevard*. She hires Joe Gillis to work on her script for her comeback, and she continues to insist he participate in her life rather than being interested in his. He dreams he is her pet chimp, and he actually becomes a victim of her Salome. Joe finds an acceptable lover in Betty, the young woman who types while he dictates, smells like soap instead of perfume, dreams of *his* career, and is content to be behind the camera instead of in front. Self-interest over devotion to a man is often the original sin of the film noir woman and metaphor for the threat her sexuality represents to him.

Another possible meaning of the many mirror shots in film noir is to indicate women's duplicitous nature. They are visually split, thus not to be trusted. Further, this motif contributes to the murky confusion of film noir: nothing and no one is what it seems. Compositions in which reflections are stronger than the actual woman, or in which mirror images are seen in odd, uncomfortable angles, help to create the mood of threat and fear.

In some films the "spider women" prove not to be so and are thus redeemed. Gilda and Laura are validated as individuals (Gilda was simply acting out the paranoid fantasies of her true love, Johnny, and Laura was an innocent catalyst for men's idealisations), but the images of sexual power they exhibit are more powerful than the narrative "explanation." The image of Gilda we remember is the close-up introduction to her, with long hair tossed back over her head to reveal her beautiful face. Her song, "Put the Blame on Mame, Boys" (for every natural and economic disaster to hit the world), is ironic, but stripping as she performs, the power she possesses as a sexually alive woman seems almost up to the task. Laura's beautiful, dominating portrait that haunts the characters and determines the action of the film when she is believed dead is the strongest visual image even when she reappears alive.

The framed portrait of a woman is a common motif in film noir. Sometimes it is contrasted with the living woman: in *Night and the City* Helen is a nagging, ambitious, destructive bitch, but her husband gazes longingly at her "safe" incarnation in the framed portrait—under control, static and powerless. Laura's portrait is compositionally dominating, inciting Mark's fantasies and giving visual expression to Waldo's idealised vision of her, but only when she unexpectedly turns up alive does further trouble ensue as she refuses to conform to the fantasies inspired by the portrait. In *Woman in the Window,* an elderly, respectable professor puts his wife and children on a train and, longing for adventure, dreams a beautiful portrait comes to life and involves him in murder. He is about to take his own life when he wakes up, cured of his longing for adventure. The lesson is obvious: only in a controlled, impotent, powerless form, powerless to move or act, is the sexual woman no threat to the film noir man.

On the rare occasions that the normal world of families, children, homes and domesticity appears in film noir it is either so fragile and ideal that we anxiously anticipate its destruction (*The Big Heat*), or, like the "good" but boring women who contrast with the exciting, sexy *femme fatales,* it is so dull and constricting that it offers no compelling alternative to the dangerous but exciting life on the fringe.

The Nurturing Woman

The opposite female archetype is also found in film noir: woman as redeemer. She offers the possibility of integration for the alienated, lost man into the stable world of secure values, roles and identities. She gives love, understanding (or at least forgiveness), asks very little in return (just that he come back to her) and is generally visually passive and static. Often, in order to offer this alternative to the nightmare landscape of film noir, she herself must not be a part of it. She is then linked to the pastoral environment of open spaces, light, and safety characterised by even, flat, high-key lighting. Often this is an idealised dream of the past and she exists only in memory; but sometimes this idealisation exists as a real alternative.

Out of the Past is one of the best of the latter type: one woman (Ann) is firmly rooted in the pastoral environment, static, undemanding and rather dull, while the other (Kathie) is exciting, criminal, very active and sexy. In this film the lack of excitement offered by the safe woman is so clearly contrasted with the sensual, passionate appeal of the other that the detective's destruction is inevitable. Kathie appears out of the misty haze of late afternoon in a little Mexican town, walking towards the detective hero as he sits in a bar, waiting for this woman whose image has already been setup for him by the man she shot and ran away from, who wants her back at any cost. They later embrace against the tumultuous sea, a sudden rainstorm, and the dark, rich textures created by low-key lighting.

The independent, active woman is often the primary noir element of noir-influenced films in other genres. In *Ramrod,* a Western, and *Beyond the Forest,* a melodrama, the initial cause of the drama which results in death is a woman who will not "stay at home"—Connie (Veronica Lake) on her father's ranch and Rosa (Bette Davis) in her small town with her doctor husband. Each woman is characterised sexually as aggressive and dangerous by the iconography and by the results of her actions. But because neither is centrally film noir, in *Ramrod* the quiet, waiting woman gets the man instead of aggressive Connie, and in *Beyond the Forest* Rosa's "unnatural" ambition is powerful enough to cause only her own destruction. The intersection of the Western and its noir influence is particularly interesting because in Westerns women are generally genre objects representing home and stability rather than actors in the drama. Other examples of noir-influenced Westerns are also characterised by active women and noir visual style: *Johnny Guitar, Rancho Notorious,* and *Forty Guns.*

The redemptive woman often represents or is part of a primal connection with nature and/or with the past, which are safe, static states rather than active, exciting ones, but she can sometimes offer the only transcendence possible in film noir. *They Live By Night* and *On Dangerous Ground* (both directed by Nicholas Ray, 1949 and 1951) are characterised by the darkly romantic element that can exist with the cynical. In the former, the young lovers are doomed, but the possibility of their love transcends and redeems them both, and its failure criticises the urbanised world that will not let them live. Their happiest moments are outdoors in the sunlight, with "normalcy" an ideal they can never realise because there is no place for them in the corrupt world. Mary (*On Dangerous Ground*) is not only cut off from the corruption of greed, money and power of the urban environment by living in a rural setting, she is further isolated (and purified) by her blindness. She teaches the badly disturbed and violent Jim to feel, and her reliance on him releases him from his emotional prison. Both characters are crippled—he emotionally and she physically—and need each other to achieve the wholeness of health. This interdependence keeps both characters and their relationship exciting, while other "innocents" of film noir who exist only to contrast with the dangerous woman simply fade into forgetfulness.

Film noir contains versions of both extremes of the female archetypes, the deadly seductress and the rejuvenating redeemer. Its special significance lies in the combination of sensuality with activity and ambition which characterises the *femme fatale,* and in the mode of control that must be exerted to dominate her. She is not often won over and pacified by love for the hero, as is the strong heroine of the 40s who is significantly less sexual than the film noir woman. Indeed, her strength is emphasised by the general passivity and impotence which characterises the film noir male, making her a far greater threat to him than the career woman of the 40s was, and thus only actual or symbolic destruction is an effective control. Even more significant is the form in which the "spider woman's" strength and power is expressed: the visual style gives her such freedom of movement and dominance that it is her strength and sensual visual texture that is inevitably printed in our memory, not her ultimate destruction.

The tendency of popular culture to create narratives in which male fears are concretised in sexually aggressive women who must be destroyed is not specific to the 40s to mid-50s in the United States, but is seen today to a degree that might help to account for the sudden popularity of these films on college campuses, on television, and in film retrospectives. But despite their regressive ideological function on a strictly narrative level, a fuller explanation for the current surge of interest in film noir must acknowledge its uniquely sensual visual style which often overwhelms (or at least acts upon) the narrative so compellingly that it stands as the only period in American film in which women are deadly but sexy, exciting and strong.

Notes

1. Often it is the films made from Raymond Chandler's novels, or films made by a director such as Fritz Lang, that have the most characteristic visual and narrative themes. Indeed, a film noir made by a strong director such as Nicholas Ray may have more in common with one of his films that is not squarely in the film noir style than with other films noirs.

2. Lighting and chiaroscuro can express the moral relationship between characters; in the still of Phyllis Dietrichson and her stepdaughter from *Double Indemnity* (p. 94) the women are contrasted and morally characterised.

3. See, for example, the still from *Double Indemnity* (p. 93) where Phyllis is putting on her lipstick.

10

Film Noir's "Femme Fatales" Hard-Boiled Women: Moving Beyond Gender Fantasies

Julie Grossman

In her essay "Professions for Women," Virginia Woolf says "It is far harder to kill a phantom than a reality" (1346). Nowhere is this insight truer than in the culture's preoccupation with the femme fatale, a figure I want to identify as a phantom, an illusion and myth that I wish not so much to kill, but to deconstruct as a category that feeds cultural gender fantasies. Feminist film critics have long recognized the ideological power of the femme fatale: first in terms of her role as a projection of male fear and desire; later, as a politically forceful symbol of unencumbered power. I want not only to extend recent emphases by critics such as Christine Gledhill, Elizabeth Cowie, and Jans Wager on how noir speaks to women but also to show the striking extent to which femme fatales—seductresses whose desires and malevolence are seemingly unmotivated—don't in fact exist in the noir movies in which so-called bad women appear. Instead film noir's lead female characters predominantly demonstrate complex psychological and social identity, resisting the spectator's habit (traced in criticism and cultural responses) of seeing past her as opaque or ambiguous (thus a screen on which to project male fears and desires) or of fixing on her as the thing, a dangerous body, to be labeled and tamed by social roles and institutions.

This essay will point to the dearth of film noir's actual femmes fatales, evil women whose raison d'être is to murder and deceive, focusing on films in which the femme fatale is presented in terms of exigency. That is, I want to call attention to the many female characters in original-cycle noir who are shown to be limited by, even trapped in, social worlds presented as psychotically gendered. Exigency for most so-called femme fatales moves these women to express—in aggressive physical and verbal gestures—an insistence on independence, which is then misread as the mark of the femme fatale. Readings of and references to the femme fatale miss the extent to which her role depends on the theme of female independence, often misconceiving her motives and serving mainly to

Reprinted from *Quarterly Review of Film and Video* 24, no. 1 (2007), by permission of Routledge.

confound our understanding of the gender fantasies that surround these so-called bad women. Such myths are propelled by the culture now both by film criticism and popular culture.

Indeed, critics have settled in their discussion of women in noir on the few female characters who conform to the notion of the quintessential femme fatale (as she is represented by Phyllis Dietrichson [*Double Indemnity*], Kathie Moffett [*Out of the Past*], and Brigid O'Shaughnessy [*The Maltese Falcon*]), who then define the category. This has two significant consequences: first, these few really bad women draw all of the attention; second the construction of a false binary opposition between femme fatales and other women means that the large majority of female characters in noir whose roles are inflected (multifaceted and interesting) are placed into the category of femme fatale without close attention paid to the complexity of the character.

Such is certainly the case with Cora Smith (Lana Turner) in Tay Garnett's *The Postman Always Rings Twice* (1946): Cora is hailed as one of the central film noir femme fatales, but the film's presentation of her is considerably more complicated than is allowed by the label. With Phyllis Dietrichson, Cora was recently dubbed "two of the [femme fatale's] most powerful screen incarnations" (Spicer, 91), and yet Cora is shown by the film to be desperately confined. This is represented most forcefully in the scene in which Nick tells her that she will be moving to northern Canada to take care of a half-paralyzed sister of Nick's. All of Cora's hopes to "be somebody" are dashed. She's trapped. Certainly, this is an important part of Cora's story. Her subjectivity, powerfully emphasized as she walks, stunned and defeated, up the stairs after the scene just alluded to, is utterly elided, however, by insisting on her being a femme fatale.

Critics and critical history have selected a specific set of narrative situations and iconic roles for the femme fatale, and canonized these women. Current critics and popular culture have then inherited a tradition that they don't really question but rather assume: Bad women are femme fatales and there will be a femme fatale in film noir movies. The inflexibility of the category of the femme fatale, despite feminist attempts to problematize and complicate the label and its various contexts, leads viewers typically to take a "Where's Waldo?" approach to the femme fatale: "She's not a real femme fatale!" "She didn't kill anyone"; or "She's not very attractive." Such exclusivity in understanding the femme fatale stalls discussion of the complexity of her represented experience, which almost always involves a woman trapped by the narrow categories on offer for understanding female social and sexual lives.

Many film noirs lend subjectivity to the independent women called femme fatales, depicting the psychological motives for becoming, or acting the role of, the femme fatale. While these motives are often clearly linked to the social conditions of women in post-war America, the depiction of femme fatales frequently attributes an "inner life" to these women that allows us to read them as sympathetic characters; these films depict femme fatales as inevitably growing out of repressive social milieus. As actress Lizabeth Scott, best known for her noir performances, such as Lewis Milestone's *The Strange Love of Martha Ivers* (1946), John Cromwell's *Dead Reckoning* (1947), and André De Toth's *Pitfall* (1948), has said,

> the femme fatale . . . was always the person, in most of the films that I did, who had the greatest understanding. She knew life better than most females of the era. She knew that life could be good and life could be bad, she knew what was right and she knew what was wrong, but . . . there were certain things she had to do. (*Noir Reader* 3, 195)

Samuel Fuller echoes Scott's remarks when he talks about the blindness and hypocrisies surrounding perceptions of Kelly, the sympathetic prostitute in Fuller's *The Naked Kiss* (1964): "When [the townspeople] find out about her past, everybody assumes she's guilty as hell." "You do what you do," Fuller adds, "out of necessity" (*Noir Reader* 3, 48). Fuller points up the two-pronged difficulty for women represented in film noir: To preserve itself, patriarchal culture projects images onto women that perpetuate a binary opposition of good girl versus femme fatale; attempts to assert independent existence, and to live beyond or to escape such projected gender fantasies, then upsets patriarchal order, and causes it to redouble its efforts to categorize these women as deviant.

This process of projection, female resistance and assertion of subjectivity, and patriarchal reinforcement is fully demonstrated in Edgar G. Ulmer's *Detour* (1945), particularly in the representation of the film's most compelling female character, Vera, played by Ann Savage. As James Naremore says, "ruthlessly hard and half-crazed," Vera "makes every femme fatale in the period look genteel by comparison" (149). However, *Detour*, reflecting on modern ambivalence toward empowered women, offers commentary on the construction of woman in terms of bifurcated images of good and evil. For example, protagonist Al Roberts says in a voiceover, as he looks at a profile of Vera: "I got the impression of beauty: not the beauty of a movie actress, mind you, or the beauty you dream about when you're with your wife, but a natural beauty, a beauty that's almost homely because it's so real . . . Then suddenly she turned to face me." The shock of recognition deflates high-grounded solipsistic projections about women.

As in Mark McPherson's struggle in Otto Preminger's *Laura* (1944) to translate his obsession with the image of Laura into mastery of the woman herself; as in Scotty Ferguson's desperate struggle in Alfred Hitchcock's *Vertigo* (1958) to maintain his ideation of Madeleine in the face of the real Judy Barton, in this scene in *Detour*, the "folksy" portrait of Vera gives way to a disappointing and threatening reality: "Then suddenly, she turned to face me." The film *Detour*'s concern with the ideal versus the real, leaving out the complexity of the actual experiences of individuals that inform or complicate their gender roles, is also emphasized in Al's later voiceover: "If this were fiction, I would fall in love with Vera, marry her and make a respectable woman of her. Or else, she'd make some supreme class-A sacrifice for me and die. Sue and I would ball a little over her grave and make some crack about there's good in all of us. But Vera unfortunately was just as rotten in the morning as she'd been the night before."

This overdetermined presentation of fictional positions on women, all of which deny her complex identity which might allow for empowered subjecthood, help to explain Vera's shrill demand to be seen for who she is. Like other honest vamps (one thinks even of the most fatale of femmes, *Out of the Past*'s Kathie Moffett, who says to Jeff Markham, "I never pretended to be anything but what I was. You just didn't see it. That's why I left you"), Vera is motivated, by exigency. As Andrew Britton says, for Vera, dying of consumption, "every word and action is designed to convince Al that she can do exactly what she likes with him ('I'm not through with you by a long shot!')" (179). Later, Vera says of the plan to steal Haskell's inheritance, "For that kind of dough, I'd let you cut my leg off."

As the desperation of this remark suggests, I think Naremore is right when he notes that while Vera is "sullen" and "dangerous," she's also, a "sympathetic figure" (149). This strangely mixed treatment of Vera is apparent in her language, "cracking like a whip," as Britton says, full of a desperate desire to claim agency in a culture that habitually denies women their subjectivity. While in simple generic terms, Vera is an absolutely unambiguous femme fatale, the nature of her presence in the film is considerably more complicated than is allowed by simply referencing her as the film's femme fatale.

Because the yoking together of sexuality, evil, and powerful women seems to me an insufficiently addressed habit in viewing film noir, I want to propose a modified perspective that builds on the work of feminists who suggest that female viewers find grounds for empathy in understanding the femme fatale. For fully engaged readings of film noir, I will argue, need to confront the simulacral fantasies that not only surround the femme fatale but that generate ideas in the culture that have very material effects. By shifting our nomenclature, for example, to talk about these trapped women as hard-boiled females rather than strictly as femme fatales, we can see more clearly the ongoing force of binary oppositions in the presentation of gender in contemporary culture and we highlight film noir's aim to destabilize gender categories.

The predominance of the idea of the femme fatale, I've been suggesting, profoundly shapes our viewing of all women in film noir. This keeps us not only from recognizing complex levels of female subjectivity but also the extent to which women are trapped in social roles they can't change and trapped particularly into performing the role of femme fatale that then perpetuates ideation surrounding these women. These traps most often take the form of simple opposition and dichotomy. Such is the case in Fritz Lang's *The Big Heat* (1953), in which the domestic angel in the house, Katie Bannion, is destroyed by the Lagana underworld and the criminal taint of the city, the public realm. In introducing his BFI book on *The Big Heat*, Colin McArthur comments on the starkness of the difference in tone between Dave Bannion's life at home and his visit to "The Retreat," the seedy bar in which he finds Lucy Chapman; McArthur juxtaposes stills of these opposite worlds (the caption reads "Counterpoint: 'the bright friendly world of Bannion home . . .' '. . . and the bleak world of The Retreat.'" [8]).

When Dave Bannion leaves the comfort of domestic contentment to follow a lead on Duncan's death, the radical shift in Bannion's affect can be seen as the character, played by Glenn Ford, dons his hat. The film abruptly shifts its attention from Dave's domestic banter with his wife Katie—"Tha's good steak"—to Bannion's detached suspicious detective-speak in the bar—"Lucy Chapman here?" In the interview that follows, Bannion shows contempt for Lucy: he reads her categorically as femme fatale because she works at "The Retreat" and because she has been involved in adultery with Duncan, one of Bannion's detective colleagues who has just committed suicide. Bannion, like most noir protagonists, has only two categories for women, angels in the house and corrupt women on the take. He mistakenly places Lucy in the latter category and by misreading her motives and character, contributes to events that lead to her brutal murder.

Bannion thus stands in for the unwitting film noir viewer who repeats this pattern almost obsessively by ignoring the often-nuanced presentation of women's experience in noir. Lang makes this point clearly when he shows Lucy's face in close-up as she reacts, wounded, to Bannon's tough-speak accusation, "What's the angle, Lucy?" Lucy says, in a broken and poignant reply, "Me?" and we are made alert to Bannion's summary blindness to her. Such failure of vision, a common theme in noir, not only looks forward to Bannion's disgusted dismissal of Debby Marsh (Gloria Grahame), thug Vince Stone's girlfriend ("I wouldn't touch anything of Vince Stone's with a ten-foot pole," says Bannion), but also anticipates Jake Gittes's naïve and at the same time brutish categorization of Evelyn Mulwray as unambiguous betrayer in Roman Polanski's *Chinatown* (1974). Jake's mistake in interpreting Evelyn Mulwray as a femme fatale, and the cynical mistrust that undergirds his reading of her, contributes, of course, to events that lead to Evelyn's gruesome death and the horrible exploitation of her daughter/sister Katherine by the evil patriarch Noah Cross (John Huston).

In her discussion of women in 40s films, Molly Haskell has suggested the close relation between the habit of reading women as image and the particularly dichotomous nature of these images of women:

> It is not the evil in women, but the mutual exclusiveness of good and evil
> that we resent, since it is a way of converting women from their ambiguous
> reality into metaphors, visitations of an angel or a devil. (199)

Haskell goes on to quote Barbara Stanwyck's comment on women in Preston Sturges' noir comedy *The Lady Eve* (1941), that "the best aren't as good as you think they are, and the bad ones aren't as bad . . . not nearly as bad." We might contrast this acknowledgment of the complexity of female experience with the exchange in Jacques Tourneur's *Out of the Past* (1947) between good-girl Ann and noir protagonist Jeff Bailey/Markham, as they discuss femme fatale Kathie Moffett: Ann says, "She can't be all bad—nobody's all bad," to which Jeff replies "She comes the closest." While on the one hand Haskell's comment critiques the binaries that cause misogyny, her alternative paradigm of "ambiguity" seems problematic, since femme fatales aren't really ambiguous any more than any complex human subject is ambiguous—ambiguity becomes here another virtual space ready to be filled by projected ideation. What so many film noir texts demonstrate in contrast is the hard-boiled reality of female experience, as these so-called femme fatales struggle to assert a power the male protagonists deny.

Through its rehearsal of binary oppositions, film noir criticizes gendered divisions of space, a strain of commentary important to look at, given contemporary culture's continuing obsession with defining social spaces as gendered (e.g. Spike TV, Super Bowl half-time shows, and the bland anodyne role modeling endorsed on Lifetime, in "chick flicks," and at Oxygen.com). Film noir has always shown the destructive nature of these boundaries by demonstrating what happens when women cross these lines: they become a severe threat to dominant male culture. Rita Hayworth's famed striptease performance of "Put the Blame on Mame" suggests the misogynist branding of women who deviate from their role as it is prescribed by cultural binary oppositions.

In Charles Vidor's *Gilda* (1946), Johnny Farrell can't abide Gilda's verbal, psychological, and sexual power over him; he reacts so violently and cruelly to her (comparing women to insects, for example), that the movie enacts in the story the annihilating process of "putting the blame on Mame." A psychotic extension of this invective against the woman for deviating from a role designed and mastered by conventional male power is seen in Cable's speech at the end of Alan J. Pakula's *Klute* (1971). Cable (Charles Cioffi) is here speaking to Bree Daniels (Jane Fonda), the call girl he blames for inciting him to become a murderer:

> There are little corners in everyone which were better left alone . . . You're too warped to do anything with your life, so you prey upon the sexual fantasies of others. There are weaknesses that should never be exposed. But that's your stock in trade: a man's weakness. And I was never fully aware of mine until you brought them out.

Bree Daniels is a femme fatale place-holder in *Klute*; her role, as is seen by the psychotic Cable, invites comparison with the many other victims of projections onto women in film noir, as in the case of Martin Scorsese's *Taxi Driver* (1976), where the potential for absolute derangement in viewing women alternately as angel and whore is explicitly demonstrated by Travis Bickle. Travis, played by Robert De Niro, idealizes Betsy (Cybil Shepherd)—who first appears as a vision in white, as Kathie Moffett did in *Out of the Past*—only to categorically devalue her several scenes later as "just like the rest." After Betsy rejects Travis when he takes her on a date to a pornographic film, he shouts that she is "going to die in hell like the rest of them." Later in the film, Travis once again shows his inability to adopt a more complex reading of female experience when he ignores the reality of twelve-year-old Iris's troubled life (as played by Jodie Foster) in order to save her from prostitution and degradation. The film shows the dramatic bifurcation in Travis's view of woman (innocent or evil) in his absurdly beatific encomium to the young prostitute as he cups her face in his hand: "Sweet Iris."

Feminist film critics have recognized that male protagonists in noir hold responsibility for their fates, but this insight hasn't led viewers to see fully the implications of these insights—mainly, that the presence of the femme fatale in film noir movies is drastically overstated and almost exclusively the result of male projection, as may be only truly obvious in the extreme case of *Klute*, as cited above. However, film noir is ripe with suggestions that the femme fatale is a projection of male gender psychosis and the women labeled as femme fatales are often struggling to escape this projection. As much as the series of films may extend sympathy toward the male crisis of identity after the destabilization of gender roles occurring in America during WWII, these films also suggest, more subversively still, the trap that society lays for women, who are branded as evil, as potentially deceptive, before they even speak.

In *Laura*, a movie that examines the habit of casting women as a priori femme fatales, Lydecker and McPherson worry throughout the film that Laura will betray her lovers—but the film presents its concern through these men's obsessive ideation, provoked, in McPherson's case quite literally, by Laura's image. The bullying Lydecker makes the point as he reveals that "the way [Laura] listened was more eloquent than speech," ratifying the idea of the good woman as the silent woman, as the image, as the portrait. "What difference," Laura says to the interrogating McPherson, "does it make what I say? You've made up your mind I'm guilty." Because McPherson has become infatuated with the portrait of Laura in this film—McPherson identifies Laura herself with the painting of her—her actual appearance disorients him into casting her as a femme fatale. Characterizing this disorientation Slavoj Zizek has said, the "'real' Laura emerges as a non-symbolized fantasmatic surplus, a ghostlike apparition" (Copjec, 220). The fantasmatic, however, threatens to be contained as Laura becomes appropriated and consumed by male desire, like the Duke's wives in Robert Browning's "My Last Duchess," a proleptically noir poem that presents woman in the form of portrait/image and explains violence against women as the result of male projection. As Angela Martin has pointed out, the expected role of Laura as this film's femme fatale is undermined by the film's insistence that Laura's mystery is entirely a result of male projection:

> Laura only expresses *anything* of the *'femme fatale'* inasmuch as that is projected through the behavior of the men around her . . . Laura herself becomes a silent and still (painted) image during her long weekend absence, which gives the other characters limitless space to recreate her in their own terms . . . But it is the male characters whose shadows are thrown; it is the male characters who produce 'the fatal': Laura just brings out what is already there (which is, of course, the real female crime in film noir). (213, 214)

As in *Laura*, the introduction of woman via portrait or image is common in noir: Diane Redfern, the real murdered victim in *Laura*, is only seen in the film in a photograph; in Fritz Lang's *The Woman in the Window* (1945), Professor Wanley (Edward G. Robinson) is seduced into noir reverie by a painting of a woman he sees in a store window; our first image of Joyce Harwood in George Marshall's *The Blue Dahlia* (1946) is in a photograph on the desk of her husband; Mona Stevens, the victimized so-called femme fatale in *Pitfall*, is also first introduced to us as a photograph in a modeling portfolio. That these women appear at first as photographic or painted images strongly suggests their initial status as images coined by male desire, "derealized," in Mary Ann Doane's terms, in the service of male fantasy.

The logic of film noir deconstructs the dichotomies that structure these gender fantasies; I am suggesting that we take this insight further to question the elevation of the femme fatale that results from these projections of desire. While feminist film critics have discussed at some length the nature of these projections, we haven't sufficiently inferred from these analyses the problems with relying on the femme fatale as the main figure in film noir. We become passive and dependent on what we think we already know about women, which evokes a femme fatale before the narrative unfolds. This model of reading women is, I've been arguing, outlined in the films themselves, as is demonstrated in a scene from *The Blue Dahlia*. Early in the film, Johnny Morrison (Alan Ladd) says thank-you and goodbye to the at-this-point anonymous woman (later identified as Joyce Harwood, played by Veronica Lake), who has picked up this disappointed war veteran in L. A. and driven him from the dark, rainy city to sunny Malibu. Johnny says, "It's hard to say goodbye." Lake's character responds "Why is it hard to say goodbye? You've never seen me before," to which Johnny replies, "Every guy's seen you. The trick is to find you."

A remarkable instance of the process of transforming a woman into an image of generalized male desire for the perfect woman, Joyce Harwood exists absolutely in Johnny's mind; a real woman couldn't ever live up to the preexisting image of Joyce as angel. In *The Blue Dahlia*, there is thus a kind of inevitability in the fact that Johnny Morrison turns on Joyce when he discovers she is married to estranged husband Harwood, played by Howard Da Silva.

Deviating at all from Johnny's ideal image of her, Joyce Harwood becomes exceedingly suspect. Instead of placing her on a pedestal, Johnny later calls her "baby"—"See you later, baby"—invoking a conventional verbal marker for sexualized woman. Joyce is even, late in the film, iconographically linked to Helen Morrison, who most nearly evokes the femme fatale: on the one hand, Helen is an adulteress who drinks, smokes, has accidentally killed her baby, and dresses in gold lamé; on the other hand, before Helen is murdered, she not only leaves clues to help Johnny discover her murderer, but her explanation of her life while Johnny was away evokes a sympathetic portrait of women struggling while their husbands were at war, a portrait made more complex by Johnny's threats to "make" Helen stop drinking. When Joyce Harwood repeats Helen's earlier habit of picking petals off the blue dahlias, Joyce is symbolically linked to Helen, the film's ostensible dangerous dark woman. In being allied with Helen, Joyce joins the ranks of women brutally dismissed by those such as Harwood's sidekick, who says about women, "they're all poison sooner or later."

Nicholas Ray's *Johnny Guitar* (1954) reveals the anxiety about female power that produces such ideation. Vienna, played by Joan Crawford, demonstrates a mannishness that elicits a comment from her employee Sam (John Carradine), striking not only for its response to gender anxiety but for its transparency in exposing this anxiety: "Never seen a woman who was more a man: She thinks like one, acts like one, and sometimes makes me feel like I'm not." Such direct commentary would be easier to take in and understand as part of a larger interpretive pattern, if viewers weren't so focused on what they expected to see in film noir. With a more open-minded reception to nuance and to the profound variety of examples on offer in noir, we see more clearly these films' exposure of the ideological contradictions in dominant culture's regulations of gender.

A critique in noir films is leveled at the continuing cultural reading of women as a projection of male desire or fear: as angel in the house or femme fatale, as two-faced, like Debby Marsh, Gloria Graham's character in *The Big Heat*, whose face, after Vince Stone (Lee Marvin) scalds her with coffee, is literally bifurcated—grotesque burn scars on one side oppose perfect angelic beauty on the other. As the fallen woman, she must die, but because she sacrifices herself so that Bannion can solve the crime and avenge his wife's murder, Lang's final shot of her is of the unscarred, angelic side of her face. Although the film in this shot seems to want to choose one side (angelic female savior) over the other (femme fatale), what the movie has shown rather methodically are the violent, even fatal, consequences of trying to define these poles as essential, and as essentially opposed.

Film noir movies demonstrate the violent consequences of these cultural oppositions, mainly enforced according to gender, by suggesting that the violent underbelly referred to in noir is itself caused by the culture's division of complex human experience into strictly circumscribed opposing realms. Further, noir reveals the ways in which structuring experience according to these dichotomies may result in palpable cynicism that keeps us from addressing social illnesses. An example might be the famous concluding lines of *Chinatown*: "Forget it Jake. It's Chinatown." But it's not just Chinatown; it's Jake's blindness and his cynicism that keep him from believing, and believing in, Evelyn Mulwray. *Chinatown* shares *The Big Heat*'s condemnation of the failures of vision. These films argue for a gray vision of the world that recognizes and responds sympathetically to the complexity of human experience; their logic calls attention to these failures of vision, suggesting an alternative model of sympathetic engagement to understand film noir narrative.

Other noir films, such as Robert Siodmak's *Phantom Lady* (1944), Fritz Lang's *The Blue Gardenia* (1953), Vincent Sherman's *The Damned Don't Cry* (1950), and *The Naked Kiss* challenge viewers' expectations of strict oppositions by placing the would-be femme fatale in the role of subject and hard-boiled female protagonist. Following this model of gender destabilization, *The Phantom Lady*, Robert Siodmak's bizarre adaptation of a Cornell Woolrich novel, introduces a male lead who is utterly emasculated (hearing that Scott's wife laughed at him, the cop says glibly, "Nothing makes a man sorer than that . . . making a patsy of you, eh?"; later in the scene, Scott begins to tear up, saying "I thought guys didn't cry."). In this film, woman takes on the role of "seeker hero," as Michael Walker notes (Cameron 110–115). To intimidate him into helping her solve the murder, Carol literally stares down the bartender, to the point where he runs from her into oncoming traffic and dies. Throughout the film, Carol role-plays, and despite some neat ideological closure, *Phantom Lady* suggests the subversive potential of the hard-boiled female protagonist.

The insistence on the femme fatale as a bad female object of fascination or investigation not only causes us as I've been arguing, to misinterpret female roles in film noir and to perpetuate unhealthy ideation in popular culture, but also leads us to draw arbitrary borders between genres whose intersections are compelling and important: *The Damned Don't Cry*, for example, is deemed melodrama, a woman's picture, but the main character shares a great many qualities with the femme fatale, if we look at that figure from a feminist perspective. As Elizabeth Cowie has suggested, film noir, not just melodrama, "afforded women roles which are active, adventurous, and driven by sexual desire" (Copjec, 135).

As in film noir, the ostensibly melodramatic *The Damned Don't Cry* also destabilizes gender categories, as well as genre categories, since its title screams melodrama. In fact, the film not only presents a noir hard-boiled female protagonist but also unequivocally presents the femme fatale as a construction of male anxiety and projection. Echoing the beginning of Michael Curtiz's *Mildred Pierce* (1945), *The Damned Don't Cry* begins with Ethel Whitehead not only trapped in the role of oppressed mother and housewife but, more significantly, victimized by the misogynist ramblings of her father, who manages to convince her husband Roy that "You'll never do enough for her." When her son is killed, Ethel decides to follow the lead of independent male loners from Sam Spade to Shane, telling Roy, who insists that he's "done the best he could," "Well it ain't good enough."

The social roles that might afford Ethel the power and independence available to male heroes are limited to modeling and prostitution, but Ethel insists on her right to determine her life. As she says to her emasculated suitor Marty Blackford: "You're a nice guy, but the world isn't for nice guys. You gotta kick and punch and belt your way up cuz nobody's going to give you a lift. You've got to do it yourself. Cuz nobody cares about us except ourselves." "The only thing that counts," says this hard-boiled woman, "is that stuff you take to the bank, that filthy buck that everybody sneers at but slugs to get."

I want to emphasize here that when a man makes this kind of speech, the myth he upholds is that of the male loner, like Chandler's detective, who minds the mean streets "a lonely man" (Chandler, qtd. in Hirsch, 33). We can expose the ideologically conservative cast of this gesture by simply pointing out that the male loner figure is never really alone. In fact, he's supported by a network of homosocial relations. The men work together, or at least believe in one another, like the family of men in *The Blue Dahlia*, or the existential partnering of Neff and Keyes in *Double Indemnity*, or the possibly sexual bond between Ballin and Johnny Farrell in *Gilda*. In all of these cases, the men have one another, and the femme fatale, like the Mame in Gilda's song, takes the blame, becomes the debased object of investigation: the inevitable by-product of a system that has constructed the femme fatale as a projection of threats to the homosocial fabric of society. Unlike the hard-boiled male detective, the hard-boiled female protagonist is truly alone, as Mae Doyle is, in Fritz Lang's *Clash by Night* (1952). "Home," she says, "is where you come when you run out of places"; Mae Doyle's expectations for domestic contentment are diminished to the point that what she finds most attractive in Jerry is that he's a man "who isn't mean and doesn't hate women."

For Ethel Whitehead in *The Damned Don't Cry*, life is also fundamentally about exigency. *The Damned Don't Cry* focuses in part on the limitations placed on Ethel's life ("Don't talk to me about self-respect. That's something you tell yourself you got when you got nothing else"). The film then portrays Ethel's aggressive response to these limitations ("All I can think of are the years I've wasted. . . . Well I want that time. I want it desperately. I'm going to drain everything out of those years there is to get . . ."). The film shows Ethel taking on the role of femme fatale, but such status is a direct result of her limitations based on gender and social roles and her hard-boiled response to those limitations—both of which are presented, for the most part, sympathetically. Because in conventional film representations of women, there is little complex understanding of a role for woman as strong and oppressed, Ethel, aggressively struggling to define her own understanding of independence and empowerment, may be seen as a femme fatale. However, Ethel Whitehead's noir identity is obscured according the classifications on offer in discussions of classic Hollywood films.

The Damned Don't Cry calls forth the label "woman's picture," which defines female space but not in a way that fosters new imaginings of female power; indeed, the labeling serves to cordon off female craving for independence as something "other" than the more meaning-ful tough work of noir, which has tended strongly to take for granted the integrity of only the male protagonist's selfhood. As Judith Walkowitz has said about women entering the public world in late nineteenth-century London, the city, for the New Woman of the late Victorian period and film noir (I would add) existed as both "a place of danger and of possibility" for women (80). By shifting our focus and critical attention from locating femme fatales to under-standing hard-boiled females, we may see more clearly how noir destabilizes gender cate-gories. We see how these female protagonists often gain our sympathy through their struggle to assume independence, as these films warn of the ongoing force of binary oppositions in the presentation and understanding of gender in culture.

In *The Damned Don't Cry*, the men read Ethel as a femme fatale, as Dave Bannion does Lucy Chapman in *The Big Heat*. Racketeer George Castleman says to Ethel (who also role-plays, as the utterly invented wealthy socialite Lorna Hansen Forbes), "You're so used to lying and cheating and double-crossing, you can almost make it seem good." While George is the one who induced Lorna to seduce Nick Prenta, George physically attacks her when she does so: "Pass out keys to all your friends," he says bitterly. Meanwhile, Nick, whom in the end Lorna is trying to protect, calls Lorna a "dirty tramp." When at the end of the film the reporters go to Ethel's home to cover the story of Prenta's and Castleman's deaths and the mystery surround-ing "Lorna Hansen Forbes," they wonder about Ethel Whitehead's future: "Well, it must be pretty tough living in a place like this." "Tougher to get out. Think she'll try again?" "Wouldn't you?" With this feminist gesture, the film provocatively ends with a strongly sympathetic tone toward Ethel's plight and status as a hard-boiled female protagonist.

Another hard-boiled female protagonist appears in Sam Fuller's bizarre *The Naked Kiss*. In this film, Kelly (played by Constance Towers) transforms herself from outcast prostitute to town heroine. After the town turns on her, then restores her image when she is vindicated for her murder of the town's philanthropist/hero, when it is proven that he was in fact a psychotic pederast, Kelly says at the end of the film, "They sure put up statues overnight around here, don't they?" This is the cultural landscape that film noir, in its most subversive gestures, ques-tions. Noir incites a consideration of the interplay between real human experience and gender expectations that are wedded to a logic of binary opposition.

Movies like the ones I've discussed in this essay take noir viewers to task for their "Where's Waldo?" approach to the femme fatale. *Chinatown* revealed the tragic implications of looking for a virtual rendering of one big containable idea of woman, as Jake Gittes, slick as he is, has no means for sympathetically imagining, thus processing, the complex victimiza-tion of Evelyn Mulwray. The seemingly mutually exclusive categories evoked by "she's my sis-ter, she's my daughter" give way to the film's plea to develop a more compassionate set of responses to the complex brutality of real human experience. *Chinatown* reveals the tragic implications of reading women as one thing or its opposite. However, this is the challenge of the paradigm of the femme fatale: ideation surrounding Evelyn Mulwray, for example, must confront the real complex experience of Evelyn Mulwray, and there must be a critical viewer present to identify the confrontation and draw insights from its presence. Such an exchange between the active viewer and critic, sensitive to the network of expectations surrounding the femme fatale and the nuanced presentation of her experience in most film noir movies, will certainly constitute a more productive model for reading film noir.

Finally, Fritz Lang's *The Blue Gardenia* presents a clear case of the productive value of deconstructing the femme fatale as a category. As E. Ann Kaplan says, "While the male discourse tried to define Norah as a femme fatale, we see rather that she is a victim of male strategies to ensnare her for something she did not do." Such insights are the fruits of questioning the femme fatale as a given. Following in the steps of Kaplan and Cowie, both of whom question the notion that noir is primarily a "male preserve" (Cowie 125), I want to shift emphases from assuming a shared understanding of femme fatales to engaging critical insight into the logic of the narrative and character development of particular texts. At that point, we can broaden our understanding of how social roles and gender fantasies (of men and women) intersect with and within film noir.

Film noir strongly indicates the problems that remain in our cultural imaginings of and about women. For as much feminist critique that has re-viewed attitudes toward gender and sexuality and for as much feminist attention that has been paid to the femme fatale as projection of male fears and desires, we remain as a culture confused about and ambivalent toward the status of women: and whether or not the arrangement of cultural experience in terms of gender is empowering or merely essentializing, thus limiting our imagination of the roles that women can play in the world.

I believe that the ongoing construction of gendered spaces in culture hasn't been resolved and that the continuities between pre-feminist, modern, and contemporary culture haven't been adequately explored. Film noir offers a window through which we see this continuity. However, we need to reframe the femme fatale not as a given but as critical apparatus for helping us to understand the limits of social roles and cultural fantasies about women. In *Women in Film Noir*, E. Ann Kaplan argues that *The Blue Gardenia* is different from other film noirs, "reversing the situation in most noir films, where women are seen only within the male discourse [whereas] here that discourse is demystified through the fact that Norah is allowed to present herself directly to us" (85).

In some sense defining the women in exceptional noir films who aren't really femme fatales begs the issue, since the comparison depends on an a priori femme fatale which is drawn from the many films that, read closely, reveal the absence of a femme fatale: she exists as an effect of problems in the culture, not as a thing in herself. Kaplan says that *The Blue Gardenia* presents "the confusion and alienation of women in a male world." I suggest that this logic pertains far more widely in film noir, permeating the representation of so-called femme fatales, than we are able to discern because of our preoccupation with categories of representation that are fixed and independent of experience rather than evolving critical tools.

Julie Grossman is associate professor and chair of the English department at Le Moyne College. Co-editor of *A Due Voci: The Photography of Rita Hammond,* she has published on the topics of film, literature, and popular culture, including essays on Thomas Hardy, Henry James, Todd Haynes, and Oscar Wilde and Karen Finley.

References

Britton, Andrew. *"Detour."* In Cameron, 174–83.

Cameron, Ian, ed. *The Book of Film Noir.* New York: Continuum, 1993.

Chandler, Raymond. "The Simple Art of Murder." In *Later Novels and Other Writings.* New York: Library of America, 1995.

Copjec, Joan, ed. *Shades of Noir.* London: Verso Press, 1993.

Cowie, Elizabeth. "Film Noir and Women." In *Copjec.* 121–66.

Doane, Mary Ann. *Femme Fatales: Feminism, Film Theory, Psychoanalysis.* New York and London: Routledge, 1991.

Gledhill, Christine. *"Klute* 2: Feminism and *Klute."* In Kaplan, 99–114.

Haskell, Molly. *From Reverence to Rape: the Treatment of Women in the Movies.* New York: Holt, Rinehart and Winston, 1974.

Hirsch, Foster. *Film Noir: The Dark Side of the Screen.* New York: Da Capo Press, 1981.

Kaplan, E. Ann, ed. *Women in Film Noir* (rev. ed.). London: British Film Institute, 1998.

Krutnik, Frank. *In a Lonely Street: Film Noir, Genre, Masculinity.* London and New York: Routledge, 1991.

Martin, Angela. "'Gilda Didn't Do Any of Those Things You've Been Losing Sleep Over!': The Central Women of 40s Films Noirs." In Kaplan, 202–228.

McArthur, Colin. *The Big Heat.* London: British Film Institute, 1992.

Naremore, James. *More Than Night: Film Noir in its Contexts.* Berkeley and Los Angeles: University of California Press, 1998.

Polan, Dana. *In A Lonely Place.* London: British Film Institute, 1993.

Porfirio, Robert, Alain Silver, and James Ursini, eds. *Film Noir Reader 3: Interviews with Filmmakers of the Classic Noir Period.* New York: Limelight, 2002.

Spicer, Andrew. *Film Noir.* Harlow, England: Longman, 2002.

Wager, Jans. *Dangerous Dames: Women and Representation in the Weimar Street Film and Film Noir.* Athens: Ohio UP, 1999.

Walker, Michael. "Robert Siodmak." In Cameron, 110–51.

Walkowitz, Judith R. *City of Dreadful Delight: Narratives of Sexual Danger in Late-Victorian London.* Chicago: University of Chicago Press, 1992.

Woolf, Virginia. "Professions for Women." *Literature By Women* (2nd ed.), ed. Sandra Gilbert and Susan Gubar. New York and London: Norton. 1996. 1345–48.

11

Whose Future? Star Wars, Alien, *and* Blade Runner

Peter Lev

Abstract

Argues that George Lucas's film "Star Wars" creates an ideologically conservative future whereas Ridley Scott's "Alien" and "Blade Runner" create futures infused with liberal and socially critical ideas. Contrasts Lucas's film with Scott's films and argues that while "Star Wars" presents a future that is clean, wholesome, and morally clear, both of Scott's films present a future of oppressive institutions and continue the socially critical American cinema of "Chinatown" (1974) and "Nashville" (1975).

The science fiction film, as a construction somewhat removed from everyday reality, is a privileged vehicle for the presentation of ideology. Because it is less concerned than other genres with the surface structure of social reality, science fiction can pay more attention to the deep structure of what is and what ought to be. In practice, this means that science fiction films vividly embody ideological positions, and that comparing science fiction films of the same era becomes an analysis of conflicting social visions. Such visions cannot, however, be reduced to a simple, discursive message. Instead, the total semiotic output of a film—images, sounds, textures, relationships—is a carrier of ideology.

As a test of this hypothesis, consider three popular films from the years around 1980: *Star Wars* (1977), *Alien* (1979), and *Blade Runner* (1982).[1] These films have much in common. All three are key moments in the renaissance of science fiction film stretching from the late 1970s to the present. And all three films are renowned for the quality of their visual design and special effects. However, *Star Wars* creates an ideologically conservative future, whereas *Alien* and *Blade Runner* create futures linked to liberal and socially critical ideas.

What factors account for *Star Wars* overwhelming success with the public? Certainly the film's narrative provides a partial answer. *Star Wars* is a modern quest narrative, blending such sources as Arthurian legend, *Paradise Lost, Lord of the Rings, the Western, The Wizard of Oz,* and the meta-discourse of Joseph Campbell's *The Hero with a Thousand Faces*.[2] Young, naive Luke Skywalker sets out on an adventure both physical and spiritual, which involves saving the princess, defeating the evil Empire, and establishing a more just government. The story has a mythic or fairytale dimension, but also a lightness of tone; Luke (Mark Hamill), Princess Leia (Carrie Fisher), and Han Solo (Harrison Ford) wisecrack their way

Reprinted by permission from *Literature/Film Quarterly* 26, no. 1.

through difficult situations. There are some weak points to the narrative. One would be a problem with character development, particularly apparent in the minor roles—e.g., Uncle Owen and Aunt Beru. Another would be the lack of emotional response to destruction of an entire inhabited planet! (Wyatt 609-10) However, the quest narrative of *Star Wars* has proved sufficiently compelling and resilient to support two film sequels (with more in process), numerous authorized novels, and a great deal of fan activity.

A second explanation is that *Star Wars* owes much of its popularity to a richness of audiovisual invention that is rare in science fiction or any other genre. Space ships, space wars, planetary ecology, alien beings (not one species of intelligent aliens, but perhaps a dozen) George Lucas and his collaborators deserve much credit for creating such a sweeping and detailed science fiction universe. John J. Pierce calls this level of invention "world creation," and notes that it is a prized aspect of science fiction novels but hard to find in science fiction films. Such worldbuilding requires a sweeping imagination that is also disciplined and thorough (Pierce 201, 209). An example from *Star Wars* would be the distinctively realized look, sound, and behavior of the two droids, R2D2 and C3PO. These two robots are original, detailed, and consistent; they may be the most interesting characters in the film. The created world in *Star Wars* is both packed with audiovisual information and given an imperfect, lived-in quality. For example, the sound effects generally start from complex natural sounds (e.g., a movie projector as the basis for the hum of the light sabers) rather than simpler, cleaner synthetic audio. Ben Burtt, the film's sound designer, explains that "The sounds of the real world are complicated and kind of dirty. They simply cannot be duplicated on a synthesizer" (Pollock 178).

John Seabrook, writing in the New Yorker, gives a more technical explanation of *Star Wars'* success. According to Seabrook, the film's "secret" is its control of the kinetic aspects of movie-making: "The first *Star Wars* movie is like a two hour image of raw speed." Lucas is not a particularly gifted director of actors, but his control of "editing and pace" creates a feeling of "pure kinetic energy which has become a part of the world's visual imagination." "Every time a studio executive tells a writer that his piercing and true story needs an "action beat" every ten minutes, the writer has George Lucas to thank" (45, 50).

This explanation seems to me far too simplistic. It leaves out *Star Wars'* most original use of kinetic filmmaking, which is genre-based: science fiction film can use the whole film frame to invent new kinds of motion. Lucas is very good at doing this, and he is a fine editor, but he does not deserve credit for singlehandedly changing the emphasis of American cinema. To take just one example from among Lucas's contemporaries, William Friedkin in *The French Connection* (1971) and *The Exorcist* (1973) is every bit as visual and kinetic as George Lucas in *Star Wars*. Yet no one would posit Friedkin as the sole inventor of contemporary film style. The increased emphasis on action and pace is undoubtedly a group creation, influenced as much by television (including commercials) as by film.

Star Wars is conservative, though not extreme right wing or Fascist, in its ideological underpinnings. Men are active heroes, Princess Leia is a damsel in distress, good and evil are clearly separated, and Luke is guided by the benevolent father figure Obiwan Kenobi. The film is very consciously a break from the anti-heroes and anti-genres of many films of the early 1970s. According to Dale Pollock's biography of Lucas, the film's return to family entertainment and traditional morality was a conscious decision by its writer-director. Lucas wanted to present positive values to the audience. In the 1970s traditional religion was out of fashion and the family structure was disintegrating. There was no moral anchor. Lucas remembered how protected he had felt growing up in the cocoonlike culture of the 1950s, a feeling he wanted to communicate in *Star Wars*. (143) Pollock lists the values of the film as "Hard work, self-sacrifice, friendship, loyalty, and a commitment to a higher purpose." Lucas himself comments, "I mean, there's a reason this film is so popular. It's not that I'm giving out propaganda nobody wants to hear" (140).

Star Wars has often been discussed as a harbinger of the renewed American conservatism of the Reagan presidency. It is certainly part of the move toward simple, optimistic genre films in the late 1970s. The clean-cut, well-spoken White youths of the film seem to come out of an idealized version of the 1950s, and the clear division between good and evil governments suggests the Cold War. Indeed, some phrases borrowed from the film became key ideological points of the Reagan years: "Star Wars" (meaning a futuristic missile defense system), "the Evil Empire" (meaning the Soviet Union). More recently, the name "Jedi Knights" was used by a U.S. Army group planning the Gulf War (Meyer 99). Lucas is not responsible for the uses politicians and governments make of his film. But the ease with which his ideas were put to political and military ends shows something about the Manichaean quality of the story.

Though *Star Wars* is part of a shift in film entertainment, away from socially critical work and toward optimistic genre films, that shift was neither simple nor complete. An alternate science fiction vision of the period can be analyzed in two films directed by Ridley Scott, *Alien* and *Blade Runner*. Both films are developments on George Lucas's combination of mythic storytelling and detailed "world creation" of the future in *Star Wars*. Ridley Scott is excellently suited for this type of science fiction filmmaking, because he is both a gifted director and a world-class art director.[3] In *Alien*, Scott takes on one part of the *Star Wars* legacy by creating an intricate and haunting portrait of a starship—the ancient Nostromo. He also develops a stunning variant on a 1950s science fiction cliche—the malevolent alien creature. In *Blade Runner*, Scott puts together a more complex version of *Star Wars*' worldbuilding project by creating a physically and emotionally convincing Los Angeles of the year 2019. *Blade Runner*, like *Alien*, draws on other influences as well, e.g., the look of 1940s film noir and the odd science fiction novels of Philip K. Dick.

The narrative premise of *Alien* is eminently simple: the monster attacks. Robbie Robertson has shown that the alien being with its savage survival logic has antecedents in science fiction literature, for example in the work of A.E. Van Vogt (175-76). Other antecedents would be science fiction films of the 1950s, including the Japanese Godzilla. Looking to mythology, the story relates to myths of the dragon, of the sea monster, of Jonah and the whale. In each case, human heroes are threatened by powerful, mysterious creatures which exaggerate the traits of known animals. In *Alien*, the monster designed by Surrealist artist H.R. Giger is reptilian, and thus related to fear of snakes, dinosaurs, and sea creatures.

Though simple, the premise of *Alien* is also trans-generic, a blend of science fiction and horror. One borrowing from the traditional horror film is a stretched-out anticipation of the monster's attack. Several scenes use silence and false cues to play with the moment of attack; this might be called the "haunted house" motif of horror film. As Scott Bukatman notes, *Alien* also presents a more contemporary (perhaps Postmodern) horror motif: the link between the monster and the human body (262-67). The alien creature in *Alien* does not merely kill humans, it uses them as hosts for a process of reproduction. This is terrifyingly shown in the scene where a small alien bursts from an astronaut's chest, killing him as a byproduct of "birth." Like the vampire, the werewolf, the zombie, the alien is thus a threat to the integrity of the human body. But in the 1979 film, the threat is more visceral, the body more subject to transformation than in classic horror films. The eruption of an alien from a human body could be seen as a disguised version of "monstrous" processes that are normally hidden, such as birth and sexuality.

Alien is unlike *Star Wars* and *Blade Runner* in that it deals with a restricted space. The main set is the human spaceship, with a few minutes spent on an uninhabited planet and in the alien ship. In the limited environment of the Nostromo, Ridley Scott and his collaborators present in a matter-of-fact way the organization and technology which make the ship work. Hibernation coffins, hospital room, airlock, gallery, control room, escape module, ship-controlling computer: all are presented simply and effectively. The ship also has a variety of hidden or "waste" spaces—vents, crawlways, corridors—and this becomes important in fighting a creature which exists apart from human spatial and conceptual logic. A particularly useful future technology invented by Scott and crew is a motion sensor that can indicate the distance of a moving object but not the direction or location.

In *Star Wars* the future is clean (though not shiny and new), wholesome, and morally clear. *Alien* reverses all three points. The starship in *Alien* is dank, dark, and messy. It is an old freighter owned by a large corporation, and therefore is maintained for utility rather than pride (compare the Millenium Falcon, *Star Wars'* version of a beloved hot rod). The unknown planet is a fiercely inhospitable environment, with strong winds and swirling gas clouds. The alien ship's scariest feature is an uncanny mixture of organic and inorganic forms. The walls and corridors of the ship seem also to be the skeleton of an organic creature, with spines and ribs and dripping mucous. Threat-as-body is thus part of the film's visual design in ways that go beyond the blatant threat of the monster itself.

Discussion of the ideological differences between *Star Wars* and *Alien* requires that we return for a moment to George Lucas's film. I have labeled *Star Wars* conservative, but it does present itself as a rebellious act. The rebels of the story have risen up against an oppressive Empire. Further, the main representative of the Empire is Darth Vader, a lightly disguised version of "Dark Father." So, *Star Wars* is a revolt against the father. However, the Rebel Alliance itself seems to be hierarchical and perhaps even authoritarian; it celebrates victory with an ending scene weirdly quoted from Leni Riefenstahl.[4] One should also remember that *Star Wars'* rebellion in no way challenges gender, race, or class relations. White male humans are "naturally" in positions of authority. The boy Luke grows up and takes his place as a responsible male leader. As Robin Wood says, the film's dominant tone is reassurance; things change so that they can return to a comfortable norm (162-65). Alien presents a more significant challenge to authority. In this film the "Company," boss and organizer of the crew, turns out to be an evil force, the malevolent twin of the monster.

The Company is represented on board by "Mother," the controlling computer; the nickname indicates the crew's dependence on the Company-programmed machine. The Company is also represented by Ash (Ian Holm), the science officer, who (unknown to other crew members) is an android. Ash's secret orders are to capture and bring back the alien; the crew is expendable. These orders are based on the commercial and military potentials of the alien creature. The Company responds to profit, and puts little value on human life. Superficially, the theme is reminiscent of *The Poseidon Adventure* (1972), where the ship owners have neglected needed repairs and put passengers and crew at risk. But in *The Poseidon Adventure* this theme seems perfunctory, a way to start the action; the film concludes with a powerful defense of patriarchal authority. In *Alien*, on the other hand, the Company's action is part of a pervasive pattern of oppression and paranoia. The film sympathizes with the outsiders on the crew, the proletarian engine mechanics and the independent-minded Ripley (Sigourney Weaver).

Blade Runner is designed around two intersecting myths. First, there is the film noir detective fighting crime and corruption in the decaying city. The detective is a version of the medieval knight, someone who embodies right values in the struggle between good and evil.[5] A complication of film noir is that good and evil may be hard to ascertain in the modern city. Further, the damsel-in-distress may not want to be saved. A second mythic plot in *Blade Runner* involves four "replicants"—androids of superior strength and intelligence who have made their way to earth. At one level, these replicants are the villains of the narrative. Deckard (Harrison Ford), the hero, is a "blade runner"—a specialized assassin hired to find and terminate replicants. But the replicants are also angels fallen to Earth; human-like beings with their own histories, needs, emotions, and morality. The link to angels is made explicit by a near-quote from William Blake uttered by Roy Batty (Rutger Hauer), leader of the replicants: "Fiery the Angels fell, while thunder roared around their shores, burning with the fires of Orc."[6]

As the conflict between the two myths suggests, Deckard's job as a blade runner is brought into question. Is he killing "skin jobs," i.e., non-human criminals? Or is he killing angels, i.e., human-like or more-than-human beings whose differences are to be respected? The film suggests that the replicants, despite differences of genesis and history, are emotionally and morally human. This point is made by the character of Rachael (Sean Young), a replicant who does not know her origins and is therefore completely human in behavior. It is reinforced when Roy Batty, who seems to be *Blade Runner*'s arch-villain, ultimately saves Deckard's life in a Christ-like gesture of compassion. The theme of android and human mixing and merging in unforeseen ways has its roots in the source novel for *Blade Runner*, Philip K. Dick's *Do Androids Dream of Electric Sheep?*

In visual design, *Blade Runner* catapults us not into an idealized 1950s, but into the darkness of 1940s film noir. Fashions are part retro-1940s, and part futuristic. The chiaroscuro lighting of film noir mixes with enormous electronic billboards of the future. The film is set in an overpopulated, highly polluted Los Angeles in the year 2019. The climate has changed drastically, so that it rains all the time (convenient for film noir). Smoke and smog mask the city, and many residents wear gas masks outdoors. Asians, Hispanics, Blacks and Eastern Europeans swarm the streets; most Caucasian Americans seem to have departed for off-world colonies. A paramilitary police force maintains order, and enormous corporate head-quarters dominate the skyline. Clearly, this is not the best of all possible worlds.

Although *Star Wars* presents a dozen alien races, it assumes pre-eminence of humans. Both the Empire and the rebels are led by humans; most of the aliens are relegated to the "freak show" of the spacefarers' bar. Even Chewbacca, the one alien among the small group of heroes, is shown as Han Solo's sidekick. In this film, man is the measure of all things. *Blade Runner*, on the other hand, entertains ideas of "not-quite-human," "different-than-human," even "more-than-human." The elusive border between machine and human is shown visually in the scene where the replicant Pris (Darryl Hannah) hides among a bunch of animated toy figures maintained by the lonely J.R. Sebastian (William Sanderson). Sebastian's toys talk and move and seem to be emotionally attached to their owner. Though Pris can hide among the toys, she is different from them because of superior intelligence and strength plus an independent spirit, a will to live. In some ways replicants are superior to humans, not just to toys. But they are limited by a built-in four-year lifespan. Because of the short lifespan, replicants can be childlike at one moment, adult and philosophical the next (Morrison 3). The film ultimately affirms the validity of replicants as thinking, feeling beings, notably via the love affair between Deckard and Rachael. It thus makes an eloquent statement for acceptance of the Other. Part II

Both *Alien* and *Blade Runner* project a future of oppressive institutions, and therefore continue the socially critical American cinema of *Chinatown* (1974), *Nashville* (1975), and *One Flew Over the Cuckoo's Nest* (1976). They are far different in ideological hue from the optimistic, Norman Rockwellish vision of the future in *Star Wars*.[7] The first part of this essay has presented an overview of the films' conflicting approaches. The second part turns from this general exposition to discuss one aspect of the science fiction film: sex.

Vivian Sobchack, in her fine essay "On the Virginity of Astronauts," suggests that the American science fiction film is characterized by an absence of women and sexuality. Astronauts are primarily male, they wear unisex coveralls and spacesuits, their environment is technological and asexual. But, says Sobchack, if the signifiers of women and sex have been omitted from the science fiction film on the surface level, they return in the deep (subconscious) layer. Space travel is often presented as a penetration; both spaceship and space itself are wombs; alien threats are often sexual, and female.

Before applying Sobchack's model to the three film examples, I would like to consider an exception to Sobchack which proves the rule. The prize-winning science fiction writer C.J. Cherryh (Carolyn J. Cherryh) has paid considerable attention to how sex and reproduction could be handled in starship-based cultures. For example, in a culture of family-operated merchant space ships, where everyone on board is likely to be blood kin, both sex and the reproduction of the culture are made possible by "dockside sleepovers." Cherryh sketches out a pattern of sexual exchange and conventions protecting the greater social good. One example of the controlling social conventions is that children take the mother's name and stay with the mother's ship. The remarkable thing about Cherryh's approach to a spacefaring culture is that almost no one, in science fiction novels or films, has considered similar questions.[8]

Let us return to our film examples. In *Star Wars* there simply is no sex. The society of the film is primarily male, or technologically neuter (the droids). The one prominent female character, Princess Leia, does not appear in sexual terms. According to Sobchack, Leia is "simultaneously protected and desexed by her social position (princesses are to fight for, not to sleep with) and by her acerbic and pragmatically critical attitude" (106). Dale Pollock quotes Marcia Lucas (ex-wife of George Lucas) as saying that *Star Wars* was conceptualized as a movie that would appeal to ten-year-old boys (142). *Star Wars* is a movie coming out of the latency period, a movie which elides the adult problem of sexuality. This is curiously confirmed by the eventual revelation in the *Star Wars* trilogy that Leia is Luke's sister.

Star Wars does not, however, strongly support Sobchack's observation that sexuality repressed on the conscious level will return in subconscious symbolism. The film is not haunted by womb imagery or female monsters. Perhaps the pre-adolescent tone is so strong that it mutes such condensed or displaced signifiers. And, of course, audiences of all ages welcomed this tone, using it to escape current malaise and to return to a simpler, more conservative time. Only two scenes in *Star Wars* suggest to me the displaced sexuality described by Sobchack. First, there is an odd scene, peripheral to the main action, where several characters are caught in a disposal chute/compactor, and they are attacked by a tentacled creature. This scene, played for laughs in *Star Wars*, nevertheless presents the threat of bodily functions and unknown organic antagonists. It thus anticipates *Alien*. Second, in the final attack on the Death Star, the one-man fighters penetrating the sphere could certainly be a representation of human reproduction, with the combination of sexual and mechanical imagery recalling *Dr Strangelove*.

Unlike *Star Wars*, *Alien* is very specifically about a female, sexual threat. The alien creature is associated with darkness, rounded spaces, eggs, slime. Its temple-like ship has doors in the shape of vaginas. The alien's offspring may be male and phallic (e.g., the thing which springs into life from a male astronaut's chest), but the original threat is female. This is made even more explicit in *Aliens* (1986), the sequel to *Alien*, where the human expedition confronts an enormous, egg-laying alien Queen.

In a reversal of the common practice of science fiction films, the protagonist in *Alien* is a female. Ripley, one of two female astronauts, is the toughest, most suspicious, most resourceful of the Nostromo's crew. She, and not the captain or the male crew members, becomes the focus of audience hopes for human survival. Is this reversal incidental, or does it have important ideological consequences for the film? Sobchack notes that Ripley was originally scripted as a male, and that for most of the film "She is not marked as either a woman or sexual" (106). In other words, Ripley is an asexual astronaut among asexual astronauts. However, at the end of the film she strips down to her underwear (preparing for a mechanically aided hibernation), and becomes clearly and challengingly a human female. Sobchack comments as follows: "Ripley no longer represents a rational and asexual functioning subject, but an irrational, potent, sexual object—a woman, the truly threatening alien generally repressed by the male-conceived and dominated genre" (107). Here I partially disagree with Sobchack. I agree that this scene reveals the irrational and sexual side of the main character, but not that it suggests an equivalence with the alien monster. Rather, the revelation is that the primary conflict of *Alien* is not technological vs. primitive, or any variation on that theme, but rather species vs. species, irrational vs. irrational. The irrational side of Ripley's character is further brought out by her determination to save the cat—not a rational calculation, but a motherly instinct. The cat represents Ripley's animal nature, and her instinct for self-preservation and the preservation of those she loves.[9] In this film, such instincts are positive, whereas the rational calculations of the Company are shown as thoroughly negative. Ripley in her underwear is affirmed as a complex human individual, not presented as "the true threatening alien."

In *Blade Runner*, the representations of femaleness run all through the mise en scene. Los Angeles, 2019, is a dank, dark place, with smoke swirling and rain constantly falling. The Nostromo and the alien ship, both ancient and womblike, have as their equivalent an entire city. Only the occasional corporate headquarters (e.g., Tyrell Corporation) have the clean, clear lines of technological masculinity.

As noted earlier, *Blade Runner* combines elements of two male-oriented genres, science fiction and film noir. The combination is important to our current thread of discussion, because film noir commonly includes rather direct, though threatening, images of female sexuality, whereas science fiction represses such images. *Blade Runner* generally follows the film noir paradigm in presenting the three female replicants, Pris, Zhora (Joanna Cassidy), and Rachael. Zhora the snake-charmer has a threatening sexuality, and Pris, despite her childlike side, is threatening as well. Rachael, though she looks like the raven-haired fatal woman of film noir, is a little different. Raised in ignorance of her replicant status, she is a mediating character between the decaying human society and the new, artificially constructed super humans. The human hero Deckard's continuing love affair with Rachael is, despite her mediating status, a break with film noir and science fiction convention and a major statement about diversity. Blade Runner is film noir/science fiction with the woman as alien not repressed.

This theme of acceptance of diversity receives an added twist via the Director's Cut of *Blade Runner*, released in 1992 and now the most readily available version of the film. In this re-edited version, Ridley Scott provides a clue that points to Deckard himself being a replicant. In an added scene, Deckard, seated at the piano in his apartment, has a brief vision of a unicorn moving through a natural landscape. This links up with a moment late in the film when Gaff (Edward James Olmos), another blade runner, leaves an origami of a unicorn in front of Deckard's door. The suggestion is that Gaff knows Deckard's visions because Deckard is programmed, Deckard is a replicant. From one point of view, the message of humanness being defined by behavior rather than by external categories gets lost here, because Deckard is now no different than Rachael. But another point of view would be that the audience's identification with Deckard in itself proves that humanness is not a matter of categories such as natural/synthetic birth (or racial, sexual, national, or political identity).

Blade Runner's theme of replicant as more-than-human brings with it some other sexual/ideological possibilities. One, unfortunately, is the possible connection between large, blond Roy Batty, played by Rutger Hauer, and the Nazi theory of an Aryan master race (Wood 187). Another, far more positive line of speculation, is that a more-than-human character can break sexual boundaries. Roy, stronger and smarter than a human, is a fiercely burning Blakean angel with a maximum four year life span. He overrides human cultural limits in a variety of ways, one of which seems to be bisexuality. He kisses his creator, Tyrell, fully on the lips, and his final duel with Deckard has a strong sexual as well as violent content. Significantly, after Roy saves Deckard and dies himself, the original release version of *Blade Runner* concludes with a voiceover of affirmation: "They just wanted what everyone else wanted. Answers to the basic questions: Who am I? Where did I come from? Where am I going?" A violent/sexual combat here melds into understanding and empathy.

Alien and *Blade Runner* are clearly descendents of *Star Wars*, works which build on the revelation that audiences would support mythic, world-creating science fiction films. But the two Ridley Scott films do not follow George Lucas's political line. Whereas *Star Wars* advocates a return to heroism and traditional morality, the Ridley Scott films show a distrust of authority and an openness to characters outside traditional definitions of heroism (e.g., Ripley and the replicants). When looked at together, these three films present a kind of debate about the (imagined) future. George Lucas sees the future as a revision of the past, as a chance to get basic moral precepts right this time. The legend of King Arthur can be replayed in a possible future. For Ridley Scott and his collaborators, on the other hand, the future provides a way to look at other issues: the place of women in society, the threat of an unexamined rationalism, the acceptance of the Other, the merging of humanity and technology. In simple terms, George Lucas is backward-looking and traditional, i.e., conservative. Ridley Scott is forward-looking and accepting of diversity, i.e., liberal. Audiences drawn to these films are thus, among other things, experiencing an ongoing political dialogue.

Notes

1. Unless otherwise noted in the text, my analysis refers to the film *Star Wars*, not to the *Star Wars* trilogy. Similarly, I will be discussing the film *Alien*, and not its sequels, with any exceptions specifically noted in the text.

2. On the literary roots of *Star Wars*, see Wyatt and Collins.

3. See Sammon 71-75 for a description of how Ridley Scott's art direction skills transformed the script for *Blade Runner*.

4. Every army presents medals with pomp and ceremony, but the music used here recalls *Triumph of the Will*.

5. The connection between Raymond Chandler's literary detective and the chivalrous knight is outlined in Durham.

6. The lines from Blake begin "Fiery the angels rose" (*America: A Prophecy*, lines 115-16). For interpretation of this near-quote, see Wood and Morrison.

7. After writing these words, I learned that George Lucas collects Norman Rockwell's work! Rockwell's work! Rockwell's paintings hang prominently on the walls of the Skywalker Ranch, Lucas's business headquarters. See Seabrook 43.

8. See, for example, Cherryh's 1982 novel *Merchanter's Luck*.

9. Thanks to Rebecca Pauly for suggesting the importance of Jonesy the cat.

Works Cited

Bukatman, Scott. *Terminal Identity*. Durham: Duke UP, 1993.

Cherryh, C.J. *Merchanter's Luck*. New York: Daw, 1982.

Collins, Robert G. "*Star Wars*: The Pastiche of Myth and the Yearning for a Past Future." *Journal of Popular Culture* 11:1 (1977): 1–10.

Durham, Philip. *Down these mean streets a man must go*. Chapel Hill: U of North Carolina P, 1963.

Meyer, David S. "Star Wars, *Star Wars*, and American Political Culture." *Journal of Popular Culture* 26:2 (1992): 99–115.

Morrison, Rachela. "*Casablanca* meets *Star Wars*: The Blakean Dialectics of *Blade Runner*." *Literature/Film Quarterly* 18:1: 2–10.

Pierce, John J. "Creative Synergy and the Art of World Creation." *Retrofitting Blade Runner*. Ed. Judith B. Keman. Bowling Green: Bowling Green: Bowling Green Popular Press, 1991.

Pollack, Dale. *Skywalking: The Life and Films of George Lucas*. Hollywood: Samuel French, 1990.

Robertson, Robbie. "The narrative sources of Ridley Scott's *Alien*." *Cinema and Fiction: New Modes of Adapting, 1950–1990*. Ed. John Orr and Colin Nicholson. Edinburgh: Edinburgh UP, 1992.

Sammon, Paul M. *Future Noir: The Making of Blade Runner*. New York: HarperCollins, 1996.

Seabrook, John. "Why is the Force Still With Us?" *New Yorker* 6 January 1997.

Sobchack, Vivian. "On the Virginity of Astronauts." *Alien Zone*. Ed. Annette Kuhn. London: Verso, 1990.

Wood, Robin. *Hollywood from Vietnam to Reagan*. New York: Columbia UP, 1986.

Wyatt, David. "*Star Wars* and the Productions of Time." *Virginia Quarterly Review* 58 (1982): 600–15.

12

Welcome to the Men's Club: Homosociality and the Maintenance of Hegemonic Masculinity

Sharon R. Bird

This study focuses on multiple masculinities conceptualized in terms of sociality, a concept used to refer to nonsexual interpersonal attractions. Through male homosocial heterosexual interactions, hegemonic masculinity is maintained as the norm to which men are held accountable despite individual conceptualizations of masculinity that depart from that norm. When it is understood among heterosexual men in homosocial circles that masculinity means being emotionally detached and competitive and that masculinity involves viewing women as sexual objects, their daily interactions help perpetuate a system that subordinates femininity and nonhegemonic masculinities. Nonhegemonic masculinities fail to influence structural gender arrangements significantly because their expression is either relegated to heterosocial settings or suppressed entirely.

To understand gender inequality, one must do more than study relations *between* genders. The nature of gender relations is such that asymmetries exist between men and women and among men and among women (Connell 1987, 1992). Recognition of masculinity as a social construct began only a couple of decades ago, and recognition of a power dynamic differentiating "normative" from "non-normative" masculinities began only a few years ago (Kimmel 1990). Investigation of the many possible types of masculinity conceptualizations has been rare (Connell 1987; Kimmel 1990). Connell's (1992) research on homosexual masculinities and their subordination to heterosexual masculinities is a notable exception. As Connell's work demonstrates, delineation of relations among masculinities is important because it facilitates a better understanding of how the structural order of gender is maintained. Hegemonic masculinity, which is "the maintenance of practices that institutionalize men's dominance over women" and is "constructed in relation to women and to subordinate masculinities"

Reprinted by permission from *Gender and Society* 10, no. 2 (April 1996).

(Connell 1987, 185–86), shapes the overall framework of gender relations. By problematizing masculinity, Connell challenges typically undisputed meanings associated with male dominance.

In this study, I focus on how meanings that correspond to hegemonic masculinity are maintained and how meanings that do not correspond to hegemonic masculinity are suppressed. Within the existing gender order, meanings associated with behaviors that challenge hegemonic masculinity are denied legitimation as *masculine;* such meanings are marginalized, if not suppressed entirely. Contradictions to hegemonic masculinity posed by male homosexuality, for example, are suppressed when homosexual masculinity is consistently rendered "effeminate" (Connell 1992).

The maintenance of hegemonic masculinity is explored here through investigation of male homosocial interactions. *Homosociality* refers specifically to the nonsexual attractions held by men (or women) for members of their own sex (Lipman-Blumen 1976). Homosociality, according to Lipman-Blumen, promotes clear distinctions between women and men through segregation in social institutions. I add, further, that homosociality promotes clear distinctions between hegemonic masculinities and nonhegemonic masculinities by the segregation of social groups. *Heterosociality,* a concept left untheorized by Lipman-Blumen, refers to nonsexual attractions held by men (or women) for members of the other sex.

Also critical to this analysis is an investigation of the relationship between sociality and the self-conceptualization of masculinity. As I argue here, homosocial interaction, among heterosexual men, contributes to the maintenance of hegemonic masculinity norms by supporting meanings associated with identities that fit hegemonic ideals while suppressing meanings associated with nonhegemonic masculinity identities. I focus specifically on the connection between individual masculinity and gender norms in small group interactions to capture subtle mechanisms of control. When personal conflicts with ideal masculinity are suppressed both in the homosocial group and by individual men, the cultural imposition of hegemonic masculinity goes uncontested (see Kaufman 1994).

The following meanings are crucial to our understanding of how homosociality contributes to the perpetuation of hegemonic masculinity: (1) *emotional detachment,* a meaning constructed through relationships within families whereby young men detach themselves from mothers and develop gender identities in relation to that which they are not (Chodorow 1978); (2) *competitiveness,* a meaning constructed and maintained through relationships with other men whereby simple individuality becomes competitive individuality (Gilligan 1982); and (3) *sexual objectification of women,* a meaning constructed and maintained through relationships with other men whereby male individuality is conceptualized not only as *different from* female but as *better than* female (Johnson 1988).

Conceptualizing Masculinities

Gender identity is distinguished from the heavily criticized concept of gender *role* in that the latter is used to refer to behavioral expectations associated with more or less static social positions, whereas the former refers to a continual *process* whereby meanings are attributed by and to individuals through social interaction. Gender, in other words, is relational. Gender identity originates in early interactions, becoming more stable through the accumulation of meanings attributed by and to the self over time (see Burke 1980; Burke and Reitzes 1981). Information received through interactions may be used either to reinforce existing self-notions of gender meanings or to weaken them. That is, mere socialization does not sufficiently explain how individuals conceptualize identity. Socialization provides the terms of social interaction but does not determine how individuals incorporate interactional meanings into their own conceptualizations of gender (Connell 1987).

The unique experiences of men, embedded within particular social institutions and subject to varying historical contexts, facilitate conceptualizations of masculinities that may differ considerably. Each male incorporates a variety of meanings into his gender identity, some of which are consistent with hegemonic masculinity and others of which are not (e.g., Connell 1992; Messner 1992b). The social ideal for masculinity, which in itself is a nonstatic notion, may be internalized (i.e., central to one's core self [see Chodorow 1980]) or simply interiorized (i.e., acknowledged by the self), enabling individuals to understand the gender norms to which they are held accountable. In either case, each male comes to understand both socially shared meanings of masculinity and the idiosyncratic meanings that comprise his unique gender identity. Internalization of hegemonic meanings provides a base of shared meanings for social interaction but also quells the expression of nonhegemonic meanings. The presumption that hegemonic masculinity meanings are the only mutually accepted and legitimate masculinity meanings helps to reify hegemonic norms while suppressing meanings that might otherwise create a foundation for the subversion of the existing hegemony. This presumption is especially prevalent in male homosocial interactions, which are critical to both the conceptualization of masculinity identity and the maintenance of gender norms.

Male Homosocial Interactions: Emotional Detachment, Competitiveness, and Sexual Objectification of Women

Three of the shared meanings that are perpetuated via male homosociality are emotional detachment, competition, and the sexual objectification of women. These meanings characterize hegemonic masculinity but are not always internalized as central to individual identity. First, emotional detachment (i.e., withholding expressions of intimacy) maintains both clear individual identity boundaries (Chodorow 1978) and the norms of hegemonic masculinity. To express feelings is to reveal vulnerabilities and weaknesses; to withhold such expressions is to maintain control (Cancian 1987). Second, competition in the male homosocial group supports an identity that depends not on likeness and cooperation but on separation and distinction (Gilligan 1982). Competition facilitates hierarchy in relationships, whereas cooperation suggests symmetry of relationships (Messner 1992a). Finally, the sexual objectification of women facilitates self-conceptualization as positively male by distancing the self from all that is associated with being female. The objectification of women provides a base on which male superiority is maintained (Johnson 1988), whereas identification with women (and what it means to be female) helps remove the symbolic distance that enables men to depersonalize the oppression of women.

Individual conceptualizations vary in the extent to which these meanings characterize one's masculinity. Masculinities that differ from the norm of hegemonic masculinity, however, are generally experienced as "private dissatisfactions" rather than foundations for questioning the social construction of gender (Thomas 1990; see also Kaufman 1994). Hegemonic masculinity persists, therefore, despite individual departures from the hegemonic form.

Method

The data collected for this study were gathered through personal interviews and field observations. Eight in-depth interviews were conducted in the fall of 1992 in a small northwestern city in the United States. Later, additional follow-up interviews were conducted with four new respondents to clarify how male homosocial and heterosexual interactions facilitate the perpetuation of hegemonic masculinity, on the one hand, but suppress nonhegemonic masculinity, on the other.

The men who participated in the interviews for this study were all selected from within the academic community of the city in which the study took place. Responses to questions, therefore, may reflect a level of education higher than that of the general population. The findings of this study, however, are consistent with findings of previous studies regarding the meanings associated with masculinity (e.g., Lehn 1992; Messner 1992a, 1992b; Phillips 1986). The men's educational level ranged from three years of undergraduate study to graduate level and post-Ph.D. The men ranged in age from 23 to 50 years. All but one of the interviewees were native-born Americans from various geographical regions of the country. The other male, a native of East Africa, had maintained residence in the United States for approximately two years before the time of the interview. Although the data received through the interview with this respondent were consistent with accounts offered by the respondents from the United States, this information was excluded from the analysis because of cultural differences that could contribute to misleading conclusions. Most of the men reported middle-class family origins, although three reported working-class backgrounds. Two of the men interviewed were Black, and the other nine were white. All of the men were raised primarily by female caretakers, and all were heterosexual.

The primary focus of the interviews was on the development of perceived consensual masculinity and the corresponding relationship between self-conceptualizations and hegemonic masculinity. Respondents were first asked questions about childhood. Each was asked to describe childhood memories of time spent with playmates, with siblings, and with parents. Responses to these questions provided general information from which more specific inquiries could be made regarding the meanings associated both with masculinity personally (i.e., identity) and with masculinity more generally (i.e., the beliefs, attitudes, and expectations of the group and of society).

To establish the parameters for the discussion during the interviews, each man was asked to consider the kinds of relationships he would find most desirable given non-work-related situations.[1] Each was then prompted to elaborate on his experiences within groups, especially those experiences within the male homosocial group. Although the men varied in how much they desired male homosocial group interaction, each explained that such groups have had a significant impact on their beliefs, attitudes, and behaviors. The men were asked to elaborate on what exactly would be considered appropriate or inappropriate, desirable or undesirable, for conversation among men and what interests were commonly or not commonly shared within their homosocial groups. The topics of sports, women, business, politics, and drinking were most commonly specified as desirable for conversation, while the topics of feelings and gossip were most frequently mentioned as undesirable. Each man was then asked to explain his views on the degree to which his personal interests corresponded to interests more generally shared by the group. I also made inquiries about why certain interests and topics are so prevalent among men in homosocial groups and whether they had experienced any repercussions when norms for male homosocial interaction were disregarded.

Additional data were collected during the fall of 1992 through field observations of male homosocial interactions in small-group contexts. Observations and interviews were conducted within the same academic community, but the men *observed* were not the same as the men *interviewed*. Approximately 25 hours of observations were conducted. The majority of the observations were made at a single location: a deli/bar frequented by men associated with the university but also visited regularly by men not associated with academia. Remaining observations were conducted at two coffee shops and three taverns, all located in the same academic community. The focus of the observations was on the interactions among male customers, including their conversations. Field notes were taken in one- to two-hour time periods at various times of the day and/or night and on various days of the week. Because the locations in which observations were made are consistently patronized by students and university faculty, the recording of observations went unnoticed. A running description was kept of interactions that transpired between men seated within hearing distance of the researcher (usually only a few feet away). Observations were made of groups ranging in size from two to eight men. Observations were also made of groups that were initially all male but were temporarily interrupted by a woman. Most of the conversations were recorded verbatim. Gestures, facial expressions, and the physical location of each group member were also noted.

The meanings described in the interviews and that emerged from the observations have been organized under the following subtopics: (1) emotional detachment, (2) competition, and (3) sexual objectification of women. The remainder of this article focuses on the processes through which these meanings are sustained and the processes through which alternative meanings are suppressed in male homosocial interaction.

Emotional Detachment: "We Were Masculine Little Kids!"

The rules that apply to homosocial friendships and to masculinity are so familiar that they are typically taken for granted by men and women alike. Rarely does anyone (other than the social scientist) seriously question the expectations associated with gender identity or gender norms. Instead, it is assumed that "boys will be boys" and will just naturally do "boy things." By the same token, "men will be men" and will continue to do "men things." Doing men things or "doing masculinity" is simply the commonplace activity of men's daily lives, recreated over and again, maintaining the norms of social behavior (West and Zimmerman 1987).

The men interviewed and those observed explained that being "one of the boys" is a key principle of symbolic and, in some cases, physical separation of "the boys" from "the girls." One man, for example, explained how, as a youngster, he and his pals "were rough and rugged . . . masculine little kids." He said,

> When you're a little boy, you hang out with other little boys and you do little boy things. You know, you burn ants and things like that. You just don't hang out with females because you don't want to be a wuss, you don't play with dolls, you don't whine, you don't cry . . . you do boy things, you know, guy stuff.

Being masculine, in other words, means being not-female. The masculinity ideal involves detachment and independence. The men interviewed indicated that emotions and behaviors typically associated with women were inappropriate within the male homosocial group. Among the emotions and behaviors considered most inappropriate, and most highly stigmatized, were those associated with feminine expressions of intimacy (e.g., talking "feelings"). As one of the men interviewed explained, "I usually talk about 'things' rather than getting into your head and asking, you know, that real intimate stuff."

This suppression of feminine emotions is more than merely a means of establishing individual masculinity. Emotional detachment is one way in which gender hierarchies are maintained. Expressing emotions signifies weakness and is devalued, whereas emotional detachment signifies strength and is valued (Cancian 1987).

In their discussions of feelings, the men hesitated; none of them made consistent use of the word *feelings*. Instead of feelings, they referred to "personal stuff," "those things," and "those matters," and when asked, many indicated that "ultimately you're doing it alone." The expectation is that "because you're going to be in situations where you're away from any support system . . . you're going to have to handle your stuff alone."

What these men explained was that within the male homosocial group, emotional detachment is viewed not only as desirable but as imperative. Those who do express their intimate emotions are excluded. On this point, the interviewees were quite clear: "If I was having a beer with a friend and they started crying, I would suspect that that person, if it were a male . . . I'd suspect that that person didn't have a very good definition of the social situation." If a guy did start crying, this interviewee was asked, where would that put him in relation to other guys? "Hmm, well, since . . . actually that would put him on the outs." The repercussion for violating the hegemonic meaning of emotional detachment, in other words, is to be "put on the outs," that is, to be ostracized from one's male homosocial group. Interviewees explained that violations of the norm of emotional detachment do not result in an alteration of the norm but instead result in the exclusion of the violator (see Schur 1984).

Data collected through observations clearly supported the pattern described by the men interviewed. Emotional detachment was exercised in even the most sensitive of topics. Two men observed, for example, appeared rather matter-of-fact as they discussed the marital problems that one of the men was experiencing: "Think of it this way, ya got a toothache. . . . You've got to have it taken out or you're gonna live with the bitch. Unless you bite the bullet and get the goddamn thing pulled out, you're gonna live with the pain." Feelings, as discussed by these two men, were something to "get over," not to experience—much less express. One man, when questioned about the possible repercussions for expressing feelings in the context of the male homosocial group, explained that feelings are "something for us all to joke about" because

> you certainly don't want to take things too seriously and have to deal with the heavy side, the heavy emotional side to it . . . Tears are a very extreme thing in these male circles, partly because it's messy . . . It has a lot to do with not looking soft and weak because if you do . . . it makes it difficult for men to have relationships with each other.

He explained that "developing emotional types of relationships with each other" is something men stereotypically do not do. Hegemonic masculinity is not expressed and maintained through excessive emotionality. This distinction separates the boys from the girls as well as the men who fit the hegemonic norm from those who do not. Through emotional detachment, the meanings formed in regard to masculinity are exaggerated so as to distinguish clearly that which all men are not, that is, female. The burden for demonstrating difference is on those trying to avoid the default meanings. Difference becomes an aspect of self in which men have a valued investment.

Departures from the norm of emotional detachment, however, do exist. Individual departures reflect an understanding of the dominant meanings but not necessarily an incorporation of them into one's self-concept. One man explained that although most men "do what the culture says and hide it" (i.e., hide their feelings), he had hoped to be able to express his feelings with other men: "A couple of times when I was hurting, uhm, I did kind of seek out a couple of male friends and I was really disappointed. . . . It was like they were embarrassed, you know, to talk about that shit, and so, uh, fuck it!" Five of the men who participated in the in-depth interviews and three of the four who participated in the follow-up interviews expressed discrepancies between hegemonic masculinity and their own masculinity. Each explained that although they knew they were *supposed* to separate themselves from things considered feminine, they did not assess their own identities to be as polarized as the hegemonic form would suggest.

> It was really unfortunate. As I grew older, I really wished that I wasn't so detached from my mom. I'm not that way now, though. After a while, I stopped caring about what everybody else thought. I mean, the intimate side got pushed aside for so long because that's not what "real" men are supposed to do. I got over it, though . . . I guess I'm not what "real" men are supposed to be.

The degree to which the masculinity meanings individuals hold for themselves correspond to the meanings of hegemonic masculinity may vary over time and from person to person. The point, however, is that although individual conceptualizations of masculinity depart from the hegemonic norm, nonhegemonic meanings are suppressed due to perceptions of "appropriate" masculinity. Even in a community where notions of the "new man" are common and where antisexist attitudes are often expected, hegemonic patterns of masculinity prevail. One whose masculinity conceptualization is nonhegemonic still understands himself as "not what 'real' men are *supposed* to be" (emphasis added).

The men who made the distinction between self-masculinity and hegemonic masculinity made three things clear. First, they explained that hegemonic masculinity was the form that prevailed in their interactions with other men throughout childhood and adolescence. Second, they asserted that when they found themselves in homosocial situations in the present, the expectation of emotional detachment continued to prevail. Third, they described themselves in the present as more heterosocially than homosocially oriented. These men explained that they did not prefer exclusively male social interaction groups. In sum, homosocial and heterosocial masculinity meanings are clearly differentiated. For these men, homosocial masculinity was characterized by emotional detachment, whereas heterosocial masculinity downplayed these factors.

Competition: "It's a Pecking Order Between Males"

Competition with other men provides a stage for establishing self both as an individual and as appropriately masculine. Competition also contributes to the perpetuation of male dominance. When asked to explain what competition meant to him, one interviewee replied,

> By nature I'm terribly competitive. I suppose one's ego gets wrapped around the things that you do. Its pretty important for me to win because I do have my ego wrapped up in that [games] and so, uhm, you know when I play a game at a party or whatever I kind of expect to win and play pretty fiercely.

To establish self as not female, young men seek out other men with whom to display "non-femaleness" (Johnson 1988). Homosocial group interactions provide feedback and support for masculinity self-conceptualization. In this sense, masculinity conceptualization is itself a form of competition. Four men described competition as a critical part of their self-conceptualizations and stressed that the competitions they preferred were those with men. Men, they believed, could understand the intensity and importance of competition, whereas women seemed less accepting and less understanding. When asked about participating in athletics with women, one interviewee responded that "women start getting angry at you and it gets ugly" when "you start getting really intense." Another added that "women typically don't want to play [basketball] or sort of want to but feel they'll be intimidated or whatever."

The men who described themselves as less competitive (or noncompetitive), on the other hand, explained that they considered the intensity with which other men engaged in competitions (especially sports) as relatively unimportant for themselves. At the same time, however, these men recognized the *expectations* of masculinity to be competitive. One man explained,

> Guys don't know what it means not to be competitive. Even those men who tell you that competition is silly know they have to [compete]. It's like otherwise you're gonna get walked on. Nobody appreciates that. I'm not as aggressive as most guys, but I can sure act it.

Again, the norms and expectations of hegemonic masculinity and individual conceptualizations do not necessarily fit; further, among the less competitive men, nonhegemonic masculinity and hegemonic masculinity meanings differ by sociality. Men whose conceptualizations of masculinity were nonhegemonic specified their lack of preference for homosocial interactions in both sporting and nonsporting activities. Men whose conceptualizations of masculinity were consistent with the hegemonic form specified a clear preference for homosocial interactions in sports. Homosociality corresponded with a focus on competitiveness, whereas heterosociality deemphasized competition. Homosocial and heterosocial meanings were clearly differentiated. In male homosocial groups, a man risks loss of status and self-esteem unless he competes. The meaning of competition is assumed under male homosocial circumstances, and violators of this norm are disadvantaged.

Sexual Objectification: "You Know, Women Were 'Othered' Early"

The competitions that support hegemonic masculinity continue throughout life in a variety of forms. Among the forms of competitions in which men engage are those that involve the objectification of women. Men often compete with one another in efforts to gain the attention and affections of women and in boasting about their sexual exploits. Observations revealed numerous stories about sexual objectification of women. In male homosocial conversations, references were made to women as "them," as clearly "other," as the nonthreatening "girl," and/or as objects to be used for sexual pleasure. While the use of these terms may or may not imply a conscious effort on the part of the speaker to objectify, they promote meanings that support hegemonic masculinity nonetheless.

The men not only explicated the objectification of women, they also explained and demonstrated the competition for objectified women. These competitions illustrate the interconnectedness of the meanings of emotional detachment, competition, and objectification. Conversations overheard at the deli/lounge, for example, shifted frequently from "shop talk" to competitive sex talk. Bantering sessions, in which one-upsmanship on stories of sexual exploits was the name of the game, were frequently overheard. For example, one man began,

> I've run across those kind. . . . I'll tell 'em, "I'll buy ya a beer." [And the hypothetical woman replies,] "Na, I'll buy you a beer." Then I'm thinkin' she's ready to get outa there with me. I just want one I can step out with, shoot up her, and get back in the bar in 5 or 10 minutes.

Another man then added his own story:

> Aw, shit, I had one down near Vegas. . . . Well, to make a long story short, when it was time to hit the rack we went back to her room. . . . We found a bucket of ice and a bottle of liquor at the door with a note from some other guy attached to it. . . . I just went ahead and drank the stuff and screwed her!

Not to be outdone, the remaining participant in the discussion followed with an account of his own:

> Yeah, one night I had a couple of beers, then went out to that country and western bar. . . . She was a bartender there. I'm tellin' ya, she was hanging all over me so much that the other bartender had to get on to her. Then later, she came knockin' on my trailer door. I thought, "What the hell, Judy won't find out, let's hop to it." She was a wicked thing.

Such conversations, according to the men interviewed, occur frequently but are less likely to be carried out with verbal explicitness when a woman or women actually join the interaction.

In this case, the conversation will likely shift; but, as my interviewees explained, the competition will continue. The question, "What happens if a woman enters the scene where you are engaging in a conversation with another man or men? prompted the following response: "Weird. Weird setup . . . because everybody is checking everybody else out. . . it's uncomfortable for everybody. You know, people are checking each other out. We'd see her as an issue of conquest." The men interviewed explained that men in homosocial groups both objectify and compete for women. When asked to describe the nature of interactions between men when an "available" woman is present among the group, one man explained, "It's competitive, you see, and it's a pecking order between men. If you do not peck, you get pecked. And so, one of the things over which there is a great deal of pecking is women."

To be "pecked" is an undesirable experience—to be avoided if a man wishes to maintain status within the male homosocial group. Objectification of women and men's competitiveness over objectified women constitute the very essence of what hegemonic masculinity means in this society (Connell 1992). Not all men view themselves in accordance with hegemonic masculinity, however, when it comes to objectifying women. Even so, men often go along with hegemonic norms to avoid being pecked. All of the men interviewed, when asked how an individual man avoids being pecked by other members of the group, explained that, on the one hand, they knew what the rules of the game were because

> there's always an assessment going on in the group. Always. . . . Some guys will go along but wouldn't make a degrading comment about women themselves. But when some guy says something, because you want to be a member of the group, it becomes, "Yeah." You follow the lead.

Some men argued, however, that these hegemonic rules did not fit their own identities:

> That stuff [sexual objectification of women] doesn't interest me terribly much because for the most part I don't really talk about those things and I don't hang out with men who do. It's a very nasty type of chat, and the goal seems to be to hurt somebody anyway.

Although the rules of hegemonic masculinity included sexual objectification, some individual conceptualizations minimized and/or disregarded its importance. Even among those men who rejected hegemonic masculinity for themselves, however, the hegemonic norm for sexual objectification prevailed in male homosocial groups. In fact, none of the men in the study, for example, mentioned ever verbally rejecting these hegemonic meanings in their all-male groups. The meanings of emotional detachment, competitiveness, and sexual objectification all were understood and behaviorally followed. Hegemonic masculinity was maintained despite individual departures from the norm, as individual departures were suppressed in homosocial settings. Nonhegemonic masculinity was subordinated through relegation to heterosocial settings. Emotional detachment, competitiveness, and the sexual objectification of women remained as the criteria to which men are held accountable, especially in all-male interactions.

Conclusions: Hegemonic Masculinity and the Gender Order

Hegemonic masculinity is consistently and continually recreated despite individual conceptualizations that contradict hegemonic meanings. Violations of the norms of hegemonic masculinity typically fail to produce alterations in the gender order; instead, they result in penalties to violators. With particular attention to the meanings that help sustain a pecking order among men, I have outlined some of the processes that pose barriers to gender equality in the United States, that is, the devaluation of meanings considered feminine, the suppression of these meanings in male heterosexual homosocial settings, and the relegation of non-hegemonic masculinity to heterosocial settings. Hegemonic masculinity, as demonstrated here, prevailed even in an academic community where ideals of gender equality are generally promoted. Reification of existing gender arrangements continues despite individual conflicts with hegemonic masculinity. The contradictions that nonhegemonic masculinity meanings (e.g., expression of intimate emotions, cooperation, and identification with women) potentially pose to dominant masculinity patterns are suppressed in male homosocial heterosexual interactions, inhibiting change. When individual departures from dominant masculinity are experienced as private dissatisfactions rather than as reason for contesting the social construction of masculinity, hegemonic patterns persist.

Because the barriers that distinguish appropriate from inappropriate masculinity generally are not accomplished through reconceptualization of individual masculinity alone, recasting the gender order in more favorable terms must also involve changes instigated at levels of social organization beyond that of social interaction. Subversion of widely accepted gender beliefs, attitudes, and expectations requires special attention to the processes that facilitate their *institutionalization.* That which must be continually challenged and ultimately eradicated in terms of masculinity, therefore, is the taken-for-granted assumption that being male means being emotionally detached, competitive, and supportive of the sexual objectification of women as well as the assumption that men whose identities do not embody these meanings are not true men. These changes must take place not only within heterosocial contexts but also within homosocial contexts and throughout all social institutions. In even broader terms, the goal yet to be accomplished is the *degenderization* of meanings. In other words, emotional detachment, competitiveness, and the sexual objectification of women must cease to exist as criteria by which being a man is measured. Indeed, the beliefs, attitudes, and expectations that decree the valuation and/or devaluation of distinctive masculine and feminine meanings in the first place must be deconstructed.

Author's Note: An earlier version of this article was presented at the 1993 annual meeting of the Pacific Sociological Association, Portland, OR. I thank Leslie Atkins, Kendal Broad, Peter Burke, Valerie Jenness, Lisa McIntyre, Margaret Andersen, Miriam Johnson, R. W. Connell, the reviewers at *Gender & Society*, and especially Lisa Broidy, Tim McGettigan, and Amy Wharton for their helpful criticisms and advice. Special thanks also to the men interviewed for this study.

Reprint Requests: Sharon R. Bird, Department of Sociology, Washington State University, Pullman, WA 99164-4020.

Note

1. Leisure situations, rather than work-related situations, were focused on to specifically highlight social interaction preferences.

References

Burke, Peter J. 1980. The self: Measurement requirements from an interactionist perspective. *Social Psychology Quarterly* 43:18–29.

Burke, Peter J., and Donald C. Reitzes. 1981. The link between identity and role performance. *Social Psychology Quarterly* 44:33–92.

Cancian, Francesca M. 1987. *Love in America: Gender and self-development.* Cambridge, UK: Cambridge University Press.

Chodorow, Nancy. 1978. *The reproduction of mothering.* Berkeley: University of California Press.

———. 1980. Gender, relation, and difference in psychoanalytic perspective. In *The future of difference,* edited by Hester Eisenstein and Alice Jardine. Boston: G. K. Hall.

Connell, R. W. 1987. *Gender and power: Society, the person, and sexual politics.* Stanford, CA: Stanford University Press.

———. 1992. A very straight gay: Masculinity, homosexual experience, and the dynamics of gender. *American Sociological Review* 57:735–51.

Gilligan, Carol. 1982. *In a different voice: Psychological theory and women's development.* Cambridge, MA: Harvard University Press.

Johnson, Miriam. 1988. *Strong mothers, weak wives.* Berkeley: University of California Press.

Kaufman, Michael. 1994. Men, feminism, and men's contradictory experiences of power. In *Theorizing masculinities,* edited by Harry Brod and Michael Kaufman. Thousand Oaks, CA: Sage.

Kimmel, Michael S. 1990. After fifteen years: The impact of the sociology of masculinity on the masculinity of sociology. In *Men, masculinities, and social theory,* edited by Jeff Hearn and David Morgan. London: Unwin Hyman.

Lehn, Gregory K. 1992. Homophobia among men: Supporting and defining the male role. In *Men's lives,* edited by Michael S. Kimmel and Michael A. Messner. New York: Macmillan.

Lipman-Blumen, Jean. 1976. Toward a homosocial theory of sex roles: An explanation of the sex segregation of social institutions. *Signs: Journal of Women and Culture and Society* 1:15–3 1.

Messner, Michael A. 1992a. Boyhood, organized sports, and the construction of masculinity. In *Men's lives,* edited by Michael S. Kimmel and Michael A. Messner. New York: Macmillan.

———. 1992b. *Power at play: Sports and the problem of masculinity.* Boston: Beacon.

Phillips, Gerald M. 1986. Men talking to men about their relationships. *American Behavioral Scientist* 29:321–41.

Schur, Edwin M. 1984. *Labeling women deviant: Gender; stigma, and social control.* New York: Random House.

Thomas, Alison. 1990. The significance of gender politics in men's accounts of their "gender identity." In *Men, masculinities, and social theory,* edited by Jeff Hearn and David Morgan. London: Unwin Hyman.

West, Candace, and Don H. Zimmerman. 1987. Doing gender. *Gender & Society* 1:125–51.

13

Men, Masculinity, and Manhood Acts

Douglas Schrock[1] and Michael Schwalbe[2]

Abstract

In the 1980s research on men shifted from studying the "male sex role" and masculinity as a singular trait to studying how men enact diverse masculinities. This research has examined men's behavior as gendered beings in many contexts, from intimate relationships to the workplace to global politics. We consider the strengths and weaknesses of the multiple masculinities approach, proposing that further insights into the social construction of gender and the dynamics of male domination can be gained by focusing analytic attention on manhood acts and how they elicit deference from others. We interpret the literature in terms of what it tells us about how males learn to perform manhood acts, about how and why such acts vary, and about how manhood acts reproduce gender inequality. We end with suggestions for further research on the practices and processes through which males construct the category "men" and themselves as its members.

Introduction

Feminism has taught sociology that no account of social life is complete if it ignores gender inequality. Sociologists of course wrote about sex roles, and about masculinity and femininity, before second-wave feminism impacted the discipline in the 1960s and 1970s. But much of this prefeminist writing, done under the influence of functionalism, treated sex roles as complementary and necessary—not as stemming from unequal power relations between women and men. Masculinity and femininity were likewise seen as sex-specific and sex-appropriate personality traits that were expressed behaviorally, rather

[1]Department of Sociology, Florida State University, Tallahassee, Florida 32306-2270; email: dschrock@fsu.edu

[2]Department of Sociology, North Carolina State University, Raleigh, North Carolina 27695-8107; email: michael_schwalbe@ncsu.edu

Annu. Rev. Sociol. 2009. 35:277–95. First published online as a Review in Advance on April 6, 2009. The *Annual Review of Sociology* is online at soc.annualreviews.org

than as attributions elicited by acts of domination and subordination. By the early 1980s, these old views had largely been superseded among sociologists of gender.

Since that time, gender scholars have created an enormous body of theory and research that goes under the rubric of "critical studies of men and masculinities." We acknowledge that defining intellectual eras by reference to decades is an oversimplification and that the emergence of this new strain in gender studies was not a discrete event. Significant changes in sociological thinking about gender, and about men and masculinity in particular, were under way before 1980 (see, e.g., Kessler & McKenna 1978, Pleck & Sawyer 1974, Tolson 1977). Yet it is possible in this case to identify a point at which the terms of the discussion shifted and the study of men and masculinity entered the mainstream. We mark this point as the publication of Carrigan et al.'s 1985 article "Toward a New Sociology of Masculinity."

Carrigan et al. debunked sex-role theory for its blindness to power, showed how masculinity was about power relations among men, not only between women and men, illuminated the link between masculinity and heterosexuality by taking gay sexuality seriously, treated masculinity not as a trait but as a form of collective male practice that has as its effect the subordination of women, and formulated the concepts of hegemonic and subordinated masculinities. Each of these ideas can be traced to earlier works (e.g., Connell 1983), but by integrating them into a coherent analysis, Carrigan et al. put the study of men and masculinities on its contemporary track.

By some measures, that track has been fruitful. Our initial search of *Sociological Abstracts* turned up 2999 articles (78.6% of them published since 1995) that listed "masculinity" or "masculinities" as a key word. There are now several textbooks and edited volumes offering overviews of the field (e.g., Clatterbaugh 1996, Messner & Kimmel 2007), four encyclopedias or handbooks on studies of men and masculinity (Flood et al. 2007, Kimmel & Aronson 2004, Kimmel et al. 2005, Whitehead 2006), and two massive bibliographies (Flood 2008, Janssen 2008). The important question, however, is not how much has been published, but, as we ask here, what has been accomplished?

It could be said that we know a great deal about men and every conventional category of social life. There are literatures on men and work, men and war, men and sports, men and race, men and health, men and aging, men and crime, men and sexuality, men and violence, men and family, and men and friendship. Viewed in these terms, the landscape of our knowledge appears vast. Yet the tendency for sociologists to embrace the men-and-(fill in the blank) pattern when studying men and masculinity has, in our view, become limiting. As we will argue, moving forward depends on reclaiming key insights from Carrigan et al. (1985) and from interactionist analyses of gender.

Our approach here is to avoid the *men and* pattern and instead look at what the literature tells us about what men do, individually and collectively, such that women as a group are subordinated to men as a group and such that some men are subordinated to others. This is meant to reassert the importance of studying practices and processes. Our approach accords with current sociological theory that sees gender not as an attribute of individuals but as the name we give to cultural practices that construct women and men as different and that advantage men at the expense of women (Lorber 1994, Martin 2003, West & Zimmerman 1987). We thus focus primarily on qualitative studies that provide insight into how males construct the category "men" and themselves as its members.[1]

---

[1]We focus primarily on qualitative research for three reasons: (*a*) Qualitative methods are those most often used in studies of masculinity; (*b*) survey-based approaches tend to reify masculinity, treating it as a static psychological trait; and (*c*) qualitative methods provide the best insight into how men present themselves as gendered beings (which is our concern here). Though beyond the scope of this paper, sociologists interested in methodological dilemmas that arise when conducting qualitative research on men have a burgeoning literature to draw on (see, for example, Butera 2006, Gatrell 2006, Hearn 2007, Messner 1990, Schwalbe & Wolkomir 2001, Schacht 1997).

Definitions

Much of the contention and confusion in the field stems from vague definitions of key concepts, inconsistent use of key concepts, or both. Although it is impossible to impose, post hoc, a set of definitions on a body of literature, it is possible to offer a set of definitions that can be used to interpret the literature. Our definitions are anchored in a social construction-ist perspective, and as such might not be congenial to all. Definitions are necessary, however, for any attempt at sense-making and for sorting out disagreements. So we begin with the basics: males, men, and masculinity.

Based on differences in reproductive anatomy, humans are sorted into the categories "male" and "female," reflecting a belief that males and females are or should become different kinds of people. Males are taught and expected to identify themselves not only as biological males, but, depending on age, as either boys or men. Females are taught and expected to iden-tify themselves not only as biological females, but, depending on age, as either girls or women. This distinction between reproductive anatomy and gender identity is crucial for understanding what men are and how to study them.

In this view, the category "males" is not equivalent to the category "men." Men are (usu-ally) biological males claiming rights and privileges attendant to membership in the domi-nant gender group. For an individual male to enjoy the benefits that derive from membership in the dominant gender group, he must present himself to others as a particular kind of social being: a man. This is, as Goffman (1977) and West & Zimmerman (1987) remind us, a dra-maturgical task. To be credited as a man, what an individual male must do, in other words, is put on a convincing manhood act (Schwalbe 2005). This requires mastering a set of conven-tional signifying practices through which the identity "man" is established and upheld in interaction.

The dramaturgical task of establishing creditability as a man and thus as a member of the dominant gender group is aided by having a male body. Because of the conventional asso-ciation between maleness and manhood, a male body is a symbolic asset. It is normally taken as a sign of qualification for membership in the category "men." However, it is neither neces-sary (females can mask their secondary sex characteristics, appear to be male, and attempt to put on a manhood act; see, e.g., Dozier 2005) nor sufficient (males can fail to muster the other signifiers necessary to establish themselves as creditable men worthy of full manhood status).

Distinguishing between sex and gender is conventional wisdom in sociology, yet the dis-tinction is worth reiterating, as it remains common to mistake males for men. Even more trouble arises in defining masculinity. Carrigan et al. (1985; see also Connell 1995) define masculinity as a "configuration of practices"—practices that have the effect of subordinating women. Although this definition usefully highlights what men do to maintain dominance, it is not without problems. It is not clear, for instance, precisely which of men's practices con-stitute masculinity (Martin 1998). The definition also tends to take the category "men" for granted, rather than treating the category as constructed by practices and the meanings given to those practices.

To avoid this problem, our definitional strategy is to say that males—if they are to do their part in maintaining men as the dominant gender group and if they wish to enjoy the privileges that come from membership in that group—must signify possession of a masculine self. This self is, however, only a virtual reality, a dramatic effect, or a consequence of how an actor's appearance and behavior are interpreted by others (Goffman 1959). In this view, as opposed to the commonsense view, a masculine self is not a psychological entity, nor a built-in feature of male bodies. It is, rather, a self imputed to an individual based on information given and given off in interaction, but it is an imputation that matters greatly.

The qualities seen as constituting a masculine self can vary historically and culturally. The practices that are interpreted as signs of a masculine self can also vary depending on other features of the actor (age, race, ethnicity, class), the audience, and the situation. In Western cultures, and in the contemporary United States especially, the essential element is a capacity to exert control or to resist being controlled (Johnson 2005). To elicit the attribution of possessing a masculine self thus requires signifying—with or without conscious awareness—that one possesses the capacities to make things happen and to resist being dominated by others.

Two further notes may be helpful here. First, to observe that males strive to claim membership in the dominant gender category by signifying a masculine self is not a moral critique. All humans learn where they are supposed to fit in a set of preexisting cultural categories, some of which are hierarchically arranged. So just as North Americans of European descent learn to think of and present themselves as white, which is the dominant racial category in U.S. culture, males learn to think of and present themselves as men, which is the dominant gender category. The root of the problem, then, if one opposes racial or gender inequality, lies in a system of privilege, not in individuals. Examining how gender is interactionally constructed, as many scholars have done and as we do here, is a matter of trying to understand how the system is reproduced, not a matter of leveling moral judgment.

Second, we acknowledge that efforts to exert control over the environment—efforts that might be part of manhood acts—can yield positive results. Survival and the quality of human life indeed depend on controlling things in the world. Thus, it is not our claim that attempts to signify a masculine self through acts of control have nothing but oppressive consequences. Our claim is that, whatever other consequences they might have, and regardless of what individual males consciously intend, manhood acts have the effect of reproducing an unequal gender order. Again, the point of taking this analytic view is not to evaluate categories of actors but to arrive at a better understanding of how the gender order works.

Problems with Plurality

Current thinking in the field treats masculinity not as singular but as plural. There is not just one form of masculinity, it is said, but rather there are multiple masculinities. This notion grew out of the distinction between hegemonic masculinity—the kind of manhood act most revered in a culture (Connell 1987, 1995, 2000)—and lower-status ways that manhood is enacted by males with fewer resources. Thinking of masculinity as plural usefully sensitizes us to differences and inequalities among groups of men, but it can also make it hard to see what it is that masculinities have in common, other than enactment by male bodies. We propose that the common theme should be seen not as a type of body but as a type of act: one that signifies a masculine self.

The multiple masculinities concept reflects a laudable desire to value diversity. It is ironic, then, that this concept has fostered a kind of categorical essentialism in studies of men. To invoke, for example, the existence of Black masculinity, Latino masculinity, gay masculinity, Jewish masculinity, working-class masculinity, and so on is to imply that there is an overriding similarity in the gender enactments of males who are Black, Latino, gay, Jewish, or working class. The implicit claim is that all members of the category practice an identifiably unique form of masculinity. This strategy of using conventional categories of race, ethnicity, sexuality, religion, or class to define masculinities into existence is dubious. It can cause us to lose sight of what these allegedly diverse gender-signifying practices have in common (again, other than enactment by male bodies) that makes them masculinity. It can also obscure important within-group variations.

The discourse of multiple masculinities has also had the effect of detaching men from their actions. Despite the ritual defining of masculinities as forms of practice, it is not uncommon to see masculinity invoked to explain men's behavior, as if masculinity were an independent variable that caused men to behave in more or less oppressive ways. This is, as some have pointed out (e.g., MacInnes 1998), circular. If the behavior in question—some form of practice being studied—is what constitutes masculinity, then masculinity cannot be used to explain that behavior. Attributing men's behavior to masculinity also tends to discount men's agency. Our preference for referring to manhood acts arises from a desire to discourage the reification of masculinity and to redirect analytic attention to what males actually do to achieve dominance.

All manhood acts, as we define them, are aimed at claiming privilege, eliciting deference, and resisting exploitation. As suggested earlier, body types are irrelevant, except inasmuch as a male body is a symbolic asset and a female body a liability, when trying to signify possession of a masculine self and put on a convincing manhood act. The view we take here also focuses attention on what males do to create, maintain, and claim membership in a dominant gender group. Our organization and discussion of the literature reflects this concern with practices and processes. We thus turn to considering what the literature tells us about (*a*) how males learn to signify masculine selves, (*b*) themes and variations in the construction of manhood acts, and (*c*) how manhood acts reproduce gender inequality.

Learning to Signify Masculine Selves

Children are born into a world in which males/boys/men are differentiated from females/girls/women. Children must learn to categorize themselves and others in these terms and learn to convey to others that they understand this system of categorization and their place within it. For young males, this means learning to identify themselves as boys and signify masculine selves. They must master, in other words, the "identity codes" (Schwalbe & Mason-Schrock 1996) that are symbolic constituents of the gender order. A great deal of research has examined how this aspect of symbolic culture is learned through childhood interaction and through exposure to media imagery.

Young males' initial adoption of the identity "boy" is micropolitical. Based on 18 months of fieldwork at a preschool, Cahill (1986) found that children and adults use the term "baby" to stigmatize children's socially immature behavior, whereas they reward more mature acts by bestowing the term "boy" or "girl." Such responses do not merely affirm that males are boys and females are girls. More than this, such responses link grown-up status and approval from others with doing gender properly.

Young males also learn that gender identities are signified by using appropriate props. Initially, much of this identity work is done by parents, as newborns and toddlers are equipped with gendered names, clothes, and toys (Pomerleau et al. 1990). Preschool boys who fail to grasp the pattern and wear dresses or pink ribbons are scolded by their peers for misbehavior (Cahill 1989). Based on 42 interviews with diverse parents of preschoolers, Kane (2006) shows that parents—especially heterosexual fathers—often censure preschool sons who play with Barbies or wear fingernail polish or pink clothing. Such policing leads young males to, as Cahill (1989, p. 290) put it, "reject and devalue . . . symbols of female identity" in order to "confirm their identities as boys."

Boys and girls are often sorted or, later, sort themselves into segregated groups. Lever's (1978) field study of 181 fifth graders revealed how girls tend to play in small groups that stress cooperation and intimacy, whereas boys play in larger groups that are more competitive, goal-directed, and rule-guided. Even when boys and girls play together, they often do so in ways that imply essential differences between boys and girls and, usually, the superiority of boys (Thorne 1993). Lever argues that this gender-segregated play can lead to differential skill development that may account for some gender inequality among adults. Our point is that participation in segregated activities comes to be understood as part of how gender identities are signified. Playing or watching sports—violent sports in particular (McBride 1995)—can thus be a way for boys and men to signify masculine selves (Messner 1992).

Another lesson for young males is that emotional display must be regulated, lest it undermine a manhood act. In their ethnographic study of a summer camp, McGuffey & Rich (1999) found that high-status boys ostracized boys who cried. Males involved in sports similarly police the expression of emotion, affirming the principle that boys should not express fear or pain (Curry 1993, Messner 1992). Parents are often complicit in this gendered training because they feel accountable—for their sons' behavior—to other adults (Kane 2006). Parents who believe that their son's masculinity is threatened may be especially inclined to encourage stoicism. For example, during one of McGuffey's (2008, p. 212) 389 interviews with 62 parents of sexually abused sons, one father said of his victimized son, "He's already been made into a woman sexually. I can't let him turn into one emotionally, too!"

Boys also learn that they should feel, or at least express, sexual desire for girls. Among preadolescent and adolescent boys, this desire is signified mainly through talk about the sexual appeal of girls and women, through sharing pin-ups and pornography, and by presenting themselves as heterosexually active and knowledgeable (Fine 1987, Thorne 1993). As Pascoe (2007, p. 114) documented in her ethnography of a high school, boys use language and sometimes violence to turn girls and women into props for signifying heterosexuality. The boys she studied sexually harassed girls with unwanted comments and touching, and talked and joked about rape (see also Renold 2007). Boys' homophobic taunting of other boys who are deemed feminine is also a means of signifying heterosexuality (Pascoe 2007).

One of the most important lessons about signifying manhood concerns aggression and violence. Young boys' play often reflects popular warrior narratives in which violence is "legitimate and justified when it occurs within a struggle between good and evil" (Jordan & Cowan 1995, p. 728). Fathers and older male relatives often encourage (subtly, if not overtly) boys to fight, and reward them for doing so (Athens 1992, Messerschmidt 2000). The importance of signifying manhood through displays of fighting spirit is reinforced in sports, as coaches and teammates celebrate aggressive play while demeaning nonaggressive play as feminine (Fine 1987, Messner 1992). The pervasiveness of bullying has been attributed to this valorization of aggression and violence (Phillips 2007). A common cultural script also portrays effective resistance to bullying as a way to assert a masculine self (Kimmel & Mahler 2003).

Learning to signify a masculine self entails learning how to adjust to audiences and situations and learning how one's other identities bear on the acceptability of a performance. Males in marginalized social groups may face special challenges in this regard (Majors & Billson 1992, Staples 1982). Research on schools shows that teachers and administrators often stereotype African American and Latino boys as unruly, prompting increased surveillance and discipline (Ferguson 2000, Morris 2005). Boys learn, however, that they can impress peers if they break rules, talk back to teachers, and disdain academics (Ferguson 2000, Fordham & Ogbu 1986, Mac an Ghaill 1994, Willis 1977). Boys socialized into urban gangs (Stretesky & Pogrebin 2007) or white supremacist groups (Kimmel 2007) learn that they can achieve manhood status through actual or symbolic acts of intimidation. The lesson—for boys who are marginalized because of class or race—is that a masculine self can be signified, and deference elicited, by evoking fear in others.

The process of learning how to signify a masculine self in situationally appropriate ways continues throughout life. Men in manual labor jobs may learn that signifying a masculine self requires displays of strength and endurance, as well as resistance to being bossed (Collinson 1992). Men training for professional jobs, such as students in traditional MBA programs (Sinclair 1995), learn to signify masculine selves by appearing to be instrumentally oriented, rational, and able to manage subordinates. Men in the military learn that toughness, in-group loyalty, and the sexual objectification of women are the marks of manhood (Higate 2007). Men entering new jobs must thus learn to signify masculine selves in ways that accord with the organization's culture and gender politics.

Media Imagery

Media imagery provides a repertoire of signifying practices that males can draw on to craft manhood acts. For example, in their fieldwork studies, Dyson (1994) shows how boys in elementary school enact superhero narratives, and Milkie (1994) shows how middle school boys discuss, identify with, exaggerate, and imitate the male heroes of Hollywood movies.

More is learned, however, than simply which models to emulate or how to do so. Media imagery also provides a shared symbolic language for identifying certain practices as signs of masculine character.

Research on children's media reveals that it often glorifies men's power. Hamilton et al. (2006) analyzed 200 of the most popular children's books and found that male characters were typically portrayed as assertive and aggressive, rarely nurturing, and more likely than female characters to work outside the home. Research on educational software for preschool children (Sheldon 2004) and comic books (Pecora 1992) similarly finds that male characters are more likely than female characters to be athletic, aggressive, and heroic. Similarly, grade school texts still overwhelmingly depict males as argumentative and competitive (Evans & Davies 2000). And whereas video games depict female characters as "victims or sexual objects," they portray male characters as "heroes and violent perpetrators" (Dietz 1998, p. 438). A lesson conveyed by much of this children's media is thus that males naturally command the attention and deference of others by virtue of their greater strength, daring, and capacity for violence.

Media targeting adolescent and adult men also create signifiers of masculine selves. Popular low-brow men's magazines (e.g., *Stuff, Maxim*) root manhood in displays of heterosexual appetite and virtuosity (Ezzell 2008, Taylor 2005). As McCaughey (2008) shows, popular culture often frames men's sexual infidelity and violence against women as biologically determined and thus inevitable. In mainstream magazines aimed at male audiences, men are most often portrayed as at work (Vigorito & Curry 1998), thus affirming productivity and breadwinning as signs of a masculine self. Even television portrayals that depart from these stereotypes, such as news stories about "Mr. Moms," typically underscore heterosexuality as a sign of genuine manhood beneath a veneer of domesticity (Vavrus 2002). The theme of the peaceful, gentle male who turns into a death-dealing warrior after suffering an unbearable outrage has been recycled often in Hollywood films (Sparks 1996). Such imagery affirms the value of a male body as a baseline signifier of a masculine self.

Media imagery also shapes the value of other signifiers. Males in marginalized groups are often represented in derogatory ways. White working-class men are often portrayed on television as "dumb, immature, irresponsible, or lacking in common sense" (Butsch 2003, p. 576). Gay men, although less disparaged in recent years, are often shown as acceptable targets of others' disapproval (Linneman 2008). Black men are often portrayed as lazy, violent, criminal, hypersexual, or naturally athletic (Entman & Rojecki 2000). Latinos too are often depicted as criminal or as illegal immigrants who cause social problems (Dixon & Linz 2002). Arab men are often depicted as decadent sheiks, religious fanatics, or terrorists (Shaheen 2001). Such imagery implicitly affirms the hegemonic ideal as white, monied, and self-possessed. It also provides symbolic resources for crafting conformist and oppositional presentations of masculine selves.

Manhood Acts: Themes and Variations

All manhood acts imply a claim to membership in the privileged gender group. To present one's self as a man is to make this claim, whether the presentation emphasizes or deemphasizes the capacity to exert control. As this point suggests and as research has shown, males can construct and present themselves as men in various ways. It is this variation that has come to be taken as evidence of multiple masculinities. A concern that has guided much research in this genre is for showing how males compensate—that is, how they modify their manhood acts—when they are unable or unwilling to enact the hegemonic ideal.

Research on transsexuals is particularly instructive. These studies have shown how adults must relearn to use their bodies, clothing, speech, and gestures to signify alternate gender identities. Female-to-male transsexuals, or transmen, flatten their chests, take hormones to grow facial hair and muscle tissue, deepen their voices, and cultivate gestures (e.g., giving firm handshakes) to publicly claim their chosen identities as men (Dozier 2005, Johnson 2007).

Transwomen likewise mask secondary sex characteristics through surgery, makeup, and vocal alteration and adopt submissive gestures and speech styles (Schrock et al. 2005). Being identified as a member of a gender category, these studies show, depends on mastering the requisite bodily, gestural, sartorial, and vocal signifiers.

Research on transsexuals also shows how the elicitation of deference depends on the type of man one is perceived to be. Based on in-depth interviews with 29 transmen, Schilt (2006) found that whereas white transmen beginning to work as men were taken more seriously, had their requests readily met, and were evaluated as more competent than they were as women, young, small Black, Latino, and Asian transmen did not gain similar advantages. Similarly, in her interview study of 18 transmen, Dozier (2005) found that, as men, white transmen reported being given more respect and more conversational space and being included in men's banter. They also experienced less public harassment. Transmen of color, on the other hand, reported being more frequently treated as criminals, and short and effeminate transmen reported being publicly harassed as gay. Gaining the full privileges of manhood is thus shown to depend not merely on being recognized as male, but on the whole ensemble of signs that are conventionally taken as evidence of a masculine self.

The multiple masculinities concept, despite its problems, has been helpful for seeing how various groups of men, using the material and symbolic resources available to them, are able to emphasize different aspects of the hegemonic ideal as means to construct effective manhood acts. For men in heterosexual relationships, occupational status and income are particularly important for eliciting deference from their partners. Middle- and upper-middle-class men can invoke job demands to avoid childcare and housework (Hochschild 1989, Pyke 1996). Based on 70 in-depth interviews with divorced and remarried men and women, Pyke (1996) showed that middle-class women's deference stems from accepting the idea that men's careers are primary. Even when women earn more than men, women "often defer to their husbands in the decision-making process" to affirm the belief that men should be in control (Tichenor 2005, p. 200). When the male is the primary breadwinner, the threat of leaving can also be used to leverage deference, as Ortiz (2006) showed in his interview-based study of 48 wives of professional athletes.

Men with fewer economic resources may use other strategies to maintain relationship control. Research shows a pattern of more frequent use of overtly coercive behavior, including verbal abuse and physical force, among poor and working-class men (Benson et al. 2004, Pyke 1996, Strauss et al. 1980). Based on in-depth interviews with 122 batterers, Cavanagh and associates (2001) show that males are more likely to be violent when they see their female partners as insufficiently submissive and not servicing their emotional and sexual desires (see also Hearn 1998). Men of all social classes may also use emotional withdrawal as a control strategy (Sattel 1976). The status of being the dominant partner can thus be achieved in different ways. Lacking one kind of resource for eliciting deference often leads to employing another kind of resource in exaggerated fashion. It is also worth noting that no control strategy is guaranteed to succeed.

Close attention to how manhood acts are actually performed shows variation in response to situations. Men in management positions, for example, can use institutional authority to elicit deference, but they must also demonstrate the qualities of rationality, resolve, and competitiveness (Collinson & Hearn 1994), and show loyalty to the male hierarchy (Jackall 1988, Martin 2001). They may sometimes adopt a paternalistic demeanor, playing the role of benevolent guide, and at other times use humiliation and threats (Kerfoot & Whitehead 1998). Professional men may also demonstrate capability by emphasizing their special knowledge (Haas & Shaffir 1977). And as Dellinger (2004) shows in her comparative ethnography of organizations that produce feminist and pornographic magazines, organizational culture influences how men present themselves at work. Manhood acts are thus strategically adapted to the realities of resource availability, individual skill, local culture, and audience expectations.

Manhood acts often entail the sexualization of women as a way to signify heterosexuality, to demarcate gender boundaries, and to challenge women's authority. A great deal of research has looked at how this occurs in workplaces (Prokos & Padavic 2002, Quinn 2002, Uggen & Blackstone 2004). Although the targets of gratuitous sexualization and harassment are often women of lower status, men also sexualize and harass women who are organizational superiors (Rospenda et al. 1998). The same phenomena can be found outside the workplace (Grazian 2007, Schacht 1996). Sexualizing women serves not only to signify heterosexuality and mark the boundary between gender groups, but it also protects males from homophobic abuse by their peers.

Men who publicly identify as gay reject heterosexuality as part of their manhood acts, yet the power of the hegemonic ideal is reflected in the creation of gay male subcultures that valorize large bodies and muscularity (Hennen 2005), sexual risk-taking and voracity (Green & Halkitis 2006), and macho fashion (Mosher et al. 2006). The subtext of these signifying acts can be read as, "Despite conventional societal standards by which we would be judged unmanly, we are indeed men and thus deserving of manhood status." Feminist analysts have suggested that misogyny among some gay men is similarly related to a desire on the part of gay men to distance themselves from women and retain a grip on male privilege (Frye 1983).

Research on men in low-status jobs shows another form of compensation: Instead of trying to control others, these men try to show that they cannot be controlled. These manhood acts rely on joking, verbal jousting, sexist talk, and sometimes sabotage to assert autonomy vis-à-vis bosses (Collinson 1992). Resistance may be heightened when men are expected to perform tasks conventionally associated with women. As Henson & Rogers (2001, p. 233) found when conducting participation observation and in-depth interviews with 68 male temporary clerical workers in Chicago and Los Angeles, despite their relative powerlessness in the workplace, the men resisted "demands for deference [such as] smiling, waiting, taking orders, and tolerating the bad moods of their supervisors." And, as Leidner (1993) shows in her field study of insurance salesmen, when work requires interactional deference with customers, the interaction is redefined as a contest for control so that men will be willing to do it.

The hegemonic ideal pervades the culture and sets a standard against which all manhood acts are measured. Because it is impossible, however, for all men to meet the hegemonic ideal, adjustments must be made, not only individually, but also subculturally. We thus find some working-class men creating bar and music cultures in which they signify masculine selves through heavy drinking and aggressive posturing (Eastman & Schrock 2008, Tilki 2006); economically marginalized men of color relying on sports, fighting, and sexual conquests (Anderson 1999, Wacquant 2003); college men turning to binge drinking and high-risk behavior (Peralta 2007); and others using crime to show that they are fearless and indomitable (Messerschmidt 1993).

Research on male subcultures has documented both wide variation in what are defined as signifiers of a masculine self and consistency in what it means to possess such a self. For example, the politically liberal, middle-class white males who populated the mythopoetic men's movement of the 1990s drew on Jungian psychology to redefine qualities conventionally associated with women—emotional expressivity, nurturance, and gentleness—as evidence of the "deep masculine" residing within all men (Schwalbe 1996). Likewise, the politically conservative Promise Keepers drew on Christian theology to validate similar qualities as masculine (Newton 2005). In both cases, however, the claim was that whereas the masculine self might need cultivation, it is naturally present in males, and its other elements—strength, courage, fierceness, and willingness to sacrifice—suit males to being warriors, leaders, and benevolent fathers.

Subcultural and historical variation in how manhood acts are performed demonstrates the fluidity of what are defined as signifiers of manhood (Kimmel 1996). Variation also arises because not all males are equally well equipped—by virtue of body type, skill, or social location—to enact the locally prevailing hegemonic ideal, thus making compensation and improvisation necessary. There remains, nonetheless, a common theme: the desire to claim an identity as a member of the privileged gender group, a desire that can be satisfied only by putting on a creditable manhood act. In competitive, hierarchical societies, especially those that are classically or vestigially patriarchal, this means signifying a capacity to exert control over one's self, the environment, and others.

The Reproduction of Gender Inequality

The original impetus for studying masculinity was to better understand the reproduction of gender inequality. Carrigan et al. (1985) were expressly concerned with masculinity as configurations of practice that have the effect of subordinating women. More recently, however, some theorists have retreated from the idea that masculinity necessarily produces inequality (see Connell & Messerschmidt 2005, p. 853). Other gender theorists have questioned the detachment of masculinity from gender inequality (Hanmer 1990, Flood 2002, Hearn 2004), arguing that the study of masculinity must remain part of a feminist project aimed at ending men's domination of women.

One reason for the loss of connection to the issue of gender inequality may be the success of the multiple masculinities concept. Eager embrace of this concept led researchers to document the diverse ways males style themselves as men, but with a loss of attention to what these styles have in common. Partly in response to this development, more critically inclined gender scholars (e.g., Jeffreys 2005, McCarry 2007) have urged a shift from the endless cataloging of masculinities to examining *how men's practices create inequality*. This is the path we take in this review. In keeping with the terms set out earlier, we consider what the literature tells us about the consequences of the practices we call manhood acts.

Differentiation is, before all else, basic to the creation and reproduction of gender inequality (Lorber 1994). Manhood acts are how males distinguish themselves from females/women and thus establish their eligibility for gender-based privilege. Indeed, the existence of the category "men" depends on the collective performance and affirmation of manhood acts. And, as argued earlier, successful manhood acts elicit deference from others in concrete situations. In these ways, manhood acts are inherently about upholding patriarchy and reproducing gender inequality. We can, however, look at research that shows how specific elements of manhood acts operate to advantage men at women's expense.

In the workplace, occupational segregation depends, first, on the manhood acts that make it possible to identify and channel different kinds of people toward different kinds of jobs (Reskin 1988). Manhood acts also have the effect of legitimating occupational segregation by upholding the illusion that men are more fit for certain kinds of jobs, especially those that involve the exercise of command. As Jackall's (1988) field study of corporate managers shows, managers must cultivate images of themselves as winners, as able to "get the job done," and as morally flexible and emotionally tough. Among defense intellectuals, a manhood act that features cold rationality may be necessary to be taken seriously (Cohn 1987). Men in some female-dominated occupations are put on a "glass escalator" toward greater authority and reward (Cognard-Black 2004, Williams 1992), whereas others are segregated horizontally in more highly valued specialties (Snyder & Green 2008, Williams 1992). Putting on a manhood act is part of how one establishes similarity to those already at the top of the hierarchy and gets through what others experience as a glass ceiling (Kanter 1977). And to the extent that jobs are designed by those who imagine the ideal occupant to be a male who fits the hegemonic ideal, those whose manhood acts come closest to the ideal are likely to be advantaged (Acker 1990).

Striving to emulate the hegemonic ideal may serve one well when seeking managerial power, but even compensatory manhood acts can make a difference for obtaining economic rewards. If the hegemonic ideal is out of dramaturgical reach, it may be possible to craft a manhood act that emphasizes self-sacrificial endurance to achieve organizational goals. Cooper (2000) shows how this was the case for the 20 computer programmers she interviewed. Much like athletes who signify a masculine self through a willingness to suffer pain

(Curry 1993), these programmers claimed manhood status by practicing "nerd masculinity" that involved suffering long hours of work to meet production goals and to establish a reputation for unique expertise.

In the political sphere, manhood acts approximating the hegemonic ideal may be crafted to achieve or consolidate power (Messner 2007). In the case of the presidency, the act must also serve an iconic function for the nation; that is, the act must represent the collectively imagined, idealized character of the nation (Hall 1979). George W. Bush, for example, refashioned his persona after the 2001 terrorist attacks to underscore his self-proclaimed role as a "war president" leading a great and powerful nation (Coe et al. 2007). Disrespecting the manhood acts of political opponents is also common. During the 2004 U.S. presidential election, the Bush campaign and much of the media framed the losing Democratic candidate, John Kerry, as feminine and French-like (Fahey 2007). Inasmuch as manhood acts are conducive to achieving positions of power—by eliciting deference over the course of a career of status-seeking—and inasmuch as executive positions are reserved for those who can serve as icons of collective power (whether of the corporation or the nation), gender inequality will be the outcome. Women who vie with men for such positions are often compelled to put on a compensatory manhood act or, as it is sometimes said, to "out-macho the boys."

Research on men in social movements, as noted in the previous section, shows that manhood acts often involve collaboration among men. This is true more generally. Even men who reject hegemonic ideals may feel compelled, when in all-male groups, to appear emotionally detached, competitive, and willing to objectify women (Bird 1996). In college fraternities, young men mutually affirm their manhood by collectively defining women as "servers" and as sexual "bait" or "prey" (Martin & Hummer 1989). In cases where men's oppressive behavior is challenged, such as batterer intervention programs (Schrock & Padavic 2007) or prison antiviolence groups (Fox 1999), men often collaborate to outwit social workers and assert a right to control women. Inequality is thus reproduced when males uncritically affirm oppressive elements of other males' manhood acts or conspire to resist challenges to those acts.

Eliciting deference by signifying a capacity to dominate can also affect the division of domestic labor. This is not to say that manhood acts always elicit compliance from female partners when the division of domestic labor is being negotiated. The acts that matter most may be those performed in the public sphere. When a manhood act yields career success, this may tip the balance of power in the household. Gender inequality created through manhood acts in the workplace can thus be translated into gender inequality—in terms of decision-making power and work distribution—within the home (Coltrane 2000). In some cases, a lack of power in the public sphere might lead to a compensatory manhood act in the home, an act that involves a refusal to do what is defined as women's work (Brines 1994). Compensatory manhood acts might also involve the use of violence to subjugate female partners (Hearn 1998).

As noted earlier, manhood acts that involve displays of heterosexual appetite and prowess often entail the sexual objectification and harassment of women. In these acts, which are often competitive and tend to escalate (Quinn 2002), women become props that men use to affirm a heterosexual identity. Gender inequality is reproduced when sexual harassment, or the threat thereof, limits women's public mobility (Gardner 1995) or undermines perceptions of women's competence as workers and professionals (Padavic & Reskin 2002). Sexual activity undertaken as part of a manhood act may also result in unwanted pregnancies that decrease young women's chances for upward mobility (Anderson 1999).[2] Even after relationships end,

---

[2]There is, of course, more to fatherhood than our brief treatment implies. Whereas our concern is mainly with fatherhood as it relates to manhood acts and the reproduction of gender inequality, others have examined the complexities of fatherhood in considerable depth. For examples, see Gavanas (2004), LaRossa (1996), and Marsiglio & Hutchinson (2002).

males may signify their uncontrollability by refusing to pay alimony and child support (Arendell 1992), acts that hurt exes economically.

Claiming a heterosexual identity as part of a manhood act may also involve homophobic taunting, especially among boys and young men. As Pascoe (2007) shows, high school boys use "fag" as an epithet to police the boundaries of acceptable manhood acts (see also Mac an Ghaill 1994). The same phenomenon has been observed among prison inmates (Thurston 1996), mental hospital patients (Leyser 2003), and athletes (Anderson 2002). Whereas this taunting mainly establishes a hierarchy among boys and men, it also reinforces sexist ideology, because the implicit insult is that a man who wants to have sex with men is like a woman—which is to say, less than a man. Homophobic taunting thus helps reproduce gender inequality by devaluing women.

Individual Liabilities and Gender-Class Advantages

The consequences of manhood acts for the reproduction of gender inequality can be contradictory. Men as a gender class can benefit from the collective upholding of sexist ideology and of images of males as possessing essential qualities that suit them for the exercise of power. Yet compensatory manhood acts can sometimes reproduce inequalities in ways that disadvantage subgroups of men. For example, a number of studies (e.g., Willis 1977, MacLeod 1995, Anderson 1999) have shown how self-protective displays of toughness by poor and working-class young men lead to disinvestment in academic work and failure in school. Young men may also distance themselves from intellectual work, which is defined as feminine, and embrace physical work, which is defined as masculine, and thus limit their chances for upward mobility via success in school (Fine et al. 1997).

Beyond school, compensatory manhood acts can undermine employment relationships. Young men who signify a capacity to resist control by others may find it difficult to get and hold jobs in the mainstream economy (Bourgois 1995). The use of crime to signify a masculine self carries the risk of getting caught and losing opportunities for conventional economic success (Messerschmidt 1993). Compensatory manhood acts that are adaptive in some contexts can thus be self-destructive in others. Much depends on who is presenting what kind of masculine self to whom and under what conditions. This suggests a need to examine how the consequences of manhood acts are shaped by racism and the class structure.

Whereas manhood acts that emphasize the defiance of authority can undermine the mobility prospects of individual men, men as a gender class may continue to enjoy privilege because of the collective image fostered by manhood acts that involve crime, violence, and interpersonal intimidation. (The use of state violence in manhood acts undertaken by elite males is also consequential in this regard.) To the extent that such acts imply the innate dangerousness of males, women may feel compelled to seek protection from males deemed safe—protection for which they exchange subservience (Schwalbe et al. 2000, pp. 426–27). Nonviolent males can thus derive privilege from the violent manhood acts of other males.

Males can also incur health damage as a consequence of manhood acts. Research has linked men's higher rates of morbidity and mortality to failure to seek help early (O'Brien et al. 2005); to higher levels of risk-taking behavior, including drinking, smoking, and reckless driving (Verbrugge 1985); and to poor social support networks (House et al. 1988). Men's sports injuries, death by violence, and suicide have also been linked to gender enactment (Sabo 2005). As with crime, much of this health-damaging behavior may be symbolic, intended to signify capacities to control one's own life, to be invulnerable and needless of help, and to be fearless and hence not easily intimidated by others. The effort to signify a masculine self, as some analysts have suggested (Courtenay 2000), can be toxic.

Conclusion

The trends noted at the outset of this review continue apace. Research continues in the men-and-(fill in the blank) pattern. New studies regularly appear that examine masculinity in still more contexts. Although these traditions of research have produced a considerable body of knowledge about the diversity of men's behavior, there has been a tendency to lose sight of the goals of trying to understand (*a*) the social construction of gender in general and (*b*) the reproduction of gender inequality. We have suggested that these problems stem in part from a tendency to reify masculinity, to erroneously see it as an essential quality of male bodies, and to treat it as if it had explanatory power.

Moving forward will require, we have suggested, reclaiming and revamping some of the basic insights of a critical sociology of gender that emphasizes practices and processes. This means maintaining distinctions between anatomy, sex and gender categories, and the identity work that both locates individuals within categories and reproduces the categories themselves. Documenting and analyzing manhood acts—the identity work that males do to claim membership in the dominant gender group, to affirm the social reality of the group, to elicit deference from others, and to maintain privileges vis-à-vis women—may prove to be more useful, we have argued, than merely cataloging more masculinities.

Refocusing our attention on practices and processes—those constitutive of what we have called manhood acts—can generate new empirical challenges. Future research might examine, for example, how males use the interaction order collaboratively to construct manhood acts, how they police and support each other's acts, and how they create and share the material and symbolic resources that enable various kinds of manhood acts. This would mean studying how manhood acts are both institutionalized and, in the face of changing conditions and threats to male supremacy, improvised. Further investigation into how subjectivity is conditioned—that is, how habits of thought and feeling are formed by and implicated in manhood acts—would also be useful.

Another challenge is to examine how the elicitation of deference in face-to-face interaction produces large-scale patterns of male domination. Such research might examine, for example, how manhood acts play a part in network formation and in maintaining regimes of organizational control. Media studies are another avenue for research, especially if attention is shifted from the consumption of images to examining how manhood acts are implicated in the production of gendered images. There is, finally, a need to study both individual and collective resistance to manhood acts, no matter who performs them, presuming an enduring concern with understanding the social processes through which gender inequality can be overcome.

Disclosure Statement

The authors are not aware of any biases that might be perceived as affecting the objectivity of this review.

Acknowledgments

The authors wish to thank Jeff Hearn, Daphne Holden, Sherryl Kleinman, Patricia Yancey Martin, and Christian Vaccaro for helpful comments on an earlier draft.

Literature Cited

Acker J. 1990. Hierarchies, jobs, bodies: a theory of gendered organizations. *Gend. Soc.* 4:139–58.

Anderson E. 1999. *Code of the Street: Decency, Violence, and the Moral Life of the Inner City*. New York: W.W. Norton.

Anderson ED. 2002. Openly gay athletes: contesting hegemonic masculinity in a homophobic environment. *Gend. Soc.* 16:860–77.

Arendell T. 1992. After divorce: investigations into father absence. *Gend. Soc.* 6:562–86.

Athens L. 1992. *The Creation of Dangerous Violent Criminals*. Urbana: Univ. Ill. Press.

Benson ML, Wooldredge J, Thistlethwaite AB. 2004. The correlation between race and domestic violence is confounded with community context. *Soc. Probl.* 51:326–42.

Bird SR. 1996. Welcome to the men's club: homosociality and the maintenance of hegemonic masculinity. *Gend. Soc.* 10:120–32.

Bourgois P. 1995. *In Search of Respect: Selling Crack in El Barrio*. Cambridge, UK: Cambridge Univ. Press.

Brines J. 1994. Economic dependency, gender, and the division-of-labor at home. *Am. J. Sociol.* 100:652–88.

Butera KJ. 2006. Manhunt: the challenge of enticing men to participate in a study on friendship. *Qual. Inq.* 12:1262–82.

Butsch R. 2003. Ralph, Fred, Archie and Homer: why television keeps recreating the white male working class buffoon. In *Gender, Race, and Class in the Media*, ed. G Dines, JM Humez, pp. 575–88. Thousand Oaks, CA: Sage.

Cahill SE. 1986. Language practices and self definition: the case of gender identity acquisition. *Sociol. Q.* 27:295–311.

Cahill SE. 1989. Fashioning males and females: appearance management and the social reproduction of gender. *Symb. Interact.* 12:281–98.

Carrigan T, Connell B, Lee J. 1985. Toward a new sociology of masculinity. *Theory Soc.* 14:551–604.

Cavanagh K, Dobash RE, Dobash RP, Lewis R. 2001. "Remedial work": men's strategic responses to their violence against intimate female partners. *Sociology* 35:695–714.

Clatterbaugh K. 1996. *Contemporary Perspectives on Masculinity: Men, Women and Politics in Modern Society*. Boulder, CO: Westview.

Coe K, Domke D, Bagley MM, Cunningham S, Van Leuven N. 2007. Masculinity as political strategy: George W. Bush, the "war on terrorism," and an echoing press. *J. Women Polit. Policy* 29:31–55.

Cognard-Black AJ. 2004. Will they stay, or will they go? Sex-atypical work among token men who teach. *Sociol. Q.* 45:113–39.

Cohn C. 1987. Sex and death in the rational world of defense intellectuals. *Signs.* 12:687–718.

Collinson D, Hearn J. 1994. Naming men as men: implications for work, organizations and management. *Gend. Work Organ.* 1:2–22.

Collinson DA. 1992. *Managing the Shopfloor: Subjectivity, Masculinity and Workplace Culture*. New York: Walter de Gruyter.

Coltrane S. 2000. Research on household labor: modeling and measuring the social embeddedness of routine family work. *J. Marriage Fam.* 62:1208–33.

Connell RW. 1983. *Which Way Is Up? Essays on Sex, Class and Culture*. Sydney: Allen & Unwin.

Connell RW. 1987. *Gender and Power: Society, the Person, and Sexual Politics*. Sydney: Allen & Unwin.

Connell RW. 1995. *Masculinities*. Sydney: Allen & Unwin.

Connell RW. 2000. *The Men and the Boys*. St Leonards, NSW: Allen & Unwin.

Connell RW, Messerschmidt JW. 2005. Hegemonic masculinity: rethinking the concept. *Gend. Soc.* 19:829–59.

Cooper M. 2000. Being the "go-to guy": fatherhood, masculinity, and the organization of work in Silicon Valley. *Qual. Sociol.* 23:379–405.

Courtenay WH. 2000. Constructions of masculinity and their influence on men's well-being: a theory of gender and health. *Soc. Sci. Med.* 50:1385–401.

Curry TJ. 1993. A little pain never hurt anyone: athletic career socialization and the normalization of sports injury. *Symb. Interact.* 16:273–90.

Dellinger K. 2004. Masculinities in "safe" and "embattled" organizations: accounting for pornographic and feminist magazines. *Gend. Soc.* 18:545–66.

Dietz TL. 1998. An examination of violence and gender role portrayals in video games: implications for gender socialization and aggressive behavior. *Sex Roles* 38:425–42.

Dixon RL, Linz D. 2002. Overrepresentation and underrepresentation of African Americans and Latinos as lawbreakers on television news. *J. Commun.* 52:131–54.

Dozier R. 2005. Beards, breasts, and bodies: doing sex in a gendered world. *Gend. Soc.* 19:297–316.

Dyson AH. 1994. The ninjas, the X-Men, and the ladies: playing with power and identity in an urban primary school. *Teach. Coll. Rec.* 96:219–39.

Eastman J, Schrock DP. 2008. Southern rock musicians' construction of white trash. *Race Gend. Class.* 15:205–19.

Entman RM, Rojecki A. 2000. *The Black Image in the White Mind: Media and Race in America.* Chicago: Univ. Chicago Press.

Evans L, Davies K. 2000. No sissy boys here: a content analysis of the representation of masculinity in elementary school reading textbooks. *Sex Roles* 41:255–70.

Ezzell MB. 2008. Pornography, lad mags, video games, and boys: reviving the canary in the cultural coal mine. In *The Sexualization of Childhood*, ed. S Olfman, pp. 7–32. Westport, CT: Praeger.

Fahey AC. 2007. French and feminine: hegemonic masculinity and the emasculation of John Kerry in the 2004 presidential race. *Crit. Stud. Mass Commun.* 24:132–50.

Ferguson AA. 2000. *Bad Boys: Public Schools in the Making of Black Masculinity.* Ann Arbor: Univ. Mich. Press.

Fine GA. 1987. *With the Boys: Little League Baseball and Preadolescent Culture.* Chicago: Univ. Chicago Press.

Fine M, Weis L, Addelston J, Marusza J. 1997. (In)secure times: constructing white working-class masculinities in the late 20th century. *Gend. Soc.* 11:52–68.

Flood M. 2002. Between men and masculinity: an assessment of the term "masculinity" in recent scholarship on men. In *Manning the Next Millennium: Studies in Masculinities,* ed. S Pearce, V Muller, pp. 203–13. Bentley, WA: Black Swan.

Flood M. 2008. *The men's bibliography: a comprehensive bibliography of writing on men, masculinities, gender, and sexualities,* 18th ed. http://mensbiblio.xyonline.net/.

Flood M, Gardiner JK, Pease B, Pringle K, ed. 2007. *International Encyclopedia of Men and Masculinities.* London/New York: Routledge.

Fordham S, Ogbu JU. 1986. Black students' school success: coping with the "burden of 'acting white.'" *Urban Rev.* 18:176–206.

Fox KJ. 1999. Changing violent minds: discursive correction and resistance in the cognitive treatment of violent offenders in prison. *Soc. Probl.* 46:88–103.

Frye M. 1983. *The Politics of Reality: Essays in Feminist Theory.* Trumansburg, NY: Crossing.

Gardner CB. 1995. *Passing By: Gender and Public Harassment.* Berkeley: Univ. Calif. Press.

Gatrell C. 2006. Interviewing fathers: feminist dilemmas in fieldwork. *J. Gend. Stud.* 15:237–51.

Gavanas A. 2004. *Fatherhood Politics in the United States.* Urbana: Univ. Ill. Press.

Goffman E. 1959. *The Presentation of Self in Everyday Life.* New York: Doubleday.

Goffman E. 1977. The arrangement between the sexes. *Theory Soc.* 4:301–31.

Grazian D. 2007. The girl hunt: urban nightlife and the performance of masculinity as collective activity. *Symb. Interact.* 30:221–43.

Green AI, Halkitis PN. 2006. Crystal methamphetamine and sexual sociality in an urban gay subculture: an elective affinity. *Cult. Health Sex.* 8:317–33.

Haas J, Shaffir W. 1977. The professionalization of medical students: developing competence and a cloak of competence. *Symb. Interact.* 1:71–88.

Hall PM. 1979. The presidency and impression management. *Stud. Symb. Interact.* 2:283–305.

Hamilton MC, Anderson D, Broaddus M, Young K. 2006. Gender stereotyping and underrepresentation of female characters in 200 popular children's picture books: a twenty-first century update. *Sex Roles* 55:557–65.

Hanmer J. 1990. Men, power, and the exploitation of women. *Women's Stud. Int. Forum.* 13:443–56.

Hearn J. 1998. *The Violences of Men.* London: Sage.

Hearn J. 2004. From hegemonic masculinity to the hegemony of men. *Fem. Theory.* 5:49–72.

Hearn J. 2007. Methods, methodology, and research. See Flood et al. 2007, pp. 433–38.

Hennen P. 2005. Bear bodies, bear masculinity: recuperation, resistance, or retreat? *Gend. Soc.* 19:25–43.

Henson KD, Rogers JK. 2001. "Why Marcia you've changed!" male clerical temporary workers doing masculinity in a feminized occupation. *Gend. Soc.* 15:218–38.

Higate P. 2007. Peacekeepers, masculinities, and sexual exploitation. *Men Masc.* 10:99–119.

Hochschild A. 1989. *Second Shift: Working Parents and the Revolution at Home.* New York: Viking Penguin.

House JS, Landis KR, Umberson D. 1988. Social relationships and health. *Science.* 241:540–45.

Jackall R. 1988. *Moral Mazes: The World of Corporate Managers.* New York: Oxford Univ. Press.

Janssen DF. 2008. *International Guide to Literature on Masculinity.* Harrison, TN: Men's Studies Press.

Jeffreys S. 2005. *Beauty and Misogyny.* New York: Routledge.

Johnson AG. 2005. *The Gender Knot: Unraveling our Patriarchal Legacy.* Philadelphia: Temple Univ. Press.

Johnson K. 2007. Changing sex, changing self: theorizing transitions in embodied subjectivity. *Men Masc.* 10:54–70.

Jordan E, Cowan A. 1995. Warrior narratives in the kindergarten classroom: renegotiating the social-contract. *Gend. Soc.* 9:727–43.

Kane EW. 2006. "No way my boys are going to be like that!" parents' responses to children's gender nonconformity. *Gend. Soc.* 20:149–76.

Kanter RM. 1977. *Men and Women of the Corporation.* New York: Basic Books.

Kerfoot D, Whitehead S. 1998. "Boys own" stuff: masculinity and the management of further education. *Sociol. Rev.* 46:436–57.

Kessler S, McKenna W. 1978. *Gender: An Ethnomethodological Approach.* New York: John Wiley.

Kimmel M. 1996. *Manhood in America: A Cultural History.* New York: Free Press.

Kimmel M. 2007. Racism as adolescent male rite of passage: ex-Nazis in Scandinavia. *J. Contemp. Ethnogr.* 36:202–18.

Kimmel M, Aronson A, ed. 2004. *A Social, Cultural, and Historical Encyclopedia.* New York: ABC-CLIO.

Kimmel M, Hearn J, Connell RW, eds. 2005. *Handbook of Studies on Men and Masculinities.* Thousand Oaks, CA: Sage.

Kimmel MS, Mahler M. 2003. Adolescent masculinity, homophobia, and violence: random school shootings, 1982–2001. *Am. Behav. Sci.* 46:1439–58.

Kimmel MS, Messner MA. 2007. *Men's Lives.* Boston: Allyn & Bacon. 7th ed.

LaRossa R. 1996. *The Modernization of Fatherhood: A Social and Political History.* Chicago: Univ. Chicago Press.

Leidner R. 1993. *Fast Food, Fast Talk.* Berkeley: Univ. Calif. Press.

Lever J. 1978. Sex differences in the complexity of children's play and games. *Am. Sociol. Rev.* 43:471–83.

Leyser H. 2003. Doing masculinity in a mental hospital. *J. Contemp. Ethnogr.* 32:336–59.

Linneman TJ. 2008. How do you solve a problem like Will Truman? The feminization of gay masculinities on Will & Grace. *Men Masc.* 10:583–603.

Lorber J. 1994. *Paradoxes of Gender.* New Haven, CT: Yale Univ. Press.

Mac an Ghaill M. 1994. *The Making of Men: Masculinities, Sexualities and Schooling.* Buckingham, UK: Open Univ. Press.

MacInnes J. 1998. *The End of Masculinity: The Confusion of Sexual Genesis and Sexual Difference in Modern Society.* Philadelphia: Open Univ. Press.

MacLeod J. 1995. *Ain't No Makin' It: Aspirations and Attainment in a Low-Income Neighborhood.* Boulder, CO: Westview.

Majors R, Billson JM. 1992. *Cool Pose: The Dilemmas of Black Manhood in America.* New York: Lexington.

Marsiglio W, Hutchinson S. 2002. *Sex, Men, and Babies: Stories of Awareness and Responsibility.* New York: New York Univ. Press.

Martin PY. 1998. Why can't a man be more like a woman? Reflections on Robert Connell's Masculinities. *Gend. Soc.* 13:472–74.

Martin PY. 2001. "Mobilizing masculinities": women's experiences of men at work. *Organization* 8:587–618.

Martin PY. 2003. "Said and done" versus "saying and doing": gendering practices, practicing gender at work. *Gend. Soc.* 17:342–66.

Martin PY, Hummer RA. 1989. Fraternities and rape on campus. *Gend. Soc.* 3:457–73.

McBride J. 1995. *War, Battering, and Other Sports: The Gulf Between American Men and Women.* New Jersey: Humanities Press.

McCarry M. 2007. Masculinity studies and male violence: critique or collusion? *Women's Stud. Int. Forum.* 30:404–15.

McCaughey M. 2008. *The Caveman Mystique: Pop-Darwinism and the Debates Over Sex, Violence, and Science.* New York: Routledge.

McGuffey CS. 2008. "Saving masculinity": gender reaffirmation, sexuality, race, and parental responses to male child sexual abuse. *Soc. Probl.* 55:216–37.

McGuffey CS, Rich BL. 1999. Playing in the gender transgression zone: race, class, and hegemonic masculinity in middle childhood. *Gend. Soc.* 13:608–27.

Messerschmidt JW. 1993. *Masculinities and Crime: Critique and Reconceptualization of Theory.* Lanham, MD: Rowman & Littlefield.

Messerschmidt JW. 2000. *Nine Lives: Adolescent Masculinities, the Body, and Violence.* Boulder, CO: Westview.

Messner MA. 1990. Men studying masculinity: some epistemological issues in sport sociology. *Soc. Sport J.* 7:136–53.

Messner MA. 1992. *Power at Play: Sports and the Problem of Masculinity.* Boston: Beacon.

Messner MA. 2007. The masculinity of the governator: muscle and compassion in American politics. *Gend. Soc.* 21:461–80.

Milkie MA. 1994. Social world approach to cultural-studies: mass-media and gender in the adolescent peer group. *J. Contemp. Ethnogr.* 23:354–80.

Morris EW. 2005. "Tuck in that shirt!" race, class, gender and discipline in an urban school. *Sociol. Perspect.* 48:25–48.

Mosher CM, Levitt HM, Manley E. 2006. Layers of leather: the identity formation of leather-men as a process of transforming meanings of masculinity. *J. Homosex.* 51:93–123.

Newton J. 2005. *From Panthers to Promise Keepers: Rethinking the Men's Movement.* Lanham, MD: Rowman & Littlefield.

O'Brien R, Hunt K, Hart G. 2005. "It's caveman stuff, but that is to a certain extent how guys still operate": men's accounts of masculinity and help seeking. *Soc. Sci. Med.* 61:503–16.

Ortiz SM. 2006. Using power: An exploration of control work in the sport marriage. *Sociol. Perspect.* 49:527–57.

Pascoe CJ. 2007. *Dude, You're a Fag: Masculinity and Sexuality in High School.* Berkeley: Univ. Calif. Press.

Pecora N. 1992. Superman/superboys/supermen: the comic book hero as socializing agent. In *Men, Masculinity, and the Media,* ed. S Craig, pp. 61–77. Newbury Park, CA: Sage.

Peralta RL. 2007. College alcohol use and the embodiment of hegemonic masculinity among European American men. *Sex Roles* 56:741–56.

Phillips DA. 2007. Punking and bullying: strategies in middle school, high school, and beyond. *J. Interpers. Violence.* 22:158–78.

Pleck JP, Sawyer J, eds. 1974. *Men and Masculinity.* Englewood Cliffs, NJ: Prentice-Hall.

Pomerleau A, Bloduc D, Cossette L, Malcuit G. 1990. Pink or blue: environmental gender stereotypes in the first two years of life. *Sex Roles* 22:359–67.

Prokos A, Padavic I. 2002. 'There oughtta be a law against bitches': masculinity lessons in police academy training. *Gend. Work Organ.* 9:439–59.

Pyke KD. 1996. Class-based masculinities: the interdependence of gender, class, and inter-personal power. *Gend. Soc.* 10:527–49.

Quinn BA. 2002. Sexual harassment and masculinity: the power and meaning of "girl watching." *Gend. Soc.* 16:386–402.

Renold E. 2007. Primary school "studs": (de)constructing young boys' heterosexual masculinities. *Men Masc.* 9:275–97.

Reskin BF. 1988. Bringing the men back in: sex differentiation and the devaluation of women's work. *Gend. Soc.* 2:58–81.

Reskin BF, Padavic I. 2002. *Women and Men at Work.* Thousand Oaks, CA: Pine Forge.

Rospenda KM, Richman JA, Nawyn SJ. 1998. Doing power: the confluence of gender, race, and class in contrapower sexual harassment. *Gend. Soc.* 12:40–60.

Sabo D. 2005. The study of masculinities and men's health: an overview. In *Handbook of Studies on Men & Masculinities,* ed. MS Kimmel, J Hearn, RW Connell, pp. 326–52. Thousand Oaks, CA: Sage.

Sattel JW. 1976. The inexpressive male: tragedy or sexual politics? *Soc. Probl.* 23:469–77.

Schacht SP. 1996. Misogyny on and off the "pitch": the gendered world of male rugby players. *Gender Soc.* 10:550–65.

Schacht SP. 1997. Feminist fieldwork in the misogynist setting of the rugby pitch: temporarily becoming a sylph to survive and personally grow. *J. Contemp. Ethnogr.* 26:338–63.

Schilt K. 2006. Just one of the guys? How transmen make gender visible at work. *Gend. Soc.* 20:465–90.

Schrock D, Padavic I. 2007. Negotiating hegemonic masculinity in a batterer intervention program. *Gend. Soc.* 21:625–49.

Schrock D, Reid L, Boyd EM. 2005. Transsexuals' embodiment of womanhood. *Gend. Soc.* 19:317–35.

Schwalbe ML. 1996. *Unlocking the Iron Cage: The Men's Movement, Gender Politics, and American Culture.* New York: Oxford Univ. Press.

Schwalbe ML. 2005. Identity stakes, manhood acts, and the dynamics of accountability. In *Studies in Symbolic Interaction,* ed. N Denzin, pp. 65–81. New York: Elsevier.

Schwalbe ML, Mason-Schrock D. 1996. Identity work as group process. In *Advances in Group Processes,* ed. B Markovsky, M Lovaglia, R Simon, pp. 113–47. Greenwich, CT: JAI.

Schwalbe ML, Godwin S, Holden D, Schrock D, Thompson S, Wolkomir M. 2000. Generic processes in the reproduction of inequality: an interactionist analysis. *Soc. Forces* 79:419–52.

Schwalbe ML, Wolkomir M. 2001. The masculine self as problem and resource in interview studies of men. *Men Masc.* 4:90–103.

Shaheen JG. 2001. *Reel Bad Arabs: How Hollywood Vilifies a People.* New York: Olive Branch.

Sheldon JP. 2004. Gender stereotypes in educational software for young children. *Sex Roles* 51:433–44.

Sinclair A. 1995. Sex and the MBA. *Organization* 2:295–317.

Snyder KA, Green AI. 2008. Revisiting the glass escalator: the case of gender segregation in a female dominated occupation. *Soc. Probl.* 55:271–99.

Sparks R. 1996. Masculinity and heroism in the Hollywood "blockbuster": the culture industry and contemporary images of crime and law enforcement. *Br. J. Criminol.* 36:348–60.

Staples R. 1982. *Black Masculinity: The Black Man's Blues in American Society.* San Francisco: Black Scholars'.

Straus MA, Gelles RJ, Steinmetz SK. 1980. *Behind Closed Doors: Violence in the American Family.* Garden City, NY: Doubleday.

Stretesky PB, Pogrebin MR. 2007. Gang-related gun violence: socialization, identity, and self. *J. Contemp. Ethnogr.* 36:85–114.

Taylor LD. 2005. All for him: articles about sex in American lad magazines. *Sex Roles* 52:153–63.

Thorne B. 1993. *Gender Play: Girls and Boys in School.* New Brunswick, NJ: Rutgers Univ. Press.

Thurston R. 1996. Are you sitting comfortably? Men's storytelling, masculinities, prison culture and violence. In *Understanding Masculinities: Social Relations and Cultural Arenas,* ed. M Mac an Ghaill, pp. 139–52. Philadelphia: Open Univ. Press.

Tichenor V. 2005. Maintaining men's dominance: negotiating identity and power when she earns more. *Sex Roles* 53:191–205.

Tilki M. 2006. The social contexts of drinking among Irish men in London. *Drugs* 13:247–61.

Tolson A. 1977. *The Limits of Masculinity.* London: Tavistock.

Uggen C, Blackstone A. 2004. Sexual harassment as a gendered expression of power. *Am. Sociol. Rev.* 69:64–92.

Vavrus MD. 2002. Domesticating patriarchy: hegemonic masculinity and television's "Mr. Mom." *Crit. Stud. Mass Commun.* 19:352–75.

Verbrugge LM. 1985. Gender and health: an update on hypotheses and evidence. *J. Health Soc. Behav.* 26:156–82.

Vigorito AJ, Curry TJ. 1998. Marketing masculinity: gender identity and popular magazines. *Sex Roles* 39:135–52.

Wacquant L. 2003. *Body and Soul: Notebooks of An Apprentice Boxer.* New York: Oxford.

West C, Zimmerman D. 1987. Doing gender. *Gend. Soc.* 1:125–51.

Whitehead S, ed. 2006. *Men and Masculinities: Critical Concepts in Sociology.* New York: Routledge.

Williams CL. 1992. The glass escalator: hidden advantages for men in the "female" professions. *Soc. Probl.* 39:253–67.

Willis P. 1977. *Learning to Labor: How Working Class Kids Get Working Class Jobs.* New York: Columbia Univ. Press.

14 | *Introduction*

Benedict Anderson

Perhaps without being much noticed yet, a fundamental transformation in the history of Marxism and Marxist movements is upon us. Its most visible signs are the recent wars between Vietnam, Cambodia and China. These wars are of world-historical importance because they are the first to occur between regimes whose independence and revolutionary credentials are undeniable, and because none of the belligerents has made more than the most perfunctory attempts to justify the bloodshed in terms of recognizable *Marxist* theoretical perspective. While it was still just possible to interpret the Sino-Soviet border clashes of 1969, and the Soviet military interventions in Germany (1953), Hungary (1956), Czechoslovakia (1968), and Afghanistan (1980) in terms of—according to taste—'social imperialism,' 'defending socialism,' etc., no one, I imagine, seriously believes that such vocabularies have much bearing on what has occurred in Indochina.

If the Vietnamese invasion and occupation of Cambodia in December 1978 and January 1979 represented the first *large-scale conventional war* waged by one revolutionary Marxist regime against another,[1] China's assault on Vietnam in February rapidly confirmed the precedent. Only the most trusting would dare wager that in the declining years of this century any significant outbreak of inter-state hostilities will necessarily find the USSR and the PRC—let alone the smaller socialist states—supporting, or fighting on, the same side. Who can be confident that Yugoslavia and Albania will not one day come to blows? Those variegated groups who seek a withdrawal of the Red Army from its encampments in Eastern Europe should remind themselves of the degree to which its overwhelming presence has, since 1945, ruled out armed conflict between the region's Marxist regimes.

Such considerations serve to underline the fact that since World War II every successful revolution has defined itself in *national* terms—the People's Republic of China, the Socialist Republic of Vietnam, and so forth—and, in so doing, has grounded itself firmly in a territorial and social space inherited from the prerevolutionary past. Conversely, the fact that the Soviet Union shares with the United Kingdom of Great Britain and Northern Ireland the rare distinction of refusing nationality in its naming suggests that it is as much the legatee of the prenational dynastic states of the nineteenth century as the precursor of a twenty-first century internationalist order.[2]

Reprinted from *Imagined Communities* (1983), by permission of Verso Books.

Eric Hobsbawm is perfectly correct in stating that 'Marxist movements and states have tended to become national not only in form but in substance, i.e., nationalist. There is nothing to suggest that this trend will not continue.'[3] Nor is the tendency confined to the socialist world. Almost every year the United Nations admits new members. And many 'old nations,' once thought fully consolidated, find themselves challenged by 'sub'-nationalisms within their borders—nationalisms which, naturally, dream of shedding this subness one happy day. The reality is quite plain: the 'end of the era of nationalism,' so long prophesied, is not remotely in sight. Indeed, nation-ness is the most universally legitimate value in the political life of our time.

But if the facts are clear, their explanation remains a matter of long-standing dispute. Nation, nationality, nationalism—all have proved notoriously difficult to define, let alone to analyze. In contrast to the immense influence that nationalism has exerted on the modern world, plausible theory about it is conspicuously meagre. Hugh Seton-Watson, author of far the best and most comprehensive English-language text on nationalism, and heir to a vast tradition of liberal historiography and social science, sadly observes: 'Thus I am *driven* to the conclusion that no "scientific definition" of the nation can be devised; yet the phenomenon has existed and exists.'[4] Tom Nairn, author of the path-breaking *The Break-up of Britain,* and heir to the scarcely less vast tradition of Marxist historiography and social science, candidly remarks: 'The theory of nationalism represents Marxism's great historical failure.'[5] But even this confession is somewhat misleading, insofar as it can be taken to imply the regrettable outcome of a long, self-conscious search for theoretical clarity. It would be more exact to say that nationalism has proved an uncomfortable *anomaly* for Marxist theory and, precisely for that reason, has been largely elided, rather than confronted. How else to explain Marx's failure to explicate the crucial adjective in his memorable formulation of 1848: 'The proletariat of each country must, of course, first of all settle matters with *its own* bourgeoisie'?[6] How else to account for the use, for over a century, of the concept 'national bourgeoisie' without any serious attempt to justify theoretically the relevance of the adjective? What is *this* segmentation of the bourgeoisie—a world-class insofar as it is defined in terms of the relations of production—theoretically significant?

The aim of this chapter is to offer some tentative suggestions for a more satisfactory interpretation of the 'anomaly' of nationalism. My sense is that on this topic both Marxist and liberal theory have become etiolated in a late Ptolemaic effort to 'save the phenomena'; and that a reorientation of perspective in, as it were, a Copernican spirit is urgently required. My point of departure is that nationality, or, as one might prefer to put it in view of that word's multiple significations, nation-ness, as well as nationalism, are cultural artifacts of a particular kind. To understand them properly we need to consider carefully how they have come into historical being, in what ways their meanings have changed over time, and why, today, they command such profound emotional legitimacy. I will be trying to argue that the creation of these artifacts towards the end of the eighteenth century[7] was the spontaneous distillation of a complex 'crossing' of discrete historical forces; but that, once created, they became 'modular,' capable of being transplanted, with varying degrees of self-consciousness, to a great variety of social terrains, to merge and be merged with a correspondingly wide variety of political and ideological constellations. I will also attempt to show why these particular cultural artefacts have aroused such deep attachments.

Concepts and Definitions

Before addressing the questions raised above, it seems advisable to consider briefly the concept of 'nation' and offer a workable definition. Theorists of nationalism have often been perplexed, not to say irritated, by these three paradoxes: (1) The objective modernity of nations to the historian's eye vs. their subjective antiquity in the eyes of nationalists. (2) The formal universality of nationality as a socio-cultural concept—in the modern world everyone can, should, will 'have' a nationality, as he or she 'has' a gender—vs. the irremediable particularity of its concrete manifestations, such that, by definition, 'Greek' nationality is sui generis. (3) The 'political' power of nationalisms vs. their philosophical poverty and even incoherence. In other words, unlike most other isms, nationalism has never produced its own grand thinkers; no Hobbeses, Tocquevilles, Marxes, or Webers. This 'emptiness' easily gives rise, among cosmopolitan and polylingual intellectuals, to a certain condescension. Like Gertrude Stein in the face of Oakland, one can rather quickly conclude that there is 'no there there'. It is characteristic that even so sympathetic a student of nationalism as Tom Nairn can nonetheless write that: '"Nationalism" is the pathology of modern developmental history, as inescapable as "neurosis" in the individual, with much the same essential ambiguity attaching to it, a similar built-in capacity for descent into dementia, rooted in the dilemmas of helplessness thrust upon most of the world (the equivalent of infantilism for societies) and largely incurable.'[8]

Part of the difficulty is that one tends unconsciously to hypostasize the existence of Nationalism-with-a-big-N (rather as one might Age-with-a-capital-A) and then to classify 'it' as *an* ideology. (Note that if everyone has an age, Age is merely an analytical expression.) It would, I think, make things easier if one treated it as if it belonged with 'kinship' and 'religion', rather than with 'liberalism' or 'fascism'.

In an anthropological spirit, then, I propose the following definition of the nation: it is an imagined political community—and imagined as both inherently limited and sovereign.

It is *imagined* because the members of even the smallest nation will never know most of their fellow-members, meet them, or even hear of them, yet in the minds of each lives the image of their communion.[9] Renan referred to this imagining in his suavely back-handed way when he wrote that 'Or l'essence d'une nation est que tous les individus aient beaucoup de choses en commun, et aussi que tous aient oublié bien des choses.'[10] With a certain ferocity Gellner makes a comparable point when he rules that 'Nationalism is not the awakening of nations to self-consciousness: it *invents* nations where they do not exist.'[11] The drawback to this formulation, however, is that Gellner is so anxious to show that nationalism masquerades under false pretences that he assimilates 'invention' to 'fabrication' and 'falsity', rather than to 'imagining' and 'creation'. In this way he implies that 'true' communities exist which can be advantageously juxtaposed to nations. In fact, all communities larger than primordial villages of face-to-face contact (and perhaps even these) are imagined. Communities are to be distinguished, not by their falsity/genuineness, but by the style in which they are imagined. Javanese villagers have always known that they are connected to people they have never seen, but these ties were once imagined particularistically—as indefinitely stretchable nets of kinship and clientship. Until quite recently, the Javanese language had no word meaning the abstraction 'society.' We may today think of the French aristocracy of the *ancien régime* as a class; but surely it was imagined this way only very late.[12] To the question "Who is the Comte de X?" the normal answer would have been, not 'a member of the aristocracy,' but 'the lord of X,' 'the uncle of the Baronne de Y,' or 'a client of the Duc de Z.'

The nation is imagined as *limited* because even the largest of them, encompassing perhaps a billion living human beings, has finite, if elastic, boundaries, beyond which lie other nations. No nation imagines itself coterminous with mankind. The most messianic nationalists do not dream of a day when all the members of the human race will join their nation in the way that it was possible, in certain epochs, for, say, Christians to dream of a wholly Christian planet.

It is imagined as *sovereign* because the concept was born in an age in which Enlightenment and Revolution were destroying the legitimacy of the divinely-ordained, hierarchical dynastic realm. Coming to maturity at a stage of human history when even the most devout adherents of any universal religion were inescapably confronted with the living *pluralism* of such religions, and the allomorphism between each faith's ontological claims and territorial stretch, nations dream of being free, and, if under God, directly so. The gage and emblem of this freedom is the sovereign state.

Finally, it is imagined as a *community,* because, regardless of the actual inequality and exploitation that may prevail in each, the nation is always conceived as a deep, horizontal comradeship. Ultimately it is this fraternity that makes it possible, over the past two centuries, for so many millions of people, not so much to kill, as willingly to die for such limited imaginings.

These deaths bring us abruptly face to face with the central problem posed by nationalism: what makes the shrunken imaginings of recent history (scarcely more than two centuries) generate such colossal sacrifices? I believe that the beginnings of an answer lie in the cultural roots of nationalism.

Notes

1. This formulation is chosen simply to emphasize the scale and the style of the fighting, not to assign blame. To avoid possible misunderstanding, it should be said that the December 1978 invasion grew out of armed clashes between partisans of the two revolutionary movements going back possibly as far as 1971. After April 1977, border raids, initiated by the Cambodians, but quickly followed by the Vietnamese, grew in size and scope, culminating in the major Vietnamese incursion of December 1977. None of these raids, however, aimed at overthrowing enemy regimes or occupying large territories, nor were the numbers of troops involved comparable to those deployed in December 1978. The controversy over the causes of the war is most thoughtfully pursued in: Stephen P. Heder, 'The Kampuchean–Vietnamese Conflict,' in David W. P. Elliott, ed., *The Third Indochina Conflict,* pp. 21–67; Anthony Barnett, 'Inter-Communist Conflicts and Vietnam,' *Bulletin of Concerned Asian Scholars,* 11: 4 (October–December 1979), pp. 2–9; and Laura Summers, 'In Matters of War and Socialism Anthony Barnett would Shame and Honour Kampuchea Too Much,' ibid., pp. 10–18.

2. Anyone who has doubts about the UK's claims to such parity with the USSR should ask himself what nationality its name denotes: Great Brito-Irish?

3. Eric Hobsbawm, 'Some Reflections on "The Break-up of Britain" ', New Left Review, 105 (September–October 1977), p. 13.

4. See his *Nations and States,* p. 5. Emphasis added.

5. See his 'The Modern Janus', *New Left Review,* 94 (November–December 1975), p. 3. This essay is included unchanged in *The Break-up of Britain* as chapter 9 (pp. 329–63).

6. Karl Marx and Friedrich Engels, *The Communist Manifesto,* in the *Selected Works,* 1, p. 45. Emphasis added. In any theoretical exegesis, the words 'of course' should flash red lights before the transported reader.

7. As Aira Kemiläinen notes, the twin 'founding fathers' of academic scholarship on nationalism, Hans Kohn and Carleton Hayes, argued persuasively for this dating. Their conclusions have, I think, not been seriously disputed except by nationalist ideologues in particular countries. Kemiläinen also observes that the word 'nationalism' did not come into wide general use until the end of the nineteenth century. It did not occur, for example, in many standard nineteenth century lexicons. If Adam Smith conjured with the wealth of 'nations,' he meant by the term no more than 'societies' or 'states.' Aira Kemiläinen, *Nationalism,* pp. 10, 33, and 48–49.

8. *The Break-up of Britain,* p. 359.

9. Cf. Seton-Watson, *Nations and States,* p. 5: 'All that I can find to say is that a nation exists when a significant number of people in a community consider themselves to form a nation, or behave as if they formed one.' We may translate 'consider themselves' as 'imagine themselves.'

10. Ernest Renan, 'Qu'est-ce qu'une nation?' in *Œuvres Complètes,* 1, p. 892. He adds: 'tout citoyen français doit avoir oublié la Saint-Barthélemy, les massacres du Midi an XIIIe siècle. Il n'y a pas en France dix familles qui puissent fournir la preuve d'une origine franque . . .'

11. Ernest Gellner, *Thought and Change,* p. 169. Emphasis added.

12. Hobsbawm, for example, 'fixes' it by saying that in 1789 it numbered about 400,000 in a population of 23,000,000. (See his *The Age of Revolution,* p. 78). But would this statistical picture of the noblesse have been imaginable under the *ancien régime?*

15 | *We Have Been Watching the Same Movie about America's Wars for 75 Years*

Peter Van Buren

In the age of the all-volunteer military and an endless stream of war zone losses and ties, it can be hard to keep Homeland enthusiasm up for perpetual war. After all, you don't get a 9/11 every year to refresh those images of the barbarians at the airport departure gates. In the meantime, Americans are clearly finding it difficult to remain emotionally roiled up about our confusing wars in Syria and Iraq, the sputtering one in Afghanistan and various raids, drone attacks and minor conflicts elsewhere.

Fortunately, we have just the ticket, one that has been punched again and again for close to a century: Hollywood war movies (to which the Pentagon is always eager to lend a helping hand). *American Sniper*, which started out with the celebratory tagline "the most lethal sniper in U.S. history" and now has the tagline "the most successful war movie of all time," is just the latest in a long line of films that have kept Americans on their war game. Think of them as war porn, meant to leave us perpetually hyped up. Now, grab some popcorn and settle back to enjoy the show.

There's Only One War Movie

Wandering around YouTube recently, I stumbled across some good old government-issue propaganda. It was a video clearly meant to stir American emotions and prepare us for a long struggle against a determined, brutal and barbaric enemy whose way of life is a challenge to the most basic American values. Here's some of what I learned: our enemy is engaged in a crusade against the West; wants to establish a world government and make all of us bow down before it; fights fanatically, beheads prisoners and is willing to sacrifice the lives of its followers in inhuman suicide attacks. Though its weapons are modern, its thinking and beliefs are 2,000 years out of date and inscrutable to us.

Of course, you knew there was a trick coming, right? This little US government–produced film wasn't about the militants of the

Reprinted by permission from the *Nation*, February 19, 2015.

Islamic State. Made by the US Navy in 1943, its subject was "Our Enemy the Japanese." Substitute" radical Islam" for "emperor worship," though, and it still makes a certain propagandistic sense. While the basics may be largely the same (us versus them, good versus evil), modern times do demand something slicker than the video equivalent of an old newsreel. The age of the Internet, with its short attention spans and heightened expectations of cheap thrills, calls for a higher class of war porn, but as with that 1943 film, it remains remarkable how familiar what's being produced remains.

Like propaganda films and sexual pornography, Hollywood movies about America at war have changed remarkably little over the years. Here's the basic formula, from John Wayne in the World War II-era *Sands of Iwo Jima* to today's *American Sniper*:

- ◆ American soldiers are good, the enemy bad. Nearly every war movie is going to have a scene in which Americans label the enemy as "savages," "barbarians," or "bloodthirsty fanatics," typically following a "sneak attack" or a suicide bombing. Our country's goal is to liberate; the enemy's, to conquer. Such a framework prepares us to accept things that wouldn't otherwise pass muster. Racism naturally gets a bye; as they once were "Japs" (not Japanese), they are now "hajjis" and "ragheads" (not Muslims or Iraqis). It's beyond question that the ends justify just about any means we might use, from the nuclear obliteration of two cities of almost no military significance to the grimmest sort of torture. In this way, the war film long ago became a moral free-fire zone for its American characters.

- ◆ American soldiers believe in God and Country, in "something bigger than themselves," in something "worth dying for," but without ever becoming blindly attached to it. The enemy, on the other hand, is blindly devoted to a religion, political faith, or dictator, and it goes without saying (though it's said) that his God—whether an emperor, Communism, or Allah—is evil. As one critic put it back in 2007 with just a tad of hyperbole, "In every movie Hollywood makes, every time an Arab utters the word Allah. . . something blows up."

- ◆ War films spend no significant time on why those savages might be so intent on going after us. The purpose of American killing, however, is nearly always clearly defined. It's to "save American lives," those over there and those who won't die because we don't have to fight *them* over here. Saving such lives explains American war: in Kathryn Bigelow's *The Hurt Locker*, for example, the main character defuses roadside bombs to make Iraq safer for other American soldiers. In the recent World War II-themed *Fury*, Brad Pitt similarly mows down ranks of Germans to save his comrades. Even torture is justified, as in *Zero Dark Thirty*, in the cause of saving our lives from their nightmarish schemes. In *American Sniper*, shooter Chris Kyle focuses on the many American lives he's saved by shooting Iraqis; his PTSD is, in fact, caused by his having "failed" to have saved even more. Hey, when an American kills in war, he's the one who suffers the most, not that mutilated kid or his grieving mother—*I got nightmares, man! I still see their faces!*

- ◆ Our soldiers are human beings with emotionally engaging backstories, sweet gals waiting at home, and promising lives ahead of them that might be cut tragically short by an enemy from the gates of hell. The bad guys lack such backstories. They are anonymous fanatics with neither a past worth mentioning nor a future worth imagining. This is usually pretty blunt stuff. Kyle's nemesis in *American Sniper*, for instance, wears all black. Thanks to that, you know he's an insta-villain without the need for further information. And speaking of lack of a backstory, he improbably appears in the film both in the Sunni city of Fallujah and in Sadr City, a Shia neighborhood in Baghdad, apparently so super-bad that his desire to kill Americans overcomes even Iraq's mad sectarianism.

◆ It is fashionable for our soldiers, having a kind of depth the enemy lacks, to express some regrets, a dollop of introspection, before (or after) they kill. In *American Sniper*, while back in the United States on leave, the protagonist expresses doubts about what he calls his "work." (No such thoughts are in the book on which the film is based.) Of course, he then goes back to Iraq for three more tours and over two more hours of screen time to amass his 160 "confirmed kills."

◆ Another staple of such films is the training montage. Can a young recruit make it? Often he is the Fat Kid who trims down to his killing weight, or the Skinny Kid who muscles up, or the Quiet Kid who emerges bloodthirsty. (This has been a trope of sexual porn films, too: the geeky looking guy, mocked by beautiful women, who turns out to be a superstar in bed.) The link, up front or implied, between sexuality, manhood and war is a staple of the form. As part of the curious PTSD recovery plan he develops, for example, Kyle volunteers to teach a paraplegic vet in a wheelchair to snipe. After his first decent shot rings home, the man shouts, "I feel like I got my balls back!"

◆ Our soldiers, anguished souls that they are, have no responsibility for what they do once they've been thrown into our wars. No baby-killers need apply in support of America's post-Vietnam, guilt-free mantra, "Hate the war, love the warrior." In the film *First Blood*, for example, John Rambo is a Vietnam veteran who returns home a broken man. He finds his war buddy dead from Agent Orange–induced cancer and is persecuted by the very Americans whose freedom he believed he had fought for. Because he was screwed over in The 'Nam, the film gives him a free pass for his homicidal acts, including a two-hour murderous rampage through a Washington State town. The audience is meant to see Rambo as a noble, sympathetic character. He returns for more personal redemption in later films to rescue American prisoners of war left behind in Southeast Asia.

◆ For war films, ambiguity is a dirty word. Americans always win, even when they lose in an era in which, out in the world, the losses are piling up. And a win is a win, even when its essence is one-sided bullying as in *Heartbreak Ridge*, the only movie to come out of the ludicrous invasion of Grenada. And a loss is still a win in *Black Hawk Down*, set amid the disaster of Somalia, which ends with scenes of tired warriors who did the right thing. *Argo*—consider it honorary war porn—reduces the debacle of years of US meddling in Iran to a high-fiving hostage rescue. All it takes these days to turn a loss into a win is to zoom in tight enough to ignore defeat. In *American Sniper*, the disastrous occupation of Iraq is shoved offstage so that more Iraqis can die in Kyle's sniper scope. In *Lone Survivor*, a small American "victory" is somehow dredged out of hopeless Afghanistan because an Afghan man takes a break from being droned to save the life of a SEAL.

In sum: gritty, brave, selfless men, stoic women waiting at home, noble wounded warriors, just causes and the necessity of saving American lives. Against such a lineup, the savage enemy is a crew of sitting ducks who deserve to die. Everything else is just music, narration and special effects. War pornos, like their oversexed cousins, are all the same movie.

A Fantasy That Can Change Reality

But it's just a movie, right? Your favorite shoot-'em-up makes no claims to being a documentary. We all know one American can't gun down fifty bad guys and walk away unscathed, in the same way he can't bed fifty partners without getting an STD. It's just entertainment. So what?

So what do you, or the typical 18-year-old considering military service, actually know about war on entering that movie theater? Don't underestimate the degree to which such films can help create broad perceptions of what war's all about and what kind of people fight it. Those lurid on-screen images, updated and reused so repetitively for so many decades, do help create a self-reinforcing, common understanding of what happens "over there," particularly since what we are shown mirrors what most of us want to believe anyway.

No form of porn is about reality, of course, but that doesn't mean it can't create realities all its own. War films have the ability to bring home emotionally a glorious fantasy of America at war, no matter how grim or gritty any of these films may look. War porn can make a young man willing to die before he's 20. Take my word for it: as a diplomat in Iraq I met young people in uniform suffering from the effects of all this. Such films also make it easier for politicians to sweet talk the public into supporting conflict after conflict, even as sons and daughters continue to return home damaged or dead and despite the country's near-complete record of geopolitical failures since September 2001. Funny thing: *American Sniper* was nominated for an Academy Award for best picture as Washington went back to war in Iraq in what you'd have thought would be an unpopular struggle.

Learning from the Exceptions

You can see a lot of war porn and stop with just your toes in the water, thinking you've gone swimming. But eventually you should go into the deep water of the "exceptions," because only there can you confront the real monsters.

There are indeed exceptions to war porn, but don't fool yourself, size matters. How many people have seen *American Sniper, The Hurt Locker* or *Zero Dark Thirty*? By comparison, how many saw the anti-war Iraq War film *Battle for Haditha*, a lightly fictionalized, deeply unsettling drama about an American massacre of innocent men, women and children in retaliation for a roadside bomb blast?

Timing matters, too, when it comes to the few mainstream exceptions. John Wayne's *The Green Berets*, a pro-Vietnam War film, came out in 1968 as that conflict was nearing its bloody peak and resistance at home was growing. (*The Green Berets* gets a porn bonus star, as the grizzled Wayne persuades a lefty journalist to alter his negative views on the war.) *Platoon*, with its message of waste and absurdity, had to wait until 1986, more than a decade after the war ended.

In propaganda terms, think of this as controlling the narrative. One version of events dominates all others and creates a reality others can only scramble to refute. The exceptions do, however, reveal much about what we don't normally see of the true nature of American war. They are uncomfortable for any of us to watch, as well as for military recruiters, parents sending a child off to war and politicians trolling for public support for the next crusade.

War is not a two-hour-and-twelve-minute hard-on. War is what happens when the rules break down and, as fear displaces reason, nothing too terrible is a surprise. The real secret of war for those who experience it isn't the visceral knowledge that people can be filthy and horrible, but that you, too, can be filthy and horrible. You don't see much of that on the big screen.

The Long Con

Of course, there are elements of "nothing new" here. The Romans undoubtedly had their version of war porn that involved mocking the Gauls as subhumans. Yet in twenty-first-century America, where wars are undeclared and Washington dependent on volunteers for its new foreign legion, the need to keep the public engaged and filled with fear over our enemies is perhaps more acute than ever.

So here's a question: if the core propaganda messages the US government promoted during World War II are nearly identical to those pushed out today about the Islamic State, and if Hollywood's war films, themselves a particularly high-class form of propaganda, have promoted the same false images of Americans in conflict from 1941 to the present day, what does that tell us? Is it that our varied enemies across nearly three-quarters of a century of conflict are always unbelievably alike, or is it that when America needs a villain, it always goes to the same script?

16 *Racial Formation*

Michael Omi and Howard Winant

In 1982–83, Susie Guillory Phipps unsuccessfully sued the Louisiana Bureau of Vital Records to change her racial classification from black to white. The descendant of an 18th-century white planter and a black slave, Phipps was designated "black" in her birth certificate in accordance with a 1970 state law which declared anyone with at least 1/32nd "negro blood" to be black.

The Phipps case raised intriguing questions about the concept of race, its meaning in contemporary society, and its use (and abuse) in public policy. Assistant Attorney General Ron Davis defended the law by pointing out that some type of racial classification was necessary to comply with federal record-keeping requirements and to facilitate programs for the prevention of genetic diseases. Phipps's attorney, Brian Begue, argued that the assignment of racial categories on birth certificates was unconstitutional and that the 1/32nd designation was inaccurate. He called on a retired Tulane University professor who cited research indicating that most Louisiana whites have at least 1/20th "Negro" ancestry.

In the end, Phipps lost. The court upheld the state's right to classify and quantify racial identity.[1]

Phipps's problematic racial identity, and her effort to resolve it through state action, is in many ways a parable of America's unsolved racial dilemma. It illustrates the difficulties of defining race and assigning individuals or groups to racial categories. It shows how the racial legacies of the past—slavery and bigotry—continue to shape the present. It reveals both the deep involvement of the state in the organization and interpretation of race, and the inadequacy of state institutions to carry out these functions. It demonstrates how deeply Americans both as individuals and as a civilization are shaped, and indeed haunted, by race.

Having lived her whole life thinking that she was white, Phipps suddenly discovers that by legal definition she is not. In U.S. society, such an event is indeed catastrophic.[2] But if she is not white, of what race is she? The *state* claims that she is black, based on its rules of classification,[3] and another state agency, the court, upholds this judgment. But despite these classificatory standards which have imposed an either-or logic on racial identity, Phipps will not in fact "change color."

Reprinted from *Racial Formation in the United States: From the 1960s to the 1990s*, Second Edition (1994), by permission of Routledge.

Unlike what would have happened during slavery times if one's claim to whiteness was successfully challenged, we can assume that despite the outcome of her legal challenge, Phipps will remain in most of the social relationships she had occupied before the trial. Her socialization, her familial and friendship networks, her cultural orientation, will not change. She will simply have to wrestle with her newly acquired "hybridized" condition. She will have to confront the "Other" within.

The designation of racial categories and the determination of racial identity is no simple task. For centuries, this question has precipitated intense debates and conflicts, particularly in the U.S.—disputes over natural and legal rights, over the distribution of resources, and indeed, over who shall live and who shall die.

A crucial dimension of the Phipps case is that it illustrates the inadequacy of claims that race is a mere matter of variations in human physiognomy, that it is simply a matter of skin color. But if race cannot be understood in this manner, how can it be understood? We cannot fully hope to address this topic—no less than the meaning of race, its role in society, and the forces which shape it—in one chapter, nor indeed in one book. Our goal in this chapter, however, is far from modest: we wish to offer at least the outlines of a theory of race and racism.

What Is Race?

There is a continuous temptation to think of race as an *essence*, as something fixed, concrete, and objective. And there is also an opposite temptation: to imagine race as a mere *illusion*, a purely ideological construct which some ideal non-racist social order would eliminate. It is necessary to challenge both these positions, to disrupt and reframe the rigid and bipolar manner in which they are posed and debated, and to transcend the presumably irreconcilable relationship between them.

The effort must be made to understand race as an unstable and "decentered" complex of social meanings constantly being transformed by political struggle. With this in mind, let us propose a definition: *race is a concept which signifies and symbolizes social conflicts and interests by referring to different types of human bodies.* Although the concept of race invokes biologically based human characteristics (so-called "phenotypes"), selection of these particular human features for purposes of racial signification is always and necessarily a social and historical process. In contrast to the other major distinction of this type, that of gender, there is no biological basis for distinguishing among human groups along the lines of race.[4] Indeed, the categories employed to differentiate among human groups along racial lines reveal themselves, upon serious examination, to be at best imprecise, and at worst completely arbitrary.

If the concept of race is so nebulous, can we not dispense with it? Can we not "do without" race, at least in the "enlightened" present? This question has been posed often, and with greater frequency in recent years.[5] An affirmative answer would of course present obvious practical difficulties: it is rather difficult to jettison widely held beliefs, beliefs which moreover are central to everyone's identity and understanding of the social world. So the attempt to banish the concept as an archaism is at best counterintuitive. But a deeper difficulty, we believe, is inherent in the very formulation of this schema, in its way of posing race as a *problem*, a misconception left over from the past, and suitable now only for the dustbin of history.

A more effective starting point is the recognition that despite its uncertainties and contradictions, the concept of race continues to play a fundamental role in structuring and representing the social world. The task for theory is to explain this situation. It is to avoid both the utopian framework which sees race as an illusion we can somehow "get beyond," and also the essentialist formulation which sees race as something objective and fixed, a biological datum.[6] Thus we should think of race as an element of social structure rather than as an irregularity within it; we should see race as a dimension of human representation rather than an illusion. These perspectives inform the theoretical approach we call racial formation.

Racial Formation

We define *racial formation* as the sociohistorical process by which racial categories are created, inhabited, transformed, and destroyed. Our attempt to elaborate a theory of racial formation will proceed in two steps. First, we argue that racial formation is a process of historically situated *projects* in which human bodies and social structures are represented and organized. Next we link racial formation to the evolution of hegemony, the way in which society is organized and ruled. Such an approach, we believe, can facilitate understanding of a whole range of contemporary controversies and dilemmas involving race, including the nature of racism, the relationship of race to other forms of differences, inequalities, and oppression such as sexism and nationalism, and the dilemmas of racial identity today.

From a racial formation perspective, race is a matter of both social structure and cultural representation. Too often, the attempt is made to understand race simply or primarily in terms of only one of these two analytical dimensions.[7] For example, efforts to explain racial inequality as a purely social structural phenomenon are unable to account for the origins, patterning, and transformation of racial difference.

Conversely, many examinations of racial difference—understood as a matter of cultural attributes *à la* ethnicity theory, or as a society-wide signification system, *à la* some poststructuralist accounts—cannot comprehend such structural phenomena as racial stratification in the labor market or patterns of residential segregation.

An alternative approach is to think of racial formation processes as occurring through a linkage between structure and representation. Racial *projects* do the ideological "work" of making these links. *A racial project is simultaneously an interpretation, representation, or explanation of racial dynamics, and an effort to reorganize and redistribute resources along particular racial lines.* Racial projects connect what race *means* in a particular discursive practice and the ways in which both social structures and everyday experiences are racially *organized*, based upon that meaning. Let us consider this proposition, first in terms of large-scale or macro-level social processes, and then in terms of other dimensions of the racial formation process.

Racial Formation as a Macro-Level Social Process

To *interpret the meaning of race is to frame it social structurally.* Consider for example, this statement by Charles Murray on welfare reform:

> My proposal for dealing with the racial issue in social welfare is to repeal every bit of legislation and reverse every court decision that in any way requires, recommends, or awards differential treatment according to race, and thereby put us back onto the track that we left in 1965. We may argue about the appropriate limits of government intervention in trying to enforce the ideal, but at least it should be possible to identity the ideal: Race is not a morally admissible reason for treating one person differently from another. Period.[8]

Here there is a partial but significant analysis of the meaning of race: it is not a morally valid basis upon which to treat people "differently from one another." We may notice someone's race, but we cannot act upon that awareness. We must act in a "color-blind" fashion. This analysis of the meaning of race is immediately linked to a specific conception of the role of race in the social structure: it can play no part in government action, save in "the enforcement of the ideal." No state policy can legitimately require, recommend, or award different status according to race. This example can be classified as a particular type of racial project in the present-day U.S.—a "neoconservative" one.

Conversely, *to recognize the racial dimension in social structure is to interpret the meaning of race.* Consider the following statement by the late Supreme Court Justice Thurgood Marshall on minority "set-aside" programs:

> A profound difference separates governmental actions that themselves are racist, and governmental actions that seek to remedy the effects of prior racism or to prevent neutral government activity from perpetuating the effects of such racism.[9]

Here the focus is on the racial dimensions of *social structure*—in this case of state activity and policy. The argument is that state actions in the past and present have treated people in very different ways according to their race, and thus the government cannot retreat from its policy responsibilities in this area. It cannot suddenly declare itself "color-blind" without in fact perpetuating the same type of differential, racist treatment.[10] Thus, race continues to signify difference and structure inequality. Here, racialized social structure is immediately linked to an interpretation of the meaning of race. This example too can be classified as a particular type of racial project in the present-day U.S.—a "liberal" one.

To be sure, such political labels as "neoconservative" or "liberal" cannot fully capture the complexity of racial projects, for these are always multiply determined, politically contested, and deeply shaped by their historical context. Thus, encapsulated within the neoconservative example cited here are certain egalitarian commitments which derive from a previous historical context in which they played a very different role, and which are rearticulated in neoconservative racial discourse precisely to oppose a more open-ended, more capacious conception of the meaning of equality. Similarly, in the liberal example, Justice Marshall recognizes that the contemporary state, which was formerly the architect of segregation and the chief enforcer of racial difference, has a tendency to reproduce those patterns of inequality in a new guise. Thus he admonishes it (in dissent, significantly) to fulfill its responsibilities to uphold a robust conception of equality. These particular instances, then, demonstrate how racial projects are always concretely framed, and thus are always contested and unstable. The social structures they uphold or attack, and the representations of race they articulate, are never invented out of the air, but exist in a definite historical context, having descended from previous conflicts. This contestation appears to be permanent in respect to race.

These two examples of contemporary racial projects are drawn from mainstream political debate; they may be characterized as center-right and center-left expressions of contemporary racial politics.[11] We can, however, expand the discussion of racial formation processes far beyond these familiar examples. In fact, we can identify racial projects in at least three other analytical dimensions: first, the political spectrum can be broadened to include racial projects, on both the left and right, as well as along other political axes. Second, analysis of racial projects can take place not only at the macro-level of racial policy-making, state activity, and collective action, but also at the micro-level of everyday experience. Third, the concept of racial projects can be applied across historical time, to identify racial formation dynamics in the past. We shall now offer examples of each of these types of racial projects.

The Political Spectrum of Racial Formation

We have encountered examples of a neoconservative racial project, in which the significance of race is denied, leading to a "color-blind" racial politics and "hands off" policy orientation; and of a "liberal" racial project, in which the significance of race is affirmed, leading to an egalitarian and "activist" state policy. But these by no means exhaust the political possibilities. Other racial projects can be readily identified on the contemporary U.S. scene. For example, "far right" projects, which uphold biologistic and racist views of difference, explicitly argue for white supremacist policies. "New right" projects overtly claim to hold "color-blind" views, but covertly manipulate racial fears in order to achieve political gains.[12] On the left, "radical democratic" projects invoke notions of racial "difference" in combination with egalitarian politics and policy.

Further variations can also be noted. For example, "nationalist" projects, both conservative and radical, stress the incompatibility of racially defined group identity with the legacy of white supremacy, and therefore advocate a social structural solution of separation, either complete or partial.[13] Nationalist currents represent a profound legacy of the centuries of racial absolutism that initially defined the meaning of race in the U.S. Nationalist concerns continue to influence racial debate in the form of Afrocentrism and other expressions of identity politics.

Taking the range of politically organized racial projects as a whole, we can "map" the current pattern of racial formation at the level of the public sphere, the "macro-level" in which public debate and mobilization takes place.[14] But important as this is, the terrain on which racial formation occurs is broader yet.

Racial Formation as Everyday Experience

At the micro-social level, racial projects also link signification and structure, not so much as efforts to shape policy or define large-scale meaning, but as the applications of "common sense." To see racial projects operating at the level of everyday life, we have only to examine the many ways in which, often unconsciously, we "notice" race.

One of the first things we notice about people when we meet them (along with their sex) is their race. We utilize race to provide clues about *who* a person is. This fact is made painfully obvious when we encounter someone whom we cannot conveniently racially categorize—someone who is, for example, racially "mixed" or of an ethnic/racial group we are not familiar with. Such an encounter becomes a source of discomfort and momentarily a crisis of racial meaning.

Our ability to interpret racial meanings depends on preconceived notions of a racialized social structure. Comments such as, "Funny, you don't look black," betray an underlying image of what black should be. We expect people to act out their apparent racial identities; indeed we become disoriented when they do not. The black banker harassed by police while walking in casual clothes through his own well-off neighborhood, the Latino or white kid rapping in perfect Afro patois, the unending *faux pas* committed by those who assume that the non-whites they encounter are servants or tradespeople, the belief that non-white colleagues are less qualified persons hired to fulfill affirmative action guidelines, indeed the whole gamut of racial stereotypes—that "white men can't jump," that Asians can't dance, etc., etc.—all testify to the way a racialized social structure shapes racial experience and conditions meaning. Analysis of such stereotypes reveals the always present, already active link between our view of the social structure—its demography, its laws, its customs, its threats—and our conception of what race means.

Conversely, our ongoing interpretation of our experience in racial terms shapes our relations to the institutions and organizations through which we are imbedded in social structure. Thus we expect differences in skin color, or other racially coded characteristics, to explain social differences. Temperament, sexuality, intelligence, athletic ability, aesthetic preferences, and so on are presumed to be fixed and discernible from the palpable mark of race. Such diverse questions as our confidence and trust in others (for example, clerks or salespeople, media figures, neighbors), our sexual preferences and romantic images, our tastes in music, films, dance, or sports, and our very ways of talking, walking, eating, and dreaming become racially coded simply because we live in a society where racial awareness is so pervasive. Thus in ways too comprehensive even to monitor consciously, and despite periodic calls—neoconservative and otherwise—for us to ignore race and adopt "color-blind" racial attitudes, skin color "differences" continue to rationalize distinct treatment of racially identified individuals and groups.

To summarize the argument so far: the theory of racial formation suggests that society is suffused with racial projects, large and small, to which all are subjected. This racial "subjection" is quintessentially ideological. Everybody learns some combination, some version, of the rules of racial classification, and of her own racial identity, often without obvious teaching or conscious inculcation. Thus are we inserted in a comprehensively racialized social structure. Race becomes "common sense"—a way of comprehending, explaining, and acting in the world. A vast web of racial projects mediates between the discursive or representational means in which race is identified and signified on the one hand, and the institutional and organizational forms in which it is routinized and standardized on the other. These projects are the heart of the racial formation process.

Under such circumstances, it is not possible to represent race discursively without simultaneously locating it, explicitly or implicitly, in a social structural (and historical) context. Nor is it possible to organize, maintain, or transform social structures without simultaneously engaging, once more either explicitly or implicitly, in racial signification. Racial formation, therefore, is a kind of synthesis, an outcome, of the interaction of racial projects on a society-wide level. These projects are, of course, vastly different in scope and effect. They include large-scale public action, state activities, and interpretations of racial conditions in artistic, journalistic, or academic fora,[15] as well as the seemingly infinite number of racial judgments and practices we carry out at the level of individual experience.

Since racial formation is always historically situated, our understanding of the significance of race, and of the way race structures society, has changed enormously over time. The processes of racial formation we encounter today, the racial projects large and small which structure U.S. society in so many ways, are merely the present-day outcomes of a complex historical evolution. The contemporary racial order remains transient. By knowing something of how it evolved, we can perhaps better discern where it is heading. We therefore turn next to a historical survey of the racial formation process, and the conflicts and debates it has engendered.

The Evolution of Modern Racial Awareness

The identification of distinctive human groups, and their association with differences in physical appearance, goes back to prehistory, and can be found in the earliest documents—in the Bible, for example, or in Herodotus. But the emergence of a modern conception of race does not occur until the rise of Europe and the arrival of Europeans in the Americas. Even the hostility and suspicion with which Christian Europe viewed its two significant non-Christian "Others"—the Muslims and the Jews—cannot be viewed as more than a rehearsal for racial formation, since these antagonisms, for all their bloodletting and chauvinism, were always and everywhere religiously interpreted.[16]

It was only when European explorers reached the Western Hemisphere, when the oceanic seal separating the "old" and the "new" worlds was breached, that the distinctions and categorizations fundamental to a racialized social structure, and to a discourse of race, began to appear. The European explorers were the advance guard of merchant capitalism, which sought new openings for trade. What they found exceeded their wildest dreams, for never before and never again in human history has an opportunity for the appropriation of wealth remotely approached that presented by the "discovery."[17]

But the Europeans also "discovered" people, people who looked and acted differently. These "natives" challenged their "discoverers" pre-existing conceptions of the origins and possibilities of the human species.[18] The representation and interpretation of the meaning of the indigenous peoples' existence became a crucial matter, one which would affect the outcome of the enterprise of conquest. For the "discovery" raised disturbing questions as to whether *all* could be considered part of the same "family of man," and more practically, the extent to which native peoples could be exploited and enslaved. Thus religious debates flared over the attempt to reconcile the various Christian metaphysics with the existence of peoples who were more "different" than any whom Europe had previously known.[19]

In practice, of course, the seizure of territories and goods, the introduction of slavery through the *encomienda* and other forms of coerced native labor, and then through the organization of the African slave trade—not to mention the practice of outright extermination—all presupposed a worldview which distinguished Europeans, as children of God, full-fledged human beings, etc., from "Others." Given the dimensions and the ineluctability of the European onslaught, given the conquerors' determination to appropriate both labor and goods, and given the presence of an axiomatic and unquestioned Christianity among them, the ferocious division of society into Europeans and "Others" soon coalesced. This was true despite the famous 16th-century theological and philosophical debates about the identity of indigenous peoples.[20]

Indeed debates about the nature of the "Others" reached their practical limits with a certain dispatch. Plainly they would never touch the essential: nothing, after all, would induce the Europeans to pack up and go home. We cannot examine here the early controversies over the status of American souls. We simply wish to emphasize that the "discovery" signalled a break from the previous proto-racial awareness by which Europe contemplated its "Others" in a relatively disorganized fashion. In other words, the "conquest of America" was not simply an epochal historical event—however unparalleled in its importance. It was also the advent of a consolidated social structure of exploitation, appropriation, domination. Its representation, first in religious terms, but soon enough in scientific and political ones, initiated modern racial awareness.

The conquest, therefore, was the first—and given the dramatic nature of the case, perhaps the greatest—racial formation project. Its significance was by no means limited to the Western Hemisphere, for it began the work of constituting Europe as the metropole, the center, of a group of empires which could take, as Marx would later write, "the globe for a theater."[21] It represented this new imperial structure as a struggle between civilization and barbarism, and implicated in this representation all the great European philosophies, literary traditions, and social theories of the modern age.[22] In short, just as the noise of the "big bang" still resonates through the universe, so the overdetermined construction of world "civilization" as a product of the rise of Europe and the subjugation of the rest of us, still defines the race concept.

From Religion to Science

After the initial depredations of conquest, religious justifications for racial difference gradually gave way to scientific ones. By the time of the Enlightenment, a general awareness of race was pervasive, and most of the great philosophers of Europe, such as Hegel, Kant, Hume, and Locke, had issued virulently racist opinions.

The problem posed by race during the late 18th century was markedly different than it had been in the age of "discovery," expropriation, and slaughter. The social structures in which race operated were no longer primarily those of military conquest and plunder, nor of the establishment of thin beachheads of colonization on the edge of what had once seemed a limitless wilderness. Now the issues were much more complicated: nation-building, establishment of national economies in the world trading system, resistance to the arbitrary authority of monarchs, and the assertion of the "natural rights" of "man," including the right of revolution.[23] In such a situation, racially organized exploitation, in the form of slavery, the expansion of colonies, and the continuing expulsion of native peoples, was both necessary and newly difficult to justify.

The invocation of scientific criteria to demonstrate the "natural" basis of racial hierarchy was both a logical consequence of the rise of this form of knowledge, and an attempt to provide a more subtle and nuanced account of human complexity in the new, "enlightened" age. Spurred on by the classificatory scheme of living organisms devised by Linnaeus in *Systema Naturae* (1735), many scholars in the 18th and 19th centuries dedicated themselves to the identification and ranking of variations in humankind. Race was conceived as a *biological* concept, a matter of species. Voltaire wrote that "the negro race is a species of men (sic) as different from ours . . . as the breed of spaniels is from that of greyhounds," and in a formulation echoing down from his century to our own, declared that

> If their understanding is not of a different nature from ours . . . , it is at least greatly inferior. They are not capable of any great application or association of ideas, and seem formed neither for the advantages nor the abuses of philosophy.[24]

Jefferson, the preeminent exponent of the Enlightenment doctrine of "the rights of man" on North American shores, echoed these sentiments:

> In general their existence appears to participate more of sensation than reflection. . . . [I]n memory they are equal to whites, in reason much inferior . . . [and] in imagination they are dull, tasteless, and anomalous. . . . I advance it therefore . . . that the blacks, whether originally a different race or made distinct by time and circumstances, are inferior to the whites. . . . Will not a lover of natural history, then, one who views the gradations in all the animals with the eye of philosophy, excuse an effort to keep those in the department of Man (sic) as distinct as nature has formed them?[25]

Such claims of species distinctiveness among humans justified the inequitable allocation of political and social rights, while still upholding the doctrine of "the rights of man." The quest to obtain a precise scientific definition of race sustained debates which continue to rage today. Yet despite efforts ranging from Dr. Samuel Morton's studies of cranial capacity[26] to contemporary attempts to base racial classification on shared gene pools,[27] the concept of race has defied biological definition.

In the 19th century, Count Joseph Arthur de Gobineau drew upon the most respected scientific studies of his day to compose his four-volume *Essay on the Inequality of Races* (1853–1855).[28] He not only greatly influenced the racial thinking of the period, but his themes would be echoed in the racist ideologies of the next one hundred years: beliefs that superior races produced superior cultures and that racial intermixtures resulted in the degradation of the superior racial stock. These ideas found expression, for instance, in the eugenics movement launched by Darwin's cousin, Francis Galton, which had an immense impact on scientific and sociopolitical thought in Europe and the U.S.[29] In the wake of civil war and emancipation, and with immigration from southern and Eastern Europe as well as East Asia running high, the U.S. was particularly fertile ground for notions such as social darwinism and eugenics.

Attempts to discern the *scientific meaning* of race continue to the present day. For instance, an essay by Arthur Jensen which argued that hereditary factors shape intelligence not only revived the "nature or nurture" controversy, but also raised highly volatile questions about racial equality itself.[30] All such attempts seek to remove the concept of race from the historical context in which it arose and developed. They employ an *essentialist* approach which suggests instead that the truth of race is a matter of innate characteristics, of which skin color and other physical attributes provide only the most obvious, and in some respects most superficial, indicators.

From Science to Politics

It has taken scholars more than a century to reject biologistic notions of race in favor of an approach which regards race as a *social* concept. This trend has been slow and uneven, and even today remains somewhat embattled, but its overall direction seems clear. At the turn of the century Max Weber discounted biological explanations for racial conflict and instead highlighted the social and political factors which engendered such conflict.[31] W. E. B. Du Bois argued for a sociopolitical definition of race by identifying "the color line" as "the problem of the 20th century."[32] Pioneering cultural anthropologist Franz Boas rejected attempts to link racial identifications and cultural traits, labelling as pseudoscientific any assumption of a continuum of "higher" and "lower" cultural groups.[33] Other early exponents of social, as opposed to biological, views of race included Robert E. Park, founder of the "Chicago school" of sociology, and Alain Leroy Locke, philosopher and theorist of the Harlem Renaissance.[34]

Perhaps more important than these and subsequent intellectual efforts, however, were the political struggles of racially defined groups themselves. Waged all around the globe under a variety of banners such as anticolonialism and civil rights, these battles to challenge various structural and cultural racisms have been a major feature of 20th-century politics. The racial horrors of the 20th century—colonial slaughter and apartheid, the genocide of the holocaust, and the massive bloodlettings required to end these evils—have also indelibly marked the theme of race as a political issue *par excellence*.

As a result of prior efforts and struggles, we have now reached the point of fairly general agreement that race is not a biologically given but rather a socially constructed way of differentiating human beings. While a tremendous achievement, the transcendence of biologistic conceptions of race does not provide any reprieve from the dilemmas of racial injustice and conflict, nor from controversies over the significance of race in the present. Views of race as socially constructed simply recognize the fact that these conflicts and controversies are now more properly framed on the terrain of politics. By privileging politics in the analysis which follows we do not mean to suggest that race has been displaced as a concern of scientific inquiry, or that struggles over cultural representation are no longer important. We do argue, however, that race is now a preeminently political phenomenon. Such an assertion invites examination of the evolving role of racial politics in the U.S. This is the subject to which we now turn.

Dictatorship, Democracy, Hegemony

For most of its existence both as European colony and as an independent nation, the U.S. was a racial dictatorship. From 1607 to 1865—258 years—most non-whites were firmly eliminated from the sphere of politics.[35] After the Civil War there was the brief egalitarian experiment of Reconstruction which terminated ignominiously in 1877. In its wake followed almost a century of legally sanctioned segregation and denial of the vote, nearly absolute in the South and much of the Southwest, less effective in the North and far West, but formidable in any case.[36] These barriers fell only in the mid-1960s, a mere quarter-century ago. Nor did the successes of the black movement and its allies mean that all obstacles to their political participation had now been abolished. Patterns of racial inequality have proven, unfortunately, to be quite stubborn and persistent.

It is important, therefore, to recognize that in many respects, racial dictatorship is the norm against which all U.S. politics must be measured. The centuries of racial dictatorship have had three very large consequences: first, they defined "American" identity as white, as the negation of racialized "otherness"—at first largely African and indigenous, later Latin American and Asian as well.[37] This negation took shape in both law and custom, in public institutions and in forms of cultural representation. It became the archetype of hegemonic rule in the U.S. It was the successor to the conquest as the "master" racial project.

Second, racial dictatorship organized (albeit sometimes in an incoherent and contradictory fashion) the "color line" rendering it the fundamental division in U.S. society. The dictatorship elaborated, articulated, and drove racial divisions not only through institutions, but also through psyches, extending up to our own time the racial obsessions of the conquest and slavery periods.

Third, racial dictatorship consolidated the oppositional racial consciousness and organization originally framed by marronage[38] and slave revolts, by indigenous resistance, and by nationalisms of various sorts. Just as the conquest created the "native" where once there had been Pequot, Iroquois, or Tutelo, so too it created the "black" where once there had been Asante or Ovimbundu, Yoruba or Bakongo.

The transition from a racial dictatorship to a racial democracy has been a slow, painful, and contentious one; it remains far from complete. A recognition of the abiding presence of racial dictatorship, we contend, is crucial for the development of a theory of racial formation in the U.S. It is also crucial to the task of relating racial formation to the broader context of political practice, organization, and change.

In this context, a key question arises: in what way is racial formation related to politics as a whole? How, for example, does race articulate with other axes of oppression and difference—most importantly class and gender—along which politics is organized today?

The answer, we believe, lies in the concept of *hegemony*. Antonio Gramsci—the Italian communist who placed this concept at the center of his life's work—understood it as the conditions necessary, in a given society, for the achievement and consolidation of rule. He argued that hegemony was always constituted by a combination of coercion and consent. Although rule can be obtained by force, it cannot be secured and maintained, especially in modern society, without the element of consent. Gramsci conceived of consent as far more than merely the legitimation of authority. In his view, consent extended to the incorporation by the ruling group of many of the key interests of subordinated groups, often to the explicit disadvantage of the rulers themselves.[39] Gramsci's treatment of hegemony went even farther: he argued that in order to consolidate their hegemony, ruling groups must elaborate and maintain a popular system of ideas and practices—through education, the media, religion, folk wisdom, etc.—which he called "common sense." It is through its production and its adherence to this "common sense," this ideology (in the broadest sense of the term), that a society gives its consent to the way in which it is ruled.[40]

These provocative concepts can be extended and applied to an understanding of racial rule. In the Americas, the conquest represented the violent introduction of a new form of rule whose relationship with those it subjugated was almost entirely coercive. In the U.S., the origins of racial division, and of racial signification and identity formation, lie in a system of rule which was extremely dictatorial. The mass murders and expulsions of indigenous people, and the enslavement of Africans, surely evoked and inspired little consent in their founding moments.

Over time, however, the balance of coercion and consent began to change. It is possible to locate the origins of hegemony right within the heart of racial dictatorship, for the effort to possess the oppressor's tools—religion and philosophy in this case—was crucial to emancipation (the effort to possess oneself). As Ralph Ellison reminds us, "The slaves often took the essence of the aristocratic ideal (as they took Christianity) with far more seriousness than their masters."[41] In their language, in their religion with its focus on the Exodus theme and on Jesus's tribulations, in their music with its figuring of suffering, resistance, perseverance, and transcendence, in their interrogation of a political philosophy which sought perpetually to rationalize their bondage in a supposedly "free" society, the slaves incorporated elements of racial rule into their thought and practice, turning them against their original bearers.

Racial rule can be understood as a slow and uneven historical process which has moved from dictatorship to democracy, from domination to hegemony. In this transition, hegemonic forms of racial rule—those based on consent—eventually came to supplant those based on coercion. Of course, before this assertion can be accepted, it must be qualified in important ways. By no means has the U.S. established racial democracy at the end of the century, and by no means is coercion a thing of the past. But the sheer complexity of the racial questions U.S. society confronts today, the welter of competing racial projects and contradictory racial experiences which Americans undergo, suggests that hegemony is a useful and appropriate term with which to characterize contemporary racial rule.

Our key theoretical notion of racial projects helps to extend and broaden the question of rule. Projects are the building blocks not just of racial formation, but of hegemony in general.

Hegemony operates by simultaneously structuring and signifying. As in the case of racial opposition, gender- or class-based conflict today links structural inequity and injustice on the one hand, and identifies and represents its subjects on the other. The success of modern-day feminism, for example, has depended on its ability to reinterpret gender as a matter of both injustice and identity/difference.

Today, political opposition necessarily takes shape on the terrain of hegemony. Far from ruling principally through exclusion and coercion (though again, these are hardly absent) hegemony operates by including its subjects, incorporating its opposition. *Pace* both Marxists and liberals, there is no longer any universal or privileged region of political action or discourse.[42] Race, class, and gender all represent potential antagonisms whose significance is no longer given, if it ever was.

Thus race, class, and gender (as well as sexual orientation) constitute "regions" of hegemony, areas in which certain political projects can take shape. They share certain obvious attributes in that they are all "socially constructed," and they all consist of a field of projects whose common feature is their linkage of social structure and signification.

Going beyond this, it is crucial to emphasize that race, class, and gender, are not fixed and discrete categories, and that such "regions" are by no means autonomous. They overlap, intersect, and fuse with each other in countless ways. Such mutual determinations have been illustrated by Patricia Hill Collins's survey and theoretical synthesis of the themes and issues of black feminist thought.[43] They are also evident in Evelyn Nakano Glenn's work on the historical and contemporary racialization of domestic and service work.[44] In many respects, race is gendered and gender is racialized. In institutional and everyday life, any clear demarcation of specific forms of oppression and difference is constantly being disrupted.

There are no clear boundaries between these "regions" of hegemony, so political conflicts will often invoke some or all these themes simultaneously. Hegemony is tentative, incomplete, and "messy." For example, gender inequality, and their frequent genuflections before the altar of hard work and upward mobility, managed to synthesize various race, gender, and class projects in a particularly explosive combination.[45]

What distinguishes political opposition today—racial or otherwise—is its insistence on identifying itself and speaking for itself, its determined demand for the transformation of the social structure, its refusal of the "common sense" understandings which the hegemonic order imposes. Nowhere is this refusal of "common sense" more needed, or more imperilled, than in our understanding of racism.

What Is Racism?

Since the ambiguous triumph of the civil rights movement in the mid-1960s, clarity about what racism means has been eroding. The concept entered the lexicon of "common sense" only in the 1960s. Before that, although the term had surfaced occasionally,[46] the problem of racial injustice and inequality was generally understood in a more limited fashion, as a matter of prejudiced attitudes or bigotry on the one hand,[47] and discriminatory practices on the other.[48] Solutions, it was believed, would therefore involve the overcoming of such attitudes, the achievement of tolerance, the acceptance of "brotherhood," etc., and the passage of laws which prohibited discrimination with respect to access to public accommodations, jobs, education, etc. The early civil rights movement explicitly reflected such views. In its espousal of integration and its quest for a "beloved community" it sought to overcome racial prejudice. In its litigation activities and agitation for civil rights legislation it sought to challenge discriminatory practices.

The later 1960s, however, signalled a sharp break with this vision. The emergence of the slogan "black power" (and soon after, of "brown power," "red power," and "yellow power"), the wave of riots that swept the urban ghettos from 1964 to 1968, and the founding of radical movement organizations of nationalist and Marxist orientation, coincided with the recognition that racial inequality and injustice had much deeper roots. They were not simply the product of prejudice, nor was discrimination only a matter of intentionally informed action. Rather, prejudice was an almost unavoidable outcome of patterns of socialization which were "bred in the bone," affecting not only whites but even minorities themselves.[49] Discrimination, far from manifesting itself only (or even principally) through individual actions or conscious policies, was a structural feature of U.S. society, the product of centuries of systematic exclusion, exploitation, and disregard of racially defined minorities.[50] It was this combination of relationships—prejudice, discrimination, and institutional inequality—which defined the concept of racism at the end of the 1960s.

Such a synthesis was better able to confront the political realities of the period. Its emphasis on the structural dimensions of racism allowed it to address the intransigence which racial injustice and inequality continued to exhibit, even after discrimination had supposedly been outlawed[51] and bigoted expression stigmatized. But such an approach also had clear limitations. As Robert Miles has argued, it tended to "inflate" the concept of racism to a point at which it lost precision.[52] If the "institutional" component of racism were so pervasive and deeply rooted, it became difficult to see how the democratization of U.S. society could be achieved, and difficult to explain what progress had been made. The result was a levelling critique which denied any distinction between the Jim Crow era (or even the whole *longue durée* of racial dictatorship since the conquest) and the present. Similarly, if the prejudice component of racism were so deeply inbred, it became difficult to account for the evident hybridity and interpenetration that characterizes civil society in the U.S., as evidenced by the shaping of popular culture, language, and style, for example. The result of the "inflation" of the concept of racism was thus a deep pessimism about any efforts to overcome racial barriers, in the workplace, the community, or any other sphere of lived experience. An overly comprehensive view of racism, then, potentially served as a self-fulfilling prophecy.

Yet the alternative view—which surfaced with a vengeance in the 1970s—urging a return to the conception of racism held before the movement's "radical turn," was equally inadequate. This was the neoconservative perspective, which deliberately restricted its attention to injury done to the individual as opposed to the group, and to advocacy of a color-blind racial policy.[53] Such an approach reduced race to ethnicity,[54] and almost entirely neglected the continuing organization of social inequality and oppression along racial lines. Worse yet, it tended to rationalize racial injustice as a supposedly natural outcome of group attributes in competition.[55]

The distinct, and contested, meanings of racism which have been advanced over the past three decades have contributed to an overall crisis of meaning for the concept today. Today, the absence of a clear "common sense" understanding of what racism means has become a significant obstacle to efforts aimed at challenging it. Bob Blauner has noted that in classroom discussions of racism, white and non-white students tend to talk past one another. Whites tend to locate racism in color consciousness and find its absence colorblindness. In so doing, they see the affirmation of difference and racial identity among racially defined minority students as racist. Non-white students, by contrast, see racism as a system of power, and correspondingly argue that blacks, for example, cannot be racist because they lack power. Blauner concludes that there are two "languages" of race, one in which members of racial minorities, especially blacks, see the centrality of race in history and everyday experience, and another in which whites see race as "a peripheral, nonessential reality."[56]

Given this crisis of meaning, and in the absence of any "common sense" understanding, does the concept of racism retain any validity? If so, what view of racism should we adopt? Is a more coherent theoretical approach possible? We believe it is.

We employ racial formation theory to reformulate the concept of racism. Our approach recognizes that racism, like race, has changed over time. It is obvious that the attitudes, practices, and institutions of the epochs of slavery, say, or of Jim Crow, no longer exist today. Employing a similar logic, it is reasonable to question whether concepts of racism which developed in the early days of the post–civil rights era, when the limitations of both moderate reform and militant racial radicalism of various types had not yet been encountered, remain adequate to explain circumstances and conflicts a quarter-century later.

Racial formation theory allows us to differentiate between race and racism. The two concepts should not be used interchangeably. We have argued that race has no fixed meaning, but is constructed and transformed sociohistorically through competing political projects, through the necessary and ineluctable link between the structural and cultural dimensions of race in the U.S. This emphasis on projects allows us to refocus our understanding of racism as well, for racism can now be seen as characterizing some, but not all, racial projects.

A racial project can be defined as *racist* if and only if it *creates or reproduces structures of domination based on essentialist[57] categories of race*. Such a definition recognizes the importance of locating racism within a fluid and contested history of racially based social structures and discourses. Thus there can be no timeless and absolute standard for what constitutes racism, for social structures change and discourses are subject to rearticulation. Our definition therefore focuses instead on the "work" essentialism does for domination, and the "need" domination displays to essentialize the subordinated.

Further, it is important to distinguish racial awareness from racial essentialism. To attribute merits, allocate values or resources to, and/or represent individuals or groups on the basis of racial identity should not be considered racist in and of itself. Such projects may in fact be quite benign.

Consider the following examples: first, the statement, "Many Asian Americans are highly entrepreneurial"; second, the organization of an association of, say, black accountants.

The first racial project, in our view, signifies or represents a racial category ("Asian Americans") and locates that representation within the social structure of the contemporary U.S. (in regard to business, class issues, socialization, etc.). The second racial project is organizational or social structural, and therefore must engage in racial signification. Black accountants, the organizers might maintain, have certain common experiences, can offer each other certain support, etc. Neither of these racial projects is essentialist, and neither can fairly be labelled racist. Of course, racial representations may be biased or misinterpret their subjects, just as racially based organizational efforts may be unfair or unjustifiably exclusive. If such were the case, if for instance in our first example the statement in question were "Asian Americans are naturally entrepreneurial," this would by our criterion be racist. Similarly, if the effort to organize black accountants had as its rationale the raiding of clients from white accountants, it would by our criterion be racist as well.

Similarly, to allocate values or resources—let us say, academic scholarships—on the basis of racial categories is not racist. Scholarships are awarded on a preferential basis to Rotarians, children of insurance company employees, and residents of the Pittsburgh metropolitan area. Why then should they not also be offered, in particular cases, to Chicanos or Native Americans?

In order to identify a social project as racist, one must in our view demonstrate a link between essentialist representations of race and social structures of domination. Such a link might be revealed in efforts to protect dominant interests, framed in racial terms, from democratizing racial initiatives.[58] But it might also consist of efforts simply to reverse the roles of racially dominant and racially subordinate.[59] There is nothing inherently white about racism.[60]

Obviously a key problem with essentialism is its denial, or flattening, of differences within a particular racially defined group. Members of subordinate racial groups, when faced with racist practices such as exclusion or discrimination, are frequently forced to band together in order to defend their interests (if not, in some instances, their very lives). Such "strategic essentialism" should not, however, be simply equated with the essentialism practiced by dominant groups, nor should it prevent the interrogation of internal group differences.[61]

Without question, any abstract concept of racism is severely put to the test by the untidy world of reality. To illustrate our discussion, we analyze the following examples, chosen from current racial issues because of their complexity and the rancorous debates they have engendered:

◆ Is the allocation of employment opportunities through programs restricted to racially defined minorities, so-called "preferential treatment" or affirmative action policies, racist? Do such policies practice "racism in reverse"? We think not, with certain qualifications. Although such programs necessarily employ racial criteria in assessing eligibility, they do not generally essentialize race, because they seek to overcome specific socially and historically constructed inequalities.[62] Criteria of effectiveness and feasibility, therefore, must be considered in evaluating such programs. They must balance egalitarian and context-specific objectives, such as academic potential or job-related qualifications. It should be acknowledged that such programs often do have deleterious consequences for whites who are not personally the source of the discriminatory practices the programs seek to overcome. In this case, compensatory measures should be enacted to vitiate the charge of "reverse discrimination."[63]

◆ Is all racism the same, or is there a distinction between white and non-white versions of racism? We have little patience with the argument that racism is solely a white problem, or even a "white disease."[64] The idea that non-whites cannot act in a racist manner, since they do not possess "power," is another variant of this formulation.[65]

For many years now, racism has operated in a more complex fashion than this, sometimes taking such forms as self-hatred or self-aggrandizement at the expense of more vulnerable members of racially subordinate groups.[66] Whites can at times be the victims of racism—by other whites or non-whites—as is the case with anti-Jewish and anti-Arab prejudice. Furthermore, unless one is prepared to argue that there has been no transformation of the U.S. racial order over the years, and that racism consequently has remained unchanged—an essentialist position *par excellence*—it is difficult to contend that racially defined minorities have attained no power or influence, especially in recent years. Having said this, we still do not consider that all racism is the same. This is because of the crucial importance we place in situating various "racisms" within the dominant hegemonic discourse about race. We have little doubt that the rantings of a Louis Farrakhan or Leonard Jeffries—to pick two currently demonized black ideologues—meet the criteria we have set out for judging a discourse to be racist. But if we compare Jeffries, for example, with a white racist such as Tom Metzger of the White Aryan Resistance, we find the latter's racial project to be far more menacing than the former's. Metzger's views are far more easily associated with an essentializing (and once very powerful) legacy: that of white supremacy and racial dictatorship in the U.S., and fascism in the world at large. Jeffries's project has far fewer examples with which to associate: no more than some ancient African empires and the (usually far less bigoted) radical phase of the black power movement.[67] Thus black supremacy may be an instance of racism, just as its advocacy may be offensive, but it can hardly constitute the threat that white supremacy has represented in the U.S., nor can it be so easily absorbed and rearticulated in the dominant hegemonic discourse on race as white supremacy can. All racisms, all racist political projects, are not the same.

◆ Is the redrawing—or gerrymandering—of adjacent electoral districts to incorporate large numbers of racially defined minority voters in one, and largely white voters in the other, racist? Do such policies amount to "segregation" of the electorate? Certainly this alternative is preferable to the pre-Voting Rights Act practice of simply denying racial minorities the franchise. But does it achieve the Act's purpose of fostering electoral equality across and within racial lines? In our view such practices, in which the post-1990 redistricting process engaged rather widely—are vulnerable to charges of essentialism. They often operate through "racial lumping," tend to freeze rather than overcome racial inequalities, and frequently subvert or defuse political processes through which racially defined groups could otherwise negotiate their differences and interests. They worsen rather than ameliorate the denial of effective representation to those whom they could not effectively redistrict—since no redrawing of electoral boundaries is perfect, those who get stuck on the "wrong side" of the line are particularly disempowered. Thus we think such policies merit the designation of "tokenism"—a relatively mild form of racism—which they have received.[68]

Parallel to the debates on the concept of race, recent academic and political controversies about the nature of racism have centered on whether it is primarily an ideological or structural phenomenon. Proponents of the former position argue that racism is first and foremost a matter of beliefs and attitudes, doctrines and discourse, which only then give rise to unequal and unjust practices and structures.[69] Advocates of the latter view see racism as primarily a matter of economic stratification, residential segregation, and other institutionalized forms of inequality which then give rise to ideologies of privilege.[70]

From the standpoint of racial formation, these debates are fundamentally misguided. They frame the problem of racism in a rigid "either-or" manner. We believe it is crucial to disrupt the fixity of these positions by simultaneously arguing that ideological beliefs have structural consequences, and that social structures give rise to beliefs. Racial ideology and social structure, therefore, mutually shape the nature of racism in a complex, dialectical, and overdetermined manner.

Even those racist projects which at first glance appear chiefly ideological turn out upon closer examination to have significant institutional and social structural dimensions. For example, what we have called "far right" projects appear at first glance to be centrally ideological. They are rooted in biologistic doctrine, after all. The same seems to hold for certain conservative black nationalist projects which have deep commitments to biologism.[71] But the unending stream of racist assaults initiated by the far right, the apparently increasing presence of skinheads in high schools, the proliferation of neo-Nazi computer bulletin boards, and the appearance of racist talk shows on cable access channels, all suggest that the organizational manifestations of the far right racial projects exist and will endure.[72] Perhaps less threatening but still quite worrisome is the diffusion of doctrines of black superiority through some (though by no means all) university-based African American Studies departments and student organizations, surely a serious institutional or structural development.

By contrast, even those racisms which at first glance appear to be chiefly structural upon closer examination reveal a deeply ideological component. For example, since the racial right abandoned its explicit advocacy of segregation, it has not seemed to uphold—in the main—an ideologically racist project, but more primarily a structurally racist one. Yet this very transformation required tremendous efforts of ideological production. It demanded the rearticulation of civil rights doctrines of equality in suitably conservative form, and indeed the defense of continuing large-scale racial inequality as an outcome preferable to (what its advocates have seen as) the threat to democracy that affirmative action, busing, and large-scale "race-specific" social spending would entail.[73] Even more tellingly, this project took shape through a deeply manipulative coding of subtextual appeals to white racism, notably in a series of political campaigns for high office which have occurred over recent decades. The retreat of social policy from any practical commitment to racial justice, and the relentless reproduction and divulgation of this theme at the level of everyday life—where whites are now "fed up" with all the "special treatment" received by non-whites, etc.—constitutes the hegemonic racial project at this time. It therefore exhibits an unabashed structural racism all the more brazen because on the ideological or signification level, it adheres to a principle of "treating everyone alike."

In summary, the racism of today is no longer a virtual monolith, as was the racism of yore. Today, racial hegemony is "messy." The complexity of the present situation is the product of a vast historical legacy of structural inequality and invidious racial representation, which has been confronted during the post-World War II period with an opposition more serious and effective than any it had faced before.

Notes

1. *San Francisco Chronicle*, 14 September 1982, 19 May 1983. Ironically, the 1970 Louisiana law was enacted to supersede an old Jim Crow statute which relied on the idea of "common report" in determining an infant's race. Following Phipps' unsuccessful attempt to change her classification and have the law declared unconstitutional, a legislative effort arose which culminated in the repeal of the law. See *San Francisco Chronicle*, 23 June 1983.

2. Compare the Phipps case of Andrew Hacker's well-known "parable" in which a white person is informed by a mysterious official that "the organization he represents has made a mistake" and that ". . . [a]ccording to their records . . . , you were to have been born black: to another set of parents, far from where you were raised." How much compensation, Hacker's official asks, would "you" require to undo the damage of this unfortunate error? See Hacker, *Two Nations: Black and White, Separate, Hostile, Unequal* (New York: Charles Scribner's Sons, 1992), pp. 31–32.

3. On the evolution of Louisiana's racial classification system, see Virginia Dominguez, *White By Definition: Social Classification in Creole Louisiana* (New Brunswick: Rutgers University Press, (1986).

4. This is not to suggest that gender is a biological category while race is not. Gender, like race, is a social construct. However, the biological division of humans into sexes—two at least, and possibly intermediate ones as well—is not in dispute. This provides a basis for argument over gender divisions—how "natural," etc.—which does not exist with regard to race. To ground an argument for the "natural" existence of race, one must resort to philosophical anthropology.

5. "The truth is that there are no races, there is nothing in the world that can do all we ask race to do for us. . . . The evil that is done is done by the concept, and by easy—yet impossible—assumptions as to its application." (Kwame Anthony Appiah, *In My Father's House: Africa in the Philosophy of Culture* [New York: Oxford University Press, 1992.]) Appiah's eloquent and learned book fails, in our view, to dispense with the race concept, despite its anguished attempt to do so; this indeed is the source of its author's anguish. We agree with him as to the non-objective character of race, but fail to see how this recognition justifies its abandonment. This argument is developed below.

6. We understand essentialism as *belief in real, true human, essences, existing outside or impervious to social and historical context*. We draw this definition, with some small modifications, from Diana Fuss, *Essentially Speaking: Feminism, Nature, & Difference* (New York: Routledge, 1989), p. xi.

7. Michael Omi and Howard Winant, "On the Theoretical Status of the Concept of Race" in Warren Crichlow and Cameron McCarthy, eds., *Race, Identity, and Representation in Education* (New York: Routledge, 1993).

8. Charles Murray, *Losing Ground: American Social Policy*, 1950–1980 (New York: Basic Books, 1984), p. 223.

9. Justice Thurgood Marshall, dissenting in *City of Richmond v. J. A. Croson Co.*, 488 U.S. 469 (1989).

10. See, for example, Derrick Bell, "Remembrances of Racism Past; Getting Past the Civil Rights Decline," in Herbert Hill and James E. Jones, Jr., eds., *Race in America: The Strug-*

gle for Equality (Madison: The University of Wisconsin Press, 1993) pp. 75–76; Gertrude Ezorsky, *Racism and Justice: The Case for Affirmative Action* (Ithaca: Cornell University Press, 1991) pp. 109–111; David Kairys, *With Liberty and Justice for Some: A Critique of the Conservative Supreme Court* (New York: The New Press, 1993) pp. 138–41.

11. Howard Winant has developed a tentative "map" of the system of racial hegemony in the U.S. circa 1990, which focuses on the spectrum of racial projects running from the political right to the political left. See Winant, "Where Culture Meets Structure: Race in the 1990s" in idem, *Racial Conditions: Politics, Theory, Comparisons* (Minneapolis: University of Minnesota Press, 1994).

12. A familiar example is use of racial "code words." Recall George Bush's manipulations of racial fear in the 1988 "Willie Horton" ads, or Jesse Helms's use of the coded term "quota" in his 1990 campaign against Harvey Gantt.

13. From this perspective, far right racial projects can also be interpreted as "nationalist." See Ronald Walters, "White Racial Nationalism in the United States," *Without Prejudice* Vol. 1, no. 1 (Fall 1987).

14. To be sure, any effort to divide racial formation patterns according to social structural location—"macro" vs. "micro," for example—is necessarily an analytic device. In the concrete, there is no such dividing line. See Winant, "Where Culture Meets Structure."

15. We are not unaware, for example, that publishing this work is in itself a racial project.

16. Antisemitism only began to be racialized in the 18th century, as George L. Mosse clearly shows in his important *Toward the Final Solution: A History of European Racism* (New York: Howard Fertig, 1978).

17. As Marx put it:

    The discovery of gold and silver in America, the extirpation, enslavement, and entombment in mines of the aboriginal population, the beginning of the conquest and looting of the East Indies, the turning of Africa into a warren for the commercial hunting of blackskins, signalized the rosy dawn of the era of capitalist production. These idyllic proceedings are the chief momenta of primitive accumulation. (Karl Marx. *Capital*. Vol. 1 (New York: International Publishers, 1967) p. 751.)

    David E. Stannard argues that the wholesale slaughter perpetrated upon the native peoples of the Western hemisphere is unequalled in history, even in our own bloody century. See his *American Holocaust: Columbus and the Conquest of the New World* (New York: Oxford University Press, 1992).

18. Winthrop Jordan provides a detailed account of the sources of European attitudes about color and race in *White Over Black: American Attitudes Toward the Negro, 1550–1812* (New York: Norton, 1977 [1968]) pp. 3–43.

19. In a famous instance, a 1550 debate in Valladolid pitted the philosopher and translator of Aristotle, Gines de Sepulveda, against the Dominican Bishop of the Mexican state of Chiapas, Bartolome de Las Casas. Discussing the native peoples, Sepulveda argued that:

    In wisdom, skill, virtue and humanity, these people are as inferior to the Spaniards as children are to adults and women to men; there is as great a difference between them as there is between savagery and forbearance, between violence and moderation, almost—I am inclined to say, as between monkeys and men (Sepulveda, *Democrates Alter*, quoted in Tsvetan Todorov, *The Conquest of America; The Question of the Other* (New York: Harper and Row, 1984), p. 153).

    In contrast, Las Casas defended the humanity and equality of the native peoples, both in terms of their way of life—which he idealized as one of innocence, gentleness, and generosity—and in terms of their readiness for conversion to Catholicism, which for him as for Sepulveda was the true and universal religion (Las Casas, "Letter to the Council of the Indies" quoted ibid, p. 163). William E. Connolly interrogates the linkages proposed by Todorov between early Spanish colonialism and contemporary conceptions of identity and difference in *Identity/Difference: Democratic Negotiations of Political Paradox* (Ithaca: Cornell University Press, 1991), pp. 40–48.

20. In Virginia, for example, it took about two decades after the establishment of European colonies to extirpate the indigenous people of the greater vicinity; fifty years after the establishment of the first colonies, the elaboration of slave codes establishing race as *prima facie* evidence for enslaved status was well under way. See Jordan, *White Over Black*.

21. Marx, *Capital*, p. 751.

22. Edward W. Said, *Culture and Imperialism* (New York: Alfred A. Knopf, 1993).

23. David Brion Davis, *The Problem of Slavery in The Age of Revolution* (Ithaca: Cornell University Press, 1975).

24. Quoted in Thomas F. Gossett, *Race: The History of an Idea in America* (New York: Shocken Books, 1965) p. 45.

25. Thomas Jefferson, *Notes on Virginia* [1787], in Merrill D. Peterson, *Writings of Thomas Jefferson* (New York: The Library of America, 1984) pp. 264–66, 270. Thanks to Kimberly Benston for drawing our attention to this passage.

26. Proslavery physician Samuel George Morton (1799–1851) compiled a collection of 800 crania from all parts of the world which formed the sample for his studies of race. Assuming that the larger the size of the cranium transited into greater intelligence, Morton established a relationship between race and skull capacity. Gossett reports that "In 1849, one of his studies included the following results: the English skulls in his collection proved to be the largest, with an average cranial capacity of 96 cubic inches. The Americans and Germans were rather poor seconds, both with cranial capacities of 90 cubic inches. At the bottom of the list were the Negroes with 83 cubic inches, the Chinese with 82, and the Indians with 79." Gossett, *Race*, p. 74. More recently, Steven Jay Gould has reexamined Morton's data, and shown that his research data were deeply, though unconsciously, manipulated to agree with his "a priori conviction about racial ranking." (Gould, *The Mismeasure of Man* [New York: W. W. Norton, 1981] pp. 50–69.

27. Definitions of race founded upon a common pool of genes have not held up when confronted by scientific research which suggests that the differences *within* a given human population are every bit as great as those *between* populations. See L. L. Cavalli-Sforza, "The Genetics of Human Populations," *Scientific American* (September 1974) pp. 81–89.

28. A fascinating summary critique of Gobineau is provided in Tsvetan Todorov, *On Human Diversity: Nationalism, Racism, and Exoticism in French Thought*, trans. Catherine Porter (Cambridge, MA: Harvard University Press, 1993), esp. pp. 129–40.

29. Two recent histories of eugenics are Alien Chase, *The Legacy of Malthus* (New York: Knopf, 1977); Daniel J. Kevles, *In the Name of Eugenics: Genetics and the Uses of Human Heredity* (New York: Knopf, 1985).

30. Arthur Jensen. "How Much Can We Boost IQ and Scholastic Achievement?" *Harvard Educational Review* 39 (1969) pp. 1–123.

31. See Weber, *Economy and Society*, Vol. I (Berkeley: University of California Press, 1978), pp. 385–87; Ernst Much Manasse, "Max Weber on Race," *Social Research*, Vol. 14 (1947) pp. 191–221.

32. Du Bois, *The Souls of Black Folk* (New York: Penguin, 1989 [1903]), p. 13. Du Bois himself wrestled heavily with the conflict between a fully sociohistorical conception of race, and the more essentialized and deterministic vision he encountered as a student in Berlin. In "The Conservation of Races" (1897) we can see his first mature effort to resolve this conflict in a vision which combined racial solidarity and a commitment to social equality. See Du Bois, "The Conservation of Races," in Dan. S. Green and Edwin D. Driver, eds., *W. E. B. Du Bois on Sociology and the Black Community* (Chicago: University of Chicago Press, 1978) pp. 238–49; Manning Marable, *W. E. B. Du Bois: Black Radical Democrat* (Boston: Twayne, 1986) pp. 35–38. For a contrary, and we believe incorrect reading, see Appiah, *In My Father's House*, pp. 28–46.

33. A good collection of Boas's work is George W. Stocking, ed., *The Shaping of American Anthropology, 1883–1911: A Franz Boas Reader* (Chicago: University of Chicago Press, 1974).

34. Robert E. Park's Race and Culture (Glencoe, IL: Free Press, 1950) can still provide insight; see also Stanford H. Lyman, *Militarism, Imperialism, and Racial Accommodation: An Analysis and Interpretation of the Early Writings of Robert E. Park* (Fayetteville: University of Arkansas Press, 1992); Locke's views are concisely expressed in Alain Leroy Locke, *Race Contacts and Interracial Relations*, ed. Jeffrey C. Stewart (Washington, DC: Howard University Press, 1992), originally a series of lectures given at Howard University.

35. Japanese, for example, could not become naturalized citizens until passage of the 1952 McCarran-Walter Act. It took over 160 years, since the passage of the Law of 1790, to allow all "races" to be eligible for naturalization.

36. Especially when we recall that until around 1960, the majority of blacks, the largest racially defined minority group, lived in the South.

37. Toni Morrison, *Playing in the Dark: Whiteness and the Literary Imagination* (Cambridge, MA: Harvard University Press, 1992); Richard Drinnon, *Facing West: The Metaphysics of Indian-Hating and Empire-Building* (Minneapolis: University of Minnesota Press, 1980); Michael Paul Rosin, *Fathers and Children: Andrew Jackson and the Subjugation of the American Indian* (New York: Knopf, 1975).

38. This term refers to the practice, widespread throughout the Americas, whereby runaway slaves formed communities in remote areas, such as swamps, mountains, or forests, often in alliance with dispossessed indigenous peoples.

39. Antonio Gramsci, *Selections from the Prison Notebooks*, edited and translated by Quintin Hoare and Geoffrey Nowell Smith (New York: International Publishers, 1971) p. 182.

40. Anne Showstack Sassoon, *Gramsci's Politics*, 2nd ed. (London: Hutchinson. 1987): Sue Golding. *Gramsci's Democratic Theory: Contributions to Post-Liberal Democracy* (Toronto: University of Toronto Press, 1992).

41. Ralph Ellison, *Shadow and Act* (New York: New American Library, 1966) p. xiv.

42. Chantal Mouffe makes a related argument in "Radical Democracy: Modern or Postmodern?" in Andrew Ross, ed., *Universal Abandon: The Politics of Postmodernism* (Minneapolis: University of Minnesota Press, 1988).

43. Patricia Hill Collins, *Black Feminist Thought: Knowledge, Consciousness, and the Politics of Empowerment* (New York and London: Routledge, 1991).

44. Evelyn Nakano Glenn, "From Servitude to Service Work: Historical Continuities in the Racial Division of Paid Reproductive Labor," *Signs: Journal of Women in Culture & Society*, Vol. 18, no. 1 (Autumn 1992).

45. Toni Morrison, ed., *Race-ing Justice, En-gendering Power: Essays on Anita Hill, Clarence Thomas, and the Construction of Social Reality* (New York: Pantheon, 1992).

46. For example, in Magnus Hirschfeld's prescient book, *Racism* (London: Victor Gollancz, 1938).

47. This was the framework, employed in the crucial study of Myrdal and his associates; see Gunnar Myrdal, *An American Dilemma: The Negro Problem and Modern Democracy*, 20th Anniversary Edition (New York: Harper and Row, 1962 [1944]). See also the articles by Thomas F. Pettigrew and George Fredrickson in Pettigrew et al., *Prejudice: Selections from The Harvard Encyclopedia of American Ethnic Groups* (Cambridge, MA: The Belknap Press of Harvard University, 1982).

48. On discrimination, see Frederickson in ibid. In an early essay which explicitly sought to modify the framework of the Mydral study, Robert K. Merton recognized that prejudice and discrimination need not coincide, and indeed could combine in a variety of ways. See "Merton, Discrimination and the American Creed," in R.M. McIver, ed., *Discrimination and National Welfare* (New York: Harper and Row, 1949).

49. Gordon W. Allport, *The Nature of Prejudice* (Cambridge, MA: Addison-Wesley, 1954) remains a classic work in the field; see also Philomena Essed, *Understanding Everyday Racism: An Interdisciplinary Theory* (Newbury Park, CA: Sage, 1991). A good overview of black attitudes toward black identities is provided in William E. Cross, Jr., *Shades of Black: Diversity in African-American Identity* (Philadelphia: Temple University Press, 1991).

50. Stokely Carmichael and Charles V. Hamilton first popularized the notion of "institutional" forms of discrimination in *Black Power: The Politics of Liberation in America* (New York: Vintage, 1967), although the basic concept certainly predated that work. Indeed, President Lyndon Johnson made a similar argument in his 1965 speech at Howard University:

    > But freedom is not enough. You do not wipe away the scars of centuries by saying: Now you are free to go where you want, do as you desire, and choose the leaders you please.
    >
    > You do not take a person who, for years, has been hobbled by chains and liberate him (sic), bring him up to the starting line of a race and then say, "You are free to compete with all the others," and still justly believe that you have been completely fair.
    >
    > Thus it is not enough just to open the gates of opportunity. All our citizens must have the opportunity to walk through those gates.
    >
    > This is the next and more profound stage of the battle for civil rights. We seek not just freedom but opportunity—not just legal equity but human ability—not just equality as a right but equality as a fact and as a result. (Lyndon B. Johnson, "To Fulfill These Rights," reprinted in Lee Rainwater and William L. Yancey, *The Moynihan Report and the Politics of Controversy* [Cambridge, MA: MIT Press, 1967, p. 125].)

    This speech, delivered at Howard University on June 4, 1965, was written in part by Daniel Patrick Moynihan. A more systematic treatment of the institutional racism approach is David T. Wellman, *Portraits of White Racism* (New York: Cambridge University Press, 1977).

51. From the vantage point of the 1990s, it is possible to question whether discrimination was ever effectively outlawed. The federal retreat from the agenda of integration began almost immediately after the passage of civil rights legislation, and has culminated today in a series of Supreme Court decisions making violation of these laws almost impossible to prove. See Ezorsky, *Racism and Justice*; Kairys, *With Liberty and Justice for Some*. As

we write, the Supreme Court has further restricted antidiscrimination laws in the case of *St. Mary's Honor Center v. Hicks*. See Linda Greenhouse, "Justices Increase Workers' Burden in Job-Bias Cases," *The New York Times*, 26 June 1993, p. 1.

52. Robert Miles, *Racism* (New York and London: Routledge, 1989), esp. chap. 2.

53. The locus classics of this position is Nathan Glazer, *Affirmative Discrimination: Ethnic Inequality and Public Policy*, 2nd ed. (New York: Basic Books, 1978); for more recent formulations, see Murray, *Losing Ground*; Arthur M. Schlesinger, *The Disuniting of America: Reflections on a Multicultural Society* (New York: W. W. Norton, 1992).

54. See Chapter 1.

55. Thomas Sowell, for example, has argued that one's "human capital" is to a large extent culturally determined. Therefore the state cannot create a false equality which runs counter to the magnitude and persistence of cultural differences. Such attempts at social engineering are likely to produce negative and unintended results; "If social processes are transmitting real differences—in productivity, reliability, cleanliness, sobriety, peacefulness [!]—then attempts to impose politically a very different set of beliefs will necessarily backfire. . . ." (Thomas Sowell, *The Economics and Politics of Race: An International Perspective* (New York: Quill, 1983) p. 252).

56. Bob Blauner "Racism, Race, and Ethnicity: Some Reflections on the Language of Race" (unpublished manuscript, 1991).

57. Essentialism, it will be recalled, is understood as belief in real, true human essences, existing outside or impervious to social and historical context.

58. An example would be the "singling out" of members of racially defined minority groups for harsh treatment by authorities, as when police harass and beat randomly chosen ghetto youth, a practice they do not pursue with white suburban youth.

59. For example, the biologistic theories found in Michael Anderson Bradley, *The Iceman Inheritance: Prehistoric Sources of Western Man's Racism, Sexism' and Aggression* (Toronto: Dorset, 1978), and in Frances Cress Welsing, *The Isis (Yssis) Papers* (Chicago: Third World Press, 1991).

60. "These remarks should not be interpreted as simply an effort to move the gaze of African-American studies to a different site. I do not want to alter one hierarchy in order to institute another. It is true that I do not want to encourage those totalizing approaches to African-American scholarship which have no drive other than the exchange of dominations—dominant Eurocentric scholarship replaced by dominant Afrocentric scholarship. More interesting is what makes intellectual domination possible; how knowledge is transformed from invasion and conquest to revelation and choice; what ignites and informs the literary imagination, and what forces help establish the parameters of criticism." (Toni Morrison, *Playing in the Dark*, p. 8; emphasis original.)

61. Lisa Lowe states: "The concept of 'strategic essentialism' suggests that it is possible to utilize specific signifiers of ethnic identity, such as Asian American, for the purpose of contesting and disrupting the discourses that exclude Asian Americans, while simultaneously revealing the internal contradictions and slippages of Asian Americans so as to insure that such essentialisms will not be reproduced and proliferated by the very apparatuses we seek to disempower." Lisa Lowe. "Heterogeneity, Hybridity, Multiplicity: Marking Asian American Differences," *Diaspora*, Vol. 1, no. 1 (Spring 1991), p. 39.

62. This view supports Supreme Court decisions taken in the late 1960s and early 1970s, for example in *Griggs v. Duke Power*, 401 U.S. 424 (1971). We agree with Kairys that only ". . . [F]or that brief period in our history, it could accurately be said that governmental discrimination was prohibited by law" (Kairys, *With Liberty and Justice For Some*, p. 144).

63. This analysis draws on Ezorsky, *Racism and Justice*.

64. See for example, Judy H. Katz, *White Awareness: Handbook for Anti-Racism Training* (Norman: University of Oklahoma Press, 1978).

65. The formula "racism equals prejudice plus power" is frequently invoked by our students to argue that only whites can be racist. We have been able to uncover little written analysis to support this view (apart from Katz, ibid., p. 10), but consider that it is itself an example of the essentializing approach we have identified as central to racism. In the modern world, "power" cannot be reified as a thing which some possess and others don't, but instead constitutes a relational field. The minority student who boldly asserts in class that minorities cannot be racist is surely not entirely powerless. In all but the most absolutist of regimes, resistance to rule itself implies power.

66. To pick one example among many: writing before the successes of the civil rights movement, E. Franklin Frazier bitterly castigated the collaboration of black elites with white supremacy. See Frazier, *Black Bourgeoisie: The Rise of a New Middle Class in the United States* (New York: The Free Press, 1957).

67. Interestingly, what they share most centrally seems to be their antisemitism.

68. Having made a similar argument, Lani Guinier, Clinton's nominee to head the Justice Department's Civil Rights Division was savagely attacked and her nomination ultimately blocked. See Guinier, "The Triumph of Tokenism: The Voting Rights Act and the Theory of Black Electoral Success," *Michigan Law Review* (March 1991). We discuss these events in greater detail in this book's Epilogue.

69. See Miles, *Racism*, p. 77. Much of the current debate over the advisability and legality of banning racist hate speech seems to us to adopt the dubious position that racism is primarily an ideological phenomenon. See Mari J. Matsuda et al., *Words That Wound: Critical Race Theory, Assaultive Speech, and the First Amendment* (Boulder, CO: Westview Press, 1993).

70. Or ideologies which mask privilege by falsely claiming that inequality and injustice have been eliminated. See Wellman, *Portraits of White Racism*.

71. Racial teachings of the Nation of Islam, for example, maintain that whites are the produce of a failed experiment by a mad scientist.

72. Elinor Langer, "The American Neo-Nazi Movement Today," *The Nation*, July 16/23, 1990.

73. Such arguments can be found in Nathan Glazer, *Affirmative Discrimination*, Charles Murray, *Losing Ground*, and Arthur M. Schlesinger, Jr., *The Disuniting of America*, among others.

17 | *White Privilege: Unpacking the Invisible Knapsack*

Peggy McIntosh

Through work to bring materials from Women's Studies into the rest of the curriculum, I have often noticed men's unwillingness to grant that they are over-privileged, even though they may grant that women are disadvantaged. They may say they will work to improve women's status, in the society, the university, or the curriculum, but they can't or won't support the idea of lessening men's. Denials which amount to taboos surround the subject of advantages which men gain from women's disadvantages. These denials protect male privilege from being fully acknowledged, lessened or ended.

Thinking through unacknowledged male privilege as a phenomenon, I realized that since hierarchies in our society are interlocking, there was most likely a phenomenon of white privilege which was similarly denied and protected. As a white person, I realized I had been taught about racism as something which puts others at a disadvantage, but had been taught not to see one of its corollary aspects, white privilege, which puts me at an advantage.

I think whites are carefully taught not to recognize white privilege, as males are taught not to recognize male[1] privilege. So I have begun in an untutored way to ask what it is like to have white privilege. I have come to see white privilege as an invisible package of unearned assets which I can count on cashing in each day, but about which I was 'meant' to remain oblivious. White privilege is like an invisible weightless knapsack of special provisions, maps, passports, codebooks, visas, clothes, tools and blank checks.

Describing white privilege makes one newly accountable. As we in Women's Studies work to reveal male privilege and ask men to give up some of their power, so one who writes about having white privilege must ask, "Having described it, what will I do to lessen or end it?"

Peggy McIntosh is Associate Director of the Wellesley College Center for Research on Women. This essay is excerpted from her working paper.
"White Privilege and Male Privilege: A Personal Account of Coming to See Correspondences Through Work in Women's Studies," copyright ©1988 by Peggy McIntosh. Available for $4.00 from address below. The paper includes a longer list of privileges. Permission to excerpt or reprint must be obtained from Peggy McIntosh, Wellesley College, Center for Research on Women, Wellesley, MA 02181: (617) 431-1453.

After I realized the extent to which men work from a base of unacknowledged privilege, I understood that much of their oppressiveness was unconscious. Then I remembered the frequent charges from women of color that white women whom they encounter are oppressive. I began to understand why we are justly seen as oppressive, even when we don't see ourselves that way. I began to count the ways in which I enjoy unearned skin privilege and have been conditioned into oblivion about its existence. I was taught to see racism only in individual acts of meanness, not in invisible systems conferring dominance on my group.

My schooling gave me no training in seeing myself as an oppressor, as an unfairly advantaged person, or as a participant in a damaged culture. I was taught to see myself as an individual whose moral state depended on her individual moral will. My schooling followed the pattern my colleague Elizabeth Minnich has pointed out: whites are taught to think of their lives as morally neutral, normative, and average, and also ideal, so that when we work to benefit others, this is seen as work which will allow "them" to be more like "us."

I decided to try to work on myself at least by identifying some of the daily effects of white privilege in my life. I have chosen those conditions which I think in my case *attach somewhat more to skin-color privilege* than to class, religion, ethnic status, or geographical location, though of course all of these other factors are intricately intertwined. As far as I can see, my African American-co-workers, friends and acquaintances with whom I come into daily or frequent contact in this particular time, place, and line of work cannot count on most of these conditions.

1. I can if I wish arrange to be in the company of people of my race most of the time.

2. If I should need to move, I can be pretty sure of renting or purchasing housing in an area which I can afford and in which I would want to live.

3. I can be pretty sure that my neighbor in such location will be neutral or pleasant to me.

4. I can go shopping alone most of the time, pretty well assured that I will not be followed or harassed.

5. I can turn on the television or open to the front page of the paper and see people of my race widely represented.

6. When I am told about our national heritage or about "civilization," I am shown that people of my color made it what it is.

7. I can be sure that my children will be given curricular materials that testify to the existence of their race.

8. If I want to, I can be pretty sure of finding a publisher for this piece on white privilege.

9. I can go into a music shop and count on finding the music of my race represented, into a supermarket with my cultural traditions, into a hairdresser's shop and find someone who can cut my hair.

10. Whether I use checks, credit cards, or cash, I can count on my skin color not to work against my financial reliability.

11. I can arrange to protect my children most of the time from people who might not like them.

12. I can swear, dress in second hand clothes, or not answer letters, without having people attribute these choices to the bad morals, the poverty, or illiteracy of my race.

13. I can speak in public to a powerful male group without putting my race on trial.

14. I can do well in a challenging situation without being called a credit to my race.

15. I am never asked to speak for all the people of my racial group.

16. I can remain oblivious of the language and customs of persons of color who constitute the world's majority without feeling in my culture any penalty for such oblivion.

17. I can criticize our government and talk about how much I fear its policies and behavior without being seen as a cultural outsider.

18. I can be pretty sure that if I ask to talk to "the person in charge" I will be facing a person of my race.

19. If a traffic cop pulls me over or if the IRS audits my tax return, I can be sure I haven't been singled out because of my race.

20. I can easily buy posters, postcards, picture books, greeting cards, dolls, toys, and children's magazines featuring people of my race.

21. I can go home from most meetings of organizations I belong to feeling somewhat tied in, rather than isolated, out-of-place, outnumbered, unheard, held at a distance, or feared.

22. I can take a job with an affirmative action employer without having co-workers on the job suspect that I got it because of race.

23. I can choose public accommodation without fearing that people of my race cannot get in, or will be mistreated in the places I have chosen.

24. I can be sure that if I need legal or medical help, my race will not work against me.

25. If my day, week, or year is going badly, I need not ask of each negative episode or situation whether it has racial overtones.

26. I can choose blemish color or bandages in "flesh" color and have them more or less match my skin.

I repeatedly forgot each of the realizations on the list until I wrote it down. For me white privilege has turned out to be an elusive and fugitive subject. The pressure to avoid it is great, for in facing it I must give up believing in democracy. If these things are true, this is not such a free country; one's life is not what one makes it: many doors open for certain people through no virtues of their own.

In unpacking this invisible knapsack of white privilege, I have listed conditions of daily experience which I once took for granted. Nor did I think of any of these perquisites as bad for the holder. I now think that we need a more finely differentiated taxonomy of privilege, for some of these varieties are only what one would want for everyone in a just society, and others give licence to be ignorant, oblivious, arrogant, and destructive.

I see a pattern running through the matrix of white privilege, a pattern of assumptions which were passed on to me as a white person. There was one main piece of cultural turf; it was my own turf, and I was among those who could control the turf. *My skin color was an asset for any move I was educated to want to make.* I could think of myself as belonging in major ways, and of making social systems work for me. I could freely disparage, fear, neglect, or be oblivious to anything outside of the dominant cultural forms. Being of the main culture, I could also criticize it fairly freely.

In proportion as my racial group was being made confident, comfortable, and oblivious, other groups were likely being made inconfident, uncomfortable, and alienated. Whiteness protected me from many kinds of hostility, distress, and violence, which I was being subtly trained to visit in turn upon people of color.

For this reason, the word "privilege" now seems to me misleading. We usually think of privilege as being a favored state, whether earned or conferred by birth or luck. Yet some of the conditions I have described here work to systematically overpower certain groups. Such privileges simply *confers dominance* because of one's race or sex.

I want, then, to distinguish between earned strength and unearned power conferred systematically. Power from unearned privilege can look like strength when it is in fact permission to escape or to dominate. But not all of the privileges on my list are inevitably damaging. Some, like the expectation that neighbors will be decent to you, or that your race will not count against you in court, should be the norm in a just society. Others, like the privilege to ignore less powerful people, distort humanity of the holders as well as the ignored groups.

We might at least start by distinguishing between positive advantages which we can work to spread, and negative types of advantages which unless rejected will always reinforce our present hierarchies. For example, the feeling that one belongs within the human circle, as Native Americans say, should not be seen as privilege for a few. Ideally it is an *unearned entitlement*. At present, since only a few have it, it is an *unearned advantage* for them. This paper results from a process of coming to see that some of the power which I originally saw as attendant on being a human being in the U.S. consisted in *unearned advantage* and *conferred dominance*.

I have met very few men who are truly distressed about systemic, unearned male advantage and conferred dominance. And so one question for me and others like me is whether we will be like them, or whether we will get truly distressed, even outraged, about unearned race advantage and conferred dominance and if so, what we will do to lessen them. In any case, we need to do more work in identifying how they actually affect our daily lives. Many, perhaps most, of our white students in the U.S. think that racism doesn't affect them because they are not people of color; they do not see "whiteness" as a racial identity. In addition, since race and sex are not the only advantaging systems at work, we need similarly to examine the daily experience of having age advantage, or ethnic advantage, or physical ability, or advantage related to nationality, religion, or sexual orientation.

Difficulties and dangers surrounding the task of finding parallels are many. Since racism, sexism, and heterosexism are not the same, the advantaging associated with them should not be seen as the same. In addition, it is hard to disentangle aspects of unearned advantage which rest more on social class, economic class, race, religion, sex and ethnic identity than on other factors. Still, all of the oppressions are interlocking, as the Combahee River Collective Statement of 1977 continues to remind us eloquently.

One factor seems clear about all of the interlocking oppressions. They take both active forms which we can see and embedded forms which as a member of the dominant group one is taught not to see. In my class and place, I did not see myself as a racist because I was taught to recognize racism only in individual acts of meanness by members of my group, never in invisible systems conferring unsought racial dominance on my group from birth.

The question is: "Having described white privilege, what will I do to end it?" Disapproving of the systems won't be enough to change them. I was taught to think that racism could end if white individuals changed their attitudes. [But] a "white" skin in the United States opens many doors for whites whether or not we approve of the way dominance has been conferred on us. Individual acts can palliate, but cannot end, these problems.

To redesign social systems we need first to acknowledge their colossal unseen dimensions. The silences and denials surrounding privilege are the key political tool here. They keep the thinking about equity incomplete, protecting unearned advantage and conferred dominance by making these taboo subjects. Most talk by whites about equal opportunity seems to me now to be about equal opportunity to try to get into a position of dominance while denying that *systems* of dominance exist.

It seems to me that obliviousness about white advantage, like obliviousness about male advantage, is kept strongly inculturated in the United States so as to maintain the myth of meritocracy, the myth that democratic choice is equally available to all. Keeping most people unaware that freedom of confident action is there for just a small number of people props up those in power, and serves to keep power in the hands of the same groups that have most of it already.

Though systemic change takes many decades, there are pressing questions for me and I imagine for some others like me if we raise our daily consciousness on the perquisites of being light-skinned. What will we do with such knowledge? As we know from watching men, it is an open question whether we will choose to use unearned advantage to weaken hidden systems of advantage, and whether we will use any of our arbitrarily-awarded power to try to reconstruct power systems on a broader base.

18

Ten Things You Should Know About Selma Before You See the Film

Emilye Crosby

In this 50th anniversary year of the Selma-to-Montgomery March and the Voting Rights Act it helped inspire, national media will focus on the iconic images of "Bloody Sunday," the words of Dr. Martin Luther King Jr., the interracial marchers, and President Lyndon Johnson signing the Voting Rights Act. This version of history, emphasizing a top-down narrative and isolated events, reinforces the master narrative that civil rights activists describe as "Rosa sat down, Martin stood up, and the white folks came south to save the day."

But there is a "people's history" of Selma that we all can learn from—one that is needed especially now. The exclusion of Blacks and other people of color from voting is still a live issue. Sheriff's deputies may no longer be beating people to keep them from registering to vote, but in 2013 the Supreme Court ruled in *Shelby v. Holder* that the Justice Department may no longer evaluate laws passed in the former Confederacy for racial bias. And as a new movement emerges, insisting that Black Lives Matter, young people can draw inspiration and wisdom from the courage, imagination, and accomplishments of activists who went before.

Here are 10 points to keep in mind about Selma's civil rights history.

1. **The Selma voting rights campaign started long before the modern Civil Rights Movement.**

    Mrs. Amelia Boynton Robinson, her husband Samuel William Boynton, and other African American activists founded the Dallas County Voters League (DCVL) in the 1930s. The DCVL became the base for a group of activists who pursued voting rights and economic independence.

Reprinted by permission from *Zinn Education Project* 3, (January 3, 2015).

2. **Selma was one of the communities where the Student Nonviolent Coordinating Committee (SNCC) began organizing in the early 1960s.**

   In 1963, seasoned activists Colia (Liddell) and Bernard Lafayette came to Selma as field staff for the Student Nonviolent Coordinating Committee (SNCC), known as "Snick." Founded by the young people who initiated the 1960 sit-in movement, SNCC had moved into Deep South, majority-black communities doing the dangerous work of organizing with local residents around voter registration.

   Working with the Boyntons and other DCVL members, the Lafayettes held Citizenship School classes focused on the literacy test required for voter registration and canvassed door-to-door, encouraging African Americans to try to register to vote. Prathia Hall, a SNCC field secretary who came to Selma in the fall of 1963, explained in *Hands on the Freedom Plow*:

   > *The 1965 Selma Movement could never have happened if SNCC hadn't been there opening up Selma in 1962 and 1963. The later nationally known movement was the product of more than two years of very careful, very slow work.*

3. **The white power structure used economic, "legal," and extra-legal means, including terrorism, to prevent African Americans from accessing their constitutional right to vote and to impede organizing efforts.**

   SNCC's organizing was necessary and extremely challenging because African Americans in Selma, despite being a majority in the community, were systematically disfranchised by the white elite who used literacy tests, economic intimidation, and violence to maintain the status quo.

   According to a 1961 Civil Rights Commission report, only 130 of 15,115 eligible Dallas County Blacks were registered to vote. The situation was even worse in neighboring Wilcox and Lowndes counties. There were virtually no Blacks on the voting rolls in these rural counties that were roughly 80 percent Black. Ironically, in some Alabama counties, more than 100 percent of the eligible white population was registered.

   Although many people are aware of the violent attacks during Bloody Sunday (when, on March 7, 1965, police brutally attacked marchers in Selma), white repression in Selma was systematic and long-standing. Selma was home to Sheriff Jim Clark, a violent racist, and one of Alabama's strongest white Citizens' Councils—made up of the community's white elite and dedicated to preserving white supremacy. The threat of violence was so strong that most African Americans were afraid to attend a mass meeting. Most of the Lafayettes' first recruits were high school students. Too young to vote, they canvassed and taught classes to adults. Prathia Hall remembers the danger in Alabama: ". . . [I]n Gadsden, the police used cattle prods on the torn feet [of young protesters] and stuck the prods into the groins of boys. Selma was just brutal. Civil rights workers came into town under the cover of darkness."

4. **Though civil rights activists typically used nonviolent tactics in public demonstrations, at home and in their own communities they consistently used weapons to defend themselves.**

   On June 12, 1963, the night Medgar Evers was assassinated in Jackson, Mississippi, whites viciously attacked Bernard Lafayette outside his apartment in Selma in what many believe was a coordinated effort to suppress Black activism.

   Lafayette believed in nonviolence, but his life was probably saved by a neighbor who shot into the air to scare away the white attackers.

This practice of armed self-defense was woven into the movement and, because neither local nor federal law enforcement offered sufficient protection, it was essential for keeping nonviolent activists alive.

5. **Local, state, and federal institutions conspired and were complicit in preventing black voting.**

   Even with the work of SNCC and the Dallas County Voters League, it was almost impossible for African Americans to register to vote. The registrar's office was only open twice a month and potential applicants were routinely and arbitrarily rejected. Some were physically attacked and others fired from their jobs. Howard Zinn, who visited Selma in the fall of 1963 as a SNCC advisor, offers a glimpse of the repression, noting that white officials had fired teachers for trying to register and regularly arrested SNCC workers, sometimes beating them in jail. In one instance, a police officer knocked a 19-year-old girl unconscious and brutalized her with a cattle prod.

   In another example, in summer 1964, Judge James Hare issued an injunction making it illegal for three or more people to congregate. This made demonstrations and voter registration work almost impossible while SNCC pursued the slow appeals process. Although the Justice Department pursued its own legal action to address discrimination against Black voters, its attorneys offered no protection and did nothing to intervene when local officials openly flaunted the 1957 Civil Rights Act.

   The FBI was even worse. In addition to refusing to protect civil rights workers attacked in front of agents, the FBI spied on and tried to discredit movement activists. In 1964, the FBI sent King an anonymous and threatening note urging him to commit suicide and later smeared white activist Viola Liuzzo, who was murdered after coming from Detroit to participate in the Selma-to-Montgomery March.

6. **SNCC developed creative tactics to highlight Black demand for the vote and the raw violence at the heart of Jim Crow.**

   To highlight African Americans' desire to vote and encourage a sense of collective struggle, SNCC organized a Freedom Day on Monday, Oct. 7, 1963, one of the monthly registration days. They invited Black celebrities, like James Baldwin and Dick Gregory, so Blacks in Selma would know they weren't alone.

   Over the course of the day, 350 African Americans stood in line to register, but the registrar processed only 40 applications and white lawmen refused to allow people to leave the line and return. Lawmen also arrested three SNCC workers who stood on federal property holding signs promoting voter registration.

   By mid-afternoon, SNCC was so concerned about those who had been standing all day in the bright sun, that two field secretaries loaded up their arms with water and sandwiches and approached the would-be voters.

   Highway patrolmen immediately attacked and arrested the two men, while three FBI agents and two Justice Department attorneys refused to intervene.

   This federal inaction was typical, even though Southern white officials openly defied both the Civil Rights Act of 1957 and constitutional protections of free assembly and speech. The FBI insisted it had no authority to act because these were local police matters, but consistently ignored such constraints to arrest bank robbers and others violating federal law.

7. **Selma activists invited Dr. King to join an active movement with a long history.**

   By late 1964, Martin Luther King Jr. and the Southern Christian Leadership Conference (SCLC) were looking for a local community where they could launch a campaign to force the country to confront the Southern white power structure's widespread discrimination against prospective Black voters.

At the same time, Mrs. Boynton, the longtime leader of the Dallas County Voters League, wanted to escalate the struggle in Selma and invited SCLC in. SCLC saw Selma as ideal because: (1) the ongoing work of SNCC and the DCVL provided a strong base of organizers and people who could be counted on to attend mass meetings, march in demonstrations, attempt to register, and canvass prospective registrants; (2) Sheriff Jim Clark's volatile white supremacy led King to believe he was likely to attack peaceful protesters in public, drawing national attention to the white violence underlying Black disfranchisement; and finally, (3) the Justice Department's own lawsuit charging racial discrimination in Dallas County voter registration reinforced the need for action.

8. **Youth and teachers played a significant role in the Selma Movement.**

An important breakthrough in the Selma Movement came when schoolteachers, angered by a physical attack on Mrs. Boynton, marched to the courthouse on Jan. 22, 1965. Despite the prominence of King and a handful of ministers in history books, throughout the South most teachers and ministers stayed on the sidelines during the movement. Hired and paid by white school boards and superintendents, teachers who joined the Civil Rights Movement faced almost certain job loss.

In Selma, the "teachers' march" was particularly important to the young activists at the heart of the Selma Movement. One of them, Sheyann Webb, was just 8 years old and a regular participant in the marches. She reflects in *Voices of Freedom*:

> *What impressed me most about the day that the teachers marched was just the idea of them being there. Prior to their marching, I used to have to go to school and it was like a report, you know. They were just as afraid as my parents were, because they could lose their jobs. It was amazing to see how many teachers participated. They follow[ed] us that day. It was just a thrill.*

9. **Women were central to the movement, but they were sometimes pushed to the side and today their contributions are often overlooked.**

In Selma, for example, Mrs. Amelia Boynton was a stalwart with the DCVL and played a critical role for decades in nurturing African American efforts to register to vote. She welcomed SNCC to town and helped support the younger activists and their work. When Judge Hare's injunction slowed the grassroots organizing, she initiated the invitation to King and SCLC.

Marie Foster, another local activist, taught citizenship classes even before SNCC arrived. In early 1965 when SCLC began escalating the confrontation in Selma, Boynton and Foster were both in the thick of things, inspiring others and putting their own bodies on the line. They were leaders on Bloody Sunday and the subsequent march to Montgomery.

Though Colia Liddell Lafayette worked side by side with husband Bernard, recruiting student workers and doing the painstaking work of building a grassroots movement in Selma, she has become almost invisible and typically mentioned only in passing, as his wife.

Diane Nash, whose plan for a nonviolent war on Montgomery inspired the initial Selma march, was already a seasoned veteran, leading the Nashville sit-ins, helping found SNCC, and taking decisive action to carry the freedom rides forward.

These are just a few of the many women who were critical to the movement's success—in Selma and across the country.

10. **Though President Lyndon Johnson is typically credited with passage of the Voting Rights Act, the Movement forced the issue and made it happen.**

    The Selma campaign is considered a major success for the Civil Rights Movement, largely because it was an immediate catalyst for the passage of the Voting Rights Act of 1965. Signed into law by President Lyndon B. Johnson on Aug. 6, 1965, the Voting Rights Act guaranteed active federal protection of Southern African Americans' right to vote.

    Although Johnson did support the Voting Rights Act, the critical push for the legislation came from the movement itself. SNCC's community organizing of rural African Americans, especially in Mississippi, made it increasingly difficult for the country to ignore the pervasive, violent, and official white opposition to Black voting and African American demands for full citizenship. This, in conjunction with the demonstrations organized by SCLC, generated public support for voting rights legislation.

This brief introduction to Selma's bottom-up history can help students and others learn valuable lessons for today. As SNCC veteran and filmmaker Judy Richardson said, "If we don't learn that it was people just like us—our mothers, our uncles, our classmates, our clergy—who made and sustained the modern Civil Rights Movement, then we won't know we can do it again. And then the other side wins—even before we ever begin the fight."

Emilye Crosby is a professor of history and coordinator of Black Studies at SUNY Geneseo. She is the author of *A Little Taste of Freedom* (University of North Carolina Press, 2005) and editor of *Civil Rights History from the Ground Up* (University of Georgia Press, 2011). She is currently a fellow at the National Humanities Center where she is working on a history of women and gender in SNCC.

19 | *Racial Microaggressions in Everyday Life: Implications for Clinical Practice*

Derald Wing Sue, Christina M. Capodilupo,
Gina C. Torino, Jennifer M. Bucceri, Aisha M. B.
Holder, Kevin L. Nadal, and Marta Esquilin
Teachers College, Columbia University

Racial microaggressions are brief and commonplace daily verbal, behavioral, or environmental indignities, whether intentional or unintentional, that communicate hostile, derogatory, or negative racial slights and insults toward people of color. Perpetrators of microaggressions are often unaware that they engage in such communications when they interact with racial/ethnic minorities. A taxonomy of racial microaggressions in everyday life was created through a review of the social psychological literature on aversive racism, from formulations regarding the manifestation and impact of everyday racism, and from reading numerous personal narratives of counselors (both White and those of color) on their racial/cultural awakening. Microaggressions seem to appear in three forms: microassault, microinsult, and microinvalidation. Almost all interracial encounters are prone to microaggressions; this article uses the White counselor—client of color counseling dyad to illustrate how they impair the development of a therapeutic alliance. Suggestions regarding education and training and research in the helping professions are discussed.

Editor's note. Lillian Comas-Díaz served as the action editor for this article before Derald Wing Sue joined the *American Psychologist* Editorial Board as an associate editor on January 1, 2007.

Authors' note. Derald Wing Sue, Christina M. Capodilupo, Gina C. Torino, Jennifer M. Bucceri, Aisha M. B. Holder, Kevin L. Nadal, and Marta Esquilin, Department of Counseling and Clinical Psychology, Teachers College, Columbia University.

Aisha M. B. Holder is now at Fordham University.

Correspondence concerning this article should be addressed to Derald Wing Sue, Department of Counseling and Clinical Psychology, Box 36, Teachers College, Columbia University, 525 West 120th Street, New York, NY 10027. E-mail: dwingsue@aol.com

Reprinted with permission from *American Psychologist* 62, no. 4 (May–June 2007).

Although the civil rights movement had a significant effect on changing racial interactions in this society, racism continues to plague the United States (Thompson & Neville, 1999). President Clinton's Race Advisory Board concluded that (a) racism is one of the most divisive forces in our society, (b) racial legacies of the past continue to haunt current policies and practices that create unfair disparities between minority and majority groups, (c) racial inequities are so deeply ingrained in American society that they are nearly invisible, and (d) most White Americans are unaware of the advantages they enjoy in this society and of how their attitudes and actions unintentionally discriminate against persons of color (Advisory Board to the President's Initiative on Race, 1998). This last conclusion is especially problematic in the mental health professions because most graduates continue to be White and trained primarily in Western European models of service delivery (D. W. Sue & Sue, 2003). For that reason, this article focuses primarily on White therapist–client of color interactions.

Because White therapists are members of the larger society and not immune from inheriting the racial biases of their forebears (Burkard & Knox, 2004; D. W. Sue, 2005), they may become victims of a cultural conditioning process that imbues within them biases and prejudices (Abelson, Dasgupta, Park, & Banaji, 1998; Banaji, Hardin, & Rothman, 1993) that discriminate against clients of color. Over the past 20 years, calls for cultural competence in the helping professions (American Psychological Association, 2003; D. W. Sue, Arredondo, & McDavis, 1992) have stressed the importance of two therapist characteristics associated with effective service delivery to racial/ethnic minority clients: (a) awareness of oneself as a racial/cultural being and of the biases, stereotypes, and assumptions that influence world-views and (b) awareness of the world-views of culturally diverse clients. Achieving these two goals is blocked, however, when White clinicians fail to understand how issues of race influence the therapy process and how racism potentially infects the delivery of services to clients of color (Richardson & Molinaro, 1996). Therapists who are unaware of their biases and prejudices may unintentionally create impasses for clients of color, which may partially explain well-documented patterns of therapy underutilization and premature termination of therapy among such clients (Burkard & Knox, 2004; Kearney, Draper, & Baron, 2005). In this article, we describe and analyze how racism in the form of racial microaggressions is particularly problematic for therapists to identify; propose a taxonomy of racial microaggressions with potential implications for practice, education and training, and research; and use the counseling/therapy process to illustrate how racial microaggressions can impair the therapeutic alliance. To date, no conceptual or theoretical model of racial microaggressions has been proposed to explain their impact on the therapeutic process.

The Changing Face of Racism

In recent history, racism in North America has undergone a transformation, especially after the post-civil rights era when the conscious democratic belief in equality for groups of color directly clashed with the long history of racism in the society (Jones, 1997; Thompson & Neville, 1999). The more subtle forms of racism have been labeled *modern racism* (McConahay, 1986), *symbolic racism* (Sears, 1988), and *aversive racism* (Dovidio, Gaertner, Kawakami, & Hodson, 2002). All three explanations of contemporary racism share commonalities. They emphasize that racism (a) is more likely than ever to be disguised and covert and (b) has evolved from the "old fashioned" form, in which overt racial hatred and bigotry is consciously and publicly displayed, to a more ambiguous and nebulous form that is more difficult to identify and acknowledge.

It appears that modern and symbolic racism are most closely associated with political conservatives, who disclaim personal bigotry by strong and rigid adherence to traditional American values (individualism, self-reliance, hard work, etc.), whereas aversive racism is more characteristic of White liberals (Dovidio & Gaertner, 1996, 2000). Aversive racists, according to these researchers, are strongly motivated by egalitarian values as well as antiminority feelings. Their egalitarian values operate on a conscious level, while their antiminority feelings are less conscious and generally covert (DeVos & Banaji, 2005). In some respects, these three forms of racism can be ordered along a continuum; aversive racists are the least consciously negative, followed by modern and symbolic racists, who are somewhat more prejudiced, and finally by old-fashioned biological racists (Nelson, 2006).

Although much has been written about contemporary forms of racism, many studies in health care (Smedley & Smedley, 2005), education (Gordon & Johnson, 2003), employment (Hinton, 2004), mental health (Burkard & Knox, 2004), and other social settings (Sellers & Shelton, 2003) indicate the difficulty of describing and defining racial discrimination that occurs via "aversive racism" or "implicit bias"; these types of racism are difficult to identify, quantify, and rectify because of their subtle, nebulous, and unnamed nature. Without an adequate classification or understanding of the dynamics of subtle racism, it will remain invisible and potentially harmful to the well-being, self-esteem, and standard of living of people of color (U.S. Department of Health and Human Services, 2001). Ironically, it has been proposed that the daily common experiences of racial aggression that characterize aversive racism may have significantly more influence on racial anger, frustration, and self-esteem than traditional overt forms of racism (Solórzano, Ceja, & Yosso, 2000). Furthermore, the invisible nature of acts of aversive racism prevents perpetrators from realizing and confronting (a) their own complicity in creating psychological dilemmas for minorities and (b) their role in creating disparities in employment, health care, and education.

The Manifestation of Racial Microaggressions

In reviewing the literature on subtle and contemporary forms of racism, we have found the term *"racial microaggressions"* to best describe the phenomenon in its everyday occurrence. First coined by Pierce in 1970, the term refers to "subtle, stunning, often automatic, and non-verbal exchanges which are 'put downs'" (Pierce, Carew, Pierce-Gonzalez, & Willis, 1978, p. 66). Racial microaggressions have also been described as "subtle insults (verbal, nonverbal, and/or visual) directed toward people of color, often automatically or unconsciously" (Solórzano et al., 2000). Simply stated, microaggressions are brief, everyday exchanges that send denigrating messages to people of color because they belong to a racial minority group. In the world of business, the term *"microinequities"* is used to describe the pattern of being overlooked, underrespected, and devalued because of one's race or gender. Microaggressions are often unconsciously delivered in the form of subtle snubs or dismissive looks, gestures, and tones. These exchanges are so pervasive and automatic in daily conversations and interactions that they are often dismissed and glossed over as being innocent and innocuous. Yet, as indicated previously, microaggressions are detrimental to persons of color because they impair performance in a multitude of settings by sapping the psychic and spiritual energy of recipients and by creating inequities (Franklin, 2004; D. W. Sue, 2004).

There is an urgent need to bring greater awareness and understanding of how microaggressions operate, their numerous manifestations in society, the type of impact they have on people of color, the dynamic interaction between perpetrator and target, and the educational strategies needed to eliminate them. Our attempt to define and propose a taxonomy of microaggressions is grounded in several lines of empirical and experiential evidence in the professional literature and in personal narratives.

First, the work by psychologists on aversive racism (Dovidio & Gaertner, 1996; Dovidio et al., 2002), studies suggesting the widespread existence of dissociation between implicit and explicit social stereotyping (Abelson et al., 1998; Banaji et al., 1993; DeVos & Banaji, 2005), the attributional ambiguity of everyday racial discrimination (Crocker & Major, 1989), the daily manifestations of racism in many arenas of life (Plant & Peruche, 2005; Sellers & Shelton, 2003;

Vanman, Saltz, Nathan, & Warren, 2004), and multiple similarities between microaggressive incidents and items that comprise measures of race-related stress/perceived discrimination toward Black Americans (Brondolo et al., 2005; Klonoff & Landrine, 1999; Utsey & Ponterotto, 1996) and Asian Americans (Liang, Li, & Kim, 2004) all seem to lend empirical support to the concept of racial microaggressions. Second, numerous personal narratives and brief life stories on race written by White psychologists and psychologists of color provide experiential evidence for the existence of racial microaggressions in everyday life (American Counseling Association, 1999; Conyne & Bemak, 2005; Ponterotto, Casas, Suzuki, & Alexander, 2001). Our analysis of the life experiences of these individuals and the research literature in social and counseling psychology led us to several conclusions: (a) The personal narratives were rich with examples and incidents of racial microaggressions, (b) the formulation of microaggressions was consistent with the research literature, and (c) racial microaggressions seemed to manifest themselves in three distinct forms.

Forms of Racial Microaggressions

Racial microaggressions are brief and commonplace daily verbal, behavioral, and environmental indignities, whether intentional or unintentional, that communicate hostile, derogatory, or negative racial slights and insults to the target person or group. They are not limited to human encounters alone but may also be environmental in nature, as when a person of color is exposed to an office setting that unintentionally assails his or her racial identity (Gordon & Johnson, 2003; D. W. Sue, 2003). For example, one's racial identity can be minimized or made insignificant through the sheer exclusion of decorations or literature that represents various racial groups. Three forms of microaggressions can be identified: microassault, microinsult, and microinvalidation.

Microassault

A microassault is an explicit racial derogation characterized primarily by a verbal or nonverbal attack meant to hurt the intended victim through name-calling, avoidant behavior, or purposeful discriminatory actions. Referring to someone as "colored" or "Oriental," using racial epithets, discouraging interracial interactions, deliberately serving a White patron before someone of color, and displaying a swastika are examples. Microassaults are most similar to what has been called "old fashioned" racism conducted on an individual level. They are most likely to be conscious and deliberate, although they are generally expressed in limited "private" situations (micro) that allow the perpetrator some degree of anonymity. In other words, people are likely to hold notions of minority inferiority privately and will only display them publicly when they (a) lose control or (b) feel relatively safe to engage in a microassault. Because we have chosen to analyze the unintentional and unconscious manifestations of microaggressions, microassaults are not the focus of our article. It is important to note, however, that individuals can also vary in the degree of conscious awareness they show in the use of the following two forms of microaggressions.

Microinsult

A microinsult is characterized by communications that convey rudeness and insensitivity and demean a person's racial heritage or identity. Microinsults represent subtle snubs, frequently unknown to the perpetrator, but clearly convey a hidden insulting message to the recipient of color. When a White employer tells a prospective candidate of color "I believe the most qualified person should get the job, regardless of race" or when an employee of color is asked "How did you get your job?", the underlying message from the perspective of the recipient may be twofold: (a) People of color are not qualified, and (b) as a minority group member, you must have obtained the position through some affirmative action or quota program and not because of ability. Such statements are not necessarily aggressions, but context is important. Hearing these statements frequently when used against affirmative action makes the recipient likely to experience them as aggressions. Microinsults can also occur nonverbally, as when a White teacher fails to acknowledge students of color in the classroom or when a White supervisor seems distracted during a conversation with a Black employee by avoiding eye contact or turning away (Hinton, 2004). In this case, the message conveyed to persons of color is that their contributions are unimportant.

Microinvalidation

Microinvalidations are characterized by communications that exclude, negate, or nullify the psychological thoughts, feelings, or experiential reality of a person of color. When Asian Americans (born and raised in the United States) are complimented for speaking good English or are repeatedly asked where they were born, the effect is to negate their U.S. American heritage and to convey that they are perpetual foreigners. When Blacks are told that "I don't see color" or "We are all human beings," the effect is to negate their experiences as racial/cultural beings (Helms, 1992). When a Latino couple is given poor service at a restaurant and shares their experience with White friends, only to be told "Don't be so oversensitive" or "Don't be so petty," the racial experience of the couple is being nullified and its importance is being diminished.

We have been able to identify nine categories of microaggressions with distinct themes: alien in one's own land, ascription of intelligence, color blindness, criminality/assumption of criminal status, denial of individual racism, myth of meritocracy, pathologizing cultural values/communication styles, second-class status, and environmental invalidation. Table 1 provides samples of comments or situations that may potentially be classified as racial microaggressions and their accompanying hidden assumptions and messages. Figure 1 visually presents the three large classes of microaggressions, the classification of the themes under each category, and their relationship to one another.

The experience of a racial microaggression has major implications for both the perpetrator and the target person. It creates psychological dilemmas that unless adequately resolved lead to increased levels of racial anger, mistrust, and loss of self-esteem for persons of color; prevent White people from perceiving a different racial reality; and create impediments to harmonious race-relations (Spanierman & Heppner, 2004; Thompson & Neville, 1999).

The Invisibility and Dynamics of Racial Microaggressions

The following real-life incident illustrates the issues of invisibility and the disguised problematic dynamics of racial microaggressions.

> I [Derald Wing Sue, the senior author, an Asian American] recently traveled with an African American colleague on a plane flying from New York to Boston. The plane was a small "hopper" with a single row of seats on one side and double seats on the other. As the plane was only sparsely populated, we were told by the flight attendant (White) that we could sit anywhere, so we sat at the front, across the aisle from one another. This made it easy for us to converse and provided a larger comfortable space on a small plane for both of us. As the attendant was about to close the hatch, three White men in suits entered the plane, were informed they could sit anywhere, and promptly seated themselves in front of us. Just before takeoff, the attendant proceeded to close all overhead compartments and seemed to scan the plane with her eyes. At that point she approached us, leaned over, interrupted our conversation, and asked if we would mind moving to the back of the plane. She indicated that she needed to distribute weight on the plane evenly.

Both of us (passengers of color) had similar negative reactions. First, balancing the weight on the plane seemed reasonable, but why were we being singled out? After all, we had boarded first and the three White men were the last passengers to arrive. Why were they not being asked to move? Were we being singled out because of our race? Was this just a random event with no racial overtones? Were we being oversensitive and petty?

Although we complied by moving to the back of the plane, both of us felt resentment, irritation, and anger. In light of our everyday racial experiences, we both came to the same conclusion: The flight attendant had treated us like second-class citizens because of our race. But this incident did not end there. While I kept telling myself to drop the matter, I could feel my blood pressure rising, heart beating faster, and face flush with anger. When the attendant walked back to make sure our seat belts were fastened, I could not contain my anger any longer. Struggling to control myself, I said to her in a forced calm voice: "Did you know that you asked two passengers of color to step to the rear of the 'bus'"? For a few seconds she said nothing but looked at me with a horrified expression. Then she said in a righteously indignant tone, "Well, I have never been accused of that! How dare you? I don't see color! I only asked you to move to balance the plane. Anyway, I was only trying to give you more space and greater privacy."

Attempts to explain my perceptions and feelings only generated greater defensiveness from her. For every allegation I made, she seemed to have a rational reason for her actions. Finally, she broke off the conversation and refused to talk about the incident any longer. Were it not for my colleague who validated my experiential reality, I would have left that encounter wondering whether I was correct or incorrect in my perceptions. Nevertheless, for the rest of the flight, I stewed over the incident and it left a sour taste in my mouth.

The power of racial microaggressions lies in their invisibility to the perpetrator and, oftentimes, the recipient (D. W. Sue, 2005). Most White Americans experience themselves as good, moral, and decent human beings who believe in equality and democracy. Thus, they find it difficult to believe that they possess biased racial attitudes and may engage in behaviors that are discriminatory (D. W. Sue, 2004). Microaggressive acts can usually be explained away by seemingly nonbiased and valid reasons. For the recipient of a microaggression, however, there is always the nagging question of whether it really happened (Crocker & Major, 1989). It is difficult to identify a microaggression, especially when other explanations seem plausible. Many people of color describe a vague feeling that they have been attacked, that they have been disrespected, or that something is not right (Franklin, 2004; Reid & Radhakrishnan, 2003). In some respects, people of color may find an overt and obvious racist act easier to handle than microaggressions that seem vague or disguised (Solórzano et al., 2000). The above incident reveals how microaggressions operate to create psychological dilemmas for both the White perpetrator and the person of color. Four such dilemmas are particularly noteworthy for everyone to understand.

Dilemma 1: Clash of Racial Realities

The question we pose is this: Did the flight attendant engage in a microaggression or did the senior author and his colleague simply misinterpret the action? Studies indicate that the racial perceptions of people of color differ markedly from those of Whites (Jones, 1997; Harris

TABLE I. EXAMPLES OF RACIAL MICROAGGRESSIONS

Theme	Microaggression	Message
Alien in own land When Asian Americans and Latino Americans are assumed to be foreign-born	"Where are you from?" "Where were you born?" "You speak good English." A person asking an Asian American to teach them words in their native language	You are not American. You are a foreigner.
Ascription of intelligence Assigning intelligence to a person of color on the basis of their race	"You are a credit to your race." "You are so articulate." Asking an Asian person to help with a math or science problem	People of color are generally not as intelligent as Whites. It is unusual for someone of your race to be intelligent. All Asians are intelligent and good in math/sciences.
Color blindness Statements that indicate that a White person does not want to acknowledge race	"When I look at you, I don't see color." "America is a melting pot." "There is only one race, the human race."	Denying a person of color's racial/ethnic experiences. Assimilate/acculturate to the dominant culture. Denying the individual as a racial/cultural being.
Criminality/assumption of criminal status A person of color is presumed to be dangerous, criminal, or deviant on the basis of their race	A White man or woman clutching their purse or checking their wallet as a Black or Latino approaches or passes A store owner following a customer of color around the store A White person waits to ride the next elevator when a person of color is on it	You are a criminal. You are going to steal/ You are poor/ You do not belong. You are dangerous.
Denial of individual racism A statement made when Whites deny their racial biases	"I'm not racist. I have several Black friends." "As a woman, I know what you go through as a racial minority."	I am immune to racism because I have friends of color. Your racial oppression is no different than my gender oppression. I can't be a racist. I'm like you.
Myth of meritocracy Statements which assert that race does not play a role in life successes	"I believe the most qualified person should get the job." "Everyone can succeed in this society, if they work hard enough."	People of color are given extra unfair benefits because of their race. People of color are lazy and/or incompetent and need to work harder.
Pathologizing cultural values/communication styles The notion that the values and communication styles of the dominant/White culture are ideal	Asking a Black person: "Why do you have to be so loud/animated? Just calm down." To an Asian or Latino person: "Why are you so quiet? We want to know what you think. Be more verbal." "Speak up more."	Assimilate to dominant culture.

TABLE 1. EXAMPLES OF RACIAL MICROAGGRESSIONS (CONTINUED)

Theme	Microaggression	Message
Pathologizing cultural values/ communication styles (cont'd)	Dismissing an individual who brings up race/culture in work/school setting	Leave your cultural baggage outside.
Second-class citizen Occurs when a White person is given preferential treatment as a consumer over a person of color	Person of color mistaken for a service worker	People of color are servants to Whites. They couldn't possibly occupy high-status positions.
	Having a taxi cab pass a person of color and pick up a White passenger	You are likely to cause trouble and/or travel to a dangerous neighborhood.
	Being ignored at a store counter as attention is given to the White customer behind you	Whites are more valued customers than people of color.
	"You people ..."	You don't belong. You are a lesser being.
Environmental microaggressions Macro-level microaggressions, which are more apparent on systemic and environmental levels	A college or university with buildings that are all named after White heterosexual upper class males	You don't belong/You won't succeed here. There is only so far you can go.
	Television shows and movies that feature predominantly White people, without representation of people of color	You are an outsider/You don't exist.
	Overcrowding of public schools in communities of color	People of color don't/shouldn't value education.
	Overabundance of liquor stores in communities of color	People of color are deviant.

Poll commissioned by the National Conference of Christians and Jews, 1992). In most cases, White Americans tend to believe that minorities are doing better in life, that discrimination is on the decline, that racism is no longer a significant factor in the lives of people of color, and that equality has been achieved. More important, the majority of Whites do not view themselves as racist or capable of racist behavior.

Minorities, on the other hand, perceive Whites as (a) racially insensitive, (b) unwilling to share their position and wealth, (c) believing they are superior, (d) needing to control everything, and (e) treating them poorly because of their race. People of color believe these attributes are reenacted everyday in their interpersonal interactions with Whites, oftentimes in the form of microaggressions (Solórzano et al., 2000). For example, it was found that 96% of African Americans reported experiencing racial discrimination in a one-year period (Klonoff & Landrine, 1999), and many incidents involved being mistaken for a service worker, being ignored, given poor service, treated rudely, or experiencing strangers acting fearful or intimidated when around them (Sellers & Shelton, 2003).

Dilemma 2: The Invisibility of Unintentional Expressions of Bias

The interaction between the senior author and the flight attendant convinced him that she was sincere in her belief that she had acted in good faith without racial bias. Her actions and their meaning were invisible to her. It was clear that she was stunned that anyone would accuse her of such despicable actions. After all, in her mind, she acted with only the best of intentions: to distribute the weight evenly on the plane for safety reasons and to give two passengers greater privacy and space. She felt betrayed that her good intentions were being questioned. Yet considerable empirical evidence exists showing that racial microaggressions become automatic because of cultural conditioning and that they may become connected neurologically with the processing of emotions that surround prejudice (Abelson et al., 1998). Several investigators have found, for example, that law enforcement officers in laboratory experiments will fire their guns more often at Black criminal suspects than White ones (Plant & Peruche, 2005), and Afrocentric features tend to result in longer prison terms (Blair, Judd, & Chapleau, 2004). In all cases, these law enforcement officials had no conscious awareness that they responded differently on the basis of race.

Herein lies a major dilemma. How does one prove that a microaggression has occurred? What makes our belief that the flight attendant acted in a biased manner any more plausible than her conscious belief that it was generated for another reason? If she did act out of hidden and unconscious bias, how do we make her aware of it? Social psychological research tends to confirm the existence of unconscious racial biases in well-intentioned Whites, that nearly everyone born and raised in the United States inherits the racial biases of the society, and that the most accurate assessment about whether racist acts have occurred in a particular situation is most likely to be made by those most disempowered rather than by those who enjoy the privileges of power (Jones, 1997; Keltner & Robinson, 1996). According to these findings, microaggressions (a) tend to be subtle, indirect, and unintentional, (b) are most likely to emerge not when a behavior would look prejudicial, but when other rationales can be offered for prejudicial behavior, and (c) occur when Whites pretend not to notice differences, thereby

Figure 1
Categories of and Relationships Among Racial Microaggressions

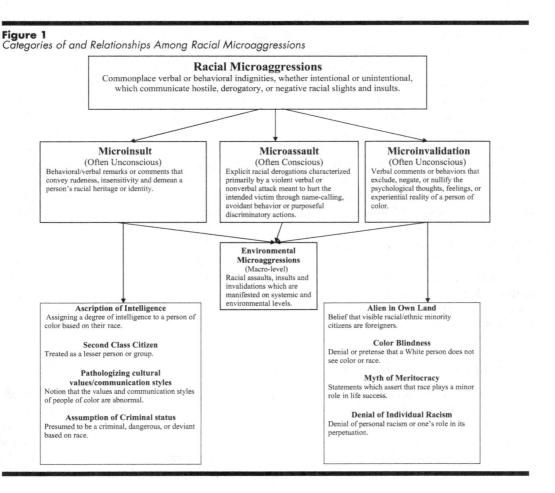

justifying that "color" was not involved in the actions taken. Color blindness is a major form of microinvalidation because it denies the racial and experiential reality of people of color and provides an excuse to White people to claim that they are not prejudiced (Helms, 1992; Neville, Lilly, Duran, Lee, & Browne, 2000). The flight attendant, for example, did not realize that her "not seeing color" invalidated both passengers' racial identity and experiential reality.

Dilemma 3: Perceived Minimal Harm of Racial Microaggressions

In most cases, when individuals are confronted with their microaggressive acts (as in the case of the flight attendant), the perpetrator usually believes that the victim has overreacted and is being overly sensitive and/or petty. After all, even if it was an innocent racial blunder, microaggressions are believed to have minimal negative impact. People of color are told not to overreact and to simply "let it go." Usually, Whites consider microaggressive incidents to be minor, and people of color are encouraged (oftentimes by people of color as well) to not waste time or effort on them.

It is clear that old-fashioned racism unfairly disadvantages people of color and that it contributes to stress, depression, shame, and anger in its victims (Jones, 1997). But evidence also supports the detrimental impact of more subtle forms of racism (Chakraborty & McKenzie, 2002; Clark, Anderson, Clark, & Williams, 1999). For example, in a survey of studies examining racism and mental health, researchers found a positive association between happiness and life satisfaction, self-esteem, mastery of control, hypertension, and discrimination (Williams, Neighbors, & Jackson, 2003). Many of the types of everyday racism identified by Williams and colleagues (Williams & Collins, 1995; Williams, Lavizzo-Mourey, & Warren, 1994) provide strong support for the idea that racial microaggressions are not minimally harmful. One study specifically examined microaggressions in the experiences of African Americans and found that the cumulative effects can be quite devastating (Solórzano et al., 2000). The researchers reported that experience with microaggressions resulted in a negative racial climate and emotions of self-doubt, frustration, and isolation on the part of victims. As indicated in the incident above, the senior author experienced considerable emotional turmoil that lasted for the entire flight. When one considers that people of color are exposed continually to microaggressions and that their effects are cumulative, it becomes easier to understand the psychological toll they may take on recipients' well-being.

We submit that covert racism in the form of microaggressions also has a dramatic and detrimental impact on people of color. Although microaggressions may be seemingly innocuous and insignificant, their effects can be quite dramatic (Steele, Spencer, & Aronson, 2002). D. W. Sue believes that "this contemporary form of racism is many times over more problematic, damaging, and injurious to persons of color than overt racist acts" (D. W. Sue, 2003, p. 48). It has been noted that the cumulative effects of racial microaggressions may theoretically result in "diminished mortality, augmented morbidity and flattened confidence" (Pierce, 1995, p. 281). It is important to study and acknowledge this form of racism in society because without documentation and analysis to better understand microaggressions, the threats that they pose and the assaults that they justify can be easily ignored or downplayed (Solórzano et al., 2000). D. W. Sue (2005) has referred to this phenomenon as "a conspiracy of silence."

Dilemma 4: The Catch-22 of Responding to Microaggressions

When a microaggression occurs, the victim is usually placed in a catch-22. The immediate reaction might be a series of questions: Did what I think happened, really happen? Was this a deliberate act or an unintentional slight? How should I respond? Sit and stew on it or confront the person? If I bring the topic up, how do I prove it? Is it really worth the effort? Should I just drop the matter? These questions in one form or another have been a common, if not a universal, reaction of persons of color who experience an attributional ambiguity (Crocker & Major, 1989).

First, the person must determine whether a microaggression has occurred. In that respect, people of color rely heavily on experiential reality that is contextual in nature and involves life experiences from a variety of situations. When the flight attendant asked the senior author and his colleague to move, it was not the first time that similar requests and situations had occurred for both. In their experience, these incidents were nonrandom events (Ridley, 2005), and their perception was that the only similarity "connecting the dots" to each and every one of these incidents was the color of their skin. In other words, the situation on the plane was only one of many similar incidents with identical outcomes. Yet the flight attendant and most White Americans do not share these multiple experiences, and they evaluate their own behaviors in the moment through a singular event (Dovidio & Gaertner, 2000). Thus, they fail to see a pattern of bias, are defended by a belief in their own morality, and can in good conscience deny that they discriminated (D. W. Sue, 2005).

Second, how one reacts to a microaggression may have differential effects, not only on the perpetrator but on the person of color as well. Deciding to do nothing by sitting on one's anger is one response that occurs frequently in people of color. This response occurs because persons of color may be (a) unable to determine whether a microaggression has occurred, (b) at a loss for how to respond, (c) fearful of the consequences, (d) rationalizing that "it won't do any good anyway," or (e) engaging in self-deception through denial ("It didn't happen."). Although these explanations for nonresponse may hold some validity for the person of color, we submit that not doing anything has the potential to result in psychological harm. It may mean a denial of one's experiential reality, dealing with a loss of integrity, or experiencing pent-up anger and frustration likely to take psychological and physical tolls.

Third, responding with anger and striking back (perhaps a normal and healthy reaction) is likely to engender negative consequences for persons of color as well. They are likely to be accused of being racially oversensitive or paranoid or told that their emotional outbursts confirm stereotypes about minorities. In the case of Black males, for example, protesting may lend credence to the belief that they are hostile, angry, impulsive, and prone to violence (Jones, 1997). In this case, the person of color might feel better after venting, but the outcome results in greater hostility by Whites toward minorities. Further, while the person of color may feel better in the immediate moment by relieving pent-up emotions, the reality is that the general situation has not been changed. In essence, the catch-22 means you are "damned if you do, and damned if you don't." What is lacking is research that points to adaptive ways of handling microaggressions by people of color and suggestions of how to increase the awareness and sensitivity of Whites to microaggressions so that they accept responsibility for their behaviors and for changing them (Solórzano et al., 2000).

Racial Microaggressions as a Barrier to Clinical Practice

In a broad sense, counseling and psychotherapy can be characterized as the formation of a deeply personal relationship between a helping professional and a client that involves appropriate and accurate interpersonal interactions and communications. For effective therapy to occur, some form of positive coalition must develop between the parties involved (D. W. Sue & Sue, 2003). Many have referred to this as the "working relationship," the "therapeutic alliance," or the "establishment of rapport" (D. W. Sue & Sue, 2003). A strong therapeutic relationship is often enhanced when clients perceive therapists as credible (trustworthy and expert) and themselves as understood and positively regarded by their therapists (Strong & Schmidt, 1970). Helping professionals are trained to listen, to show empathic concern, to be objective, to value the client's integrity, to communicate understanding, and to use their professional knowledge and skills to aid clients to solve problems (Grencavage & Norcross, 1990).

As a therapeutic team, therapist and client are better prepared to venture into problematic areas that the client might hesitate to face alone. Research suggests that the therapeutic alliance is one of the major common factors of any helping relationship and is correlated with successful outcome (Lui & Pope-Davis, 2005; Martin, Garske, & Davis, 2000). More important, however, are findings that a client's perception of an accepting and positive relationship is a better predictor of successful outcome than is a similar perception by the counselor (Horvath & Symonds, 1991). Thus, when clients do not perceive their therapists as trustworthy and when they feel misunderstood and undervalued, therapeutic success is less likely to occur. Oftentimes, the telltale signs of a failed therapeutic relationship may result in clients being less likely to self-disclose, terminating prematurely, or failing to return for scheduled visits (Burkard & Knox, 2004; Kearney, Draper, & Baron, 2005).

Although the task of establishing an effective therapeutic relationship applies to the entire helping spectrum, working with clients who differ from the therapist in race, ethnicity, culture, and sexual orientation poses special challenges. White therapists who are products of their cultural conditioning may be prone to engage in racial microaggressions (Locke & Kiselica, 1999). Thus, the therapeutic alliance is likely to be weakened or terminated when clients of color perceive White therapists as biased, prejudiced, or unlikely to understand them as racial/cultural beings. That racism can potentially infect the therapeutic process when working with clients of color has been a common concern voiced by the President's Commission on Mental Health (1978) and the Surgeon General's Report on *Mental Health: Culture, Race and Ethnicity* (U.S. Department of Health and Human Services, 2001). It has been postulated that therapist bias might partially account for the low utilization of mental health services and premature termination of therapy sessions by African American, Native American, Asian American, and Latino/Hispanic American clients (U.S. Department of Health and Human Services, 2001).

Yet research also reveals that most people in our nation believe in democracy, fairness, and strong humanistic values that condemn racism and the inequities that it engenders (Dovidio et al., 2002). Such a statement is arguably truer for mental health professionals, whose goals are to help rather than hinder or hurt clients of color. Both the American Psychological Association and the American Counseling Association have attempted to confront the biases of the profession by passing multicultural guidelines or standards that denounce prejudice and discrimination in the delivery of mental health services to clients of color (American Psychological Association, 2003; D. W. Sue et al., 1992). Like most people in society, counselors and therapists experience themselves as fair and decent individuals who would never consciously and deliberately engage in racist acts toward clients of color. Sadly, it is often pointed out that when clinician and client differ from one another along racial lines, however, the relationship may serve as a microcosm for the troubled race relations in the United States. While many would like to believe that racism is no longer a major problem and that the good intentions of the helping profession have built safeguards against prejudice and discrimination, the reality is that they continue to be manifested through the therapeutic process (Utsey, Gernat, & Hammar, 2005). This is not to suggest, however, that positive changes in race relations have not occurred. Yet, as in many other interactions, microaggressions are equally likely to occur in therapeutic transactions (Ridley, 2005).

The Manifestation of Racial Microaggressions in Counseling/Therapy

Microaggressions become meaningful in the context of clinical practice, as relational dynamics and the human condition are central aspects of this field. The often unintentional and unconscious nature of microaggressions (Dilemma 2: Invisibility) poses the biggest challenge to the majority of White mental health professionals, who believe that they are just, unbiased, and nonracist. Further, mental health professionals are in a position of power, which renders them less likely to accurately assess (Dilemma 1: Conflict of Racial Realities) whether racist acts have occurred in their sessions. Thus, the harm they perpetrate against their clients of color is either unknown or minimized (Dilemma 3: Minimal Harm). Microaggressions not only oppress and harm, but they place clients of color in the unenviable position of a catch-22 (Dilemma 4).

In clinical practice, microaggressions are likely to go unrecognized by White clinicians who are unintentionally and unconsciously expressing bias. As a result, therapists must make a concerted effort to identify and monitor microaggressions within the therapeutic context. This process is reminiscent of the importance of becoming aware of potential transference and countertransference issues between therapist and client and how they may unintentionally interfere with effective therapy (Woodhouse, Schlosser, Crook, Ligiero, & Gelso, 2003). The inherent power dynamic in the therapeutic relationship further complicates this issue, as therapists are in a position of power to make diagnoses and influence the course of treatment. The power dynamic between therapist and client also effects the catch-22 of responding to microaggressions because clients may be less likely to confront their therapists and more likely to question their own perceptions in the event of a microaggression.

Table 2 provides a few examples of microaggressions in counseling practice under each of the nine categories identified earlier. Under Color Blindness, for example, a client of color stresses the importance of racial experiences only to have the therapist reply, "We are all unique. We are all individuals." or "We are all human beings or the same under the skin." These colorblind statements, which were intended to be supportive, to be sympathetic, and to convey an ability to understand, may leave the client feeling misunderstood, negated, invalidated, and unimportant (especially if racial identity is important to the client). Moreover these statements presume that the therapist is *capable* of not seeing race and impose a definition of racial reality on the client (Neville et al., 2000).

Under Denial of Individual Racism, a common response by Whites to people of color is that they can understand and relate to experiences of racism. In Table 2, under this category, we provide the following anecdote: A client of color expresses hesitancy in discussing racial issues with his White female therapist. She replies, "I understand. As a woman, I face discrimination too." The message is that the therapist believes her gender oppression is no different from the client's experiences of racial/ethnic oppression. This response is problematic because such attempts by the therapist to explain how he or she can understand a person of color's experience with racism may be perceived by the client as an attempt to minimize the importance of his or her racial identity, to avoid acknowledging the therapist's racial biases, or to communicate a discomfort with discussing racial issues. Furthermore, the therapist excuses himself or herself from any blame or fault in perpetuating racism and the power of racism. This failure to acknowledge the significance of racism within and outside of the therapy session contributes to the breakdown of the alliance between therapist and client. A therapist's willingness to discuss racial matters is of central importance in creating a therapeutic alliance with clients of color (Cardemil & Battle, 2003).

Under the category "Alien in Own Land," many Asian Americans and Latino/Hispanic Americans report that they are commonly seen as perpetual foreigners. For example, a female Asian American client arrives for her first therapy session. Her therapist asks her where she is from, and when told "Philadelphia," the therapist further probes by asking where she was born. In this case, the therapist has assumed that the Asian American client is not from the United States and has imposed through the use of the second question the idea that she must be a foreigner. Immediately, a barrier is created in the helping relationship because the client feels invalidated by the therapist (she is perceived as a foreigner, not a U.S. citizen). Unfortunately, the Asian American client is unlikely to question her therapist or point out the bias because of the power dynamic, which causes her to harbor resentment and ill feelings toward the therapist.

We contend that clients of color are at increased risk of not continuing in the counseling/therapy session when such microaggressions occur. Worse yet, they will not receive the help they need and may leave the session feeling worse than when they first sought counseling. Because it is unlikely that clinicians intentionally create hostile and unwelcoming environments for their ethnic minority clients, it can be assumed that these biases are being expressed through microaggressions. Therapists can convey their bias to their ethnic minority clients in myriad ways, such as by minimizing symptoms for Asian Americans on the basis of a false belief in the "model" minority (D. W. Sue & Sue, 2003) or by placing greater emphasis on symptoms such as paranoid delusions and substance abuse in Native Americans and African Americans, who are believed to suffer from these afflictions (U.S. Department of Health and Human Services, 2001).

Last, White counselors and therapists can impose and value their own cultural worldview while devaluing and pathologizing the cultural values of their ethnic minority clients. Previous research has shown that pathologizing clients' cultural values has been a major determinant of clients of color discontinuing psychotherapy (S. Sue, Fujino, Hu, & Takeuchi, 1991). Many clients of color may feel misunderstood by their therapists because of a lack of cultural understanding. Asian American or Latino American clients who enter therapy to discuss family issues such as feeling obligated, stressed, or overwhelmed with excess family responsibilities may be encouraged by therapists to speak out against their families or to make decisions regardless of family support or expectations. Therapists may be unaware that they may be directly invalidating cultural respect for authority and imposing an individualistic view over a collectivist one.

Future Directions in the Understanding of Racial Microaggressions

With respect to racism, D. W. Sue (2004, p. 762) has stated that the greatest challenge society and the mental health professions face is "making the 'invisible' visible." That can only be accomplished when people are willing to openly and honestly engage in a dialogue about race and racism. In that respect, the education and training of mental health professionals must incorporate issues of race and culture. One would ordinarily expect that mental health professionals would be more willing than most to dialogue on this topic, but studies suggest that White clinicians receive minimal or no practicum or supervision experiences that address race and are uncomfortable broaching the topic (Knox, Burkard, Johnson, Suzuki, & Ponterotto, 2003). Many White trainees in therapy dyads experience anxiety in the form of poor articulation, faltering and/or trembling voices, and mispronunciation of words when directly engaged in discussions about race (Utsey et al., 2005). It is interesting that such nonverbal behaviors also serve as a form of racial microaggression. When helping professionals have difficulty addressing race issues, they cut off an avenue for clients of color to explore matters of bias, discrimination, and prejudice.

Education and Training and Racial Microaggressions

It is clear that mental health training programs must support trainees in overcoming their fears and their resistance to talking about race by fostering safe and productive learning environments (Sanchez-Hucles & Jones, 2005). It is important that training programs be structured and facilitated in a manner that promotes inquiry and allows trainees to experience discomfort and vulnerability (Young & Davis-Russell, 2002). Trainees need to be challenged to explore their own racial identities and their feelings about other racial groups. The prerequisite for cultural competence has always been racial self-awareness. This is equally true for understanding how microaggressions, especially those of the therapist, influence the therapeutic process. This level of self-awareness brings to the surface possible prejudices and biases

TABLE 2. EXAMPLES OF RACIAL MICROAGGRESSIONS IN THERAPEUTIC PRACTICE

Theme	Microaggression	Message
Alien in own land When Asian Americans and Latino Americans are assumed to be foreign-born	A White client does not want to work with an Asian American therapist because "she will not understand my problem." A White therapist tells an American-born Latino client that he/she should seek a Spanish-speaking therapist.	You are not American.
Ascription of intelligence Assigning a degree of intelligence to a person of color on the basis of their race	A school counselor reacts with surprise when an Asian American student had trouble on the math portion of a standardized test. A career counselor asking a Black or Latino student, "Do you think you're ready for college?"	All Asians are smart and good at math. It is unusual for people of color to succeed.
Color blindness Statements which indicate that a White person does not want to acknowledge race	A therapist says "I think you are being too paranoid. We should emphasize similarities, not people's differences" when a client of color attempts to discuss her feelings about being the only person of color at her job and feeling alienated and dismissed by her co-workers. A client of color expresses concern in discussing racial issues with her therapist. Her therapist replies with, "When I see you, I don't see color."	Race and culture are not important variables that affect people's lives. Your racial experiences are not valid.
Criminality/assumption of criminal status A person of color is presumed to be dangerous, criminal, or deviant on the basis of their race	When a Black client shares that she was accused of stealing from work, the therapist encourages the client to explore how she might have contributed to her employer's mistrust of her. A therapist takes great care to ask all substance abuse questions in an intake with a Native American client, and is suspicious of the client's nonexistent history with substances.	You are a criminal. You are deviant.
Denial of individual racism A statement made when Whites renounce their racial biases	A client of color asks his or her therapist about how race affects their working relationship. The therapist replies, "Race does not affect the way I treat you." A client of color expresses hesitancy in discussing racial issues with his White female therapist. She replies "I understand. As a woman, I face discrimination also."	Your racial/ethnic experience is not important. Your racial oppression is no different than my gender oppression.

TABLE 2. EXAMPLES OF RACIAL MICROAGGRESSIONS IN THERAPEUTIC PRACTICE (CONTINUED)

Theme	Microaggression	Message
Myth of meritocracy Statements which assert that race does not play a role in succeeding in career advancement or education.	A school counselor tells a Black student that "if you work hard, you can succeed like everyone else." A career counselor is working with a client of color who is concerned about not being promoted at work despite being qualified. The counselor suggests, "Maybe if you work harder you can succeed like your peers."	People of color are lazy and/or incompetent and need to work harder. If you don't succeed, you have only yourself to blame (blaming the victim).
Pathologizing cultural values/communication styles The notion that the values and communication styles of the dominant/White culture are ideal	A Black client is loud, emotional, and confrontational in a counseling session. The therapist diagnoses her with borderline personality disorder. A client of Asian or Native American descent has trouble maintaining eye contact with his therapist. The therapist diagnoses him with a social anxiety disorder. Advising a client, "Do you really think your problem stems from racism?"	Assimilate to dominant culture. Leave your cultural baggage outside.
Second-class citizen Occurs when a White person is given preferential treatment as a consumer over a person of color	A counselor limits the amount of long-term therapy to provide at a college counseling center; she chooses all White clients over clients of color. Clients of color are not welcomed or acknowledged by receptionists.	Whites are more valued than people of color. White clients are more valued than clients of color.
Environmental microaggressions Macro-level microaggressions, which are more apparent on a systemic level	A waiting room office has pictures of American presidents. Every counselor at a mental health clinic is White.	You don't belong/Only white people can succeed. You are an outsider/You don't exist.

that inform racial microaggressions. A first step for therapists who want to integrate an understanding of racism's mental health effects into the conceptualization of psychological functioning is to undergo a process of learning and critical self-examination of racism and its impact on one's life and the lives of others (Thompson & Neville, 1999). For White clinicians, it means addressing the question "What does it mean to be White?" and being fully cognizant of their own White racial identity development and how it may intrude on people of color (Helms, 1992, 1995). In addition, it has been suggested that articulating a personal theory of reality and of therapeutic change in the context of an environment of racism is one way to begin integrating knowledge of racism with the practice of psychotherapy (Thompson & Neville, 1999). Education and training must aid White clinicians to achieve the following: (a) increase their ability to identify racial microaggressions in general and in themselves in particular; (b) understand how racial microaggressions, including their own, detrimentally impact clients of color; and (c) accept responsibility for taking corrective actions to overcome racial biases.

Research on Racial Microaggressions

A major obstacle to understanding racial microaggressions is that research is in a nascent state. Researchers continue to omit subtle racism and microaggressions from their research agendas, and this absence conveys the notion that covert forms of racism are not as valid or as important as racist events that can be quantified and "proven." In fact, omitting microaggressions from studies on racism on the basis of a belief that they are less harmful encourages the profession to "look the other way." Moreover, the fact that psychological research has continued to inadequately address race and ethnicity (Delgado-Romero, Rowland, & Galvin, 2005) is in itself a microaggression. Pursuing a line of research examining how cross-racial dyadic compositions impact the process and outcome of counselor/client interactions would be a tremendous contribution to the field of counseling and clinical psychology. Helms and Cook (1999) noted that racial consciousness is a critical consideration in determining White therapists' ability to operate effectively in cross-racial dyads.

For mental health purposes, it would be useful to explore the coping mechanisms used by people of color to stave off the negative effects of microaggressions. The fact that people of color have had to face daily microaggressions and have continued to maintain their dignity in the face of such hostility is a testament to their resiliency (D. W. Sue, 2003). What coping strategies have been found to serve them well? A greater understanding of responses to microaggressions, both in the long term and the short term, and of the coping strategies employed would be beneficial in arming children of color for the life they will face. Such research is necessary because without documentation and analysis to help better understand microaggressions, the threats that they pose and the assaults that they justify can be easily ignored or downplayed (Solórzano et al., 2000). Studying the long-term impact that microaggressions have on mental health functioning, self-esteem, self-concept, and racial identity development appears crucial to documenting the harm microaggressions inflict on people of color. The taxonomy of microaggressions proposed here may make it easier to explore other social psychological questions as well.

First, it is highly probable that microaggressions vary in their severity and impact. As indicated, a microassault does not evoke a guessing game because the intent of the perpetrator is clear. However, the racist intent of microinsults and microinvalidations is less clear and presents different dilemmas for people of color. Some questions to ponder include the following: (a) Are the three forms of racial microaggressions equal in impact? Are some themes and their hidden messages more problematic than others? Although all expressions may take a psychological toll, some are obviously experienced as more harmful and severe than others. (b) Is there a relationship between forms of racial microaggressions and racial identity development? Recent research and formulations on White racial identity development and the psychosocial costs of racism to Whites (Helms, 1995; Spanierman, Armstrong, Poteat, & Beer, 2006) imply that forms of racial microaggressions may be associated with certain statuses or trait clusters. (c) Finally, is it possible that different racial/ethnic groups are more likely to encounter certain forms of racial microaggressions than others? A preliminary study suggests that Asian Americans are prone to be victims of microinvalidations with themes that revolve around "alien in one's own land" (D. W. Sue, Bucceri, Lin, Nadal, & Torino, 2007) rather than microinsults with themes of "criminality." Is it possible that Blacks are more likely to be subjected to the latter than to the former? What about Latinos and American Indians?

Second, the challenge in conducting research aimed at understanding microaggressions involves measurement. Adequate assessment tools need to be created to effectively explore the new and burgeoning field of microaggression research. Although there are several promising race-related stress and discrimination measures, such as the Perceived Ethnic Discrimination Questionnaire (PEDQ; Brondolo et al., 2005), the Color-Blind Racial Attitude Scale (COBRAS; Neville et al., 2000), the Index of Race Related Stress (IRRS; Utsey & Ponterotto, 1996), and the Schedule of Racist Events (SRE; Klonoff & Landrine, 1999), none of them is directly aimed at distinguishing between categories of racial microaggressions or their intentional or unintentional nature. The PEDQ uses four subscales that broadly measure stigmatization, harassment, workplace discrimination, and social exclusion; the COBRAS is specific to a person's minimization of race and racism; the IRRS uses Jones's (1997) framework to measure individual, institutional, and societal racism; and the SRE is aimed at measuring frequency of racist incidents. All contain examples of racial microaggressions that support our taxonomy, but none makes conceptual distinctions that allow for categorical measurements of this phenomenon. It seems imperative that specific instruments be developed to aid in understanding the causes, consequences, manifestations, and elimination of racial microaggressions.

Conclusion

Nearly all interracial encounters are prone to the manifestation of racial microaggressions. We have chosen mainly to address the therapeutic relationship, but racial microaggressions are potentially present whenever human interactions involve participants who differ in race and culture (teaching, supervising, training, administering, evaluating, etc.). We have purposely chosen to concentrate on racial microaggressions, but it is important to acknowledge other types of microaggressions as well. Gender, sexual orientation, and disability microaggressions may have equally powerful and potentially detrimental effects on women, gay, lesbian, bisexual, and transgender individuals, and disability groups. Further, racial microaggressions are not limited to White-Black, White-Latino, or White-Person of Color interactions. Interethnic racial microaggressions occur between people of color as well. In the area of counseling and therapy, for example, research may also prove beneficial in understanding cross-racial dyads in which the therapist is a person of color and the client is White or in which both therapist and client are persons of color. Investigating these combinations of cross-racial dyads would be useful, because it is clear that no racial/ethnic group is immune from inheriting the racial biases of the society (D. W. Sue, 2003). We encourage future research in these two areas because all forms of microaggressions have detrimental consequences.

References

Abelson, R. P., Dasgupta, N., Park, J., & Banaji, M. R. (1998). Perceptions of the collective other. *Personality and Social Psychology Review, 2,* 243–250.

Advisory Board to the President's Initiative on Race. (1998). *One America in the 21st century: Forging a new future.* Washington, DC: U.S. Government Printing Office.

American Counseling Association. (1999). *Racism: Healing its effects.* Alexandria, VA: Author.

American Psychological Association. (2003). Guidelines on multicultural education, training, research, practice, and organizational change for psychologists. *American Psychologist, 58,* 377–402.

Banaji, M. R., Hardin, C., & Rothman, A. J. (1993). Implicit stereotyping in person judgment. *Journal of Personality and Social Psychology, 65,* 272–281.

Blair, I. V., Judd, C. M., & Chapleau, K. M. (2004). The influence of afrocentric facial features in criminal sentencing. *Psychological Science, 15,* 674–679.

Brondolo, E., Kelly, K. P., Coakley, V., Gordon, T., Thompson, S., & Levy, E. (2005). The Perceived Ethnic Discrimination Questionnaire: Development and preliminary validation of a community version. *Journal of Applied Social Psychology, 35,* 335–365.

Burkard, A. W., & Knox, S. (2004). Effect of therapist color-blindness on empathy and attributions in cross-cultural counseling. *Journal of Counseling Psychology, 51,* 387–397.

Cardemil, E. V., & Battle, C. L. (2003). Guess who's coming to therapy? Getting comfortable with conversations about race and ethnicity in psychotherapy. *Professional Psychology: Research and Practice, 34,* 278–286.

Chakraborty, A., & McKenzie, K. (2002). Does racial discrimination cause mental illness? *British Journal of Psychiatry, 180,* 475–477.

Clark, R., Anderson, N. B., Clark, V. R., & Williams, D. R. (1999). Racism as a stressor for African Americans. *American Psychologist, 54,* 805–816.

Conyne, R. K., & Bemak, F. (2005). *Journeys to professional excellence: Lessons from leading counselor educators and practitioners.* Alexandria, VA: American Counseling Association.

Crocker, J., & Major, B. (1989). Social stigma and self-esteem: The self-protective properties of stigma. *Psychological Review, 96,* 608–630.

Delgado-Romero, E. A., Rowland, M., & Galvan, N. (2005). The continuing and evolving challenge of race and ethnicity in empirical counseling and counseling psychology research: A reply. *Counseling Psychologist, 33,* 559–564.

DeVos, T., & Banaji, M. R. (2005). American = White? *Journal of Personality and Social Psychology, 88,* 447–466.

Dovidio, J. F., & Gaertner, S. L. (1996). Affirmative action, unintentional racial biases, and intergroup relations. *Journal of Social Issues, 52,* 51–75.

Dovidio, J. F., & Gaertner, S. L. (2000). Aversive racism and selective decisions: 1989–1999. *Psychological Science, 11,* 315–319.

Dovidio, J. F., Gaertner, S. L., Kawakami, K., & Hodson, G. (2002). Why can't we all just get along? Interpersonal biases and interracial distrust. *Cultural Diversity and Ethnic Minority Psychology, 8,* 88–102.

Franklin, A. J. (2004). *From brotherhood to manhood: How Black men rescue their relationships and dreams from the invisibility syndrome.* Hoboken, NJ: Wiley.

Gordon, J., & Johnson, M. (2003). Race, speech, and hostile educational environment: What color is free speech? *Journal of Social Philosophy, 34,* 414–436.

Grencavage, L. M., & Norcross, J. C. (1990). Where are the commonalities among the therapeutic common factors? *Professional Psychology: Research and Practice, 21,* 372–378.

Helms, J. E. (1992). *A race is a nice thing to have: A guide to being a white person or understanding the white persons in your life.* Topeka, KS: Content Communications.

Helms, J. E. (1995). An update of Helms's White and people of color racial identity models. In J. G. Ponterotto, J. M. Casas, L. A. Suzuki, & C. M. Alexander (Eds.), *Handbook of multicultural counseling* (pp. 181–191). Thousand Oaks, CA: Sage.

Helms, J. E., & Cook, D. (1999). *Using race and culture in counseling and psychotherapy: Theory and process.* Needham Heights, MA: Allyn & Bacon.

Hinton, E. L. (2004, March/April). Microinequities: When small slights lead to huge problems in the workplace. *DiversityInc.* (Available at http://www.magazine.org/content/files/Microinequities.pdf).

Horvath, A. O., & Symonds, B. D. (1991). Relationship between working alliance and outcome in psychotherapy: A meta-analysis. *Journal of Counseling Psychology, 38,* 139–149.

Jones, J. M. (1997). *Prejudice and racism* (2nd ed.). Washington, DC: McGraw-Hill.

Kearney, L. K., Draper, M., & Baron, A. (2005). Counseling utilization by ethnic minority college students. *Cultural Diversity and Ethnic Minority Psychology, 11,* 272–285.

Keltner, D., & Robinson, R. J. (1996). Extremism, power, and imagined basis of social conflict. *Current Directions in Psychological Science, 5,* 101–105.

Klonoff, E. A., & Landrine, H. (1999). Cross-validation of the Schedule of Racist Events. *Journal of Black Psychology, 25,* 231–254.

Knox, S., Burkard, A. W., Johnson, A. J., Suzuki, L. A., & Ponterotto, J. G. (2003). African American and European American therapists' experiences of addressing race in cross-racial psychotherapy dyads. *Journal of Counseling Psychology, 50,* 466–481.

Liang, C. T. H., Li, L. C., & Kim, B. S. K. (2004). The Asian American Racism-Related Stress Inventory: Development, factor analysis, reliability, and validity. *Journal of Counseling Psychology, 51,* 103–114.

Locke, D. C., & Kiselica, M. S. (1999). Pedagogy of possibilities: Teaching about racism in multicultural counseling courses. *Journal of Counseling and Development, 77,* 80–86.

Lui, W. M., & Pope-Davis, D. B. (2005). The working alliance, therapy ruptures and impasses, and counseling competence: Implications for counselor training and education. In R. T. Carter (Ed.), *Handbook of racial-cultural psychology and counseling* (pp. 148–167). Hoboken, NJ: Wiley.

Martin, D. J., Garske, J. P., & Davis, M. K. (2000). Relations of the therapeutic alliance with outcome and other variables: A meta-analytic review. *Journal of Counseling and Clinical Psychology, 66,* 832–837.

McConahay, J. B. (1986). Modern racism, ambivalence, and the Modern Racism Scale. In J. F. Dovidio & S. L. Gaertner (Eds.), *Prejudice, discrimination and racism* (pp. 91–126). Orlando, FL: Academic Press.

National Conference of Christians and Jews. (1992). *Taking America's pulse: A summary report of the National Conference Survey on Inter-Group Relations.* New York: Author. (Available at http://eric.ed.gov/ERICDocs/data/ericdocs2/content_storage_01/0000000b/80/23/84/59.pdf)

Nelson, T. D. (2006). *The psychology of prejudice.* Boston: Pearson.

Neville, H. A., Lilly, R. L., Duran, G., Lee, R., & Browne, L. (2000). Construction and initial validation of the Color Blind Racial Attitudes Scale (COBRAS). *Journal of Counseling Psychology, 47,* 59–70.

Pierce, C. (1995). Stress analogs of racism and sexism: Terrorism, torture, and disaster. In C. Willie, P. Rieker, B. Kramer, & B. Brown (Eds.), *Mental health, racism, and sexism* (pp. 277–293). Pittsburgh, PA: University of Pittsburgh Press.

Pierce, C., Carew, J., Pierce-Gonzalez, D., & Willis, D. (1978). An experiment in racism: TV commercials. In C. Pierce (Ed.), *Television and education* (pp. 62–88). Beverly Hills, CA: Sage.

Plant, E. A., & Peruche, B. M. (2005). The consequences of race for police officers' responses to criminal suspects. *Psychological Science, 16,* 180–183.

Ponterotto, J. G., Casas, J. M., Suzuki, L. A., & Alexander, C. M. (2001). *Handbook of multicultural counseling.* Thousand Oaks, CA: Sage.

President's Commission on Mental Health. (1978). *Report of the President's Commission on Mental Health.* Washington, DC: U.S. Government Printing Office.

Reid, L. D., & Radhakrishnan, P. (2003). Race matters: The relations between race and general campus climate. *Cultural Diversity and Ethnic Minority Psychology, 9,* 263–275.

Richardson, T. Q., & Molinaro, K. L. (1996). White counselor self-awareness: A prerequisite for multicultural competence. *Journal of Counseling & Development, 74,* 238–242.

Ridley, C. R. (2005). *Overcoming unintentional racism in counseling and therapy* (2nd ed.). Thousand, Oaks, CA: Sage.

Sanchez-Hucles, J., & Jones, N. (2005). Breaking the silence around race in training, practice, and research. *Counseling Psychologist, 33,* 547–558.

Sears, D. O. (1988). Symbolic racism. In P. A. Katz & D. A. Taylor (Eds.), *Eliminating racism: Profiles in controversy* (pp. 53–84). New York: Plenum.

Sellers, R. M., & Shelton, J. N. (2003). The role of racial identity in perceived racial discrimination. *Journal of Personality and Social Psychology, 84,* 1070–1092.

Smedley, A., & Smedley, B. D. (2005). Race as biology is fiction, racism as a social problem is real. *American Psychologist, 60,* 16-26.

Solórzano, D., Ceja, M., & Yosso, T. (2000, Winter). Critical race theory, racial microaggressions, and campus racial climate: The experiences of African American college students. *Journal of Negro Education, 69,* 60–73.

Spanierman, L. B., Armstrong, P. I., Poteat, V. P., & Beer, A. M. (2006). Psychosocial Costs of Racism to Whites: Exploring patterns through cluster analysis. *Journal of Counseling Psychology, 53,* 434–441.

Spanierman, L. B., & Heppner, M. J. (2004). Psychosocial Costs of Racism to Whites Scale (PCRW): Construction and initial validation. *Journal of Counseling Psychology, 51,* 249–262.

Steele, C. M., Spencer, S. J., & Aronson, J. (2002). Contending with group image: The psychology of stereotype and social identity threat. In M. Zanna (Ed.), *Advances in experimental social psychology* (Vol. 23, pp. 379–440). New York: Academic Press.

Strong, S. R., & Schmidt, L. D. (1970). Expertness and influence in counseling. *Journal of Counseling Psychology, 17,* 81–87.

Sue, D. W. (2003). *Overcoming our racism: The journey to liberation.* San Francisco: Jossey-Bass.

Sue, D. W. (2004). Whiteness and ethnocentric monoculturalism: Making the "invisible" visible. *American Psychologist, 59,* 759–769.

Sue, D. W. (2005). Racism and the conspiracy of silence. *Counseling Psychologist, 33,* 100–114.

Sue, D. W., Arredondo, P., & McDavis, R. J. (1992). Multicultural competencies/standards: A call to the profession. *Journal of Counseling & Development, 70,* 477–486.

Sue, D. W., Bucceri, J., Lin, A. I., Nadal, K. L., & Torino, G. C. (2007). Racial microaggressions and the Asian American experience. *Cultural Diversity and Ethnic Minority Psychology, 13,* 72–81.

Sue, D. W., & Sue, D. (2003). *Counseling the culturally diverse: Theory and practice* (4th ed.). New York: Wiley.

Sue, S., Fujino, D. C., Hu, L., & Takeuchi, D. (1991). Community mental health services for ethnic minority groups: A test of the cultural responsiveness hypothesis. *Journal of Consulting and Clinical Psychology, 59,* 533–540.

Thompson, C. E., & Neville, H. A. (1999). Racism, mental health, and mental health practice. *Counseling Psychologist, 27,* 155–223.

U.S. Department of Health and Human Services. (2001). *Mental health: Culture, race, and ethnicity—A supplement to Mental Health: A Report of the Surgeon General.* Rockville, MD: U.S. Department of Health and Human Services, Substance Abuse and Mental Health Services Administration, Center for Mental Health Services.

Utsey, S. O., Gernat, C. A., & Hammar, L. (2005). Examining White counselor trainees' reactions to racial issues in counseling and supervision dyads. *Counseling Psychologist, 33,* 449–478.

Utsey, S. O., & Ponterotto, J. G. (1996). Development and validation of the Index of Race-Related Stress (IRRS). *Journal of Counseling Psychology, 43,* 490–502.

Vanman, E. J., Saltz, J. L., Nathan, L. R., & Warren, J. A. (2004). Racial discrimination by low-prejudiced Whites. *Psychological Science, 15,* 711–719.

Williams, D. R., & Collins, C. (1995). US socioeconomic and racial differences in health: Patterns and explanations. *Annual Review of Sociology, 21,* 349–386.

Williams, D. R., Lavizzo-Mourey, R., & Warren, R. C. (1994). The concept of race and health status in America. *Public Health Reports, 109,* 26–41.

Williams, D. R., Neighbors, H. W., & Jackson, J. S. (2003). Racial/ethnic discrimination and health: Findings from community studies. *American Journal of Public Health, 93,* 200–208.

Woodhouse, S. S., Schlosser, L. Z., Crook, R. E., Ligiero, D. P., & Gelso, C. J. (2003). Client attachment to therapist: Relations to transference and client recollections of parental caregiving. *Journal of Counseling Psychology, 50,* 395–408.

Young, G., & Davis-Russell, E. (2002). The vicissitudes of cultural competence: Dealing with difficult classroom dialogue. In E. Davis-Russell (Ed.), *The California School of Professional Psychology handbook of multicultural education, research, intervention, and training* (pp. 37–53). San Francisco: Jossey-Bass.

20

Naturalizing Racial Differences through Comedy: Asian, Black, and White Views on Racial Stereotypes in Rush Hour 2

Ji Hoon Park, Nadine G. Gabbadon &
Ariel R. Chernin

In this paper, we examine the ideological implications of racial stereotypes in comedy through a textual and audience analysis of Rush Hour 2. *Although Asian, Black, and White focus group participants differentially engaged with racial stereotypes in the film, most participants, regardless of race, found the film's racial jokes inoffensive. Many Asian and Black participants found a positive source of pleasure in the negative portrayals of their own race and did not produce oppositional discourse. Our study suggests that the generic conventions and textual devices of comedy encourage the audience to naturalize racial differences rather than to challenge racial stereotypes.*

Rush Hour 2 (2001), the sequel to *Rush Hour* (1998), achieved enormous commercial success, grossing over $226 million in the United States and $329 million worldwide.[1] As of March 2005, the film ranked 45th in the all-time U.S. box office.[2] The movie follows two police officers, one from Los Angeles (Chris Tucker as "Carter") and one from Hong Kong (Jackie Chan as "Lee"), as they pursue Asian gang members attempting to execute an elaborate counterfeiting plot. Although *Rush Hour* and *Rush Hour 2* can be classified as action-comedy "buddy movies," the films depart from convention by pairing an African American and an Asian in the lead roles. Although such a casting decision could have alienated White viewers, the film's incredible mainstream success suggests that it appealed to both minority and White audiences. Perhaps inspired by the success of the *Rush Hour* franchise, the current film

Corresponding author: Ji Hoon Park; e-mail: jpark@asc.upenn.edu

Reprinted from the *Journal of Communication* 56, no. 1 (2006), by permission of John Wiley & Sons, Inc.

landscape reveals a growing number of comedies that feature Asian and/or Black leading men, among them *I Spy* (2002), *Shanghai Knights* (2003), and *Harold and Kumar Go to White Castle* (2004).

It is possible to argue that the growing number of comedies starring racial minorities has facilitated racial tolerance, as well as the acceptance of Asian men, in particular, who have been consistently marginalized from mainstream cultural representation in the United States. However, it is premature to claim that these films represent a substantial shift in the cultural representation of race. A critical investigation reveals that not only is the racial hierarchy a crucial part of these films' narratives but also the characters consistently conform to negative minority stereotypes that can be deemed racist. The relationship between explicitly stereotypical portrayals of race and commercial success seems highly problematic and contradictory. If blatant stereotypes are embodied in films, why do people enjoy them? *Rush Hour 2*'s enormous commercial success makes it an ideal example through which to explore the apparent paradox between potentially racist representations in comedy and its widespread popularity transcending racial boundaries.

Through *Rush Hour 2*, we examine the ideological implications of racial stereotypes in comedy and discuss how the genre of comedy privileges a reading of racial stereotypes as harmless, despite the potential negative consequences of such representations. Our textual analysis of *Rush Hour 2* identifies the kinds of stereotypes and the textual devices that attempt to diffuse viewers' critical interpretations. Through a cross-racial reception analysis, we investigate how Asian, Black, and White viewers react to racial jokes in *Rush Hour 2* and examine if they differentially engage with the film's racial stereotypes. Although the present study is specific to *Rush Hour 2*, the findings provide valuable insight into how racial stereotypes in comedy naturalize racial differences.

Racial Stereotypes in Comedy

Stereotyping serves multiple purposes, both cognitive and motivational, and it "emerges in various contexts to serve particular functions necessitated by those contexts" (Hilton & von Hippel, 1996, p. 238). A wide range of situations, such as cognitive overload, group conflict, power differences, or a desire to justify the status quo, can give rise to the formation and activation of stereotypes (Hilton & von Hippel). From a media industry perspective, stereotyping results from the need to quickly convey information about characters and to instill in audiences expectations about characters' actions (Casey, Casey, Calvert, French, & Lewis, 2002; Omi, 1989; Wilson, Gutiérrez, & Chao, 2003). Stereotypes are important in comedy because not only do they help to establish instantly recognizable character types but such character traits and stereotype-based jokes also constitute a source of humor (Bowes, 1990; King, 2002).

Critical attention has been paid to the ideological implications of the stereotypical treatment of racial minorities in comedy, whether stereotypes are "read as a symptom of existing social relations or as a more active component of the politics of representation" (King, 2002, p. 129). With regard to the disruptive potential of comedy, King notes that comic representations of race (i.e., exaggerated portrayals of racial traits) can be identified as a parody of the stereotype and a strategy of subversion, thereby opening up the possibility of critiquing the racial norm and rejecting prejudice. Denzin (2002) suggests that the conventional narrative in the interracial buddy films, where two men of different races develop trust and friendship, can be read as an imaginary utopia in which racial differences do not matter. In fact, comedy often inverts stereotypes to generate humor. For instance, in the *Lethal Weapon* (1987) film series, the Black character is middle class, conservative, and family oriented, and the White character is unpredictable and dangerous (Malanowski, 2002). Jewish and Black comedians tell jokes about their own race to criticize social injustice and racial inequalities (Haggins, 1995; King).

Scholars, however, concede that it is often difficult to distinguish social commentary and satire from the ideological reproduction of racial stereotypes in comedy. The most frequently debated question is whether viewers laugh at stereotyped minority figures or *with* them (Bowes, 1990; Hall, 1990). For critical scholars, the distinction is less important than the negative social consequences of seemingly harmless racial jokes. Critical views on race in comedy posit that racial stereotyping serves an ideological function, normalizing racially defined characteristics and legitimating the racial hierarchy (Bogle, 2001; Hall; King, 2002; Means Coleman, 2000; Omi, 1989; Wilson et al., 2003). Critical scholars claim that in a social environment in which racism is deeply rooted, racial jokes and stereotypes inevitably reinforce hierarchically structured racial differences (Hall; Omi). Omi argues that racial jokes told across the color lines "will, despite its 'purely' humorous intent, serve to reinforce stereotypes and rationalize the existing relations of racial inequality" (p. 121). Schulman (1992) questions the satirical use of racial humor as a tool for criticizing racism. She argues that an attempt to critique racism through comedy results in unintended consequences, namely, the reinforcement of the very stereotypes that the humor attempts to ridicule. Race-based comedy often juxtaposes racially characterized non whites against socially dominant Whites: "[racial humor] appears at the same time to have internalized something of the very despicable images that oppressors of the black community have harbored for centuries, however blatantly it parodies their absurdity and illogic" (Schulman, 1992, p. 6). Bogle claims that although comedy is perceived as having the potential to comment on the problematic nature of stereotyping, it rarely capitalizes on the opportunity. In the world of the film, minority characters rarely resist or reject the stereotypes that are forced upon them. In his discussion of *48 Hrs.* (1982), Bogle argues that the character Reggie Hammond (played by Eddie Murphy, a Black actor/comedian) never gets mad at Jack Cates (played by Nick Nolte, a White actor) for making racially insulting comments, thus "greatly neutralizes the inherent racism" (p. 282).

Scholars also highlight the harmful effects of minority actors embodying stereotypes associated with their own race. King (2002) points to the enactment of racist stereotypes, particularly that of the "coon," by Black comedians, such as Eddie Murphy, Martin Lawrence, and Chris Tucker, and notes that their performances are uncomfortably reminiscent of racist ideologies that have been used to justify racial discrimination in the past. Means Coleman (2000) also claims that Black actors appearing in what she terms "neominstrelsy" sitcoms, such as *Martin* (1992–1997), *The Fresh Prince of Bel Air* (1990–1996), and *The Wayans Bros.* (1995–1999), are "taking part in their own racial ridicule by adopting Jim Crow, coon, and Sambo characterizations" (p. 130). She argues that Black sitcoms emphasize self-deprecating humor, physical comedy, provocative and flashy clothing, and "ghettocentric" characterizations, all of which contribute to a narrowly defined portrait of African American men and women.

Theories of genre suggest that the naturalization of racial difference through stereotyping is more likely to occur in a comedic format because generic conventions discourage viewers' critical engagement with the racial discourse. Feuer (1992) argues that "the genre positions the interpretive community in such a way as to naturalize the dominant ideologies expressed in the text" (p. 145). Genres structure viewers' expectations, which, in turn, limit the ways in which viewers can interpret the film (Altman, 1987; Feuer; Neale, 1980). Comedy as a genre essentially extends the alleged harmlessness of interpersonal jokes, which allows controversial content in mainstream films to be considered acceptable (King, 2002, p. 149). The nature of the genre and the comedic performance dictate that audiences should not take stereotypes seriously because they are intentionally humorous and that taking offense to stereotypic representations simply signals a misreading of the filmmakers' intent (Bowes, 1990; Casey et al., 2002; Malanowski, 2002). Bowes argues that comedy affirms the dominant ideological positions because it diffuses viewers' critical interpretations. Hall (1990) characterizes race-based comedy as "a licensed zone, disconnected from the serious" and argues that its generic convention "ultimately protects and defends viewers from acknowledging their incipient racism" (p. 17).

We contend that seemingly innocuous racial jokes and stereotypes in comedy need critical attention in the current social climate. Most people claim to be color blind and antiracist; however, race continues to serve as an important cognitive category with which people make sense of their social world (Myers & Williamson, 2001). Much of the existing scholarship expands the understanding of racism and racial differences in conjunction with racial stereotypes as representational devices or cognitive categories. Racial stereotypes play a significant role in maintaining the racial ideology in post–civil rights America where blatant declarations of racist views, bigotry, and violence have become uncommon and unacceptable (Essed, 1991; Myers & Williamson; van Dijk, 1984, 1987). Racial stereotypes ultimately reduce and naturalize racial differences and, thus, preclude alternative ways to think about the category of race (Hall, 1997). Once the beliefs of racial differences are naturalized as objectively existent and immutable, these differences provide insight into how people see their world. Given that racial stereotypes are most frequently used to represent people of color, the reified racial beliefs help maintain the racial hierarchy and White privileges. These beliefs also lead to social consequences, including the negative judgments of racial minorities and social injustice (see Schaufer, 2003). We argue that racial stereotypes in comedy should be taken seriously because of their potential to naturalize racial differences through humor. However, the potential of comedy to subvert racial stereotypes cannot be underestimated. The purpose of the present study is to examine the ideological implications of racial stereotypes in comedy and to determine whether they humorously naturalize or possibly disrupt the beliefs of racial differences that constitute the ideological basis of the racial hierarchy.

Textual Analysis

The textual analysis that follows has three parts. First, a descriptive synopsis of *Rush Hour 2* situates racially stereotypical moments in the specific situations where they occur in order to examine how race is configured through dialogue and how racial jokes are related to the film narrative. We identify the stereotype-based racial jokes in *Rush Hour 2* that are consistent with previous scholars' discussions of the dominant representations of Asians and Blacks in American mass media (see Bogle, 2001; Hamamoto, 1994; King, 2002; Lee, 1999; Shim, 1998). The descriptive narrative analysis of the film is followed by a critical analysis that attempts to decode the racial ideology embedded in the film. The ideological analysis of *Rush Hour 2* was conducted in conjunction with the two important theoretical categories, character and narrative, as suggested in the work of Fiske (1987) and White (1992). Fiske claims that character is a crucial category of textual analysis because characters are discursive constructs embodying ideological positions and values; they are not individuals existing independent of textual and broader social relations. Narrative serves as another significant category of textual analysis in that narrative orients viewers' understanding of stories and naturalizes meanings and events that are ideological (Fiske; White). Finally, we examine the ideological limitations and possibilities of several textual devices in the film narrative.

Rush Hour 2 features the character James Carter (Chris Tucker), who is a detective in the Los Angeles Police Department, and his friend, Lee (Jackie Chan), who is chief inspector of the Hong Kong Police Department. The movie begins in Hong Kong, where Carter is visiting Lee on vacation. Amidst Carter's preoccupation with picking up women, Lee receives a call from his boss, who informs him that the Hong Kong Police suspect that Ricky Tan (played by John Lone), the cunning head of the Fu-Cang-Long Triads gang, is responsible for an explosion in the American embassy that killed two Americans. Carter's desire to enjoy a stress-free vacation leads him to warn Lee that, if Lee takes the case, "I'll slap you so hard that you'll end up in the Ming Dynasty." Throughout the movie, Carter is high pitched, childish, irresponsible, and hypersexual. When Carter sees a few Chinese women in the car next to theirs, he yells, "Let's get some sushi!" to the women, revealing his cultural ignorance.

Disguising his intentions to begin investigating the case, Lee brings Carter to a club where the Triad gang has gathered. When Lee tells Carter to act like a tourist, Carter replies, "I'm two feet taller than everybody in here." Carter impulsively decides to roust the bar and demands that people reveal Ricky Tan's whereabouts. Carter's irrational antics alert Ricky Tan's beautiful but deadly henchwoman, Hu Li (played by Zhang Ziyi) and her fellow gangsters, resulting in a fight between Chan and the gang members.

After their first scuffle with the Triads, Lee takes Carter to an upscale massage parlor called "Heaven on Earth" to perform another undercover operation. Carter is shown a group of scantily clad Chinese women and the hostess assures Carter that he can pick any girl to perform his massage. When Lee tells Carter to speed up his selection process, Carter exclaims, "You don't jump in front of a black man in a buffet line!" Instead of choosing one girl, Carter greedily selects five. Later at the massage parlor when Lee and Carter find Ricky Tan, Carter starts another fight with the Asian gang members, despite Lee's attempt to verbally reason with Tan. During the fight, Carter exclaims to a gang member, "No wonder you're mad!" after the man's towel falls off and he is standing fully naked. Carter accidentally punches Lee instead of a gang member and explains, "You all look alike." Defeated, Lee and Tucker are kidnapped and later tossed out onto the highway.

Circumstances lead Carter to a yacht party hosted by Ricky. Carter meets and immediately begins flirting with a Latina woman named Isabella Molina (played by Roselyn Sanchez) who ignores his advances. Carter discovers that she is affiliated with Steven Reign, a wealthy White businessman from Los Angeles who claims that he is in Hong Kong to sightsee. When Carter meets Lee on the boat, he says, "No one understands the words coming out of your mouth" due to his accent. Carter shares with Lee his theory of investigation, which is, in sum, "follow the rich white man," stating that every major crime has a rich, White man behind it expecting to make large financial gains. After seeing Reign on the yacht, Carter becomes convinced that he is involved in the smuggling and that he is the key to solving the crime.

Lee and Carter follow Reign to Los Angeles where they run into Isabella Molina, who they learn is an undercover Secret Service agent. Molina tells them that Steven Reign and the Triads are involved in producing and shipping hundreds of millions of dollars in counterfeit "superbills." Isabella asks Lee and Carter to help find the plates used to counterfeit the money, and they agree. Carter boasts, "She chose me because I'm tall, dark and handsome, and you're third-world-ugly." Lee responds, "I'm not third-world-ugly. Women like me, they think I'm cute. Like Snoopy." Tucker then says, "Snoopy is six inches taller than you."

In pursuit of the plates, Lee and Carter are captured by Hu Li. Trapped and tied up inside a truck, Carter and Lee discover thousands of counterfeit bills and Carter takes some of the money, saying it is for "evidence." Lee and Carter start fighting. Carter exclaims, "I will slap the hell out of you right now!" Lee responses, "I'll bitch-slap you back to Africa!" They eventually work together to escape, only to find themselves in Las Vegas.

In Las Vegas, Carter and Lee see a casino called the "Red Dragon" (the same name as Ricky Tan's yacht) and realize that this is where the money is being laundered. When they enter the casino, Carter tells Lee to look for the plates and that he distracts the security guards. Carter uses some of the counterfeit money that he got from the truck and starts gambling at one of the craps tables in his usual loud-mouthed fashion. He complains to the White dealer that he gets $500 chips instead of $1,000 chips because he is Black. Carter then brings up the issue of Black slavery, exclaiming, "You gave me $500 chips because I'm black? You think my people suffered 362 years of slavery so you could send us to cotton fields with $500 chips? Do I look like Chicken George to you?" During the film's climax, Lee and Carter once again face Hu Li and Ricky Tan. Both gang members die, and the counterfeiting plates are recovered.

Rush Hour 2 promotes numerous Black and Asian stereotypes through characters that personify and verbalize these racial myths. Lee is a respectful but culturally ignorant and asexual Asian man who excels at Kung Fu. Henchwoman Hu Li serves as the Asian "dragon lady" who is desirable but dangerous (Ogunnaike, 2003, p. E1). The Chinese women at the massage parlor embody the stereotype of obedient Oriental dolls readily fulfilling Americans' sexual desire and fantasies. These two images of Asian women may seem contradictory, but they reflect two major stereotypes of Asian women frequently found in the mass media. Omi (1989) suggests that although it is possible for racial minorities to be stereotyped in multiple ways within the same text, such contradictions do not challenge the one dimensionality of minority images. Carter is a loud, impulsive, hypersexual yet childish Black man who is often portrayed as ignorant and causing trouble. He constantly reinforces stereotypes associated with his own race. He tells a Chinese woman that he likes his chicken "dead and deep fried," as if it is natural that a Black man likes fried chicken. He also furthers the African American stereotype in his manner of speaking, such as "she's the bomb," "mack out," and "look fly."

A critical reading of *Rush Hour 2* indicates that racial ideology is coded both in the characters and in the narrative. First, Jackie Chan and Chris Tucker both portray likeable characters that do not problematize or transgress mainstream racial images and boundaries. Their characters are buffoons or "symbolically castrated men" that do not challenge White masculinity (Lo, 2001, p. 474). In contrast to Chan's Hong Kong–made action movies, where his characters are not only affable but also masculine and tough (Teo, 1997), Chan's Hollywood films, such as *Shanghai Noon* (2000) and *Shanghai Knights* (2003), cast him in the role of the funny, desexualized, and unthreatening Oriental male. Lo argues that Chan's masculinity has been toned down in Hollywood in order to ensure that his characters conform to racial conventions. Tucker as Carter is an infantile Black man who, despite his masculine physical presence, is incapable of protecting himself without Chan's help. King (2002) indicates that the Black comedian's high-pitched voice and childish tone are unthreatening to the racial status quo because they help "reduce any threat created by the spectacle of a seemingly dominating Black character" (p. 149). Most of the racial jokes in *Rush Hour 2* are directed toward minorities, which strengthens Whites' positive self-image and their dominant position in the racial order.

Second, the narrative's binary opposition of powerful Whites and subordinate minorities contains the symbolic threats to the racial hierarchy. The contrast between the powerful and the powerless becomes a "metaphor for power relationships in society and thus a material practice through which the dominant ideology works" (Fiske, 1987, p. 9) because a binary opposition in narrative naturalizes and universalizes the hierarchy implied by the opposition. Although White characters only have small roles in *Rush Hour 2*, they still occupy key "overseeing" positions in the storyline, regardless of whether they are good or evil. Steven Reign, the billionaire hotel owner, funds gang leader Ricky Tan's operation and provides his casino as a means of money laundering, and agent Sterling of the U.S. Secret Service supervises the criminal investigation into Tan's and Reign's activities. The main villains of the film are Asian. Ricky Tan, Hu Li, and the team of Chinese gangsters all threaten American interests by blowing up the American embassy in Hong Kong and by circulating counterfeit U.S. currency. Although Lee and Carter play a crucial role in avenging the Chinese villains and maintaining justice, they act in service of White America by defeating those who challenge White patriarchal power. Ultimately, the violence of and against Asian gangsters does not constitute a threat to White masculinity and domination but helps maintain the racial status quo.

In addition to generic conventions that communicate the innocuousness of racial stereotypes, several textual devices in *Rush Hour 2* diffuse viewers' potential claims of racism and promote the acceptability of racial stereotypes. First, the minority status of two main characters signals that their racial jokes are acceptable and not racist. Because people of color are usually portrayed as victims rather than perpetrators of racism, they are not perceived as having power over the others (as opposed to a White character having power over a minority character).

Second, racial jokes in the film cross color lines, creating an impression that all races are subject to stereotypes. Although there are only a couple of instances in the film that could potentially be interpreted as promoting White stereotypes, the inclusion of these few quips creates the impression that all racial groups are targeted by the film's racial humor. Marchetti (1991) argues that "Hollywood films often play various positions one against the other, so that a text can appear to espouse rather liberal attitudes toward race" (p. 279).

Third, the film's stereotypes are coded as realistic and natural and based on the characters' personality differences and the execution of the plot. For instance, Carter's impulsive behavior is used to propel the plot and causes Lee to engage in fights with the Triad gang members. Carter is also always the funny distraction when Lee is responsibly investigating the crime. The relevance of stereotypes to the plot and characterization makes the racially stereotyped content acceptable and realistic.

Fourth, the two leading men are portrayed as good friends. Because neither Carter nor Lee is hurt by the racial remarks, the film encourages viewers to interpret the humor as acceptable. They are seen singing together in the car, and they often help each other out of difficult situations. At the end of the movie, Lee gives Carter his father's badge as a symbol of friendship. This also implies that despite all of Carter's racial jokes and comments, Lee was still a true friend and there were indeed no hard feelings between them.

Although a critical analysis suggests that these textual devices serve an ideological function by promoting the acceptability and believability of racial stereotypes, such devices can simultaneously be read as strategies to subvert or disrupt the racial status quo. For instance, the friendship between Carter and Lee can signify two conflicting meanings to the audience. Although it communicates the acceptability of negative racial jokes by suggesting that "in this world of racial integration, ugly racial slurs are reserved only for the bad buys" (Denzin, 2002, p. 101), it may also change viewers' racial attitudes by cultivating favorable views on Blacks or Asians. Lee can be read as subservient to the (White) authority, but he can also be considered respectful and responsible. Kenny, Carter's African American informant, who owns a Chinese restaurant, wears traditional Chinese clothing, and is married to an Asian woman, may, through juxtaposition, make Carter appear to be the "normal" Black man. Kenny's unusual traits may also challenge viewers' preconceived images of African Americans. There are many other aspects of the film that can be read as potentially subversive: People from two different cultures developing friendship and trust, two good guys learning about each other in life and death situations and overcoming cultural misunderstandings, and so forth.

A discussion of the ideological limitations and possibilities of racial stereotypes in comedy cannot be complete without exploring audiences' interpretation of the text. We now turn our attention to the viewers. We examine how viewers of different races make sense of the racial stereotypes in relation to the genre of comedy and the textual devices that we discussed above. How do audiences interpret *Rush Hour 2*'s racial stereotypes? Are White, Black, or Asian audiences offended by any content in the film? Do White, Black, and Asian American audiences differ in their sensitivity to the portrayal of race in this film?

Researching the Audience

Method

The focus group interviews were conducted with White, Black, and Asian participants. Several studies have demonstrated the strengths of focus groups in identifying audiences' response to the media portrayal of race beyond their surface attitudes and in mapping out a subtle picture of audience reaction (see Bird, 1996, 2003; Bobo, 1989, 1995; Jhally & Lewis, 1992). Blacks, Asians, and White viewers were placed in separate focus groups with a moderator of their racial group. We felt this approach created an atmosphere where participants would feel comfortable discussing potentially sensitive topics, such as racism. It also facilitated comparisons between racial groups.

There were eight focus groups with three to eight people per group: two groups of White Americans, three groups of Black Americans, and three groups of Asian Americans. Of the

40 volunteers who participated in the groups,[3] race and gender were as follows: 11 White (7 males, 4 females), 18 Asian (7 males, 11 females), and 11 Black (6 males, 5 females). Age ranges were as follows: White participants, 18–21 years (mean 19.7 years); Black participants, 18–28 years (mean 21.2 years); and Asian participants, 18–31 years (mean 21.6 years). The majority of the participants were recruited from the undergraduate population of a large East Coast university through e-mail, in classrooms, and by word-of-mouth. One Asian participant had a graduate degree; two Asian participants and one Black participant were graduate students.

For each focus group, the participants were brought together either in someone's home or in a classroom. They watched *Rush Hour 2* together, and then, the moderator facilitated a discussion about their views on the movie, including questions about their opinions on the characters, what they thought about the stereotypes in the movie and whether they were offended. The moderator also asked participants to comment on issues of racial stereotypes in general in order to explore how they made sense of the film's stereotypes in relation to their own actual beliefs on race. The semistructured discussions were relaxed and informal so that much of the information shared emerged from the natural flow of conversation. The moderators asked questions to keep the discussion on track and to probe participants to explain their comments in more detail. Discussions, which lasted about 30–60 minutes, were tape recorded and transcribed at a later date. Pseudonyms are used to protect participants' anonymity.

In analyzing the focus group data, we looked at two overarching areas: offensiveness and perceptions of stereotypes. With regard to offensiveness, we assessed whether or not the participants were offended by *Rush Hour 2* and why. With regard to stereotypes, we explored which stereotypes the participants noticed in the movie and which, if any, they perceived as true. Instead of simply reiterating how participants of different races responded to racial stereotypes in the movie, we provide accounts of why they responded in the ways that they did. Radway (1986) notes that researchers' critical accounts of informants' own interpretation of a text is a crucial task because audiences "live ideology . . . they are produced by it to accept a particular limited view of their situation. *Their self-understanding, when seen from some other perspective, then, might be constructed as 'false'*" (pp. 106–107, emphasis added).

Offensiveness

Irrespective of race, the majority of the focus group participants laughed throughout their viewing of *Rush Hour 2*. They stated explicitly that they enjoyed *Rush Hour 2*, and that the film's racial humor did not offend them. Although participants gave numerous reasons for why they were not offended, several common themes emerged. First, Black, White, and Asian participants mentioned that *Rush Hour 2*'s status as a comedy dictated that the film should not be taken seriously. Many participants stated that they would have taken offense at racial jokes and stereotypes if they had been conveyed in different generic forms, such as drama.

> Jeff (White male, 19): It's not as offensive when you know it's supposed to be funny, as opposed to just coming out of nowhere, and you're like, "what?"

> Justin (Asian male, 18): I think since it's in a comedy movie, people can let it go.

> Aaron (Black male, 20): The context of putting the whole interaction with the comedy so people aren't necessarily offended when Lee says, I'm gonna bitch-slap you back to Africa or something. Like, that was funny because of the context but if he said it anywhere else, it wouldn't.

Most participants in all three racial groups acknowledged, however, that even within the context of a comedy, racial humor could potentially be racist. Several participants said that the race of the person telling a joke can dictate whether or not the joke is racist. In comedy, it is often considered acceptable for racial minorities to tell racial jokes, whereas the same jokes told by Whites would be considered racist. Most participants agreed that if a White character told the same jokes as Carter and Lee, audiences would probably be offended.

> Vanessa (Black female, 20): Well, I guess culturally people would be less inclined to take offense, in my opinion, [because of] the fact that Chris Tucker is black and Jackie Chan is Chinese . . . . They're both minorities . . . . Whereas I feel that if one of the characters had been White, there's a historical stigma of White oppressor that could maybe just not let people think his intentions don't have any racial prejudice or racial hatred or patronizing feelings in any way.

> Ryan (Asian male, 19): I think it's more acceptable I think. There's one line when Jackie Chan was in a truck, he's like "I'll slap you back to Africa." There's no way that a White character would ever say that in the movie because . . . . You can't say that.

> Ethan (White male, 20): The movie works because it's two minorities. They can rag on each other. It wouldn't be acceptable if one of them was White because . . . . It just wouldn't work out. People would be offended and stuff.

The White participants' discussion of racial stereotypes revealed that they were keenly aware of Whites' stigmatized position as perpetrators of racism. One White participant explained that the main characters' minority status allowed White people to enjoy the jokes without feeling guilty.

> Amy (White female, 20): Maybe the jokes are more politically correct because . . . . you're making fun of your race against someone who can also make fun of their race and White people don't have to stand back and be, like, "Oh, shit, sorry." Like, I'm sorry I'm an oppressor, or something.

Second, several of the Black, Asian, and White participants stated that the movie was not offensive because the jokes were targeted at Blacks, Asians, and Whites—and not at one group in particular.

> Stacey (White female, 20): I think a lot of it has to do with that they ragged on every race in this movie. I think if it was just focused in on one race, and they only made fun of that one race, it would start to get a little racist . . . . If it was just only Black jokes or only Asian jokes, or only White jokes . . .

Even when Lee told Carter that he would "bitch-slap him back to Africa," some Black participants stated that there was no need to be offended by the comment because earlier in the film Carter had said he would slap Lee back to the Ming Dynasty. One Black participant suggested that making jokes about every race was a deliberate move by the filmmakers. Our textual analysis, however, shows that Whites were portrayed differently than Blacks and Asians in *Rush Hour 2*. The film successfully creates the impression among the viewers that all races are objects of mockery, distortion, and exaggeration.

Third, in assessing the offensiveness of the film's racial humor, Asian, Black, and White participants considered the movie's internal context of two close friends making fun of each other's race. Participants felt this type of racial humor was acceptable because neither Carter nor Lee seemed offended by any of the comments. Their banter was interpreted as harmless "inside jokes."

Nathan (Black male, 18): I think a lot of the joking about the stereotypes in the movie was kind of softened by the fact that Jackie and Tucker are friends . . . and they're cool.

An interesting aspect of the discussions within the Black and Asian focus groups is the fact that although most participants denied being offended by *Rush Hour 2*, many were still able to label the film as offensive on an intellectual level. We propose that this happened in part because of the nature of the focus group experience; participants were forced to think about the film and its implications. However, even after they acknowledged the movie's potential offensiveness, most were still accepting of the film and insisted that they were not offended.

Stereotypes

Although not offended by *Rush Hour 2*, White participants made reference to the implicit stereotypes expressed in the film, including the Asian man skilled in martial arts who cannot speak proper English, Asian women as seductresses, and the Black cop with "street credibility." White participants also commented on the stereotypes verbalized by the main characters, including the idea that a rich White man is behind most crimes, Asian men are short, and Black people like fried chicken. Most White participants felt that both the implicit and the explicit stereotypes were not only blatant and contrived but also very funny.

White viewers' interpretations of the film characters were structured around racial stereotypes. Jackie Chan's character was read along the line of typical Asian male stereotypes. White participants found Lee entertaining but did not consider him attractive. Chris Tucker's character was also perceived of in terms of particular Black stereotypes (i.e., loud and childish) but to a lesser extent than Chan's. Many of the White participants felt that Chris Tucker's acting was intentionally over the top, and they assessed his performance not only in terms of Black stereotypes but also in terms of his previous roles and general acting style. Overall, White participants' reading of *Rush Hour 2* was straightforward in that their understanding of Black and Asian characters did not go beyond their stereotypical depictions. For White participants, Lee and Carter were no more than typical Asian and Black men in their imagination. We did not see any alternative or creative engagement with the movie among White participants. We proposed that this is because White viewers were comfortably aligned with the dominant racial ideology that promotes White invisibility and minority stereotypes (see Dyer, 1997) and thus readily adopted the reading strategy privileged by the film. We argue that the White participants felt no need to contest or negotiate with the film's representation of race since their relation to the racial ideology is much less resistive. The racial imagery in the film did not challenge prevailing notions of race and did not provoke feelings of discomfort or anxiety in White viewers. The absence of a major White character did not alienate White viewers because the inclusion of a White character verbalizing racial stereotypes could have implicated White people as perpetrators of racism and thus would have made White viewers uncomfortable and resistant.

As the most stereotyped and joked about group in *Rush Hour 2*, Asian participants were quick to point out the Asian and Black stereotypes in the film, including culturally ignorant Asian men, submissive Asian women, and impulsive Black men. The recognition of negative and objectionable Asian stereotypes, however, did not prevent participants from enjoying the film. We argue that Asian participants were uncritical of the film because of the unique way Asian characters were interpreted. For Asians, who have long been under- and misrepresented in the American media,[4] *Rush Hour 2* could be perceived as a sign of progress. Unlike previous Hollywood films where Asian men play subservient or villainous roles, *Rush Hour 2* presents a self-confident, successful, and heroic Asian man. Thus, while the film promotes numerous Asian stereotypes that are potentially racist, it nonetheless offers a positive image of an Asian man in a leading role that Asian viewers can be proud to cheer for and support.

> Sandra (Asian female, 22): I think you always cheer for the Asian guy. I am not saying that "Oh, I relate with Jackie Chan." But when he does something good, I'm like "Yes! Fight for the Asians!"

Bobo's (1989, 1995) study of Black female viewers' positive engagement with *The Color Purple* suggests that non white audiences are not necessarily critical of a racially controversial film because they quickly sift through contentious parts of the film and identify positive elements that resonate with their own experiences. We found such evidence in our Asian and Black focus groups. Asian and Black viewers overlooked the negative stereotypes of their races and instead focused on positive aspects of minority representations. In *Rush Hour 2*, minority characters are not just sidekicks but good guys who end up winning. Asian and Black participants also recognized that two men of color were positioned in a nonhierarchical relationship. For Asian and Black participants, the sense of cross-racial equality and friendship expressed in the film outweighed the negative minority stereotypes.

> Justin (Asian male, 18): Chris Tucker and Jackie Chan complement each other. Obviously Jackie Chan is better in fighting and stuff. But Chris Tucker is better at talking and everything. So they kind of cancel each other out. They are a good combo. But I think with a White person and an Asian person, it always feels like the White person is better than the Asian person.

We observed that Asian participants' positive interpretations of Chan's character extended to their view of the portrayal of Asian women. Despite the film's stereotypical representation of Asian women as submissive and seductive and as ruthless "dragon ladies," none of the Asian participants raised the issue of racialized sexism. In contrast, several of the female participants stated that they were empowered by Zhang Ziyi's character in the film.

In general, the Asian participants accepted and found humor in the potentially racist comments directed toward Lee and other Asian characters in *Rush Hour 2*. We suspect that this occurred because the participants perceived important differences between themselves and Lee with regard to national identity. The Asian participants felt that they could laugh at Lee, a Chinese man, because the stereotypes associated with him, such as poor English-language skills and cultural ignorance, did not apply to them as Asian Americans. Overall, Asian participants read the Asian characters in *Rush Hour 2* as Chinese more so than Asian American. As a result, although Asian participants were glad that Asians had prominent roles in the film, they simultaneously distanced themselves from Lee and other "Chinese" characters and felt comfortable laughing at the jokes directed toward Asians; Asian participants depersonalized the Asian stereotypes. It should be noted that although Asian participants were keenly aware of the Asian characters' national origins, White and Black participants read the characters much more broadly, that is, as generically Asian.

Black participants recognized many racial stereotypes in the film and characterized them as exaggerated racial traits, which they found to be funny and entertaining. They acknowledged Chris Tucker as representing the loud Black man who is always after women and is essentially placed in the film to elicit laughter from the audience. The participants saw Jackie Chan as a stereotypical Asian man who knows martial arts, is not fluent in English, and is calm and respectful. The participants also recognized Carter's statement that a rich White man is behind most crimes. Although Black participants did not feel empowered by Tucker's character, a few of them identified with him and suggested that they would have reacted the same way he did in several of the film's scenes. Although *Rush Hour 2* presents numerous Black stereotypes that can be deemed offensive, Black participants did not seem critical of nor did they take them seriously. We propose that this is because Black participants were inclined to see the positive aspects of the film's representations of African Americans instead of being upset by unpleasant portrayals. For instance, Black participants concentrated on the fact that the ideas perpetuated are ones that most people do not get upset over or that are usually considered humorous (e.g., Black people like fried chicken, all Asians know karate). They contrasted these ideas with joking about serious stereotypes, such as poverty and drug use, claiming that had the movie made light of these issues, it likely would have offended them. In addition, several participants remarked that in contrast to films that position Black characters as criminals, Tucker's character does not commit a crime but solves one. Some participants also considered Tucker's character as more important than Chan's in the narrative. We also argue that Black participants were often accepting of Carter's comments about Black people because they are accustomed to Black entertainers capitalizing on their own racial stereotypes (Means Coleman, 2000). Having recognized the importance of Tucker's role, several Black participants commented that White viewers would have enjoyed *Rush Hour 2* the least because there is no positive portrayal of Whites and White viewers are not entitled to laugh at Black stereotypes like Black viewers. They also felt sorry for Asian viewers because Asians were the most joked about in the film.

Regardless of race, the majority of focus group participants did not take *Rush Hour 2*'s portrayal of race seriously, stating it was only a comedy and thus not intended to offend viewers. Throughout the discussions, participants frequently commented that it would be unusual to discuss a *fictional* comedy like *Rush Hour 2* at length and that the moderators were reading too much into it. Although participants made light of the racial stereotypes in *Rush Hour 2*, they perceived and accepted many of its racial portrayals as *real*. Participants in all three racial groups felt that the racial stereotypes in the film were humorous and acceptable because they were based on a "kernel of truth" that had been exaggerated.

> Moderator: What are some of the stereotypes in the movie?
> Stacey (White female, 20): Tucker kicks Jackie Chan in the face and says all Asians look alike.
> [People laugh]
> Josh (White male, 21): Or that all Asians are short.
> Emily (White female, 20): [Quoting movie]: "I'm two feet taller than everyone else in the room."
> [People laugh]
> Moderator: And why is that funny? I can see everyone sort of giggling when they remember it.
> Anthony (White male, 18): It's just so true.
> [People laugh]
> Moderator: So you think there's truth in it. Is there truth in the stereotypes?
> Stacey (White female, 20): Yeah.
> Moderator: Do you remember "Carter's theory of criminal investigation"?
> Richard (Asian male, 23): Follow a [rich] White guy. [There's always a rich White guy behind every crime].
> Sandra (Asian female, 22): When I heard that, [I thought] "Oh my God. It's kind of funny" because I guess . . .
> Steve (Asian male, 22): Because it's true.
> Ken (Asian male, 19): Stereotypes are based on some types of truth.
> Mark (Black male, 21): I think most stereotypes Tucker brings out are true. They are things that you don't usually think about or just say. But they are kind of true . . . .

> In general, of course you can't stereotype every single Black person, but I think Carter is supposed to be that average Black person from the ghetto.

Despite participants' emphasis on the fictional nature of *Rush Hour 2*, they perceived a sense of realism in its racial representations; few participants stated that racial stereotypes in the film were unreal or incorrect. Although many participants claimed that they could distinguish between fiction and reality, we observed strong continuity between the film's representations of race and participants' general opinions about racial traits. As participants' comments suggest, many revealed (likely without realizing it) that they thought many of the stereotypes expressed in the film were based on truth.

Throughout the focus group discussions, many participants displayed a blurring of the distinction between the fictional characters and the actors who play them, using Lee and Chan, or Carter and Tucker interchangeably. One White participant implied that Black stereotypes in *Rush Hour 2* are likely to be true because Chris Tucker (as an actor) plays off of stereotypes and he makes jokes about his own race. As Jhally and Lewis (1992) note, fictional media are simultaneously real and unreal and therefore have a significant impact on how we perceive the social world. Fiske (1987) argues that realism in the media encourages viewers to incorporate on-screen attitudes and beliefs into the real world. Although it is beyond the scope of our study to determine whether participants of our study transformed *Rush Hour 2*'s racial characterizations into their everyday common sense, we found evidence that the movie influenced how participants made sense of racial differences. We observed several incidents in which participants used *Rush Hour 2* as a reference to validate their own actual racial beliefs.

> Amy (White female, 20): It was funny, because in the outtakes, Jackie Chan got his lines wrong, and Chris Tucker's phone goes off, and he's like, "No, brother, get off the phone. Get off the phone." The outtakes almost played into the stereotypes and it's the actual people, not their characters. I don't know if that was a very politically correct thing for me to say.

The sense of realism participants perceived in *Rush Hour 2* has ideological effects because it authenticates the racial stereotypes in the film and grants them an objective status. We claim that a comedy like *Rush Hour 2* can contribute to viewer's sense of the real and foster the believability of different racial characteristics. Although not all participants stated explicitly that the film's stereotypes are based on truth, most of them hesitated to claim that they were false, confessing that their first-hand experience of different races is limited. We argue that the humorous portrayal of racial traits and the sense of realism in *Rush Hour 2* encouraged participants to see or seek "true" components in racial stereotypes rather than to challenge or argue against the exaggerated and totalizing nature of stereotypes. Most participants in all three racial focus groups agreed that there are certain characteristics about different racial groups that are more common than others and that the film simply exaggerated these traits to make them funny and entertaining. In addition, the participants of all three racial groups rarely talked about White stereotypes while preoccupied with minority stereotypes. Although participants identified several jokes about White people in the film, they did not see a strong association between Whiteness and stereotypes. In the general discussion of racial stereotypes, participants of all races infrequently mentioned stereotypes associated with Whites. Our study suggests that *Rush Hour 2* successfully promotes a sense of normality of Whiteness among viewers while encouraging them to see non whites as racially marked and different.

Conclusion

The fact that almost none of our focus group participants were offended by *Rush Hour 2*'s explicit racial jokes is revealing but potentially misleading. Viewers' claims that racial stereotyping in comedy is funny, inoffensive, and therefore acceptable do not automatically establish that it is harmless. Racial stereotypes in comedy are problematic precisely because they help validate racial differences through humor, thus rendering them natural and unchallengeable. Inoffensiveness in comedy is a necessary condition for the naturalization of racial differences because if overly antagonistic racist remarks or assumptions were presented in ways that were offensive, they would likely trigger an oppositional reading, resulting in a straightforward rejection and critical evaluation of the cultural construction of racial differences. Because racial stereotypes in comedy rarely offend the audiences and are presented in an enjoyable way, audiences are able to naturalize specific knowledge about racial minorities without resistance. The generic conventions and textual devices of comedy ensure that viewers actively consume and derive pleasure from racial jokes and stereotypes without critical and interrogative engagement with them. Comedy ultimately controls and limits audiences' critical reflection of potentially racist characterizations, thereby making viewers susceptible to the beliefs of racial difference. Our study suggests that not only do different racial audiences enjoy racial jokes and humor in comedy but they are also much more inclined to see truth in racial stereotypes than to cast doubt on them.

We also gathered evidence that audiences of different races do not engage with racial stereotypes in comedy in uniform ways. In comparison to White viewers who interpreted minority characters strictly within the confines of stereotypes, Black and Asian participants found a positive source of pleasure in the seemingly offensive portrayals of their own race. However, we claim that it is inaccurate to take this as an indication of comedy's potential to disrupt the racial status quo. Viewers' creative and positive engagement with racial stereotypes does not necessarily indicate that the text's subversive potential is realized by audiences, for their negotiation with racial stereotypes does not always work to disrupt the racial ideology. Communication scholars note that the selective and creative activity of the audience may not constitute critical viewing (Condit, 1989; Morley, 2005; Schudson, 1998). Morley suggests that the notion of interpretative freedom often leads us to underestimate the power of the media to shape our social reality, arguing that "the power of viewers to reinterpret meanings is hardly equivalent to the discursive power of the centralized media institutions to construct the texts which the viewer then interprets, and to imagine otherwise is simply foolish" (p. 175). Condit claims that audience pleasure is not sufficient "to certify a positive role for mass media in the process of social change" (p. 103). We are skeptical of the disruptive potential of race-based comedy because in our study, minority participants' pleasure did not transcend but occurred *within* the discursive confines of the racial ideology. Although participants of different racial groups employed different hermeneutic strategies to negotiate their readings, such negotiated readings involved rearticulating the genesis of each racial stereotype (e.g., kernel of truth). In other words, participants' active viewing and pleasure were based on the self-validation of racial characteristics rather than on the subversion of stereotypes. Bird (2003) would describe this as "constrained cultural activity" (p. 167) in that although the audiences do many unexpected things with the images provided by the media, their meaning making is constrained by the boundaries set by the media. Audiences' pleasure in viewing racial humor tends to require the acceptance of the beliefs of racial differences because there would be little pleasure if viewers perceived racial stereotypes in comedy as unreal or false. We claim that viewers' validation of racial stereotypes is the ideological effect of comedy that encourages them to perceive racial differences as essential and natural, not culturally constructed. Although creative, none of our focus group participants produced any oppositional discourse with regard to the problematic aspects of racial characterizations in *Rush Hour 2*. The absence of a critical discourse and the validation of racial stereotypes among the viewers suggest that racial stereotypes in comedy successfully enable viewers of all races to naturalize the beliefs of racial differences while allowing them to enjoy the humor.

Notes

1. Box Office Prophets. (n.d.). *Rush hour 2*. Retrieved March 3, 2005, from http://www.boxofficeprophets.com/tickermaster/listing.cfm?TMID = 169

2. Internet Movie Database. (n.d.). *All-time USA box office*. Retrieved March 3, 2005, from http://www.imdb.com/Charts/usatopmovies

3. Except for one Black participant who was born abroad and migrated to the United States at an early age, all the White and Black participants were American born. "Asian Americans" refers to Americans of East Asian decent. All Asian participants were of Chinese, Korean, or Japanese descent and used English as their first language. Among the 18 Asian participants, 14 were American born and 4 were foreign born. Two foreign-born Asian participants were adopted and raised by White families, and the other two foreign-born participants immigrated to American at their early age.

4. For discussions of the representations of Asian Americans in American film and television, see Hamamoto (1994), Shim (1998), and Wong (1978).

Acknowledgments

This study was presented at the annual conference of the National Communication Association in Chicago in November 2004. The authors thank Paul Messaris, Oscar Gandy, Barbie Zelizer, Larry Gross, Toby Miller, and two anonymous reviewers for their comments and suggestions on previous drafts of this paper.

References

Altman, R. (1987). *The American film musical*. Bloomington: Indiana University Press.

Bird, S. E. (1996). Not my fantasy: The persistence of Indian imagery in Dr. Quinn, Medicine Woman. In S. E. Bird (Ed.), Dressing in feathers: *The construction of the Indian in American popular culture* (pp. 245–261). Boulder, CO: Westview Press.

Bird, S. E. (2003). *The audience in everyday life: Living in a media world*. New York: Routledge.

Bobo, J. (1989). Sifting through the controversy: Reading *The Color Purple*. *Callaloo*, 39, 332–342.

Bobo, J. (1995). *Black women as cultural readers*. New York: Columbia University Press.

Bogle, D. (2001). *Toms, coons, mulattoes, mammies, and bucks: An interpretive history of blacks in American films*. New York: Continuum.

Bowes, M. (1990). Only when I laugh. In A. Goodwin & G. Whannel (Eds.), *Understanding television* (pp. 128–140). London: Routledge.

Bowman, J., Lawrence, M., Milmore, J., Carew, T., & Williams, S.-A. (Executive producers). (1992–1997). *Martin* [Television series]. Los Angeles, CA: Fox.

Box Office Prophets. (n.d.). *Rush hour 2*. Retrieved March 3, 2005, from http:// www.boxofficeprophets.com/tickermaster/listing.cfm?TMID=169

Casey, B., Casey, N., Calvert, B., French, L., & Lewis, J. (2002). *Television studies: The key concepts*. London: Routledge.

Condit, C. M. (1989). The rhetorical limit of polysemy. *Critical Studies in Mass Communication*, 6, 103–122.

Denzin, N. K. (2002). *Reading race: Hollywood and the cinema of racial violence*. London: Sage.

Dey, T. (Director). (2000). *Shanghai noon* [Motion picture]. United States: Touchstone Pictures.

Dobkin, D. (Director). (2003). *Shanghai knights* [Motion picture]. United States: Buena Vista Motion.

Donner, R. (Director). (1987). *Lethal weapon* [Motion picture]. United States: Warner Bros.

Dyer, R. (1997). *White*. New York: Routledge.

Essed, P. (1991). *Understanding everyday racism: An interdisciplinary theory*. London: Sage.

Feuer, J. (1992). Genre study and television. In R. C. Allen (Ed.), *Channels of discourse, reassembled: Television and contemporary criticism* (pp. 138–160). Chapel Hill: University of North Carolina Press.

Fiske, J. (1987). *Television culture*. New York: Routledge.

Haggins, B. L. (1995). Laughing mad: The black comedian's place in American comedy of the post-Civil Rights era. In F. Krutnik (Ed.), *Hollywood comedians: The film reader* (pp. 171–186). London: Routledge.

Hall, S. (1990). The whites of their eyes: Racist ideologies and the media. In M. Alvarado & J. O. Thompson (Eds.), *The media reader* (pp. 7–23). London: BFI.

Hall, S. (1997). The spectacle of the 'other.' In S. Hall (Ed.), *Representation: Cultural representations and signifying practices* (pp. 223–290). London: Sage.

Hamamoto, D. Y. (1994). *Monitored peril: Asian Americans and the politics of TV representation*. Minneapolis: University of Minnesota Press.

Hill, W. (Director). (1982). *48 hrs.* [Motion picture]. United States: Paramount.

Hilton, J., & von Hippel, W. (1996). Stereotypes. *Annual Review of Psychology*, 47, 237–271.

Internet Movie Database, (n.d.). *All-time USA box office*. Retrieved March 3, 2005, from http://www.imdb.com/Charts/usatopmovies

Jhally, S., & Lewis, J. (1992). *Enlightened racism: The Cosby show, audiences, and the myth of the American dream*. Boulder, CO: Westview Press.

Jones, Q., Smith, W., & Hervey, W. (Director). (1990–1996). *The fresh prince of Bel Air* [Television series]. New York: NBC.

King, G. (2002). *Film comedy*. London: Wallflower Press.

Lee, R. G. (1999). *Orientals: Asian Americans in popular culture*. Philadelphia: Temple University Press.

Leiner, D. (Director). (2004). *Harold and Kumar go to White Castle* [Motion picture]. United States: New Line Cinema.

Lo, K. (2001). Double negations: Hong Kong cultural identity in Hollywood's transnational representations. *Cultural Studies*, 15, 464–485.

Malanowski, J. (2002, November 10). Colorblind buddies in black and white. *New York Times*. Retrieved March 30, 2005, from http://www.nytimes.com

Marchetti, G. (1991). Ethnicity, the cinema and cultural studies. In L. D. Friedman (Ed.), *Unspeakable images: Ethnicity and the American cinema* (pp. 277–307). Urbana: University of Illinois Press.

Means Coleman, R. R. (2000). *African American viewers and the black situation comedy: Situating racial humor*. New York: Garland.

Morley, D. (2005). Theoretical orthodoxies: Textualism, constructivism and the 'new ethnography.' In P. Leistyna (Ed.), *Cultural studies: From theory to action* (pp. 171–187). Malden, MA: Blackwell.

Myers, K. A., & Williamson, P. (2001). Race talk: The perpetuation of racism through private discourse. *Race & Society*, 4(1) 3–26.

Neale, S. (1980). *Genre*. London: British Film Institute.

Ogunnaike, L. (2003, October 13). The perks and pitfalls of a ruthless-killer role. *The New York Times*, p. E1.

Omi, M. (1989). In living color: Race and American culture. In I. Angus & S. Jhally (Eds.), *Cultural politics in contemporary America* (pp. 111–122). London: Routledge.

Radway, J. A. (1986). Identifying ideological seams: Mass culture, analytical method, and political practice. *Communication*, 9, 93–123.

Ratner, B. (Director). (1998). *Rush hour* [Motion picture]. United States: New Line Cinema.

Ratner, B. (Director). (2001). *Rush hour 2* [Motion picture]. United States: New Line Cinema.

Schaufer, F. (2003). *Profiles, probabilities and stereotypes.* Cambridge, MA: Belknap Press.

Schudson, M. (1998). The new validation of popular culture: Sense and sentimentality in academia. In J. Storey (Ed.), *Cultural theory and popular culture: A reader* (pp. 495–503). London: Prentice Hall.

Schulman, N. M. (1992). Laughing across the color barrier: In living color. *Journal of Popular Film and Television*, 20(1), 2–5.

Shim, D. (1998). From yellow peril through model minority to renewed yellow peril. *Journal of Communication Inquiry*, 22, 385–409.

Teo, S. (1997). *Hong Kong cinema: The extra dimensions.* London: British Film Institute.

Thomas, B. (Director). (2002). *I spy* [Motion picture]. United States: Columbia Pictures.

van Dijk, T. (1984). *Prejudice in discourse: An analysis of ethnic prejudice in cognition and conversation.* Philadelphia, PA: John Benjamins.

van Dijk, T. (1987). *Communicating racism: Ethnic prejudice in thought and talk.* London: Sage.

Wayans, M., Van Zandt, B., Milmore, J., Kellard, P., Moore, T., & Hawkins, R. (Director). (1995–1999). *The Wayans bros.* [Television series]. United States: WB.

White, M. (1992). Ideological analysis and television. In R. C. Allen (Ed.), *Channels of discourse, reassembled: Television and contemporary criticism* (pp. 161–202). Chapel Hill: University of North Carolina Press.

Wilson, C. C., Gutiérrez, F., & Chao, L. M. (2003). *Racism, sexism, and the media: The rise of class communication in multicultural America.* Thousand Oaks, CA: Sage.

Wong, E. F. (1978). *On visual media racism: Asians in the American motion pictures.* New York: Arno Press.

21 | *The Meritocracy Myth*

Stephen J. McNamee and Robert K. Miller, Jr.

According to the ideology of the American Dream, America is the land of limitless opportunity in which individuals can go as far as their own merit takes them. According to this ideology, you get out of the system what you put into it. Getting ahead is ostensibly based on individual merit, which is generally viewed as a combination of factors including innate abilities, working hard, having the right attitude, and having high moral character and integrity. Americans not only tend to think that is how the system should work, but most Americans also think that is how the system does work (Huber and Form 1973, Kluegel and Smith 1986, Ladd 1994).

In our book *The Meritocracy Myth* (Rowman & Littlefield, 2004), <http://www.rowmanlittlefield.com/isbn/0742510565>, we challenge the validity of these commonly held assertions, by arguing that there is a gap between how people think the system works and how the system actually does work. We refer to this gap as "the meritocracy myth," or the myth that the system distributes resources—especially wealth and income—according to the merit of individuals. We challenge this assertion in two ways. First, we suggest that while merit does indeed affect who ends up with what, the impact of merit on economic outcomes is vastly overestimated by the ideology of the American Dream. Second, we identify a variety of nonmerit factors that suppress, neutralize, or even negate the effects of merit and create barriers to individual mobility. We summarize these arguments below. First, however, we take a brief look at what is at stake. That is, what is up for grabs in the race to get ahead?

There are a variety of ways to depict America's unequal distributions of income and wealth. Income refers to how much one earns and wealth refers to how much one owns. Although Americans tend to think of income as coming from wages and salaries, there are actually two sources of income. In addition to income from wages and salaries, income also includes sources of revenue that are unrelated to jobs, such as income from capital gains, dividends, interest payments, and some forms of government aid ("welfare" including food stamps and the like). In some cases, these sources of income are related to prior but not current employment (e.g. social security payments, pensions). Wealth does not refer to a revenue stream, but to assets that one owns such as houses, cars, personal belongings, businesses, nonresidential real estate, stocks and bonds, trusts, and other financial assets. These

Reprinted by permission from *Sociation Today,* spring 2004.

TABLE 1. SHARE OF TOTAL AVAILABLE HOUSEHOLD INCOME, 2002*

Income Group	Share of Income
Top Fifth	49.7%
Second Fifth	23.3%
Third Fifth	14.8%
Fourth Fifth	8.8%
Bottom Fifth	3.5%
Total	100.0%
Top 5 Percent	21.7%

Source: DeNavas-Walt et al. 2003. See U.S. Current Population Reports for details.

TABLE 2. SHARE OF TOTAL AVAILABLE HOUSEHOLD NET WORTH, 2001*

Wealth Group	Share of Net Worth
99–100th percentile	32.7%
95–99th percentile	25.0%
90–95th percentile	12.1%
50th–90th percentile	27.1%
0–50th percentile	2.8%
Total	100.0%

Source: Kennickell, 2003. See data from the Federal Reserve Board for details.

assets can further be distinguished between those that tend to depreciate in value (e.g. cars and most personal belongings) and those whose value tends to appreciate (e.g. business, real estate, stocks, etc.). In general, the more wealth one has, the more likely that wealth derives from sources of ownership that tend to appreciate in value. Net worth refers to the difference between assets (what one owns) and liabilities (what one owes). Net worth is an accurate measure of what one is really "worth." Table 1 depicts the distributions of income and Table 2 depicts distributions of net worth.

These tables show that the distributions of income and especially wealth are highly skewed. The top 20 percent of American households, for instance, receive a large portion of the total amount of available income (49.7%) while the lowest 20 percent of American households receive a much smaller portion of available income (3.5%). The top 5% percent of households alone receive 21.7 percent of all available income. The distribution of wealth measured by net worth is even more highly skewed. The richest 1% of households (99th–100th percentile) account for nearly a third of all available net worth while the bottom half of households (0–50th percentile) account for only 2.8% of all available net worth. In other words, the American distributions of income and wealth are "top heavy" (Wolff 2002) and represent a level of economic inequality that is the highest among industrial countries of the world.

These distributions are relevant to the myth of meritocracy in several ways. First, despite the widely held perception that America is a "middle class" society, most of the money is highly concentrated at the top of the system. Second, many of the arguments suggesting that "merit" is behind the distribution of income and wealth also make the case that merit is distributed "normally" in the population. That is, that the shape of the distribution of merit resembles a "bell curve" with small numbers of incompetent people at the lower end, most people of average abilities in the middle and small numbers of talented people at the upper end. The highly skewed distribution of economic outcomes, however, appears quite in excess of any reasonable distribution of merit. Something that is distributed "normally" cannot be the direct and proportional cause of something with such skewed distributions. There has to be more to the story than that.

On Being Made of the Right Stuff

When factors associated with individual "merit" are related to income and wealth, it turns out that these factors are often not as uniquely individual or as influential as many presume. Most experts point out, for instance, that "intelligence," as measured by IQ tests, is partially a reflection of inherent intellectual capacity and partially a reflection of environmental influences. It is the combination of capacity and experience that determines "intelligence." Even allowing for this "environmental" caveat, IQ scores only account for about 10% of the variance in income differences among individuals (Fisher et al. 1996). Since wealth is less tied to achievement than income, the amount of influence of intelligence on wealth is much less. Other purportedly innate "talents" cannot be separated from experience, since any "talent" must be displayed to be recognized and labeled as such (Chambliss 1989). There is no way to determine for certain, for instance, how many potential world-class violinists there are in the general population but who have never once picked up a violin. Such "talents" do not spontaneously erupt but must be identified and cultivated.

Applying talents is also necessary. Working hard is often seen in this context as part of the merit formula. Heads nod in acknowledgment whenever hard work is mentioned in conjunction with economic success. Rarely is this assumption questioned. But what exactly do we mean by hard work? Does it mean the number of hours expended in the effort to achieve a goal? Does it mean the amount of energy or sheer physical exertion expended in the completion of tasks? Neither of these measures of "hard" work is directly associated with economic success. In fact, those who work the most hours and expend the most effort (at least physically) are often the most poorly paid in society. By contrast, the really big money in America comes not from working at all but from owning, which requires no expenditure of effort, either physical or mental. In short, working hard is not in and of itself directly related to the amount of income and wealth that individuals have.

What about attitudes? Again, the story here is mixed. First, it is not clear which particular mix of attitudes, outlooks, or frames of mind are associated with economic success. The kind of mental outlook that would be an advantage in one field of endeavor, may be a disadvantage in another field of endeavor. A different set of "proper attitudes," for instance, may be associated with being a successful artist than being a successful accountant. Second, the direction of influence is not always clear. That is, are certain attitudes a "cause" of success or are certain attitudes the "effect" of success?

An example of the difficulty in discerning the impact and direction of these influences is reflected in the "culture of poverty" debate. According to the culture of poverty argument, people are poor because of deviant or pathological values that are then passed on from one generation to the next, creating a "vicious cycle of poverty." According to this perspective, poor people are viewed as anti-work, anti-family, anti-school, and anti-success. Recent evidence reported in this journal (Wynn, 2003) and elsewhere (Barnes, 2002; Gould, 1999; Wilson, 1996), however, indicates that poor people appear to value work, family, school, and achievement as much as other Americans. Instead of having "deviant" or "pathological" values, the evidence suggests that poor people adjust their ambitions and outlooks according to realistic assessments of their more limited life chances.

An example of such an adjustment is the supposed "present-orientation" of the poor. According to the culture of poverty theory, poor people are "present-oriented" and are unable to "defer gratification." Present orientation may encourage young adults to drop out of school to take low wage jobs instead staying in school to increase future earning potential. However, the present orientation of the poor can be an "effect" of poverty rather than a "cause." That is, if you are desperately poor, you may be forced to be present oriented. If you do not know where your next meal is coming from, you essentially have no choice but to be focused on immediate needs first and foremost. By contrast, the rich and middle class can "afford" to be more future oriented since their immediate needs are secure. Similarly, the poor may report more modest ambitions than the affluent, not because they are unmotivated, but because of a realistic assessment of limited life chances. In this sense, observed differences in outlooks between the poor and the more affluent are more likely a reflection of fundamentally different life circumstances than fundamentally different attitudes or values.

Finally, we challenge the idea that moral character and integrity are important contributors to economic success. Although "honesty may be the best policy" in terms of how one should conduct oneself in relations with others, there is little evidence that the economically successful are more honest than the less successful. The recent spate of alleged corporate ethics scandals at such corporations as Enron, WorldCom, Arthur Andersen, Adelphia, Bristol-Myers Squibb, Duke Energy, Global Crossing, Xerox as well as recent allegations of misconduct in the vast mutual funds industry reveal how corporate executives often enrich themselves through less than honest means. White-collar crime in the form of insider trading, embezzlement, tax fraud, insurance fraud and the like is hardly evidence of honesty and virtue in practice. And neither is the extensive and sometimes highly lucrative so-called "irregular" or "under the table" economy—much of it related to vice in the form of drug trafficking, gambling, pornography, loan sharking, or smuggling. Clearly, wealth alone is not a reflection of moral superiority. To get ahead in America, it no doubt helps to be bright, shrewd, to work hard, and to have the right combination of attitudes that maximize success within given fields of endeavor. Playing by the rules, however, probably works to suppress prospects for economic success since those who play by the rules are more restricted in their opportunities to attain wealth and income than those who choose to ignore the rules.

Nonmerit Barriers to Mobility

There are a variety of social forces that tend to suppress, neutralize, or even negate the effects of merit in the race to get ahead. We might collectively refer to these forces as "social gravity." These forces tend to keep people in the places they already occupy, regardless of the extent of their individual merit.

First and foremost among these nonmerit factors is the effect of inheritance, broadly defined as the effects of initial class placement at birth on future life chances. Inheritance is not just bulk estates that are transferred upon the death of parents. Inheritance refers more broadly to unequal starting points in the race to get ahead. The race to get ahead is like a relay race in which we inherit an initial starting point from parents. For a while, we run alongside our parents as the baton is passed, and then we take off on our own. In this relay race, those born into great wealth start far ahead of those born to poor parents, who have a huge deficit to overcome if they are to catch up. Indeed, of all the factors that we might consider, where we start out in life has the greatest effect on where we end up. In the race to get ahead, the effects of inheritance come first and merit second, not the other way around.

Inheritance provides numerous cumulative nonmerit advantages that are available in varying degrees to all those born into at least some relative advantage, excluding only those at the very bottom of the system. Included among these nonmerit advantages are high standards of living from birth, inter vivos gifts (gifts between the living) such as infusions of cash and property bestowed by parents on their children at critical junctures in the life course (going to college, getting married, buying a home, having children, starting a business, etc.), insulation from downward mobility (family safety nets which prevent children from skidding in times of personal crises, setbacks, or as the result of personal failures), access to educational opportunities as well as other opportunities to acquire personal merit or to have merit identified and cultivated, better health care and consequently longer and healthier lives (which increases earning power and the ability to accumulate assets during the life course).

Another advantage of inheritance is access to high-powered forms of social and cultural capital. Social capital is one's "social resources" and refers essentially to the value of whom you know. Cultural capital is one's cultural resources and refers essentially to the social value of what you know. Everyone has friends, but those born into privilege have friends in high places with resources and power. Everyone possesses culture—bodies of knowledge and information needed to navigate through social space. Full acceptance into the highest social circles, however, requires knowledge of the ways of life of a particular group, a kind of "savoir faire" that includes expected demeanor, manners, and comportment associated with the upper class. Those born into these high powered circles are trained from an early age in the cultural ways of the group, which allows them to travel comfortably in these circles and to "fit in." Outsiders who aspire to become part of these high-powered circles must learn these cultural ways of life from the outside in a more difficult and daunting task that continually carries the risk of being exposed as an imposter or pretender.

Besides the nonmerit effects of inheritance, just plain bad luck can suppress the effects of merit. Bad luck can take many forms but two very common forms of bad luck are to be laid off from a job that you are good at or to spend many years preparing for a job for which demand either never materializes or declines. In looking at jobs and job opportunities, Americans tend to focus on the "supply" side of markets for labor; that is, the pool of available people in the labor force. Much less attention is paid to the "demand" side, or the number and types of jobs available. In the race to get ahead, it is possible and all too common for meritorious individuals to be "all dressed up with no place to go." For the past twenty years, the "growth" jobs in America have disproportionately been in the low wage service sector of the economy. At the same time, more Americans are getting more education, especially higher education. Simply put, these trends are running in opposite directions: the economy is not producing as many high-powered jobs as the society is producing highly qualified people to fill them (Collins 1979, Livingstone 1998).

In addition to the number and types of jobs available, the locations of jobs both geographically and within different sectors of the economy also represent non-merit factors in the prospects for employment. For instance, a janitor who works for a large corporation in New York City may get paid much more for doing essentially the same job as a janitor who works for a small family business in a small town in Mississippi. These effects are independent of the demands of the jobs or the qualifications or merit of the individuals holding them. Differences in benefits and wages between such jobs are often substantial and may mean the difference between a secure existence and poverty.

If poverty were exclusively due to individual differences, we would expect rates of poverty to be randomly distributed throughout the country. Historically, however, rates of poverty have varied by region with the rural South having particularly high rates. These differences have been reduced in recent decades as Northern and Midwest states in the so-called "rust belt" have experienced plant closings and "deindustrialization" while Southern and Southwest states in the so-called "sun belt" have experienced greater economic diversity and development. Despite these trends, research recently reported in this journal (Wimberley and Morris, 2003) shows that rates of poverty in the United States continue to vary by region and locations within regions suggesting that geography is still a major factor in the distribution of economic opportunity.

Education is another factor widely seen as responsible for where people end up in the system. The role of education in getting ahead in America, however, is not as simple as is often assumed. On the one hand, those with more education, on average, have higher income and wealth. Education is thus often seen as the primary means of upward social mobility. In this context, education is widely perceived as a gatekeeper institution which sifts and sorts individuals according to individual merit. Grades, credits, diplomas, degrees, and certificates are clearly "earned," not purchased or appropriated. But, as much research has demonstrated, educational opportunity is not equally distributed in the population (Bowles and Gintis 1976, 2002, Bourdieu and Passeron 1990, Aschaffenburg and Maas 1997, Kozol 1991, Sacks 2003, Ballantine 2001). Upper class children tend to get upper class educations (e.g. at elite private prep schools and ivy league colleges), middle class children tend to get middle class educations (e.g. at public schools and public universities), and working class people tend to get working class educations (e.g. public schools and technical or community colleges), and poor people tend to get poor educations (e.g. inner city schools that have high drop out rates and usually no higher education). Educational attainment clearly depends on family economic standing and is not simply a major independent cause of it. The quality of schools and the quality of educational opportunity vary according to where one lives, and where one lives depends on familial economic resources and race. Most public schools, for instance, are supported by local property taxes. The tax base is higher in wealthy communities and proportionally lower in poorer areas. These discrepancies give rise to the perpetual parental scramble to locate in communities and neighborhoods that have reputations for "good schools," since parents want to provide every possible advantage to their children that they can afford. To the extent that parents are actually successful in passing on such advantages, educational attainment is primarily a reflection of family income. In sum, it is important to recognize that individual achievement occurs within a context of unequal educational opportunity.

Besides education, self-employment is popularly perceived as a major route to upward mobility. Opportunities to get ahead on the basis of being self-employed or striking out on one's own to start a new business, however, have sharply declined. In colonial times, about three fourths of the non-slave American population was self-employed most as small family farmers. Today, only seven percent of the labor force is self employed (U.S. Census Bureau 2002). The "family farm," in particular, is on the brink of statistical extinction. As self-employment has declined, the size and dominance of corporations has increased. This leaves many fewer opportunities for "self-made" individuals to enter existing markets or to establish new ones. America has witnessed the sharp decline of "mom and pop" stores, restaurants, and retail shops and the concomitant rise of Wal-Marts, Holiday Inns, and McDonalds. As more Americans work for someone else in increasingly bureaucratized settings, the prospects of rapid "rags to riches" mobility decline.

In addition to the decline of self-employment, manufacturing has also experienced drastic workforce reduction as production facilities have increasingly moved to foreign countries in efforts to reduce costs of production. This is a significant trend since the United States became a world power based on its industrial strength, which supported a large and relatively prosperous working and middle class. Some service jobs, such as customer service and computer programming, are also being moved to foreign countries in increasing numbers. All of these trends are occurring quite independent of the merit of individuals but nevertheless profoundly impact the opportunities of individuals to get ahead.

The most obvious and widely recognized nonmerit barrier to achievement is discrimination. Discrimination not only suppresses merit; it is the antithesis of merit. Race and sex discrimination have been the most pervasive forms of discrimination in America. The good news is that such discrimination is declining. The bad news is that these forms of discrimination are down but not out. Besides ongoing discrimination, there are still inertial effects of past discrimination that create disadvantage in the present. The divisive debate over affirmative action in America highlights the continuing disagreements about the size and importance of these residual effects and how to best address them.

Most Americans agree that race and sex discrimination are wrong and that a "level playing field" should be established. Indeed, it is often assumed that we would have true equality of opportunity in American if only these forms of discrimination were eliminated. This position is naïve, however, because it overlooks the effects of other nonmerit factors identified here (especially inheritance). Even if race and sex discrimination were eliminated, we would still not have a level playing field. This position also overlooks other forms of discrimination that, while less pervasive in America, nevertheless suppress or neutralize the affects of merit: discrimination on the basis of sexual orientation, religion, age, physical disability (unrelated to job performance), physical appearance, and region (discrimination against Southerners and preference for Yankees). That these forms of discrimination affect fewer people than sex and race discrimination is little comfort to those who are victimized by it. For them, the effective rate of discrimination is 100 percent.

Some of these forms of discrimination are not well-recognized or generally acknowledged. "Lookism," for instance, is a subtle form of discrimination in which attractive people get numerous nonmerit advantages over less attractive people (e.g., more attention, more help, more recognition and credit for accomplishments, more positive evaluation of performance and the like) (Etcoff 1999). These nonmerit advantages have profound and independent effects on life chances and individual merit.

What Now?

In *The Meritocracy Myth,* we do not suggest that "merit" is a myth. Rather, we argue that meritocracy, the idea that societal resources are distributed exclusively or primarily on the basis of individual merit, is a myth. It is a myth because of the combined effects of non-merit factors such as inheritance, social and cultural advantages, unequal educational opportunity, luck and the changing structure of job opportunities, the decline of self-employment, and discrimination in all of its forms. If meritocracy is a myth, how can the system be made to operate more closely according to meritocratic principles that Americans so uniformly endorse?

We suggest four ways in which American society could be made more genuinely meritocratic.

1. Current forms of discrimination could be reduced or eliminated.
2. The wealthy could be encouraged to redistribute greater amounts of their accumulated wealth through philanthropy in ways that would provide greater opportunity for the less privileged.
3. The tax system could be redesigned to be genuinely progressive in ways that would close the distance between those at the top and the bottom of the system.
4. More government resources could be allocated to provide more equal access to critical services such as education and health care.

All of these measures would reduce the overall extent of inequality in society and at the same time allow individual merit to have a greater effect on economic outcomes. Such fundamental change in the distribution of societal resources and opportunity, however, are predicated on the assumption that these goals would be widely seen as both desirable and politically feasible.

It is generally acknowledged that a pure meritocracy is probably impossible to achieve. What is less generally acknowledged is that such a system may not be entirely desirable. The limits and dangers of a system operating purely on the basis of merit were dramatically portrayed in *The Rise of the Meritocracy* (1961), a novel by British sociologist Michael Young. Young envisioned a society in which those at the top of the system ruled autocratically with a sense of righteous entitlement while those at the bottom of the system were incapable of protecting themselves against the abuses leveled against them from the merit elite above. Instead of a fair and enlightened society, the meritocracy became cruel and ruthless.

One possible advantage of a nonmeritocratic society is that at any point in time there are, for whatever combination of reasons, at least some of those at the top of the system who are less capable and competent than at least some of those at the bottom. Such discrepancies should render humility for those at the top and hope and dignity for those at the bottom. But this can only happen if it is widely acknowledged that inheritance, luck, and a variety of other circumstances beyond the control of individuals are important in affecting where one ends up in the system. While meritocracy may be neither possible nor even desirable, we argue that the myth of meritocracy is itself harmful because by discounting the most important causes of inequality, it leads to unwarranted exaltation of the rich and unwarranted condemnation of the poor. We may always have the rich and poor among us, but we need neither exalt the former nor condemn the latter.

References

Aschaffenburg, Karen, and Ineke Maas. 1997. "Cultural and Educational Careers: The Dynamics of Social Reproduction." *American Sociological Review* 62: 573–87.

Ballantine, Jeanne H. 2001. *The Sociology of Education.* Upper Saddle River, NJ: Prentice Hall.

Barnes, Sandra L. 2002. "Achievement or Ascription Ideology? An Analysis of Attitudes about Future Success for Residents in Poor Urban Neighborhoods." *Sociological Focus.* 35:207–25.

Bourdieu, Pierre, and Jean-Claude Passeron. 1990. *Reproduction in Education, Society, and Culture.* London: Sage.

Bowles, Samuel, and Herbert Gintis. 1976. *Schooling in Capitalist America.* NY: Basic Books.

———. 2002. "Schooling in Capitalist America Revisited." *Sociology of Education* 75: 1–18.

Chambliss, William. 1989. "The Mundanity of Excellence." *Sociological Theory* 7:70–86.

Collins, Randall. 1979. *The Credential Society.* NY: Academic Press.

DeNavas-Walt, Carmen, Robert Cleveland, and Bruce H. Webster, Jr. 2003. "Income In the United States, 2002" in *Current Population Reports,* U.S. Census Bureau, P60–221. Washington, D.C.: U.S. Government Printing Office.

Etcoff, Nancy. 1999. *Survival of the Prettiest: The Science of Beauty.* NY: Doubleday.

Fischer, Claude S., Michael Hout, Martin Sanchez Jankowski, Samuel R. Lucas, Ann Swidler, and Kim Voss. 1996. *Inequality by Design: Cracking the Bell Curve Myth.* Princeton, NJ: Princeton University Press.

Gould, Mark, 1999. "Race and Theory: Adaptation to Discrimination." In *Sociological Theory.* Wilson and Ogbu, eds. 17:171–20.

Huber, Joan, and William Form. 1973. *Income and Ideology: An Analysis of the American Political Formula.* NY: Free Press.

Kennickell, Arthur B. 2003. *A Rolling Tide: Changes in the Distribution of Wealth in the U.S. 1989–2001.* Washington, D.C.: Federal Reserve Board.

Kluegel, James R., and Eliot R. Smith. 1986. *Beliefs about Inequality: Americans' Views of What Is and What Ought to Be.* NY: de Gruyter.

Kozol, Jonathan. 1991. *Savage Inequalities: Children in America's Schools.* NY: Harper-Perennial.

Ladd, Everett Carll. 1994. *The American Ideology.* Storrs, CT: The Roper Center for Public Opinion Research.

Livingstone, D. W. 1998. *The Education-Jobs Gap: Underemployment or Economic Democracy.* Boulder, CO: Westview.

McNamee, Stephen J. and Robert K. Miller, Jr. 2004. *The Meritocracy Myth.* Lanham, MD: Rowman & Littlefield.

Sacks, Peter. 2003. "Class Rules: The Fiction of Egalitarian Higher Education." *The Chronicle of Higher Education* 49 (July 25): B7–10.

U.S. Department of Labor. 2002. "Self Employed in 2000." *Monthly Labor Review.* January 28, 2002.

Wilson, William Julius. 1996. *When Work Disappears: The World of the New Urban Poor.* New York: Knopf.

Wimberley, Ronald C. and Libby V. Morris. *U.S. Poverty in Space and Time: Its Persistence in the South. Sociation Today.* Volume 1, Number 2, Fall 2003.

Wolff, Edward N. 2002. *Top Heavy: The Increasing Inequality of Wealth in America and What Can Be Done About It.* NY: The New Press.

Wynn, Lyndelia Burch. 2003. *The Attitude of AFDC Recipients Towards Work. Sociation Today.* Volume 1, Number 2, Fall 2003.

Young, Michael. 1961. *The Rise of the Meritocracy, 1870–2033: An Essay on Education and Equality.* Baltimore, MD: Penguin Books.

22

Business as Usual: The American Dream in Hollywood Business Films

Mary S. Pileggi, Maria Elizabeth Grabe,
Lisa B. Holderman & Michelle de Montigny

Using reviews of 120 top-grossing Hollywood films about business released from 1927 to 1995, in this study we examine the American dream myth's structure and analyze how the relative dominance of 2 seemingly contradictory tales, the cautionary and the hopeful, varies over time. We further investigate the influence of a particular tale's dominance on class and occupational mobility, character demographics, and keys to success. Finally, we evaluate the correlation between a tale's dominance and social conditions. Findings reveal that with a dominant hopeful tale, mobility is low; mobility is significantly higher when the cautionary tale dominates. A particular tale's prevalence does not correlate with keys to success or demographics. Moreover, a dominant hopeful tale correlates with a society's economic climate. The cautionary tale appears when the social order is threatened.

Myths, the stories we tell about who we are and about how we are, have played an important role in culture formation for centuries. De Certeau (1980/1988) put it concisely in saying that myths "have the function of founding and articulating space" (p. 123). Through their narrative structure and actions, myths organize space by setting boundaries, "creating a field" (p. 125), where we engage in our quotidian practices. In this sense "spatial practices . . . structure the determining conditions of social life" (p. 96). Researchers have argued that the American dream, or what Jhally and Lewis (1992) called the myth of classlessness, defines social life in American society (Berk, 1977; Edington, 1995; Gray, 1989; Horton, 1982; Levy, 1991; Manly, 1990). The American dream promotes social mobility or the notion that

Reprinted from *Mass Communication and Society* 3, no. 2 (2000), by permission of Taylor & Francis.

"although everyone may not start with the same income and wealth, everyone has the same chance to reach the top of the income hierarchy because a person's class background does not limit a person's chances of economic success" (Jhally & Lewis, 1992, p. 68). Although few American lives exemplify the dream, media content perpetuates the myth that achieving the American dream is within everyone's reach. Structural barriers to social mobility such as demographic heritage and the limits on potential financial gain are underplayed. Ultimately, this narrative structure provides a social space that benefits the economic system (see Jarvie, 1982).

The majority of systematic research on media portrayals of social mobility focuses on television (Berk, 1977; Bettie, 1995; Butsch, 1992; DeFleur, 1964; Freeman, 1992; Gentile&Miller, 1961; Gray, 1989; Steeves & Smith, 1987; Theberge, 1981; Thomas & Callahan, 1982), not film. James (1996) called for more focus on film in studies that consider constructions of social class mobility. Indeed, given the working-class origins of the film medium (Sklar, 1975; Stead, 1995) relatively little systematic research has focused on social class in film, and focus on portrayals of class mobility in film is virtually absent. The body of literature on social class portrayals in film comprises textual analyses of class in specific Hollywood films (Butsch, 1979; Byers, 1987; Conroy, 1996; Desser, 1991; Giroux, 1980; Jameson, 1977; Lebow, 1986; Nichols, 1996; Parshall, 1991; Pfeil, 1993; Sandell, 1995; Traube, 1989, 1992), analyses of film genres (Arthur, 1996; Kellner, 1996; Kleinhans, 1996; Levy, 1991) and made-for-television movies (Rapping, 1992), portrayals of specifically the working class in Hollywood films (Bergman, 1971/1993; Garafola, 1980; Quart & Auster, 1991; Ryan & Kellner, 1988; Stead, 1995), and wealthy and business classes (Powers, Rothman, & Rothman, 1996; Thomas & Leshay, 1992). Audience research has addressed TV and film audiences in terms of their class positions and attitudes toward TV shows and films (DiMaggio & Useem, 1978; Hall, 1980; Jhally & Lewis, 1992; Morely, 1992; Press, 1995; Robinson, 1975), and Lewis (1985) and Powers et al. (1996) empirically studied the social class origins, attitudes, and perceptions of Hollywood elites. What remains unclear is how the finer nuances of the American dream, including social mobility, have been played out in films over time. Using plot summaries, in this study we examine dimensions and fluctuations of the American dream in Hollywood sound films about corporate business over a period of 68 years.

The American Dream: A Nuanced Prescription for Social Mobility

As its various manifestations attest, the American dream myth has a rich history. The American dream "existed before the actual continent was known" (Ruland & Bradbury, 1991, p. 4), and descended from the utopian desire for a new world, a land ripe with opportunity, that permeated the European Renaissance. As evidenced in the writings of Edwards (1995) and of Mather (1967), the American dream may claim even older ancestry, tracing its lineage to biblical myth: It is the displaced narrative of "the Pilgrim, entering new space and new history . . . the tale of the Chosen People and the Promised Land" (Ruland & Bradbury, 1991, p. 9). Our Puritan forefathers imbued the American dream with the belief that through hard work and effort we may earn riches and good fortune. Indeed, the dream's moral dimension, which saw "worldly success . . . as a sign of salvation . . . [and] failure . . . [as] damnation" (Edington, 1995, p. 63) is our legacy from this Puritan past.

Although it has circulated since the first Europeans colonized the New World, the American dream is not a monolithic, static myth. Manly (1990) argued that the myth is "a compromise of the democratic and elitist dreams" (p. 90). Although it champions the "legal and political equality" (p. 90) necessary in a democracy, it nonetheless privileges those individuals who have achieved success. Furthermore, as Traube (1992) noted, the myth's multiple versions have changed over time, registering and responding to historically engendered cultural tensions. Moreover, Horton (1982) demonstrated that versions of the myth have been mobilized to support both liberal ideologies, as a speech delivered by Martin Luther King exemplifies, as well as more conservative ends, as witnessed in the trial of Dan White, who was convicted of murdering San Francisco Mayor George Moscone and San Francisco City Supervisor Harvey Milk.

Historically, certain factors seemed to sustain the dream. Perhaps most notable was the belief that land was plentiful and resources were abundant in America. This belief lured many immigrants to America in search of prosperity. In conjunction with the doctrine of manifest destiny, this notion of America the bountiful sparked western expansion and fostered the myth of the rugged frontier individual whose success depended on personal qualities (e.g., self-reliance, talent, virtue, industry, etc.). Livesay (1984) also credited geographic mobility with bolstering the myth. He observed that Americans, in keeping with their immigrant heritage, always tended to equate movement with change, and change with progress. The freedom to pick up and move "helped keep aspirations alive, for no one had to feel tied to a place where he couldn't move up the ladder" (p. 162). As the United States shifted from an agrarian to an industrialized society, the success of a few individuals such as Carnegie and Rockefeller lent credence to the belief that living the American dream was indeed possible. To varying degrees, industrial development provided American workers with the means necessary to capitalize on what could be called the consumer version of the dream. In this version acquiring material possessions became the measure of one's success (Leach, 1993). With the rise of the professional and managerial class, a focus on public image and personality as stepping stones to attaining the American dream have displaced "the entrepreneurial values of self-reliance, effort, and achievement" (Traube, 1992, p. 278).

American media have fueled the myth of individualism in attaining the American dream. Research confirms that the media typically emphasize a character's individual action as the avenue to social mobility and success (Byers, 1987; Desser, 1991; Freeman, 1992; Giroux, 1980; Lebow, 1986; Lipsitz, 1986; Thomas & Callahan, 1982; Traube, 1992). The self-made person who rises from poverty to respectability, the "rags-to-riches" version of the dream, was perhaps best portrayed in the tales of 19th-century novelist Horatio Alger. Alger's heroes, as Cawelti (1965) noted, embodied "the values that middle-class Americans have been taught to revere: honesty, hard work, loyalty; good manners; neatness of appearance; generosity . . . respect for education and self-culture" (p. 121). The biography of television talk show host Oprah Winfrey offers one of many contemporary expressions of this myth, suggesting that "despite the structural economic and political obstacles to achievement and survival posed in a racist society" (Cloud, 1996, p. 116), the dream is a reality for Black Americans. During presidential debates candidates regularly appeal to voters' belief in the American dream in their political rhetoric.

The media also provide examples of the American dream gone awry in versions of the money-can't-buy-happiness narrative. Dreiser's (1954) *An American Tragedy* and Fitzgerald's (1958) *The Great Gatsby* are classic literary examples. The money-can't-buy-happiness narrative also surfaces in nonfiction as Beers's (1996) *Blue Sky Dream*, a look at the crash of the aerospace industry, exemplifies. The recent *Philadelphia Inquirer* series "Who Stole the American Dream" (Barlett & Steele, 1996) and readers' responses to the articles illustrate that the myth in its different manifestations is alive in contemporary American society.

The American dream is clearly a nuanced myth that often intertwines ingredients for success and failure in the quest for financial success and social mobility. Two seemingly contradictory narratives, rags-to-riches and money-can't-buy-happiness, articulate these different dimensions of the American dream. Often concomitantly, the two narratives extend the promise of upward social mobility and offer a warning against upward mobility. The rags-to-riches or underdog-succeeding narrative, a dimension of what we call the hopeful tale, focuses on the prosperous dimension of the American dream, building on the idea that, irrespective of an individual's socioeconomic background, dreams, ambitions, and goals can be actualized (Berk, 1977; Giroux, 1980; Gray, 1989; Horton, 1982; Lebow, 1986; Levy, 1991). This dimension of the American dream myth posits hard work and personal integrity as the key ingredients for unlimited spiritual, social, and financial growth (Freeman, 1992; Weiss, 1969). It also applauds ambition, which is often characterized as a hunger or desire for self-improvement that ultimately benefits the larger society.

On the other hand, the money-can't-buy-happiness narrative, a dimension of what we call the cautionary tale, portrays the American dream gone awry. Whereas the rags-to-riches narrative promotes individual advancement, money-can't-buy-happiness presents the need for personal advancement as greed, an irrational and excessive appetite for power and material gain. Hence, individuals are characterized as greedy and unscrupulous, stretching beyond self-improvement into the realm of exploitation and ultimately suffering sweeping losses (Edington, 1995). Conspicuous-consumption and poor-little-rich-person narratives are common outcomes of the cautionary tale. This latter narrative, in particular, paints the wealthy as unhappy individuals who are lacking the sincerity and warmth of family relations, romance, and friendship (Cawelti, 1975; Thomas, 1986, 1990). Perhaps the most extreme version of the cautionary tale is the power-corrupts narrative. It suggests that social class mobility and financial gain are inherently evil and corruptive processes that result in tragedy, misery, and self-destruction (Levy 1991; Powers, Rothman, & Rothman, 1992; Thomas, 1986; Thomas & Leshay, 1992). In this study, we investigate the prevalence of these different dimensions of the American dream myth, the prescriptive stepping stones for success and failure, and the demography of social mobility in films about business. The central research question guiding this study asks: How do the dimensions of the American dream myth vary over time? Assuming that different dimensions dominate at different times, we also asked the following questions: How do these variations relate to the descriptive characteristics (genre, character demographics, and type of business) of the films employed to tell stories about business? How do these variations affect the dynamics of class and occupational mobility of characters in these films? How do these variations affect the prevalence of portrayed keys to success in the business world? Is there a correlation between the variation of the dimensions of the American dream myth and contemporaneous social, economic, and political conditions?

Method

In this content analysis of 120 Hollywood sound films (made from 1927 to 1995), we used plot summaries of films for two reasons. First, we investigate the broad narrative structures underlying business films and not the minutiae of things such as set design or dialogue. Second, using plot summaries for the content enabled us to study 68 years of filmmaking. Inquiry into the availability of the 120 business films in our population revealed that more than half the films released between 1927 and 1940 were not available on video.

Of the variety of summary sources considered, *The Motion Picture Guide* (Manzon, 1992–1995; Nash & Ross, 1985–1991) provided the most comprehensive and detailed account of the film plots used in this analysis. Not one of the sampled movies is absent from this source. Unlike reviews in *Variety Magazine* or *The New York Times*, *The Motion Picture Guide* provided plot summaries rather than critical evaluations of films. For 104 films we exclusively used *The Motion Picture Guide*. This source provided sufficient information about the story structure and major characters to make informed coding decisions about these films. However, for 16 films *Variety Film Reviews* (1983) and *The New York Times Film Reviews* (1968) were consulted as supplementary sources to guide coding decisions.

To assess the reliability of using plot summaries for data collection, 12 films (10% of the sample) and 40 characters in these films were coded based on viewing the films on video. The 12 films were selected based on availability but at least 1 film per decade was included in this sample.[1] The data were compared to coding decisions about the same films based on plot summary information. The overall Krippendorff alpha indicating agreement between data collected from reading plot summaries and data collected from viewing the same films was .93. For categories pertaining to the demography and social or occupational mobility of plot functional characters the reliability was .92. Reliability for items pertaining to broader structural variables, such as the prevalence of myths, was .94. These reliability results reveal that the plot summaries were indeed a dependable source of information for making coding decisions about films.

We purposefully sampled business films because the pursuit of financial gain is unmistakably part of the business world and achieving success at it is central to social mobility in American society. We are not suggesting that the American dream is unique to stories about business, but we do argue that by examining stories about the business world we optimize the presence of the social mobility theme in the sample. For research purposes we defined business as a profit-seeking enterprise such as a company, corporation, or factory, but we excluded smaller family businesses (corner stores, restaurants, etc.) and illegitimate commercial ventures (*The Random House Dictionary of the English Language*, 1968). We also omitted films in which professions such as law, medicine, education, and architecture were the central commercial venture, for as Greisman (1976) argued, professionals in these fields differentiate themselves from business people, often elevating their practices to a "higher plane than the entrepreneur or executive" (p. 73).

To arrive at the final list of films, we consulted annual lists of top 50 grossing feature films (1927 to 1995) and selected films with companies, corporations, or factories central to their plots. We reasoned that the top 50 grossing films are the most widely viewed by contemporary audiences, therefore they potentially act as agents of socialization (Levy, 1991). To generate a comprehensive list of annual top-grossing films over a period of 68 years, we consulted a variety of sources. Because all of these sources did not provide equally comprehensive lists of top-grossing films, focusing on the top 50 films allowed us to consider the same number of films for each year.

In our list of 3,414 top-grossing films, we included all films tying for the annual 50th place in the population. Rereleases were not included. Since 1942, with the exception of 1944, 1945, and 1956, annual lists of top-grossing films were published in *Variety Magazine's Anniversary Edition* (1942–1943; 1946–1955; 1957–1995). Steinberg (1980) provided information about top-grossing films for the years 1940, 1941, 1944, 1945, and 1956 as well as for the years 1927 through 1929. *That Was Hollywood: The 1930s* (Eyles, 1987) provided the annual top 50 grossing films for 1930 through 1939. Out of 3,414 films, 120 films fit our definition of a business film.

For coding purposes we used two units of analysis: the single business film and the individual plot functional character. Using the single business film as a unit of analysis, we addressed broad structural questions about the films. The coding instrument consisted of 22 categories regarding film genre,[2] types of business,[3] and dimensions of the American dream myth.[4]

A plot functional character, the second unit of analysis, is one who received more than a mere mention in the film review and who is instrumental to the filmic narrative. This definition resulted in a data set of 337 characters. The coding instrument consisted of 58 categories related to plot functional characters including demography,[5] keys to success in business,[6] and character development.[7]

The 120 business films were randomly assigned to four coders. Each analyzed 30 film summaries. We also randomly selected 10% of the population for coder reliability tests. We achieved an overall .91 agreement (Krippendorff's α) among coders across all items. Yet, some categories required interpretative evaluations (e.g., coding for the presence of myths like rags-to-riches, money-can't-buy-happiness, good-triumphs-over-evil, and coding the social class of characters). Coder reliability for these items was slightly lower (.86) than for categories that involved simple categorical counts (.95).

Myth Index

A central aim of this study was to investigate variations in the structure of the American dream myth over time. More specifically, we asked whether there were significant and systematic differences in the prevalence of the various dimensions of the American dream myth during certain historical periods over the past 68 years. We asked, for example, if and when cautionary tales dominate. Given that it is possible to distinguish historical periods where the cautionary or hopeful tale dominates, we sought to establish if there was a significant difference in the representation of class mobility and keys to success in these respective periods. Finally, we looked at correlations between specific dimensions of the American dream and political or economic events over the 68-year period under study.

To determine whether there were variations in the American dream myth over time, we constructed a myth index. First, we sorted films by year of their release and indexed them from 1 to 120. Next, we assessed the strength of the 10 dimensions of the American dream myth (see footnote 4) contemporaneous with each film. To assess a dimension's strength, we averaged its score using the four films before a specific film, the specific film, and the four films after that specific film. This yielded a modified score, a number for each film between 0 and 1, that measures the frequency of a particular dimension's presence in the nine films averaged around a specific film. Using nine films allowed us to refine our analysis with a minimum loss of data. We then calculated the grand average and standard deviation of these modified scores to determine the probability distribution of a dimension's presence. Assuming normal distribution, we rejected dimensions with a probability presence of less than 99%. The following three dimensions were identified: good-over-evil (99.99%), money-can't-buy-happiness (99.9%), and rags-to-riches (99.42%). For each of these dimensions we constructed a cumulative distribution function that plots the number of times the strength of a specific dimension exceeds its expected level as a function of the film index.

Using the Kolmogorov–Smirnov test, we executed a 2×2 distribution comparison. Results showed that at a .01 alpha level the distribution of good-over-evil and rags-to-riches were statistically equivalent, $D(N = 112) = .0625$ (they tell a hopeful tale), whereas money-can't-buy-happiness was different from both rags-to-riches, $D(N = 112) = .2143$, and good-over-evil, $D(N = 112) = .2598$ (it tells a cautionary tale). Although good-over-evil is the dominant dimension, we noted that it exhibits nonstationary patterns (see Figure 1). Specifically, from the early 1970s through the late 1980s this dimension consistently takes on values well below the level observed between the 1930s and the 1960s. Given this phenomenon, we opted to consider good-over-evil at a later phase and were left with two statistically different dimensions: rags-to-riches (hopeful tale) and money-can't-buy-happiness (cautionary tale). The myth index was then defined as the difference between the relative strength of the hopeful tale and that of the cautionary tale at a particular point in time. With this instrument we were not only able to identify fluctuations in the prominence of the hopeful or cautionary tales, but we were able to determine when one of the two tales dominated the other. When the myth index was positive, the relative strength of the hopeful tale is stronger than the cautionary tale. When it was negative the inverse is true. Figure 2 shows the variation of the myth index over time.

Figure 1

Evolution of Good-Over-Evil and Power-Corrupts Over Time

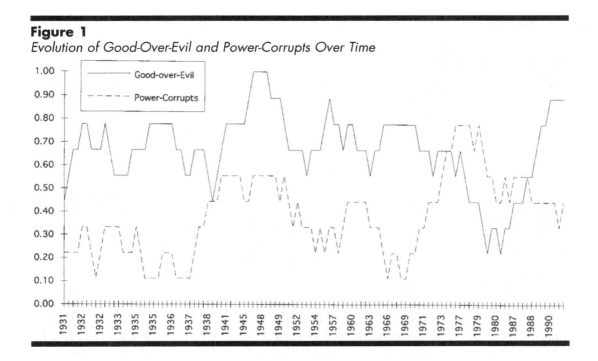

Figure 2

Myth Index Over Time

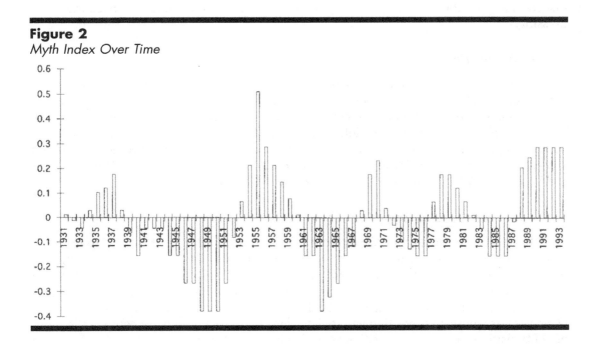

Results

Having identified when either the cautionary tale or the hopeful tale of the American dream myth was prevalent, we first considered the general characteristics of the films according to the two groups (cautionary tale or hopeful tale) in terms of genre and the types of business represented. We also examined characters' demographics, class mobility, occupational mobility, and keys to success.

Films

There were no significant differences between cautionary tale and hopeful tale populations in terms of genre and business representation. However, a number of descriptive insights into the general characteristics of films about the business world and the characters inhabiting this world emerged from this study. For example, we found that 81% of business films fell into either the drama (41%) or comedy (40%) categories. Not a single business film fit the horror, disaster, mystery, science fiction, or fantasy genre. The combined frequencies of action adventure, thriller, musical, biography, and western genres represented a mere 14% of all coded business films. This finding is not surprising: America's economic well-being rests on commitment to honest hard work and belief in the promise of social mobility. Horror, disaster, mystery, science fiction, and fantasy films typically scare or bewilder audiences. Telling stories about the legitimate business world within the framework of these genres could be counterproductive to promoting the hard reality of dedicating oneself to labor and believing in the American dream.

We found that manufacturing (37%) and nonfinancial services (27%) were the two business sectors most frequently portrayed in films. This emphasis on manufacturing and nonfinancial services is evenly distributed over the 68 years. The portrayal of financial services such as banking and brokering is scarce. Only 12% of businesses fell into this category. Interestingly, 50% of financial services (banks, stock brokerage, insurance, real estate) portrayals are dispersed around the Great Depression years (1930 to 1939) when financial need was most pressing.

Demography

We found no significant differences in demographics between the characters in the two populations (cautionary tale and hopeful tale). The majority of plot functional characters in top-grossing sound films about business are White (96%), male (64%), and American (89%). Most characters are either upper middle or upper class: At the beginning of films 61% of characters comprise these classes, rising to 72% of characters by the end of films. Our study's demographic profile of business people corroborates the findings of DeFleur (1964), Seggar and Wheeler (1973), Thomas and Leshay (1992), and Weigel and Loomis (1981).

Class and Occupational Mobility

To answer the research question about how the variations in the myth index affect the dynamics of class and occupational mobility of film characters, we tested if the representation of class and occupational mobility differs when different tales dominate. First, we identified two distinct groups of characters: those from films in which the cautionary tale dominates ($n = 128$) and those from films in which the hopeful tale dominates ($n = 129$). We eliminated 60 characters whose class position was undetermined. For each group, we counted the number of transitions from a class position at the beginning of the films to a class position at the end of the films. We then compared characters' class mobility within and across these groups.

An alpha level of .01 was used for all statistical tests, unless otherwise stated. First, we tested if there was a significant difference between the distribution of class at the beginning of the films and the distribution of class at the end of the films for each group. We found that the distribution at the beginning and end of films where the hopeful tale dominates was not significant, $\chi^2(4, N = 129) = 8.52, p = .07$. In contrast the difference between the class distribution at the beginning and end of films in which the cautionary tale dominates was significant, $\chi^2(4, N = 128) = 22.36, p = .001$. Next, we tested if there was a significant difference between the distribution of class at the beginning of films for both groups. We found that the difference between the distribution of class at the beginning of films for the two groups was significant, $\chi^2(4, N = 129) = 13.4765, p = .009$. We also tested if there was a significant difference between the distribution of class at the end of films for both groups. We found that the difference between the distribution of class at the end of films for the two groups was also significant, $\chi^2(4, N = 129) = 14.4787, p = .006$. Finally, we compared the three distributions whose chi squares were significant in terms of their means using a t test. The difference between the means was significant when we compared characters' average class position at the beginning ($M = 3.88$) and the end ($M = 4.27$) of films when the cautionary tale was dominant, $t(126) = 3.00, p = .002$. The average character position moved upward. All other comparisons between means were insignificant. These results suggest a higher degree of mobility in films with a dominant cautionary tale than in films with a dominant hopeful tale.

To refine our analysis of class mobility, we looked at class position at the beginning and end of films in another way. First, we counted the number of characters who stayed in the same class, those who moved up, and those who moved down. We compared these distributions and found a significant difference, $\chi^2(N = 129) = 29.439, p = .001$. Specifically, we found that films with a dominant hopeful tale exhibit a higher degree of class stability: 82% of characters stay in the same class. In contrast, only 67% of characters in dominant cautionary tales maintained their class position. Furthermore, we found that upward mobility is common to both types of tales. Of the 18% of characters who move in the hopeful tales, 91% move up. Of the 33% of characters who move in cautionary tales, 81% move up. Although the overall number of characters who move down is low (10 of 257), we noted that of all the characters who move down, 80% are characters in films in which cautionary tales dominate.

We repeated this analysis to assess occupational mobility, identifying two distinct groups of characters: those from films in which the cautionary tale dominates ($n = 100$) and those in which the hopeful tale dominates ($n = 126$), dropping 109 characters whose occupations were unknown. Occupational mobility mirrored class mobility. There was no significant change in occupation distribution when a hopeful tale was prevalent, $\chi^2(6, N = 129) = 10.035, p = .123$, whereas changes in occupation distribution were significant when cautionary tales were prevalent, $\chi^2(6, N = 128) = 28.99, p = .001$. We also noted that occupation distributions were significantly different ($p < .01$) depending on which tale dominated. These results confirm a higher degree of occupational mobility when the cautionary tale dominates.

We also looked at characters' occupational position at the beginning and end of films for the two character populations by counting the number of characters that stayed in the same occupation as well as those that moved up and those that moved down the occupational ladder. When comparing these distributions, we found their difference significant for an alpha level of .05, $\chi^2(6, N = 106) = 7.73, p = .021$. At this significance level we still found that films with a dominant hopeful tale marginally exhibit a higher degree of occupational stability; 70% of characters stay in the same occupation. In contrast, only 66% of characters in cautionary tales maintained their occupation. Furthermore, we found that upward mobility was common to both types of tales. Of the 17% of characters that moved in the hopeful tales, 56% moved up and 44% moved down. Of the 26% of characters that moved in cautionary tales, 78% moved up and 22% moved down.

Keys to Success

To evaluate how variation of the American dream myth affects keys to success, we counted the number of occurrences of each key to success for characters appearing in films in which either a hopeful tale or a cautionary tale dominated. A *t* test comparing each of the 18 keys to success in cautionary and in hopeful tales revealed no significant difference ($p > .01$). However, 4 keys to success appeared considerably more often than the others: ambition (47%), hard work (35%), risk (25%), and sacrifice (23%). Moreover, these 4 keys to success were used as stepping stones in the majority of cases (79%, 86%, 67%, and 43%, respectively). Risk and sacrifice were more often presented as impediments to success (23% and 26% of the time) than ambition (9%) and hard work (1%).

Consistent with past research (Freeman, 1992; Horton, 1982), these results indicate a general emphasis on the Protestant work ethic as exemplified in the rags-to-riches myth. Business films seem to advance the promise that the hard-working individual who has the proper level of ambition, makes the necessary sacrifices, and is open to taking risk has the best chance of attaining success.

Five variables associated with an antisocial or deviant route to success were also investigated. These include betrayal (18%), breaking the law (15%), sex (14%), misrepresentation (12%), and violence (7%). These potential keys to success were used as stepping stones most frequently (41%, 39%, 71%, 76%, and 43%, respectively) except for the category of breaking the law, which was an impediment to success in as many cases as it was a stepping stone. Finally, betrayal and violence served as impediments to success far more frequently (26% and 22% of the time) than sex or misrepresentation (13% and 11% of the time).

Also noteworthy is that these antisocial routes to success characterize successful women in business films. Of the 93 female characters, 24 (26%) moved upward, and 18 (75%) of the 24 were coded as good people. Yet, they broke the law ($n = 4$; 17%), misrepresented themselves ($n = 4$; 17%), betrayed people ($n = 3$; 13%), and used sex ($n = 10$; 42%) to climb the ladder of success in the business world.

In addition to the aforementioned variables that require a character's active participation, we investigated two passive or accidental keys to success: luck and inheritance. Our findings indicated that success through luck (9%) or inheritance (7%) is rare. Such a message reinforces the belief that success comes to those who are active and who work hard. Finally, of all coded keys to success, education (although never an impediment to success) appeared the least (2%). This may be because, as Bidney (1968) suggested, intelligence and education are destructive and divisive forces that often threaten the solidarity among members of a society.

Myth Over Time

With the myth index we established that there are periods when either the hopeful or cautionary tale dominates. We then considered if there was a correspondence between the variation of the myth index and contemporaneous economic, social, or political conditions. To do this we defined an index of well-being that included both unemployment and federal deficit figures.[8] We chose these economic indicators because class and occupational mobility relates to employment and the federal deficit may be an indicator of economic well-being. To compare these two series (the myth and economic indexes), we used a correlation analysis. We repeated this analysis, shifting the economic index forward from 1 to 4 years. The correlation between the series reached its maximum with a 3-year shift (e.g., the 1950 economic index is matched with the 1952 myth index). We note that this shift may account for the time necessary for a film to reach its audience. More important, it suggests that these Hollywood films tend to replicate existing economic conditions rather than promote changes in economic conditions. Overall, we found a positive, albeit statistically weak correlation $r = .46$ between the value of the myth index and the value of the well-being index. However if we only consider those periods that have both a positive myth index and a positive well-being index, the relation is stronger $r = .65$. This suggests that during periods of economic stability or general well-being (1953 to 1960, 1969 to 1971, 1990 to 1994) the hopeful tale is dominant and perhaps acts to maintain social order. During other times the influence of economic well-being on the tale being told is minimal, as shown in Figure 3. Specific instances of economic, social, or political instability may affect the relation between economic well-being and the myth index. This occurs notably during the Great Depression, World War II, the 1970s, and the period following the stock market crash of 1987.

A dominant hopeful tale coupled with high unemployment prevailed during the Depression. On the one hand, a dominant hopeful tale makes sense: The 1929 stock market crash may be seen as a reification of the cautionary tale and, as such, it is redundant to retell this tale. On the other hand, this is a period of what Gans (1979) called social disorder. Focusing on news narratives, he argued that during such times there is a concern for the "restoration of order" (p. 54) as well as a need to preserve social cohesion. It makes sense then, to promote the hopeful tale during these trying economic times, particularly if these tales are correlated with social stability or little class mobility in films.

During and shortly after World War II, the myth index is strongly negative and the well-being index is strongly positive. This is primarily driven by the frequency of the rags-to-riches narrative, which is well below its average and by the frequency of money-can't-buy-happiness, which is well above its average. Such a strongly negative myth index may be a reflection of the war effort as portrayed by Hollywood, where the focus was on the collective rather than on the individual. A strong money-can't-buy-happiness and a weak rags-to-riches narrative discourages individual achievement, which must be subsumed to the needs of national defense. This effect may in fact be reinforced through the direct collaboration between Washington and Hollywood at the time. In the years following the war (1946 to 1951) the myth index takes on large negative values (see Figure 2). This reflects the extreme dominance of the cautionary tale, which is exacerbated by the drastic decline in the rags-to-riches tale. Interestingly, this drastic fluctuation coincides with social pressure on women who took jobs during the war to return home, creating employment opportunities for the returning soldiers. The hopeful tale for men is reified in the social arena (e.g., as with the GI bill) which effectively promoted a

Figure 3
Economic Index versus Myth Index

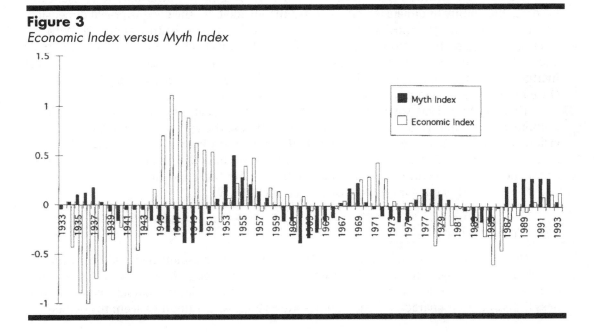

rags-to-riches mentality. However, because the social order was reconfigured by the war, the cautionary tale appears to help rechannel women to traditional ways of living. Although the tale is different from that told during the Depression, its function is similar: reestablishing social order (Gans, 1979).

From 1953 through 1960 myth and well-being indexes are positively correlated. This was a time of relative domestic stability and thus the hopeful tale dominates. However, unlike the Depression, the hopeful tale here serves to support domestic order. In addition, the hopeful tale encourages individual achievement, which had been discouraged during the war.

During the 1960s the myth index is strongly negative and the well-being index is average. A strongly negative myth index may reflect the political environment at the time, which was ideal for a dominant cautionary tale. Labor disputes and work stoppages were prominent events during 1959. The steel industry experienced a strike that lasted for 116 days, negatively affecting other industries (Denison, 1974). The Cold War was in full swing, as evidenced by the Bay of Pigs and the Cuban missile crisis. Kennedy was assassinated in 1963. American involvement in Vietnam escalated and civil unrest fomented. Again, the United States experienced social disorder, but the upheaval, unlike the Depression or World War II, was closer to civil unrest. Again, we see a caution against disrupting the social field and perhaps a call for moderatism (Gans, 1979).

The opening of the Nixon administration brought a brief respite from the turmoil of the 1960s. With Nixon's promises of peace and the restoration of law and order came the return of the hopeful tale with a strong well-being index. However, among Hollywood filmmakers, the cautionary tale promptly returned in 1972 and with it a recession, not to mention extreme moral and political corruption, in the form of Watergate and the end of the Vietnam war. Again, in this period of disorder, the cautionary tale may be seen as a promotion of political as well as moral order.

During the following five years (1976 to 1980) the hopeful tale resurges despite threatening economic conditions including high unemployment and the oil embargo. This situation is comparable to the Depression era when, despite a high unemployment rate, the hopeful tale was prevalent. This return of the hopeful tale is also associated with the end of moral disorder represented by the Nixon administration and Carter's election to office. Although the power-corrupts dimension was not statistically significant overall, we did notice an interesting effect of this dimension on the myth index between 1972 and 1980. Power-corrupts essentially becomes the dominant dimension during this time. In addition, the good-over-evil dimension, which we noted was the most significant, is weakest during this historical period. With the election of Reagan, the cautionary tale returns, in part motivated by poor economic conditions and perhaps by the perception of this period as a time of greed. The crash of the stock market in 1987 triggers a reaction somewhat similar to 1929 and the hopeful tale again dominates. Once more we see this tale operating to restore economic chaos.

From 1990 to 1994 we enter a period in which the hopeful tale correlates with strong economic well-being. This corresponds to a celebration of the end of the Cold War and to the vision of a strong and prosperous America. Perhaps the crushing national debt, which topped $4 trillion, and the deficit, which reached $300 billion, may have had an influence on the prevalence of the hopeful tale (Dow Jones, 1999). Under these conditions, the hopeful tale could be expected to encourage increased economic activity.

Conclusions

Our study of reviews of Hollywood films about business established that over time the American dream myth fluctuates between cautionary or hopeful tales. However, the differences between these tales did not have any effect on the descriptive characteristics of business films and their character demographics. Nevertheless, our findings seem to corroborate research about business and class in other media (Berk, 1977; Butsch, 1992; Byers, 1987; Desser, 1991; Freeman, 1992; Gentile & Miller, 1961; Giroux, 1980; Lipsitz, 1986; Thomas & Callahan, 1982; Traube, 1992). We found that upper middle and upper class White men are disproportionately overrepresented in these films. Indeed, these popular films suggest that an individual's socioeconomic position has little bearing on achieving success and upward mobility.

We also noted that business films exhibit different patterns of class and occupational mobility depending on the dominance of the hopeful or cautionary tales. During the periods when the hopeful tale dominated, the degree of class and occupational mobility in films was low. Conversely, we found that when the cautionary tale dominated, the degree of class and occupational mobility in films was high. Although in films there are more opportunities for mobility during times of turmoil, the risk of downward class mobility is increased. The cautionary tale perhaps reflects the turmoil in society conveying the increased opportunities the situation affords and cautioning against the risk inherent in these uncertain opportunities. The hopeful tale is somewhat different. Celebrating the positive aspects of the American dream, it essentially suggests that the dream is a reality, that we will all live happily ever after as we are.

Keys to success in business do not seem to be correlated with fluctuations in the hopeful or cautionary tales. Nonetheless, business films were quite specific in prescribing the keys to social mobility. Individuals who worked hard, were ambitious, and were willing to make sacrifices were most likely to achieve the dream. These values are far more likely to bring about success in the world of business films than antisocial actions (betrayal, breaking the law, etc.), accidental or passive events (luck or inheritance), or knowledge. Finally, we found that the prevalence of the hopeful tale is influenced by a society's economic climate. Specifically, when economic conditions are good, the hopeful tale reinforces social stability. When financial conditions are unstable, as, for example, with the Great Depression, the hopeful tale may serve to restore order. The cautionary tale, on the other hand, appears when the social order is threatened or reconfigured because of internal or external threats. In those cases, the cautionary tale helped deflect the effect of the threat and redirect society to a more stable place. We observed this effect during World War II and the postwar years as well as during the 1960s civil unrest and the moral corruption of the Nixon era.

Given our findings, it is important to reflect on how the myth-making function of Hollywood operates within American society. It is clear that the measure of economic well-being does not correlate well with the characteristics of the American dream myth as presented in business films. It is also clear that the forces that seem to influence the characteristics of the American dream myth are complex and varied. For example, in the 1960s, civil unrest precipitated by labor, race, and gender relations as well as reactions to the Vietnam War are only some of the myriad forces at work in the social field. Except for the years during World War II when a clear collaboration between Hollywood and the U.S. government was evident, there is no apparent social elite forcing specific myths on the public. Although Hollywood does not act as the regulator of a social system, it does participate in the social field by engaging in strategies that serve its own interests. If, for instance, Hollywood needs a strong consumer base it makes sense to circulate tales audiences can relate to and that reflect the social conditions of the time. Concomitantly, if social stability is necessary for consumption, then Hollywood needs to circulate a tale that promotes stability. How the relations between Hollywood and other forces in the social field are articulated warrants further study.

Acknowledgments

We thank Sari Thomas for her comments on an earlier version of this article, Dominique Richard for his help with statistical matters, and the reviewers for their guidance.

Notes

1. One film from each of the following years was coded based on viewing it: 1936, 1938, 1941, 1949, 1954, 1967, 1979, 1980, 1987, 1988, 1990, and 1994.

2. Using *The Motion Picture Guide's* (Manzon, 1992–1995; Nash & Ross, 1985–1991) classification of film genre we coded each film in one of the following categories: action adventure, thriller, comedy, horror, disaster, musical, mystery, science fiction, drama, fantasy, biography, Western, and other.

3. Based on the *Business Today* ("Career Survey Listing," 1990) options within this category were manufacturing (factory production of material goods such as chemical, pharmaceutical, clothing, electronic, energy, and entertainment production industries), distribution (e.g., trucking companies, retail outlets, publishing companies), nonfinancial services (companies that do not manufacture or exchange material goods, including hospitals, advertising agencies, and other services), financial services (companies concerned directly with the exchange of economic capital, including banks, brokerage firms, insurance, and real estate companies), other (anything that does not fit the preceding options), and undetermined (when the kind of business could not be determined).

4. Ten dimensions of the American dream were coded: rags-to-riches, money-can't-buy-happiness, power-corrupts, good-triumphs-over-evil, crime-doesn't-pay, the American reality, money-can-buy-happiness, power-is-good, evil-triumphs-over-good, and crime pays. With rags-to-riches we mean a narrative based on the idea that, irrespective of an individual's socioeconomic background, his or her dreams, ambitions, and goals can be actualized. Hard work and personal integrity are presented as the key ingredients for unlimited spiritual, social, and financial growth. Ambition is applauded as a hunger or desire for personal self-improvement that also impacts positively on the larger society. The inverse of this, the American reality, was defined as a narrative implying that even though people work hard, are ambitious, and have integrity, they stay where they are socially and economically. Money-can't-buy-happiness was defined as a narrative based on the idea that financial gain is inherently bad and results in tragedy, misery, and self-destruction. The wealthy are typically presented as individuals who are lacking the sincerity and warmth of family relations, romance, and friendship. Money-can-buy-happiness was defined as narratives about financial gain as central to happiness in family relations, romance, and friendship. Power-corrupts was defined as a narrative about those who achieve a position of power compromising their values or acting in unscrupulous or uncaring ways, whereas power-is-good was defined as stories about people who achieve positions of power behaving in prosocial ways. Good-triumphs-over-evil was defined as stories about good people beating out bad people, whereas evil-triumphs-over-good was defined as bad people beating out the good people. Crime-doesn't-pay, a more contemporary version of "As ye sow, so shall ye reap," is a story about breaking the law and being punished for it. Punishment does not necessarily imply the intervention of the criminal law system, but could result from personal tragedy or loss of wealth. The idea that "what comes around goes around" illustrates punishment without the necessity of criminal justice intervention. Crime-doesn't-pay rejects "an eye for an eye," the oldest and simplest human conception of justice (Cawelti, 1975). With crime-pays, those who break the law succeed.

5. Race, gender, age, social class, and occupation were determined from the listing of actors and descriptions of characters in the plot summaries. Social class was coded for each plot functional character at the beginning and end of the film using the Papazian (1984) category system: upper class (if the character can be considered a member of the "old rich," or the "nouveau riche" successful elite), upper middle class (if the character is wealthier than average but not extraordinarily rich), middle class (if the character appears to be of average comforts and living standards), working class (if the character is

just getting along or barely can make ends meet), underclass (if character is below poverty level or destitute), undetermined (if social class status cannot be determined), or other (if the character does not fall into the preceding categories). We coded a character as a youth (if the character appears to be in the under-20 age group), a young adult (if the character appears to be in the 21–30 age group), an adult (if the character appears to be in the 31–60 age group), a mature adult (if the character appears to be in the over-60 age group), undetermined (if age cannot be determined), or other (if age is known to be none of the preceding). We also coded the occupation (from Papazian, 1984) for each plot functional character at the beginning and at the end of the film as an assessment of occupational mobility. Options within the occupational category were service (if the character is a service or clerical worker), white-collar managerial (if the character is a business manager in middle management, a non-gold-collar executive, or a project leader), white-collar nonmanagerial (if the character is employed as a professional in the academe, sciences, law, computer programming, laboratory technology, sales, etc.), blue-collar (if the character is a skilled, semiskilled, or manual laborer, artisan, operator, etc.), gold-collar (if the character is an executive or proprietor of a large concern or a major professional such as a chief executive officer, president, chair of board, etc.), financially independent (if the character is not working and has sufficient means so that he or she does not need to work), unemployed (if the character is not by choice unemployed), undetermined (if the occupation of the character cannot be determined), or other (with open-ended comments if the preceding categories do not apply).

6. Eighteen keys to success were coded individually using yes or no options within categories. Each key to success was also coded as a stepping stone, an impediment, or irrelevant to success. The keys were wanting to improve financial or material situation, education, sex, hard work, misrepresentation of self, risk taking, luck, inheritance, ambition, invent something, having an idea someone else wants, having a skill someone else wants, having information someone else wants, having something concrete that someone else wants, betraying someone, committing a crime, acting violently, and making a sacrifice.

7. Ethical challenges to plot functional characters and their role in the struggle between good and evil were coded.

8. To calculate the index of well-being, we first calculated the average value of unemployment and of the federal deficit. We then estimated the ratio of the actual value of unemployment and of the federal deficit to their respective averages. This operation provided a relative measure of unemployment and federal deficit. We then combined these two measures linearly by associating a weight with each measure: 21 for unemployment and 1.1 for the federal deficit. To define the normalized well-being index, we calculated the average value of the compound measure and determined the difference between the value of the compound measure and its average. With this method, a positive well-being index indicates periods of relative economic prosperity and a negative index indicates poor economic conditions. For coherence the calculation of this index was done on data reported by the U.S. Bureau of Labor Statistics (1948–1995). Because the Bureau of Labor Statistics did not collect data prior to 1947, data for those years was obtained from the U.S. Bureau of the Census (1975). Unemployment figures before 1947 include people 14 years of age and up. After 1947, they include people 16 years of age and up.

References

Arthur, P. (1996). The Gun in the Briefcase; Or, The Inscription of Class in Film Noir. In D. E. James & R. Berg (Eds.), *The Hidden Foundation: Cinema and the Question of Class* (pp. 90–113). Minneapolis: University of Minnesota Press.

Barlett, D., & Steele, J. (1996, September 8). Who Stole the American Dream? *The Philadelphia Inquirer*, p. A1.

Beers, D. (1996). *Blue Sky Dream*. New York: Doubleday.

Bergman, A. (1993). *We're in the Money: Depression America and Its Films*. New York: Harper Colophon. (Original work published 1971.)

Berk, L. M. (1977). The Great Middle American Dream Machine. *Journal of Communication, 27*(3), 27–31.

Bettie, J. (1995). Class Dismissed? *Roseanne* and the Changing Face of Working-Class Iconography. *Social Text, 45*(14) 125–149.

Bidney, D. (1968). Myth, Symbolism, and Truth. In T. A. Sebeok (Ed.), *Myth: A Symposium* (pp. 3–24). Bloomington: Indiana University Press.

Butsch, R. (1979). Legitimations of Class Structures in *Gone With the Wind. Qualitative Sociology, 2,* 63–79.

Butsch, R. (1992). Class and Gender in Four Decades of Television Situation Comedy: Plus Ça Change. *Critical Studies in Mass Communication, 9,* 387–399.

Byers, T. (1987). Commodity Futures: Corporate State and Personal Style in Three Recent Science-Fiction Movies. *Science Fiction Studies, 14,* 326–339.

Career survey listings. (1990, Fall). *Business Today, 27*(3), 84.

Cawelti, J. (1965). *Apostles of the Self-Made Man.* Chicago: University of Chicago Press.

Cawelti, J. (1975). Myths of Violence in American Popular Culture. *Critical Inquiry, 1,* 521–541.

Charting the Dow Jones Averages. [Chart]. Retrieved April 3, 1999 from the World Wide Web: http://averages.dowjones.com/chrt1930.html

Cloud, D. (1996). Hegemony or concordance? The Rhetoric of Tokenism in "Oprah" Winfrey's Rags-to-Riches Biography. *Critical Studies in Mass Communication, 13,* 115–137.

Conroy, M. (1996). No Sin in Lookin Prosperous: Gender, Race, and the Class Formations of Middlebrow Taste in Douglas Sirks' *Imitation of Life*. In D. E. James & R. Berg (Eds.), *The Hidden Foundation: Cinema and the Question of Class* (pp. 114–137). Minneapolis: University of Minnesota Press.

de Certeau, M. (1988). *The Practice of Everyday Life* (S. Rendall, Trans.). Berkeley: University of California Press. (Original work published 1980)

DeFleur, M. L. (1964). Occupational Roles as Portrayed on Television. *Public Opinion Quarterly, 28,* 57–74.

Denison, E. (1974). *Accounting for United States Economic Growth 1929–1969.* Washington, DC: Brookings Institution.

Desser, D. (1991). Race, Space and Class: The Politics of the SF Film from *Metropolis* to *Blade Runner*. In J. B. Kerman (Ed.), *Retrofitting* Blade Runner: *Issues in Ridley Scott's* Blade Runner *and Phillip K. Dick's* Do Androids Dream of Electric Sheep? Bowling Green, OH: Popular.

DiMaggio, P., & Useem, M. (1978). Social Class and Arts Consumption. *Theory and Society, 5,* 141–161.

Dreiser, T. (1954). *An American Tragedy.* New York: Heritage.

Edington, K. (1995). The Hollywood Novel: American Dream, Apocalyptic Vision. *Literature/Film Quarterly, 23,* 63–67.

Edwards, J. (1995). *A Jonathan Edwards Reader.* New Haven, CT: Yale University Press.

Eyles, A. (1987). *That Was Hollywood: The 1930s.* London: Batsford.

Fitzgerald, F. S. (1958). *The Great Gatsby.* New York: Scribner.

Freeman, L. (1992). Social Mobility in Television Comedies. *Critical Studies in Mass Communication, 9,* 400–406.

Gans, H. (1979). *Deciding What's News: A Study of* CBS Evening News, NBC Nightly News, Newsweek, *and* Time. New York: Vintage.

Garafola, L. (1980). Hollywood and the Myth of the Working Class. *Radical America, 14*(1), 7–15.

Gentile, F., & Miller, S. M. (1961). TV and Social Class. *Sociology and Social Research, 45*(2), 202–209.

Giroux, H. A. (1980, May). Norma Rae: Character, Culture and Class. *Jump Cut, 22,* 1–7.

Gray, H. (1989). Television, Black Americans, and the American Dream. *Critical Studies in Mass Communication, 6,* 376–386.

Greisman, H. C. (1976, Autumn). The Image of the Business Executive on Television. *Journal of Contemporary Business, 5,* 71–89.

Hall, S. (1980). Encoding/Decoding. In S. Hall, D. Hobson, A. Lowe, & P. Willis (Eds.), *Culture, Media, Language* (pp. 128–138). London: Hutchinson.

Horton, J. (1982). Class Struggle and the American Dream: A Marxist Analysis of Communication. *Studies in Communications, 2,* 111–141.

James, D. E. (1996). Introduction: Is There Class in This Text? In D. E. James & R. Berg (Eds.), *The Hidden Foundation: Cinema and the Question of Class* (pp. 1–25). Minneapolis: University of Minnesota Press.

Jameson, F. (1977). Class and Allegory in Contemporary Mass Culture: *Dog Day Afternoon* as a Political Film. *College English, 38,* 843–859.

Jarvie, I. (1982). The Social Experience of Movies. In S. Thomas (Ed.), *Film/culture: Explorations of Cinema in Its Social Context* (pp. 247–268). Metuchen, NJ: Scarecrow.

Jhally, S., & Lewis, J. (1992). *Enlightened Racism:* The Cosby Show, *Audiences, and the Myth of the American Dream.* Boulder, CO: Westview.

Kellner, D. (1996). Poltergeists, Gender, and Class in the Age of Reagan and Bush. In D. E. James & R. Berg (Eds.), *The Hidden Foundation: Cinema and the Question of Class* (pp. 217–239). Minneapolis: University of Minnesota Press.

Kleinhans, C. (1996). Class in Action. In D. E. James & R. Berg (Eds.), *The Hidden Foundation: Cinema and the Question of Class* (pp. 240–263). Minneapolis: University of Minnesota Press.

Leach, W. (1993). *Land of Desire: Merchants, Power, and the Rise of a New American Culture.* New York: Pantheon.

Lebow, J. (1986). *Flashdance:* Eroticism and the American Dream. In D. Fowler (Ed.), *The Kingdom of Dreams in Literature and Film* (pp. 40–45). Tallahassee: Florida State University Press.

Levy, M. (1991). The American Dream of Family in Film: From Decline to Comeback. *Journal of Comparative Family Studies, 22,* 187–204.

Lewis, J. M. (1985). Social Class Origins of Academy Award Winners, 1940 to 1982. *Free Inquiry in Creative Sociology, 13,* 80–82.

Lipsitz, G. (1986). The Meaning of Memory: Family, Class and Ethnicity in Early Network Television Programs. *Cultural Anthropology, 1,* 355–387.

Livesay, H. (1984). The "Rags to Riches" Mentality in the Corporate Age. *Actes du Groupe de Recherche et d'Etudes Nord-Americaines Colloque, 2–4,* 155–166.

Manly, J. (1990). American Liberalism and the Democratic Dream: Transcending the American Dream. *Policy Studies Review, 10*(1), 89–102.

Manzon, M. (Ed.). (1992–1995) *The Motion Picture Guide* (Vols. 9–10). New York: Baseline.

Mather, C. (1967). *Magnalia Christi Americana.* New York: Russell & Russell.

Morely, D. (1992). *Television, Audiences, and Cultural Studies.* London: Routledge.

Nash, J. R., & Ross, S. R. (Eds.). (1985–1991). *The Motion Picture Guide* (Vols. 1–8). Chicago: Cine.

New York Times Film Reviews. (1968). New York: The New York Times.

Nichols, B. (1996). *Strike* and the Question of Class. In D. E. James & R. Berg (Eds.), *The Hidden Foundation: Cinema and the Question of Class* (pp. 72–89). Minneapolis: University of Minnesota Press.

Papazian, C. J. (1984). *A Content Analysis of the Portrayal of Social Class on Prime Time Television Drama*. Unpublished master's thesis, Temple University, Philadelphia.

Parshall, P. F. (1991). *Die Hard* and the American Mythos. *Journal of Popular Film and Television, 18*(4), 134–144.

Pfeil, F. (1993). From Pillar to Postmodern: Race, Class, and Gender in the Male Rampage Film. *Socialist Review, 23*(2), 123–152.

Powers, S., Rothman, D. J., & Rothman, S. (1992). Hollywood's Class Act. *Society, 29*(2), 47–64.

Powers, S., Rothman, D. J., & Rothman, S. (1996). *Hollywood's America: Social and Political Themes in Motion Pictures*. Boulder, CO: Westview.

Press, A. L. (1995). Women Watching Television: Issues of Class, Gender, and Mass Media Receptions. In P. d'Agostino & D. Tafler (Eds.), *Transmission: Toward a Post-Television Culture* (2nd ed., pp. 53–89). Thousand Oaks, CA: Sage.

Quart, L., & Auster, A. (1991). *American Film and Society Since 1945*. New York: Praeger.

The Random House Dictionary of the English Language. (1968). New York: Random House.

Rapping, E. (1992). *The Movie of the Week: Private Stories, Public Events*. Minneapolis: University of Minnesota Press.

Robinson, D. C. (1975). Television/Film Attitudes of Upper-Middle Class Professionals. *Journal of Broadcasting, 19*, 195–209.

Ruland, R., & Bradbury, M. (1991). *From Puritanism to Postmodernism: A History of American Literature*. New York: Penguin.

Ryan, M., & Kellner, D. (1988). *Camera Politica: The Politics and Ideology of Contemporary Hollywood Film*. Bloomington: Indiana University Press.

Sandell, J. (1995). Out of the Ghetto and into the Marketplace: Hoop Dreams and the Commodification of Marginality. *Socialist Review, 25*(2), 57–82.

Seggar, J., & Wheeler, P. (1973). World of Work on TV: Ethnic and Sex Representations in TV Drama. *Journal of Broadcasting, 17*, 201–204.

Sklar, R. (1975). *Movie-Made America*. New York: Vintage.

Stead, P. (1995). *Film and the Working Class: The Feature Film in British and American Society*. London: Routledge.

Steeves, H. L., & Smith, M. C. (1987). Class and Gender on Prime Time Television Entertainment: Observations from a Socialist Feminist Perspective. *Journal of Communication Inquiry, 11*(1), 43–63.

Steinberg, C. S. (1980). *Film Facts*. New York: Facts on File.

Theberge, L. J. (Ed.). (1981). *Crooks, Conmen and Clowns: Business Men in TV Entertainment*. Washington, DC: Media Institute.

Thomas, S. (1986). Mass Media and the Social Order. In G. Gumpert & R. Cathcart (Eds.), *Inter/Media: Interpersonal Communication in a Media World* (pp. 611–627). New York: Oxford University Press.

Thomas, S. (1990). Myths in and about Television. In J. Downing, A. Mohammadi, & A. Sreberny-Mohammadi (Eds.), *Questioning the Media: A Critical Introduction* (pp. 330–344). Newbury Park, CA: Sage.

Thomas, S., & Callahan, B. P. (1982). Allocating Happiness: TV Families and Social Class. *Journal of Communication, 32*(3), 184–189.

Thomas, S., & Leshay, S. V. (1992). Bad Business? A Reexamination of Television's Portrayal of Businesspersons. *Journal of Communication 42*(1), 95–105.

Traube, E. G. (1989). Secrets of Success in Postmodern Society. *Cultural Anthropology, 4,* 273–300.

Traube, E. G. (1992). *Dreaming Identities: Class, Gender, and Generation in 1980s Hollywood Movies.* Boulder, CO: Westview.

U.S. Bureau of the Census. (1975). *Historical Statistics of the United States: Colonial Times to 1970, Part 1.* Washington, DC: U.S. Department of Commerce.

Variety Film Reviews (Vol. 5). (1983). New York: Garland.

Variety Magazine's Anniversary Edition. (1942–1943; 1946–1955; 1957–1995). New York: Variety.

Weigel, R. H., & Loomis, J. W. (1981). Televised Models of Female Achievement Revisited: Some Progress. *Journal of Applied Social Psychology, 11,* 58–63.

Weiss, R. (1969). *The American Myth of Success: From Horatio Alger to Norman Vincent Peale.* New York: Basic.

23 | *The Destructive Power of Money*

Karl Marx

Marx advances the thesis that money is the alienated form of labor process as well as a "disruptive power," which undermines all social relations. This argument is presented in the present selection, the first part of which is taken from Marx's notes of 1844 on James Mill's Treatise of Political Economy, *and the second part is from the* Third of the Economic and the Philosophical Manuscripts *of the same year.*

The essence of money is not primarily that it externalizes property but that the *mediating activity* or process—the *human* and social act in which man's products reciprocally complement one another—becomes *alienated* and takes on the quality of a *material thing*, money, external to man. By externalizing this mediating activity, man is active only as he is lost and dehumanized. The very *relationship* of things and the human dealings with them become an operation beyond and above man. Through this *alien mediation* man regards his will, his activity, and his relationships to others as a power independent of himself and of them—instead of man himself being the mediator for man. His slavery thus reaches a climax. It is clear that this *mediator* becomes an *actual god*, for the mediator is the *actual power* over that which he mediates to me. His worship becomes an end in itself. Apart from this mediation, objects lose their value. They have value only insofar as they *represent* it while originally it appeared that the mediation would have value only insofar as *it* represents *objects*. This inversion of the original relationship is necessary. The *mediation*, therefore, is the lost, alienated *essence* of private property, exteriorated and *externalized* private property, just as it is the *externalized exchange* of human production with human production, the *externalized* species-activity of man. All qualities involved in this activity are transmitted to the mediator. Man as separated from this mediator thus becomes so much the poorer as the mediator becomes *richer*. . . .

Reprinted from *Basic Writings on Politics and Philosophy*, edited by Lewis S. Feuer (1967), by permission of Robin Feuer Miller.

Why must private property end up in *money?* Because man as a social being must resort to *exchange* and because exchange—under the presupposition of private property—must end up in value. The mediating process of man making exchanges is no social, no *human process,* no human relationship; rather, it is the *abstract relationship* of private property to private property, and this *abstract* relationship is the *value* whose actual existence as value is primarily *money.* Because men making exchanges do not relate to one another as men, *things* lose the significance of being human and personal property. The social relationship of private property to private property is a relationship in which private property has alienated itself. The reflexive existence of this relationship, money, is thus the externalization of private property, an abstraction from its *specific* and personal nature. . . .

[. . . Money is] the *pander* between need and object, between human life and the means of subsistence. But *that which* mediates *my* life mediates also the existence of other men for me. It is for me the *other* person.

> *"Why, Zounds! Both hands and feet are, truly—*
> *And head and virile forces—thine:*
> *Yet all that I indulge in newly,*
> *Is't thence less wholly mine?*
> *If I've six stallions in my stall,*
> *Are not their forces also lent me?*
> *I speed along completest man of all,*
> *As though my feet were four-and-twenty*
> (Goethe, Faust—Mephistopheles)[1]

Shakespeare in Timon of Athens:

> *Gold? yellow, glittering, precious gold? No, gods,*
> *I am no idle votarist: roots, you clear heavens!*
> *Thus much of this will make black, white; foul, fair;*
> *Wrong, right; base, noble; old, young; coward, valiant.*
> *. . . . . Why this*
> *Will lug your priests and servants from your sides;*
> *Pluck stout men's pillows from below their heads:*
> *This yellow slave*
> *Will knit and break religious; bless th' accurst;*
> *Make the hoar leprosy ador'd; place thieves,*
> *And give them title, knee, and approbation,*
> *With senators on the bench: this is it*
> *That makes the wappen'd widow wed again;*
> *She whom the spital-house and ulcerous sores*
> *Would cast the gorge at, this embalms and spices*
> *To th'April day again. Come, damned earth,*
> *Thou common whore of mankind, that putt'st odds*
> *Among the rout of nations, I will make thee*
> *Do thy right nature."[2]*

And later on:

> *"O thou sweet king-killer and dear divorce*
> *'Twixt natural son and sire! Thou bright defiler*
> *Of Hymen's purest bed! thou valiant Mars!*
> *Thou ever young, fresh, loved, and delicate wooer,*
> *Whose blush doth thaw the consecrated snow*
> *That lies on Dian's lap! thou visible god,*

That solder'st close impossibilities
And mak'st them kiss! that speak'st with every tongue,
To every purpose! O thou touch of hearts!
Think, thy slave man rebels; and by the virtue
Set them into confounding odds, that beasts
May have the world in empire!"[3]

Shakespeare portrays admirably the nature of *money*. To understand him, let us begin by expounding the passage from Goethe.

That which exists for me through the medium of *money*, that which I can pay for (i.e., which money can buy), that I *am*, the possessor of the money. My own power is as great as the power of money. The properties of money are my own (the possessor's) properties and faculties. What I *am* and *can do* is, therefore, not at all determined by my individuality. I *am* ugly, but I can buy the *most beautiful* woman for myself. Consequently, I am not *ugly*, for the effect of *ugliness*, its power to repel, is annulled by money. As an individual I am *lame*, but money provides me with twenty-four legs. Therefore, I am not lame. I am a detestable, dishonorable, unscrupulous and stupid man, but money is honored and so also is its possessor. Money is the highest good, and so its possessor is good. Besides, money saves me the trouble of being dishonest; therefore, I am presumed honest. I am *stupid*, but since money is the *real mind* of all things, how should its possessor be stupid? Moreover, he can buy talented people for himself, and is not he who has power over the talented more talented than they? I who can have, through the power of money, *everything* for which the human heart longs, do I not possess all human abilities? Does not my money, therefore, transform all my incapacities into their opposites?

If *money* is the bond which binds me to *human* life, and society to me, and which links me with nature and man, is it not the bond of all *bonds?* Is it not, therefore, also the universal agent of separation? It is the real means of both *separation* and *union*, the galvano-*chemical* power of society.

Shakespeare emphasizes particularly two properties of money: (1) it is the visible deity, the transformation of all human and natural qualities into their opposites, the universal confusion and inversion of things; it brings incompatibles into fraternity; (2) it is the universal whore, the universal pander between men and nations.

The power to confuse and invert all human and natural qualities, to bring about fraternization of incompatible, the *divine* power of money, resides in its *character* as the alienated and self-alienating species-life of man. It is the alienated *power of humanity*.

What I as a *man* am unable to do, and thus what all my individual faculties are unable to do, is made possible for me by *money*. Money, therefore, turns each of these faculties into something which it is not, into its *opposite*.

If I long for a meal, or wish to take the mail coach because I am not strong enough to go on foot, money provides the meal and the mail coach; i.e., it transforms my desires from representations into *realities*, from imaginary being into *real being*. In mediating thus, money is a *genuinely creative* power.

Demand also exists for the individual who has no money, but his demand is a mere creature of the imagination which has no effect, no existence for me, for a third party . . . and which thus remains unreal and without object. The difference between effective demand, supported by money, and ineffective demand, based upon my need, my passion, my desire, etc., is the difference between being, and thought, between the merely inner representation and the representation which exists outside myself as a real object.

If I have no money for travel I have no *need—no* real and self-realizing need—for travel. If I have a *vocation* for study but no money for it, then I have *no* vocation, i.e., no *effective, genuine* vocation. Conversely, if *I* really have *no* vocation for study, but have money and the urge for it, then I have an *effective* vocation. *Money* is the external, universal *means* and *power* (not derived from man as man or from human society as society) to change *representation* into *reality* and *reality* into *mere representation.* It transforms *real human and natural faculties* into mere abstract representations, i.e., *imperfections* and tormenting chimeras; and on the other hand, it transforms *real imperfections and fancies,* faculties which are really important and which exist only in the individual's imagination, into *real faculties and powers.* In this respect, therefore, money is the general inversion of *individualities,* turning them into their opposites and associating contradictory qualities with their qualities.

Money, then, appears as a *disruptive* power for the individual and for the social bonds, which claim to be self-subsistent *entities.* It changes fidelity into infidelity, love into hate, hate into love, virtue into vice, vice into virtue, servant into master, stupidity into intelligence and intelligence into stupidity.

Since money, as the existing and active concept of value, confounds and exchanges everything, it is the universal *confusion and transposition* of all things, the inverted world, the confusion and transposition of all natural and human qualities.

He who can purchase bravery is brave, though a coward. Money is not exchanged for a particular quality, a particular thing, or a specific human faculty, but for the whole objective world of man and nature. Thus, from the standpoint of its possessor, it exchanges every quality and object for every other, even though they are contradictory. It is the fraternization of incompatibles; it forces contraries to embrace.

Let us assume *man* to be *man,* and his relation to the world to be a human one. Then love can only be exchanged for love, trust for trust, etc. If you wish to enjoy art you must be an artistically cultivated person; if you wish to influence other people you must be a person who really has a stimulating and encouraging effect upon others. Every one of your relations to man and to nature must be a *specific expression,* corresponding to the object of your will, of your *real individual* life. If you love without evoking love in return, i.e., if you are not able, by the *manifestation* of yourself as a loving person, to make yourself a *beloved person,* then your love is impotent and a misfortune.

Notes

1. Goethe, *Faust.* Part I, Scene 4. This passage is taken from the translation by Bayard Taylor; the Modern Library, New York, 1950.—*Tr. Note*

2. Shakespeare, *Timon of Athens.* Act IV, Scene 3. Marx quotes from the Schlege-Tieck translation.—*Tr. Note*

3. *Ibid.*

24

Gender as a Social Structure: Theory Wrestling with Activism

Barbara J. Risman

In this article, the author argues that we need to conceptualize gender as a social structure, and by doing so, we can better analyze the ways in which gender is embedded in the individual, interactional, and institutional dimensions of our society. To conceptualize gender as a structure situates gender at the same level of general social significance as the economy and the polity. The author also argues that while concern with intersectionality must continue to be paramount, different structures of inequality have different constructions and perhaps different influential causal mechanisms at any given historical moment. We need to follow a both/and strategy to understand gender structure, race structure, and other structures of inequality as they currently operate while also systematically paying attention to how these axes of domination intersect. Finally, the author suggests we pay more attention to doing research and writing theory with explicit attention to how our work can indeed help transform as well as inform society.

Gender has become a growth industry in the academy. In the years between my own college education and today, we have moved from not enough having been published in 1972 to justify my writing a literature review for an undergraduate course paper to more sociologists' studying and teaching about gender than any other single substantive area in American society. In 1998, I published *Gender Vertigo: American Families in Transition* (Risman 1998), which offered both a historical narrative about how the field of gender had developed and an integrative theoretical explanation for the tenacity of gender stratification in families. In this article, I briefly summarize my earlier argument that gender should be conceptualized as a social structure (Risman 1998) and extend it with an attempt to classify the mechanisms that help produce gendered outcomes within each dimension of the social structure. I then provide evidence from my own and others' research to support the usefulness of this theoretical schema. Finally, using gender structure as a starting point, I engage in conversation with ideas currently emerging about intersectionality and wrestle with how we might use theory in the service of social change.

Reprinted by permission from *Gender and Society* 18, no. 4 (August 2004).

Gender as a Social Structure

With this theory of *gender as a social structure,* I offer a conceptual framework, a scheme to organize the confusing, almost limitless, ways in which gender has come to be defined in contemporary social science. Four distinct social scientific theoretical traditions have developed to explain gender. The first tradition focuses on how individual sex differences originate, whether biological (Udry 2000) or social in origin (Bern 1993). The second tradition, perhaps portrayed best in Epstein's (1988) *Deceptive Distinctions,* emerged as a reaction to the first and focuses on how the social structure (as opposed to biology or individual learning) creates gendered behavior. The third tradition, also a reaction to the individualist thinking of the first, emphasizes social interaction and accountability to others' expectations, with a focus on how "doing gender" creates and reproduces inequality (West and Zimmerman 1987). The sex-differences literature, the doing gender interactional analyses, and the structural perspectives have been portrayed as incompatible in my own early writings as well as in that of others (Fuchs Epstein 1988; Kanter 1977; Ferree 1990; Risman 1987; Risman and Schwartz 1989). England and Browne (1992) argued persuasively that this incompatibility is an illusion: All structural theories must make assumptions about individuals, and individualist theories must make presumptions about external social control. While we do gender in every social interaction, it seems naive to ignore the gendered selves and cognitive schemas that children develop as they become cultural natives in a patriarchal world (Bern 1993). The more recent integrative approaches (Connell 2002; Lorber 1994; Ferree, Lorber, and Hess 1999; Risman 1998) treat gender as a socially constructed stratification system. This article fits squarely in the current integrative tradition.

Lorber (1994) argued that gender is an institution that is embedded in all the social processes of everyday life and social organizations. She further argued that gender difference is primarily a means to justify sexual stratification. Gender is so endemic because unless we see difference, we cannot justify inequality. Lorber provided much cross-cultural, literary, and scientific evidence to show that gender difference is socially constructed and yet is universally used to justify stratification. She wrote that "the continuing purpose of gender as a modem social institution is to construct women as a group to be subordinate to men as a group" (p. 33). I share this presumption that the creation of difference is the very foundation on which inequality rests.

Martin (forthcoming) extended Lorber's (1994) use of the term "institution" in her argument that gender should be conceptualized as such. She identified the criteria for a social institution as follows: (1) Characteristic of groups; (2) persists over time and space; (3) includes distinct social practices; (4) constrains and facilitates behavior/action; (5) includes expectations, rule/norms; (6) is constituted and reconstituted by embodied agents; (7) is internalized as identities and selves; (8) includes a legitimating ideology; (9) is contradictory, rife with conflict; (10) changes continuously; (11) is organized by and permeated with power; and (12) is mutually constituted at different levels of analysis. I build on this notion of gender as an institution but find the institutional language distracting. The word "institution" is too commonly used to refer to particular aspects of society, for example, the family as an institution or corporations as institutions. My notion of gender structure meets the criteria offered by Martin (forthcoming) as well. While the language we use may differ, our goals are complementary, as we seek to situate gender as embedded not only in individuals but throughout social life (Patricia Martin, personal communication).

I prefer to define gender as a social structure because this brings gender to the same analytic plane as politics and economics, where the focus has long been on political and economic structures. While the language of structure suits my purposes, it is not ideal because despite ubiquitous usage in sociological discourse, no definition of the term "structure" is widely shared. Smelser (1988) suggested that all structuralists share the presumption that social structures exist outside individual desires or motives and that social structures at least partially explain human action. Beyond that, consensus dissipates. Blau (1977) focused solely on the constraint collective life imposes on the individual. In their influential work, Blau and his colleagues (e.g., Blau 1977; Rytina et al. 1988) argued that the concept of structure is trivialized if it is located inside an individual's head in the form of internalized norms and values. Blau focused solely on the constraint collective life imposes on the individual; structure must be conceptualized, in his view, as a force opposing individual motivation. Structural concepts must be observable, external to the individual, and independent of individual motivation. This definition of "structure" imposes a clear dualism between structure and action, with structure as constraint and action as choice.

Constraint is, of course, an important function of structure, but to focus only on structure as constraint minimizes its importance. Not only are women and men coerced into differential social roles; they often choose their gendered paths. A social structural analysis must help us understand how and why actors choose one alternative over another. A structural theory of action (e.g., Burt 1982) suggests that actors compare themselves and their options to those in structurally similar positions. From this viewpoint, actors are purposive, rationally seeking to maximize their self-perceived well-being under social-structural constraints. As Burt (1982) suggested, one can assume that actors choose the best alternatives without presuming they have either enough information to do it well or the options available to make choices that effectively serve their own interests. For example, married women may choose to do considerably more than their equitable share of child care rather than have their children do without whatever "good enough" parenting means to them if they see no likely alternative that the children's father will pick up the slack.

While actions are a function of interests, the ability to choose is patterned by the social structure. Burt (1982) suggested that norms develop when actors occupy similar network positions in the social structure and evaluate their own options vis-a-vis the alternatives of similarly situated others. From such comparisons, both norms and feelings of relative deprivation or advantage evolve. The social structure as the context of daily life creates action indirectly by shaping actors' perceptions of their interests and directly by constraining choice. Notice the phrase "similarly situated others" above. As long as women and men see themselves as different kinds of people, then women will be unlikely to compare their life options to those of men. Therein lies the power of gender. In a world where sexual anatomy is used to dichotomize human beings into types, the differentiation itself diffuses both claims to and expectations for gender equality. The social structure is not experienced as oppressive if men and women do not see themselves as similarly situated.

While structural perspectives have been applied to gender in the past (Epstein 1988; Kanter 1977), there has been a fundamental flaw in these applications. Generic structural theories applied to gender presume that if women and men were to experience identical structural conditions and role expectations, empirically observable gender differences would disappear. But this ignores not only internalized gender at the individual level (which indeed purely structural theorists deny exists) but the cultural interactional expectations that remain attached to women and men because of their gender category. A structural perspective on gender is accurate only if we realize that gender itself is a structure deeply embedded in society.

Giddens's (1984) structuration theory adds considerably more depth to this analysis of gender as a social structure with his emphasis on the recursive relationship between social structure and individuals. That is, social structures shape individuals, but simultaneously, individuals shape the social structure. Giddens embraced the transformative power of human action. He insisted that any structural theory must be concerned with reflexivity and actors' interpretations of their own lives. Social structures not only act on people; people act on social structures. Indeed, social structures are created not by mysterious forces but by human action. When people act on structure, they do so for their own reasons. We must, therefore, be concerned with why actors choose their acts. Giddens insisted that concern with meaning must go beyond the verbal justification easily available from actors because so much of social life is routine and so taken for granted that actors will not articulate, or even consider, why they act.

This nonreflexive habituated action is what I refer to as the cultural component of the social structure: The taken for granted or cognitive image rules that belong to the situational context (not only or necessarily to the actor's personality). The cultural component of the social structure includes the interactional expectations that each of us meet in every social encounter. My aims are to bring women and men back into a structural theory where gender is the structure under analysis and to identify when behavior is habit (an enactment of taken for granted gendered cultural norms) and when we do gender consciously, with intent, rebellion, or even with irony. When are we doing gender and re-creating inequality without intent? And what happens to interactional dynamics and male-dominated institutions when we rebel? Can we refuse to do gender or is rebellion simply doing gender differently, forging alternative masculinities and femininities?

Connell (1987) applied Giddens's (1984) concern with social structure as both constraint and created by action in his treatise on gender and power. In his analysis, structure constrains action, yet "since human action involves free invention ... and is reflexive, practice can be turned against what constrains it; so structure can deliberately be the object of practice" (Connell 1987, 95). Action may turn against structure but can never escape it. We must pay attention both to how structure shapes individual choice and social interaction and to how human agency creates, sustains, and modifies current structure. Action itself may change the immediate or future context.

A theory of gender as a social structure must integrate this notion of causality as recursive with attention to gender consequences at multiple levels of analysis. Gender is deeply embedded as a basis for stratification not just in our personalities, our cultural rules, or institutions but in all these, and in complicated ways. The gender structure differentiates opportunities and constraints based on sex category and thus has consequences on three dimensions: (1) At the individual level, for the development of gendered selves; (2) during interaction as men and women face different cultural expectations even when they fill the identical structural positions; and (3) in institutional domains where explicit regulations regarding resource distribution and material goods are gender specific.

Advantages to Gender Structure Theory

This schema advances our understanding of gender in several ways. First, this theoretical model imposes some order on the encyclopedic research findings that have developed to explain gender inequality. Thinking of each research question as one piece of a jigsaw puzzle, being able to identify how one set of findings coordinates with others even when the dependent variables or contexts of interest are distinct, furthers our ability to build a cumulative science. Gender as a social structure is enormously complex. Full attention to the web of interconnection between gendered selves, the cultural expectations that help explain interactional patterns, and institutional regulations allows each research tradition to explore the growth of their own trees while remaining cognizant of the forest.

A second contribution of this approach is that it leaves behind the modernist warfare version of science, wherein theories are pitted against one another, with a winner and a loser in every contest. In the past, much energy (including my early work; Risman 1987) was devoted to testing which theory best explained gender inequality and by implication to discounting every alternative possibility.[1] While this is perhaps an effective technique for building academic careers, as a model for explaining complex social phenomena, it leaves much to be desired. Theory building that depends on theory slaying presumes parsimony is always desirable, as if this complicated world of ours were best described with simplistic monocausal explanations. While parsimony and theory testing were the model for the twentieth century science, a more postmodern science should attempt to find complicated and integrative theories (Collins 1998). The conceptualization of gender as a social structure is my contribution to complicating, but hopefully enriching, social theory about gender.

A third benefit to this multidimensional structural model is that it allows us to seriously investigate the direction and strength of causal relationships between gendered phenomena on each dimension. We can try to identify the site where change occurs and at which level of analysis the ability of agentic women and men seem able, at this historical moment, to effectively reject habitualized gender routines. For example, we can empirically investigate the relationship between gendered selves and doing gender without accepting simplistic unidirectional arguments for inequality presumed to be either about identities or cultural ideology. It is quite possible, indeed likely, that socialized femininity does help explain why we do gender, but doing gender to meet others' expectations, surely, over time, helps construct our gendered selves. Furthermore, gendered institutions depend on our willingness to do gender, and when we rebel, we can sometimes change the institutions themselves. I have used the language of dimensions interchangeably with the language of levels because when we think of gender as a social structure, we must move away from privileging any particular dimension as higher than another. How social change occurs is an empirical question, not an a priori theoretical assumption. It may be that individuals struggling to change their own identities (as in consciousness-raising groups of the early second-wave women's movement) eventually bring their new selves to social interaction and create new cultural expectations. For example, as women come to see themselves (or are socialized to see themselves) as sexual actors, the expectations that men must work to provide orgasms for their female partners becomes part of the cultural norm. But this is surely not the only way social change can happen. When social movement activists name as inequality what has heretofore been considered natural (e.g., women's segregation into low-paying jobs), they can create organizational changes such as career ladders between women's quasi-administrative jobs and actual management, opening up opportunities that otherwise would have remained closed, thus creating change on the institutional dimension. Girls raised in the next generation, who know opportunities exist in these workplaces, may have an altered sense of possibilities and therefore of themselves. We need, however, to also study change and equality when it occurs rather than only documenting inequality.

Perhaps the most important feature of this conceptual schema is its dynamism. No one dimension determines the other. Change is fluid and reverberates throughout the structure dynamically. Changes in individual identities and moral accountability may change interactional expectations, but the opposite is possible as well. Change cultural expectations, and individual identities are shaped differently. Institutional changes must result from individuals or group action, yet such change is difficult, as institutions exist across time and space. Once institutional changes occur, they reverberate at the level of cultural expectations and perhaps even on identities. And the cycle of change continues. No mechanistic predictions are possible because human beings sometimes reject the structure itself and, by doing so, change it. Much time and energy can be wasted trying to validate which dimension is more central to inequality or social change. Instead, the feminist project is better served by finding empirical answers to particular questions and by identifying how particular processes explain outcomes in need of change. If our goal is to do scholarship that contributes to transforming society, the identification of the processes that explain particular outcomes is the first step in effectively changing those processes and subsequently the outcomes themselves.

Social Processes Located by Dimension in the Gender Structure

When we conceptualize gender as a social structure, we can begin to identify under what conditions and how gender inequality is being produced within each dimension. The "how" is important because without knowing the mechanisms, we cannot intervene. If indeed gender inequality in the division of household labor at this historical moment were primarily explained (and I do not suggest that it is) by gendered selves, then we would do well to consider the most effective socialization mechanisms to create fewer gender-schematic children and resocialization for adults. If, however, the gendered division of household labor is primarily constrained today by cultural expectations and moral accountability, it is those cultural images we must work to alter. But then again, if the reason many men do not equitably do their share of family labor is that men's jobs are organized so they cannot succeed at work and do their share at home, it is the contemporary American workplace that must change (Williams 2000). We may never find a universal theoretical explanation for the gendered division of household labor because universal social laws may be an illusion of twentieth-century empiricism. But in any given moment for any particular setting, the causal processes should be identifiable empirically. Gender complexity goes beyond historical specificity, as the particular causal processes that constrain men and women to do gender may be strong in one institutional setting (e.g., at home) and weaker in another (e.g., at work).

The forces that create gender traditionalism for men and women may vary across space as well as time. Conceptualizing gender as a social structure contributes to a more postmodern, contextually specific social science. We can use this schema to begin to organize thinking about the causal processes that are most likely to be effective on each dimension. When we are concerned with the means by which individuals come to have a preference to do gender, we should focus on how identities are constructed through early childhood development, explicit socialization, modeling, and adult experiences, paying close attention to the internalization of social mores. To the extent that women and men choose to do gender-typical behavior cross-situationally and over time, we must focus on such individual explanations. Indeed, much attention has already been given to gender socialization and the individualist presumptions for gender. The earliest and perhaps most commonly referred to explanations in popular culture depend on sex-role training, teaching boys and girls their culturally appropriate roles. But when trying to understand gender on the interactional/cultural dimension, the means by which status differences shape expectations and the ways in which in-group and out-group membership influence behavior need to be at the center of attention. Too little attention has been paid to how inequality is shaped by such cultural expectations during interaction. I return to this in the section below. On the institutional dimension, we look to law, organizational practices, and formal regulations that distinguish by sex category. Much progress has been made in the post-civil rights era with rewriting formal laws and organizational practices to ensure gender neutrality. Unfortunately, we have often found that despite changes in gender socialization and gender neutrality on the institutional dimension, gender stratification remains.

What I have attempted to do here is to offer a conceptual organizing scheme for the study of gender that can help us to understand gender in all its complexity and try to isolate the social processes that create gender in each dimension. This is necessary before we can begin to imagine how to change these processes and thus to change the way we socially construct gender. Table 1 provides a schematic outline of this argument.[2]

Cultural Expectations during Interaction and the Stalled Revolution

In *Gender Vertigo* (Risman 1998), I suggested that at this moment in history, gender inequality between partners in American heterosexual couples could be attributed particularly to the interactional expectations at the cultural level: the differential expectations attached to being a mother and father, a husband and wife. Here, I extend this argument in two ways. First, I propose that the stalled gender revolution in other settings can similarly be traced to the interactional/cultural dimension of the social structure. Even when women and men with feminist identities work in organizations with formally gender-neutral rules, gender inequality is reproduced during everyday interaction. The cultural expectations attached to our sex category, simply being identified as a woman or man, has remained relatively impervious to the feminist forces that have problematized sexist socialization practices and legal discrimination. I discuss some of those processes that can help explain why social interaction continues to reproduce inequality, even in settings that seem ripe for social change.

Contemporary social psychological writings offer us a glimpse of possibilities for understanding how inequality is reconstituted in daily interaction. Ridgeway and her colleagues (Ridgeway 1991, 1997, 2001; Ridgeway and Correll 2000; Ridgeway and Smith-Lovin 1999)

Table 1 Dimensions of Gender Structure, by Illustrative Social Processes

		Dimensions of the Gender Structure	
	Individual Level	Interactional Cultural Expectations	Institutional Domain
Social Processes[a]	Socialization	Status expectations	Organizational practices
	Internalization	Cognitive bias	Legal regulations
	Identity work	Othering	Distribution of resources
	Construction of selves	Trading power for patronage	Ideology
		Altercasting	

[a]These are examples of social processes that may help explain the gender structure on each dimension. They are meant to be illustrative and not a complete list of all possible social processes or causal mechanisms.

showed that the status expectations attached to gender and race categories are cross-situational. These expectations can be thought of as one of the engines that re-create inequality even in new settings where there is no other reason to expect male privilege to otherwise emerge. In a sexist and racist society, women and all persons of color are expected to have less to contribute to task performances than are white men, unless they have some other externally validated source of prestige. Status expectations create a cognitive bias toward privileging those of already high status. What produces status distinction, however, is culturally and historically variable. Thus, cognitive bias is one of the causal mechanisms that help to explain the reproduction of gender and race inequality in everyday life. It may also be an important explanation for the reproduction of class and heterosexist inequality in everyday life as well, but that is an empirical question.

Schwalbe and his colleagues (2000, 419) suggested that there are other "generic interactive processes through which inequalities are created and reproduced in everyday life." Some of these processes include othering, subordinate adaptation, boundary maintenance, and emotion management. Schwalbe and his colleagues suggested that subordinates' adaptation plays an essential role in their own disadvantage. Subordinate adaptation helps to explain women's strategy to adapt to the gender structure. Perhaps the most common adaptation of women to subordination is "trading power for patronage" (Schwalbe et al. 2000, 426). Women, as wives and daughters, often derive significant compensatory benefits from relationships with the men in their families. Stombler and Martin (1994) similarly showed how little sisters in a fraternity trade affiliation for secondary status. In yet another setting, elite country clubs, Sherwood (2004) showed how women accept subordinate status as "B" members of clubs, in exchange for men's approval, and how when a few wives challenge men's privilege, they are threatened with social ostracism, as are their husbands. Women often gain the economic benefits of patronage for themselves and their children in exchange for their subordinate status.

One can hardly analyze the cultural expectations and interactional processes that construct gender inequality without attention to the actions of members of the "dominant group." We must pay close attention to what men do to preserve their power and privilege. Schwalbe et al. (2000) suggested that one process involved is when superordinate groups effectively "other" those who they want to define as subordinate, creating devalued statuses and expectations for them. Men effectively do this in subversive ways through "politeness" norms, which construct women as "others" in need of special favors, such as protection. By opening doors and walking closer to the dirty street, men construct women as an "other" category, different and less than independent autonomous men. The cultural significance attached to male bodies signifies the capacity to dominate, to control, and to elicit deference, and such expectations are perhaps at the core of what it means for men to do gender (Michael Schwalbe, personal communication).

These are only some of the processes that might be identified for understanding how we create gender inequality based on embodied cultural expectations. None are determinative causal predictors, but instead, these are possible leads to reasonable and testable hypotheses about the production of gender. I offer them as part of a conceptual scheme to help us think about how different kinds of processes are implicated at each dimension of the gender structure. Martin's (2003) research on men and women workers in a corporate setting can help illustrate how such a conceptual scheme might work. She wrote about a male vice-president's asking his female counterpart to pick up a phone call, which she does unreflectively, but she soon thereafter identifies this request as problematic. Martin presented this as an example of how interactional status expectations attached to sex category create inequality within professional relationships. This empirical example supports the thesis that shared but routine cultural expectations re-create inequality even without the conscious intent of the actors. Gender structure theory does not presume that this man and woman do not bring gendered selves to the office to accept Martin's analysis. In fact, one might suggest that a vice-president who had more thoroughly internalized traditional femininity norms would not have noticed the inequity at all. Nor does one need to have a company that has purged all discriminatory practices from its policies to see the import of the cultural expectations that Martin identified. A meta-analysis that looks at the effects of gender inequality in the workplace should integrate findings about social processes at the level of individual identities, cultural expectations, and organizational practices. In the next section of this article, I provide empirical illustrations of this conceptual scheme of gender as a social structure.

Empirical Illustrations

I begin with an example from my own work of how conceptualizing gender as a social structure helps to organize the findings and even push forward an understanding of the resistance toward an egalitarian division of family work among contemporary American heterosexual couples. This is an area of research that incorporates a concern with nurturing children, housework, and emotional labor. My own question, from as early as graduate school, was whether men could mother well enough that those who care about children's well-being would want them to do so. Trained in the warfare model of science, my dissertation was a test of structural versus individualist theories (Kanter 1977) of men's mothering. As someone who considered herself a structuralist of some generic sort, I hypothesized (Risman 1983) that when men were forced into the social role of primary parent, they could become just like mothers: The parenting role (e.g., a measure of family structure) would wipe out the effects of individual gendered selves in my models. What I found was, alas, more complicated. At the time, I concluded that men could "mother" but did not do so in ways identical to women (Risman 1983). After having been influenced by studies showing that tokenism worked differently when men were the tokens (Williams 1992; Zimmer 1988) and that money could not buy power in marriage for women quite as it seemed to for men (Brines 1994; Ferree 1990), I came to the realization that gender itself was a structure and would not disappear when men and women were distributed across the variety of structural positions that organize our social world.

To ask the question, Can men mother, presuming that gender itself is a social structure leads us to look at all the ways that gender constrains men's mothering and under what conditions those change. Indeed, one of my most surprising, and unanticipated, findings was that single fathers who were primary caretakers came to describe themselves more often than other men with adjectives such as "nurturant," "warm," and "child oriented," those adjectives we social scientists use to measure femininity. Single fathers' identities changed based on their experiences as primary parents. In my research, men whose wives worked full-time did not, apparently, do enough mothering to have such experiences influence their own sense of selves. Most married fathers hoard the opportunity for leisure that frees them from the responsibilities of parenting that might create such identity change. My questions became more complicated but more useful when I conceptualized gender as a social structure. When and under what conditions do gendered selves matter? When do interactional expectations have the power to overcome previous internalized predispositions? What must change at the institutional level allow for expectations to change at the interactional level? Does enough change on the interactional dimension shift the moral accountability that then leads to collective action in social organizations? Could feminist parents organize and create a social movement that forces workplaces to presume that valuable workers also have family responsibilities?

These questions led me to try to identify the conditions that enable women and men to actually succeed in creating egalitarian relationships. My next research project was an in-depth interview and qualitative study of heterosexual couples raising children who equally shared the work of earning a living and the family labor of child care, homemaking, and emotion work. The first interesting piece of data was how hard it was to find such people in the end of the twentieth century, even when recruiting at daycare centers, parent-teacher associations, university venues, and feminist newsletters (all in the southeastern United States). Three out of four volunteer couples failed the quite generous criteria for inclusion: Working approximately the same number of hours in the labor force (within five hours per week), sharing the household labor and child care tasks within a 60/40 split, and both partners' describing the relationship as equitable. There are clearly fewer couples who live equal lives than those who wish fervently that they did so.

What I did find from intensive interviews and home observations with 20 such couples was that the conditions that enabled their success spread across each dimension of the gender structure. Although I would have predicted otherwise (having once been committed to a purely structural theory of human behavior), selves and personalities matter. The women in my sample were strong, directive women married to relatively laidback men. Given the overwhelming gendered expectations for men's privilege in heterosexual marriage, this should have been expected, but to someone with my theoretical background, it was not. Less surprising to me, the women in these couples also had at least the income and career status of their partners and often bettered them. But this is not usually enough to dent men's privilege, or we would have far more egalitarian marriages by now. In addition, these couples were ideologically committed to equality and to sharing. They often tried explicitly to create social relationships with others who held similar values, for example, by joining liberal churches to meet like-minded others. Atypical gendered selves and shared feminist-inspired cultural expectations were important conditions for equality, but they were not enough. Men's workplace flexibility mattered as well. Nearly every father in this sample was employed in a job with flexible working hours. Many women worked in jobs with flexibility as well, but not as uniformly as their male partners. These were privileged, educated workers for whom workplace flexibility was sometimes simply luck (e.g., a father who lost a corporate job and decided to sell real estate) but more often was a conscious choice (e.g., clinical psychologists choosing to teach at a small college to have more control over working hours despite decreased earning power). Thus, these couples experienced enabling contexts at the level of their individual selves, feminist ideology to help shape the cultural expectations in their most immediate environments (within the dyad and among at least some friends), and the privilege within the economy to have or find flexible jobs. By attending to each dimension of the gender structure, I amassed a more effective explanation for their ability to negotiate fair relationships than I could have without attention to selves, couple interaction, and their workplaces. The implications for feminist social change are direct: We cannot simply attend to socializing children differently, nor creating moral accountability for men to share family work, nor fighting for flexible, family-friendly workplaces. We must attend to all simultaneously.

The research on gender in occupational settings (Williams 1992; Zimmer 1988) and quantitative studies of household division of labor (Brines 1994; Greenstein 2000) also provide good examples of how using gender structure as a conceptual framework can help organize meta-analytic reviews of the literature to create cumulative knowledge. Kanter's (1977) early structural hypotheses presumed that tokenism per se was an important mechanism that explained women's and men of color's continued subordination in the labor force. But as research testing this tokenism hypothesis expanded to include men in women's jobs, it became clear that the theory was not indeed only about numbers. Tokenism did not work the same way for white men. Men tokens rode glass escalators while women and racial minorities hit glass ceilings (Reskin 1998; Williams 1992; Yoder 1991). Gender and race remained important; the cultural interactional expectations remained different even in integrated work settings. Status expectations (Ridgeway 1991; Ridgeway et al. 1998) favored men and devalued women, whatever their numbers. We can conceptualize this as the interactional cultural level impeding further changes that realignments on the institutional dimension would predict.

Similarly, quantitative research findings about the household division of labor have made it quite clear that even when women work outside the home full-time, they shoulder the majority of household and child care. Over time, researchers have tested a variety of theories for why, sometimes presuming that as time pressures and resources equalized between husbands and wives, so too would the burden of household labor (Bianchi et al. 2000; Coverman 1985; Pleck 1985; Presser 1994; Shelton 1992). Not so. The data are unequivocal. Even in dual worker families, women do considerably more work and retain the majority of responsibility, even if they do share (or perhaps delegate) some of the family work to husbands and children. Sociology has provided solid evidence (Fenstermaker Berk 1985; Greenstein 1996, 2000; Robinson and Milkie 1998; Twiggs, McQuillan, and Ferree 1999) that domestic work, whether cleaning toilets or changing diapers, is as much about the production and display of gender as it is about clean toilets and dry bottoms. But such information only gets us so far analytically. We can integrate such research by asking questions about when and how the different effects of the gender structure remain resistant to change and when some progressive feminist change has occurred. Do young women in the twenty-first century, raised by feminists, successfully negotiate fair families? Or does the moral accountability to do gender as mothers and wives combined with devalued status in the workplace still defeat even women socialized for equality? Does workplace flexibility for men allow feminist women more success in their negotiations at the family level? The conceptualization of gender as a structure, and attention to the mechanisms at work in each dimension of the gender structure, helps to frame the kind of research that might answer such queries.

Gender structure theory allows us to try to disentangle the "how" questions without presuming that there is one right answer, for all places, times, and contexts. It is easy to illustrate that a combination of gender wage gap and the organization of careers requiring inflexible hours and full-time commitment pushes married mothers outside the labor force and creates stressful lives for mothers who remain within it, married or not. But we must still ask why this is true for women but not men. Perhaps, under some conditions, women socialized for emphasized femininity do indeed hold themselves accountable for being personally responsible for more than good enough mothering and sparkling households. Research should identify under what conditions and to what extent gendered selves help to account for objective inequalities (e.g., women working more hours a day than their partners) and when other factors are more significant. My own hypothesis is that feminist women are often defeated in their attempt at egalitarian heterosexual relationships by cultural gendered interactional expectations. Within the past year, memoirs have been written by young feminists, academics, and daughters of famous women's movement leaders (Fox 2003; Hanauer 2002) bemoaning the impossible expectations facing career women who choose motherhood as well. Similarly, a recent feminist cyberspace conversation on the Listserve of Sociologists for Women in Society described the struggle to combine motherhood and career in the academy in nearly as despairing a tone as did Arlie Hochschild (1975) in her classic article first published three decades ago. I have yet to see recent memoirs, or hear of painful listserver conversations, among twenty-first-century fathers. Little cultural change has occurred around fathering. Most men are still not morally responsible for the quality of family life, and women have yet to discover how to avoid being held accountable.

Gender structures are even more complicated than my discussion suggests thus far because how gender identities are constructed on the individual and cultural dimensions vary tremendously over time and space. Even within contemporary American society, gender structures vary by community, social class, ethnicity, and race.

Gender Structure and Intersectionality

Perhaps the most important development in feminist thought in the last part of the twentieth century was the increasing concern with intersectionality (Andersen and Collins 1994; Baca Zinn and Thornton Dill 1994; Collins 1990). Women of color had been writing about intersectionality from nearly the start of the second wave of feminist scholarship. It was, however, not until several decades into the women's movement when they were heard and moved from margin closer to center (Myers et al. 1998). There is now considerable consensus growing that one must always take into consideration multiple axes of oppression; to do otherwise presumes the whiteness of women, the maleness of people of color, and the heterosexuality of everyone.

I concur with this consensus that gender must be understood within the context of the intersecting domains of inequality. The balkanization of research and theory into specializations of race or ethnicity or gender or stratification has undermined a sophisticated analysis of inequality (but see Reskin 2002; Schwalbe et al. 2000; Tilly 1999). I do not agree, however, with an operational strategy for scholarship that suggests the appropriate analytic solution is to only work within an intersectionality framework. While various axes of domination are always intersecting, the systems of inequality are not necessarily produced or re-created with identical social processes. The historical and current mechanisms that support gender inequality may or may not be those that are most significant for other kinds of oppression; whether this is the case is an empirical question. Gender research and theory can never again ignore how women's subordination differs within racial and ethnic communities or is constructed within class dynamics. Yet we should not therefore only study gender, race, and class simultaneously. There is a difference between an analysis of psychological, historical, or sociological mechanisms that construct inequality and the subjective experience of the outcomes of such mechanisms. There may be similarity of outcomes (e.g., experiences of oppression) along axes of oppression that arise from different causal mechanisms, but that is an empirical question, not a logical necessity. To focus all investigations into the complexity or subjective experience of interlocking oppressions would have us lose access to how the mechanisms for different kinds of inequality are produced. Feminist scholarship needs a both/and strategy (Collins 1998). We cannot study gender in isolation from other inequalities, nor can we only study inequalities' intersection and ignore the historical and contextual specificity that distinguishes the mechanisms that produce inequality by different categorical divisions, whether gender, race, ethnicity, nationality, sexuality, or class.

Calhoun (2000) exemplifies this both/and strategy in her argument that heterosexism cannot simply be understood as gender oppression and merged into feminist theory. She argued that we must study heterosexism as a separate system of oppression. While it is clearly the case that gender subordination and heterosexism support one another, and a gendered analysis of homophobia is critical, the two oppressions should not be conflated. It is often presumed that Rich's (1980) argument about "compulsory heterosexuality and lesbian existence" suggests that heterosexism is primarily a product of men's dominance, an attempt to ensure sexual access to women by men, and that this is a primary explanation for lesbian oppression.

While this is surely an important component of heterosexism, Calhoun argued that it is a mistake to presume that it is the whole of it. She suggested instead that challenging men's dominance is a necessary condition of ending the subordination of lesbians and gay men but not a sufficient condition to end such oppression. It is important for analytic clarity, and therefore to the scholarly contribution to social change, to identify causal mechanisms for heterosexism and gender oppression distinctly.

Other examples also illustrate the analytic usefulness of paying attention to the distinct properties of different axes of oppression. Gendered images support racial domination, but racial domination can hardly be attributed to gender inequality. For example, Black men's inferiority gets promoted through constructions of hyper-sexuality (Collins 2004), and Black women's inferiority gets promoted through sexualized images such as Jezebel or welfare queen (Collins 2000). Similarly, Asian American men's autonomy and even citizenship rights were abrogated by constructions of effeminacy (Espiritu 1997). Yet it is implausible to argue that racial domination is nothing but a product of gender oppression. While we must pay attention to how axes of oppression affect one another and how the experience of their oppressions are simultaneous, we must continue to study and work to transform each one independently as well as in conjunction with one another.

Each categorical inequality (Tilly 1999) that is deeply embedded in society can be conceptualized as a social structure. Bonilla-Silva (1997) has made this argument persuasively for conceptualizing race as a social structure. He argued that race is a social structure that influences identities and attitudes but is also incorporated into how opportunities and constraints work throughout every societal institution. According to Bonilla-Silva, to conceptualize race as a social structure forces us to move beyond seeing racial inequality as constructed simply by racist attitudes and to understand the ways in which our society embeds white privilege at every level of analysis. I hardly need to argue that class inequality should be conceptualized as a structure as the economic structure of society has long been a primary concern of social scientists. Similarly, political structures have long been studied both at the national and comparative level because here too, politics are routinely considered a basic component of human society. My argument is that race, gender, and sexuality are as equally fundamental to human societies as the economy and the polity. Those inequalities that are fundamentally embedded throughout social life, at the level of individual identities, cultural expectations embedded into interaction, and institutional opportunities and constraints are best conceptualized as structures: The gender structure, the race structure, the class structure, and the sexuality structure. This does not imply that the social forces that produced, nor the causal mechanisms at work in the daily reproduction of inequality within each structure, are of similar strength or type at any given historical moment. For example, gender and race structures extend considerably further into everyday life in the contemporary American context, at home and at work, than does the political structure.[3] I propose this structural language as a tool to help disentangle the means by which inequalities are constructed, recreated, and—it is hoped—transformed or deconstructed. The model for how gender structure works, with consequences for individuals, interactions/cultural expectations, and institutions, can be generalized to the study of other equally embedded inequalities such as race and sexuality. Each structure of inequality exists on its own yet coexists with every other structure of inequality. The subjective experience of actual human beings is always of intersecting inequalities, but the historical construction and contemporary reproduction of inequality on each axis may be distinct. Oppressions can be loosely or tightly coupled, can have both common and distinct generative mechanisms.

Theory Wrestling with Activism

Within any structure of inequality, perhaps the most important question a critical scholar must ask is, What mechanisms are currently constructing inequality, and how can these be transformed to create a more just world? If as critical scholars, we forget to keep our eye on social transformation, we may slip without intention into the implicitly value-free role of social scientists who study gender merely to satisfy intellectual curiosity (Risman 2003). The central questions for feminists must include a focus on social transformation, reducing inequality, and improving the status of women. A concern with social change brings us to the thorny and as yet too little explored issue of agency. When do subordinate groups collectively organize to challenge their oppression? When do superordinate groups mobilize to resist? How do we know agency when we see it, and how can we support feminist versions of it?

Feminist scholarship must seek to understand how and why gender gets done, consciously or not, to help those who hope to stop doing it. I end by focusing our attention on what I see as the next frontier for feminist change agents: A focus on the processes that might spur change at the interactional or cultural dimension of the gender structure. We have begun to socialize our children differently, and while identities are hardly postgender, the sexism inherent in gender socialization is now widely recognized. Similarly, the organizational rules and institutional laws have by now often been rewritten to be gender neutral, at least in some nations. While gender-neutral laws in a gender-stratified society may have short-term negative consequences (e.g., displaced homemakers who never imagined having to support themselves after marriage), we can hardly retreat from equity in the law or organizations. It is the interactional and cultural dimension of gender that have yet to be tackled with a social change agenda.

Cognitive bias is one of the mechanisms by which inequality is re-created in everyday life. There are, however, documented mechanisms for decreasing the salience of such bias (Bielby 2000; Reskin 2000; Ridgeway and Correll 2000). When we consciously manipulate the status expectations attached to those in subordinate groups, by highlighting their legitimate expertise beyond the others in the immediate social setting, we can begin to challenge the nonconscious hierarchy that often goes unnoticed. Similarly, although many subordinates adapt to their situation by trading power for patronage, when they refuse to do so, interaction no longer flows smoothly, and change may result. Surely, when wives refuse to trade power for patronage, they can rock the boat as well as the cradle.

These are only a few examples of interactive processes that can help to explain the reproduction of inequality and to envision strategies for disrupting inequality. We need to understand when and how inequality is constructed and reproduced to deconstruct it. I have argued before (Risman 1998) that because the gender structure so defines the category woman as subordinate, the deconstruction of the category itself is the best, indeed the only sure way, to end gender subordination. There is no reason, except the transitional vertigo that will accompany the process to dismantle it, that a utopian vision of a just world involves any gender structure at all. Why should we need to elaborate on the biological distinction between the sexes? We must accommodate reproductive differences for the process of biological replacement, but there is no a priori reason we should accept any other role differentiation simply based on biological sex category. Before accepting any gender elaboration around biological sex category, we ought to search suspiciously for the possibly subtle ways such differentiation supports men's privilege. Once two salient groups exist, the process of in-group and out-group distinctions and in group opportunity hoarding become possible. While it may be that for some competitive sports, single-sex teams are necessary, beyond that, it seems unlikely that any differentiation or cultural elaboration around sex category has a purpose beyond differentiation in support of stratification.

Feminist scholarship always wrestles with the questions of how one can use the knowledge we create in the interest of social transformation. As feminist scholars, we must talk beyond our own borders. This kind of theoretical work becomes meaningful if we can eventually take it public. Feminist sociology must be public sociology (Burawoy forthcoming). We must eventually take what we have learned from our theories and research beyond professional journals to our students and to those activists who seek to disrupt and so transform gender relations. We must consider how the knowledge we create can help those who desire a more egalitarian social world to refuse to do gender at all, or to do it with rebellious reflexiveness to help transform the world around them. For those without a sociological perspective, social change through socialization and through legislation are the easiest to envision. We need to shine a spotlight on the dimension of cultural interactional expectations as it is here that work needs to begin.

We must remember, however, that much doing gender at the individual and interactional levels gives pleasure as well as reproduces inequality, and until we find other socially acceptable means to replace that opportunity for pleasure, we can hardly advocate for its cessation. The question of how gender elaboration has been woven culturally into the fabric of sexual desire deserves more attention. Many of our allies believe that "viva la difference" is required for sexual passion, and few would find a postgender society much of a feminist utopia if it came at the cost of sexual play. No one wants to be part of a revolution where she or he cannot dirty dance.

In conclusion, I have made the argument that we need to conceptualize gender as a social structure, and by doing so, we can analyze the ways in which gender is embedded at the individual, interactional, and institutional dimensions of our society. This situates gender at the same level of significance as the economy and the polity. In addition, this framework helps us to disentangle the relative strength of a variety of causal mechanisms for explaining any given outcome without dismissing the possible relevance of other processes that are situated at different dimensions of analysis. Once we have a conceptual tool to organize the encyclopedic research on gender, we can systematically build on our knowledge and progress to understanding the strength and direction of causal processes within a complicated multidimensional recursive theory. I have also argued that our concern with intersectionality must continue to be paramount but that different structures of inequality have different infrastructure and perhaps different influential causal mechanisms at any given historical moment. Therefore, we need to follow a both/and strategy, to understand gender structure, race structure, and other structures of inequality as they currently operate, while also systematically paying attention to how these axes of domination intersect. Finally, I have suggested that we pay more attention to doing research and writing theory with explicit attention to how our work can come to be "fighting words" (Collins 1998) to help transform as well as inform society. If we can identify the mechanisms that create gender, perhaps we can offer alternatives to them and so use our scholarly work to contribute to envisioning a feminist utopia.

Author's Note: There are too many scholars who have read this work and helped to improve it to thank each and every one. I do owe a great deal to the feminist intellectual community of Sociologists for Women in Society. Special thanks are due to Shannon Davis, Patricia Yancey Martin, Michael Schwalbe, Donald Tomaskovic-Devey, and the students in my 2003 and 2004 graduate seminars in sociology of the family, sociology of gender, and feminist thought. All of them have helped improve my argument, but of course I alone remain responsible for the content, flaws and all.

Notes

1. See Scott (1997) for a critique of feminists who adopt a strategy where theories have to be simplified, compared, and defeated. She too suggested a model where feminists build on the complexity of each others' ideas.

2. I thank my colleague Donald Tomaskovic-Devey for suggesting the visual representation of these ideas as well as his usual advice on my ideas as they develop.

3. One can certainly imagine a case where political structures extend far into everyday life, a nation in the midst of civil war or in the grips of a fascist state. One can also envision a case when race retreats to the personal dimension, as when the Irish became white in twentieth-century America.

References

Andersen, Margaret, and Patricia Hill Collins. 1994. *Race, class, and gender: An anthology.* Belmont, CA: Wadsworth.

Baca Zinn, Maxine, and Bonnie Thornton Dill. 1994. *Women of color in U.S. society.* Philadelphia: Temple University Press.

Bern, Sandra. 1993. *The lenses of gender.* New Haven, CT: Yale University Press.

Bianchi, Suzanne M., Melissa A. Milkie, Liana C. Sayer, and John P. Robinson. 2000. Is anyone doing the housework? Trends in the gender division of household labor. *Social Forces* 79 (1): 191–228.

Bielby, William T. 2000. Minimizing workplace gender and racial bias. *Contemporary Sociology* 29 (1): 120–29.

Blau, Peter. 1977. *Inequality and heterogeneity.* New York: Free Press.

Bonilla-Silva, Eduardo. 1997. Rethinking racism: Toward a structural interpretation. *American Sociological Review* 62 (3): 465–80.

Brines, Julie. 1994. Economic dependency, gender, and the division of labor at home. *American journal of Sociology* 100 (3): 652–88.

Burawoy, Michael. Forthcoming. Public sociologies contradictions, dilemmas and possibilities. *Social Forces.*

Burt, Ronald S. 1982. *Toward a structural theory of action.* New York: Academic Press.

Calhoun, Cheshire. 2000. *Feminism, the family, and the politics of the closet: Lesbian and gay displacement.* New York: Oxford University Press.

Collins, Patricia Hill. 1990. *Black feminist thought: Knowledge, consciousness, and the politics of empowerment.* New York: Routledge.

———. 1998. *Fighting words: Black women and the search for justice.* Minneapolis: University of Minnesota Press.

———. 2004. *Black sexual politics: African Americans, gender, and the new racism.* New York: Routledge.

Connell, R. W. 1987. *Gender and power: Society, the person, and sexual politics.* Stanford, CA: Stanford University Press.

———. 2002. *Gender: Short introductions.* Malden, MA: Blackwell.

Coverman, Shelley. 1985. Explaining husbands' participation in domestic labor. *Sociological Quarterly* 26 (1): 81–97.

England, Paula, and Irene Browne. 1992. Internalization and constraint in women's subordination. *Current Perspectives in Social Theory* 12:97–123.

Espiritu, Yen Le. 1997. *Asian American women and men: Labor, laws, and love.* Thousand Oaks, CA: Sage.

Fenstermaker Berk, Sarah. 1985. *The gender factory: The apportionment of work in American households.* New York: Plenum.

Ferree, Myra Marx. 1990. Beyond separate spheres: Feminism and family research. *Journal of Marriage and the Family* 53 (4): 866–84.

Ferree, Myra Marx, Judith Lorber, and Beth Hess. 1999. *Revisioning gender.* Thousand Oaks, CA: Sage.

Fox, Faulkner. 2003. *Dispatches from a not-so-perfect Life: On how I learned to love the house, the man, the child.* New York: Harmony Books.

Fuchs Epstein, Cynthia. 1988. *Deceptive distinctions: Sex, gender, and the social order.* New Haven, CT: Yale University Press.

Giddens, Anthony. 1984. *The constitution of society: Outline of the theory of structuration.* Berkeley: University of California Press.

Greenstein, Theodore N. 1996. Husbands' participation in domestic labor: Interactive effects of wives' and husbands' gender ideologies. *Journal of Marriage and the Family* 58: 585–95.

———. 2000. Economic dependence, gender, and the division of labor in the home: A replication and extension. *Journal of Marriage and the Family* 62 (2): 322–35.

Hanauer, Cathi. 2002. *The bitch in the house: 26 women tell the truth about sex, solitude, work, motherhood, and marriage.* New York: William Morrow.

Hochschild, Arlie. 1975. Inside the clockwork of male careers. In *Women and the power to change,* edited by Florence Howe. New York: McGraw Hill. Repr. in *The commercialization of intimate life.* Berkeley: University of California Press, 2003.

Kanter, Rosabeth. 1977. *Men and women of the corporation.* New York: Basic Books.

Lorber, Judith. 1994. *Paradoxes of gender.* New Haven, CT: Yale University Press.

Martin, Patricia. 2003. "Said and done" versus "saying and doing": Gendering practices, practicing gender at work. *Gender & Society* 17:342–66.

———. Forthcoming. Gender as a social institution. *Social Forces.*

Myers, Kristen A., Cynthia D. Anderson, and Barbara J. Risman, eds. 1998. *Feminist foundations: Toward transforming society.* Thousand Oaks, CA: Sage.

Pleck, Joseph H. 1985. *Working wives/working husbands.* Beverly Hills, CA: Sage.

Presser, Harriet B. 1994. Employment schedules among dual-earner spouses and the division of household labor by gender. *American Sociological Review* 59 (3): 348–64.

Reskin, Barbara. 1998. *The realities of affirmative action in employment.* Washington, DC: ASA.

———. 2000. The proximate causes of employment discrimination. *Contemporary Sociology* 29 (2): 319–28.

———. 2002. How did the poison get in Mr. Bartlett's stomach? Motives and mechanisms in explaining inequality. Presidential address given at the 97th annual meetings of the American Sociological Association, Chicago, August.

Rich, Adrienne. 1980. Compulsory heterosexuality and lesbian existence. *Signs: Journal of Women in Culture and Society* 5 (4): 631–60.

Ridgeway, Cecilia L. 1991. The social construction of status value: Gender and other nominal characteristics. *Social Forces* 70 (2): 367–86.

———. 1997. Interaction and the conservation of gender inequality: Considering employment. *American Sociological Review* 62 (2): 218–35.

———. 2001. Gender, status, and leadership. *Journal of Social Issues* 57 (4): 637–55.

Ridgeway, Cecilia L., and Shelley J. Correll. 2000. Limiting inequality through interaction: The end(s) of gender. *Contemporary Sociology* 29:110–20.

Ridgeway, Cecilia L., Kathy J. Kuipers, Elizabeth Heger Boyle, and Dawn T. Robinson. 1998. How do status beliefs develop? The role of resources and interactional experience. *American Sociological Review* 63:331–50.

Ridgeway, Cecilia L., and Lynn Smith-Lovin. 1999. The gender system and interaction. *Annual Review of Sociology* 25:191–216.

Risman, Barbara J. 1983. Necessity and the invention of mothering. Ph.D. diss, University of Washington.

———. 1987. Intimate relationships from a microstructural perspective: Mothering men. *Gender & Society* 1:6–32.

———. 1998. *Gender vertigo: American families in transition.* New Haven, CT: Yale University Press.

———. 2003. Valuing all flavors of feminist sociology. *Gender & Society* 17:659–63.

Risman, Barbara J., and Pepper Schwartz. 1989. *Gender in intimate relationships.* Belmont, CA: Wadsworth.

Robinson, John P., and Melissa A. Milkie. 1998. Back to the basics: Trends in and role determinants of women's attitudes toward housework. *Journal of Marriage and the Family* 60 (1): 205–18.

Rytina, Steve, Peter Blau, Jenny Blum, and Joseph Schwartz. 1988. Inequality and intermarriage: Paradox of motive and constraint. *Social Forces* 66:645–75.

Schwalbe, Michael, Sandra Godwin, Daphne Holden, Douglas Schrock, Shealy Thompson, and Michele Wolkomir. 2000. Generic processes in the reproduction of inequality: An interactionist analysis. *Social Forces* 79 (2): 419–52.

Scott, Joan Wallach. 1997. Comment on Hawkesworth's "Confounding Gender." *Signs: Journal of Women in Culture and Society* 22 (3): 697–702.

Shelton, Beth Anne. 1992. *Women, men and time: Gender differences in paid work, housework and leisure.* Westport, CT: Greenwood.

Sherwood, Jessica. 2004. Talk about country clubs: Ideology and the reproduction of privilege. Ph.D. diss., North Carolina State University.

Smelser, Neil J. 1988. Social structure. In *Handbook of sociology,* edited by Neil J. Smelser. Beverly Hills, CA: Sage.

Staples, Robert. 1990. Social inequality and Black sexual pathology: The essential relationship. *Black Scholar* 21 (3): 29–37.

Stombler, Mindy, and Patricia Yancey Martin. 1994. Bring women in, keeping women down: Fraternity "little sister" organizations. *Journal of Contemporary Ethnography* 23: 150–84.

Tilly, Charles. 1999. *Durable inequality.* Berkeley: University of California Press.

Twiggs, Joan E., Julia McQuillan, and Myra Marx Ferree. 1999. Meaning and measurement: Reconceptualizing measures of the division of household labor. *Journal of Marriage and the Family* 61 (3): 712–24.

Udry, J. Richard. 2000. Biological limits of gender construction. *American Sociological Review* 65:443–57.

West, Candace, and Don Zimmerman. 1987. Doing gender. *Gender & Society* 1: 125–51.

Williams, Christine. 1992. The glass escalator: Hidden advantages for men in the "female" professions. *Social Problems* 39:253–67.

Williams, Joan. 2000. *Unbending gender: Why family and work conflict and what to do about it*. New York: Oxford University Press.

Yoder, Janice. 1991. Rethinking tokenism. *Social Problems* 5:178–92.

Zimmer, Lynn. 1988. Tokenism and women in the workplace: The limits of gender-neutral theory. *Social Problems* 35:64–77.

Barbara J. Risman is Alumni Distinguished Research Professor of Sociology at North Carolina State University. She studies gender in intimate and family relationships. She is the author of Gender Vertigo: American Families in Transition *(1998, Yale University Press). She also edits* The Gender Lens *book series with Judith Howard and Joey Sprague, designed to transform the discipline of sociology by mainstreaming a gender perspective throughout the curriculum. She is past president of Sociologists for Women in Society and is currently co-chair of the Council on Contemporary Families. Her current research focuses on gender and sexual ideology among teenagers.*

25

We (Still) Need a Woman for the Job: The Warrior Woman, Feminism, and Cinema in the Digital Age

Lee-Jane Bennion-Nixon

Lee-Jane Bennion-Nixon is lecturer in the Film Program, Victoria University of Wellington and a filmmaker. Her PhD project explored the figure of the warrior woman in contemporary film and media and its use as a pedagogical tool. Her films include To the End *and* Back Again.

Recent developments in cinema show that we are in the midst of a shift to a digital future. The advances in computer generated imagery (CGI) have provided filmmakers with the potential to explore new and exciting worlds, characters, and narrative trajectories. Distribution formats and patterns are altering our engagement with cinema. The success of James Cameron's *Avatar* (2009) has resulted in a resurgence of interest in 3D technology as filmmakers attempt to create a more immersive viewing experience. However, despite these innovations and possibilities, the creative teams that make content are still rooted in a cultural world that has specific ideological limits. For example, while digital technology provides the capacity to manipulate gender identities, contemporary digital representations of women often seem to belong to an analogue world, as a discussion of the warrior woman will demonstrate.

The warrior woman can be understood as a representational figure who exemplifies and embodies a range of contested meanings about femininity, especially physically capable and resourceful women. Although the notion of a warrior-like woman has been around in our cultural imaginaries for some time, she has until recently been more an anomaly than an archetype.[1] Over the last decade the warrior woman has been visible in many places and across several genres.[2] Understandably, the warrior woman has become the focus of increasing academic attention. The concept of a heroic female figure is permeating our cultural imagination, as Hilary Neroni states, she has become 'an established presence in the universe of contemporary media.'[3] There is even

Reprinted by permission from *Senses of Cinema* 56, no. 3 (2010).

a compendium that highlights 187 different warrior women, with the authors proclaiming her 'a multifaceted symbol of 'womanhood'.[4] Moreover, the warrior woman is not confined to western popular culture. Anne Billson argues us that this kind of female figure can also be seen in Chinese action cinema, with action heroines who are "more than mere side kicks, girl-friends or sisters; they [are] heroines with a purpose, using their martial-arts skills to combat evil."[5]

The figure that I have designated as the 'warrior woman' has also been called a 'tough girl',[6] 'action girl',[7] 'feisty heroine',[8] 'violent femme'[9] and 'violent woman'.[10] What anchors this figure is her propensity towards violence. The warrior woman can also be recognised by the physical and/or mental strength she displays in the face of adversity. It is this combination of strength and tendency towards violence that makes her a distinct manifestation of 'woman-hood'. Some of the more familiar manifestations of the warrior woman include 'The Avenging Mother' of *The Long Kiss Goodnight* (1996), the 'English Lady-cum-Pirate' in the *Pirates of the Caribbean* trilogy (2003, 2006, 2007), the 'Avenging Bride' of Quentin Tarantino's *Kill Bill* films (2003/2004), the 'Rogue Spy' of *Salt* (2010), or the CGI alien Neytiri, the 'Heroic Lover' from *Avatar*.

The continuing emergence of new warrior women indicates that debates about representation within feminist film and media studies remain relevant. As Hilary Neroni comments, "it is rarer to see a woman who can't fight for herself, or help out in a fight, than one who can."[11] For example, the advertising tag line for *Elizabeth: The Golden Age* (2007) reads "Woman Warrior Queen." The film's trailer also depicts Elizabeth (Cate Blanchett) in full armour, this time riding a white horse and addressing her army as they prepare for the battle-field. This type of advertising strategy suggests that the notion of women as national warriors is widely understood by a general audience. The figure of a violent, fighting, brave, heroic woman is not only culturally legible, it is familiar. This representation of 'womanhood' high-lights changing ideas of what it means to be 'woman', marking a major shift in the way women can be portrayed in mainstream popular culture, and expanding the realms of what 'woman' can represent.[12]

The warrior woman also challenges our understanding of the conventions of gender representation. If, as Judith Halberstam argues, codes of masculinity conjure up "notions of power, legitimacy and privilege," thereby "naturalising" relations between men and power in our western society, then the warrior woman questions this process.[13] The warrior woman offers a more progressive idea of what it is to be heroic and female to the collective imagination. She is a dynamic representation of a female figure that combines masculine and feminine traits. She is also a site of contention over what can be regarded as 'acceptably female'. The female heroism of the warrior woman is both masculine and feminine which subverts cultural tendencies to represent gender categories in rigid, binary terms. I want to suggest that she signifies a 'potent fusion'[14] between feminine and masculine attributes in a female sexed body. She is recognizably female, even maternal, yet she is also a highly effective 'sol-dier' whose adept use of weaponry and technology or capacity for strategy and leadership is as good as any man's. Furthermore, her feminine qualities do not inhibit her fighting prowess in any way, while her masculine traits do not diminish her humanity.

The warrior woman is, therefore, a heroic female figure that embodies and represents a hybridised gender identity that transcends conventional gender identities and iconography. This suggests that this apparently progressive figure of womanhood from the pre-digital age could provide the basis for extraordinary digital women to emerge. One such figure might have been Neytiri in *Avatar*, who I will discuss shortly. The director of *Avatar*, James Cameron, is a notable figure in the screen history of the warrior woman because his previous films included two memorable examples: Sarah Connor (Linda Hamilton) in *The Terminator* (1984) and *Terminator 2: Judgment Day* (1991), and Ellen Ripley (Sigourney Weaver) in *Aliens* (1986). The portrayal of Sarah Connor pushed the limits of what 'motherhood' had been portrayed as. Starting out as a terrified waitress in the first film, she becomes a fully fledged warrior woman in the sequel as she tries to protect her son from futuristic robotic assassins. In *Terminator 2* her muscular, yet feminine body points to a notion of motherhood that is active and unrestrained by gender conventions.[15] In *Aliens* Cameron transformed the somewhat compromised female protagonist of *Alien* (1979) into an explicitly feminist figure.[16] Judith Newton comments on Ripley in *Alien* that, far from being a feminist hero, she is 'robbed of radical thrust' because the narrative attributes to her stereotypical feminine characteristics; 'impulsive, nurturing, and sexually desirable'.[17] Cameron's version of Ripley merged masculine aggression with 'mothering' instincts to overcome the alien threat but also to protect Newt, a young female survivor. Ripley faces her mirror image—the monstrous alien 'queen'—and triumphs.[18]

Given Cameron's interest in strong female characters, one might have hoped that Neytiri would signify a new phase in the warrior woman's trajectory. Despite the opportunity for aesthetic innovation, Cameron has created a conventional, even stereotypical, Hollywood leading lady. Neytiri has more in common with Rose from *Titanic* (1997) than Sarah Connor, Ellen Ripley, or Lindsay Brigman (Mary Elizabeth Mastrantonio) in *The Abyss* (1989). An attractive and exotic figure, Neytiri fulfils the role of love interest and indigenous beauty. Although she is presented as a warrior within the context of the narrative, her story arc recalls figures such as Pocahontas in the eponymous Disney film. Neytiri's concerns are subordinate to those of the protagonist Jake (Sam Worthington); she is depicted as scantily clad with animal-like qualities. As such, she conforms to the racist stereotype of the 'dusky maiden'.

The role played by digital technology in this process is important. Like many of the characters in *Avatar*, Neytiri was created through the digital manipulation of the performance of a live actor via motion capture technology. In the case of Neytiri, Zoe Saldana, known for her work in *Pirates of the Caribbean: The Curse of the Black Pearl* (2003) and *Star Trek* (2009) provided the original 'performance'. Saldana's voice was subsequently synchronised with the digitally projected body of Neytiri. This combination (arguably) provided the character with an authenticity because she seems grounded in the 'real'. Of course, all of Neytiri's physical features, the manner in which her digital body moved through space, and how 'she' interacted with her environment and displayed emotional responses was developed through the effort of a large team of CGI artists. The result is a sexual and racial stereotype, but one which has been naturalised by the actor's corporeal presence. However, digitalisation functions differently within the film's narrative context because it enables the 'real' or 'human' Jake to adopt an artificial persona or avatar which provides him with the opportunity to overcome his disability. *His* story arc is a fantasy of transcendence with erotic fulfillment.

The representation of gender and race in *Avatar* is hardly surprising because it is, after all, a mainstream Hollywood film. However, its representations remind us that the struggles over representation continue irrespective of the medium, and that rhetoric about the creative freedom remains just that, rhetoric. Such claims always carry an ideological dimension. In this respect, the warrior woman has a vital role to play in the ongoing battle over gender and representation. Her various qualities can be read as a metaphor for the different roles women occupy in contemporary society—mother, worker, breadwinner, family head—or problems they face: discrimination, violence, inequality and so on. The warrior woman also embodies the very notion of struggle through her hands on, action packed, physically demanding existence. She is a reminder, a challenge, and a call to arms, an empowered figure that projects a representation of 'womanhood' who is more than capable of being heroic no matter what comes her way.

The proliferation of the warrior woman can also be regarded as an index of feminist contestations of popular culture and gender identity. Following post-feminism, it is perhaps fashionable to believe that myth that empowerment for women has been achieved, and that feminism is defunct. In her exploration of feminism's position in the so-called post-feminist period, Angela McRobbie argues that while elements of feminism have been incorporated into political and institutional life, this has been only a nominal form of empowerment that seeks to appease women rather than remove serious inequalities faced by them.[19] As Joanne Hollows suggests, 'This 'progress' can never be assumed but is still a site of struggle, and rights which have been won are not guaranteed'.[20] Diane Negra argues similarly that 'post-feminism continually hypes empowerment, but a closer examination of popular culture reveals a sense of stern disapproval and judgment for any manifestations of 'off-script' femininity'.[21] She asserts that post-feminism in popular culture is marked by an idealisation of traditional femininities that promote 'homemaker chic', and warns that 'post-feminism offers the pleasure and comfort of (re)claiming an identity uncomplicated by gender politics, postmodernism, or institutional critique.[22]

Tina Chanter claims that feminists need to "take a lead in forging a new politics and ethics, new ways of relating to one another, both among women and between men and women."[23] If McRobbie and Negra are correct in their assessments that feminism in contemporary popular culture is in some ways outmoded, then this points to the need for innovative and effective action so that 'progress' does not unravel, and the gains of previous struggles are maintained. The warrior woman can play a dynamic role in this process. While the warrior woman's progressiveness is constrained by her combination of binary gender characteristics, she has the capacity to reveal the hierarchical dimensions of gender in contemporary society and culture. The hybridity, fluidity and frequent changes and manifestations associated with this figure all gesture towards the artifice of gender positions and the possibilities of change.

Chanter reminds us that merely reversing the existing power dynamics of masculine and feminine roles is not an adequate project for feminism; becoming militant and 'calling all the shots' is not the answer.[24] However, calling some of the *shoots* might be a good place to start in the era of digital cinema. Despite all of the collaborative work that went into *Avatar*, it is worth remembering that not only is it the vision of one man, but that, if anecdotal evidence is anything to go by, James Cameron was responsible for much of the minutiae of the film. There is little doubt that he played Pygmalion to Saldana's Neytiri. One wonders, for example, what Neytiri (or, indeed, the film as a whole) might have been like if it had been directed by, say, Cameron's ex-wife and Oscar rival, Kathryn Bigelow. While Bigelow has denied being a feminist, her films have often displayed an interest in reworking the conventions of gender and genre—*Blue Steel* (1989), *Point Break* (1991) and *Strange Days* (1995) for example.

If we are going to surpass the limits of analogue representation in digital technology, then we will need to do more than manipulate pixels. We need to put *thought* itself into flux. At a time when many women, especially young women, do not see the need for a feminist politics, the warrior woman can function as a means to stimulate debates around the representation of gender from a feminist perspective. However, she is only a figure or a tool, one strategy for creating and sustaining engagement. Digital technology is increasingly affordable: camera equipment and special effects packages are now reasonably accessible, and animation software may become so in the near future. It is foreseeable that we can move beyond the creative hierarchies that structure the production of blockbusters towards the democratisation of the moving image.

In this respect it is worth exploring Lara Croft's potential as a digital woman because she indicates how the figure of the warrior woman can operate as a site of complex negotiations. Croft is an unusual, hybrid creature who first appeared in the 1990s as a computer generated character created by a British computer game designer. Lara is an adventurer and pursues traditionally masculine goals of finding hidden artifacts and buried treasure—she is a re-imagining of the male adventurer figure like Indiana Jones. Lara is physically strong, an excellent fighter, and a great markswoman. She can drive cars, ride motorcycles and handle all manner of vehicles. Her exceptional gymnastic abilities enable her to climb and negotiate terrain that is normally impassable. Since her first manifestation Lara Croft has become an iconic figure spanning video games, comic books and films. While the casting and performance of Angelina Jolie as Lara in the two *Tomb Raider* films (2001, 2003) have provided a recognisable cinematic version of Croft, Lara remains a popular and fluid cultural figure.

Maja Mikula claims that Lara Croft's appeal for her fans lies precisely in the open or flexible quality of the character: "She is drag queen and female automaton, dominatrix and queer babe, at the same time, in different ways, for different audiences."[25] Like Lara Croft, all warrior women are sites of negotiated meanings; their social and cultural meanings are difficult to fix. We can draw parallels between the ability to manipulate digital imagery and the pliable, even slippery qualities of the warrior woman. Mikula contends that this makes Lara Croft an empty sign.[26]

However, while the warrior woman is a shape-shifter, Croft's multiple presences demonstrate, the warrior woman can circulate within culture as a discursive conversation about what can potentially be portrayed and identified as female. Lara Croft is a representation of femininity that is flexible and adaptable for audiences, a site of contested negotiations that gives her subversive potential. Mikula acknowledges that different gamers view Lara Croft in a variety of ways. Some women express how great it is to 'be' Lara—adventurous, strong and independent—whilst male gamers talk of controlling Lara.[27] Some feminist activists, Mikula notes, have even used her image in performances as a political sign of gender bending.[28] Croft is therefore a playful figure that can, to some degree, interact with her fans. It does not matter that as a filmic image she has been attached to a certain star body, she remains malleable according to the wants, needs and/or desires of her fans, as well as where and in what way she appears. This flexibility also acts as a metaphor for a feminist politics of digital representation. The digital (warrior) woman does not float freely above or beyond gender: each of her appearances is a performance of gender identity and representation that can be traced and analysed, especially in terms of the cinematic and televisual warrior women who have preceded her.

This article has been peer reviewed.

Notes

1. Hilary Neroni traces her back to early cinema in *The Violent Woman: Femininity, Narrative, and Violence in Contemporary American Cinema* (Albany: State University of New York Press, 2005).

2. *ibid.*

3. *ibid*, p. 36.

4. Dominique Mainon and James Ursini, *The Modern Amazons: Warrior Women On-Screen* (New Jersey: Limelight Editions, 2006), p. 1. Although this book was published in 2006, there is already a need for a revised version.

5. Anne Billson, *Buffy the Vampire Slayer* (London: BFI Publishing, 2005), p. 12.

6. Sherrie A. Inness, *Tough Girls: Women Warriors and Wonder Women in Popular Culture* (University of Pennsylvania Press, 1999).

7. Bill Osgerby and Anna Gough-Yates, *Action TV: Tough-Guys, Smooth Operators and Foxy Chicks* (London and New York: Routledge, 2001).

8. Yvonne Tasker, *Working Girls: Gender and Sexuality in Popular Cinema* (London and New York: Routledge, 1998).

9. Stephanie Mencimer, *Washington Monthly*, (September, 2001).

10. Hilary Neroni, *The Violent Woman: Femininity, Narrative, and Violence in Contemporary American Cinema* (Albany: State University of New York Press, 2005).

11. *ibid*. p. 38.

12. However, not all examples of the warrior woman are clearly feminist, as the recent reworking of the television program Nikita demonstrates. See http://www.wired.com/ underwire/2010/09/nikita/?utm_source=feedburner&utm_medium=feed&utm

_campaign=Feed%3A+wired%2Findex+%28Wired%3A+Index+3+%28Top+Stories +2%29%29.

13. Judith Halberstam, *Female Masculinity* (Durham and London: Duke University Press, 1998), p. 2.

14. Donna Haraway, 'A Cyborg Manifesto: Science, Technology, and Socialist-Feminism in the Late Twentieth Century,' in *Simians, Cyborgs and Women: The Reinvention of Nature* (New York & London: Routledge, 1991), p. 154.

15. Yvonne Tasker, *Spectacular Bodies: Gender Genre and the Action Cinema* (London & New York: Routledge, 1993). The continuing cultural interest in the figure of Sarah Connor was demonstrated by the production of the television series *Terminator: The Sarah Connor Chronicles* (2008–2009).

16. For example, Judith Newton argues that in *Alien* Ripley is "robbed of radical thrust" because of her stereotypical feminine traits, while Sherrie Inness suggests that the ending of *Alien* resexualises Ripley because she is seen undressing as she prepares for hibernation. See Judith Newton, 'Feminism and Anxiety, in Alien', *Alien Zone: Cultural Theory and Contemporary Science Fiction Cinema*, A. Kuhn (ed.), (London: Verso, 1990), p. 87, and Sherrie Inness, *Tough Girls: Women Warriors and Wonder Women in Popular Culture*, (Pennsylvania: University of Pennsylvania Press, 1999), p. 107.

17. Judith Newton, 'Feminism and Anxiety in Alien', *Alien Zone: Cultural Theory and Contemporary Science Fiction Cinema*, A. Kuhn (ed.), (London: Verso, 1990), p. 87.

18. For feminist critics this representation is not without it's issues and numerous work has been written on Ripley, most notably Barbra Creed, *The Monstrous-Feminine: Film, Feminism, Psychoanaylsis* (London & New York: Routledge, 1993), pp. 16–30. However, for these purposes I have kept my discussion brief.

19. Angela McRobbie, *The Aftermath of Feminism: Gender, Culture and Social Change* (Los Angeles & London: Sage, 2009).

20. Joanne Hollows, and Stacy Gillis, (eds.), *Feminism, Domesticity and Popular Culture*, New York: Routledge, 2009.

21. Diane Negra, *What A Girl Wants: Fantasizing the Reclamation of Self in Postfeminism*, (London & New York: 2009), p. 152.

22. *ibid.* p. 2.

23. Tina Chanter, *Gender: Key Concepts in Philosophy* (London: Continuum, 2009), p. 127.

24. *ibid.*

25. Maja Mikula, 'Gender and Videogames: the political valency of Lara Croft', *Continuum: Journal of Media & Cultural Studies*, (Vol. 17, Number 1, pp. 79–87(9), 2003), pp. 84–85.

26. *ibid.* p. 84.

27. *ibid.* p. 81.

28. *ibid.* p. 85.

26

Sexual Orientations in Perspective

Linda D. Garnets

This article presents a new paradigm for understanding the complexity of human sexual, affectional, and erotic attractions—commonly known as sexual orientation. This new paradigm recognizes that there is great diversity among sexual orientations, erotic and emotional attractions, behaviors, and identities and that there are complex inter-relations among these dimensions. Sexual orientation is determined by multiple influences, including a wide range of sociocultural factors. The development of sexual orientation is arrived at through multiple pathways. Individuals with the same sexual orientation may have little else in common. Thus, a model of sexual orientation is presented that is based on multiplicity, not sameness, and that examines the overlapping identities and statuses of culture, gender, age, race, ethnicity, class, disability, and sexuality.

◆ *sexual orientation* ◆ *gay* ◆ *lesbian* ◆ *bisexual* ◆ *heterosexual*
◆ *gender* ◆ *sexuality* ◆ *cultural diversity* ◆ *racial/ethnic identity*

This article presents a new conceptual paradigm that analyzes the complexity of human sexual, affectional, and erotic attractions—commonly known as sexual orientation. This paradigm synthesizes findings from the growing base of scientific research on gender, sexuality, and sexual orientation conducted in many fields over the past 30 years. Plural terms such as *sexualities* and *sexual orientations* are used to signal the importance of encompassing the full range of people's desires, love, and relationships. In addition, throughout the article, sometimes *LGB* is used as a shorthand term for lesbian/gay/ bisexual. Four issues are of central importance to the new paradigm: (a) conceptualization of sexual orientations; (b) development of sexual orientations; (c) new perspectives on gender and sexual orientations; and (d) convergences, divergences, and intersections of sexual orientation with other aspects of human diversity.

Cultural Diversity and Ethnic Minority Psychology Vol. 8, No. 2, 115–129
Copyright 2002 by the Educational Publishing Foundation 1099-9809/02/$5.00
DOI: 10.1037//1099-9809.8.2.115

Conceptualization of Sexual Orientations

How should sexual orientation be conceptualized? An old paradigm put people into rigid categories of heterosexual versus homosexual. In contrast, scientific research points to a new continuous, multidimensional conceptualization of sexual orientation. Four features of the old and new models highlight how the new paradigm advances our understanding.

First, the old paradigm assumed that individuals can be readily categorized as heterosexual or homosexual. In other words, it viewed sexual orientation as a dichotomous construct that exists only in two opposite, discrete categories. In fact, human experience rarely fits either/or categories. For example, the old paradigm either ignored or denied the existence of bisexuality or viewed bisexuality as a transitory or transitional state. As one bisexual man expressed it: "I'm simply trying to live a both/and life in an either/or world" (Bennett, 1992, p. 205).

Bisexuality challenges this either/or assumption that sexual orientation comes in only two mutually exclusive categories. Recent research has documented the existence of bisexuals and examined the diverse ways that bisexual men and women construct their sexual identity and relationships (Fox, 1996; Rust, 2000). This, in turn, has shown that sexual orientation is not reducible to bipolar dichotomies.

In contrast, the new paradigm conceptualizes sexual orientations as flexible, complex, and multifaceted. Sexual orientation reflects the diversity of sexual, affectional, and erotic attractions and love toward persons of the same gender, other gender, or both genders. In the new paradigm, attraction to females and attraction to males are conceptualized as two separate and independent dimensions. An individual's sexual orientation reflects the combination of his or her location on each of these dimensions. The combinations of these independent dimensions, in turn, reflect a spectrum of distinct sexual orientations that differ in degree and intensity (Garnets & Kimmel, 1991; Rothblum, 2000). This model also makes it possible to view bisexuality as an identity.

Second, the old paradigm assumed that sexual behavior is the defining feature of a person's sexual orientation. In contrast, research has found that sexual orientations encompass not only sexual behavior but also erotic–affectional behaviors and fantasies, emotional attachments, self-identification, and current relationship status. In fact, sexual behavior by itself is not always a good indicator of a person's sexual orientation. For example, a woman may identify as lesbian or bisexual but not engage in same-gender sexual behavior. Or an individual may engage in sexual acts without self-identifying as a member of a particular sexual orientation. In fact, many more people engage in same-gender sexual behavior than identify as gay, lesbian, or bisexual (Rothblum, 2000). Each individual has a distinctive combination of erotic and affectional feelings, fantasies, activities, and relationships that is as unique as one's fingerprint or voiceprint. Money (1987) termed this template a *lovemap*. For example, some men view themselves as heterosexual but recognize strong attractions to other men. Many middle-aged lesbians had sexual relationships with men in their youth. Two people with similar personal histories may define their sexuality differently.

Third, the old paradigm assumed that there is congruence among sexual identity, behavior, and desire. Some individuals do report complete consistency: A woman might identify as lesbian, be attracted exclusively to women, and be sex partners with women only. However, research has shown that sexual activity, fantasy, and identity are not always congruent (Baumeister, 2000; Diamant, Schuster, McGuigan, & Lever, 1999). Exceptions are common. For example, a woman who identifies as a bisexual might never develop a strong attraction to a man. A man who identifies as gay might have been married and had a strong attraction to a woman. For some women, explicit sexuality is not particularly important; emotional bonding with a partner is what counts. A heterosexual man may use homoerotic fantasies when having sex with his female partner. A woman may experience strong attractions to both men and women but identify as heterosexual rather than bisexual. Or a man may have strong sexual desires without self-identifying as a member of a specific sexual orientation.

Fourth, the old paradigm asserted that sexual orientation is an enduring disposition that forms at an early age and is then fixed and unchanging. New empirical findings present a very different picture. Sexual development appears to be potentially fluid and changeable over time (Peplau & Garnets, 2000). Its pattern varies across social contexts and cultures. Identification as bisexual, gay, lesbian, or heterosexual and actual behavior can vary over time. It need not be the same at age 15, 25, 45, or 70. There is considerable evidence, for example, that attractions toward both women and men change over time and characterize the experience of some men and women who may, or may not, call themselves bisexual (Rust, 2000). For example, women who have had exclusively heterosexual experiences may develop an attraction to other women at any time in their lives, and vice versa (Blumstein & Schwartz, 1976; Kitzinger & Wilkinson, 1995). Such fluidity is more characteristic of women than men (Baumeister, 2000; Diamond, 1998; Laumann, Gagnon, Michael, & Michaels, 1994; Weinberg, Willliams, & Pryor, 1994). It is important to emphasize that the capacity for erotic fluidity does not mean that most men or women will actually exhibit significant change over time. The key point is that some people experience variation and change in their lovemap.

Development of Sexual Orientations

Until recently, those interested in the development of sexual orientation asked why some people become gay or lesbian. Today's new paradigm expands this question to ask what leads all individuals—heterosexual as well as LGB—to form a particular sexual orientation.

Biological Antecedents

Despite the popularity of ideas about gay brains and gay genes, the actual scientific evidence for biological influences on sexual orientation in humans is quite limited and has generally been based only on studies of men. For example, consider the work attempting to identify differences in brain structures between heterosexuals and homosexuals. To date, this research is based on a total of four studies, each with different findings (Allen & Gorski, 1992; Allen, Hines, Shryne, & Gorski, 1989; LeVay, 1991; Swaab & Hofman, 1990), and all studying gay men. This research has been widely reported in the popular press as the "discovery of a gay brain." In the scientific community, however, the replicability of these findings has been questioned and their interpretations remain controversial (Byne, 1995). This fact alone should warrant caution in placing too much weight on biological influences for individuals.

Further, there appear to be important sex differences in potential biological influences. Current findings suggest that male homosexuality may be more strongly linked to genetic or other biological determinants (Bailey, 1995; Baumeister, 2000; Peplau & Garnets, 2000). As one of many possible examples, there is some evidence of a potential genetic linkage for sexual orientation in men but not in women (Bailey, Pillard, Neale, & Agyei, 1993; Hamer, Magnuson, Hu, & Pattatucci, 1993; Hu et al., 1995). Available evidence suggests that biological factors play only a minor and indirect role in the development of women's sexual orientation, and it is therefore unwise to generalize from the male to the female situation (Schneider, 2001; Veniegas & Conley, 2000).

Most scientists now agree that human behavior invariably reflects both biological and environmental or experiential factors. In other words, there is no biological influence—be it a gene or prenatal hormones— that flips a switch and changes an individual's sexual orientation from heterosexual to homosexual. So, whatever possible influence hormones and genes may have on the development of human sexual orientation, they will invariably be indirect and strongly influenced by the social environment.

Childhood Antecedents

It is often believed that sexual orientation is strongly influenced by early childhood experiences. Empirical research has not supported this view. Efforts to verify psychoanalytic theories about the family history antecedents of sexual orientation have failed (Bell, Weinberg, & Hammersmith, 1981; Downey & Friedman, 1988; Magee & Miller, 1997). Furthermore, the sexual orientation of parents appears to have little impact on the sexual orientation of their children: Most lesbians and gay men were raised by heterosexual parents, and most children raised by gay or lesbian parents become heterosexual adults (Bailey & Dawood, 1998; Patterson, 1997). A recent analysis by Stacey and Biblarz (2001) reviewed 21 studies on this topic and found that more children from gay or lesbian households said they had considered a same-gender relationship, but they were not statistically more likely to identify themselves as lesbian, gay, or bisexual.

As with biological antecedents, childhood experiences appear to have stronger and more lasting effects on male than female sexuality (Baumeister, 2000; Veniegas & Conley, 2000). For example, the correlation between adult sexual orientation and retrospective reports of childhood gender nonconformity is significantly higher among men than among women (Bailey & Zucker, 1995; Peplau, Spalding, Conley, & Veniegas, 1999). Moreover, available empirical research has so far failed to identify events or activities that predictably point a girl in U.S. culture on the path toward lesbian or bisexual attractions (Bohan, 1996).

Multiple Causal Factors and Multiple Pathways to the Development of Sexual Orientations

Although some might appreciate the simplicity of identifying the "gay gene" or a single formative experience that leads one person to be heterosexual and another to be lesbian, gay, or bisexual, reality is far more complex. Recent research suggests sexual orientation is multiply determined by many influences (Peplau & Garnets, 2000). No single factor reliably predicts whether a man or a woman will embark on a path toward heterosexuality, homosexuality, or bisexuality or some other pattern. For example, some youthful tomboys who like so-called masculine games and activities grow up to become lesbians, but many become heterosexuals (Peplau et al., 1999). Some gender-nonconforming boys grow up to be bisexual or heterosexual—many may remain gender nonconforming men as adults.

In addition, there are multiple developmental pathways that lead to similar outcomes (Diamond & Savin-Williams, 2000; Savin-Williams, 1998). Just as people become psychotherapists through multiple pathways and for diverse personal reasons, so too people may adopt their sexual orientations and identities through different developmental trajectories. Also, men and women may be drawn to particular orientations and identities for different reasons. Knowing how some people label their sexual identity does not necessarily inform us about the patterns of their life experiences or the nature of their current erotic behavior, thoughts, and feelings (Peplau & Garnets, 2000).

The new paradigm views the development of sexual identities as diverse and complex. Instead of a single step-by-step sequence, development may be nonlinear (Rust, 1996a). Research has challenged stage models that hypothesized a linear process involving a specific sequence of steps moving toward the establishment of a stable identity as lesbian or gay. Instead, research has found that many individuals do not follow the steps outlined in these models (Diamond, 2000; Savin-Williams & Diamond, 2000; Weinberg et al., 1994). For example, Diamond (1998, 2000) studied the sexual attractions, behaviors, and identities of sexual minority youths over a 2-year period. Nearly 40% of participants reported having undergone changes in their sexual attractions that they did not attribute to changes in awareness. Furthermore, 50% of the young women had changed their identity label more than once since first relinquishing their heterosexual identity. The new paradigm recognizes the highly individualized and personal process of arriving at a sexual identity for each person.

Sexual Prejudice

The developmental experiences of LGB individuals must be understood in the context of widespread prejudice against sexual minorities in U.S. society. Sexual prejudice, according to Herek (2000), refers to "negative attitudes toward an individual because of her or his sexual orientation . . . . It is used to characterize heterosexuals' negative attitudes toward (a) homosexual behavior; (b) people with a homosexual or bisexual orientation; and (c) communities of gay, lesbian, and bisexual people" (p. 19). A related concept is heterosexism, which refers to the belief that heterosexuality is the only acceptable sexual orientation. Any nonheterosexual form of behavior, identity, relationship, or community is denied, denigrated, and stigmatized (Herek, 1990). Heterosexism serves to legitimize both individual and institutional prejudice and discrimination. For example, a common, recurrent issue for many LGBs is that when one's partner is dying, some hospitals only let the other partner see the patient when she or he pretends to be a sister or brother. Lesbian, gay, and bisexual partners are often not considered "immediate family" by the hospital's visitation rules.

Bisexual men and women often encounter negative attitudes from heterosexuals and homosexuals, a form of prejudice called *monosexism* (Eliason, 1997; Istvan, 1983; Ochs, 1996). Examples include the belief that bisexuality does not exist, bisexuals are promiscuous, and the pressure that bisexuals experience to identify as either heterosexual or gay/lesbian (Spalding & Peplau, 1997). On the one hand, they may be seen as trying to avoid the stigma of being homosexual; on the other hand, they may be viewed as being less trustworthy than a heterosexual (Rust, 1993).

New Perspectives on Gender and Sexual Orientation

A growing body of research on gender and sexuality indicates that there may be important differences between lesbians and gay men (Garnets & Peplau, 2000). Empirical findings strongly suggest that patterns of sexual thoughts, behaviors, and attractions appear to be strongly linked to gender but not to sexual orientation (Baldwin & Baldwin, 1997; DeLamater, 1987; Diamond & Savin-Williams, 2000; Ellis & Symons, 1990; Garnets & Kimmel, 1993; Hatfield, Sprecher, Pillemer, Greenberger, & Wexler, 1989; Keating & Over, 1990; Oliver & Hyde, 1993; Paroski, 1987; Sprecher & McKinney, 1993). For example, gay men and lesbians bring to love relationships many of the same expectations, values, and interests as heterosexuals of the same gender (Garnets & Kimmel, 1991; Klinkenberg & Rose, 1994). These similarities among men and similarities among women are currently recognized as based on some combination of biology, gender socialization, and social status.

Regardless of sexual orientation, there are gender differences between the sexualities of women and men. Girls and women tend to have a relational or partner-centered orientation to sexuality, and boys and men tend to have a recreational or body-centered orientation (Baldwin & Baldwin, 1997; Peplau, 2001; Weinberg et al., 1994). For example, Regan and Berscheid (1996, p. 116) asked young heterosexual adults, "What is sexual desire?" These comments are illustrative.

Man: "Sexual desire is wanting someone . . . in a physical manner. No strings attached. Just for uninhibited sexual intercourse."
Woman: "Sexual desire is the longing to be emotionally intimate and to express love for another person."

Parallel responses were found among a sample of gay men and lesbians. A lesbian in Sears' (1989) study defined a homosexual as a person who "has intimate love for a person of the same sex." A gay man in the study defined a homosexual as "someone who has sex with the same sex." Of course, not everyone fits exclusively into their gender pattern all of the time.

A few other research examples highlight this point. In a study comparing gay/lesbian and heterosexual young adults, Bailey, Gaulin, Agyei, and Gladue (1994) found male–female differences on seven aspects of "mating psychology," including an interest in uncommitted sex, frequency of causal sex, and the importance of the partner's physical attractiveness, youth, or status. In contrast, lesbian and heterosexual women as well as gay men and heterosexual men were indistinguishable on most measures.

In another comparative study of heterosexual and homosexual single and cohabiting men, Guido (1981) found that there were relatively few differences in the masturbation and sexual fantasies among these groups. The most commonly reported masturbation fantasy themes were of "unknown people or situation" and "past sexual experiences." High amounts of sexual fantasies were found to be correlated with high amounts of sexual behaviors. In contrast, both lesbian and heterosexual sexual fantasies more commonly include a familiar partner, affection, and commitment and describe the setting for the sexual encounter (Blumstein & Schwartz, 1989; Ellis & Symons, 1990; Vetere, 1983).

Among both heterosexuals and homosexuals, males report a significantly greater numbers of sex partners than do females (e.g., Bell & Weinberg, 1978; Laumann et al., 1994; Oliver & Hyde, 1993). For example, Paroski (1987) found that 95% of gay men compared with 16% of lesbians learned about homosexuality through sexual encounters. Similarly, he reported that 81% of males and 31% of females visited locations thought or known to be gay or lesbian (many of these places, such as public rest rooms, are used by men for sexual purposes). In sum, the available data indicate that gender appears to be more powerful than sexual orientation in influencing men and women's sexualities.

Recent research has also questioned the role that gender plays in partner choice. In particular, data about bisexual men and women challenge the old view that gender is the primary criterion for selecting a sexual or romantic partner. The findings suggest that bisexuals seem to be less restricted by gender in their sexual and affectional attraction than heterosexuals, gay men, or lesbians. They appear to attend more to characteristics of the person than to his or her gender. One woman describes it this way: "I've tried to define myself using labels of lesbian, straight, bisexual, and I didn't feel that any of them were mine. I think of it in terms of people I could love, not sexes I could love" (Rosenbaum & Sanford, 1998, p. 236). The central point is that for many people bisexuality is not a combination of attractions to women and men but rather an attraction to individuals regardless of their gender (Rust, 2000).

In other words, neither biological sex nor socially defined gender is necessarily the basis for attraction to a partner. For example, a bisexual woman currently in a monogamous relationship with another woman explained, "My sexual orientation is toward creative people of color who can cook" (Som, 1991, p. 142). There are many other dimensions along which the sexual activity of one person can be differentiated from that of another besides the gender of object choice (Sedgwik, 1990).

Recent research has also brought to light problems inherent in narrow and rigid societal dichotomous definitions of gender (Fausto-Sterling, 1993; Lorber, 1996; Rust, 2000). Just what does it mean to be a "man" or to be a "woman"? Some people view their own gender as defying simplistic bimodal categories of male versus female and of masculine versus feminine (Gainor, 2000; Rothblum, 2000). *Transgendered* is a broad term used today to describe the continuum of individuals whose gender identity and gendered behavior do not correspond with their biological sex. As one woman explains, "Some of us who have been raised as women may choose to dress in ways that men customarily dress. We may cut our hair very short . . . We may bind our breasts or take male hormones. Some of us live our public lives as women and our private lives as men, or vice versa" (Sanford, 1998, p. 181). It is important to emphasize that there is no inherent connection between being transgendered and sexual orientation. Transgendered people may be gay, bisexual, or heterosexual—or attracted primarily to other transgendered people. Today, a movement among transgendered individuals is working to redefine their experiences as a form of gender nonconformity, not a form of psychopathology (Dean et al., 2000; Gainor, 2000).

In finding a better framework for thinking about gender, it is important to look at how other cultures have incorporated gender diversity into their traditions. Native American notions of sexuality and gender, for example, tend to be conceptualized very differently from Euro American ones. Tafoya (1997) reported that of the approximately 250 Native languages still spoken in the United States, at least 168 have been identified as having terms for people who are not considered male or female. These cross-gender individuals are often viewed as blessed, possessing both a male and a female spirit, as *two-spirited*. The role is one of a spiritual/social identity for some Native American people, rather than a psychosexual identity. Tafoya (1997) suggested that a useful way to compare these views would be to

> see European concepts of gender and sexuality as being bipolar opposites, or different ends of the same stick. One is either/or male or female, gay or straight. Native American concepts usually prefer circles to lines. If one takes the line of male/female, gay/straight, and bends it into a circle, there are an infinite number of points. Just so, there are theoretically an infinite number of possible points of gender and sexual identity for an individual that can shift and differ over time and location. (pp. 7–8)

The concept of "two-spirited" people among some Native Americans is an excellent example of ways other cultures can provide models of gender diversity that may be more useful than the dominant Western models.

Convergences, Divergences, and Intersections with Sexual Orientation and Other Aspects of Human Diversity

The sexual minority community encompasses great diversity. Lesbians, gay men, and bisexuals are young and old, rich and poor, physically able and challenged. They live in urban centers and rural areas and come from all racial and ethnic groups. Three facets of the relationship between sexual minorities and other minority groups are discussed: (a) convergences and similarities between sexual and other minority groups, (b) divergences or the distinctive challenges for sexual minorities, and (c) intersections of sexual minorities with race/ethnicity.

Convergences

As a stigmatized minority group, lesbians, bisexuals, and gay men share certain elements in common with other minority groups. Five important issues, discussed below, affect not only LGB individuals but also individuals from many other social groups, including racial and ethnic minorities, individuals from different class backgrounds, women, and those with disabilities.

STEREOTYPES. Individuals from all of these groups confront stereotypes based on group membership. For example, just as stereotypes have often depicted racial minorities as hypersexual "breeders," so too stereotypes of homosexuals have also emphasized sexuality. In the public eye, homosexuals are first and foremost interested in sex rather than love or commitment. The stereotype is particularly negative about gay men, who are seen as constantly "on the cruise," ready to prey on children and straight men (Tinney, 1986).

DISCRIMINATION. A second parallel is discrimination—and the substantial barriers that it creates to equal opportunities and resources for members of minority groups. Just as ethnic minorities have faced discrimination in employment and housing, so have LGBs. Just as laws once prevented marriages that crossed racial lines, today gays and lesbians are prevented from marrying partners deemed to be of the "wrong" sex. Likewise, discrimination against sexual minorities may mean that they lose their jobs, lose custody of their children, face eviction from their homes, and are alienated from and rejected by their families, friends, and coworkers (D'Augelli & Garnets, 1995). Federal civil rights laws do not apply to sexual orientation, so that sexual minorities are not a protected category against discrimination.

HOSTILITY AND VIOLENCE. Members of all these groups are vulnerable to acts of hostility and violence. These may range from the daily hassles of hearing jokes or derogatory names to extreme acts of personal violence and hate crimes. Reports of hate crimes based on race/ethnicity, immigrant status, gender, and sexual orientation have increased dramatically in recent years. In some measure, these acts of hatred reflect societal attitudes that tolerate or encourage group antagonisms.

IDENTITY DEVELOPMENT. To form a positive identity, individuals from each minority group must assess, confront, and reject the negative, devalued identity reinforced by society and transform it into a positive and viable identity. As a result, LGBs, like other minority groups, have developed strategies to manage their differences from the mainstream and to respond to overt and covert oppression (Garnets & Kimmel, 1991).

GROUP SOLIDARITY. Sexual minorities like other minorities develop group solidarity among their members based on shared experiences and are committed to working toward the elimination of prejudice and discrimination. As members of groups, they have worked together to form support networks and communities to facilitate group identity. For example, there are parallels between the efforts of African American leaders to foster "Black pride" and the idea that "Black is beautiful" and efforts by lesbian, gay, and bisexual activists to foster "LGBT pride," the idea that "gay is good," to hold annual national LGBT Pride Day and National Coming Out Day events.

Divergences

Although there are many parallels between sexual orientation and other aspects of human diversity, there are also distinctive challenges for gay men, lesbians, and bisexuals.

First, lesbians, gay men, and bisexuals continually confront decisions about whether to reveal or conceal their identity. Second, sexual orientation is an "achieved identity" that is not recognized or acknowledged from birth, but rather is generally recognized only in adolescence or adulthood. This is in contrast to other minority groups who have an "ascribed status" that is recognized and acknowledged from birth (Garnets & Kimmel, in press).

Third, families of lesbians, gay men, and bisexuals typically are heterosexual. They thus generally do not provide useful role models for normal transitions and developmental periods of LGB individuals' lives. Moreover, family disruption frequently results when a gay, lesbian, or bisexual sexual orientation is revealed.

Finally, in contrast to other minority groups, there is the potential for permeability of the boundaries separating heterosexuals from LGBs. For example, heterosexuals cannot be unequivocally assured that they will never feel romantic or sexual desire for a person of the same gender (Rust, 1996a). Research that has been discussed throughout this article has shown that everyone is not 100% heterosexual all of the time. Heterosexuals may—or fear they may—explore same-gender sexual fantasies and engage in same-gender behavior at some point in their lives. This complex reality about a person's unique sexual desires, feelings, and behaviors heightens fears and prejudice toward sexual minorities. The description of these unique characteristics of sexual minorities is a reminder that every minority group has its own distinctive challenges.

Intersections of Sexual Orientation and Other Aspects of Human Diversity

For analytic purposes, one often separates the experiences of sexual minorities and people of color, the old and the young, those who are physically able and those who are physically challenged, and so on. But in reality, each individual occupies a unique life space that locates him or her on all these dimensions of human diversity. A lesbian may also be African American, highly educated, and elderly. A gay man may also be biracial and blind. Why is the examination of intersections across diverse groups so important? The realities of human lives involve interconnections among the individual's various identities. Because of the powerful influence of minority status on daily life, intersections among minority statuses are especially important.

No single element of identity, be it class, race, gender, disability, or sexual orientation, can truly be understood except in relation to the others (Greene, 2000). When individuals are forced to separate these aspects of themselves from one another, they experience a sense of alienation. Audre Lorde (1990) phrased it well:

> As a Black lesbian feminist comfortable with the many different ingredients of my identity, and a woman committed to racial and sexual freedom from oppression, I find I am constantly being encouraged to pluck some one aspect of myself and present this as the meaningful whole, eclipsing or denying other aspects of myself. (p. 285)

This comment reminds us of the need for a model of sexual orientation based on multiplicity, not sameness, and examines the overlapping identities and statuses of culture, gender, age, race, ethnicity, class, disability, and sexuality. Three issues illustrate this important point: sociocultural influences on sexual orientation, the relationship between sexual minority status and the heterosexual majority, and the intersection of sexual orientation and race/ethnicity.

SOCIOCULTURAL INFLUENCES ON SEXUAL ORIENTATION. It is all too easy for the public and psychologists to ignore the many powerful ways that cultural and historical forces influence sexual orientations (Blackwood & Wierenga, 2000; Faderman, 1991; Peplau et al., 1999). Although passion and sexual desire are experienced as intensely personal and unique, they are in fact shaped by cultural beliefs about gender and sexuality, by kinship systems, by men's and women's economic and social status, by whether or not sexual identities are recognized in a given culture, and by attitudes of acceptance versus rejection toward sexual minorities (Blackwood, 2000; Peplau & Garnets, 2000). For example, in some cultures, same-sex attachments are socially approved and widespread, whereas elsewhere they are stigmatized and hidden. In some settings, same-gender relationships for women coexist with heterosexual marriage; in other settings, women are more likely to form exclusive relationships with either a same-gender or other-gender partner. Elements assumed by American psychologists to be basic to the nature of sexual orientation may be unique to our contemporary culture and not necessarily related to sexual orientation in other social contexts.

RELATIONSHIP BETWEEN SEXUAL MINORITY STATUS AND THE HETEROSEXUAL MAJORITY. The stigma of homosexuality harms everyone, regardless of their sexual orientation. Two examples illustrate ways sexual prejudice affects the heterosexual majority. First, there are strong cultural pressures toward heterosexuality based on fears of being labeled gay. Research has shown, for example, how sexual prejudice is used to put pressures on teenage girls to adopt traditional gender roles and to become heterosexual adults. As Hyde and Jaffee (2000) explained:

> All four sources of cultural influence—peers, parents, the media, and the schools—shape girls into heterosexual adults through three processes: (a) displaying overtly anti-gay or homophobic attitudes, leading adolescents to believe that homosexuality is

wrong, disgusting, and abnormal; (b) making homosexuality and homosexual persons invisible; and (c) encouraging traditional gender roles, a strong component of which is heterosexuality. (p. 288)

These social pressures are aimed at ensuring heterosexual adults and thereby limiting the rich range of sexualities and sexual orientations possible for any individual.

Second, heterosexuals may experience social pressure to conform to traditional gender roles to avoid the stigmatizing label of homosexuality. Regardless of their sexual orientation, women and men who manifest characteristics inconsistent with those culturally prescribed for their gender are likely to be labeled as gay. Girls and women who seem to be masculine in their appearance or interests, who resist a man's sexual advances, who work in nontraditional occupations, who fight for their rights as a woman, or who appear assertive risk being called lesbians (Kite, 1994; Kite & Deaux, 1987). Because of more restricted gender role socialization of boys, this influence appears to be especially strong for men (Herek 1991; Pleck, 1981). For example, attempts to avoid the stigma of being labeled gay inhibit heterosexual men's ability to form close, intimate relationships with members of their own gender. There is a high cost to society for the restrictive constraints of heterosexist bias that limits behavior to rigid gender roles, requires 100% heterosexuality, and defines one's value as a man or woman by one's rejection of homosexuality.

INTERSECTION OF SEXUAL ORIENTATION AND RACE/ETHNICITY. The experiences of lesbians, gay men, and bisexuals of color often differ from the Anglo American experience. The process of forming multiple identities (e.g., Asian American, female, and bisexual) involves reconciling one's ethnicity, gender, and sexual orientation as well as other identities. It is important to remember that ethnic/racial minorities are highly heterogeneous as well as multidimensional in terms of their cultural beliefs and practices. Education, socioeconomic status, and generation of migration in particular can lead to important variations in such cultural beliefs. It would be inaccurate to generalize from the examples used in this discussion to all racial/ethnic minority individuals or cultures. Moreover, ethnicity is relevant to the identities of many White people. Not all White Americans are Anglo-Saxon Protestants or espouse the values of the dominant group (Fygetakis, 1997). As Cornell West (1995) described, "There's something called whiteness that was constructed, that hides and conceals a very rich multiculturalism among brothers and sisters of European descent in America." For example, White people who are also members of ethnic groups that are less tolerant of lesbian and gay sexual orientations are less likely to be out and thereby less visible (Fygetakis, 1997).

The challenges for LGB people of color is to integrate multiple identities, each of which can be disparaged and can result in social disadvantage. This challenge can affect the ties LGB individuals maintain with their racial/ethnic cultures and communities and the way they manage conflicting allegiances among different communities.

CHALLENGES FOR LGBS' TIES TO THEIR RACIAL/ETHNIC COMMUNITIES. Racial/ethnic communities and extended families often serve as the primary reference groups providing social networks and support for their members (Greene, 2000; Rust, 1996b). When a person of color discloses a gay, lesbian, or bisexual identity to his or her family, the person risks several types of criticism. Like other LGBs, the person may be criticized for rejecting the path of heterosexuality expected by his or her family. But in addition, the person may be viewed as selfishly placing personal desires above the needs of his or her ethnic community. A LGB identity may be perceived as a betrayal of one's own people, a loss of connection with one's own heritage, a public statement about something that reflects badly on one's culture or religion, a violation of gender role expectations of the culture, or a sign of assimilation into White mainstream culture (Garnets & Kimmel, 1993). As an African American lesbian explained:

The family is very contradictory for us. There are emotional involvements, there are ties, the roots that it represents for us all as individuals in a fundamentally racist/sexist society. That's why Black people may decide not to come out as lesbians or gay for fear of being rejected by a group of people whom you not only love but who represent a real source of security, foundation. (Carmen, Gail, Neena, & Tamara, 1991, p. 217)

MANAGING CONFLICTING ALLEGIANCES AMONG DIFFERENT COMMUNITIES. Racial/ethnic minorities who are lesbian, gay, or bisexual must participate in divergent social worlds, balancing demands and crossing boundaries of different groups, including the LGB communities, one's ethnic/racial group, and the majority culture (Garnets & Kimmel, 1991; Greene, 2000; Rust, 1996b). Individuals with double and triple minority status may experience discrimination and prejudice as outsiders in each of these communities. This may be especially acute for recent immigrants and their families. As one Greek American woman describes it,

There's a part of me that likes being different, unique and special. But what's difficult is to not fit in anywhere. Not as a Greek single parent or a lesbian single parent. Most lesbians who are moms are in couples. My sense of self is constantly from within. I don't get the benefit of either community. (Fygetakis, 1997, pp. 182–183)

Another example of managing conflicting allegiances occurs in the experiences of ethnic/racial minority bisexuals. On the one hand, this process appears to be more challenging for racial or ethnic minority bisexuals than for lesbians and gay men, because bisexuals are a political and social minority within the gay and lesbian community (Blasingame, 1992; Rust, 1996b). On the other hand, as Rust (1996b) pointed out,

Many bisexuals of mixed race or ethnicity feel a comfortable resonance between their mixed heritage and their bisexuality. In a society where both racial-ethnic and sexual categories are highly elaborated, individuals of mixed heritage or who are bisexual find themselves straddling categories that are socially constructed as distinct from one another. (p. 69)

As one Asian European woman explained it:

Being multiracial, multicultural has always made me aware of nonbipolar thinking. I have always been outside people's categories, and so it wasn't such a big leap to come out as bi, after spending years explaining my [racial and cultural] identity rather than attaching a single label [to it]. (Rust, 1996b, p. 71)

In sum, all of us are affected by multiple, intersecting identities and allegiances. Failure to recognize the complexity of contemporary identities will seriously limit the effectiveness of psychologists' work. Instead, psychologists who focus their research and practice on the lives of sexual minorities must incorporate other forms of diversity into their research, theoretical analyses, teaching, and practices. Similarly, those who focus their research and practice on ethnic minorities and other areas of diversity must consider how sexual orientation fits into their work. No single element of identity be it race, ethnicity, class, disability, gender, or sexual orientation can truly be understood except in relation to the others. Psychologists must use models that are based on multiplicity, not sameness. And all psychologists need to open their minds to individuals' multiple identities and the full range of diversity.

References

Allen, L. S., & Gorski, R. A. (1992). Sexual orientation and the size of the anterior commissure in the human brain. *Proceedings of the National Academy of Sciences, USA, 89,* 7199.

Allen, L. S., Hines, M., Shryne, J. E., & Gorski, R. A. (1989). Two sexually dimorphic cell groups in the human brain. *Journal of Neuroscience, 9,* 497–506.

Bailey, J. M. (1995). Biological perspectives on sexual orientation. In A. R. D'Augelli & C. J. Patterson (Eds.), *Lesbian, gay and bisexual identities over the lifespan* (pp. 104–135). New York: Oxford University Press.

Bailey, J. M., & Dawood, K. (1998). Behavioral genetics, sexual orientation, and the family. In C. J. Patterson & A. R. D'Augelli (Eds.), *Lesbian, gay, and bisexual identities in families* (pp. 3–18). New York: Oxford University Press.

Bailey, J. M., Gaulin, S., Agyei. Y., & Gladue, B. A. (1994). Effects of gender and sexual orientation on evolutionary relevant aspects of human mating psychology. *Journal of Personality and Social Psychology, 66,* 1081–1093.

Bailey, J. M., Pillard, R. C., Neale, M. C., & Ageyi, Y. (1993). Heritable factors influence sexual orientation in women. *Archives of General Psychiatry, 50,* 217–223.

Bailey, J. M., & Zucker, K. J. (1995). Childhood sex-typed behavior and sexual orientation: A conceptual analysis and quantitative review. *Developmental Psychology, 31,* 43–55.

Baldwin, J. D., & Baldwin, J. I. (1997). Gender differences in sexual interest. *Archives of Sexual Behavior, 26,* 181–210.

Baumeister, R. F. (2000). Gender differences in erotic plasticity: The female sex drive as socially flexible and responsive. *Psychological Bulletin, 126,* 347–374.

Bell, A. P., & Weinberg, M . S. (1978). *Homosexualities: A study of diversity among men and women.* New York: Simon & Schuster.

Bell, A. P., Weinberg, M. S., & Hammersmith, S. K. (1981). *Sexual preference.* Bloomington: Indiana University Press.

Bennett, K. (1992). Feminist bisexuality: A both/and option for an either/or world. In E. R. Weise (Ed.), *Closer to home: Bisexuality and feminism* (pp. 205–231). Seattle, WA: Seal Press.

Blackwood, E. (2000). Culture and women's sexualities. *Journal of Social Issues, 56,* 223–238.

Blackwood, E., & Wierenga, S. E. (2000). *Female desires: Same-sex relations and transgender practices across cultures.* New York: Columbia University Press.

Blasingame, B. M. (1992). The roots of biphobia: Racism and internalized heterosexism. In E. R. Weise (Ed.), *Closer to home: Bisexuality and feminism* (pp. 47–53). Seattle, WA: Seal Press.

Blumstein, P. W., & Schwartz, P. (1976). Bisexuality in women. *Archives of Sexual Behavior, 5,* 171–181.

Blumstein, P. W., & Schwartz, P. (1989). Intimate relationships and the creation of sexuality. In B. Risman & P. Schwartz (Eds.). *Gender in intimate relationships: A microstructural approach* (pp. 120–129). Belmont, CA: Wadsworth.

Bohan, J. S. (1996). *Psychology and sexual orientation.* New York: Routledge.

Byne, W. (1995). Science and belief: Psychobiological research on sexual orientation. *Journal of Homosexuality, 28,* 303–344.

Carmen, Gail, Neena, & Tamara. (1991). Becoming visible: Black lesbian discussions. In Feminist Review (Eds.), *Sexuality: A reader* (pp. 216–244). London: Virago.

D'Augelli, A. R., & Garnets, L. D. (1995). Lesbian, gay, and bisexual communities. In C. J. Patterson & A. R. D'Augelli (Eds.), *Lesbian, gay, and bisexual identities over the lifespan: psychological perspectives* (pp. 293–320). New York: Oxford University Press.

Dean, L., Meyer, I. H., Robinson, K., Sell, R. L., Sember, R., Silenzio, V. M. B., et al. (2000). Lesbian, gay, bisexual, and transgender health: Findings and concerns. *Journal of the Gay and Lesbian Medical Association, 4*, 101–151.

DeLamater, J. (1987). Gender differences in sexual scenarios. In K. Kelley (Ed.), *Females, males and sexuality: Theories and research* (pp. 127–129). Albany: State University of New York Press.

Diamant, A. L., Schuster, M. A., McGuigan, K., & Lever, J. (1999). Lesbians' sexual history with men. *Archives of Internal Medicine, 159*, 2730–2736.

Diamond, L. M. (1998). Development of sexual orientation among adolescent and young women. *Developmental Psychology, 34*, 1085–1095.

Diamond, L. M. (2000). Sexual identities, attractions, and behavior among young sexual-minority women over a two-year period. *Developmental Psychology, 36*, 241–250.

Diamond, L. M., & Savin-Williams, R. C. (2000). Explaining diversity in the development of same-sex sexuality among young women. *Journal of Social Issues, 56*, 297–313.

Downey, J. I., & Friedman, R. C. (1998). Female homosexuality: Classical psychoanalytic theory reconsidered. *Journal of the American Psychoanalytic Association, 46*, 471–506.

Eliason, M. J. (1997). The prevalence and nature of biphobia in heterosexual undergraduate students. *Archives of Sexual Behavior, 26*, 317–326.

Ellis, B. J., & Symons, D. (1990). Sex differences in sexual fantasy. *Journal of Sex Research, 27*, 527–555.

Faderman, L. (1991). *Odd girls and twilight lovers*. New York: Columbia University Press.

Fausto-Sterling, A. (1993, March/April). The five sexes: Why male and female are not enough. *The Sciences*, 20–24.

Fox, R. (1996). Bisexuality in perspective: A review of theory and research. In B. Firestein (Ed.), *Bisexuality: The psychology and politics of an invisible minority* (pp. 3–50). Thousand Oaks, CA: Sage.

Fygetakis, L. M. (1997). Greek American lesbians: Identity odysseys of honorable good girls. In B. Greene (Ed.), *Ethnic and cultural diversity among lesbians and gay men* (pp. 152–190). Thousand Oaks, CA: Sage.

Gainor, K. A. (2000). Including transgender issues in lesbian, gay, and bisexual psychology: Implications for practice and training. In B. Greene & G. L. Croom (Eds.), *Education, research, and practice in lesbian, gay, bisexual, and transgendered psychology* (pp. 131–160). Thousand Oaks, CA: Sage.

Garnets, L. D., & Kimmel, D. C. (1991). Lesbian and gay male dimensions in the psychological study of human diversity. In J. Goodchilds (Ed.), *Psychological perspectives on human diversity in America* (pp. 137–192). Washington, DC: American Psychological Association.

Garnets, L. D., & Kimmel, D. C. (1993). Cultural diversity among lesbians and gay men. In L. D. Garnets & D. C. Kimmel (Eds.), *Psychological perspectives on lesbian and gay male experiences* (pp. 331–337). New York: Columbia University Press.

Garnets, L. D., & Kimmel, D. C. (in press). *Psychological perspectives on lesbian, gay, and bisexual experiences* (2nd ed.). New York: Columbia University Press.

Garnets, L. D., & Peplau, L. A. (2000). Understanding women's sexualities and sexual orientations. *Journal of Social Issues, 56*, 181–192.

Greene, B. (2000). Beyond heterosexism and across the cultural divide: Developing an inclusive lesbian, gay, and bisexual psychology: A look to the future. In B. Greene & G. L. Croom (Eds.), *Education, research, and practice in lesbian, gay, bisexual, and transgendered psychology* (pp. 1–45). Thousand Oaks, CA: Sage.

Guido, P. A. (1981). A comparison of heterosexual and homosexual single and cohabiting male masturbation fantasies. *Dissertation Abstracts International, 42*(05), 2056.

Hamer, D. H., Magnuson, V. L., Hu, N., & Pattatucci, A. M. L. (1993, July 16). A linkage between DNA markers on the X chromosome and male sexual orientation. *Science, 261,* 321–327.

Hatfield, E., Sprecher, S., Pillemer, J. T., Greenberger, D., & Wexler, P. (1989). Gender differences in what is desired in the sexual relationship. *Journal of Psychology and Human Sexuality, 1*(2), 39–52.

Herek, G. M. (1990). The context of antigay violence: Notes on cultural and psychological heterosexism. *Journal of Interpersonal Violence, 5,* 316–333.

Herek, G. M. (1991). Stigma, prejudice, and violence against lesbians and gay men. In J. C. Gonsiorek & J. D. Weinrich (Eds.), *Homosexuality: Research findings for public policy* (pp. 60–80). Newbury Park, CA: Sage.

Herek, G. M. (2000). The psychology of sexual prejudice. *Current Directions in Psychological Science, 9,* 19–22.

Hu, S., Pattatucci, A. M., Patterson, C., Li, L., Fulker, D. W., Cherny, S. S., Kruglyak, L., & Hamer, D. (1995). Linkage between sexual orientation and chromosome Xq28 in males but not in females. *Nature Genetics, 11,* 248–256.

Hyde, J. S., & Jaffee, S. R. (2000). Becoming a heterosexual adult: The experiences of young women. *Journal of Social Issues, 56,* 283–296.

Istvan, J. (1983). Effects of sexual orientation on interpersonal judgment. *Journal of Sex Research, 19,* 173–191.

Keating, J., & Over, R. (1990). Sexual fantasies of heterosexual and homosexual men. *Archives of Sexual Behavior, 19,* 461–475.

Kite, M. E. (1994). When perceptions meet reality: Individual differences in reactions to gay men and lesbians. In B. Greene & G. Herek (Eds.), *Lesbian and gay psychology: Theory, research, and clinical applications* (pp. 25–53). Thousand Oaks, CA: Sage.

Kite, M. E., & Deaux, K. (1987). Gender belief systems: Homosexuality and the implicit inversion theory. *Psychology of Women Quarterly, 11,* 83–96.

Kitzinger, C., & Wilkinson, S. (1995). Transitions from heterosexuality to lesbianism. *Developmental Psychology, 31,* 95–104.

Klinkenberg, D., & Rose, S. (1994). Dating scripts of gay men and lesbians. *Journal of Homosexuality, 26*(4), 23–45.

Laumann, E. O., Gagnon, J. H., Michael, R. T., & Michaels, S. (1994). *The social organization of sexuality: Sexual practices in the United States.* Chicago: University of Chicago Press.

LeVay, S. (1991). A difference in hypothalamic structure between heterosexual and homosexual men. *Science, 253,* 1034–1037.

Lorber, J. (1996). Beyond the binaries: Depolarizing the categories of sex, sexuality, and gender. *Sociological Inquiry, 66,* 143–159.

Lorde, A. (1990). Age, race, class and sex: Women redefining difference. In R. Ferguson, M. Gever, T. Minh-ha, & C. West (Eds.), *Out there: Marginalization and contemporary cultures* (pp. 281–87). New York: New Museum of Contemporary Art.

Magee, M., & Miller, D. C. (1997). *Lesbian lives: Psychoanalytic narratives old and new.* Hillsdale, NJ: Analytic Press.

Money, J. (1987). Sin, sickness, or status? Homosexual gender identity and psychoneuroendocrinology. *American Psychologist, 42,* 384–399.

Ochs, R. (1996). Biphobia: It goes more than two ways. In B. Firestein (Ed.), *Bisexuality: The psychology and politics of an invisible minority* (pp. 217–239). Thousand Oaks, CA: Sage.

Oliver, M. B., & Hyde, J. S. (1993). Gender differences in sexuality: A meta-analysis. *Psychological Bulletin, 114,* 29–51.

Paroski, P. (1987). Healthcare delivery and the concerns of gay and lesbian adolescents. *Journal of Adolescent Health Care, 8*, 188–192.

Patterson, C. J. (1997). Children of lesbian and gay parents. In T. H. Ollendick & R. J. Prinz (Eds.), *Advances in clinical child psychology, 19* (pp. 235–282). New York: Plenum Press.

Peplau, L. A. (2001). Rethinking women's sexual orientation: An interdisciplinary, relationship-focused approach. *Personal Relationships, 8*, 1–19.

Peplau, L. A., & Garnets, L. D. (2000). A new paradigm for understanding women's sexuality and sexual orientation. *Journal of Social Issues, 56*, 329–350.

Peplau, L. A., Spalding, L. R., Conley, T. D., & Veniegas, R. C. (1999). The development of sexual orientation in women. *Annual Review of Sex Research, 10*, 70–99.

Pleck. J. H. (1981). *The myth of masculinity*. Cambridge, MA: MIT Press.

Regan, P. C., & Berscheid, E. (1996). Beliefs about the state, goals, and objects of sexual desire. *Journal of Sex and Marital Therapy, 22*, 110–120.

Rosenbaum, L., & Sanford, W. (1998). Sexuality. In Boston Women's Health Book Collective (Eds.), *Our bodies, our selves for the new century* (pp. 229–262). New York: Simon & Schuster.

Rothblum, E. D. (2000). Sexual orientation and sex in women's lives: Conceptual and methodological issues. *Journal of Social Issues, 56*, 193–204.

Rust, P. C. (1993). Neutralizing the political threat of the marginal woman: Lesbians' beliefs about bisexual women. *Journal of Sex Research, 30*, 214–228.

Rust, P. C. (1996a). Finding a sexual identity and community: Therapeutic implications and cultural assumptions in scientific models of coming out. In E. D. Rothblum & L. A. Bond (Eds.), *Preventing heterosexism and homophobia* (pp. 87–123). Thousand Oaks, CA: Sage.

Rust, P. C. (1996b). Managing multiple identities: Diversity among bisexual men and women. In B. Firestein (Ed.), *Bisexuality: The psychology and politics of an invisible minority* (pp. 53–83). Thousand Oaks, CA: Sage.

Rust, P. C. (2000). Bisexuality: A contemporary paradox for women. *Journal of Social Issues, 56*, 205–221.

Sanford, W. (1998). Relationships and sexuality. In Boston Women's Health Book Collective (Eds.), *Our bodies, our selves for the new century* (pp. 179–184). New York: Simon & Schuster.

Savin-Williams, R. C. (1998). *". . . And then I became gay": Young men's stories*. New York: Routledge.

Savin-Williams, R. C., & Diamond, L. M. (2000). Sexual identity trajectories among sexual-minority youths: Gender comparisons. *Archives of Sexual Behavior, 29*, 419–440.

Schneider, M. J. (2001). Toward a reconceptualization of the coming-out process for adolescent females. In A. R. D'Augelli & C. J. Patterson (Eds.), *Lesbian, gay, and bisexual identities and youth: Psychological perspectives* (pp. 71–96). New York: Oxford University Press.

Sears, J. T. (1989). The impact of gender and race on growing up lesbian and gay in the South. *National Women's Studies Association Journal, 1*, 422–457.

Sedgwik, E. K. (1990). *Epistemology of the closet*. Berkeley: University of California Press.

Som, I. (1991). The queer kitchen. In M. Silvera (Ed.), *Piece of my heart: A lesbian of color anthology* (pp. 142–146). Toronto, Ontario, Canada: Sister Vision Press.

Spalding L. R., & Peplau, L. A. (1997). The unfaithful lover: Heterosexuals' perceptions of bisexuals and their relationships. *Psychology of Women Quarterly, 21*, 611–625.

Sprecher, S., & McKinney, K. (1993). *Sexuality*. Newbury Park, CA: Sage.

Stacey, J., & Biblarz, T. (2001). (How) does the sexual orientation of parents matter? *American Sociological Review, 66,* 159–203.

Swaab, D. F., & Hofman, M. A. (1990). An enlarged suprachiasmatic nucleus in homosexual men. *Brain Research, 537,* 141.

Tafoya, T. (1997). Native gay and lesbian issues: The two-spirited. In B. Greene (Ed.), *Ethnic and cultural diversity among lesbians and gay men* (pp. 1–9). Thousand Oaks, CA: Sage.

Tinney, J. (1986). Interconnections. *Interracial Books for Children Bulletin, 14*(3–4), 24–27.

Veniegas, R. C., & Conley, T. D. (2000). Biological research on women's sexual orientations: Evaluating the scientific evidence. *Journal of Social Issues,* 56, 267–282.

Vetere, V. A. (1983). The role of friendship in the development and maintenance of lesbian love relationships. *Journal of Homosexuality, 8*(2), 51–65.

Weinberg, M. S., Williams, C. J., & Pryor, D. W. (1994). *Dual attraction: Understanding bisexuality.* New York: Oxford University Press.

West, C. (Speaker). (1995). *The radical democratic tradition* [Transcript]. Boulder, CO: Alternative Radio.

Many of the features of the new paradigm presented in this article were developed in collaboration with Douglas Kimmel and Anne Peplau. I thank Martha Bernal, Connie Chan, Jacqueline Goodchilds, Douglas Kimmel, Barrie Levy, Anne Peplau, Esther Rothblum, and Nancy Toder for their valuable comments on an earlier version of the article.

Correspondence concerning this article should be addressed to Linda D. Garnets, Department of Psychology, Box 951563, University of California, Los Angeles, California 90095-1563. E-mail: lgarnets@ucla.edu

27 Queer Feelings

Sara Ahmed

As the immigrant makes visible the processes of production, she also exemplifies the idea that the family is in need of protection because it is losing its viability, increasingly posed in the horrors of the imaginary as needing ever more fierce strategies of security to ensure its ideal of reproducing itself. It is this connection that is hidden—a relation between the production of life (both discursive and reproductive) and global production. (Goodman 2001: 194)

As I argued in the previous two chapters, the reproduction of life itself, where life is conflated with a social ideal ('life as we know it') is often represented as threatened by the existence of others: immigrants, queers, other others. These others become sources of fascination that allow the ideal to be posited as ideal through their embodiment of the failure of the ideal to be translated into being or action. We might note that 'reproduction' itself comes under question. The reproduction of life—in the form of the future generation—becomes bound up with the reproduction of culture, through the stabilization of specific arrangements for living ('the family'). The family is idealisable through the narrative of threat and insecurity; the family is presented as vulnerable, and as needing to be defended against others who violate the conditions of its reproduction. As Goodman shows us, the moral defence of the family as a way of life becomes a matter of 'global polities'. I have already considered how the defence of the war against terrorism has evoked 'the family' as the origin of love, community and support (see Chapter 3). What needs closer examination is how heterosexuality becomes a script that binds the familial with the global: the coupling of man and woman becomes a kind of 'birthing', a giving birth not only to new life, but to ways of living that are already recognisable as forms of civilisation. It is this narrative of coupling as a condition for the reproduction of life, culture and value that explains the slide in racist narratives between the fear of strangers and immigrants (xenophobia), the fear of queers (homophobia) and the fear of miscegenation (as well as other illegitimate couplings).

These narratives or scripts do not, of course, simply exist 'out there' to legislate the political actions of states. They also shape bodies and lives, including those that follow and depart from such narratives in the ways in which they love and live, in the decisions that they make and take within the intimate spheres of home and work. It is important to consider how

Reprinted from *The Cultural Politics of Emotion* (2004), Taylor & Francis.

Queer Feelings is taken from Chapter 7 of *The Cultural Politics of Emotion*, by Sarah Ahmed. All references to other chapters are in said book.

compulsory heterosexuality—defined as the accumulative effect of the repetition of the narrative of heterosexuality as an ideal coupling—shapes what it is possible for bodies to do,[1] even if it does not contain what it is possible to be. Bodies take the shape of norms that are repeated over time and with force. The work of repetition involves the concealment of labour under the sign of nature. In this chapter, I want to argue that norms surface *as* the surfaces of bodies; norms are a matter of impressions, of how bodies are 'impressed upon' by the world, as a world made up of others. In other words, such impressions are effects of labour; how bodies work and are worked upon shapes the surfaces of bodies. Regulative norms function in a way as 'repetitive strain injuries' (RSIs). Through repeating some gestures and not others, or through being orientated in some directions and not others, bodies become contorted; they get twisted into shapes that enable some action only insofar as they restrict capacity for other kinds of action.

I would suggest that heteronormativity also affects the surfaces of bodies, which surface through impressions made by others. Compulsory heterosexuality shapes bodies by the assumption that a body 'must' orient itself towards some objects and not others, objects that are secured as ideal through the fantasy of difference (see Chapter 6). Hence compulsory heterosexuality shapes which bodies one 'can' legitimately approach as would-be lovers and which one cannot. In shaping one's approach to others, compulsory heterosexuality also shapes one's own body, *as a congealed history of past approaches*. Sexual orientation is not then simply about the direction one takes towards an object of desire, as if this direction does not affect other things that we do. Sexual orientation involves bodies that leak into worlds; it involves a way of orientating the body towards and away from others, which affects how one can enter different kinds of social spaces (which presumes certain bodies, certain directions, certain ways of loving and living), even if it does not lead bodies to the same places. To make a simple but important point: orientations affect what it is that bodies can do.[2] Hence, the failure to orient oneself 'towards' the ideal sexual object affects how we live in the world, an affect that is readable as the failure to reproduce, and as a threat to the social ordering of life itself.

Of course, one does not have to do what one is compelled to do: for something to be compulsory shows that it is not necessary. But to refuse to be compelled by the narratives of ideal heterosexuality in one's orientation to others is still to be affected by those narratives; they work to script one's orientation as a form of disobedience. The affects of 'not following' the scripts can be multiple. We can consider, for example, the psychic as well as social costs of loving a body that is supposed to be unloveable for the subject I am, or loving a body that I was 'supposed to' repudiate, which may include shame and melancholia (Buder 1997b; Braidotti 2002: 53; see Chapter 5). The negative affects of 'not quite' living in the norms show us how loving loves that are not 'normative' involves being subject to such norms precisely in the costs and damage that are incurred when not following them. Do queer moments happen when this failure to reproduce norms as forms of life is embraced or affirmed as a political and ethical alternative? Such affirmation would not be about the conversion of shame into pride, but the enjoyment of the negativity of shame, an enjoyment of that which has been designated shameful by normative culture (see Barber and Clark 2002: 22-9).

In this chapter, I could ask the question: How does it feel to inhabit a body that fails to reproduce an ideal? But this is not my question. Instead, I wish to explore 'queer feelings' without translating such an exploration into a matter of 'feeling queer'. Such a translation would assume 'queerness' involves a particular emotional life, or that there are feelings that bodies 'have' given their failure to inhabit or follow a heterosexual ideal. Of course, one can feel queer. There are feelings involved in the self-perception of 'queerness', a self-perception that is bodily, as well as bound up with 'taking on' a name. But these feelings are mediated and they are attached to the category 'queer' in ways that are complex and contingent, precisely because the category is produced in relation to histories that render it a sign of failed being or 'non-being'.[3] In examining the affective potential of queer, I will firstly consider the relationship between norms and affects in debates on queer families. I will then discuss the role of grief in queer politics with specific reference to queer responses to September 11. And finally,

I will reflect on the role of pleasure in queer lifestyles or countercultures, and will ask how the enjoyment of social and sexual relations that are designated as 'non-(re)productive' can function as forms of political disturbance in an affective economy organised around the principle that pleasure is only ethical as an incentive or reward for good conduct.

(Dis)comfort and Norms

It is important to consider how heterosexuality functions powerfully not only as a series of norms and ideals, but also through emotions that shape bodies as well as worlds: (hetero)norms are investments, which are 'taken on' and 'taken in' by subjects. To practise heterosexuality by following its scripts in one's choice of some love objects—and refusal of others—is also to become invested in the reproduction of heterosexuality. Of course, one does not 'do' heterosexuality simply through who one does and does not have sex with. Heterosexuality as a script for an ideal life makes much stronger claims. It is assumed that all arrangements will follow from the arrangement of the couple: man/woman. It is no accident that compulsory heterosexuality works powerfully in the most casual modes of conversation. One asks: 'Do you have a boyfriend?' (to a girl), or one asks: 'Do you have a girlfriend?' (to a boy). Queer subjects feel the tiredness of making corrections and departures; the pressure of this insistence, this presumption, this demand that asks either for a 'passing over' (a moment of passing, which is not always available) or for direct or indirect forms of self-revelation ('but actually, he's a she' or 'she's a he', or just saying 'she' instead of 'he' or 'he' instead of 'she' at the 'obvious' moment). No matter how 'out' you may be, how (un)comfortably queer you may feel, those moments of interpellation get repeated over time, and can be experienced as a bodily injury; moments which position queer subjects as failed in their failure to live up to the 'hey you too' of heterosexual self-narration. The everydayness of compulsory heterosexuality is also its affectiveness, wrapped up as it is with moments of ceremony (birth, marriage, death), which bind families together, and with the ongoing investment in the sentimentality of friendship and romance. Of course, such sentimentality is deeply embedded with public as well as private culture; stories of heterosexual romance proliferate as a matter of human interest. As Lauren Berlant and Michael Warner argue: 'National heterosexuality is the mechanism by which a core national culture can be imagined as a sanitised space of sentimental feeling' (Berlant and Warner 2000: 313).

We can consider the sanitised space as a comfort zone. Normativity is comfortable for those who can inhabit it. The word 'comfort' suggests wellbeing and satisfaction, but it also suggests an ease and easiness. To follow the rules of heterosexuality is to be at ease in a world that reflects back the couple form one inhabits as an ideal.[4] Of course, one can be made to feel uneasy by one's inhabitance of an ideal. One can be made uncomfortable by one's own comforts. To see heterosexuality as an ideal that one might or might not follow—or to be uncomfortable by the privileges one is given by inhabiting a heterosexual world—is a less comforting form of comfort. But comfort it remains and comfort is very hard to notice when one experiences it. Having uncomfortably inhabited the comforts of heterosexuality for many years, I know this too well. Now, living a queer life, I can reflect on many comforts that I did not even begin to notice despite my 'felt' discomforts. We don't tend to notice what is comfortable, even when we think we do.

Thinking about comfort is hence always a useful starting place for thinking. So let's think about how it feels to be comfortable. Say you are sinking into a comfortable chair. Note I already have transferred the affect to an object ('it is comfortable'). But comfort is about the fit between body and object: my comfortable chair may be awkward for you, with your differently-shaped body. Comfort is about an encounter between more than one body, which is the promise of a 'sinking' feeling. It is, after all, pain or discomfort that return one's attention to the surfaces of the body *as body* (see Chapter 1). To be comfortable is to be so at ease with one's environment that it is hard to distinguish where one's body ends and the world begins.

One fits, and by fitting, the surfaces of bodies disappear from view. The disappearance of the surface is instructive: in feelings of comfort, bodies extend into spaces, and spaces extend into bodies. The sinking feeling involves a seamless space, or a space where you can't see the 'stitches' between bodies.

Heteronormativity functions as a form of public comfort by allowing bodies to extend into spaces that have already taken their shape. Those spaces are lived as comfortable as they allow bodies to fit in; the surfaces of social space are already impressed upon by the shape of such bodies (like a chair that acquires its shape by the repetition of some bodies inhabiting it: we can almost see the shape of bodies as 'impressions' on the surface). The impressions acquired by surfaces function as traces of bodies. We can even see this process in social spaces. As Gill Valentine has argued, the 'heterosexualisation' of public spaces such as streets is naturalised by the repetition of different forms of heterosexual conduct (images on billboards, music played, displays of heterosexual intimacy and so on), a process which goes unnoticed by heterosexual subjects (Valentine 1996: 149). The surfaces of social as well as bodily space 'record' the repetition of acts, and the passing by of some bodies and not others.

Heteronormativity also becomes a form of comforting: one feels better by the warmth of being faced by a world one has already taken in. One does not notice this *as a world* when one has been shaped by that world, and even acquired its shape. Norms may not only have a way of disappearing from view, but may also be that which we do not consciously feel.[5] Queer subjects, when faced by the 'comforts' of heterosexuality may feel uncomfortable (the body does not 'sink into' a space that has already taken its shape). Discomfort is a feeling of disorientation: one's body feels out of place, awkward, unsettled. I know that feeling too well, the sense of out-of-place-ness and estrangement involves an acute awareness of the surface of one's body, which appears *as* surface, when one cannot inhabit the social skin, which is shaped by some bodies, and not others. Furthermore, queer subjects may also be 'asked' not to make heterosexuals feel uncomfortable by avoiding the display of signs of queer intimacy, which is itself an uncomfortable feeling, a restriction on what one can do with one's body, and another's body, in social space.[6] The availability of comfort for some bodies may depend on the labour of others, and the burden of concealment. Comfort may operate as a form of 'feeling fetishism': some bodies can 'have' comfort, only as an effect of the work of others, where the work itself is concealed from view.[7]

It is hence for very good reasons that queer theory has been defined not only as anti-heteronormative, but as anti-normative. As Tim Dean and Christopher Lane argue, queer theory 'advocates a politics based on resistance to all norms' (Dear and Lane 2001: 7). Importantly, heteronormativity refers to more than simply the presumption that it is normal to be heterosexual. The 'norm' is regulative, and is supported by an 'ideal' that associates sexual conduct with other forms of conduct. We can consider, for example, how the restriction of the love object is not simply about the desirability of *any* heterosexual coupling. The couple should be 'a good match' (a judgement that often exercises conventional class and racial assumptions about the importance of 'matching' the backgrounds of partners) and they should exclude others from the realm of sexual intimacy (an idealisation of monogamy, that often equates intimacy with property rights or rights to the intimate other as property). Furthermore, a heterosexual coupling may only approximate an ideal through being sanctioned by marriage, by participating in the ritual of reproduction and good parenting, by being good neighbours as well as lovers and parents, and by being even better citizens. In this way, normative culture involves the differentiation between legitimate and illegitimate ways of living whereby the preservation of what is legitimate ('life as we know it') is assumed to be necessary for the well-being of the next generation. Heteronormativity involves the reproduction or transmission of culture through how one lives one's life in relation to others.

For queer theorists, it is hence important that queer lives do not follow the scripts of heteronormative culture: they do not become, in Judith Halberstam's provocative and compelling term, 'homonormative' lives (Halberstam 2003: 331). Such lives would not desire access to comfort; they would maintain their discomfort with all aspects of normative culture in how they live. Ideally, they would not have families, get married, settle down into unthinking coupledom, give birth to and raise children, join neighbourhood watch, or pray for the nation in times of war. Each of these acts would 'support' the ideals that script such lives as queer, failed and unliveable in the first place. The aspiration to ideals of conduct that is central to the reproduction of heteronormativity has been called, quite understandably, a form of assimilation.

Take, for instance, the work of Andrew Sullivan. In his *Virtually Normal* he argues that most gay people want to be normal; and that being gay does not mean being not normal, even if one is not quite as normal as a straight person (to paraphrase Homi Bhabha, 'almost normal, but not quite'). So he suggests that one can aspire to *have* a heterosexual life without *being* heterosexual: the only difference would be the choice of one's love object. As he puts it:

> *It's perfectly possible to combine a celebration of the traditional family with the celebration of a stable homosexual relationship. The one, after all, is modelled on the other. If constructed carefully as a conservative social ideology, the notion of stable gay relationships might even serve to buttress the ethic of heterosexual marriage, by showing how even those excluded from it can wish to model themselves on its shape and structure.*
> *(Sullivan 1996: 112)*

Here, gay relationships are valued and celebrated insofar as they are 'modelled' on the traditional model of the heterosexual family. Indeed, Sullivan explicitly defines his project as a way of supporting and extending the ideal of the family by showing how those who are 'not it' seek to 'become it'. Gay relationships, by miming the forms of heterosexual coupling, hence pledge their allegiance to the very forms they cannot inhabit. This mimicry is, as Douglas Crimp (2002) has argued, a way of sustaining the psychic conditions of melancholia insofar as Sullivan identifies with that which he cannot be, and indeed with what has already rejected him. As Crimp remarks, Sullivan is 'incapable of recognising the intractability of homophobia because his melancholia consists precisely in his identification with the homophobe's repudiation of him' (Crimp 2002: 6). Assimilation involves a desire to approximate an ideal that one has already failed; an identification with one's designation as a failed subject. The choice of assimilation—queer skin, straight masks—is clearly about supporting the violence of heteronormative distinctions between legitimate and illegitimate lives.[8]

As Judith Butler has argued, one of the biggest problems in campaigns for gay marriage is precisely the way that they may strengthen the hierarchy between legitimate and illegitimate lives. Rather than the hierarchy resting on a distinction between gay and straight, it becomes displaced onto a new distinction between more and less legitimate queer relationships (Butler 2002a: 18). As she asks, does gay marriage 'only become an "option" by extending itself as a norm (and thus foreclosing options), one which also extends property relations and renders the social forms for sexuality more conservative'? (Butler 2002a: 21). In other words, if some of the rights of heterosexuality are extended to queers, what happens to queers who don't take up those rights; whose life choices and sexual desires cannot be translated into the form of marriage, even when emptied of its predication on heterosexual coupling? Do these (non-married) queers become the illegitimate others against which the ideal of marriage is supported?

Of course, the question of gay marriage remains a political dilemma. For not to support the extension of the right of marriage to gay relationships could give support to the status quo, which maintains the distinction between legitimate and illegitimate lives on the grounds of sexual orientation. As Judith Butler (2002a) argues, the social and psychic costs of not having one's relationship recognised by others (whether or not the recognition is determined by law) are enormous especially in situations of loss and bereavement (see the following section). I want to enter this debate by considering how the political choice of being queer or straight (or an assimilated queer) can be contested. Butler herself contests the choice through adopting a position of ambivalence. Whilst I recognise the value of such ambivalence, I want to suggest that more reflection on queer attachments might allow us to avoid positing assimilation or transgression as choices.

To begin with, we can return to my description of what we might call a queer life. I suggested that 'ideally' such lives will maintain a discomfort with the scripts of heteronormative existence. The reliance on this word is telling. For already in describing what may be queer, I am also defining grounds of an ideality, in which to have an ideal queer life, or even to be legitimately queer, people must act in some ways rather than others. We need to ask: How does defining a queer ideal rely on the existence of others who fail the ideal? Who can and cannot embody the queer ideal? Such an ideal is not equally accessible to all, even all those who identify with the sign 'queer' or other 'signs' of non-normative sexuality. Gayatri Gopinath (2003), for example, reflects on how public and visible forms of 'queerness' may not be available to lesbians from South Asia, where it may be in the private spaces of home that bodies can explore homo-erotic pleasures. Her argument shows how queer bodies have different access to public forms of culture, which affect how they can inhabit those publics. Indeed, whilst being queer may feel uncomfortable within heterosexual space, it does not then follow that queers always feel comfortable in queer spaces. I have felt discomfort in some queer spaces, again, as a feeling of being out of place. This is not to say that I have been *made* to feel uncomfortable; the discomfort is itself a sign that queer spaces may extend some bodies more than others (for example, some queer spaces might extend the mobility of white, middle-class bodies). At times, I feel uncomfortable about inhabiting the word 'queer', worrying that I am not queer enough, or have not been queer for long enough, or am just not the right kind of queer. We can feel uncomfortable in the categories we inhabit, even categories that are shaped by their refusal of public comfort.

Furthermore, the positing of an ideal of being free from scripts that define what counts as a legitimate life seems to presume a negative model of freedom; defined here as *freedom from norms*. Such a negative model of freedom idealises movement and detachment, constructing a mobile form of subjectivity that could escape from the norms that constrain what it is that bodies can do. Others have criticised queer theory for its idealisation of movement (Epps 2001: 412; Fortier 2003). As Epps puts it: 'Queer theory tends to place great stock in movement, especially when it is movement against, beyond, or away from rules and regulations, norms and conventions, borders and limits . . . it makes fluidity a fetish' (Epps 2001: 413). The idealisation of movement, or transformation of movement into a fetish, depends upon the exclusion of others who are already positioned as *not free in the same way*. Bodies that can move with more ease may also more easily shape and be shaped by the sign 'queer'. It is for this reason that Biddy Martin suggests that we need to 'stop defining queerness as mobile and fluid in relation to what then gets construed as stagnant and ensnaring' (Martin 1996: 46). Indeed, the idealisation of movement depends upon a prior model of what counts as a queer life, which may exclude others, those who have attachments that are not readable as queer, or indeed those who may lack the (cultural as well as economic) capital to support the 'risk' of maintaining antinormativity as a permanent orientation.

Queer lives do not suspend the attachments that are crucial to the reproduction of heteronormativity, and this does not diminish 'queerness', but intensifies the work that it can do. Queer lives remain shaped by that which they fail to reproduce. To turn this around, queer lives shape what gets reproduced: in the very failure to reproduce the norms through how they inhabit them, queer lives produce different effects. For example, the care work of lesbian parents may involve 'having' to live in close proximity to heterosexual cultures (in the negotiation with schools, other mothers, local communities), whilst not being able to inhabit the heterosexual ideal. The gap between the script and the body, including the bodily form of 'the family', may involve discomfort and hence may 'rework' the script. The reworking is not inevitable, as it is dependent or contingent on other social factors (especially class) and it does not necessarily involve conscious political acts.

We can return to my point about comfort: comfort is the effect of bodies being able to 'sink' into spaces that have already taken their shape. Discomfort is not simply a choice or decision—'I feel uncomfortable about this or that'—but an effect of bodies inhabiting spaces that do not take or 'extend' their shape. So the closer that queer subjects get to the spaces defined by heteronormativity the more *potential* there is for a reworking of the heteronormative,[9] partly as the proximity 'shows' how the spaces extend some bodies rather than others. Such extensions are usually concealed by what they produce: public comfort. What happens when bodies fail to 'sink into' spaces, a failure that we can describe as a 'queering' of space?[10] When does this potential for 'queering' get translated into a transformation of the scripts of compulsory heterosexuality?

It is important, when considering how this potential is translated into transformation, that we do not create a political imperative; for example, by arguing that all lesbian parents should actively work to interrupt the scripts of compulsory heterosexuality. As Jacqui Gabb shows, some lesbian parents may perceive their families to be 'just like other families' (Gabb 2002: 6; see also Lewin 1993). Now, is this a sign of their assimilation and their political failure? Of course, such data could be read in this way. But it also shows the lack of any direct translation between political struggle and the contours of everyday life given the ways in which queer subjects occupy very different places within the social order. Maintaining an active positive of 'transgression' not only takes time, but may not be psychically, socially or materially possible for some individuals and groups given their ongoing and unfinished commitments and histories. Some working-class lesbian parents, for example, might not be able to afford being placed outside the kinship networks within local neighbourhoods: being recognised as 'like any other family' might not simply be strategic, but necessary for survival. Other working-class lesbian parents might not wish to be 'like other families': what might feel necessary for some, could be impossible for others. Assimilation and transgression are not choices that are available to individuals, but are effects of how subjects can and cannot inhabit social norms and ideals.[11] Even when queer families may wish to be recognised as 'families like other families', their difference from the ideal script produces disturbances—moments of 'non-sinking'—that will require active forms of negotiation in different times and places.

To define a family as queer is already to interrupt one ideal image of the family, based on the heterosexual union, procreation and the biological tie. Rather than thinking of queer families as an extension of an ideal (and hence as a form of assimilation that supports the ideal), we can begin to reflect on the exposure of the failure of the ideal as part of the work that queer families are doing. As Weeks, Heaphy and Donovan suggest, we can consider families as social practices, and 'more as an adjective or, possibly, a verb' (Week, Heaphy and Donovan 2001: 37). Families are *a doing word and a word for doing*. Indeed, thinking of families as what people do in their intimate lives allows us to avoid positing queer families as an alternative ideal, for example, in the assumption that queer families are necessarily more egalitarian (Carrington 1999: 13). Queer lives involve issues of power, responsibility, work and inequalities and, importantly, do not and cannot transcend the social relations of global capitalism (Carrington 1999: 218). Reflecting on the work that is done in queer families, as well as what queer families do, allow us to disrupt the idealisation of the family form.

This argument seems to suggest that queer families may be just like other families in their shared failure to inhabit an ideal. But of course such an argument would neutralise the differences between queer and non-queer families, as well as the differences between queer families. Families may not 'be' the ideal, which is itself an impossible fantasy, but they have a different relation of proximity to that ideal. For some families the ideal takes the shape of their form (as being heterosexual, white, middle-class, and so on). The 'failure' to inhabit an ideal may or may not be visible to others, and this visibility has effects on the contours of everyday existence. Learning to live with the effects and affects of heterosexism and homophobia may be crucial to what makes queer families different from non-queer families. Such forms of discrimination can have negative effects, involving pain, anxiety, fear, depression and shame, all of which can restrict bodily and social mobility. However, the effects of this failure to embody an ideal are not simply negative. As Kath Weston has argued, queer families often narrate the excitement of creating intimacies that are not based on biological ties, or on established gender relations: 'Far from viewing families we choose as imitations or derivatives of family ties created elsewhere in their society, many lesbians and gay men alluded to the difficulty and excitement of constructing kinship in the *absence* of what they called "models"' (Weston 1991: 116, see also Weston 1995: 93). The absence of models that are appropriate does not mean an absence of models. In fact, it is in 'not fitting' the model of the nuclear family that queer families can work to transform what it is that families can do. The 'non-fitting' or discomfort opens up possibilities, an opening up which can be difficult and exciting.

There remains a risk that 'queer families' could be posited as an ideal within the queer community. If queer families were idealised within the queer community, then fleeting queer encounters, or more casual forms of friendship and alliance, could become seen as failures, or less significant forms of attachment. Queer politics needs to stay open to different ways of doing queer in order to maintain the possibility that differences are not converted into failure. Queer subjects do use different names for what they find significant in their lives and they find significance in different places, including those that are deemed illegitimate in heteronormative cultures. The word 'families' may allow some queers to differentiate between their more and less significant bonds, where significance is not assumed to follow a form that is already given in advance. For others, the word 'families' may be too saturated with affects to be usable in this way. Eve Kosofsky Sedgwick's vision of the family, for instance, is 'elastic enough to do justice to the depth and sometimes durability of nonmarital and/or nonprocreative bonds, same-sex bonds, nondyadic bonds, bonds not defined by genitality, "step"-bonds, adult sibling bonds, nonbiological bonds across generations, etc' (Sedgwick 1994: 71). But hope cannot be placed simply in the elasticity of the word 'family': that elasticity should not become a fetish, and held in place as an object in which we must all be invested. The hope of 'the family' for queer subjects may exist only insofar as it is not the only object of hope (see Chapter 8, for an analysis of hope). If we do not legislate what forms queer bonds take—and presume the ontological difference between legitimate and illegitimate bonds—then it is possible for queer bonds to be named as bonds without the demand that other queers 'return' those bonds in the form of shared investment.

It is, after all, the bonds between queers that 'stop' queer bodies from feeling comfortable in spaces that extend the form of the heterosexual couple. We can posit the effects of 'not fitting' as a form of queer discomfort, but a discomfort which is generative, rather than simply constraining or negative. To feel uncomfortable is precisely to be affected by that which persists in the shaping of bodies and lives. Discomfort is hence not about assimilation or resistance, *but about inhabiting norms differently*. The inhabitance is generative or productive insofar as it does not end with the failure of norms to be secured, but with possibilities of living that do not 'follow' those norms through. Queer is not, then, about transcendence or freedom from the (hetero)normative. Queer feelings are 'affected' by the repetition of the scripts that they fail to reproduce, and this 'affect' is also a sign of what queer can do, of how it can work by *working on* the (hetero)normative. The failure to be non-normative is then not the failure of queer to be queer, but a sign of attachments that are the condition of possibility for queer. Queer feelings may embrace a sense of discomfort, a lack of ease with the available scripts for living and loving, along with an excitement in the face of the uncertainty of where the discomfort may take us.

Queer Grief

The debate about whether queer relationships should be recognised by law acquires a crucial significance at times of loss. Queer histories tell us of inescapable injustices, for example, when gay or lesbian mourners are not recognised as mourners in hospitals, by families, in law courts. In this section, I want to clarify how the recognition of queer lives might work in a way that avoids assimilation by examining the role of grief within queer politics. There has already been a strong case made for how grief supports, or even forms, the heterosexuality of the normative subject. For example, Judith Butler argues that the heterosexual subject must 'give up' the potential of queer love, but this loss cannot be grieved, and is foreclosed or barred permanently from the subject (Butler 1997b: 135). As such, homosexuality becomes an 'ungrievable loss', which returns to haunt the heterosexual subject through its melancholic identification with that which has been permanently cast out. For Butler, this ungrievable loss gets displaced: heterosexual culture, having given up its capacity to grieve its own lost queerness, cannot grieve the loss of queer lives; it cannot admit that queer lives are lives that could be lost.

Simply put, queer lives have to be recognised as lives in order to be grieved. In a way, it is not that queer lives exist as 'ungrievable loss', but that queer losses cannot 'be admitted' as forms of loss in the first place, as queer lives are not recognised as lives 'to be lost'. One has to recognise oneself as having something before one can recognise oneself as losing something. Of course, loss does not simply imply having something that has been taken away. The meanings of loss slide from 'ceasing to have', to suffering, and being deprived. Loss implies the acknowledgement of the desirability of what was once had: one may have to love in order to lose. As such, the failure to recognise queer loss *as* loss is also a failure to recognise queer relationships as significant bonds, or that queer lives are lives worth living, or that queers are more than failed heterosexuals, heterosexuals who have failed 'to be'. Given that queer becomes read as a form of 'non-life'—with the death implied by being seen as non-reproductive—then queers are perhaps even already dead and cannot die. As Jeff Nunokawa suggests, heteronormative culture implies queer death, 'from the start' (Nunokawa 1991: 319). Queer loss may not count *because it precedes a relation of having*.

Queer activism has consequently been bound up with the politics of grief, with the question of what losses are counted as grievable. This politicisation of grief was crucial to the activism around AIDS and the transformation of mourning into militancy (see Crimp 2002). As Ann Cvetkovich puts it: 'The AIDS crisis, like other traumatic encounters with death, has challenged our strategies for remembering the dead, forcing the invention of new forms of mourning and commemoration' (Cretkovich 2003a: 427). The activism around AIDS produced works of collective mourning, which sought to make present the loss of queer lives within public culture: for example, with the Names Project Quilt, in which each quilt signifies a loss that is joined to others, in a potentially limitless display of collective loss. But what are the political effects of contesting the failure to recognise queer loss by displaying that loss?

In order to address this question, I want to examine public forms of grief displayed in response to September 11 2001. As Marita Stukern has argued, the rush to memorialise in response to the event not only sought to replace an absence with a presence, but also served to represent the absence through some losses and not others. On the one hand, individual losses of loved others were grieved, and surfaced as threads in the fabric of collective grief. The individual portraits of grief in the *New York Times*, and the memorials to individual losses posted around the city, work as a form of testimony; a way of making individual loss present to others. Each life is painted in order to transform a number into a being, one who has been lost to someone; so the person who is lost *is not only missing, but also missed*. But at the same time, some losses more than others came to embody the collective loss. Sturken suggests that a 'hierarchy of the dead' was constructed: 'The media coverage of September 11 establishes a hierarchy of the dead, with, for instance, the privileging of the stories of public servants, such as firefighters over office workers, of policemen over security guards, and the stories of those with economic capital over those without, of traders over janitors' {Sturken 2002: 383-4). Whilst some losses are privileged over others, some don't appear as losses at all. Some losses get taken in (as 'ours'), thereby excluding other losses from counting as losses in the first place.[12]

Queer losses were among the losses excluded from the public cultures of grief. As David L. Eng has argued, the public scripts of grief after September 11 were full of signs of heteronormativity: 'The rhetoric of the loss of "fathers and mothers", "sons and daughters", and "brothers and sisters" attempts to trace the smooth alignment between the nation-state and the nuclear family, the symbolics of blood relations and nationalist domesticity' (Eng 2002: 90). It is because of this erasure that some queer groups have intervened, by naming queer losses. The president of the National Lesbian and Gay Journalists Association,[13] for example, names queer loss both by naming individual queers who were lost in September 11, and by describing that event as a loss for the queer community. What is interesting about this response is how it addresses two communities: the nation and the queer community, using inclusive pronouns to describe both. The first community is that of all Americans: 'This unimaginable loss has struck at the very core of our sense of safety and order.' Here, September 11 is viewed as striking 'us' in the same place. But even in this use of inclusive language, the difference of GLBT Americans is affirmed: 'Even on a good day, many GLBT Americans felt unsafe or at least vulnerable in ways large and small. Now, that feeling has grown even more acute and has blanketed the nation.' The feelings of vulnerability that are specific to queer communities are first named, and then get extended into a feeling that blankets the nation, covering over the differences. The extension relies on an analogy between queer feelings (unsafety, vulnerability) and the feelings of citizens living with the threat of terrorism (see Chapter 3). The narrative implies that the nation is almost made queer by terrorism: heterosexuals 'join' queers in feeling vulnerable and fearful of attack. Of course, in 'becoming' queer, the nation remains differentiated from those who 'are' already queer.

This tension between the 'we' of the nation and the 'we' of the queer community is also expressed through the evocation of 'hate': 'Like others, our community knows all too well the devastating effects of hate.' This is a complicated utterance. On the one hand, this statement draws attention to experiences of being hated that trouble the national imaginary, which assumes a distinction between tolerant multicultural subjects who 'love' and fundamentalists and racists who 'hate' (see Chapter 6). By showing how queers are a community 'that is hated' by the imagined nation, the statement breaches the ideal image the nation has of itself ('America can hate others (queers), as well as be hated by others'). But at the same time, this narrative repeats the dominant one: the tragedy of the event is the consequence of 'their hate' for 'us' ('Why do they hate us?'). The construction of the queer community as a hated community, which splits the nation, slides into a construction of the nation as 'being' hated by others. The nation is reinstalled as a coherent subject within the utterance: together, we are hated, and in being hated, we are together.

Within this queer response, mourning responds to the loss of 'every life', which includes 'members of our own community'. Individual names are given, and the losses are named as queer losses: 'They include an American Airlines co-pilot on the flight that crashed into the Pentagon; a nurse from New Hampshire; a couple travelling with their 3-year old son.' Furthermore, the losses are evoked through the language of heroism and courage: 'Father Mychal Judge, the New York Fire Department chaplain, who died whilst administering last rites to a fallen fire fighter, and Mark Bingham, a San Francisco public relations executive, who helped thwart the hijackers'. Certainly, the call for a recognition of queer courage and queer loss works to 'mark' the others already named as losses. That is, the very necessity of identifying some losses *as* queer losses reveals how most losses were narrated as heterosexual losses in the first place. The apparently unmarked individual losses privileged in the media are here marked by naming these other losses *as* queer losses. The risk of the 'marking' is that queer loss is then named as loss *alongside* those other losses; the use of humanist language of individual courage and bravery makes these losses *like the others*. Hence, queer loss becomes incorporated into the loss of the nation, in which the 'we' is always a 'we too'. The utterance, 'we too', implies both a recognition of a past exclusion (the 'too' shows how the 'we' must be supplemented), and a claim for inclusion (we are like you in having lost). Although such grief challenges the established 'hierarchy between the dead' (Sturken 2002: 384), it also works as a form of covering; the expression of grief 'blankets' the nation. Queer lives are grieved *as* queer lives only to support the grief of the nation, which perpetuates the concealment of other losses (such as, for example, the losses in Afghanistan, Iraq, Palestine).

So whilst the NLGJA response to September 11 challenges the way in which the nation is secured by making visible some losses more than others, it allows the naming of queer losses to support the narrative it implicitly critiques. But our response cannot be to suspend the demand for the recognition of queer grief. We have already registered the psychic and social costs of unrecognised loss. The challenge for queer politics becomes finding a different way of grieving, and responding to the grief of others. In order to think differently about the ethics and politics of queer grief, I want to reconsider the complexity of grief as a psycho-social process of coming to terms with loss.

Freud's distinction between mourning and melancholia might help us here. For Freud, mourning is a healthy response to loss, as it is about 'letting go' of the lost object, which may include a loved person or an abstraction which has taken the place of one (Freud 1934b: 153). Melancholia is pathological: the ego refuses to let go of the object, and preserves the object 'inside itself' (Freud 1934b: 153). In the former 'the world becomes poor and empty', whilst in the latter, 'it is the ego itself' (Freud 1934b: 155). Melancholia involves assimilation: the object persists, but only insofar as it is taken within the subject, as a kind of ghostly death. The central assumption behind Freud's distinction is that it is good or healthy to 'let go' of the lost object (to 'let go' of that which is already 'gone'). Letting go of the lost object may seem an ethical as well as 'healthy' response to the alterity of the other.

But the idea that 'letting go' is 'better' has been challenged. For example, the collection *Continuing Bonds*, 'reexamines the idea that the purpose of grief is to sever the bonds with the deceased in order to free the survivor to make new attachments' (Silverman and Klass 1996: 3). Silverman and Klass suggest that the purpose of grief is not to let go, but lies in 'negotiating and renegotiating the meaning of the loss over time' (Silverman and Klass 1996: 19). In other words, melancholia should not be seen as pathological; the desire to maintain attachments with the lost other is enabling, rather than blocking new forms of attachment. Indeed, some have argued that the refusal to let go is an ethical response to loss. Eng and Kazanjian, for example, accept Freud's distinction between mourning and melancholia, but argue that melancholia is preferable as a way of responding to loss. Mourning enables gradual withdrawal from the object and hence denies the other through forgetting its trace. In contrast, melancholia is 'an enduring devotion on the part of the ego to the lost object', and as such is a way of keeping the other, and with it the past, alive in the present (Eng and Kazanjian 2003: 3). In this model, keeping the past alive, even as that which has been lost, is ethical: the object is not severed from history, or encrypted, but can acquire new meanings and possibilities in the present. To let go might even be to kill again (see Eng and Han 2003: 365).

Eng and Han's work points to an ethical duty to keep the dead other alive. The question of how to respond to loss requires us to rethink what it means to live with death. In Freud's critique of melancholia, the emphasis is on a lost external object, that which is other to me, being preserved by becoming internal to the ego. As Judith Butler puts it, the object is not abandoned, but transferred from the external to the internal (Butler 1997b: 134). However, the passage in grief is not simply about what is 'outside' being 'taken in'. For the object to be lost, *it must already have existed within the subject*. It would be too narrow to see this 'insideness' only in terms of a history of past assimilation ('taking in' as 'the making of likeness'), although assimilation remains crucial to love as well as grief, as I have already suggested. We can also think of this 'insideness' as an effect of the 'withness' of intimacy, which involves the process of being affected by others. As feminist critics in particular have argued, we are 'with others' before we are defined as 'apart from' others (Benjamin 1995). Each of us, in being shaped by others, carries with us 'impressions' of those others. Such impressions are certainly memories of this or that other, to which we return in the sticky metonymy of our thoughts and dreams, and through prompting either by conversations with others or through the visual form of photographs. Such 'withness' also shapes our bodies, our gestures, our turns of phrase: we pick up bits and pieces of each other as the effect of nearness or proximity (see Diprose 2002). Of course, to some extent this proximity involves the making of likeness. But the hybrid work of identity-making is never about pure resemblance of one to another. It involves a dynamic process of perpetual resurfacing: the parts of me that involve 'impressions' of you can never be reduced to the 'you-ness' of 'you', but they are 'more' than just me. The creation of the subject hence depends upon the impressions of others, and these 'impressions' cannot be conflated with the character of 'others'. The others exist within me and apart from me at the same time. Taking you in will not necessarily be 'becoming like you', or 'making you like me', as other others have also impressed upon me, shaping my surfaces in this way and that.

So to lose another is not to lose one's impressions, not all of which are even conscious. To preserve an attachment is not to make an external other internal, *but to keep one's impressions alive*, as aspects of one's self that are both oneself and more than oneself, as a sign of one's debt to others. One can let go of another as an outsider, but maintain one's attachments, by keeping alive one's impressions of the lost other. This does not mean that the 'impressions' stand in for the other, as a false and deadly substitute. And nor do such 'impressions' have to stay the same. Although the other may not be alive to create new impressions, the impressions move as I move: the new slant provided by a conversation, when I hear something I did not know; the flickering of an image through the passage of time, as an image that is both your image, and my image of you. To grieve for others is to keep their impressions alive in the midst of their death.

The ethical and political question for queer subjects might, then, not be *whether* to grieve but *how* to grieve. In some queer responses to September 11, the public display of grief installs queer loss as an object, alongside other losses, and in this way constructs the nation as the true subject of grief. But queer subjects can also share their impressions of those they have lost without transforming those impressions into objects that can be appropriated or taken in by the nation. For some, this was precisely the work of the Names Project Quilt, despite the reservations theorists such as Crimp have expressed about the way it sanitised loss for the mainstream audience (Crimp 2002: 196). As Ken Plummer has argued, the Project might matter not because of how it addresses the nation, as an imagined subject who might yet take this grief on as its own, but because of the process of working through loss with others. He suggests that 'stories help organise the flow of interaction, binding together or disrupting the relation of self to other and community' (Plummer 1995: 174). Perhaps queer forms of grief sustain the impressions of those who have been lost by sharing impressions with others. Sharing impressions may only be possible if the loss is not transformed into 'our loss', or converted into an object: when the loss becomes 'ours', it is taken away from others. Not to name 'my' or 'your' loss as 'our loss' does not mean the privatisation of loss, but the generation of a public in which sharing is not based on the presumption of shared ownership. A queer politics of grief needs to allow others, those whose losses are not recognised by the nation, to have the space and time to grieve, rather than grieving for those others, or even asking 'the nation' to grieve for them. In such a politics, recognition does still matter, not of the other's grief, but of the other as a griever, as the subject rather than the object of grief, a subject that is not alone in its grief, since grief is both about and directed to others.[14]

It is because of the refusal to recognise queer loss (let alone queer grief), that it is important to find ways of sharing queer grief with others. As Nancy A. Naples shows us in her intimate and moving ethnography of her father's death, feeling pushed out by her family during her father's funeral made support from her queer family of carers even more important (Naples 2001: 31). To support others as grievers—not by grieving for them but allowing them the space and time to grieve—becomes even more important when those others are excluded from the everyday networks of legitimation and support. The ongoing work of grief helps to keep alive the memories of those who have gone, provide care for those who are grieving, and allow the impressions of others to touch the surface of queer communities. This queer community resists becoming one, and aligned with the patriotic 'we' of the nation, only when loss is recognised as that which cannot simply be converted into an object, and yet is with and for others. Here, your loss would not be translated into 'our loss', but would prompt me to turn towards you, and allow you to impress upon me, again.

Queer Pleasures

Of course, queer feelings are not simply about the space of negativity, even when that negativity gets translated into the work of care for others. Queer politics are also about enjoyment, where the 'non' offers hope and possibility for other ways of inhabiting bodies. How do the pleasures of queer intimacies challenge the designation of queer as abject, as that which is 'cast out from the domain of the liveable' (Butler 1993: 9), or even as the 'death' made inevitable by the failure to reproduce life itself? This is a risky question. Whilst queers have been constructed as abject beings, they are also sources of desire and fascination. Michael Bronski explores the tension between 'heterosexual fear of homosexuality and gay culture (and the pleasure they represent) and the equally strong envy of and desire to enjoy that freedom and pleasure' (Bronski 1998: 2). Žižek also examines the ambivalence of the investment in 'the other' as the one 'who enjoys', and whose enjoyment exceeds the economies of investment and return (Žižek 1991: 2). The racist or homophobe tries to steal this enjoyment, which he assumes was taken from him, through the aggression of his hatred (see also Chapters 2 and 6). To speak of queer pleasure as potentially a site for political transformation risks confirming constructions of queerness that sustain the place of the (hetero)normative subject.

Equally though, others can be envied for their lack of enjoyment, for the authenticity of their suffering, their vulnerability, and their pain. I have examined, for example, how the investment in the figure of the suffering other gives the Western subject the pleasures of being charitable (see Chapter 1). Within the Leninist theory of the vanguard party, or the work of the Subaltern Studies group, there also seems to be an investment in the pain and struggle of the proletariat or peasant. Here the investment allows the project of speaking for the other, whose silence is read as an injury (Spivak 1988). In other words, the other becomes an investment by providing the normative subject with a vision of what is lacking, whether that lack is a form of suffering or deprivation (poverty, pain), or excess (pleasure, enjoyment). The other is attributed with affect (as being *in* pain, or *having* pleasure) as a means of subject constitution. I will not suggest that what makes queers 'queer' is their pleasure (from which straight subjects are barred), but will examine how the bodily and social practices of queer pleasure might challenge the economies that distribute pleasure as a form of property—as a feeling we have—in the first place.

In mainstream culture, it is certainly not the case that pleasure is excluded or taboo (there are official events—and places where the public is required to display pleasure—where pleasure is a matter of being 'a good sport'). Indeed within global capitalism the imperative is to have more pleasure (through the consumption of products designed to tantalise the senses). And yet alongside this imperative to enjoy, there is a warning: pleasures can distract you, and turn you away from obligations, duties and responsibilities. Hedonism does not get a good press, certainly. Pleasure becomes an imperative only as an incentive and reward for good conduct, or as an 'appropriate outlet' for bodies that are busy being productive ('work hard play hard'). This imperative is not only about having pleasure as a reward, but also about having the right kind of pleasure, in which rightness is determined as an orientation towards an object. Pleasure is 'good' only if it is orientated towards some objects, not others. The 'orientation' of the pleasure economy is bound up with heterosexuality: women and men 'should' experience a surplus of pleasure, but only when exploring each other's bodies under the phallic sign of difference (pleasure as the enjoyment of sexual difference). Whilst sexual pleasure within the West may now be separated from the task or duty of reproduction, it remains tied in some way *to the fantasy of being reproductive*: one can enjoy sex with a body that it is imagined one *could be* reproductive with. Queer pleasures might be legitimate here, as long as 'the queer' is only a passing moment in the story of heterosexual coupling ('queer as an enjoyable distraction'). The promise of this pleasure resides in its convertability to reproduction and the accumulation of value.

We might assume that queer pleasures, because they are 'orientated' towards an illegitimate object, will not return an investment. But this is not always or only the case. As Rosemary Hennessy has argued, 'queer' can be commodified, which means that queer pleasures can be profitable within global capitalism: the pink pound, after all, does accumulate value (Hennessy 1995: 143). Hennessy argues that money and not liberation is crucial to recent gay visibility. As she puts it: 'The freeing up of sensory-affective capacities from family alliances was simultaneously rebinding desire into new commodified forms' (Hennessy 2000: 104). The opening up of non-familial desires allows new forms of commodification; the 'non' of the 'non-normative' is not outside existing circuits of exchange, but may even intensify the movement of commodities, which converts into capital (see Chapter 2). Global capitalism involves the relentless search for new markets, and queer consumers provide such a market. The production of surplus value relies, as Marx argued, on the exploitation of the labour of others. The commodification of queer involves histories of exploitation: the leisure industries that support queer leisure styles, as with other industries, depend upon class and racial hierarchies. So it is important not to identify queer as outside the global economy, which transforms 'pleasures' into 'profit' by exploiting the labour of others.

Such an argument challenges the way in which sexual pleasure is idealised—as almost revolutionary in and of itself—within some versions of queer theory. For example, Douglas Crimp offers a vision of gay male promiscuity as 'a positive model of how sexual pleasures might be pursued' (Crimp 2002: 65), while Michael Warner defines sexual autonomy as 'access to pleasures' (Warner 1999: 7). Michael Bronski sees the 'pleasure principle' as the reason for the fear of homosexuality and also for its power: 'Homosexuality offers a vision of sexual pleasure completely divorced from the burden of reproduction: sex for its own sake, a distillation of the pleasure principle' (Bronski 1998: 8). This idealisation of pleasure supports a version of sexual freedom that is not equally available to all: such an idealisation may even extend rather than challenge the 'freedoms' of masculinity. A negative model of freedom is offered in such work, according to which queers are free to have pleasure as they are assumed to be free *from* the scripts of (hetero)normative existence: 'Because gay social life is not as ritualised and institutionalised as straight life, each relation is an adventure in nearly uncharted territory' (Warner 1999: 115; see also Bell and Binnie 2000: 133). Ironically, such a reading turns queer pleasure into a discovery narrative that is not far off genres that narrated the pleasures of colonialism: as a journey into uncharted territory. Who is the explorer here? And who provides the territory?

And yet, despite the way in which queer pleasures can circulate as commodities within global capitalism, I want to suggest that they can also work to challenge social norms, as forms of investment. To make this argument, we need to reconsider how bodies are shaped by pleasure and take the shape of pleasures. I have already addressed the phenomenology of pain (see Chapter 1), arguing that pain reshapes the surfaces of the body through the way in which the body turns in on itself. Pleasure also brings attention to surfaces, which surface as impressions through encounters with others. But the intensification of the surface has a very different effect in experiences of pleasure: the enjoyment of the other's touch opens my body up, opens me up. As Drew Leder has argued, pleasure is experienced in and from the world, not merely in relation to one's own body. Pleasure is expansive: 'We fill our bodies with what they lack, open up to the stream of the world, reach out to others' (Leder 1990: 75).

Pleasures open bodies to worlds through an opening up of the body to others. As such, pleasures can allow bodies to take up more space. It is interesting to consider, for example, how the display of enjoyment and pleasure by football fans can take over a city, excluding others who do not 'share' their joy, or return that joy through the performance of pleasure. Indeed, the publicness of pleasure can function as a form of aggression; as a declaration of 'We are here.' Beverley Skeggs (1999) shows how the display of pleasure by heterosexuals in queer space can also work as a form of colonisation; a 'taking over' of queer space, which leaves queer subjects, especially lesbians, feeling unsettled, displaced and exposed. These examples demonstrate an important spatial relation between pleasure and power. Pleasure involves not only the capacity to enter into, or inhabit with ease, social space, but also functions as a form of entitlement and belonging. Spaces are claimed through enjoyment, an enjoyment that is returned by being witnessed by others. Recalling my argument in the first section of this chapter, the display of queer pleasure may generate discomfort in spaces that remain premised on the 'pleasures' of heterosexuality. For queers, to display pleasure through what we do with our bodies is to make the comforts of heterosexuality less comfortable.

Further, pleasure involves an opening towards others; pleasure orientates bodies towards other bodies in a way that impresses on the surface, and creates surface tensions. But pleasure is not simply about any body opening up to any body. The contact is itself dependent on differences that already impress upon the surfaces of bodies. Pleasures are about the contact between bodies that are already shaped by past histories of contact. Some forms of contact don't have the same effects as others. Queer pleasures put bodies into contact that have been kept apart by the scripts of compulsory heterosexuality. I am not sure that this makes the genitals 'weapons of pleasure against their own oppression' (Berlant and Freeman 1997: 158). However queer pleasures in the enjoyment of forbidden or barred contact engender the possibility of different kinds of impressions. When bodies touch and give pleasure to bodies that have been barred from contact, then those bodies are reshaped. The hope of queer is that the reshaping of bodies through the enjoyment of what or who has been barred can 'impress' differently upon the surfaces of social space, creating the possibility of social forms that are not constrained by the form of the heterosexual couple.

Queer pleasures are not just about the coming together of bodies in sexual intimacy. Queer bodies 'gather' in spaces, through the pleasure of opening up to other bodies. These queer gatherings involve forms of activism; ways of claiming back the street, as well as the spaces of clubs, bars, parks and homes. The hope of queer politics is that bringing us closer to others, from whom we have been barred, might also bring us to different ways of living with others. Such possibilities are not about being free from norms, or being outside the circuits of exchange within global capitalism. *It is the non-transcendence of queer that allows queer to do its work*. A queer hope is not, then, sentimental. It is affective precisely in the face of the persistence of forms of life that endure in the negative attachment of 'the not'. Queer maintains its hope for 'non-repetition' only insofar as it announces the persistence of the norms and values that make queer feelings queer in the first place.

Notes

1. I borrow this phrase, of course, from Adrienne Rich. I am indebted to her work, which demonstrates the structural and institutional nature of heterosexuality.

2. A queer phenomenology might offer an approach to 'sexual orientation' by rethinking the place of the object in sexual desire, attending to how bodily directions 'towards' some objects and not others affects how bodies inhabit spaces, and how spaces inhabit bodies.

3. To reflect on queer feelings is also to reflect on 'queer' as a sticky sign. As Butler points out, the word 'queer' is performative: through repetition, it has acquired new meanings (Butler 1997c). Queer, once a term of abuse (where to be queer was to be not us, not straight, not normal, not human) has become a name for an alternative political orientation. Importantly, as a sticky sign, 'queer' acquires new meanings not by being cut off from its previous contexts of utterance, but by preserving them. In queer politics, the

force of insult is retained; 'the not' is not negated ('we are positive'), but embraced, and is taken on as a name. The possibility of generating new meanings, or new orientations to 'old' meanings, depends on collective activism, on the process of gathering together to clear spaces or ground for action. In other words, it takes more than one body to open up semantic as well as political possibilities. Furthermore, we should remember that queer still remains a term of abuse, and that not all those whose orientations we might regard as queer, can or would identify with this name, or even be able to 'hear' the name without hearing the history of its use as an injurious term: 'Now, the word *queer* emerges. But other than referring to it in quotations, I will never use the term *queer* to identify myself or any other homosexual. It's a word that my generation—and my companion, who's twenty-five years younger than I am, feels the same way—will never hear without evoked connotations—of violence, gay-bashings, arrest, murder' (Rechy 2000: 319). What we hear when we hear words such as 'queer' depends on complex psychobiographical as well as institutional histories.

4. See Chapter 5 on shame, where I discuss the way in which normative bodies have a 'tautological' relation to social ideals: *they feel pride at approximating an ideal that has already taken their shape*.

5. My analysis in Chapter 8, section 2, of the relation between wonder and the departure from what is ordinary takes this argument forward.

6. Of course, heterosexual subjects may experience discomfort when faced by queers, and queer forms of coupling, in the event of the failure to conceal signs of queerness. A queer politics might embrace this discomfort: it might seek to make people feel uncomfortable through making queer bodies more visible. Not all queers will be comfortable with the imperative to make others uncomfortable. Especially given that 'families of origin' are crucial spaces for queer experiences of discomfort, it may be in the name of love, or care, that signs of queerness are concealed. Thanks to Nicole Vittelone who helped me to clarify this argument. See also Chapter 5 on shame for a related discussion of queer shame within families.

7. Global capitalism relies on the 'feeling fetish' of comfort: for consumers to be comfortable, others must work hard, including cleaners as well as other manual workers. This division of labour and leisure (as well as between mental and manual labour) functions as an instrument of power between and within nation states. But the 'work' relation is concealed by the transformation of comfort into property and entitlement. We can especially see this in the tourism industry: the signs of work are removed from the commodity itself, such as the tourist package, as a way of increasing its value. See McClintock (1995) for an analysis of commodification and fetishism and Hochschild (1983: 7) for an analysis of the emotional labour that is required for the well-being of consumers.

8. I am, of course, paraphrasing Frantz Fanon's *Black Skin, White Masks*. The analogy has its limits: assimilation into whiteness and assimilation into straightness cannot be assumed to be equivalent, partly given the different relation of race and sexuality to signs of visibility. See Lorde 1984.

9. Thanks to Jackie Stacey whose astute comments during a conversation helped me to formulate this argument.

10. Of course, some queer bodies can pass, which means passing into straight space. Passing as a technology entails the work of concealment: to pass might produce an effect of comfort (we can't see the difference), but not for the subject who passes, who may be feeling a sense of discomfort, or not being at ease, given the constant threat of 'being seen' or caught out. See Ahmed (1999).

11. The debate about queer families has also been defined in terms of the opposition between assimilation and resistance (Goss 1997; Sandell 1994; Phelan 1997: l; Weston 1991: 2; Weston 1998).

12. Of course, a question remains as to whether 'others' would want collective grief to be extended to them. What would it mean for the ungrieved to be grieved? The other might not want my grief precisely because such a grief might 'take in' what was not, in the first place, 'allowed near'. Would Iraqis, Afghanistanis want the force of Western grief to transform them into losses? Would this not risk another violent form of appropriation, one which claims their losses as 'ours', a claim that conceals rather than reveals our responsibility for loss? Expressions of nostalgia and regret by colonisers for that which has been lost as an effect of colonisation are of course mainstream (see hooks 1992). Recognising the other *as* grieving, as having experienced losses (for which we might have responsibility) might be more ethically and politically viable than grieving for the other, *or claiming their grief as our own*. See my conclusion, 'Just Emotions', for an analysis of the injustice that can follow when the ungrievable is transformed into the grieved.

13. The National Lesbian and Gay Journalists Association 'is an organization of journalists, online media professionals, and students that works from within the journalism industry to foster fair and accurate coverage of lesbian, gay, bisexual and transgender issues. NLGJA opposes workplace bias against all minorities and provides professional development for its members.' Their web site is available on: http://www.nlgja.org/ Accessed 22 December 2003.

14. The political and legal battle for the recognition of queer partners in claims for compensation post September 11 is crucial. However, so far no such recognition has been offered. Recognising queer losses, and queers as the subjects of grief would mean recognising the significance of queer attachments. Bill Berkowitz interprets the 9/11 Victim Compensation Fund, which leaves the determination of eligibility for compensation to states, as follows: 'In essence, in a rather complicated and convoluted decision, families of gays and lesbians will not be given federal compensation unless they have wills, or the states they live in have laws recognizing domestic partnerships, which of course most states do not.' 'Victims of 9/11 and Discrimination', http://www.workingforchange.com/article.cfm?ItemId=13001 Accessed 6 January 2004.

28

To Commend or To Critique?: The Question of Religion and Film Studies

John Lyden

Abstract

This paper examines two approaches to popular film to come out of religious studies. The first assumes popular culture is as valid as any culture, in which case "religious" analysis of films seeks to identify the iconography and mythology of film as expressive of a viable popular religion. The second method critiques popular film as a form of hegemonic discourse to be unmasked as supportive of classist, racist, and sexist ideologies. This paper accepts the validity of both methods and seeks to balance them by asserting that all films should be seen both as viable expressions of culture and also as ideology. Films are both to the extent that all contain multiple "texts" and multiple meanings, held together in an aporial and not entirely rational fusion. We do not need to decide which meaning is fundamental, as all are present in the film.

Article

The study of film from a religious studies vantage point has produced a broad consensus. Films include religious symbolism, consciously or unconsciously, and films may project a world-view which functions much like a religion in our culture.

Films are a creation and a reflection of the popular culture which produces and sustains them. They support this culture through creating myths, icons, and values which are celebrated and reinforced in a ritualized fashion. A variety of methods are used by religious scholars to study films. There are representative of the range of methods available within film studies generally: semiotics, textual or formalistic studies, psychoanalytic methods, ideological or political critiques, reader-response theories, genre and auteur studies, and so on.

There is a fundamental tension, however, between two basic approaches to the study of film as exemplative of a popular religious tradition. On the one hand, popular culture may be accepted as a culture which is as valid as any other, and which expresses its own values through media such as film. Even though the films are not produced by the people but by a technological industry, they are produced for the people and (in part) out of response to what people believe in and hope

---

Reprinted by permission from *Journal of Religion and Film* 1, no. 2 (October 1997).

for. An analysis of their religious impact will then seek to identify the mythology of popular film with the purpose of establishing how it contributes to the religion of popular culture, and will often (at least implicitly) celebrate the values expressed by this mythology.

On the other hand, the opposed method views films' presentation of popular culture and its religious aspects with great suspicion. The films are defined as a form of hegemonic discourse which ultimately supports the status quo of classist, racist, and sexist ideologies (to name the most significant). In this case, popular film is to be unmasked as this hegemonic discourse and deconstructed in order to reveal how it influences our society in negative ways. This method has been shaped by liberationist and feminist approaches to culture and religion.

Of course, this typology presents an oversimplification (as all typologies do), as there will be few interpreters of film who rigidly conform to either model. Most will "commend" the values of some films, and "critique" those of others. After all, like everybody else, religion scholars are prone to disagree about what constitutes a "good" or a "bad" movie. But my point here is that one's methodological assumptions may at the outset give one a bias either for or against popular film. As a result, one may either uncritically accept the values of the culture (arguing that they are as valid as any other), or uncritically reject those same values (arguing that nothing good can come out of Hollywood). And I do not think that one can avoid this question by claiming to bracket value judgments while one examines popular culture, as one's values will still affect how one views the phenomenon, implicitly or otherwise.

There is a parallel here with the study of non-Christian religions by western Christian scholars of religion. It is only recently that western theologians and historians of religion have been able to enter into genuine dialogue with other religions, listening to what they are saying rather than uncritically rejecting their views or uncritically accepting them (usually without really understanding them, in either case). I would argue that the study of popular film by religion scholars is at a similar place, as it is only very recently that they have begun to seriously examine how the whole range of popular films function, religiously and culturally. And yet the question still lurks in the background as to whether this popular filmic religion should be accepted in tolerance or torn down like an idol.

Many have tended towards the latter view; but I will argue it is too easy to condemn without analyzing the texts of popular film, and perhaps there is something to commend in them even as we critique them. I will argue that it is possible to balance the two approaches insofar as the films themselves can be considered both forms of viable religion, and ideology. We do not need to decide which "meaning" is fundamental, as many may exist in the same film in an aporial and not entirely rational fusion.

First let us examine those who "commend" popular film. In this view, one seeks to appreciate the values of popular film as a valid expression of the culture they mirror. As Catherine Albanese has observed in regard to the study of religion and American popular culture in general, no American scholar of popular culture can exist outside of the culture she or he describes, and so there are no "Olympian heights," of superior knowledge or taste, to which one might escape to level value judgments on the culture.[1] There is really no way to "bracket" value-judgments regarding one's own culture, so that the scholar (as participant/observer of it) will probably at least tacitly accept its values—unless he or she consciously rejects them.

In regard to the study of film, religious scholars have accepted some of what films do for the culture, as they have experienced some sense of the power of the movies to convey a distinctive religious vision of the world. Thus Darrol Bryant writes that "the profoundly spiritual significance of film lies not so much in content or subject matter as in our experience of the film itself—an experience of order and harmony that stands in counterpoint to our experience of the everyday world.[2]

Michael Bird has said that a film can be a "hierophany," a manifestation of the sacred in our midst, drawing on Paul Tillich's view of culture as "open" to the transcendent which it may symbolically reflect.[3] Even the earlier studies which were primarily interested in connections with Christianity mirrored this appreciation of the religious power of film. In 1970, Carl

Skrade wrote that "contemporary film-makers force their audiences not only to examine the structures of destruction and peer into the depths of the human predicament, but they also offer filmic forms of symbols of renewal."[4]

Recent studies of religion and film also evidence this approach. In *New Image of Religious Film*, editor John May notes that in viewing popular films as being worthy of theological consideration, the essays in the book acknowledge but regret the tendency of many theologians to "distrust" popular film. May, in contrast, argues that popular culture should be considered an "ally in the process of evangelization."[5] Further, the predominantly Roman Catholic authors in May's volume see film as expressing the sense of mystery and of the sacred to the modern world in an especially effective way. For example, Joseph Marty here claims that "cinema awakens *homo religious*" because

> "It brings back to life the sense of mystery by making us love what is not immediately perceivable, what is beyond appearance and evidence. It suggests the invisible . . . Thus, cinema binds us again with the poetic and religious expression of humanity . . . Everything that is human, every relationship to the world and to nature, treated artistically by the cinema becomes a poem, a tale, a re-reading, a proposal of meaning, a celebration—in short, something that resembles a first religious step."[6]

Another example of a collection of essays which includes some that "commend" the religious aspects of popular films is *Screening the Sacred: Religion, Myth, and Ideology in Popular American Film*, edited by Joel Martin and Conrad Ostwalt. In this volume there are a number of articles which indicate some appreciation for the "mythologies" of popular film. Thus Avent Childress Beck writes of *Platoon* that the film is: "a mythic reinvention of the war that displaces grand historical statement on the involvement of the United States with an assertion instead of the primacy of an individual's or a small group's religious or psychological experience of the war" so that "in dark theaters, we are treated to the balms of religious myth; in the case of *Platoon*, to the ordered familiarities and emotive comfort of the Christian narrative."[7]

Similarly, in the same volume, Caron Schwartz Ellis writes in regard to Science Fiction films which feature "saviors" from the sky that "our spacemen are important to us. They give us hope in a world in which our vision of the stars is obscured by pollution and the potential for nuclear holocaust."[8] And Andrew Gordon's essay, written in 1978, analyzes the mythological form of *Star Wars* (which George Lucas developed out of Joseph Campbell's work) and so argues that the film is a "myth for our times." He then concludes:

"The fact is that each generation must create its own myths and heroes or regenerate those of the past. We are in a period in which the heroes have been cast down through such national catastrophes as Vietnam and Watergate, when the lines between good and evil grow cloudy, and when sexual identities have been redefined by the women's movement. Meanwhile, we have created a machine world for ourselves, a world that seems drained of spiritual values, a world in which we feel impotent and alien. We desperately need a renewal of faith in ourselves as Americans, as good guys on the world scene, as men and women, as human beings who count, and so we return to the simpler patterns of the past."[9]

It is Gordon's remarks in particular which show the problematic nature of this sort of analysis. In being ready to applaud the fact that the film makes the viewer "feel good," he has concluded it is valuable precisely because it offers an easy dualism between good and evil, so avoiding the ambiguity of world politics and feminism. Americans fall into this sort of dualism easily enough in any case. Should one commend those films which encourage in our "popular culture" a dualistic attitude of "us versus them"? Are such films flawed in seeking to avoid any challenge to our hegemonic structures? It can be asked whether *Star Wars* really does this (or whether it only does this), but the question here is, are the values Gordon cites really the sort one should uncritically accept as an aspect of popular film?

This question leads to the other type of approach to the values of popular films, and it is probably the more common among scholars of religion. Drawing on liberationist and feminist critiques of hegemonic discourse, religious scholars trained in these approaches have viewed popular American films as a prime example of that which secures and perpetuates ideology in America. As scholars of religion, they have been able to identify the theological or mythological forms used to secure this ideology. This approach has also been able to draw on much in film studies proper, as ideological critique of popular film is a well-established method in that field. Again from *Screening the Sacred*, Joel Martin's treatment of *Rocky* engages in this sort of analysis by viewing the film as one which scapegoats blacks as the cause of America's economic problems. The film appealed to white working-class Americans precisely because it engages in this sort of racism which "aggressively and ideologically reinterprets recent history.[10] Similarly, Janice Hocker Rushing interprets *Aliens* as an anti-feminist film which pits the "Good Mother/goddess" against the "Bad Mother/monster/goddess" and so reaffirms conservative visions of femininity which have bifurcated the feminine consciousness and so stigmatized certain types of women who do not accept their "proper" role in the patriarchy.[11]

Brandon Scott has also critiqued the ideology of popular films in his book *Hollywood Dreams and Biblical Stories*. His method is to establish a dialogue between the Bible and popular film and so he juxtaposes texts from both "canons" in regard to particular themes (e.g., gender, war, apocalyptic, etc.). He shows that the mythology transmitted by popular film works to legitimate (for example) violence and revenge (in the *Dirty Harry* films),[12] racism (in *The Birth of a Nation* and *Gone with the Wind*),[13] and female embeddedness (in *Mr. Mom* and *Fatal Attraction*).[14] In this sense, mythology functions as ideology, as it reinforces cultural hegemonies by suppressing conflict through an overarching narrative structure. Here Scott is drawing on the work of Roland Barthes (as expressed in his book, *Mythologies*,[15] which has influenced numerous film theorists). Scott also cites Claude Levi-Strauss' understanding of myth, which lies behind Barthes' application of the notion to popular culture. In Levi-Strauss' view, cited by Scott, "the purpose of myth is to provide a logical model capable of overcoming contradiction (an impossible achievement if, as it happens, the contradiction is real)."[16] We use myths to hide contradictions in the beliefs of our societies. As film genre analysis sees it, the film western, for example, mediates the contradiction between civilization and savagery in American society. That is, we approve of violence in our need to keep order. But the contradiction is overcome in film when the violence is evacuated from civilization after its occurrence: hence the need for the hero to leave after he saves the family in *Shane, The Searchers*, and innumerable other westerns.[17]

Although myth may be the dominant form in popular film, Scott also recognizes that popular films sometimes challenge and even subvert the myths of society. For example, he analyzes *Bronco Billy* as a myth-subverting western,[18] and *Private Benjamin* as a film which attacks the myth of female embeddedness[19]—though one might note that it does so by reinforcing myths about the military. John May has also noted that non-mythological films exist, and he draws a parallel between these and the form of parable (drawing on John Dominic Crossan's work), in that such films do not reassure us but challenge us to change our world-view.[20] He cites the work of Kubrick and Altman as examples of this form of parabolic cinema.[21]

Margaret Miles, in her book, *Seeing and Believing: Religion and Values in the Movies*, evidences yet another approach by a scholar of religious studies. She utilizes a cultural studies (rather than a textual-based) approach to assess the values projected by films within the socio-politico-cultural matrix in which the film is produced, distributed, and seen.[22] In doing so she seeks to avoid the automatic rejection of the values of the movies (which so often is the approach of conservative religion) as well as some of the assumptions of some ideological critics.[23] And yet, even though she claims she wishes to avoid "cultural pessimism,[24] her analysis draws considerably on ideological criticism in its rejection of the values of popular film. Out of all the films evaluated in her book, Miles seems able to approve the values only of one: *Daughters of the Dust* (1992).[25] And this one is hardly typical of popular films as it was an independent film made by an African-American woman.

Even films such as *Jesus of Montreal*, *Thelma and Louise*, and *Jungle Fever*, which could all be seen as challenging hegemonic structures, finally end up in Miles' analysis as films which make white males comfortable and do not deliver on the challenges they begin.[26] In her analysis, the cultural context in which such films are produced and received, as well as the content of the film images, disqualify them from being legitimate sources of values. "The many choices made in the production of a film," she writes in conclusion, "often undercut the radical topic filmmakers intended to present sympathetically," thus indicating the "profound conservativism" of Hollywood films.[27] The main value of popular films therefore lies merely in their ability to articulate the problems and anxieties of society, not to provide solutions.[28]

Miles' tendency to reject the values of almost all popular films and to embrace mainly independent films made outside the Hollywood system also mirrors a tendency of ideological criticism. Popular films tend to be lumped together as ideological, largely due to the fact that they are created by a major American capitalist industry which is more interested in profit and producing pleasing fantasies than in making challenging and subversive art films. This judgment can be traced to the analysis of "mass culture" developed by Theodor Adorno and Max Horkheimer, German intellectuals of the Frankfurt School who fled Nazi Germany only to come to Hollywood. Ready to see the seeds of totalitarianism everywhere, they viewed all Hollywood films as commodities of capitalism which injected their ideologies into passive audiences, discouraging thought or questioning of authority. In fact, Adorno and Horkheimer viewed all popular films as having basically the same plot and the same characters, as mass production eliminated any significant artistic individuality of the filmmakers.[29] The only films which could be viewed as legitimate were avant-garde art films made outside the Hollywood system, as these did not participate in its decadence but could critique it.

In spite of the fact that the study of film has developed beyond Adorno and Horkheimer's analyses, many film theorists have been unable to shake their view that popular film is by nature ideological and that only avant-garde cinema has value.[30] But Pierre Bourdieu has argued that this denigration of popular film is just another form of elitism, as cultural elites reject the taste of the "masses" in order to defend their own tastes, and hence secure their own cultural hegemony as the supposedly "legitimate" evaluators of culture.[31]

Besides being a not-too-subtle form of classism, this dualism between "popular" and "avant-garde" over-generalized about the content of films. If one is to evaluate popular film fairly, one cannot force a monolithic judgment on it without reference to individual films. Sometimes ideological film analysts are so certain of the content of the films they are discussing that they utilize a priori categories of interpretation which are in principle non-falsifiable and ignore details of the individual films; e.g., in Barbara Creed's psychoanalytic feminist analysis, all movie monsters are symbols of the feminine (because the female is defined as "monstrous" by our culture), even when the monsters are literally male in the film narrative.[32] This sort of analysis has determined what the film has said before ever examining the text, and so has identified all popular film with ideology rather than letting popular films speak for themselves.

This is not to say that all ideological film critics over-generalize in this way, nor to suggest that the religion scholars cited here have necessarily done so in every case. Rather, my purpose is to point out the danger present in ideological criticism if it is the primary method of interpretation. Just as Andrew Gordon's mythological analysis of *Star Wars* (see fn. 9, above) demonstrates the dangers of uncritical acceptance of the visions of popular film, so ideological critique may fall into an uncritical rejection of the worldview of popular film. Many interpreters have engaged in forms of both types of methods, and so have balanced them; but what principles should determine when one method is employed, and when the other? What criteria found in the films themselves might assist us in deciding whether to make peace or war on a particular film? Is it all just a matter of "taste" based on idiosyncrasies of our own worldviews, or are there principles that can guide the religious interpreter of film in regard to this question?

I would suggest that another look at the idea of "myth" may help solve this puzzle. Although mythology has been identified with ideology by some (e.g. Roland Barthes), even in following Levi-Strauss's basic definition of myth one need not conflate mythology with the original Marxist sense of ideology (as that which maintains hegemony). Myth holds together contradictions that cannot be mediated logically, but those contradictions are not always or merely accepted in order to conserve hegemonic structures. The Christian myth of the atonement holds together the aporia of a just-yet-loving God. How can God avoid sanctioning sin, and yet forgive it? The myth of God's Son dying for our sins is designed to overcome this aporia, but it does not do so in an entirely rational way. Though Anselm and others have tried to reduce the myth to a series of logical axioms, the effort has never been fully successful; one cannot logically explain how one person's death can pay for another's sins. There is something irreducible about the myth, the narrative of the story itself, which does not allow itself to be fully "explained" by any doctrine. Hence there has been no "authoritative" doctrine of the atonement in the history of Christian thought, and rival views have stood side by side.[33] This could be said of all religious myths, and the newer narrative theologies would support this non-rational mythological core of religion as essential to its nature. Indeed, it has been observed that there is something about classical narrative itself which contains a contradiction, as it seeks to resolve a conflict and so "end"—but in reality, there would be no end, as more events would transpire after the story finishes, upsetting the neat conclusion.[34]

All narrative then asserts a myth of wholeness which does not jar with our experiences in life. However, this does not in itself imply the reinforcement of hegemonic power structures; it only shows that we need the illusion of myth to make sense of our lives, which do not conform to the neatness of narrative. Myths can then exercise a positive function for societies by giving us a meaningful structure to live by, hopes to aspire to, ideas to believe in. *Star Wars*, for example, is not merely a movie that reinforces ideological dualism. It promotes a cosmic confidence in reality as governed by a higher power in which we can share, in spite of evidence to the contrary. Myths seek to reconcile the disparities and contradictions in our experience not by eliminating them, but by holding them together in a paradoxical and non-rationalizable fusion. And although myths may be inherently conservative of culture, cultures do need conserving and not simply critiquing.

Of course, there are times when popular film critiques itself, at least to some extent (as Scott and others have observed). At this level, the myth exposes some of its own aporial nature, even though this is usually suppressed by the end of the film. Still, in raising questions about itself, the myth grows and develops to incorporate the changing values of society. This also serves to conserve society (which myths do best) but in this case by allowing the myth to stretch with society as it seeks to develop its values. In this way, films of the 50's and 60's began to critique racism, even though the issues were dealt with in a carefully controlled fashion. For example, the harmonious liberal vision of interracial romance expressed in Stanley Kramer's *Guess Who's Coming to Dinner* (1967) is a far cry from the critique of the same in Spike Lee's *Jungle Fever* (1991), as Kramer's vision belittles racial tension through the myth of integration and assimilation. Yet Kramer's vision is also equally far from the overtly racist depiction of predatory black men attacking chaste white women in D. W. Griffith's *The Birth of a Nation* (1915). The values of films develop as society develops, and they reflect and encourage that development.

Affirming the importance of film as myth, however, should not erase the need to see film as ideology. In reality, films are both. As films already contain contradictory messages within them—as they both support and subvert established structures, or conserve society's values even while they critique them—so also the multiple texts within a film may be seen as conserving and developing society's values in a valid way, as well as illegitimately preserving power structures which ought to be dismantled. I would borrow a concept from my own Lutheran theological background to elucidate this, that of the Christian as "simul justus et peccator." According to this idea, the Christian has been justified by God even as and while a sinner, and so can be a subject and vehicle of God's grace in spite of human imperfection. Similarly, popular films may act as windows to transcendence which express messages seen as valuable by those of us in religious studies, as they open us to new visions or reassert what is valid in old ones—and films may also support class, race, and gender structures which deserve deconstruction. They may do both simultaneously, even within the same film, so that it is not a question of dichotomizing "good" vs. "bad" films, or "popular" vs. "avant-garde." The same film can convey both sorts of messages, and although some readers will be more sensitive to one than the other, neither can be discounted as present.

This does not mean all films are created equal. We may regard some as more or less valid than others. But we need at least to accept the possibility that any film can convey valid messages even while it contributes to ideology. And the presence of ideological content in a film does not somehow invalidate what the film might be said legitimately to accomplish as mythology of a popular religion which preserves values of society at least some of us might commend. Both the myth and the ideology are present in the film, and neither can be regarded as "the" fundamental meaning.

In evaluating a popular film, then, we should look at the ways in which it may provide not only an ideology, but a mythology which can provide the basis for meaningful life and action—in spite of, or even (like religion?) perhaps because of, its illusionism and idealism.

Endnotes

1. Catherine L. Albanese, "Religion and American Popular Culture: An Introductory Essay," in *Journal of the American Academy of Religion*, Vol. LXIV, number four (Winter 1996), p. 737.

2. M. Darrol Bryant, "Cinema, Religion, and Popular Culture" in *Religion in Film*, John R. May and Michael Bird, eds. (Knoxville: University of Tennessee Press, 1982), p. 112.

3. Michael Bird, "Film as Hierophany," in *Religion in Film*, pp. 322.

4. Carl Skrade, "Theology and Films" in *Celluloid and Symbols*, eds. John C. Cooper and Carl Skrade (Philadelphia: Fortress Press, 1970), p. 21.

5. Introduction to *New Image of Religious Film*, ed. John R. May (Kansas City: Sheed & Ward, 1997), p. ix.

6. Joseph Marty, "Toward a Theological Interpretation and Reading of Film: Incarnation of the Word of God—Relation, Image, Word," in *New Image*, pp. 135–136.

7. Avent Childress Beck, "The Christian Allegorical Structure of *Platoon*" in *Screening the Sacred: Religion, Myth, and Ideology in Popular American Film*, Joel W. Martin and Conrad E. Ostwalt, eds. (Boulder, CO: Westview Press, 1995), p. 54.

8. Caron Schwartz Ellis, "With Eyes Uplifted: Space Aliens as Sky Gods" in *Screening the Sacred*, p. 93.

9. Andrew Gordon, "Star Wars: A Myth for Our Times" in *Screening the Sacred*, p. 82.

10. Joel W. Martin, "Redeeming America: *Rocky* as Ritual Racial Drama" in *Screening the Sacred*, p. 130.

11. Janice Hocker Rushing, "Evolution of 'The New Frontier' in *Alien* and *Aliens*: Patriarchal Co-Optation of the Feminine Archetype" in *Screening the Sacred*, p. 114.

12. Bernard Brandon Scott, *Hollywood Dreams and Biblical Stories* (Minneapolis: Fortress Press, 1994), pp. 102–117.

13. Scott, pp. 158–165.

14. Scott, p. 247. Numerous other films receive this indictment, including *Working Girl* and *Baby Boom*.

15. Roland Barthes, *Mythologies* (New York: Hill and Wang, 1957).

16. Claude Levi-Strauss, "The Structural Study of Myth" in *Structural Anthropology* (New York: Harper & Row, 1963), p. 229, quoted in Scott, p. 5.

17. Thomas Schatz, *Old Hollywood/New Hollywood: Ritual, Art, and Industry* (Ann Arbor, MI: UMI Research Press, 1983), pp. 9–10.

18. Scott, pp. 118–123.

19. Scott, pp. 225–227.

20. John R. May, "Visual Story and the Religious Interpretation of Film" in *Religion in Film*, pp. 32–33.

21. May, "Visual Story," pp. 38, 41.

22. Margaret R. Miles, *Seeing and Believing: Religion and Values in the Movies* (Boston: Beacon Press, 1996), p. xiii.

23. She rejects Laura Mulvey's thesis, for example (proposed in an article which influenced almost all subsequent feminist film analysis, "Visual Pleasure and Narrative Cinema," *Screen* 16, 3 (1975), pp. 6–18), that in order to challenge the values of mainstream film, one must "destroy" the pleasure produced by it. Miles finds Mulvey's approach unacceptable as she believes it to be based on the ascetic notion that only what has overcome pleasure has value. Miles, p.10.

24. Miles, p. 22.

25. Miles, pp. 127–134.

26. For Miles' analysis of *Jesus*, see pp. 40–47; *Thelma*, pp. 141–149; *Jungle*, pp. 158–167.

27. Miles, p. 190.

28. Miles, pp. 192–193.

29. Joanne Hollows, "Mass Culture Theory and Political Economy," in *Approaches to Popular Film*, eds. Joanne Hollows and Mark Jancovich (Manchester: Manchester University Press, 1995), pp. 18–23.

30. Mark Jancovich gives this criticism of recent screen theory (Jancovich, "Screen Theory," in *Approaches to Popular Film*, p. 126, 144, and passim).

31. Joanne Hollows and Mark Jancovich, "Introduction: Popular Film and Cultural Distinctions," in *Approaches to Popular Film*, pp. 4–5.

32. Noted by Mark Jancovich in "Screen Theory," *Approaches*, p. 147; he refers to Barbara Creed's *The Monstrous-Feminine: Film, Feminism, Psychoanalysis* (London: Routledge, 1993).

33. It may have been Gustaf Aulen who first recognized the impossibility of rationally explaining the myth of the atonement, in his classic book, *Christus Victor: An Historical Study of the Three Main Types of the Idea of the Atonement*, tr. A. G. Hebert (New York: Macmillan, 1966).

34. The view of Colin McCabe, "Realism and the Cinema: Notes on Some Brechtian Theses," *Screen*, 15:2 (summer 1974), pp. 21–27, referenced in Jancovich, "Screen Theory," *Approaches*, pp. 128–129.

29

Real or Not Real: The Hunger Games *as Transmediated Religion*[1]

Yonah Ringlestein

Abstract

Transmedia is a powerful mode of mediated storytelling. Resembling the mythic imaginaries of Jewish mysticism and Christian Gnosticism, transmedia encourages fans to perform their desire for wholeness and ultimate reality. The Hunger Games franchise does religious work of shaping desire for wholeness through fan culture by promising fans they can overcome fragmentation and experience reintegration. Cultural analyses of transmedia franchises have yet to look at the mythic pattern of fragmentation, negotiation, and reunification of self through transmedia and fan-based activities. What makes The Hunger Games distinctive is how it functions as a transmediated world and also exposes the necessity of negotiation with media to recognize the difference between artifice and reality. I conclude that The Hunger Games eschews both the singular reality of modernity and the fluid realities of postmodernity, instead advocating for a persistently critical perspective of all kinds of constructed worlds and all realities.

On 2 May 2012, 13-year-old Julia Bluhm led a protest outside the Hearst Tower in New York City, pressuring *Seventeen Magazine* to stop airbrushing young women. Julia argued that the magazine should portray real women because "[n]obody's photoshopped in real life" (Krupnick 2012). Media brands themselves have responded to the artifice that permeates the media, revealing behind-the-scenes manipulations of reality and encouraging consumers to engage in a process of negotiation between reality and unreality. In 2006, the Dove Campaign for Real Beauty released the Evolution of Beauty video, which shows a normally attractive woman transformed by cosmetics and Photoshop until she is unrecognizable. Dove concludes the video with the artificially beautified woman on a billboard followed by the statement, "No wonder our perception of beauty is distorted" (Dove 2006). TLC's newest reality

Reprinted from the *Journal of Religion and Popular Culture* 25, no. 3 (2013), University of Toronto Press.

show *Here Comes Honey Boo Boo*, which portrays the life of a self-proclaimed "redneck" family from Georgia, engages with the same issues and has incited controversy over its insistence on being overtly real, refusing to conceal the vulgar behaviour of the Thompson family.

These three examples—Julia's protest against airbrushing, Dove's revelation of photoshopped models, and TLC's *Honey Boo Boo*—all point to what we might call a yearning for reality in the construction of media and necessitate viewer responsibility in negotiating between artifice and reality. There is a paradoxical tension inherent in these developments—an awareness and acknowledgement of media construction, and at the same time, a desire to negotiate media construction to discover what is *really* reality. In this essay, I will argue that this hunger for reality[2] is a form of religious work, occupying us not only in commercial engagement or reality TV, but in our most popular emerging franchised storyworlds.[3] Indeed, the call to engage in the process of negotiation between artifice and reality is nowhere better illustrated than in the aptly named popular culture phenomenon *The Hunger Games*.

What makes *The Hunger Games* franchise especially worthy of our attention? Statistics show that *Hunger Games* fans are just as, if not more, enthusiastic than *Harry Potter* or *Avatar* fans: *The Hunger Games* film adaptation released in March 2012 broke Fandango's record for highest first-day advance tickets sales (Bethune 2012b). But what makes this fan frenzy so curious is that *The Hunger Games* franchise originally derives from Suzanne Collins's young adult novel in which a totalitarian government forces children to battle each other to the death. This dystopia is clearly a far cry from the Hogwarts and Pandora realms, so it seems it should not generate the same desire for imaginative entry. Fans of the older franchises had mantras like "Quitting school. Going to Hogwarts!" and "Wish I could live on Pandora!" Despite their intense devotion, *Hunger Games* fans do not generally seem to desire to imaginatively live in Panem, where they could potentially be placed in a deadly arena. Commenting on the peculiar popularity of *The Hunger Games*, one schoolteacher noted that many readers cannot see themselves in the arena despite their intense interest in the franchise. When asked if they would survive the arena, fans always respond "no, no way" (Dunne 2012). *Entertainment Weekly* similarly registers consternation about the seemingly bizarre fan attraction to *The Hunger Games*:

> [T]here's almost no element of escapism [in The Hunger Games]. Everyone who saw the Harry Potter films dreamed of going to Hogwarts, and the Twilight franchise offered its besotted female fan base a sparkly array of male eye candy. But the uncompromising universe of The Hunger Games, where children as young as 12 are sacrificed for entertainment, isn't exactly one you'd want to imagine your way into. (Staskiewicz and Bell 2012)

Thus we have a striking paradox: while *The Hunger Games* presents a fictional world that is undesirable to inhabit, fans eagerly immerse themselves in this world. For the opening weekend of the film's release, 3 a.m. IMAX movie screenings had to be added because midnight screenings were sold out (McNary 2012). If the fictional world of *The Hunger Games* is deadly and uninhabitable, then why are fans attempting to enter it using any medium they can get their hands on?

There are some obvious reasons why the franchise might be popular right now. Film scholar Mark Fisher has noted that the first book in *The Hunger Games* trilogy was first published in 2008 amidst the worst of the American financial crisis, and thus reflects contemporary concerns about intense social stratification in which the rich are carefree and the poor live in a state of "precariousness" and "anxiety" (Fisher 2012). Indeed, the trilogy's commentary on social stratification has led to the series being called a "parable of the Occupy Wall Street movement" (Zeitchik 2012) in which the "fantastically-coiffed and couture-clad denizens of the Capitol" represent the one percent (Cvetkovic 2012). Although concerns about class conflict undoubtedly resonate with many fans, I propose that *The Hunger Games* is best understood as a compelling mode of self-critical, reflexive transmediated world-building, significant because it proposes useful modes of coping with current anxieties about "reality."

Transmedia, World-Building, and "Wholeness-Hunger"

Transmedia is one of the most powerful modes of mediated storytelling today. *The Hunger Games* is an emerging transmedia world with, at the time of writing, a completed trilogy of books, one film released, a second film in production, and a plethora of online and offline mediums created by both media producers and fans themselves. As consumers engage with *The Hunger Games* transmedia franchise through multiple access points, they actively participate in a form of complex world-building, and in so doing, perform the desire for unification of identity and articulation of "real reality" that marks this franchise as distinctive.

Henry Jenkins explains that transmedia "integrate[s] multiple texts to create a narrative so large that it cannot be contained within a single medium" (Jenkins 2008, 97). These mediums could be books, films, games, clothing, posters, events, and anything else related to the franchise. As a result of this multiplicity of platforms, "each new text mak[es] a distinctive and valuable contribution to the whole" (Jenkins 2008, 97–8). To fully immerse in a transmedia world like *The Hunger Games*, then, consumers "must assume the role of hunters and gatherers, chasing down bits of story across media channels" (Jenkins 2008, 21). Any element in the transmedia franchise can serve as a "point of entry" into the larger fictional world (Jenkins 2008, 98). Transmedia storytelling is, in short, "the art of world making" (Jenkins 2008, 21).

Transmedia franchises, even the dystopic *The Hunger Games*, that build entire worlds through diverse media platforms are engaged in a "quintessentially religious endeavor" (Wagner 2012, 208). Religions have long engaged in "cosmos construction" or the "imagining of a world in which we are in control, in which things make sense, in which what we do has profound meaning, and in which we can enact our ideal selves" (Wagner 2012, 2). Rachel Wagner identifies the connection between transmedia, religion, and world-building:

> If religion is like a Katamari ball, then each manifestation of it is a combination, a "sticky-ball," of a variety of these facets [of religion]—and the more things have been rolled up together, the more people will likely see the same phenomenon as "religion" even if they experience it in different ways . . . Traditional religions have been remarkably good at rolling together a host of different components or "streams" that all flow together to a central core. (Wagner 2012, 206–7)

Like traditional religions, transmedia producers "are in the business of 'rolling up' rituals, stories and traditions in their production and marketing new 'sticky balls' of their own" (Wagner 2012, 208). Transmedia also "functions like religion in its ability to engender hunger in consumers," a desire to inhabit a world that is ordered and has meaning (Wagner 2012, 13). Devoted fan participation in a transmedia franchise can even be compared to traditional religious rituals, each operating as a "performance of belief" (Wagner 2012, 13). Transmedia, then, is powerful in the way it constructs worlds for people seeking meaning, order, purpose, and a sense of belonging.

This life-orienting activity may explain the immense popularity of recent transmedia franchises, such as *Harry Potter* and *Avatar*, that construct highly desirable worlds that fans imagine themselves inhabiting. The fact that *The Hunger Games* world is a violent dystopia, of course, raises the question of why fans are so devoted to it. But as I argue here, the very popularity of *The Hunger Games* franchise is due to the way it forces us to think critically before we plunge into media worlds. In other words, we still desire entry into transmediated worlds as an escape from the chaos of life, but at the same time we are hungry for "reality" and question the role that artificial mediated spaces play in our quest for meaning. *The Hunger Games* meets us in this paradoxical space of desire, especially in the movie version, as will be shown.

David Chidester argues that every form of religious expression, including popular culture that works *like* religion, has its own "logic of desire," but he does not provide a satisfactory explanation of *what* is being desired (Chidester 2005, 26). Yet if transmedia can work like religion, we can ask: What do we desire from transmedia? Wade Clark Roof's discussion of American "quest culture" helps to provide an explanation for the widespread appeal of transmedia franchises like *The Hunger Games*. Roof explains that modernity "severs connections to place and community, alienates people from their natural environments, separates life and work, dilutes ethical values, all of which makes the need for unifying experience so deeply felt" (Roof 1999, 62).

"Wholeness-hunger," a concept that Roof borrows from John Murray Cuddihy, is caused by these severing forces, which push spiritual seekers to engage in "processes of 'de-differentiation'—that is, in constructive efforts at reintegrating life experiences . . . [these efforts] are all aimed at healing the wounds of minds, bodies, and souls" (Roof 1999,62–3). Roof's description of the scattered pieces of life closely resembles the scattered *Hunger Games* transmedia story spread across a multiplicity of mediums. Therefore, part of the appeal of transmedia is how it enables consumers to perform their desire for unity—the more points of entry you engage with, the closer you are to grasping the entire story. Consumers must constantly negotiate with thousands of transmedia elements as they attempt to achieve a sense of wholeness. Transmedia, then, feeds our desire for reality *and* completeness.

This process of negotiation is necessitated by the contemporary media climate. Heidi Campbell explains,

> *the religious-social shaping of technology calls for investigation of the* negotiation process *religious communities undergo when faced with a new form of media. Here religious communities draw on their history, tradition, and their core beliefs as the basis for established patterns of media use . . . [I]f the technology is significantly new in its form or in the social conditions it creates so that it raises challenges for the community, the community must enter into a negotiation process to see what factors or uses of the technology can be accepted and which ones might need to be rejected.* (Campbell 2010, 61)

The fragmentation of modernity is itself expressed in the vast array of new media technologies with which we are faced today, and we are challenged with negotiating how we will live and engage with these media in our daily lives. Stewart M. Hoover also emphasizes the process of negotiation with media; in contrast to the "effects theory" in which media are "determinative ideological constructions." Hoover argues that media influence is better understood through the theory of "interactionism," in which "media objects" are "symbolic resources" self-consciously integrated into daily life for "meaning-making" (Hoover 2006, 40–41).

This process of negotiation and meaning-making is part of the search for wholeness as media consumers take each media fragment, negotiate with it, and appropriately incorporate it into their personal religious narratives. Transmedia is especially appealing, then, because the more points of entry with which the individual negotiates and subsequently incorporates, the closer that person is to the sense of satisfaction derived from overcoming their "wholeness-hunger." As no one medium can contain the entire story, a transmedia world like *The Hunger Games* achieves integrity and actualization only in the mind of each individual who encounters it—and the more devoted the expression of fandom, the more likely the fan is to experience that wholeness. The desire for wholeness, for the completion of the transmedia world, is thus a way of expressing the hunger for reality.

Mythic Hunger for Reality

The search for wholeness as a hunger for reality is surprisingly not a new religious concept. It can be found in the Jewish concept of *tikkun*, the notion of restoration or restitution as expressed in late-sixteenth-century Lurianic Kabbalism. In both Jewish mysticism and *The Hunger Games* transmedia franchise, there are scattered narrative and ritual "pieces," material and symbolic elements that must be sought out and negotiated by individual devotees. In addition, the mythic formulation of *tikkun*, which directs human desire toward the completion not of a storyworld, but of God himself, suggests that this desire for unified wholeness is a deeply religious endeavour, expressed in powerful forms of religious practice. Transmedia, as a popular form of world-building and an expression of desire for unity, echoes this mystical narrative, even if it makes far fewer ultimate promises about what reunification entails.

A recitation of the myth of *tikkun* will help to illustrate this resemblance. In Lurianic Kabbalism, God is believed to have originally filled the entire universe. In order to make room for creation, God had to contract himself into himself. This process of withdrawal required God to contract his divine emanations into ten vessels called *sefirot*. The weaker vessels, the myth says, were not strong enough to contain God's brilliance and so they broke, shattering the universe and scattering sparks of divine light. As a result of this cosmic catastrophe, God desires reunification, and the Jewish people must play an essential role in the reunification process. Each individual is charged with the responsibility of doing *tikkun*, which literally means "restoration" or "restitution." He or she must direct his or her "whole inner purpose towards the restoration of the original harmony" and unity of God (Scholem 1941, 275). To put it crudely, each worshipper must be a fully devoted fan of the *tikkun* universe and invest in its rituals with full commitment. In fact, the "fulfillment of each and every commandment was to be accompanied by a formula declaring" that the action was done for the purpose of working toward the unity of God (Scholem 1941, 275–76).

It may seem an odd comparison at first, but the religious mode of world-building in Jewish Kabbalah has a popular analogue in contemporary transmedia, suggesting that the human desire for storyworlds is old, deep, and incredibly powerful. While one can certainly argue that the myth of *tikkun* reveals a "true" state of the universe and *The Hunger Games* is purely fictional, the *functional* mode of reconstructing a meaningful world through narrative reintegration and committed practice is a common element in both forms of devotion. Just as God is fragmented and cannot be contained in any one fragment, no one platform can contain the entire *Hunger Games* transmedia world. As the Jewish people were charged with negotiating the material world to unify and realize God, so the consumer today negotiates with numerous transmedia platforms, engaging the fictional world at as many points of entry as possible to fulfill the desire for wholeness and reality. These extensive functional similarities between *tikkun* and contemporary franchises suggest that the religious tradition of Lurianic Kabbalism was actually an early form of transmedia. As Wagner explains, we should "think of transmedia as religion, and religion as transmedia" in the way that they both provide ways of negotiating with the mediums of life with the goal of unification and actualization of ultimate reality (Wagner 2012, 208).

Another place that transmediated elements appear in established religious history is in early Christian Gnosticism, which itself has ancient roots in the strands of Neoplatonic mystical thought that also influenced the development of Jewish mysticism. The religious beliefs that ultimately resulted in both Gnosticism and Jewish mysticism were initially developed in the tumultuous time of the Roman Empire, and each presents a mythic imaginary of the processes of fragmentation, negotiation, and reunification. Indeed, the connections between Gnostic principles and transmedia are so strong that we can see both of these in *The Matrix* franchise, showing one of the first fully developed attempts at transmedia world-building in the post-Internet age. *The Matrix* franchise functions as a form of transmedia through its cultivation of desire for related points of entry into the film's storyline via comic books, anime, video games, and apparel. But it also demonstrates in its own plotline the anxiety about media and the hunger for reality that blossoms in full form in *The Hunger Games*.

In Gnosticism, humans are charged with a personal responsibility to rise above "ignorance" to "gnosis" or wisdom. *The Matrix* demonstrates a similar process:

> *Neo is "saved" through gnosis or secret knowledge . . . Neo learns about the true structure of reality and about his own true identity, which allows him to break the rules of the material world he now perceives to be an illusion . . . He functions as a Gnostic Redeemer, a figure from another realm who enters the material world in order to impart saving knowledge about humanity's true identity and the true structure of reality, thereby setting free anyone able to understand the message.* (Flannery-Dailey and Wagner 2001)

The theme of fragmentation appears quite literally in Neo's defeat of Agent Smith when Neo enters Smith's body and visibly shatters him into pieces "by means of pure luminosity, portrayed through special effects as light shattering Smith from the inside out" (Flannery-Dailey and Wagner 2001). In conquering Smith, Neo reunified all of creation by dispersing, then regathering, the shattered elements of identity expressed in the multiplication of "Smiths." Neo's final moments in the third film, plugged into the matrix system and serving as a saviour figure, reveal that the goal of Smith's shattering is in fact a reintegration of the fragmented pieces represented by the "Smiths." The symbolism shows us that Neo's *gnosis* or enlightenment of the true reality, his literal luminosity, defeats the fragmentation of the material world in which media *claims* to be the true reality, but is only an illusion.

The Matrix, then, argues that individuals must strive for awakening so that they can discover the truth and in so doing achieve reunification—a message that is repeated in another form in *The Hunger Games*. Each person is charged with the responsibility to negotiate with multiple elements of media (the material world) in order to discover the "real" reality. *The Matrix* is a transmedia franchise in which negotiating with media and striving for wholeness by defeating fragmentation leads to knowledge of ultimate reality—prized religious knowledge. It is no coincidence, then, that the myth of Gnosticism is employed by the creators, nor that the medium of transmedia world-building is also employed. As evidenced by Jewish mysticism and Christian Gnosticism, humans have long been involved in working religiously toward unification. Transmedia today should be viewed as a contemporary outgrowth of this very old mythic hunger for reality.

It is true that *The Hunger Games* appears to present a fully secularized world. But whether we see contemporary transmedia franchises as engaging with "authentic" modes of religious expression or not, they certainly appear to be gesturing toward the same deep forms of human desire, feeding these with promises of reintegration and wholeness. *The Hunger Games* performs this mythic gesture toward wholeness and ultimate religious reality in taking shape as a transmedia franchise across multiple media platforms, functioning as an "authentic fake" that is "doing real religious work in forging a community" and "focusing desire" in a manner that closely resembles religion (Chidester 2005, viii). *The Hunger Games*, then, operates *like* religion by gesturing toward communal wholeness in addition to self-wholeness. At the same time, it drives fan desire for a sense of belonging, a characteristic that has long been recognized as a form of religious work.

Hunger in *The Hunger Games* Fan Community

The Hunger Games franchise nurtures what Chidester calls a "community of allegiance," which intensifies the desire for entry into otherworldly narrative spaces, reinforcing the work of transmedia as religion (Chidester 2005, 33). Even before the film was released, fans gathered for *Hunger Games*–themed events at libraries and bookstores across the country. There were trivia contests, survival challenges, costume parties, mock battles, community readings, art exhibits, and book discussions (Dunne 2012; Cawthon 2012). A "Run for Your Life" 5K even took place in North Carolina near Shelby, the site of *The Hunger Games* movie set (Cawthon 2012). Participation in these *Hunger Games* rituals develops social bonds between fans and reinforces feelings of "sacred solidarity" in a "sacred collectivity" (Chidester 2005, 33). The performance of desire was exceptionally powerful during the *Hunger Games* mall tour, which gave fans the opportunity to meet the film's stars. Intensely devoted fans sat on the floor for more than ten hours waiting for the stars to arrive (Crandell 2012). During this ritual of waiting, a powerful sense of community emerged as "friendships were being made over conversations about the books" (Crandell 2012). Fans even went through embarrassing rites of passage, such as dancing like monkeys, to win coveted personal meet-and-greets with the actors.

This dedicated community of allegiance reached fever pitch when the *Hunger Games* film was released on 23 March 2012. Chidester notes that popular culture creates sacred time, and no time is more sacred for franchise fans than the midnight movie screening (Chidester 2005, 2). During a midnight release, the movie theatre is transformed into a sacred space for fans where they know the most dedicated fan community will gather to celebrate. One fan described her feeling of belonging: "It's fantastic being able to see something you love with all the people who love the exact same thing" (Staskiewicz and Bell 2012). The sacred space and time of the movie theatre encourages this sense of solidarity and supports a "sense of uniformity, a sense of belonging to a vast . . . family that attends the same church" (Chidester 2005, 36). And just as religious worshippers would not usually wear casual clothing to church, the movie theatre becomes a church-like place where fans don costumes as ritual attire to embody their favourite characters from the story and perform their desire to be a part of *The Hunger Games* community.

Related ritualized fan events reinforce this sense of belonging. One fansite, The Hob, organized a midnight movie event that included a raffle of an autographed copy of the book. When the raffle ticket was drawn, the winner yelled out a poignant line from the book and fans burst out laughing (Staskiewicz and Bell 2012). As only fans would understand the joke, this raffle is an insider ritual performance that mimics a ritual event within the books—the reaping of tributes to fight in the arena—and reinforces a strong sense of "sacred collectivity" between all those gathered for the real-life performance of belief in the fictional world (Chidester 2005, 33). By inviting similar ritual performances, New York Sports Clubs morphed into sacred spaces with the introduction of *Hunger Games*–themed classes where devoted fans could gather and "Train Like a Tribute" with moves like "Katniss Kickbacks," "Peeta Presses," and "Sprint to the Cornucopia," and potentially be declared the "victor" of the workout by the teacher or "Gamemaker." By participating in the sacred time of such an exercise class, fans ritually enact events from the transmedia storyworld and gather together to express their desire for communal wholeness.

Of course, transmediated world-building is fueled by consumerist tendencies, as exhibited by the film-release events and the host of items for sale connected to the franchise. *Hunger Games* transmedia directs desire for products that will enable consumers to display their membership in the sacred collective, effectively selling the wish for belonging. Chidester argues that such desire-driven consumer products can nonetheless become "invested with transcendent power and sacred significance" (Chidester 2005, 3). Moreover, "even ordinary objects can be transformed into icons, extraordinary magnets of meaning with a religious cast" (Chidester 2005, 34). Transmedia consumer products have the ability to transcend their utilitarian function and become symbolic representations of the fuller meaning of the transmedia story.

As Emile Durkheim explains, "collective feelings can be embodied" in a totemic symbol, which serves to unite a group of people by tapping into a belief in a higher reality (Durkheim

2001, 177). Totemic *Hunger Games* products abound, including clothing, jewellery, action figures, nail polish, and phone cases. But the product that has garnered the most attention is Katniss's mockingjay pin, the central totemic symbol of the entire franchise. The official licensed mockingjay pin alone has made over eight million dollars, and it was ranked number one in "Pins and Accessories" on Amazon for four weeks (Graser 2012a). As Durkheim argues, the "best way of attesting to oneself and to others that we are part of the same group is to imprint the same distinctive mark on the body" (Durkheim 2001, 177). Thus this highly desired pin functions totemically—fans wear it proudly, displaying their affiliation with and loyalty to *The Hunger Games* community.

The cultivation of desire for wholeness was integral to the marketing strategies for other *Hunger Games* memorabilia. Target, Walmart, Best Buy, and Costco all sold DVD or Blu-ray discs with exclusive content or products. John Butcher, vice president of entertainment at Target, even said that it is "important to make sure we provide product[s] to our guests that they can only find at Target" (Graser 2012b). Consumers find themselves in a position where, in order to complete the story narrative, they must literally go to multiple stores, because without the exclusive content, their fictional world will remain incomplete, thus failing to fulfill their desire for reality. Consumerism, then, becomes implicated in world-building and the sense of wholeness it promises.

The desire for communal wholeness is not limited to *The Hunger Games* community in the United States: the franchise community transcends physical boundaries in its utilization of virtual space. People around the world are invited to inhabit Panem, the North American nation in *The Hunger Games*, in cyberspace—Panem has its own Web site and even its own Web domain (thecapitol.pn). This digital occupation is significant because Web sites can also function as "virtual sacred spaces" with a "threshold" demarcating the sacred and profane locations (Jacobs 2007). On the Panem Web site, you are in "profane" space until you pass the threshold (i.e., create your own District Identification Pass), which assigns you to a District and allows you access to the "sacred" parts of the Web site. This rite of passage symbolically places users within the *Hunger Games* universe, demonstrating their membership in the transmedia world. The Capitol.PN Network has more than ten affiliated Web sites, where fans around the globe engage with the *Hunger Games* world, including official movie sites, Capitol TV YouTube page, and Capitol Couture fashion blog.

For fans who feel that inhabiting Panem in cyberspace does not fully address their communal "wholeness-hunger," there are opportunities to go on pilgrimage to *Hunger Games* sites. Traditional religions usually emphasize the importance of such physical travel to specific sacred sites, which Eliade calls forms of an *axis mundi*, a symbolic "center" of the world where earth and divine realms meet (Eliade 1965, 12). Francis Lawrence, director of the second *Hunger Games* film, developed a sweepstakes offering twelve lucky fans a trip to the set of *Catching Fire*. *The Hunger Games* Facebook page celebrates the promise of communal wholeness to be achieved through just such a pilgrimage: "This is your chance to hang out with fans from across the world on the set of Catching Fire!" (*The Hunger Games* Facebook page 2012). Fans who are *already* participants in the Capitol.PN Network are at an advantage, because the sweepstakes entrance video must include the submitter's "District number." Here we have an explicit example of transmedia storytelling—fans cannot go on pilgrimage, cannot perform their desire to really "be"in Panem, if they are not already engaged with other points of entry. Desire is distributed across the franchise, urging the performance of wholeness through greater fan devotion.

Fans who do not win the sweepstakes are not completely out of luck. Hunger Games Fan Tours offers an immersive experience at DuPont State Recreational Forest, where enthusiasts can visit set locations from the first *Hunger Games* film, "be part of the lottery and get separated into [their] own District," "join other Tributes for a welcoming banquet," learn survival skills like archery, fire building, and shelter building, zip-line to see "what it's like to be in the tree tops at night like Katniss and Rue," and simulate *The Hunger Games* with "timed trials of the skills [they have] learned over the weekend" ("Adventure Weekends" 2012). Fans yearn for communal wholeness from these on-location experiences, arriving at the sites in "enthusiastic packs"(Bethune 2012a). By being physically present at the film set and ritually performing actions from the story, fans immerse themselves into the *Hunger Games* world as a community, transforming it from fiction to reality.

"Real or Not Real?": Reality TV and *The Hunger Games*[3]

What is unique about *The Hunger Games* franchise, however, is that, while these religious-like fans struggle to make their transmedia storyworld whole through intense immersion, *The Hunger Games* story in which they are immersed brings to the fore the issue of constructed transmedia worlds themselves and their reality or unreality. *The Hunger Games* constantly juxtaposes media artifice and true reality, raising questions about what is real and what is not. Indeed, the author of *The Hunger Games*, Suzanne Collins, described the construction of television media as her original inspiration for writing the trilogy:

> *I was channel surfing between reality TV programming and actual war coverage when Katniss's story came to me. One night I'm sitting there flipping around and on one channel there's a group of young people competing for, I don't know, money maybe? And on the next, there's a group of young people fighting an actual war. And I was tired, and the lines began to blur in this very unsettling way, and I thought of this story.* ("A Conversation: Suzanne Collins" 2012)

What makes *The Hunger Games* different, then, from all the previous transmedia franchises is its inclusion of reality television as a key element in the story. The relative lack of "fantastical elements" demonstrates that, instead of the franchise being escapist, it is rather displaying a "direct relationship"with the realities of the contemporary world (Zeitchik 2012). The brutal battle in the arena is entirely televised for the entertainment of Capitol citizens and is mandatory viewing in the Districts. The events in the Capitol leading up to and during the Hunger Games, "the 'close-up,' personal interviews, the audience reactions, the commentators' analysis," are reminiscent of some of the most popular reality TV series in recent years, especially *Survivor* and *American Idol* (Cvetkovic 2012). There certainly is a striking similarity between these reality TV shows and *The Hunger Games*. As film reviewer Katharine Krupp remarks: "The televised interviews conducted in conjunction with the [opening] ceremonies [of the Hunger Games] introduce the doomed children to the viewing public as celebrities. These scenes also give readers a look at the preparation that goes on behind the scenes, including the practice interviews, wardrobe design, and styling" (Krupp 2011). Collins herself was deeply affected by the blurring between the artifice of media and reality today, explaining that she is "fearful that today people see so many reality shows and dramas that when real news is on, its impact is completely lost on them" (Blasingame 2009).

Suzanne Collins is not alone in her concerns about contemporary media consumption. Media scholars register concern about reality television, which often contains little to no "reality" at all. Jack Z. Bratich argues that reality television is "less about representing reality than intervening in it" and is "more accurately a television version of 'reality programming'" (Bratich 2007, 6–7). Bratich says we should think of reality television as more like "reality software" in which subjects on the show have "partial access to that code" and can participate in programming reality (Bratich 2007, 13). Audiences too can participate in creating reality as "co-programmers" and "co-producers" (Bratich 2007, 10). Consequently, reality television indicates that reality *itself* is no longer characterized by its fixedness, but rather by its malleability.

Though today's adults were alive to see the emergence of reality television and the drastic changes it made to the television landscape, the younger generation has never known television without reality TV. Mark Fisher is troubled by this generational discrepancy and points out how the "manipulations [of reality TV] are taken for granted by a generation that has grown up on reality TV" (Fisher 2012). Despite the violence of the story, Collins is justified in gearing *The Hunger Games* trilogy toward young adults because "there is evidence that young people emulate the behavior of reality stars and that reality programs influence their buying behavior" (Patino, Kaltcheva, and Smith 2011). The young people who watch reality television view the celebrities and participants in these shows as "opinion leaders and role models" (Patino, Kaltcheva, and Smith 2011). The dangerous confusion between artifice and reality has been exacerbated by reality shows aimed at a young audience, like MTV's *Made*, which portrays teenagers' dramatic identity transformations as nearly instantaneous, concealing the reality that complex skills take time and repetitive practice to master (Riley and Rosen 2011). Though Suzanne Collins's target audience is the young adult cohort, the need to negotiate "reality" is in no way limited by age. By appealing to all of us and asking us to consider the issues behind reality TV and media in general as we read, watch, and immerse in transmedia, *The Hunger Games* story forces us to become more aware of our experience of and negotiation with media and calls on us to take on the responsibility of questioning whether what we are looking at is reality or just "reality software."

Negotiating the Media of Panem

Representative examples from *The Hunger Games* books and film will be instructive in illuminating how the content of the story itself raises these issues of media construction for both the story's characters and its readers/viewers. For instance, as soon as Katniss Everdeen, the protagonist heroine, is swept off to the seat of the totalitarian government, she is immediately confronted with situations that demonstrate the Capitol's propensity for manipulating reality for a TV audience. The first place Katniss is forced to go is the "Remake Center." Reminiscent of popular reality TV shows such as TLC's *What Not to Wear* and the heavy-handed airbrushing that Julia Bluhm and Dove responded to, Katniss undergoes a comprehensive bodily makeover before her televised "reveal" as District 12 tribute. She vividly describes the work of her "prep team":

> *[The makeover] has included scrubbing down my body with a gritty foam that has removed not only dirt but at least three layers of skin, turning my nails into uniform shapes, and primarily, ridding my body of hair. My legs, arms, torso, underarms, and parts of my eyebrows have been stripped of the stuff, leaving me like a plucked bird, ready for roasting.* (Collins 2008, 61)

Upon seeing Katniss after this radical makeover, Flavius, a member of the prep team, tells her, "You almost look like a human being now!" (Collins 2008, 62). To the citizens of the Capitol, Katniss cannot fit into their "reality" until her body is manipulated almost beyond recognition. Katniss is a "human being" only insofar as she is constructed like all Capitol citizens. Indeed, the Capitol will not ceremonially display Katniss on TV until she is made over. It is her manipulated, waxed, tweezed, and perfected body that will be televised for all to view as "reality."

Another episode in which both characters and readers/viewers must confront media construction occurs just before Katniss enters the arena. The realization that the Capitol's reality TV is in fact a form of "reality software" overwhelms Katniss before her televised tribute interview. Her mentor, Haymitch Abernathy, attempts to help her prepare for the interview by having her pretend to be someone she is not. Katniss becomes frustrated, admitting that she "is not good at lying" (Collins 2008, 117) and "can't be one of [the] people [Haymitch] wants [her] to be" (Collins 2008, 121). Though Katniss wants to remain authentic, Haymitch explains that this is not possible in the Hunger Games if she wants to survive. He tells her that reality is irrelevant because "It's all a big show. It's all how you're perceived" on the television screen (Collins 2008, 135). Haymitch highlights the Capitol's obsession with media construction and how, too often, appearances matter more than reality—a lesson that we real-life viewers could stand to learn as well and one that Katniss learns to practice in her own rebellious way.

Both Katniss and readers/viewers are again jolted back to reality upon encountering one of the most devastating events in the Hunger Games arena. Katniss deftly negotiates between reality and artifice as she repeatedly refuses to be part of the Capitol's televised machinations. She struggles to survive the deadly arena, and at the same time remain true to herself. Joseph Foy describes the emotional scene in which Katniss rebels against the televised constructions of the Gamemakers by placing flowers on the body of her dead ally, Rue, in an attempt to reveal the reality of the arena to the enraptured Capitol audience (and, presumably, to us viewers as well). Foy writes:

> Demonstrating . . . her moral autonomy, Katniss acknowledges the human
> dignity of her slain companion, letting the Capitol know that she is more
> than just a piece in their Game, more than a slave to survival instincts that
> the Capitol can manipulate for its own purposes. (Foy 2012, 215)

By placing flowers on Rue's body, Katniss shows that a real person has died—indeed, that death is real—and that neither she nor Rue will consent to being pawns in a mediated game. This ultimate reality of death is especially powerful in the movie version, as Katniss is shown demonstrating a hand signal of solidarity to Rue's family using the Capitol's own surveillance cameras, which are usually for filming the "game," to convey the horrible truth of the tragedy that has occurred. The Capitol can manipulate the arena, but Katniss sends the message that they cannot manipulate her, nor the horrifying reality she faces. Katniss again rejects the artifice of the televised arena at the end of the first book in the trilogy. When the Gamemakers change the rules of the game to manipulate Katniss into killing her fellow tribute, Peeta, she and Peeta both place deadly berries in their mouths to defy the Capitol's manipulation of the game. Katniss chooses suicide rather than consenting to obeying the Gamemakers' rules for the production of "reality software."

As individuals who stream ourselves through technology today, we are invited to pay close attention when Katniss attempts to become a media object. Her most important characteristic, though, is her "inability to behave in ways that *don't* come natural to her" (Coatney 2012, 179). In short, Katniss represents *reality*, because despite all the artifice and construction around her, she is consistently incapable of being a fake, especially in the third book of the trilogy, *Mockingjay*. During her first performance as the rebellion's symbolic Mockingjay, the filming of a propaganda spot, she inevitably fails as an actor. The episode is significant because the "setting for this failure couldn't illustrate the problem more perfectly: it is literally a *set*. Complete with lights, camera, and action, the fake smoke and sound effects are . . . far from real combat" (Coatney 2012, 179). Katniss is unable to deliver a good performance because the words are not from her heart, and she is completely removed from the reality of war. The only effective television Katniss does produce is when she is being real, her words are spontaneous and unscripted, and she is caught in the midst of horrifyingly real events on the ground during the war. Even when she agrees to become a media object for the ostensibly "good guys," Katniss remains real and is literally unable to be manipulated into a "reality software" role that does not mesh with her authentic self. Because we identify so closely with Katniss, Collins urges us as readers and viewers to examine our voyeurism of the real people whose lives we see on "reality television," suggesting that mediated events can have real consequences for both participants and viewers, for both must negotiate media or be consumed by it.

Though the book trilogy certainly makes the reader uncomfortable with media consumption and voyeurism, *The Hunger Games* film amplifies this feeling by providing additional dimensions to the negotiations between artifice and reality. Director Gary Ross knows he is translating from novel to film and uses this transformation to his advantage. First, the film adds new material: it allows us to view the Gamemakers' control room as they manipulate the arena, sending fireballs and genetically engineered creatures to harm Katniss and the other tributes. The film, then, makes us even more aware of the constructed nature of the arena than the novels do, positioning the audience in a visual God's eye view above the arena, forcing us periodically to view the arena from the perspective of the media manipulators themselves. Second, the most significant scene in the film is when Katniss is in the Hunger Games arena hiding in a tree. She suspects she is being watched by the cameras and suddenly turns around and looks into a hole in the tree trunk. Ross chose his camera angle for this moment wisely. Instead of positioning the camera behind Katniss so that the audience can observe what she is peering into, Ross keeps the camera directly in front of Katniss's face so that we are positioned inside the camera, inside the tree trunk, the same spot as the voyeuristic viewers of the televised events in the Capitol. In an instant of movie-making genius, Ross has conflated the film's audience with the Capitol Gamemakers and with the audience of Panem.

Video game theorist Cindy Poremba could have been sitting in the movie theatre watching that scene in *The Hunger Games* when she was writing about video games and their relationship to reality. She argues that "brink games" are unique in the way they force players to reflect on the non-game realm, the realm of reality:

> *What forbidden or brink games do* specifically *is draw attention to the border, and implicate it in their unfolding. In doing so, they destabilize immersion and force reflection on the construct of the game: the explicit and implicit rules and goals. This requires observation of both the game and non-game, marked and unmarked states. As such, a brink game forces second-order observation that includes the game frame . . . [T]hey additionally self-critique what it means to be a game. But perhaps more importantly, by pulling back the frame of observation, they also reveal the non-game social rules that are implicated in the game.* (Poremba 2007)

In this framework, the Hunger Games becomes a kind of "brink" game, and when we view the film we are purposefully positioned on the border between game and reality. As director, Ross cleverly calls our attention to negotiate this border: we must decide if the media in front of us is game (just a movie) or reality (we are just like the Capitol citizens and fail to see the horrific reality of the arena that is gilded in entertaining artifice). In either case, Katniss is our eyes and ears in the arena, our avatar. As Miroslaw Filiciak says, "avatars are not an escape from our 'self,' they are, rather, a longed-for chance of expressing ourselves beyond physical limitations" (Filiciak 2003, 100). Katniss, then, is not just our proxy; she is *us* projected onto the screen, so when she stares at us through the camera, the moment is literally *us* looking at *us*. In this way, *The Hunger Games* demands viewer responsibility, urging us to engage in a process of self-reflexivity, persistently negotiating between fiction and reality like Katniss and constantly asking ourselves if the media we are looking at is artifice or reality, and inviting us to think deeply about the consequences of our mindless consumption.

Conclusion

In postmodern novels, characters like Katniss "often seem confused as to which world they are in, and how they should act with respect to it" (Harvey 1990, 41). In the words of author Jorge Luis Borges, these characters might ask: "Who was I? Today's self, bewildered, yesterday's forgotten; tomorrow's unpredictable?" (Harvey 1990, 41). Katniss is constantly asking just these kinds of questions as she is confused and surrounded by manipulated and multiplying realities, seeking to bring all the disparate elements in her life back into a unified whole, and serving as a proxy for the viewer hoping for the same thing. At the same time that Katniss's and our realities multiply out of control, the desire for some kind of grounding arises.

Indeed, *The Hunger Games* can be viewed as a response to the most troubling aspects of postmodernism as it filters into popular consciousness. As David Harvey explains, "the greater the ephemerality, the more pressing the need to discover or manufacture some kind of eternal truth" (Harvey 1990, 292). Postmodern fragmentation causes us to "search for more secure moorings and longer-lasting values in a shifting world" (Harvey 1990, 292). For *Hunger Games* enthusiasts, fan culture provides these "moorings" that anchor fans to a community, providing them with an identity and sense of belonging, as well as a story from which they derive meaning and values. Most important, however, is the unified wholeness that the *Hunger Games* transmedia franchise promises, the "eternal truth" and ultimate reality that can only be actualized by the most intensely devoted fans.

What is most unique about *The Hunger Games*, though, is that while there is this religious fan culture itching to complete the transmedia world, at the same time *The Hunger Games* sends a prophetic warning message to consumers that they must be critical not just of reality television but of constructed systems as a whole. *The Hunger Games* neither accepts the singular reality of modernity, nor the plural, fluid, malleable realities of postmodernity. Rather, it advocates for a persistently critical perspective of *all* kinds of constructed worlds and *all realities*. *The Hunger Games* transmedia world forces us to look at our own world with this critical gaze. Thus by combining a captivating fictional world with the manipulations and constructions of reality TV, *The Hunger Games* represents the first transmedia phenomenon to expose the negotiation with media and to call for *critical* reflexivity in that negotiation process. *The Hunger Games* challenges media consumers to be seekers, to be questioning fans, to be constantly searching for reality, like Katniss. But the enduring paradoxical tension is that while the transmedia franchise promises to deliver this reality through potential wholeness, it is in intense mediated story-world immersion that the franchise reveals its own fabrication. The violent dystopic vision in *The Hunger Games* thus serves as a prophetic warning about what could happen if we fail to remain vigilant and critical in our negotiations with media, if we become too comfortable with our transmediated worlds, if we let others define reality for us. The onus, then, is not on transmedia producers or advertisers, because both the book trilogy and Katniss's gaze into the camera demand that each individual ask: *What am I doing?*

Notes

1. The title of the essay refers to a game that Katniss and Peeta play in the third book of the trilogy, *Mockingjay*. Peeta is captured by the Capitol and subjected to torturous injections of tracker jacker (genetically enhanced wasp) venom, which replaces most of his memories with Capitol-constructed illusions. To aid in recovering his *real* memories, Peeta asks Katniss repeatedly "Real or Not Real?" and she responds accordingly to help him sort out artifice from reality. The larger transmedia franchise is encouraging us to ask the same question.

2. The idea of "hunger for reality" is borrowed from a chapter in Rachel Wagner's book *Godwired* (2012). Wagner uses the idea to describe the structured and ordered world of both religion and transmedia, but my usage in the paper adds an additional layer of meaning to the phrase.

3. I wish to express my gratitude to Dr. Rachel Wagner for introducing me to the concept of transmedia and for her insightful comments and suggestions that were instrumental in shaping my ideas for this essay.

References

"A Conversation: Suzanne Collins; Author of *The Hunger Games* trilogy." http://www .scholastic.com/ thehungergames/media/qanda.pdf (accessed 15 November 2012).

"Adventure Weekends." *Hunger Games* fan tours. http://hungergamesunofficialfantours .com/#! adventure-weekends/ (accessed 1 December 2012).

Advertising Age. 2012. "Top 5: Hunger Games' Special." 83: 27.

Bethune, Brian. 2012a. "'The Hunger Games': Your kids are angrier than you think." *Maclean's* 125 (April 2), http://www2.macleans.ca/2012/04/02/dystopia-now/ (accessed 1 December 2012).

Bethune, Brian. 2012b. "The odds are ever in their favour." *Maclean's* 125: 64.

Blasingame, James. 2009. "An interview with Suzanne Collins." *Journal of Adolescent & Adult Literacy* 52: 726–727.

Bratich, Jack Z. 2007. "Programming reality: Control societies, new subjects and the powers of transformation." In *Makeover television: Realities remodelled*, ed. Dana Heller, 6–22. New York: Palgrave Macmillan.

Campbell, Heidi. 2010. *When religion meets new media*, New York: Routledge.

Cawthon, Graham. 2012. "County-wide events build to "Hunger Games" premiere." *McClatchy-Tribune Business News*, January 6.

Chidester, David. 2005. *Authentic fakes: Religion and american popular culture*, Los Angeles: University of California Press.

Coatney, Dereck. 2012. "Why does Katniss fail at everything she fakes? Being versus seeming to be in the *Hunger Games* trilogy." In *The Hunger Games and philosophy: A critique of pure treason*, ed. George A. Dunn and Nicolas Michaud, 178–92. Hoboken, NJ: John Wiley & Sons.

Collins, Suzanne. 2008. *The Hunger Games*, New York: Scholastic.

Crandell, Ben. 2012. "They're hungry to see stars: Kids flock to mall to share "Hunger Games" excitement." *South Florida Sun-Sentinel*, March 9.

Cvetkovic, Vibiana Bowman. 2012. "*The Hunger Game*: Katniss in Oz." *Red Feather: An International Journal of Children's Visual Culture* 3: 37–9.

Dove. 2006. "The Evolution of Beauty." 2006. http://www.youtube.com/watch?v=knEIM16NuPg (accessed 1 December 2012).

Dunne, Susan. 2012. "Hunger Games" trivia challenge and activities." *McClatchy-Tribune Business News*, March 21.

Durkheim, Emile. 2001. *The elementary forms of religious life*, Trans. Carol Cosman. New York: Oxford University Press.

Eliade, Mircea. 1965. *The myth of the eternal return or, cosmos and history*, Trans. Willard R. Trask. Princeton, NJ: Princeton University Press.

Filiciak, Miroslaw. 2003. "Hyperidentities: Postmodern identity patterns in massively multiplayer online role-playing games." In *The Video Game Theory Reader*, ed. Mark J.P. Wolf and Bernard Perron, 87–102. New York: Routledge.

Fisher, Mark. 2012. "Precarious dystopias: *The Hunger Games, In Time, and Never Let Me Go.*" *Film Quarterly* 65 (4): 27–33. http://dx.doi.org/10.1525/FQ.2012.65.4.27.

Flannery-Dailey, Frances, and Rachel Wagner. 2001. "Wake up! Gnosticism and Buddhism in *The Matrix.*" *Journal of Religion and Film 5*, http://www.unomaha.edu/jrf/gnostic.htm (accessed 1 December 2012).

Foy, Joseph J. 2012. "Safe to do what? Morality and the war of all against all in the arena." In *The Hunger Games and philosophy: A critique of pure treason*, ed. George A. Dunn and Nicolas Michaud, 206–21. Hoboken, NJ: John Wiley & Sons.

Graser, Marc. 2012a. "Hunger Games' mockingjay pin." *Variety* 427: 4.

Graser, Marc. 2012b. "Pricey push for 'Hunger.'" *Daily Variety* 1 (August 6): 13.

Harvey, David. 1990. *The condition of postmodernity*, Cambridge: Blackwell Publishers.

Hoover, Stewart M. 2006. *Religion in the media age*, New York: Routledge.

The Hunger Games Facebook page, September 15 2012, https://www.facebook.com/TheHungerGamesMovie (accessed 1 December 2012).

Jacobs, Stephen. 2007. "Virtually sacred: The performance of asynchronous cyber-rituals in online spaces." *Journal of Computer-Mediated Communication* 12 (3): 1103–21. http://dx.doi.org/10.1111/ j.1083-6101.2007.00365.x.

Jenkins, Henry. 2008. *Convergence culture: Where old and new media collide*, New York: New York University Press.

Krupnick, Ellie. 2012. "Julia Bluhm protests airbrushing outside Seventeen HQ with other teen girls." *The Huffington Post*, May 2, http://www.huffingtonpost.com/2012/05/02/julia-bluhm-protestairbrushing-seventeen-magazine_n_1471876.html (accessed 1 December 2012).

Krupp, Katharine. 2011. "Review of *The Hunger Games, Catching Fire,* and *Mockingjay*, by Suzanne Collins." *Journal of the American Academy of Child and Adolescent Psychiatry* 50: 1295–96. http:// dx.doi.org/10.1016/j.jaac.2011.10.003.

McNary, Dave. 2012. "Imax feeds 'Games' hunger." *Daily Variety*, March 15: 5.

Patino, Anthony, Velitchka D. Kaltcheva, and Michael F. Smith. 2011. "The appeal of reality television for teen and pre-teen audiences: The power of 'connectedness' and psycho-demographics." *Journal of Advertising Research*, 51 (1): 288–97. http://dx.doi.org/10.2501/JAR-51-1-288-297.

Poremba, Cindy. 2007. "Critical potential on the brink of the magic circle." Paper presented at the Third Digital Games Research Association International Conference, Tokyo, Japan, September 21–23, 2007. http://www.digra.org/wp-content/uploads/digital-library/07311.42117.pdf (accessed 1 December 2012).

Riley, Naomi Schaefer, and Christine Rosen. 2011. "Myths and reality TV." *Christianity Today*, September 7. http://www.christianitytoday.com/ct/2011/septemberweb-only/mythsreality.html? paging=off (accessed 8 November 2011).

Roof, Wade Clark. 1999. *Spiritual marketplace: Baby boomers and the remaking of American religion*, Princeton, NJ: Princeton University Press.

Scholem, Gershom G. 1941. *Major trends in Jewish mysticism*, New York: Schocken Books.

Staskiewicz, Keith, and Carrie Bell. 2012. "Hunger Strikes!" *Entertainment Weekly*, April 6.

Wagner, Rachel. 2012. *Godwired: Religion, ritual and virtual reality*, New York: Routledge.

Zeitchik, Steven. 2012. "What "The Hunger Games" really means." *Los Angeles Times*, March 24.

30 The Sigh of the Oppressed?: Marxism and Religion in America Today

Kathryn Lofton

A 2008 survey by the Pew Forum on Religion and Public Life found that more than half of Americans rank the importance of religion very highly in their lives, attend religious services regularly, and pray daily.[1] Despite the predictions of some eighteenth- and nineteenth-century social observers, the riotous success of capitalism and the democratization of higher education did not diminish religious life. If anything, the modes of capital have merely incited religious energies, with the markets of one feeding off of the promises of another. This is fertile territory for the Marxist observer, since it seems to fulfill Marx's prophecies as well as resist his plotted rebellions. For Marx, capitalism was a systematic misrecognition. Individuals are taken not as human beings, but as means of production. To comfort themselves amid their objectification as labor, individuals may embrace a variety of false ideologies, none of which—according to Marx—finally resolve the primal misrecognition of capitalism. Marx imagined that if their alienation grew great enough, workers might, finally, resist all such ideological distraction and seize the modes of production themselves. To live in the contemporary United States is to live in an era of extraordinary income disparity and abundant religious life. Is this a disappointment of Marx's prophecies? Or a fulfillment of them?

If I know religion to be man's alienated self-consciousness, then what I know to be confirmed in it as religion is not my self-consciousness but my alienated self-consciousness.[2]

The monk belongs to the world, but the world belongs to him insofar as he has dedicated himself totally to liberation from it in order to liberate it.[3]

The conjunction of these italicized quotations intends to establish the complexities found in the concept of religion as described by Marx. If we focus on the first quotation, we find ourselves in familiar Marxist territory. This is the Marx that argued for the abolition of religion as a

Reprinted from *New Labor Forum* 21, no. 3 (October 1, 2012), by permission of Taylor & Francis.

form of illusory happiness. In his writings, Marx explained how people came to believe certain confused ideas about themselves in the world, and how those ideas were successful precisely because they seemed liberating, and not oppressing. This is how ideology finally works in a capitalist society: not as bold-faced barking propaganda, but as cheerful reminders to be joyful in the light of Jesus, or to be made well by wearing the rightly-fitting jeans. Whether it is talk about a divinity or a consumer good, the seduction of such ideology results in you (as worker, believer, or consumer) being alienated from the real material facts of things, and, consequently, from real happiness. You may *feel* conscious, but you are not. You are alienated from your wakefulness by competing claims to your consciousness. One word for such a proxy consciousness is religion.

Yet Marx is hardly totalizing in his dismissal of religion. He famously wrote: "Religious suffering is at one and the same time the expression of real suffering and a protest against real suffering. Religion is a sigh of the oppressed creature, the heart of a heartless world and the soul of soulless conditions." Here we see Marx consider religion as a reply to the world as it truly is. Religion is an "opium" insofar as it is a wrongheaded fix for a true experience—the wrong way of protesting something that deserves to be protested.[4] In the early twentieth century, Antonio Gramsci argued that religion need not only be understood as an ideology for the elites to suppress those that materially support their power.[5] He suggested that popular forms of religion could function as subaltern protests against hegemony: against the hegemony of clergy, of industrialists, of the structures that seem to determine consciousness through delimiting freedom. In the second quotation, we see another speaker reaching for the same conceptual point, as he suggests that whatever religions exist—wherever and however they exist—they may contain the possibility of real consciousness.

Over the last two centuries, religious figures have considered the writings of Karl Marx to be more kin than nemesis. Those believers found that within religion itself there may be the possibility of ridding oneself of ideological illusions. For example, the speaker in the second quotation, Trappist monk Thomas Merton, wrote about Marxism during his travels in Asia, where he encountered communists, as well as Buddhist monks living within communism. In his reflections on the relationship between monasticism and Marxism, he cited student Marxists who had claimed, "We are the true monks." How could the ardently atheistic Marxist claim any association with the most committed Christian? "The monk is essentially someone who takes up a critical attitude toward the world and its structures," Merton would write. The criticisms of the monk and the Marxist are different, Merton concedes, as are the ultimate ends of their critique. But they share a common recognition that the claims of the world are fraudulent.[6] And they each work for the revolution of real consciousness to begin.

I begin with the conjunction of these perspectives to consider the strange bedfellows Marxism and religion make, and to wonder whether it is even conceivable to find their most productive relation—as seen in the Merton quotation—anywhere else in the American context. Most of contemporary religion in America is hardly monastic, and to most observers it would seem that no place better exemplifies the fulfillment of Marx's critical predictions about the effects of capitalism than America. In the United States, consumer culture has effectively become the primary articulation of human values, and religious life has rightly been described as a marketplace.[7] This is not merely a contemporary history of the pervasion of consumer culture. The constitutional disestablishment of religions produced largely free markets of religion in which any sect or prophet might have circulation.[8] To be sure, the resultant commodity religions created their own economic strictures. Religions prescribe dietary restrictions that create alternative consumer markets; religions advocate Sabbath days that influence the work-week calendar; religions recommend certain careers and criticize others. Yet the limits religions place on the American marketplace are only conceivable in a free marketplace. The United States has simultaneously (and not coincidentally) supported a marketplace of religions and a free market; it has, in so doing, produced an environment in which Marx would identify an abundance of "alienated self-consciousness."

It is tempting, then, to conclude any consideration of religion and Marxism in America with claims of absolute apposition, placing religion on the side of capital and Marxism on the side of its upending. In the mid-twentieth century, for instance, religious belief was understood as an essential weapon in the struggle to preserve American capitalism against communism. James German writes, "The pairing of the terms godless and communism implied its opposite: the pairing of religion and capitalism."[9] Even prior to the Cold War, many Americans understood prosperity itself as a God-given right, and interpreted those who were successful in their pursuit of capital as touched by God. The dominant idiom of American religious history, evangelicalism, possesses an especially analogous relationship to capitalism, insofar as the primary definition of evangelicalism is that of communicating the good word to anyone you can, through whatever medium possible. "Few religious groups in modern America have been as enthusiastic about free-market capitalism as evangelicalism," writes historian Catherine Brekus, suggesting too that few religions have been so gleefully capitalist as those denominations, leaders, and sects animated by evangelicalism.[10] Finally, in their study of General Social Survey data from the 1980s and 1990s, the sociologists Christian Smith and Robert Faris conclude that the "American religious system at the end of the twentieth century reflected major socioeconomic differences between groups within that system."[11] With Americans believing there to be a correlation between theism and prosperity, with evangels proposing good news like advertising copy, and with the resultant class structure mapping onto denominational difference, how could Marxism be found in concert with any American religion? It seems that America is an apotheosis of Marxist critique, while lacking any of its alienated resistance.

Nevertheless, encounters between religious actors and Marxist writings recur throughout American religious history, as individuals articulated dissent from the given economic structures through religious activism. Indeed, dissent seems uniquely possible in American religious life, as no individual parishioners in the United States imagine themselves simply obedient to religious elites; most surveys suggest that Americans pick and choose what they like from whatever religious repository they like. Thus the interaction between the devotedly religious and the critical Marxist suggests that apposition is not the right description for their American relation. Even without the writings of Marx in hand, many religious groups in America have creatively reimagined economic institutions, arguing that religious life might be the grounds for new social structures. For some religious groups, this has involved the development of alternative sects that possessed their own internal market principles, such as the Puritans, Moravians, or Shakers in early America, or the communities founded at Amana, Koinonia Farm, Oneida, or Rajneeshpuram in the nineteenth and twentieth centuries. Each of these experimental sects countered commonplace concepts of property ownership and inheritance with commitments to alternative consumer cultures, industrial economies, and communal property. Short on duration and demographics, these groups possessed more power as emblems of cultural dissension than as indicators of broader economic shifts.

More successful would be individuals whose writings or preaching superseded sectarian borders. For instance, a loose confederation of Protestant theologians advocated on behalf of a new "Social Gospel" in the late-nineteenth and early-twentieth centuries. The theology emphasized the importance of reforming the world in preparation for the final coming of the Kingdom of God. Walter Rauschenbusch, a Baptist seminary professor in New York, called for the "spiritual force of Christianity" to be turned against "the materialism and mammonism of our industrial and social order." He condemned religious men as being too "cowed by the prevailing materialism and arrogant selfishness of our business world."[12] While it would be hard to enumerate parishioners of this new gospel, the millennial ambition and social critique of this movement would continue to be taken up by a variety of progressive liberal thinkers over the next century, including leaders of the civil rights movement.

"Our industrial order . . . makes property the end, and man the means to produce it," Rauschenbusch would write. "Man is treated as a thing to produce more things." Rauschenbusch's worry about man as a thing is strikingly similar to a description Marx offered when he wrote: "The peak of slavery is this: It is only as a worker that he can maintain himself as a physical subject, while as a worker he is only a physical subject."[13] Many participants in the labor movement were motivated by new readings of scripture that emphasized the importance of individual human beings and their full self-realization as democratic citizens. In 1891, Pope Leo XIII published "On the Condition of the Working Classes," in which he advocated a series of reforms including limits on the length of the work day, a living wage, and the elimination of child labor. Most significantly, he argued for the right of labor to organize, an advocacy that inspired many participants in the diffuse labor movement to galvanize their efforts. "In a fundamental sense," according to historian Jama Lazerow, "the early American labor movement was something of a Christian movement, too."[14] Participation in groups like the Industrial Workers of the World (IWW) became a kind of religious devotion for some workers, who believed their value as humans was produced through their consciousness as laborers.[15] Attending meetings, proselytizing to colleagues, and reciting creed-like mission statements, workers involved with the IWW would later recount that their involvement replaced other forms of church and ethnic community, creating a global movement for the betterment of humanity. That the IWW offered such a context for its participants carried some irony, since organized religion was a pronounced enemy to their efforts, insofar as it was implicated with the perpetuation of the bourgeoisie.[16]

Labor organizing inspired many religious thinkers to reject church authority and revise their tradition. On May 1, 1933, The *Catholic Worker* newspaper made its debut with a first issue of 2,500 copies. The newspaper advocated, first, a viewpoint: "The Catholic Worker Movement is grounded in a firm belief in the God-given dignity of every human person." Second, the newspaper represented committed activists who promoted that belief through their own voluntary poverty, pronounced advocacy of nonviolence, and hospitality for "the homeless, exiled, hungry, and forsaken."[17] Dorothy Day served as the headlining figure of the movement, writing about her own personal experiences as well as her broader philosophical commitment to protest injustice and violence in all forms. In her memoir, she writes that she became a socialist for essentially religious reasons, believing that "the poor and oppressed were going to rise up, they were collectively the new Messiah, and they would release the captives."[18]

Such a Christian frame pervaded the experience of the Depression-era working poor. Recent historical research by Jarod Roll and others has illuminated the new forms of religious activity that emerged to serve the disenfranchised working class. Roll has especially focused on the relationship between political movements and grassroots religious revivals in the American South. He argues that the burgeoning Pentecostal movement offered spiritual vigor and democratic energy to farm workers seeking to secure economic futures in a rapidly changing agricultural economy.[19] A Presbyterian named Claude Williams is especially indicative of this "gospel of the working class." Originally inspired by modernist and Social Gospel theologies emerging from mainline denominations, Williams became disenchanted with the institutional church, believing it cooperated with wealthy interests rather than engaging the struggles of working men and women to achieve a fair standard of living. Radicalized by his activism in the Southern Tenant Farmers' Union, Williams began to study Marxist thought, and while he never ascribed to Marxism, he used it to sharpen his faith, and to found a Proletarian Labor Church and Temple that served as a spiritual and political base of operations for his activism.[20]

Even as mainline Protestants and Catholic groups seemed never to equal the revolutionary spirit of the labor movement, during the later twentieth century many within seminaries organized in reply to American economic colonization. In the wake of the Vietnam War, many Americans became increasingly aware of the relationship between their economic prosperity and the colonization of what had come to be called the Third World. The effort to contain "godless" communism encouraged American imperialism, and the U.S. government consistently supported autocratic regimes that were friendly to American economic and geopolitical interests on the grounds of spreading democracy. Yet those same regimes denied their own people the political and economic rights touted in the American Constitution. Christian thinkers in these post-colonial spaces developed a "theology of liberation" that sought to enlist the gospel on behalf of the material needs of the poor and oppressed. This new social gospel compelled many American religious leaders—like Catholic priests Daniel and Philip Berrigan, Virgilio Elizondo, and William Stringfellow—and during the 1980s a number of Christian churches in the United States gave sanctuary to refugees from political oppression in Latin America. Those same churches were often mobilized to face anew the ongoing inequalities of de facto segregation in post-civil rights American cities.

Liberation theology did not overtake the majority of American churches, however. In the wake of 1960s countercultural efforts, any talk of revolutions seemed an adolescent fantasy. Liberal activist solidarity transformed into the "Me" generation and its neoliberal self-help solipsism. What happened? Why did the social gospels of 1960s radicalism not transfigure the economies of the '70s and '80s?

Many answers might be and have been mounted, focusing on the effects of deindustrialization, segregated suburbanization, and the expansion of information technologies over every aspect of the human experience. Marx might note the increasingly fetishistic power attributed to money itself during the late twentieth century, as signaled by the diversification of financial industries and pervasive governmental acceptance of supply-side economic theories alongside the expansion of state lotteries and payday lenders. These patterns were reflected in religious life, so that by the late 1990s, any worries about economic inequality had turned inward, with American parishioners seeking religion to revive their wealth rather than consider its redistribution. Contemporary evangelists like Creflo Dollar, Joyce Meyer, Joel Osteen, and T.D. Jakes espouse variants of the prosperity gospel, the belief that material wealth is God's desire for the faithful. The luxurious lifestyles of these evangelists are, then, not ironic counterpanes to their Christian proposals, but "material rewards of a life committed to spiritual discipleship."[21] For the past several decades, this strain of Christianity has gone by several names (Word of Faith, The Faith, Faith Formula, Health and Wealth, Word Movement, Name It and Claim It, Prosperity Theology), but no matter the particular invocation, the pastor espousing its ideas emphasizes the same dream of physical and spiritual wellness through accessing God's abundance. Appealing to the disadvantaged and the middle class alike, this is a global theological phenomenon with constituencies in Brazil, Guatemala, Scandinavia, South Africa, and South Korea.[22] In Ghana, the "new Faith churches subscribe to a political theology by praying for a God-fearing leader who brings his people prosperity."[23] The Global South that had been the theater for a Marxist Christianity now becomes a major mission field for a Christianity bent on capital.

The prosperity gospel is an odd climax in a discussion on Marxism and religion. On the one hand, with its obsessive enchantment of "the money form," prosperity gospels may seem antithetical to Marxist hope of proletariat solidarity. However, as a component of the broader evangelical tradition, the prosperity gospel is an idiom of individual uplift and individual access. Individuals might be seen, then, as designers of their own hegemony, styling a prosperity consciousness through consumer practice rather than through orthodox obedience to elites. In such a landscape, participants imagine they are the ultimate agents of their religious life and their economic life.

Yet this, too, is another illusion. Whereas once ecclesiastical authority colluded with the maintenance of the bourgeoisie, now we might see corporate authority as in similar cahoots, managing individual choice through the matrices of Facebook profiles, Amazon.com recommendations, and Wal-Mart superstores. It could seem that we are left in the apposition where we began, wondering whether any productive conversation between Marxism and religion in America is conceivable, since Americans seem succored by social media and trapped by vast financial bureaucracies.

Yet as the recent Occupy Wall Street protests show, there is a discomfort with the economic status quo. While the story of Marxism and religion in America may seem to have come to a dead end in denominational and sectarian life, there are other locations for creative thinking about the structures of experience and the values we share. And as religion itself develops within and through consumer culture and celebrity adulation, we may find that new sources of revelation, and new modes of protest, may emerge from the magic embedded in commodity fetish. Consider the seething critique of capital embedded in Suzanne Collins's young adult *Hunger Games* trilogy. In that series, the messianic heroine is pitted not against an amorphous monster, but against Capitol City, the most elite region in a country suffering from starvation. An annual sacrificial ritual—the Hunger Games—is designed largely for the pleasure of the viewing wealthy in that city. "To make it humiliating as well as torturous, the Capitol requires us to treat the Hunger Games as a festivity, a sporting event pitting every district against the others," the heroine observes, explaining that at the end of this event the winning district will receive a year of bread as repayment for its successful circuses. Upon arriving for the first time in Capitol, the heroine observes decadence. In other works of fiction, such an urbane vision might elicit wonder from the provincial girl, but for her it only produces discomfort. "All the colors seem artificial, the pinks too deep, the greens too bright, the yellows painful to the eyes," she explains. To be sure, the basic myth is familiar, plotting precocious children to triumph despite personal disadvantage and adult manipulation. The violence of the story, however, organized around a potential rebellion against Capitol, encourages an exploration of the precise ideology that this particular myth exposes and encourages. In an era without common scripture, popular serial fictions become the premise of new communities, and new discussions of familiar values. Toward the end of Book One in the trilogy, the heroine reflects: "The Hunger Games are their weapon and you are not supposed to be able to defeat it. So now the Capitol will act as if they've been in control the whole time . . . But that will only work if I play along with them."[24] Even as the *Hunger Games* magnifies itself as a commodity (through spinoff texts, films, and figurines), it also contains a plot to deconstruct the power of those commodities. This was always the hope of religion: not that it is merely a tool of authority, but that it was also the way we named authority, practiced submission, and interpreted life itself. Popular culture, like religion, could be merely another emblem of alienated self-consciousness. Or it could incite the beginning of new self-consciousness, for liberation from the very obsessions it compels.

Notes

1. "Summary of Key Findings," U.S. Religious Landscape Survey, Pew Forum on Religion and Public Life, available at http:// religions.pewforum.org/reports#.

2. Karl Marx, "From the Paris Notebooks (1844)," in *Marx: Early Political Writings*, ed. Joseph O'Malley (Cambridge: Cambridge University Press, 1944), 90.

3. Thomas Merton, "Marxism and Monastic Perspectives," in *The Asian Journal of Thomas Merton* (New york: New Directions Books, 1973), 341.

4. Karl Marx, "Contribution to the Critique of Hegel's *Philosophy of Right*: Introduction," in *The Marx-Engels Reader*, ed. Robert C. Tucker (New York: W. W. Norton, 1978), 54.

5. Dwight B. Billings, "Religion as Opposition: A Gramscian Analysis," *American Journal of Sociology* 96, no. 1 (July 1990): 6–9.

6. Merton, "Marxism and Monastic Perspectives," 329.

7. For an elaboration of this argument, see Kathryn Lofton, *Oprah: The Gospel of an Icon* (Berkeley: University of California Press, 2011).

8. For descriptions of the limits to this model, see David Sehat, *The Myth of American Religious Freedom* (New York: Oxford University Press, 2010); Winnifred Fallers Sullivan, *The Impossibility of Religious Freedom* (Princeton: Princeton University Press, 2007).

9. James German, "Economy," in *Themes in Religion and American Culture*, eds. Philip Goff and Paul Harvey (Chapel Hill: University of North Carolina Press, 2004), 286–287.

10. Catherine Brekus, "The Perils of Prosperity: Some Historical Reflections on Christianity, Capitalism, and Consumerism in America," in *American Christianities: A History of Dominance and Diversity*, eds. Catherine A. Brekus and W. Clark Gilpin (Chapel Hill: University of North Carolina Press, 2011), 280.

11. Christian Smith and Robert Faris, "Socioeconomic Inequality in the American Religious System: An Update and Assessment," *Journal for the Scientific Study of Religion* 44 (2005): 100.

12. Walter Rauschenbusch, *Christianity and the Social Crisis* (New York: Macmillan, 1913), 369, 372.

13. Rauschenbusch, *Christianity and the Social Crisis*, 369; Marx, Early Political Writings, 73.

14. Jama Lazerow, *Religion and the Working Class in Antebellum America* (Washington, D.C.: Smithsonian Institution Press, 1995), 31.

15. Donald E. Winters, *The Soul of the Wobblies: The IWW, Religion, and American Culture in the Progressive Era, 1905–1917* (Westport, CT: Greenwood Press, 1985); Kevin J. Christiano, "Religion and Radical Labor Unionism," *Journal for the Scientific Study of Religion* 27, no. 3 (1988): 378–88.

16. Richard Callahan, "Class and Labor," in *Blackwell Companion to Religion in America*, ed. Philip Goff (Malden, MA: Wiley-Blackwell, 2010), 79–80.

17. See the Catholic Worker Movement's website, available at www.catholicworker.org.

18. Dorothy Day, *The Long Loneliness* (New York: HarperCollins, 1952), 46.

19. Jarod Roll, *Spirit of Rebellion: Labor and Religion in the New Cotton South* (Urbana: University of Illinois Press, 2010).

20. Erik S. Gellman and Jarod Roll, *The Gospel of the Working Class: Labor's Southern Prophets in New Deal America* (Urbana: University of Illinois Press, 2011), 45–46.

21. Jonathan L. Walton, *Watch This! The Ethics and Aesthetics of Black Televangelism* (New York: New York University Press, 2009), xi.

22. Simon Coleman, "America Loves Sweden: Prosperity Theology and the Cultures of Capitalism," in *Religion and the Transformations of Capitalism*, ed. Richard H. Roberts (London: Routledge, 1995), 161–79; Rosalind Hackett, "The Gospel of Prosperity in West Africa," *Religion and the Transformations of Capitalism*, 199–214; David Hollinger, "Enjoying God Forever: An Historical/Sociological Profile of the Health and Wealth Gospel in the USA," *Religion and Power, Decline and Growth: Sociological Analyses of Religion in Britain, Poland, and the Americas*, eds. Peter Gee and John Fulton (Twickenham: British Sociological Association, Sociology of Religion Study Group, 1991), 53–66.

23. Simon Coleman, *The Globalisation of Charismatic Christianity* (Cambridge: Cambridge University Press, 2000), 33.

24. Suzanne Collins, *The Hunger Games* (New york: Scholastic Books, 2008), 19, 59, 358.

31 | *Treat Students Right by Valuing Their Diversity*

Matthew Meuleners

The human body has more than 200 different types of cells. Each cell develops to maturity differently, just as each person grows up in a different environment. Cells work towards different goals, just as each of us does.

Some cells tell us we are hungry, while others help us digest the food we eat. They deal with different challenges—stomach cells adapt to resist the harsh acidic environment around them, while muscle cells maintain a delicate chemical balance to create motion.

Each cell looks very different, just as every human being is distinctive. A human egg cell is the size of the period at the end of this sentence, while some nerve cells stretch the length of your leg. Millions of unique cells are working together to make it possible for you to read this article right now.

Yet, even the great diversity of cells in the human body is nothing when it is compared to the diversity of background, thought, experience, and expression which exists in the minds of just one classroom of students. This variety is a wonderful thing when we respond to it in ways which are appropriate, but we can cause serious problems if we deal with diversity in the wrong way.

Picture a ladder with three rungs on it. Each of these rungs is spaced widely from the next, making it impossible to reach one without first reaching the one directly below it. Rising to the next rung requires a big stretch that would be difficult for someone who is stiff and inflexible, while someone who is limber could more easily make the ascent. The way we each deal with diversity develops in a progression like this ladder.

The first stage is recognition, when we make contact with "it" and compare "it" to ourselves. In this first stage, we don't understand what "it" is, and we are often afraid. The next stage is tolerance. In this stage, we understand "it" better, but are still uncomfortable. We often try to distance ourselves from "it." In the final stage, which is called celebration, we accept "it" fully and acknowledge that "it" adds value to our life.

This progression is not determined by our age or by our intelligence, but by our attitude and our experience. Some people spend all their lives in the recognition stage, growing stiff and locked in their

Reprinted by permission from *Education Digest* 67, no. 4 (2001).

ways. Others arrive at the stage of celebration while still very young, developing open, limber minds in an environment where diversity is the norm.

Where on the ladder are you located? How can you help guide your school to climb to higher levels?

1. Recognition. "Racist," "bigot," and "ignorant" are some of the words which are aimed at those who are locked in the stage of recognition. These are people who respond negatively when they come in contact with someone they don't understand or who is different from them. The problem here is a lack of information. This ignorance can cause trouble in two ways.

First, when we don't have any knowledge of something that is new, our brain will often use our past experiences of something that is similar to fill in the gaps. Psychologists call this a schema reaction. A schema is a blueprint for how we see the world.

When a new experience fits with this blueprint for how we see the world, then that new experience is added to memory, but when something new disagrees with the blueprint, it is rejected and replaced with data from a past experience. Does this sound familiar? This is how a stereotype is formed.

For example, if the only Hispanic person you ever met had stolen from you, you might tend to be less trusting of the next Hispanic person you meet. These stereotypes can build into a vicious cycle, and, unfortunately, a person's schema doesn't even have to be based upon his or her own experiences.

Attitudes are often passed down from parents, peers, and other role models. Advisers and student leaders are role models, whether they realize it or not. For this reason it is important for them to be conscious of the actions and the attitudes which they are passing on to others.

The second way in which it is possible for ignorance to cause trouble is by creating fear. People are sometimes afraid of what they don't understand. Too often, this terror transforms into feelings of anger and hate. These powerful emotions can lead people to do things that they wouldn't even consider doing if they were in other circumstances.

Everything from verbal harassment to physical hate crimes can result from the discomfort and fear of the unknown. In middle-level and high schools, this often takes the form of rejection and verbal abuse between cliques. Encouraging an open-minded attitude within your school organization can indirectly create a more tolerant attitude in your school community by setting a model for others to follow.

2. Tolerance. Remember that what keeps people locked in the recognition stage is a lack of information. So, in order for one to move on to the second stage, that of tolerance, one must ask questions. As we learn about the unknown, it becomes easier to accept as reality, like adjusting the focus control on a camera. When we make the effort, we can see details that we might otherwise have missed.

For people who are in the tolerance stage, the different people are accepted, but they are not welcomed. A good way to describe it might be respectful distance. They respect the other person's right to exist as long as they keep their distance.

People in the tolerance stage don't want to be directly affected by diversity. These are the people who create policies like the military department's "Don't ask, don't tell." The government tells people, "It's okay to be gay as long as nobody ever knows." In high school, people in the tolerance stage include the guy who doesn't have anything against black people, but avoids making black friends or taking black lab partners.

This attitude can be just as destructive as direct confrontation. Those who are stuck in the tolerance stage often miss many opportunities for friendship, growth, and fresh ideas. By making a real effort to go outside of your comfort zone and to interact with people who make you feel uncomfortable, you can push yourself away from this stage.

People in the tolerance stage have to overcome difficult obstacles in order to move on to the stage of celebration. They have to learn to see the qualities about each person that are worthy of praise and attention. They also have to realize the value of true synergy, and the path to take in order to achieve it.

No matter how a person looks on the surface, or how they view the world, it is important to realize that we are all connected by our heritage as human beings. Each one of us brings value to the equation, and each one of us is worthy of love and praise.

True synergy is a state of being where a community, family, or team works together to create more than they could create if each was working alone. The only way in which to accomplish this state of smooth, enhanced interaction is to utilize each person's unique talents, nurture the reduction of their unique limitations, and empower them to reach their full potential.

3. Celebration. Imagine that your school organization is making plans for a year-end celebration banquet. Kris is an organizational whiz, and Montel is the best speaker in the group. Obviously, each is going to work more on their area of specialty than they will be working on the rest of the planning which is to be done. This utilization of unique talents will make your event planning more efficient and more effective, but the celebration still won't quite reach its full potential.

What about when Kris has to tell the rest of the organization about your progress? She isn't exactly the best communicator. Montel could deliver the information beautifully, but he can't keep all of it straight in his head. Everyone has shortcomings, skills that could be improved.

As a team, it is important to nurture the reduction of individual limitations by teaching and learning from each other. When Montel gives Kris a few tips on eye contact and provides her with a pep talk, she can do the briefing in a clear, concise way. Kris could also help Montel to organize his speech notes for the purpose of ensuring that the presentation flows through the agenda smoothly.

Celebrating diversity is the equation for true synergy, whether you happen to be a smooth-talking student leader or a well-organized adviser. By acknowledging that every member of your community, organization, or family has something to contribute and recognizing that his or her contributions add value to your life, you are moving toward the stage of celebration.

When you celebrate the many differences in those around you, you will be able to utilize, nurture, and empower others to achieve more than ever before. But how do you empower?

You start the process by being flexible. Remember that the ladder is difficult to climb if you are stiff and intolerant. However, when you are flexible—and you adapt to other people's preferences, opinions, and needs—this allows them to create at their full potential. This is often the most difficult barrier for people to cross because it means thinking about your life as cooperation rather than competition.

Modern American society pushes individual strength and independence. We are taught not to rely on or help other people, but rather that we will be less successful if others are more so. We must unlearn these attitudes if we are to ever achieve real synergy in our society by empowering those around us.

To return to the analogy from the introduction, the human body is an example of synergy that has been amazing scientists for centuries. Vastly dissimilar cells work in teams to form tissues and organs that carry out the functions of life.

If you think of each person around you as being like a cell, you can imagine that your entire organization makes up an organ that provides some of the functions which are necessary for the lift of our society. Each of the groups that are in your school works together to support the human race like organ systems which are cooperating to support a single body.

The near perfection of the human body's synergy is what makes us the most advanced creatures on the planet. Nerve cells trigger muscle cells to fire. Muscle cells contract in the heart to keep our blood cells circulating. Blood cells carry essential nutrients to cells in our glands that release protective immune cells to fight disease. Hundreds of systems cooperate and sustain each other for the purpose of achieving a common goal. If our society were to run like that, just imagine what we would accomplish.

What happens when the synergy in our bodies fails? What happens when, for some reason, one system stops working with another system? Sometimes in our society, two or more cultures of communities stop working together.

What if, like a group of older people who refuse to interact with today's "crazy" youth, our brain's reflex reaction center stopped working with our muscles? The next time our hand touched a hot burner on a stove, we wouldn't move it off until we smelled smoke!

What about when our fellow human beings attack each other, through hate crimes and ridicule, destroying the lives of innocent people just because they are different? This is like when our own body cells turn against each other, invading, reprogramming, and destroying healthy cells around them. This is a virus called AIDS, and it is no less frightening and destructive when applied to our model of society.

The virus invades the protective barriers of healthy cells, like a bigot who breaks down someone's self-esteem through taunts and abuse. Then the virus reprograms the cell's DNA to produce copies of the AIDS virus itself. In the same way, a victim of prejudice and intolerance can sometimes believe that their abusers are right, that they deserve that treatment because they are lesser human beings.

Finally, the virus causes the once-healthy cell to destroy itself, releasing thousands of copies of the disease to attack other healthy cells. Remember that intolerance and false schemas are easily passed on to those who are close to us—like children, friends, and organization members.

As of today, there is no cure for AIDS, just as there is no cure for the intolerance of diversity. Both of these diseases are reaching epidemic proportions across the world. The only way to restrict the growth of these outbreaks is by carefully regulating our own behavior and encouraging others to do the same.

Challenge yourself to ascend the ladder. Ask questions to help you understand the unknown. Keep a flexible mind that is open to new ideas and opinions. Utilize the talents of others while nurturing the reduction of the problem areas where they need help. Empower each other by cooperating instead of competing.

Remind yourself every day of the consequences of intolerance and work to celebrate the powerful strength that comes from the diversity of thought, experience, and expression in those around you.

32

A Revolution of Values: The Promise of Multicultural Change

bell hooks

Two summers ago I attended my twentieth high school reunion. It was a last minute decision. I had just finished a new book. Whenever I finish a work, I always feel lost, as though a steady anchor has been taken away and there is no sure ground under my feet. During the time between ending one project and beginning another, I always have a crisis of meaning. I begin to wonder what my life is all about and what I have been put on this earth to do. It is as though immersed in a project I lose all sense of myself and must then when the work is done rediscover who I am and where I am going. When I heard that the reunion was happening, it seemed just the experience to bring me back to myself, to help in the process of rediscovery. Never having attended any of the past reunions, I did not know what to expect. I did know that this one would be different. For the first time we were about to have a racially integrated reunion. In past years, reunions had always been segregated. White folks had their reunion on their side of town and black folks had it on ours.

None of us was sure what it would be like to have an integrated reunion. Those periods in our adolescent lives of racial desegregation had been full of hostility, rage, conflict, and loss. We black kids had been angry that we had to leave our beloved all-black high school Crispus Attucks and be bussed halfway cross town to integrate white schools. We had to make the journey and thus bear the responsibility of making desegregation a reality. We had to give up the familiar and enter a world that seemed cold and strange, not our world, not our school. We were certainly on the margin, no longer at the center, and it hurt. It was such an unhappy time. I still remember my rage that we had to awaken an hour early so that we could be bussed to school before the white students arrived. We were made to sit in the gymnasium and wait. It was believed that this practice would prevent outbreaks of conflict and hostility since it removed the possibility of social contact before classes began. Yet once again the burden of this transition was placed on us. The white school was desegregated, but in the classroom, in the cafeteria, and in most social spaces racial apartheid prevailed. Black and white students who considered ourselves progressive

Reprinted from *Teaching to Transgress: Education as the Practice of Freedom* (1994), by permission of the author.

rebelled against the unspoken racial taboos that were meant to sustain white supremacy and racial apartheid even in the face of desegregation. The white folks never seemed to understand that our parents were no more eager for us to socialize with them than they were to socialize with us. Those of us who wanted to make racial equality a reality in every area of our life were threats to the social order. We were proud of ourselves, proud of our willingness to transgress the rules, proud to be courageous.

Part of a small integrated clique of smart kids who considered ourselves "artists," who believed we were destined to create outlaw culture where we would live as bohemians forever free, we were certain of our radicalness. Days before the reunion, I was overwhelmed by memories and shocked to discover that our gestures of defiance had been nowhere near as daring as they had seemed at the time. Mostly they were acts of resistance that did not truly challenge the status quo. One of my best buddies during that time was white and male. He had an old gray Volvo that I loved to ride in. Every now and then he would give me a ride home from school if I missed the bus—an action which angered and disturbed those who saw us. Friendship across racial lines was bad enough, but friendship across gender was unheard of and dangerous. We found out one day just how dangerous when grown white men in a car tried to run us off the road. Ken's parents were religious. Their faith compelled them to live out a belief in racial justice. They were among the first white folks in our community to invite black folks to come to their house, to eat at their table, to worship with them. As one of Ken's best buddies, I was welcome in their house. After hours of discussion and debate about possible dangers, my parents agreed that I could go there for a meal. It was my first time to eat together with white people. I was sixteen years old. I felt then as though we were making the new history of America, that we were in the process of living the dream of democracy, of creating a culture where equality, love, justice, and peace would be the values that would shape and form our nation's destiny.

After graduation I lost touch with Ken even though he always had a warm place in my memory. I thought of him when meeting and interacting with liberal white folks who believed that having a black friend meant that they were not racist, who sincerely believed they were doing us a favor by extending offers of friendly contact for which they felt they should be rewarded. I thought of him during years of watching white folks play at unlearning racism but walking away when they encountered obstacles, rejection, conflict, pain. Our high school friendship had been forged not because we were black and white but because we shared a similar take on reality. Racial difference meant that we had to struggle to claim the integrity of that bonding. We had no illusions. We knew there would be obstacles, conflict, and pain. In white supremacist capitalist patriarchy, words we never used then, we knew we would have to pay a price for this friendship, that we would need to possess the courage to stand up for our belief in democracy, in racial justice, in the transformative power of love. We valued the bond between us enough to meet the challenge. Remembering the sweetness of our friendship days before the reunion, I felt humbled by the knowledge of what we give up when we are young, believing either that we will find something just as good or better someday only to find that not to be so. I wondered just how it could have been that Ken and I could ever have lost contact with one another. Along the way I had not found white folks who understood as well the depth and complexity of racial injustice, who were as willing to practice the art of living a non-racist life as folks were then. In my adult life I have seen few white folks who are really willing to go the distance to create a world of racial equality—white folks willing to take risks, to be courageous, to live against the grain. I went to the reunion hoping that I would have a chance to see Ken face to face, to tell how much I cherished all that we shared, to tell him in words which I never dared to say to any white person back then, simply that I loved him.

Remembering this past, I am most struck by our passionate commitment to a vision of social transformation that was rooted in the fundamental belief in a radically democratic idea of freedom and justice for all. Our notions of social change were not fancy. There was no elaborate postmodern political theory shaping our actions. We were simply trying to change the way we went about our everyday lives so that our values and habits of being would reflect our commitment to freedom. Then our major concern was ending racism. That concern was coupled with other concerns for freedom: we wanted sexual freedom, we wanted an end to gender boundaries. As I grew up politically, I placed alongside the struggle to end racism a commitment to ending sexism and sexism oppression, to eradicating systems of class exploitation. Aware that we are living in a culture of domination I ask myself now as I did more than twenty years ago as I go about my daily life: what values and habits of being reflect my/our commitment to freedom?

In retrospect I see that in the last twenty years of my life I have encountered many folks who say they are committed to freedom and justice for all even though the way they live, the values and habits of being they institutionalize in public and private rituals daily help maintain the culture of domination, help create an unfree world. With prophetic insight Martin Luther King, in the book entitled *Where Do We Go from Here: Chaos or Community*, told the citizens of this nation that we would be unable to go forward if we did not experience a "true revolution of values." He assured us that "The stability of the large world house which is ours will involve a revolution of values to accompany the scientific and freedom revolutions engulfing the earth. We must rapidly begin the shift from a 'thing'-oriented society to a 'person' oriented society. When machines and computers, profit motives and property rights are considered more important than people, the giant triplets of racism, materialism, and militarism are incapable of being conquered. A civilization can flounder as readily in the face of moral and spiritual bankruptcy as it can through financial bankruptcy." Today we live in the midst of that floundering. We live in chaos, uncertain about the possibility of building and sustaining community. The public figures who speak the most to us about a return to old-fashioned values embody the evils King describes. They are most committed to maintaining systems of domination—racism, sexism, class exploitation, and imperialism. They promote a perverse vision of freedom that makes it synonymous with materialism. They teach us to believe that domination is "natural," that it is right for the strong to rule over the weak, the powerful over the powerless. What amazes me is that so many people claim not to embrace these values and yet our collective rejection of them cannot be complete as they prevail in our daily lives.

These days I am compelled to consider what forces keep us from moving forward, from having that revolution of values that would enable us to live differently. King taught us to understand that if "we are to have peace on earth," "our loyalties must transcend our race, our tribe, our class, and our nation." Long before the word multi-culturalism became fashionable, he encouraged us to "develop a world perspective." Yet what we are witnessing today in our everyday life is not an eagerness on the part of neighbors and strangers to develop a world perspective but a return to narrow nationalisms, isolationisms, and xenophobia. These shifts are usually explained in New Right and neo-conservative terms as attempts to bring order to chaos, to return to an idealized past. The notion of family evoked in these discussions is one in which sexist defined roles for males and females are upheld as stabilizing traditions. Not surprising, this idealized vision of family life is coupled with a notion of security and safety that suggests we are always most safe with people of our own group, who are of the same race, class, religion, etc. No matter how many statistics on domestic violence, homicide, rape, child abuse, etc. indicate that in fact the idealized patriarchal family is not a "safe" space; that those of us who experience any form of assault are more likely to be victimized by those who are like us rather than by some mysterious strange outsiders, these realities are denied. Considering these circumstances, it becomes apparent that one of the primary reasons for not having experienced a revolution of values is that a culture of domination necessarily promotes addiction to lying and denial.

That lying takes the presumably innocent form for many white people (and even some black folks) to suggest that racism does not exist anymore and that conditions of social equality are solidly in place that would enable any black person who works hard to achieve economic self-sufficiency. Forget about the fact that capitalism requires the existence of a mass underclass of surplus labor. It takes the form of mass media creating the myth that the feminist movement has completely transformed society, so much so that the politics of patri-archal power have been inverted and that men, particularly white men, like emasculated black men, have become the victims of dominating women, so that all men, white and black in particular, must pull together (e.g., the Clarence Thomas hearings) to support and reaf-firm patriarchal domination. Add to this the widely held assumption on the part of many peo-ple that blacks, other minorities, and white women are taking jobs from white men, that people are poor and unemployed because they want to be, and it becomes most evident that part of our contemporary crisis is created by a lack of meaningful access to truth. When this collective cultural consumption of and attachment to misinformation is coupled with the layers of lying individuals do in their personal lives, our capacity to face reality is severely diminished as is our will to intervene and change unjust circumstances.

When we critically examine the traditional role of the university in the pursuit of truth and the sharing of knowledge and information, it becomes painfully clear that biases that uphold and maintain white supremacy, imperialism, sexism, racism, etc. have distorted edu-cation so that it has not been about the practice of freedom. The call for a recognition of cul-tural diversity, a re-thinking of ways of knowing, a deconstruction of old epistemologies, and the concomitant demand that there be a transformation in our classrooms, in how we teach and what we teach, has been a necessary revolution—one that seeks to restore life to a corrupt and dying academy. When everyone first began to speak about cultural diversity it was excit-ing. For those of us on the margins (many of us people of color, folks from working-class back-grounds, and/or gay), who had always felt ambivalent about our presence in institutions where knowledge was shared in ways that re-inscribed colonialism, domination, it was thrilling to think that the vision of justice and democracy that was at the very heart of the civil rights movement would be realized in the academy. At last there was the possibility of a learn-ing community, a place where difference could be acknowledged, where we would finally all understand, accept, and affirm that our ways of knowing are forged in history and relations of power. Finally we were all going to break through collective academic denial and acknowledge that the education most of us had received and were giving was not and is never politically neutral. Though it was evident that change would not be immediate, there was tremendous hope that this process we had set in motion would lead to a fulfillment of the dream of educa-tion as the practice of freedom.

Initially, many of our colleagues were reluctant participants in this change. Yet many of them tried, and are still trying, to open their minds, to shift their paradigms. The greatest motivating catalyst for professorial change was and is the joy in our students, who for the most part sincerely desire a liberatory education. Change is difficult—particularly when we are called to uproot familiar ways of thinking and behaving and replace them with new thought and action.

Many folks found that as they tried to respect "cultural diversity" they had to confront the limitations of their training, knowledge, and possible loss of "authority." Indeed, exposing certain truths and biases in the classroom often created chaos and confusion. The idea that the classroom should always be a "safe" harmonious place was challenged. It was hard for individuals to fully grasp the idea that recognition of difference might also require of us a will-ingness to see and experience the classroom change, to allow for shifts in relations between students. A lot of people panicked. What they saw happening was not the comforting "melting pot" idea of cultural diversity, the rainbow coalition where we would all be grouped together, in our difference, but wearing the same "have a nice day" smile. This was the stuff of coloniz-ing fantasy, a perversion of the progressive vision of cultural diversity. Critiquing this longing in a recent interview entitled "Critical Multiculturalism and Democratic Schooling," Peter McLaren asserts: "Diversity that somehow constitutes itself as a harmonious ensemble of benign cultural spheres is a conservative and liberal model of multiculturalism that, in my mind, deserves to be jettisoned because, when we try to make culture an undisturbed space of harmony and agreement where social relations exist within cultural forms of uninterrupted accord, we ascribe to a form of social amnesia in which we forget that all knowledge is forged in histories that are played out in the held of social antagonisms."[1] Many professors lacked strategies to deal with antagonisms in the classroom. When this fear joined with the refusal to change that characterized the stance of an old, predominantly white male guard, it created a space for disempowered collective backlash.

All of a sudden professors who had taken issues of multiculturalism and cultural diversity seriously were backtracking, expressing doubts, casting votes in directions that would restore biased traditions or prohibit changes in faculty and curriculum that were to bring diversity of representation and perspective. Joining forces with the old guard, previously open professors condoned senior colleagues using tactics of ostracization, belittlement, etc. to dissuade junior faculty members from making paradigm shifts that would lead to changes in curriculum, scholarly research, writing, and teaching practices. This week in my Toni Morrison seminar, as we went around our circle voicing critical reflections on Morrison's language, a sort of classically white, blondish J Crew kinda coed shared that one of her other English professors, an older white man (whose name none of us wanted her to mention) confided that he was so pleased to find a student still interested in reading literature—words—the language of texts and "not that race and gender stuff." Somewhat amused by the assumption he had made about her, she was disturbed by his conviction that conventional ways of critically approaching a novel could not co-exist in classrooms that also offered new perspectives.

I shared my recent experience of being at a Halloween party where a new white male colleague with whom I was chatting for the first time at the mere mention of my Toni Morrison seminar went on a tirade emphasizing that *Song of Solomon* was a weak re-write of Hemingway's *For Whom the Bell Tolls*. Passionately full of disgust for Morrison, being a Hemingway scholar, he seemed to be covertly sharing the often heard concern that black women writers/thinkers are just poor imitations of "great" white men. Not wanting at that moment to launch into Unlearning Colonialism, Divesting of Racism and Sexism 101, I opted for the strategy taught to me by that in-denial-of-institutionalized-patriarchy self-help book *Women Who Love Too Much*. I just said, Oh! Later, I assured him that I would read again *For Whom the Bell Tolls* to see if I would see the same connection. Both of these seemingly trivial incidents reveal how deep-seated the fear is that any de-centering of Western civilization, of the white male canon, is really an act of cultural genocide.

Some folks think that everyone who supports cultural diversity wants to replace one dictatorship of knowing with another, changing one set way of thinking for another. This is perhaps the gravest mis-perception of cultural diversity. Even though there are those overly zealous among us who hope to replace one set of absolutes with another, this perspective does not accurately represent progressive visions of the way commitment to cultural diversity can constructively transform the academy. In all cultural revolutions there are periods of chaos and confusion, times when grave mistakes are made. If we fear mistakes, doing things wrongly, having to be constantly evaluating, introducing new ideas and strategies, we will never transform the academy into a culturally diverse place with scholars and curriculum addressing every dimension of that difference.

As backlash swells, as budgets are cut, as jobs become even more scarce, many of the few progressive interventions that were made to change the academy, to create an open climate for cultural diversity are in danger of being undermined and/or eliminated. These threats should not be ignored. Nor should our collective commitment to cultural diversity change because we have not yet devised and implemented perfect strategies that would enable smooth transformation. To create a culturally diverse academy we must commit ourselves fully. Learning from other movements for social change, from civil rights and feminist liberation efforts, we must accept the protracted nature of our struggle and be willing to remain both patient and vigilant. To commit ourselves to the work of transforming the academy into a place where cultural diversity informs every aspect of our learning, we must embrace struggle and sacrifice. We cannot be easily discouraged, we cannot despair when there is conflict. Our solidarity must be affirmed by shared belief in a spirit of intellectual openness that celebrates diversity, welcomes dissent, and rejoices in collective dedication to truth.

Drawing strength from the life and work of Martin Luther King, I am often reminded of the profound inner struggle that took place within him when he felt spiritually called by his religious beliefs to oppose the war in Vietnam. Fearful of alienating conservative bourgeois supporters, of alienating the Black Church, King meditated on a passage from the Book of Romans which reminded him of the necessity of dissent, challenge, and change. That passage begins: "Be not conformed to this world but be ye transformed by the renewal of your minds. . . ." All of us in the academy and in the culture as a whole are called to renew our minds if we are to transform educational institutions and society, so that the way we live, teach, and work can reflect our joy in cultural diversity, our passion for justice, and our love of freedom.

Oberlin College

Endnote

1. Shirley Steinberg, "Critical Multiculturalism and Democratic Schooling: An Interview with Peter McLaren and Joe Kincheloe," International Journal of Educational Reform 1.4 (October 1992): 399.

33 *National Identity and the Politics of Multiculturalism*

Henry A. Giroux

Global changes have provided the conditions for the emergence of new theoretical discourses that pose a powerful challenge to modern assumptions regarding the unity of nationalism and culture, the state and the nation, and national identity and the universal imperatives of a common culture. The changes that have, in part, produced new forms of theorizing about globalization, the politics of diaspora, immigration, identity politics, multiculturalism, and postcolonialism are as profound intellectually as they are disruptive politically. Judith Squires captures the scope of these changes, while expressing some reservations about what they have come to mean as they are rapidly absorbed into new theoretical discourses:

> The global economy is a given in our life now: transnational corporations cross borders to maximize productivity and transnational intellectuals cross academic boundaries to maximize knowledge. The academic discipline, along with the national state, is subject to powerful forces of change. And, as we might acknowledge the failings of the old model of state sovereignty and hegemonic nationalism but nonetheless remain deeply skeptical about the gains to be had from the free movement of international capital around the globe in pursuit of profit, so we must be attuned to the benefits of jettisoning the status of empirical area studies, the constricting patriarchal academic canons and oppressive hierarchical department structures, but also the pitfalls. (v)

The pitfalls to which Squires refers are the lack of specificity and theoretical blurriness that sometimes accompany the scholarly rush to take up issues of the politics of globalization, diaspora, multiculturalism, and postcolonialism (see also Grewal and Kaplan, Ien, Calhoun, "Nationalism," and Parry). I am particularly concerned here with a position that does not differentiate among radical, liberal, and conservative forms of multiculturalism within the politics of the nation state. Such generalizations often recycle or reproduce colonialist discourse. What must be resisted is the assumption that the politics of national identity is necessarily complicitous with a reactionary discourse of nationalism and has been superseded by theories which locate identity politics squarely within the discourses of postnational, diasporic globalism, or what Arjun Appadurai calls the "search for nonterritorial principles of solidarity" (417).

This is not to suggest that diverse nationalisms can be addressed outside of their transnational links, or that the mechanisms of a dominant and oppressive politics of assimilation can be abstracted from the pain, anguish, and suffering experienced by those diasporic groups who define themselves through "nonnational identities and aspirations" (Appadurai 418). What I am resisting is the claim that nationalism can only be associated with ethnic conflict, that nationalism is witnessing its death knell, or that the relationship between nationalism and national identity can only be framed within a transnational discourse. The importance of such arguments must be acknowledged, but at the same time it is important to recognize in the context of the current conservative ideological offensive in the United States that it is crucial for critical educators and others to "locate our theorizing in the grounded sites of cultural and political resistance" within the United States, on the one hand, and to guard against the tendency to "overgeneralize the global current of so-called nomadic, fragmented and deterritorialized subjectivity" (Squires vi).

Nationalism is crucial to understanding the debates over identity and multiculturalism in the United States. As important as the discourse of globalization might be, it cannot be used to overlook how national identity reasserts itself within new discourses and sites of learning. More specifically, I want to argue that rather than dismissing the politics of identity as another essentialist discourse, progressives need to address how the politics of identity and difference are being constructed around new right wing discourses and policies. Central to the construction of a right wing nationalism is a project of defining national identity through an appeal to a common culture that displaces any notion of national identity based upon a pluralized notion of culture with its multiple literacies, identities, and histories and erases histories of oppression and struggle for the working class and minorities. Stuart Hall is right in arguing that the 1990s is witnessing the return of recharged nationalism in big and small societies that serves to restore national culture as the primordial source of national identity ("Culture" 353). But this should not suggest that the relationship between nationalism and culture manifests itself exclusively in terms of oppression or domination or that any attempt to develop an insurgent multiculturalism through an appeal to radical democracy necessarily assumes or leaves intact the boundary of the nation as an unproblematic historical, political, and spatial formation. At stake here is the need to acknowledge the existence of the nation state and nationalism as primary forces in shaping collective identities while simultaneously addressing how the relationship between national identity and culture can be understood as part of a broader struggle around developing national and postnational forms of democracy.

The relationship between culture and nationalism always bears the traces of those historical, ethical, and political forces that constitute the often shifting and contradictory elements of national identity. To the degree that the culture of nationalism is rigidly exclusive and defines its membership in terms of narrowly based common culture, nationalism tends to be xenophobic, authoritarian, and expansionist. The latter reflects the most commonly cited example of a nationalism steeped in the practices of ethnic cleansing, genocide, or imperialist aggression. On the other hand, nationalism moves closer toward being liberal and democratic to the degree that national identity is inclusive and respectful of diversity and difference. And yet, a civic nationalism that makes a claim to respecting cultural differences does not guarantee that the state will not engage in coercive assimilationist policies. In other words, democratic forms of nationalism cannot be defended simply through a formal appeal to abstract, democratic principles. How nationalism and the nation state embrace democracy must be determined, in part, through the access diverse cultural groups have to shared structures of power that organize commanding legal, economic, and cultural institutions on the local, state, and national level (see Kymlicka).

Cultural differences and national identity stand in a complex relationship to each other and point to progressive as well as totalitarian elements of nationalism that provide testimony to its problematic character and effects. On the negative side, recent history bears witness to the second world war steeped in forms of national identity that mobilized racial hatred and supported right wing, anti-democratic governments in Germany, Italy, and Japan. Following 1945, one of the most flagrant legacies of such a poisonous nationalism is evident in the long-standing apartheid regime that, until recently, dominated South African politics as well as in the continuing attempt on the part of Turkey to deny the Kurds any status as a national group.

Representations of national identity constructed through an appeal to racial purity, militarism, anti-semitism, and religious orthodoxy have once again surfaced aggressively in Western Europe and can be seen in the rise of neo-nazi youth movements in Germany, the neo-Fascist political parties that won the recent election in Italy, and the ethnic cleansing that has driven Serbian nationalism in the former Republic of Yugoslavia. This highly selective list merely illustrates how national identity can be fashioned around appeals to a monolithic cultural identity that affirms intolerance, bigotry, and an indifference to the precepts of democratic pluralism. Needless to say, these forms of demagogic nationalism emerge from a diverse set of conditions and circumstances, the roots of which lie in a complex history of racial conflict, the unstable economic conditions that have gripped Europe, and the dismantling of the Soviet Union and its empire. As a social construction, nationalism does not rest upon a particular politics; it takes its form within, rather than outside of, specific historical, social, and cultural contexts.

The more positive face of nationalism has emerged in a number of countries through a legacy of democratic struggles and can be seen not only in various anti-colonialist struggles in Asia and Africa, but also in diverse attempts on the part of nation-states to mobilize popular sentiment in the interest of expanding human rights and fighting against the encroachments of undemocratic social forces. While many of these movements of national struggle are far from unproblematic, particularly during periods in which they assume state control, they do provide credibility to the emancipatory power of nationalism as a defining principle in world politics.[1] A progressive notion of nationalism requires the coordination of a democratic politics of difference and multiculturalism with a notion of border crossing, diasporic politics, and postnationalism that recognizes the transits, flows, and social formations being produced on a global scale. It is precisely in the interaction of the national and global that a borderline space exists for generating new forms of transnational literacy, social relations, and cultural identities that expand the meaning of democratic citizenship beyond national borders.

Mythic National Identity

For many Americans, questions of national identity seem to elude the complex legacy of nationalism and take on a mythic quality. Informed by the powerful appeal to assimilation and the legitimating discourse of patriotism, national identity often operates within an ideological register untainted by the historical and emerging legacies of totalitarianism. Rather than being viewed cautiously as a potential vehicle for undermining democracy, national identity in the United States has been defined more positively in commonsensical terms as deeply connected to the mythic march of progress and prosperity at home and the noble effort to export democracy abroad. Hence, national identity has all too often been forged within popular memory as a discourse that too neatly links nation, culture, and citizenship in a seamless and unproblematic unity. Invoking claims to the past in which the politics of remembering and forgetting work powerfully to legitimate a notion of national belonging that "constructs the nation as an ethnically homogeneous object" (Gilroy 3), national identity is rewritten and purged of its seamy side. Within this narrative, national identity is structured through a notion of citizenship and patriotism that subordinates ethnic, racial, and cultural differences to the assimilating logic of a common culture, or, more brutally, the "melting pot." Behind the social imaginary that informs this notion of national identity is a narrowly defined notion of history that provides a defense of the narratives of imperial power and dominant culture and legitimates an intensely narrow and bigoted notion of what it means to be an American.

In an era of recharged nationalist discourse in the United States, the populist invocation of national identity suggests that social criticism itself is antithetical to both the construction of national identity and the precepts of patriotism. Of course, national identity, like nationalism itself, is a social construction that is built upon a series of inclusions and exclusions regarding history, citizenship, and national belonging. As the social historian Benedict Anderson has pointed out, the nation is an "imagined political community" that can only be understood within the intersecting dynamics of history, language, ideology, and power. In other words, nationalism and national identity are neither necessarily reactionary nor necessarily progressive politically. They give rise to communities which, as Anderson points out, are "to be distinguished, not by their falsity/genuineness, but by the style in which they are imagined" (6).

The insight that national identity must be addressed according to the ways in which it is imagined signals for me the importance of pedagogical practices that are central to the current debates around questions of identity characterizing much political debate in the United States. It is the pedagogical processes at work in framing the current debates on national identity that interest me most. More specifically, the questions I want to raise are: what forms of address, images, texts, and performances are being produced and used in popular discourses to construct what it means to be an American, and what are the implications of these dominant representations for extending or undermining a substantive plural democracy?

The current debate over national identity represents not only a conservative backlash fueled by the assumption that "those common values and consensual freedoms that have defined the 'American' way of life, circa Norman Rockwell" (Bhabha, "A Good Judge" 233) are now under attack by racial, sexual, and political minorities. Moreover, the current conservatism produces a new nationalism rooted in an imaginary construction of national identity that is dangerous to any viable notion of democracy. This is not meant to suggest that the discourse of national unity voiced through an appeal to shared language of difference (not the assimilationist language of a common culture) should be summarily dismissed as Eurocentric, racist, or patriarchal. The vision of national identity steeped in a shared vision of social justice and a respect for cultural differences is to be applauded. At the same time, the healing grace of a national identity based on a respect for "lived cultures in the plural" (Graff and Robbins 434) should not be confused with a politically reactionary notion of national identity whose primary purpose is to restrict the terms of citizenship and community to a discourse of monoculturalism and nativism. National identity in the service of a common culture recognizes cultural differences only to flatten them out in the conservative discourse of assimilation and the liberal appeal to tolerance (see Ien, Hage). However, the relationship between national identity and nationalism is not bound by any particular politics, and by definition is not intrinsically oppressive. Hence, it is both important and necessary as part of a progressive politics of national identity to provide a theoretical space to address the potential of both a pedagogy and politics that can pluralize cultural differences within democratic relations of power as part of an effort to develop an emancipatory politics of national identity and nationalism. This is especially important at a time in the United States when the discourses of nationalism and national identity have taken a decidedly reactionary political turn.

The appropriation of national identity as a vehicle to foster racism, nativism, and political censorship is not specific to the 1990s, but has a long history in the United States. What is somewhat new are the conditions, contexts, and content through which the discourse of national identity is being produced and linked to virulent forms of nationalism. For example, media culture with its new cable technologies coupled with the proliferation of radio and television talk channels has created a public sphere that vastly expands the intrusion into daily life of mainstream discourses that greatly restrict the possibility for real debate, exchange, and diversity of opinions. These electronic media, largely driven by corporate conglomerates, have no precedent in American life in terms of their power both to disseminate information and to shape how national identity is configured, comprehended, and experienced as part of everyday life. Secondly, popular culture has become a powerful site for defining nationalism and national identity against diversity and cultural differences, the latter rendered synonymous with disruption, disunity, and separatism. In this populist discourse, there is a theoretical slippage that equates national identity with a common identity and the assertion of cultural pluralism with an assault on the very character of what it means to be an American. At issue here is a politics of forgetting that erases how disparate social identities have been produced, legitimated, and marginalized within different relations of power. But there is more at stake than the erasure of social memory; there is also the emergence of a racially saturated discourse that mobilizes national identity as the defining principle for a national community that is under siege. Similarly, the new nationalism in foreign policy employs the chauvinistic bravado of the marketplace with its call for the United States to be number one in the world while simultaneously stigmatizing internal social criticism as unpatriotic and a threat to American culture and civility.

Media Culture and the Populist Construction of Nationalist Identity

I want to examine briefly some populist examples of the new nationalism that speak from different places in the cultural apparatuses that shape public opinion. In different ways, these populist voices advocate a pedagogy and politics of national identity that serve to reproduce some reactionary elements of the new nationalism. For example, expressions of the new nationalism can be found in several sites: in the backlash against multiculturalism in the public schools and universities; in the rise of the English Only movement; in the notion of the state as a "stern parent" willing to inflict harsh measures on welfare mothers; and in educational reforms demanding a national curriculum. Ideological signposts pointing to the new nationalism can be found in analogies invoking metaphors of battle, invasion, and war, which increasingly shape the debates over immigration in the United States, as in the passing of anti-immigration legislation such as California's Proposition 187. Crime is represented in the dominant white media as a black issue, implying that race can only be understood through a reductionist correlation of culture and identity. Representations of black men appear ad nauseam on the covers of magazines such as *Newsweek, The New York Times Sunday Magazine,* and *Time* whenever a signifier is needed to mobilize and draw upon the general public's fear of crime and urban decay. Recent Hollywood films abound with racist representations that link criminality to skin color. Some of the most popular examples include *Pulp Fiction* (1994) and *Just Cause* (1995) (see Giroux). All of these examples underscore how nationalism is currently being shaped to defend a beleaguered notion of national identity read as white, heterosexual, middle-class, and allegedly threatened by contamination from cultural, linguistic, racial, and sexual differences.

The power of the new nationalism and its centrality to American political life can also be seen in its growth and popularity in a number of popular and public spaces. One example can be found in the written and television commentaries of Republican presidential hopeful Patrick Buchanan on shows such as CNN's *Crossfire*. Buchanan represents a new version of the public intellectual speaking from such critical public sites as the news media, especially the growing number of news programs on cable television that are largely dominated by right-wing commentary. For Buchanan, the new nationalism is defined through a bellicose nativism that views cultural differences as a threat to national unity. Buchanan argues that the reality of cultural difference, with its plurality of languages, experiences, and histories, poses a serious threat to both national unity and what he defends as Judeo-Christian values. According to Buchanan, calls for expanding the existing potential of political representation and self-determination are fine in so far as they enable white Americans to "take back" their country. In this reactionary discourse, difference becomes a signifier for racial exclusivity, segregation, or, in Buchanan's language, "self determination." For Buchanan, public life in the United States has deteriorated since 1965 because "a flood tide of immigration has rolled in from the Third World, legal and illegal, as our institutions of assimilation . . . disintegrated." Ushering in the discourse of nativism, Buchanan asks: "Who speaks for the Euro-Americans? Is it not time to take America back?" (qtd. in Krauthammer A4). Similarly, populist right-wing conservative Rush Limbaugh, who describes himself as the "Doctor of Democracy," rails against the poor and disadvantaged minorities because they do not act like "real" Americans who "rely upon their own resources, skills, talents, and hard work" (26). Limbaugh has become the populist equivalent of Beavis and Butt-Head. Combining humor, unrestrained narcissism, and outright buffoonery with a virulent and mean-spirited attack on progressive causes, Limbaugh accentuates the current appeal of the talk-show that is part of a broader reactionary, conservative offensive through popular media. Perhaps the only thing interesting about Limbaugh is that he exemplifies how right wing conservatives no longer limit their political agenda to the traditional channels of policy, news, and information. They have now extended their influence to the more populist cultural realms of radio and television talk shows, the world of stand-up comics, and other texts of media culture.

Rush Limbaugh, Howard Stern, Andrew Dice Clay, and other popular media figures represent a marriage of media culture and the lure of extremist attacks in what appears as a legitimation of a new form of public pathology dressed up as entertainment.[2] Limbaugh echoes the increasingly popular assumption that an "ethnic upsurge" threatens both the American model of assimilation and the unity of America as a single culture. Extending rather than challenging the ideological assumptions that buttress the old racism and Social Darwinism, Limbaugh and others echo a view of cultural unity less as an overt marker for racial superiority than as a discourse for privileging a white "minority." Within this populist discourse, racism is couched in the critique of the welfare state but serves primarily as a signifier for cultural containment, homogeneity, and social and structural inequality. Just as Charles Murray and Richard Herrnstein warn in *The Bell Curve* against the effects of immigration on the gene pool of white, middle-class Americans, and the religious right calls for a "holy war" to be waged in the schools to preserve the identity of the United States as a "Christian" nation, right wing populist commentators add a twist to the new nationalism and its racial coding by appealing to a nostalgic, romanticized view of history as the "good old days" in which white men ruled, blacks knew their place in the social and political hierarchy, and women attended to domestic work. The appeal is no longer simply to racial supremacy but also to cultural uniformity parading as the politics of nationalism, national identity, and patriotism. These anti-multicultural attacks organize themselves around a view of nationalism that eschews any disagreement by simply labelling critics as "America-bashers."

In the world of TV spectacles and mass entertainment, the Buchanans and Limbaughs represent the shock-troops of the new nationalism. On the academic front, a more "refined" version of the new nationalism has been advanced. Two examples will suffice, though they are hardly inclusive. In the first instance, public intellectuals writing in conservative periodicals such as *The New Republic, The New Criterion,* and *The American Spectator* increasingly put forth an argument for the new nationalism in terms that both dismiss multiculturalism and reproduce the discourse of assimilation and common culture. Rather than analyzing multiculturalism as a complex, legitimate, and necessary "ongoing negotiation among minorities against assimilation" (Bhabha, "Beyond the Pale" 15), the new nationalists see in the engagements of cultural difference less a productive tension than a debilitating divisiveness. John B. Judis and Michael Lind echo this sentiment in their own call for a new nationalism:

> [T]here is a constructive and inclusive current of American nationalism that runs
> from Alexander Hamilton through Abraham Lincoln and Theodore Roosevelt. It

emphasizes not the exclusion of foreigners, but rather the unification of Americans of different regions, races and ethnic groups around a common national identity. It stands opposed not only to nativism, but also to today's multiculturalism and economic or strategic globalism. (21)

Nationalism in this discourse becomes the marker of certainty; it both affirms monoculturalism and restores the racially coded image of "Americanness" as a beleaguered national identity (Hall, "Culture" 357). The new nationalism also posits national identity against the ability of different groups to articulate and affirm their histories, languages, cultural identities, and traditions through the shifting and complex relations in which people imagine and construct national and postnational social formations. This is evident in the attack being waged by the right and the Republican Congress on affirmative action, quotas, immigration, bilingualism, and multiculturalism in the public schools. But the new nationalism is not confined to right wing conservatives and evangelical Christians.

A more moderate version of the new nationalism can be found in the work of writers like Richard Rorty, a prominent liberal philosopher from the University of Virginia. While Buchanan, Limbaugh, and their followers might be dismissed as simply populist demagogues, public intellectuals such as Rorty command enormous respect from the academic community and the established press. Moreover, such intellectuals travel between academic and popular public spheres with enough influence to bring professional legitimacy to the new nationalism as it is taken up in television and talk radio programs, the electronic media, and in the major newspapers and magazines in the United States. Hence, it is all the more important that arguments that reinforce the logic of the new nationalism and parade under the banner of a "tough" or "patriotic" liberalism be critically engaged, especially for individuals who find in such arguments a semblance of reason and restraint.

Richard Rorty, Liberalism, and the Problem of National Identity

Writing in the Op-Ed section of *The New York Times,* Rorty has argued under the headline, "The Unpatriotic Academy," that left-wing academics who support multiculturalism are "unpatriotic." For Rorty, the litmus test for patriotism is not to be found in social criticism that holds a country up to its professed ideals, but in a refusal on the part of "this left . . . to rejoice in the country it inhabits. It repudiates the idea of a national identity, and the emotion of national pride." Speaking for an unspecified group of "patriotic" Americans, Rorty, in this instance, insists that "We take pride in being citizens of a self-invented, self-reforming, enduring constitutional democracy" (E15). One wonders: for whom do intellectuals such as Rorty speak? Have they appointed themselves as spokespersons for all Americans who disassociate themselves from the left? And does this generalization further suggest that one gives up respect and love of one's country if one engages in criticism that can be conveniently labeled as left-wing? Does a public assertion of patriotism, as ritualistically invoked by all manner of demagogues, suggest that such rhetoric provides a certified stamp of legitimacy regarding one's own politics?

Of course, Limbaugh and Buchanan consistently engage in the rhetoric of love for their country while simultaneously baiting gays, blacks, feminists, and others. Moreover, one must consider the implications of Rorty's attack on the left social critics in light of the ways in which the United States engaged in red-baiting during the 1920s and the McCarthy witch-hunts of the 1950s. Is he suggesting that left-wing theorists (as if they could be grouped homogeneously) should be policed and punished for their lack of patriotism? There is a recklessness in Rorty's charges that places him squarely in the camp of those who would punish dissenters rather than support free speech, especially if it is speech that one disagrees with. Maybe Rorty was simply being rambunctious in his use of the term "unpatriotic," but given the way in which the term has been used historically in this country to squelch social criticism, such a lapse of historical memory seems unlikely. So what is the point?

Rorty seems to be caught between liberal guilt and the appeal of a rabid conservatism that equates cultural differences with a threat to national unity, a threat that has to be overcome. Equating the politics of difference with a threat to national unity, Rorty then takes the extraordinary step of identifying all those academics who support some version of multiculturalism as posing a threat to the social order. For Rorty, there is no contradiction in feeling one's heart swell with patriotism and "national hope" and feeling "shame at the greed, the intolerance and the indifference to suffering that is widespread in the United States" (E15). In this theoretical sweep, multiculturalism is not addressed in its complexity as a range of theoretical positions that run the ideological gamut extending from calls for separatism to new forms of cultural democracy. Multiculturalism for Rorty is simply a position that exists under some absolute sign. In this reductionistic perspective, there are no theoretical differences between multicultural positions espoused by academic leftists such as Hazel Carby, Guillermo Gomez-Pena, June Jordan, and bell hooks, on the one hand, and liberals such as James Banks, Gregory Jay, or Stanley Fish on the other. But there is more at stake here than Rorty's suspect appeal to patriotism. Social criticism is not the enemy of patriotism, it is the bedrock of a shared national tradition that allows for many voices to engage in a dialogue about the dynamics of cultural and political power. In fact, national identity must be understood within a broader concern for the expansion and deepening of democratic public life itself.

I believe that Rorty's notion of national identity closes down, rather than expands, the principles that inform a multicultural and multiracial democracy. However, Rorty is important in terms of exemplifying the limits of the reigning political philosophy of liberalism. Rorty's gesture towards tolerance "presupposes that its object is morally repugnant, that it really needs to be reformed, that is, altered" (Goldberg, *Racist Culture* 7). As David Theo Goldberg points out:

> Liberals are moved to overcome the racial differences they tolerate and have been so instrumental in fabricating by diluting them, by bleaching them out through assimilation or integration. The liberal would assume away the difference in otherness maintaining thereby the dominant of a presumed sameness, the universally imposed similarity in identity. (Racist Culture 7)

National identity cannot be constructed around the suppression of dissent. Nor should it be used in the service of a new fundamentalism by appealing to a notion of patriotism that equates left-wing social criticism with treason, and less critical forms of discourse with a love of nationalism or national identity. It is precisely this type of binarism that has been used, all too frequently throughout the twentieth century, to develop national communities that make a virtue of intolerance and exclusion. Moreover, this kind of logic prevents individuals and social groups from understanding and critically engaging national identity not as a cultural monument but as a living set of relations that must be constantly engaged and struggled over.

Rorty's facile equating of national identity with the love of one's country, on the one hand, and the dismissal of forms of left social criticism that argue for various forms of multiculturalism, on the other, are simply an expression of the new nationalism, one which views cultural differences and the emergence of multiple cultures as a sign of fragmentation and a departure from, rather than an advance toward, democracy. Rorty's mistake is that he assumes that national identity is to be founded on a single culture, language, and history when in fact it can't. National identity is always a shifting, unsettled complex of historical struggles and experiences that are cross-fertilized, produced, and translated through a variety of cultures. As such, it is always open to interpretation and struggle. As Hall points out, national identity "is a matter of 'becoming' as well of 'being.' . . . [It] is never complete, always in process. . . . [It] is not eternally fixed in some essentialized past [but] subject to the continuous 'play' of history, culture, and power" ("Cultural Identity" 225).

The discourse of multiculturalism represents, in part, the emergence of new voices that have generally been excluded from the multiple histories that have defined our national identity. Far from being a threat to social order, multiculturalism in its various forms has challenged notions of national identity that equate cultural differences with deviance and disruption. Refusing a notion of national identity constructed on the suppression of cultural differences and social dissent, multiculturalism, especially its more critical and insurgent versions, explores how dominant views of national identity have been developed around cultural differences constructed within hierarchical relations of power that authorize who can or cannot speak legitimately as an American. Maybe it is the insertion of politics and power back into the discourse on difference that threatens Rorty so much that he responds to it by labelling it as unpatriotic.

Pitting national identity against cultural difference not only appeals to an oppressive politics of common culture, but reinforces a political moralism that polices "the boundaries of identity, encouraging uniformity and ensuring intellectual inertia" (Rutherford 17). National identity based on a unified cultural community suggests a dangerous relationship between the ideas of race, intolerance, and the cultural membership of nationhood. Not only does such a position downplay the politics of culture at work in nationalism, but it erases an oppressive history forged in an appeal to a common culture and a reactionary notion of national identity. As Will Kymlicka points out, liberals and conservatives often overlook the fact that the American government "forcibly incorporated Indian tribes, native Hawaiians, and Puerto Ricans into the American state, and then attempted to coercively assimilate each group into the common American culture. It banned the speaking of Indian languages in school and forced Puerto Rican and Hawaiian schools to use English rather than Spanish or Hawaiian" (132).

What is problematic about Rorty's position is not simply that he views multiculturalism as a threat to a totalizing notion of national identity. More important is his theoretical indifference to counter-narratives of difference, diaspora, and cultural identity that explore how diverse groups are constructed within an insurgent multiculturalism, which engage the issue both of what holds us together as a nation and of what constitutes our differences from each other. Viewing cultural differences only as a problem, Rorty reveals a disturbing lacuna in his notion of national identity. It is a view that offers little defense against the forces of ethnic absolutism and cultural racism that are so quick to seize upon national identity as a legitimating discourse for racial violence. There is an alarming defensiveness in Rorty's view, one that reinforces rather than challenges a discourse of national community rooted in claims to cultural and racist supremacy.

Pedagogy, National Identity, and the Politics of Difference

Critical educators need a notion of national identity that addresses its political, cultural, and pedagogical components. In the first instance, national identity must be addressed as part of a broader consideration linking nationalism and postnational social formations to a theory of democracy. That is, the relationship between nationalism and democracy must address not only the crucial issue of whether legal rights are provided for all groups irrespective of their cultural identity, but also how structures of power work to ensure that diverse cultural communities have the economic, political, and social resources to exercise "both the capacity for collective voice and the possibility of differentiated, directly interpersonal relations" (Calhoun, "Nationalism" 311). Rather than waging war against the pluralization of cultural identities and the crucial spheres in which they are nurtured and engaged, educators must address critically how national identity is constructed in the media, through the politics of state apparatuses, and through the mobilization of material resources and power outside of the reach of the state (see Goldberg, "Introduction"). As part of a broader politics of representation, this suggests the need for progressive cultural workers to provide the pedagogical conditions and sites "open to competing conceptualizations, diverse identities, and a rich public discourse" necessary to expand the conditions for democracy to flourish on both a national and global level (Calhoun, "Nationalism" 327).

Secondly, national identity must be inclusive and informed by a democratic pluralization of cultural identities. If the tendency towards a universalizing, assimilative impulse is to be resisted, educators must ensure that students engage varied notions of an imagined community by critically addressing rather than excluding cultural differences. While the approach toward such a pedagogy is culturally inclusive and suggests expanding the varied texts that define what counts as knowledge in public schools and institutions of higher education in the United States, there is also a need to create institutionalized spaces obligated to transdisciplinarity and multicultural studies. But such pedagogical spaces must be firmly committed to more than a politics of inclusive representation or simply aimed at helping students to understand and celebrate cultural difference (Martin Luther King, Jr. Day, for example). The politics of cultural difference must be a politics of more than texts: it must also understand, negotiate, and challenge differences as they are defined and sustained within oppressive networks of power. Critically negotiating the relationship between national identity and cultural differences, as Homi Bhabha has pointed out, is a negating activity that should be valued for *making a difference* in the world rather than merely reflecting it ("Beyond" 22).

What educators need is a pedagogy that redefines national identity not through a primordial notion of ethnicity or a monolithic conception of culture, but as part of a postmodern politics of cultural difference in which identities are constantly being negotiated and reinvented within complex and contradictory notions of national belonging. A collective dialogue over nationalism, national identity, and cultural differences is not going to be established by simply labelling certain forms of social criticism as unpatriotic or national identity as a shared tradition that exists outside of the struggles over representation, democracy, and social justice. If American society is to move away from its increasing defensiveness about cultural differences, it will have to advocate a view of national identity that regards bigotry and intolerance as the enemy of democracy and cultural differences as one of its strengths. However, even where such differences are acknowledged and affirmed, it is important to recognize that they cannot be understood exclusively within the language of culture and identity, but rather as a part of an ethical discourse that contributes to a viable notion of democratic public life. In part, this suggests a pedagogy and language through which values and social responsibility can be discussed not simply as a matter of individual choice, reduced to complacent relativism, but as a social discourse and pedagogical practice grounded in public struggles. Goldberg is right in arguing that educators need a "robustly nuanced conception of relativism underpinning the multicultural project [one that] will enable distinctions to be drawn between more or less accurate truth claims and more or less justifiable values (in contrast to absolute claims to the truth or the good)" ("Introduction" 15). The issue here is not merely the importance of moral pragmatism in developing a pedagogy that addresses national identity as a site of resistance and reinvention. Equally important is the political and pedagogical imperative of developing a postmodern notion of democracy in which students and others will be attentive to negotiating and constructing the social, political, and cultural conditions for diverse cultural identities to flourish within an increasingly multicentric, international, and transnational world.

In short, if national identity is not to be used in the service of demagogues, it must be addressed pedagogically and politically to unravel how cultural differences have been constructed within the unequal distribution of resources, how such differences need to be understood around issues of power and struggle, and how national identity must be taken up in ways that challenge economic and cultural inequality.

Giroux is Waterbury Chair Professor of Education at Penn State. He writes in the fields of critical pedagogy, cultural studies, and popular culture. His most recent books include *Border Crossings, Living Dangerously, Disturbing Pleasures*, and his forth-coming *Fugitive Cultures: Race, Violence, and Youth* (Routledge).

Notes

1. The literature on nationalism and national identity is much too voluminous to cite here, but excellent examples can be found in Anderson; Chatterjee; Bhabha's *Nation and Narration;* Said; Parker, Russo, Sommer, and Yaeger; and Balibar and Wallerstein. Some recent sources can be found in Calhoun's *Social Theory and the Politics of Identity.*

2. For a brilliant analysis of this phenomenon, especially the marketing of Beavis and Butt-Head, see Kellner.

References

Anderson, Benedict. *Imagined Communities.* 2nd ed. London: Verso, 1991.

Appadurai, Arjun. "Patriotism and Its Futures," *Public Culture* 5.3 (1993): 411–29.

Balibar, Etienne, and Immanuel Wallerstein. *Race, Nation, Class: Ambiguous Identities.* London: Verso, 1991.

Bhabha, Homi K. "Beyond the Pale: Art in the Age of Multicultural Translation." *Kunst and Museum Journal* 5.4 (1994): 15–23.

———. "A Good Judge of Character: Men, Metaphors, and the Common Culture." *Race-ing Justice, En-Gendering Power: Essays on Anita Hill, Clarence Thomas, and the Construction of Social Reality.* Ed. Toni Morrison. New York: Pantheon, 1992.

———. ed., *Nation and Narration.* New York: Routledge, 1990.

Calhoun, Craig. "Nationalism and Civil Society: Democracy, Diversity, and Self-Determination." Calhoun, ed. 304–35.

———. ed., *Social Theory and the Politics of Identity.* Cambridge: Blackwell, 1994.

Chatterjee, Partha. *The Nation and Its Fragments.* Princeton: Princeton UP, 1993.

Gilroy, Paul. *The Black Atlantic: Modernity and Double Consciousness.* Cambridge: Harvard UP, 1993.

Giroux, Henry A. "Racism and the Aesthetic of Hyper-Real Violence: *Pulp Fiction* and Other Visual Tragedies." *Social Identities* 1.2 (forthcoming).

Goldberg, David Theo. "Introduction: Multicultural Conditions." *Multiculturalism: A Critical Reader.* Ed. Goldberg. Cambridge: Blackwell, 1994.

———. *Racist Culture.* Cambridge: Blackwell, 1993.

Graff, Gerald, and Bruce Robbins. "Cultural Criticism." *Redrawing the Lines.* Ed. Stephen Greenblatt and Giles Gunn. New York: MLA, 1992.

Grewal, Inderpal, and Caren Kaplan. "Introduction: Transnational Feminist Practices and Questions of Postmodernity." *Scattered Hegemonies.* Ed. Grewal and Kaplan. Minneapolis: U of Minnesota P, 1994. 1–33.

Hage, Ghassan. "Locating Multiculturalism's Other: A Critique of Practical Tolerance." *New Formations* 24 (Winter 1994): 19–34.

Hall, Stuart. "Cultural Identity and Diaspora." Rutherford, ed.

———. "Culture, Community, Nation." *Cultural Studies* 7.3 (Oct. 1993).

Ien Ang. "On Not Speaking Chinese: Postmodern Ethnicity and the Politics of Diaspora." *Social Formations* 24 (March 1995): 1–18.

Judis, John B., and Michael Lind. "For A New Nationalism." *New Republic* 27 (Mar. 1995): 19–27.

Kellner, Douglas. *Media Culture: Cultural Studies, Identity, and Politics—Between The Modern and the Postmodern.* New York: Routledge, forthcoming.

Krauthammer, Charles. "The Real Buchanan is Surfacing." *Cincinnati Enquirer* 3 Mar. 1990: A4.

Kymlicka, Will. "Misunderstanding Nationalism." *Dissent* (Winter 1995): 130–37.

Limbaugh, Rush H., III. *See, I Told You So.* New York: Pocket, 1993.

Parker, Andrew, Mary Russo, Doris Sommer, and Patricia Yaeger, eds. *Nationalisms and Sexualities.* New York: Routledge, 1992.

Parry, Benita. "Signs of Our Times: A Discussion of Homi Bhabha's *The Location of Culture*." *Third Text* 28/29 (Autumn/Winter 1994): 5–24.

Rorty, Richard. "The Unpatriotic Academy." *New York Times.* Op-Ed Section, Sunday (13 Feb. 1994): E15.

Rutherford, Jonathan, ed. *Identity, Community, Culture, Difference.* London: Lawrence and Wishart, 1990.

———. "A Place Called Home: Identity and the Cultural Politics of Difference." Rutherford, ed.

Said, Edward. *Culture and Imperialism.* New York: Knopf, 1993.

Squires, Judith. "Editorial." *New Formations* 24 (Winter 1994): v–vi.

Bibliography

Ahmed, Sara. "Queer Feelings." *The Politics of Emotion*. Edinburgh University Press, 2004. 144–167.

Althusser, Louis. "Ideology and Ideological State Apparatuses (Notes: toward an Investigation)." *Lenin and Philosophy and Other Essays*. New York: Monthly Review Press, 1991.

Anderson, Benedict. "Introduction." *Imagined Communities*. New York: Verso Books, 2006.

Andre, Judith. "Stereotypes: Conceptual and Normative Considerations." *Racism and Sexism: An Integrated Study*. Ed. Paula S. Rothenburg. New York: St. Martin's Press, 1998.

Bennion-Nixon, Lee-Jane. "We (Still) Need a Woman for the Job: The Warrior Woman, Feminism, and Cinema in the Digital Age." *Senses of Cinema* 56.3 (2010).

Bird, Sharon R. "Welcome to the Men's Club: Homosociality and the Maintenance of Hegemonic Masculinity." *Gender and Society* 10.2 (1996): 120–132.

Crosby, Emilye. "Ten Things You Should Know About Selma Before You See the Film." *The Zinn Education Project*, 3 January 2015. Web. 10 March 2015.

Garnets, Linda D. "Sexual Orientations in Perspective." *Cultural Diversity and Ethnic Minority Psychology* 8.2 (2002): 115–129.

Giroux, Henry A. "National Identity and the Politics of Multiculturalism." *College Literature* 22.2 (1995): 42–57.

Grossman, Julie. "Film Noir's 'Femme Fatales' Hard Boiled Women: Moving Beyond Gender and Fantasies." *Quarterly Review of Film and Video* 24.1 (2007): 19–30.

Hall, Stuart. "Representation, Meaning and Language." *Representation: Cultural Representations and Signifying Practices*. London: Sage, 1997.

hooks, bell. "A Revolution of Values: The Promise of Multicultural Change." *Teaching to Transgress: Education as the Practice of Freedom*. New York: Routledge, 1994. 23–34.

Kellner, Douglas. "Cultural Studies, Multiculturalism, and Media Culture." *Gender, Race, and Class in Media*. Eds. Gail Dines and Jean M. Humez. Thousand Oaks, CA: Sage, 2003. 9–20.

Lev, Peter. "Whose Future? *Star Wars, Alien,* and *Blade Runner.*" *Literature/Film Quarterly* 26.1 (1998): 30–7.

Lofton, Kathryn. "The Sigh of the Oppressed?: Marxism and Religion in America Today." *New Labor Forum* 21.3 (2012): 58–65.

Lull, James. "Hegemony." *Media, Communication, Culture: A Global Approach*. New York: Columbia University Press, 1995.

Lyden, John. "To Commend or To Critique? The Question of Religion and Film Studies." *Journal of Religion and Film Studies* 1.2 (1997).

Marx, Karl. "The Destructive Power of Money." *Marx's Concept of Man*. Ed. Erich Fromm. Trans. T.B. Bottomore. New York: F. Ungar Publishing, 1963.

McIntosh, Peggy. "White Privilege: Unpacking the Invisible Knapsack." *Peace and Freedom* July/August (1989): 10–12.

McNamee, Stephen and Robert K. Miller, Jr. "The Meritocracy Myth." *Sociation Today* 2.1 (2004).

Mirrlees, Tanner. "The Economics, Geopolitics and Ideology of an Imperial Film Commodity." *Cineaction* 92.2 (2014) 4–11.

Mueleners, Matthew. "Treat Students Right By Valuing Their Diversity." *The Education Digest* (2001): 46–51.

Omi, Michael and Howard Winant. "Racial Formation." *Racial Formation in the United States: From the 1960s to the 1990s*. Routledge, 1994.

Park, J. H., N. G. Gabbadon, and A. R. Chernin. "Naturalizing Racial Differences through Comedy: Asian, Black, and White Views on Racial Stereotypes in *Rush Hour 2*." *Journal of Communication* 56.1 (2006): 157–77.

Pileggi, Mary S., Maria Elizabeth Grabe, Lisa B. Holderman, and Michelle de Montigny. "Business as Usual: The American Dream in Hollywood Business Films." *Mass Communication and Society* 3.2 (2000): 207–28.

Place, Janey. "Women in Film Noir." *Women in Film Noir*. Ed. E. Ann Kaplan. London: BFI, 1989. 35–68.

Ringlestein, Yonah. "Real or Not Real: *The Hunger Games* as Transmediated Religion." *Journal of Religion and Popular Culture* 25.3 (2013): 372–87.

Risman, Barbara J. "Gender as a Social Structure: Theory Wrestling with Activism." *Gender and Society*. Thousand Oaks, CA: Sage, 2004.

Schrock, Douglas and Michael Schwalbe. "Men, Masculinity, and Manhood Acts." *Annual Review of Sociology* 35 (2009): 277–95.

Shaheen, Jack G. "Reel Bad Arabs: How Hollywood Vilifies a People." *Annals of the American Academy of Political and Social Science*. 588 (2003): 171–193.

Soles, Carter. "Team Apatow and the Tropes of Geek-Centered Romantic Comedy." *Bright Lights Film Journal*, 31 October 2015. Web. 10 March 2015.

Sue, Derald Wing, Christina M. Capodilupo, Gina C. Torino, Jennifer M. Bucceri, Aisha M. B. Holder, Kevin L. Nadal, and Marta Esquilin. "Racial Microagressions in Everyday Life: Implications for Clinical Practice." *American Psychologist* 62.4 (2009): 271–86.

Van Buren, Peter. "We Have Been Watching the Same Movie About America's Wars for 75 Years." *The Nation*, 19 February 2015. Web. 10 March 2015.